ROBERT BRESSON

ROBERT BRESSON:
A PASSION FOR FILM

Tony Pipolo

OXFORD
UNIVERSITY PRESS
2010

OXFORD
UNIVERSITY PRESS

Oxford University Press, Inc., publishes works that further
Oxford University's objective of excellence
in research, scholarship, and education.

Oxford New York
Auckland Cape Town Dar es Salaam Hong Kong Karachi
Kuala Lumpur Madrid Melbourne Mexico City Nairobi
New Delhi Shanghai Taipei Toronto

With offices in
Argentina Austria Brazil Chile Czech Republic France Greece
Guatemala Hungary Italy Japan Poland Portugal Singapore
South Korea Switzerland Thailand Turkey Ukraine Vietnam

Published by Oxford University Press, Inc.
198 Madison Avenue, New York, New York 10016

www.oup.com

Oxford is a registered trademark of Oxford University Press

Library of Congress Cataloging-in-Publication Data
Pipolo, Tony.
Robert Bresson : a passion for film / Tony Pipolo.
    p. cm.
Includes bibliographical references and index.
ISBN 978-0-19-531980-4; 978-0-19-531979-8 (pbk.)
1. Bresson, Robert—Criticism and interpretation.   I. Title.
PN1988.3.B755P57   2010
791.4302'33092—dc22   2009018997

Frontispiece image courtesy of PhotoFest, New York

9 8 7 6 5 4 3 2 1

Printed in the United States of America
on acid-free paper

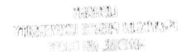

To Carole Pipolo and Isabel Pipolo

Acknowledgments

The films of Robert Bresson have been an important part of my life for over forty years. Inevitably this means that conversations, debates, and discussions with numerous people, inside and outside academia, helped to form the impressions that have made their way, for better or worse, into this book. Among those who shared their thoughts and reacted to mine over these many years are the late Paul Arthur, who read and commented comprehensively and vigorously on several chapters; George Amberg, Robert Beavers, Noël Carroll, Barry Gillam, Tom Gunning, Ira Hozinsky, Kent Jones, Jane Kupersmidt, Jay Leyda, Stuart Liebman, Babette Mangolte, Richard Porton, Adam Reilly, and Amy Taubin.

Dudley Andrew, Gilberto Perez, and Malcolm Turvey were kind enough to invite me to speak on Bresson at Yale University and Sarah Lawrence. Gary Crowdus, Ted Perry, and James Quandt invited me to publish earlier versions of two chapters. The essay on *Les Anges du péché* in chapter 1, "The Rules of the Game," is a modified version of an essay published in the anthology *Robert Bresson*, edited by James Quandt (1998); the essay on *Au hasard Balthazar* (chapter 5) is an expanded version of the one in *Masterpieces of Modernist Cinema,* edited by Ted Perry (2006).

From my first years in the graduate film program at New York University in the early 1970s to the present, I benefited from countless exchanges with Annette Michelson who shared personal recollections of her meetings with Bresson. For these and reasons too numerous to mention, she remains not only an invaluable mentor but a cherished friend.

Mylène Bresson received me kindly and answered my questions when I visited her on the Ile St. Louis where she lived with Bresson for many years. Nadia Margulies shared her expertise on Joan of Arc, read over the chapter on Bresson's film, and corrected historical errors as well as my French. Further thanks to Babette Mangolte for submitting my questions to and relaying responses from Claude Laydu at a Bresson conference in Paris and for sharing her experiences while filming her documentary *The Models of Pickpocket.*

I am grateful to Andrew Lampert and John Mhiripiri of Anthology Film Archives who allowed me to view films on a steenbeck from which I selected some of the images that appear in this book. Arunas Kaulikauskas photographed the frames chosen, and Isabel Pipolo, as always, was indispensable in making them presentable for printing. Photofest supplied stills from *Four Nights of a Dreamer* as well as the image of Bresson at the beginning of the book, and has been inordinately patient about having these returned. Thanks to Shannon McLachlan, my editor at Oxford, for urging me to complete the book and for understanding when I exceeded several deadlines. Thanks also to Brendan O'Neill at Oxford for his assistance and support; and to Jessica Ryan, whose copyediting taught me more about my peculiarities of style than she may realize.

No single individual contributed more to the completion of this book than P. Adams Sitney of Princeton University. He read every chapter as it was written and offered the kind of critical scrutiny that only one who knows and admires Bresson's work could provide. While his enthusiasm and support were unflagging, he never failed to point out contradictions, inaccuracies, or vague reasoning that forced me to rethink and sharpen my readings of Bresson's films. Whatever flaws remaining in the pages that follow are due to clumsiness or stubbornness on my part.

This book took many years to complete, during which time I received only encouragement and patience from my wife Carole and my daughter Isabel. Both took time either to listen to ideas as they were being honed or to perform some task that made progress possible. For these and countless reasons, I dedicate this book to them.

Contents

ROBERT BRESSON

The artist's essential task is not simply to make the most effective work possible, as viewed *in* its kind. It is rather to achieve a view of the world superior to all other views.

—Wayne C. Booth, introduction to Mikhail Bakhtin, *Problems of Dostoevsky's Poetics*, characterizing Bakhtin's position

Introduction

Perhaps the most highly regarded French filmmaker after Jean Renoir, Robert Bresson sustained a reputation as an uncompromising artist throughout his career. In 1957 the director Jacques Rivette remarked, "There is only one [French] film-maker left who has not sold out, and that's Bresson."[1] At the time Bresson had made only four films, but the claim proved prophetic. Few filmmakers have clung so tenaciously to the same thematic concerns, exerted such obsessive control over every aspect of their work, and adhered to as harsh a vision of the world. Like Carl-Theodor Dreyer, another idiosyncratic filmmaker sometimes drawn to religious subjects and whose career also spanned nearly half a century, Bresson's rigorous standards limited his production. In forty years he made only thirteen films.

This book is a highly personal response to these films and to the artistry of their maker. It presumes that Bresson was an extraordinary and unique figure and that the products of his creative imagination, devotion to craft, and lifelong commitment to filmmaking are expressions and extensions of his beliefs, his convictions, and his perceptions of the world. As with Pier Paolo Pasolini or Jean Cocteau, the latter of whom once collaborated with

Bresson, or any other idiosyncratic film artist, to study his films is to study the person. It is as true of Bresson as it is of these others to say that "a film, whatever it might be, is always its director's portrait."[2] Because of this I have found it useful to adopt the tenets and tools of psychoanalytic investigation in an effort to understand this connection in a richer, more productive way. It is neither my desire nor my intent to apply this approach indiscriminately. At all times it is the aesthetic and thematic values of the work with which I am concerned and how these values reflect the person and philosophy of Bresson. As there is not yet a biography of Bresson, even in French, one must look to the films themselves for insights along these lines. Having admired them for more than half of my life, studied them closely over the past twenty years, and taught them to graduate and undergraduate students, it is my conviction that they are as close to providing an aesthetic biography of the filmmaker as is the work of any great artist.

Bresson occupied a singular position in international cinema. His pursuit of a "pure" film aesthetic not only placed him outside the mainstream, but led him to renounce even those pleasures afforded by the art cinema of his contemporaries. No star personalities grace his work as they do those of Roberto Rossellini (Ingrid Bergman), Michelangelo Antonioni (Monica Vitti), or Federico Fellini (Marcello Mastroianni). Determined to free the cinema of any residue of the theater, Bresson rejected professional actors, minimized dialogue, and eschewed the angst-ridden psychology typical of Ingmar Bergman and Bernardo Bertolucci. His films display neither the self-conscious malaise of Antonioni nor the Brechtian/Marxist reflexivity of Godard. And in his mission to purge the cinema of visual excess, he avoided the elaborate mise-en-scène and extended camera movements so beloved of Claude Chabrol, Kenji Mizoguchi, Max Ophuls, and Luchino Visconti.

Bresson's films once divided audiences and critics alike, even those who patronized film festivals. Susan Sontag, an early American admirer, declared that he had been "firmly labeled as an esoteric director [who] has never had the attention of the art-house audience that flocks to Buñuel, Bergman, Fellini—though he is a far greater director than these."[3] This was before *Au hasard Balthazar* (1966), perhaps his strangest film. Judging from the success of an international retrospective in 1998, the situation has changed. Yet the bleakness of Bresson's vision did not abate, as his last films, *Lancelot of the Lake* (1974), *The Devil Probably* (1977), and *L'Argent* (1983), confirm. The continued resistance to his work still seems tied to a moral rigor completely averse to the permissive relativism of contemporary life.

Bresson's concern with ethical behavior and how to conduct a moral life was consistent with the climate in the aftermath of the Second World War, when traditional value systems were challenged by philosophies such as Sartrean existentialism. But he was not the only filmmaker who witnessed the crises brought on by that war and whose works have a religious cast. Rossellini's *Flowers of St. Francis*, released around the time of *Diary of a Country Priest* (1951), was preceded and followed by a series of films, in which the director explored existential conditions from a deeply spiritual point of view.[4] It was perhaps in response to this atmosphere that Bresson's protagonists of the 1940s and 1950s—in *Les Anges du péché* (1943), *Diary*, and *A Man Escaped* (1956)—are moved to alter the inner lives of others. Although this theme seems to disappear in his later films, a crucial component of it remains: Bresson's attraction to young people is as indisputable as their iconographic importance to his work. If, amid his darkest conjurations, there is a glimpse of light and hope, it is carried by the radiant faces and indelible presences of the young, even those, such as the wife in *Une femme douce* (1969) and Charles in *The Devil Probably*, haunted by death.

As this might suggest, from *Les Anges du péché* to *L'Argent*, Bresson explored the theme of innocence and corruption, the dividing line of which is frequently sexual initiation. Although sex is not in the foreground of the films, its presence is often cause for distress. It torments Chantal's adolescence in *Diary of a Country Priest*, thrusts Marie into shame and humiliation in *Au hasard Balthazar*, and leads to the young protagonist's suicide in *Mouchette* (1967). But though sex may be the bridge between a state of relative innocence and the fallen world, Bresson did not, like Georges Bernanos, one of his literary sources, harbor an idealized view of early childhood. As his unfulfilled project to film the Book of Genesis attests, he appeared to acknowledge the concept of original sin.

It should not be surprising, then, that several of his characters are virgins, most notably the protagonist of *The Trial of Joan of Arc* (1962), the fifteenth-century heroine who, from all reports, convinced a horde of military figures, politicians, court royalty, and theologians that she could lead an army and drive the English out of France. No small part of the political considerations that both Church and State figures exploited was Joan's confirmed virginity, a state believed by ecclesiastics and common people alike to permit privileged access to God. Later, in order for the Church and its English allies to condemn her as a witch so as to tarnish the legitimacy of the king she crowned, they needed to falsify her claim or deprive her of her virginity.

The virginal was also a quality that Bresson sought in those who impersonate his characters. Not only should they lack sufficient life experience to preclude an embittered demeanor, but they had to be equally inexperienced in front of the camera. So adamant was he about this that he virtually never used the same people twice. Having taken something precious from them, he once said, he could no longer see them as "unspoiled." How this bears directly on his aesthetic and his approach to actors and acting will be discussed later.

Never wholly innocent, however, Bresson's characters manifest that hubris identified by Aristotle as the tragic flaw of the protagonists of Sophoclean drama, and in Catholic theology as the most serious of the seven deadly sins. Even, in fact especially those bent on saving the spiritual lives of others must wrestle with the prideful aspect of religious fervor. The novice Anne-Marie, the country priest, and Joan are stubbornly devoted to their missions, thorns in the side of everyone around them. This speaks to a primary tension in Bresson's narratives between the relationship of individual will and destiny. The idea that human history follows a prescribed course, fairly explicit in the films up to 1962, remains discernible, I believe, in all subsequent films. The struggle is between the apparent course of this plan and each character's acceptance of or resistance to it, played out in terms of how he or she comes to recognize and renounce pride. Perhaps because of this, some of Bresson's narratives have been described as tracing a "negative route to God."

Just as Sophocles' characters defy the gods until they accept their destiny, Bresson's move through scenarios, the ends of which have already been written. From first film to last the relationship between free will and determinism is dynamic, even when it is not always immediately evident. Bresson does not so much pose the question of whether lives are ruled by independent will or design as he assumes the paradoxical fusion of the two, echoing the contradiction at the heart of Sophoclean tragedy. When the chorus asks the protagonist at the end of *Oedipus the King* who is responsible for his blindness, he exclaims that it was Apollo who ordained his agonies but "my hand…and mine alone" that dealt the blow.

In both his first film, *Les Anges du péché*, and his last, *L'Argent*, there is a reversal of character behavior in the final moments, something also true of *Les Dames du bois de Boulogne* (1945) and *Pickpocket* (1959). In each film the sense of design is both reinforced *and* contradicted by the inflexible trajectory of Bresson's narrative structures and the compression of his filmic style. That is to say, the driven quality of the narrative and the style appears to personify a character's independent will while, *at the same time,* each film moves inexorably to a foregone conclusion. This seeming contradiction, I would argue, is at the heart of Bresson's cinema: the driven nature of his narratives is mirrored in the driven nature of his style.

Related to this is the role of coincidence, or seeming coincidence, in Bresson's work. Peter Brooks notes an interesting contrast between Balzac and Flaubert and the role of coincidence in their plot structures. Whereas

Balzac turns a coincidental meeting into an "essential confrontation, where the actors play out everything that they represent, bringing a crisis and a change of position," Flaubert's coincidences in *Sentimental Education* are "non-essentialized, as they are de-dramatized: they are not confrontations, but simple encounters, unfolding the narrative as something close to pure metonymy without metaphoric arrest."[5]

The precision of Bresson's work is closer to Flaubert's, yet coincidence in his films is tinged with destiny, the consequences, no doubt, of living in a world stained by original sin. His films may be "de-dramatized" and close to "pure metonymy," but they are hardly "non-essentialized." Chance encounters in Bresson are saturated with the taint of human cruelty and indifference, evidence of the flawed human condition and the fall from grace.

The Question of God

The question of Bresson's personal convictions about God and the Catholic faith in which he was raised is difficult to answer, since, without a biography, one can only conjecture from the work and from remarks he made in interviews over the years. The more immediate question concerns the relationship of Bresson's art to belief in God, and more specifically to the tenets of Catholic doctrine. Many critics and admirers of Bresson would prefer that such questions just go away. But as the words *design*, *destiny*, *inevitable course*, and *prescribed plan*—all of which have been used by critics of every stripe—suggest, Bresson's cinema has always evoked the question of God. Whether convenient or not, politically correct or not, fashionable or not, or simply awkward for those who write about him, the question is unavoidable. God is not a side issue that surfaces in some films and not others in terms of its relevance to plot or a specific character. My argument in this book is that the question of God's existence and everything that ensues from it bears directly and pervasively on Bresson's thematic preoccupations, on his overall philosophy of human life and behavior, on the stylistic rigor of his films, and even on his use of *models* rather than professional actors.

Consider the moral severity of the films mentioned earlier. Although such a stance has been attributed to his Catholicism, there is no hard evidence that Bresson practiced the faith in his adult life. Nevertheless it would be difficult to deny that both Catholicism and faith left their marks on his thinking and his art, along with a perhaps heretical belief in predestination, as the implacable nature of his narratives strongly supports. Even his late films suggest an inability or an unwillingness to relinquish the idea of design inflected by the Christian theory of history. This is something Bresson shared with Georges Bernanos, Feodor Dostoevsky, and Leo Tolstoy, whose works inspired more than half of his films. Like them, he was preoccupied with questions of good and evil, the existence of God, the relationship between body and soul, and that between personal and social morality. For him, as for Bernanos and Dostoevsky, the world is fallen and evil is intrinsic to the human condition, as present in the provinces as it is in the city, in the old as well as the young, the rich as well as the poor, the powerful as well as the weak. It was this obstinate posture that infuriated Leftist critics in such journals as *Positif* who declared Bresson out of touch with social and political reality.

The relation between God's will and human willfulness, and whether the latter is merely the unwitting instrument of the former, is central to Bresson's cinema. It is as true of his first film, *Les Anges du péché*, in which the protagonist hears "the word" that directs her actions and the course of the narrative, as it is of *L'Argent*, his last and most cynical film, in which there are subtle hints, as a minor character puts it, that "someone is looking out for [the protagonist] from afar." That the former is an original screenplay and the latter based on a novella by Tolstoy suggests that Bresson's interest in this theme predated and no doubt determined his choices of literary sources. Indeed, it would appear that he is merely echoing Christ when the latter prays to avoid the inevitable passion and death for which, according to Christian teaching, he came into the world.[6]

In Bresson's first six films the rigid stance was mitigated by a final moral or spiritual victory, which implied that the evils of the world could be "transcended," as Paul Schrader, another of Bresson's American admirers, expressed it. Beginning with *Au hasard Balthazar*, the possibility of such redemption seemed precluded; indeed, among the seven films in the later group, three, possibly four, end in the suicide of the protagonist. Though one might conclude that Bresson's vision had darkened considerably, the darkness, in fact, was always there. The images of French provincial life in *Balthazar* and *Mouchette* are no harsher than that of the village in *Diary of a Country Priest*, made sixteen years earlier. It is in *Diary* that we find the first apparent suicide, the character of the doctor, and enough evidence to wonder if the priest's spare diet and consumption of bad alcohol is also a form of slow suicide.

When Bresson was questioned upon the release of *Balthazar* about an alleged change in his thinking, whereby God was now absent from his work, he denied it: "Pronouncing the name of God isn't what makes him present. If he [Marie's father in that film] rejects God, then God exists, and therefore God is present."[7] Perhaps he shared Bernanos's sense that "the feeling of God's absence was the only sign left of his existence."[8] Indeed, Bresson's films, thematically and formally, have always been about *apparent* absences, silences, and the invisible. The only "evidence" of God's existence in *Diary* is the intense look on the face of Claude Laydu as he stares into a powerfully charged off screen space. The idea takes a different form in *Balthazar*, for what could be more indicative of the remoteness of God and redemption from contemporary life than making an animal a Christ figure, a fictional construct that, presumably, could no longer be convincingly embodied by a human being? In his incommunicability, no less than his saintliness, Balthazar embodies this remote, invisible, unknowable God.

Bresson's work therefore bears the signs of one raised Catholic as well as the doubts of a deeply engaged modern thinker. Pivoting on the line between the two, his cinema reflects an authentic mind-set of mid-twentieth-century thought. Wondering how committed he was to a religious point of view seems an inescapable aspect of watching his films. One might say that the psychological tension in which the viewer is held is a result of the sense one has of Bresson's ambivalence toward Catholicism along with his attraction to the vision it embodies. More strikingly and ambiguously than Ingmar Bergman's, his films mirror the crisis of faith, moving relentlessly toward catharsis without relieving existential doubt.

The Catholic aspect of this vision is evident not only in the many allusions to specific rites of the Church, but in the way suffering is deemed an inevitable part of the fallen world and necessary for salvation, and death, far from a state to be feared, provides passage to the other world where the soul is freed from the prison house of the body and can achieve eternal life. This ruling idea in Christianity, from St. Paul to John Calvin, is implied even as late as *The Devil Probably* in which Charles, though contemplating suicide, admits a belief in eternal life. Those too quick to declare the cynicism in Bresson's later films as proof of his renunciation of the faith they take for granted in the earlier ones underestimate the force of both tendencies in his work.

I would argue that the perceived shift in Bresson's perspective is more a matter of emphasis and style than an alteration of fundamental convictions, and that the religious dimension is no more unmitigated up to *The Trial of Joan of Arc* than it is entirely absent from those films that defy or question the existence or relevance of God.[9] It is my view that from *Mouchette* on, Bresson found a way to insinuate religious or spiritual motifs in his films through aspects of the narrative or cinematographic strategies without making their meaning explicit. Although such allusions might escape us initially, on closer examination they are discernible enough to warrant acknowledgment. In the analyses of the later films, I refer to these tendencies and the associations they evoke as Bresson's *sacred indirections*, a term that allows such phenomena to be understood as part rhetorical and part cinematographic and does not presume that they are conscious and deliberate in every case.

This does not preclude the paradox of his films, the grimness of which would *almost* not be out of place in the world of Maldoror, whose gaze encompasses the most hideous workings of nature, human and otherwise, and whose image of the Creator is that of a cruel and perverse torturer who revels in the sufferings of his creatures.[10] So unredeemable does the world seem that "Maldoror will want to kill a child so that it may never reach the complete repulsiveness of the adult."[11] Bresson's view of the unavoidable corruption of childhood, similar to that of Bernanos, could be reconciled with this sentiment were it not for his presumed faith in a different Creator.

Indeed, in *Lancelot of the Lake* and *L'Argent* the idea of design is no less difficult to dismiss, as if both were enactments of that "theo-rhetoric" in which "primary religious dramas emerge *through the texture* of literary texts—they appear fleetingly but continually, in fragmentary and degraded forms but with constant urgency."[12] Though God and faith are still at issue in *Lancelot*, it is less easy to see *L'Argent* in this vein. Yet it can be argued, contrary to what seems final evidence of Bresson's doubt, that faith can counter the evils of the world, that the tendency toward sacred indirection affects the trajectory of this narrative as well. Perhaps more than any other film, *L'Argent* challenges the tension between a spiritual perspective and an aesthetics that remained a constant force of Bresson's work. Anne-Marie's unwavering determination to alter the life of the recalcitrant Thérèse in *Les Anges du péché* metamorphoses in *L'Argent* into the relentless drive of the film's form and editing structure to reach its apotheosis, in which another last-minute surrender to the Law is the external sign of internal spiritual rupture. That Bresson said while shooting *L'Argent*, "I felt I was doing things more intuitively," suggests how persistent and deeply embedded his moral and aesthetic convictions were.[13]

What compels the viewer, then, in Bresson's work? Is it an example, as Nietzsche said of higher culture, of the "spiritualization of cruelty"? Or is it closer to the severest of Athenian and Shakespearean tragedies, in which the light and ritual of art transform the suffering of the world into a contemplative spectacle? In the *Poetics* Aristotle tells us that although the sight of certain things gives us pain, we enjoy looking at imitations of them. Films are capable of mimesis beyond what Aristotle could have imagined, yet Bresson's work, though committed to the inherent realism of the medium, places the concept of imitation in question. It is therefore, as with any great artist, to his style that we must look for the key to his unparalleled achievement.

The Question of Style

Significant form is a matter, above all, of reduction—of saying complex

things in the fewest syllables, with nuance and implication doing most

of the work. Economy is the guarantor not simply of aesthetic

force—the lapidary, the aphoristic—but of truth.... Why should

one brush mark be necessary when twenty would do.

—T. J. Clark, *The Sight of Death: An Experiment in Art Writing*

What should we call the style of a filmmaker who was sometimes drawn to religious subjects, determined to rid his work of dramatic and narrative excess, and bent on perfecting filmic form through the refinement of cinematographic properties? Can one word or concept embrace all of these aims and the entire body of work? The filmmaker Eric Rohmer said he "didn't know what category to put Bresson in. You could very well say that he is above categories."[14] Thus while Bresson was bent on distilling and stripping down filmic form and purging it of dependence on the theatrical, he was nevertheless deeply committed to literature.

In addition to Diderot, Bernanos, Dostoevsky, and Tolstoy, he adapted a prison memoir for *A Man Escaped* and used historical documents for *The Trial of Joan of Arc* and various medieval legends for *Lancelot of the Lake*. Of the films credited with original screenplays, only *Les Anges du péché*, with a screenplay by the playwright Jean Giradoux, and *The Devil Probably*, written by Bresson, are virtually free of preexisting sources. *Au hasard Balthazar* draws much of its plot, theme, and cast of characters from Dostoevsky's *The Idiot* and Apuleius' *The Golden Ass*; *Pickpocket* barely disguises its debt to *Crime and Punishment*. In every case Bresson cut to the essence of the work, casting away everything that distracted from the fundamental questions with which all of his films are concerned.

Writing about the first half of Bresson's career, Susan Sontag distinguished the "spiritual" quality that she believed resulted from his stripping down to essentials, from the "explicit religious point of view" to which she believed he was committed.[15] In light of subsequent film history, this must be qualified. Over the past thirty years the work of many filmmakers, mostly European, has assimilated key elements of Bresson's films: tightness of narrative and editing structure, paucity of dialogue, intensity of focus, minimal acting, and overall spareness.[16] This late twentieth-century European film style is convincing evidence of Bresson's influence, a testament to his ambition to chasten the art of the cinema or, as he put it, to distinguish the *cinema* as it was generally practiced from *cinematography*, his word for the art he practiced.

Not surprisingly, what is not prevalent in the work of those he influenced but is all over the place in Bresson is God. One must wonder, then, whether describing his style as "spiritual," however abstrusely we use the word, would have occurred to anyone had there not also been an implicit religious dimension. The Catholic André Bazin, writing eloquently on *Diary of a Country Priest*, was more struck by Bresson's marriage of literature and cinema, using words like abstraction and stylization and reserving spiritual to describe three specific moments in that film.[17]

Before becoming a filmmaker, Paul Schrader wrote a study of what he called "transcendental style" in film, which included Bresson.[18] Describing the films as pursuing a certain stasis linked to sacred art, this style seems more connected to the religious in that the films climax in a transcending of the everyday that bestows spiritual meaning retroactively. Like Sontag, Schrader does not examine Bresson's films after *Joan of Arc* and implies that they might not qualify as "transcendental," which suggests that the category is not comprehensive enough to account for all of Bresson's art. I would argue that the endings of Bresson's films do achieve a transformative *effect*, which, through the coalescence of moral, emotional, and psychological tensions that pervade the narrative, leads the viewer to a higher plane of comprehension. The last words of the priest, read over the soundtrack as a cross fills the screen in *Diary of a Country Priest*; the triumphant walk of Fontaine and Jost into the night paced to the "Kyrie" of Mozart's *Mass in C-minor* in *A Man Escaped*; the disappearance of Joan's body from the stake accompanied by a drum roll in *The Trial of Joan of Arc*; the gentle movement of the water over Mouchette's drowned body to the strains of Monteverdi's *Magnificat*; the sheep and their clanging bells surrounding the dying Balthazar: these are memorable crystallizations of thematic and aesthetic resonance, although none of them involves a character reversal. The effect differs from the idea of "transcendence" in that it does not preclude psychological credibility and, particularly in the later films, may coexist with a certain cynicism.

Recent studies indicate that terms such as spiritual and transcendental have not been abandoned, although the more ambiguous nature of the later films has made it even more difficult to define the terms clearly.[19] As a result, a cloud of unknowing has enshrouded the Bresson persona and filmography, making it difficult to see, much less write about, the roles played by psychology and sexuality in the films. An investigation of these sheds light not only on the subject matter and moral tenor of Bresson's work, but on the asceticism of his style, his insistent use of nonprofessionals, his "models," and on the filmmaker himself.

From *Diary* on, in fact, we might say that Bresson did not simply discover the means by which he would impose his vision of the world; he became a God-like author of that vision, whose compulsive control over every facet of each film—a stance by definition antithetical to the egoistic personalities of actors—effectively *re-created* the world in the image and manner in which he believed it *was* created. That nothing is left to chance in the construction of his films echoes the idea that human lives are predetermined. In light of this, it is not an exaggeration to suggest that Bresson, like Bernanos, may have felt "called" to his vocation and that, regardless of what he believed, he behaved as if he were one of God's chosen messengers.

The only way to justify such a claim is to examine in depth the narrative, thematic, psychological, stylistic, and cinematographic richness of Bresson's work. My approach in this book is to consider every film a chapter in the unfolding of Bresson's convictions and in the refinement of his craft, even the early films often characterized as not yet "Bressonian." Though they might be seen within the grand tradition of classic French cinema, *Les Anges du péché* and *Les Dames du bois de Boulogne* are underrated gems that reveal Bresson's efforts to infuse the conventions of the cinema with a quality that elevates both above the confines of melodrama. As a result, they already embody, thematically and structurally, the theme of spiritual regeneration.

As Bresson moved on, the drive to hone those conventions became inseparable from the moral convictions underlying the work. The rigorous results of the former allow us to view him in the context of modernism, as it was defined by Clement Greenberg, one of its foremost witnesses: "The essence of modernism lies, as I see it, in the use of the characteristic methods of a discipline to criticize the discipline itself, not in order to subvert it, but in order to entrench it more firmly in its area of competence."[20] Consider this in light of a declaration in Bresson's own small bible of film aesthetics: "A sigh, a silence, a word, a sentence, a din, a hand, the whole of your model, his face, in repose, in movement, in profile, full face, an immense view, a restricted space, each thing exactly in its place: your only resources."[21]

Although Bresson's style increasingly distilled or eliminated much of what comprised conventional narrative cinema, few narrative filmmakers have so persistently worked toward the "entrenchment" Greenberg notes. His aim was neither to subvert the illusionism of film nor to create an aesthetic of deficits. As his statement conveys, he wanted to clarify and intensify what we see and hear, to sharpen our appreciation of film's powers of articulation. The list just cited evidences not only the discipline Bresson brought to his craft but *the sense of equality* he ascribed to each and every element of a film. This cannot be overstated. Bresson never formally theorized his ideas about the cinema, but if his approach can be said to have an affinity with anyone's theory, it might be Pasolini's idea that "cinema expresses reality with reality....It is nothing more than the 'written' manifestation of a natural, total language, which is the acting of reality."[22]

In regard to the second point, that the urge to discipline the medium was inseparable from his underlying moral convictions, consider the words often used to characterize Bresson's efforts: *chastening, cleansing, purging, purifying, renunciation*. They might easily apply to the labors of a novice entering the religious life, fired by the belief that to reach spiritual perfection one must renounce the world and its pleasures. It is the theme and guiding principle of great mystics such as John of the Cross and Teresa of Avila. Such words remind us that Bresson was on a mission to create a form of cinema that would be the perfect instrument of his view of the world. In order to create it, he had to give up familiar pleasures. In the process he merged two missions: first, by ridding the cinema of what he believed did not belong to it, he created an object more suited to the interior core of his stories and the moral imperative that motivated them; second, in the process he provided a model of how to narrate a film in purely cinematographic terms. Although, like Pasolini, he founded his approach on the "natural" language of the world—the language of action, behavior, corporeality, and written and spoken words—he strove to concentrate the means of the cinema toward a more forceful enunciation of that *given* language to which we are generally indifferent.

Bresson's artistic method was not only about de-theatricalizing and refining the filmic object, but also about focusing the material world into a pristine embodiment of a singular idea: the progress of an individual, or "soul" as he might say, *through* the world. To this end, every image, every action, every word, every sound is in service. The paradox is that the more he disciplined the methods of his craft, the closer he came to creating a genuinely materialist cinema, and the more materialist it became, the closer it approached that condition some have labeled "spiritual" because it was sparer than the style of anyone else. As we will see, this strategy characterized his approach to acting as well; character is revealed not through the actor's expansive methods of internalizing and projecting feelings, but through the external, material signs of action and gesture. These are the idiosyncratic means of a truly unique modernist.

Cinematography in Action

Rapports, Bresson asserts in an early interview, is the essence of cinema. Although the word in French has a variety of connotations, he was referring to the way everything in a film relates to everything else, that *rapports* were at the heart of the art of film. This may sound commonplace, but the fact that the average narrative movie includes actors, sets, and props, is lit in various ways, shot from specific camera angles, and edited in a particular order does not guarantee that all of these things relate meaningfully to each other. During their dominant years, Hollywood movies, with notable exceptions, shared the same look and moved at the same pace because studio films were designed, dressed, shot, and cut by art directors, set designers, cameramen, and editors under contract. These conditions did not always doom a film to predictability. In the hands of strong directors, those we call *auteurs*, the system could produce a more personal, high-quality product. A similar distinction was true of the European cinema.

When Bresson stressed the importance of the relationships of a film's concept to its images, its edits, its sounds, and its structure, he was drawing attention to what a work of film art *should* be, and so, though he used the same conventions that other filmmakers did, he concentrated their individual strengths, controlled their specific roles, and held them accountable to the aesthetic of necessity. To this end, his reduction of the material before the camera and his tailoring of every element to a specific purpose were ways to diminish the impact of those out-of-bound features to which most narrative films are prone. Cinematography and sound are thus also diluted in order to bring visual and audio elements to a condition purified of extraneous "chemicals."

Unlike most classic narrative cinema, Bresson's films after *Diary of a Country Priest* do not lay out settings and lead us from the general to the particular. They often begin with a detail in close-up, for example a hand engaged or about to be engaged in an action. The approach favors metonymy over the metaphorical resonance we see in the earlier films. In *Les Dames*, for example, the lovers meet for the first time by a waterfall, the site of a later, critical rendezvous that transforms their relationship; Hélène, the woman who engineers the plot, is seen ascending in the elevator while her victims are seen descending.

The great stylists of the medium use strong visual compositions to accumulate emotional and thematic impact. To recall the "Rembrandt" lighting and mise-en-scène of Dreyer's *Day of Wrath* (1943) or the deep focus shots in Welles's *Citizen Kane* (1941) is to confirm how brilliantly photographed compositional design, charged with symbolic significance, imprints an indelible picture on the eye and mind of the spectator. An entire sequence can be summoned by gazing at a still from such films. Though it would be presumptuous to insist that this is never true of Bresson, even after *Diary* it is much less common; more important, it would not be a result of elaborate mise-en-scène, as is the case with Welles, Dreyer, and any number of filmmakers, in which a totalizing picture can be formed from a still that captures a moment. The very juxtaposition of these terms is instructive: *picture* connotes stasis, whereas *moment* connotes a temporal fragment. Bresson's films, moving unwaveringly in time, resist the seductive forces of inertia.

Mobile framing can be similarly distinguished. Tracking shots in *Day of Wrath* or in Mizoguchi's films deepen the connotations of the mise-en-scène, metaphorically linking the moving camera to such themes as fate, desire, or the transience of life, providing authorial commentary on the action. An example of this in early Bresson is the somberly paced tracking shot preceding the lovers who have ended their affair in *Les Dames*. In accord with the scaling down of stylistic flourish, Bresson eliminated such gestures by the mid-1950s, moving the camera only in brief runs to reframe a shot, and always in conjunction with a character's movements or perspective, creating what one scholar has called "the two-part shot."[23]

Yet certain moments in later films suggest that his work was not *exclusively* metonymic. In the spirit of Peter Brooks's subtle distinction—namely, "narrative as something *close to* pure metonymy without metaphoric arrest" (italics mine)—some elements and objects in the films, though belonging to the world of the fiction, nevertheless assume metaphoric or symbolic value. The woods in *Mouchette* are a primal image of the harshness of provincial life, where animals are trapped and killed and Mouchette loses her virginity. Balthazar is a real animal, but also the repository of virtues of which the film's characters are bereft. But in those films with a documentary-like aspect—*A Man Escaped*, *Pickpocket*, *Joan of Arc*—the metonymic dominates, linked to the increased economy and precision Bresson pursued in the late 1950s and early 1960s.

Editing and Framing

Of all the elements of film that Bresson sought to refine, editing is perhaps the most critical, a category of *rapports* important not only to the rhythm of his films but to their underlying ethos. Bresson employed continuity editing, shot-countershot, and crosscutting, but they all take on an urgency that is anything but standard. Here lies the critical importance of *looks* in his films. With fierce clarity, their effect, figuratively speaking, is to empty the frame of any static pictorial tendency and direct us to the ongoing energies of the work, to each moment's *rapport* with the next. Gathering impetus befitting the surge of the narrative and its interstitial connection to form, looks are not just the eyes but also the pulse of each film, "bind[ing] persons to each other and to objects."[24] It is through Fontaine's looks in *A Man Escaped*, including those not actually directed at an object but registering an alertness to a distant sound, that we experience the environment of the prison, attuned to every move and anticipating every cut that leads to his freedom. Looks are not the only generators of the cut, but they carry enough intensity even to penetrate and linger past a fade-out between shots. Along with hands and doors, looks achieve an iconographic status in Bresson's work well beyond the norm.

An equally important, no less elevated convention is the elliptical cut. As early as *Les Anges* we see that this technique is used not only to collapse space and time in the interest of narrative economy, but as an instrument of each film's thematic trajectory. In *Les Anges* key developments are elided, as if the film's structure were ruled by the same urgency that seizes the protagonist, Anne-Marie. The moral force underlying this welding of narrative and filmic form is an important aspect of Bresson's cinema.

Not least of the forces behind the effectiveness of editing in Bresson is the way each shot is framed to isolate an action that by its very thrust anticipates a cut. This becomes more prominent after *Diary*, when the style, drained of atmospheric and ornamental potential, concentrates on the primary action of a shot. Its centrality is enforced by a more exacting concern for the right- ness of a camera angle and of the moment to cut, both dictated by the essence of an action and its connection to an adjacent action. The action, as implied above, may be simply the look of a protagonist so forcefully projected off screen by what Bresson called "the ejaculatory force of the eye" that it antici- pates the cut. This efficient use of filmic elements creates the *impression* of the unrepeatability of each shot, a remarkable feature of Bresson's work and no small contribution to its realistic dimension. Rather than depict, describe, or elaborate on action, the films are synonymous with action. A description of thirty or forty sequential shots from virtually any section of his films from the mid-1950s on would require one, two, or three transitive verbs per shot.

A Man Escaped and *Pickpocket* are exemplary in this respect, but even *Balthazar*, a more leisurely narrative with the most passive of protagonists, follows suit. The prologue, consisting of twenty-eight shots, contains twice as many actions and includes dialogue in only six shots. By this point (1966), the midriff of the body was as important as the face, since it privileges the pivotal section of the anatomy that governs movement and often displays what hands are doing. The action of the prologue is not primarily conveyed through expositional dialogue, but through each gesture, look, and action in succession.

The Sounds of the (Filmic) World

The leanness of Bresson's style is bound to his use of sound, which he made especially acute in order to avoid visual redundancy and further condense the style: "When a sound can replace an image, cut the image or neutralize it."[25] In the last twenty minutes of *A Man Escaped* sound measures the spatial distances between the two prisoners and the guards and between the prisoners and the world beyond the prison. It marks the intervals between movements of the escapees as it does the duration of the entire operation. It materializes the dangers of the environment—the gravel crunched on the roof surface, the wires stretched across the walls. It both displaces and conceals action, such as the murder of a guard.

Beginning with his first color film, *Une femme douce*, sound assumes, more emphatically than it had previously, the critical role of bridging shots, replacing fades and dissolves, which color made it impossible to control. Overlapping sounds affect how we perceive the past and present of that narrative. In the tournament sequence of *Lancelot of the Lake*, the sound sometimes collapses the distinction between cause and effect, reinforcing the sense of the inevitable. In his late work sound is often the most pronounced of Bresson's strategies, the primary carrier of design, an instrument so intimately linked with editing as to further intensify the propulsion of the action. At several junctures in *L'Argent* the juxtaposition of sound and image or sound and sound carries the greater implications of the action.

Apart from their importance to narrative and theme, sounds have a startling eloquence. In *Lancelot* and *L'Argent* the tonic physicality of sounds bestows tactility to objects. Their resistance to being swallowed up in an illusory, nebulous flow renders them preternatural. From the first image of *L'Argent*, a close-up of an outdoor ATM machine, over which we hear street traffic, sounds are as calculated and isolated as images, their registration and textural effects precisely controlled. We cannot tune them out as we do the sounds of the world around us or in conventional movies. In some instances a sound beginning at the end of one shot belongs to and overlaps into the next. At other times the sound in a shot is fazed out before the cut, leaving a second or two of silence as if to prepare us inwardly for the next shot. This too is apparent in the first shot of *L'Argent*, as the sounds of traffic diminish before the end of the credits. These moments, though brief, provide caesurae within the architecture of the soundtrack. Silent only in relation to what we hear before and after, they function as stressed intervals in a musical composition and assail the idea of an illusionary continuum in which the viewer is indifferently immersed.

It should not be surprising that spoken dialogue is subject to the same control. Bresson felt that voices were of paramount importance. He told more than one interviewer that he often telephoned a potential model even after seeing him or her to be sure that the voice suited the character he had in mind. One way to perceive the distinct quality of speech of Bresson's models is to listen to the dialogue without watching the film. The contrast between *Les Anges du péché* or *Diary of a Country Priest*, for example, and *Balthazar* or *Lancelot of the Lake* is the most obvious indicator of how this element changed. One senses in the first two an integration of speech and action; there is little or no disparity between the expression, tone, and projection of an utterance and its immediate effect on listeners. As a staple of classical cinema, speech, fusing the skills of acting and locution that we expect from highly trained professionals, belongs quite naturally to the world depicted. In the latter two films, however, dialogue has an estranged quality, not only because it is spoken by nonprofessionals, but as a result of the director's insistence that it be emptied of familiar expressivity. The meaning is clear, but the delivery tends to be directed past its target, "as if it were reported by someone else...where the character speaks as if he were listening to his own words...hence achieving a *literalness* of the voice, cutting it off from any direct resonance."[26] This is often compounded by the nature of the dialogue itself, composed of broken or unfinished phrases, sentences that seem to emerge from or go nowhere, and sudden, blunt exclamations. Here, as he has in every facet of his art, Bresson refuses to concede the ground to the naturalistic norm, making the sounds of the world, human and otherwise, as important as shots and editing, potent instruments of artistic signification.

Color

An important element of Bresson's last five films is color. As any film scholar concerned with style and aesthetics knows, trying to describe the role of color can be a doomed exercise since one must contend with the sad fact of film's mortality. Without access to mint-condition prints, or as close to that as possible, one is forced to watch prints with faded or distorted color. Even excellent quality DVDs are a mixed blessing, since they too are based on prints of varying quality, and, because DVDs are a different technology, they cannot duplicate the accuracy, density, subtlety, or temperature of a color as these are registered on celluloid. Often one must rely on memory and notes of the original to identify colors as accurately as possible. I have seen the rarest of Bresson's color films (*Four Nights of a Dreamer* [1971], *The Devil Probably*) several times in original, pristine, or near pristine prints and have seen each film many times since in less than perfect prints, or on VHS or DVD. I have seen the others (*Une femme douce*, *Lancelot of the Lake*, and *L'Argent*) many more times in excellent quality prints as well as in other conditions and formats. No less than sound, color is carefully articulated, whether it establishes a pattern of thematic association, infuses a scene with an emotion suppressed in the dialogue and acting, or simply lends a vibrant sensuality to the world of the narrative. Although I make observations along these lines throughout the book where relevant, there is no gainsaying the difficulty of making confident assertions about this dimension of Bresson's last five films. If nothing else, I hope that this book plays a small part in encouraging producers and distributors to make new prints of all of Bresson's films and make them widely available.

The Model and Characterization

Commercial narrative films are often evaluated in terms of whether or not characters are realistically conceived and behave credibly, even though we know that actors have ready-made personas, including publicized private lives, that unavoidably bear upon their fictive incarnations and on the way audiences perceive characters and performances. This strange, unquestioned situation would not do for Bresson, whose initial experiences convinced him that the professional "actor in cinematography might as well be in a foreign country. He does not speak its language."[27]

Certain films of the 1940s—*Brief Encounter* (1945), *Bicycle Thieves* (1947), and *Louisiana Story* (1948), all three of which once made Bresson's list of "the ten best movies" of all time and all released between *Les Dames* and *Diary*—must have influenced his thoughts about actors.[28] The first, with professionals, brought a new realism to the British cinema; the other two used nonactors as part of the neorealist and documentary movements, as did Rossellini in *Open City* (1945) and *Paisa* (1946). Rossellini used real monks to play the saint and his followers in *Flowers of St. Francis*. More than likely, Bresson was affected by such developments, although his idea of the actor differs from these examples since he also discouraged the "natural" expressivity endemic to the amateur and typical of Italian neorealist cinema. Bresson almost never used the same actors twice and avoided those familiar through other filmmakers' works.[29] This was contrary to the practice not only of classical Hollywood filmmakers such as John Ford and Howard Hawks, but also of independents such as John Cassavetes, who made the interactions of the private lives and cinematic personas of his friends and relatives the subject of his films.

In short, Bresson opposed not just professional actors, but *acting* itself. He thought it generated a false effect at odds with the medium. Acting interfered with the execution of the filmic text—an ensemble of image, sound, and the relation between shots—by disrupting the rhythm and tone that made it work. If cinema was a matter of *rapports*, nothing should stand out at the expense of anything else. In traditional movies, the actor unavoidably disrupts this *rapport*; he or she does not just occupy the image, but dominates it, often rendering other features irrelevant or invisible. By definition, the professional actor draws attention to personality and invites the viewer, according to Bresson, "to search for talent on his or her face" rather than look at the film as a whole.

It was critical, therefore, to find the right "soul," as Gregory Markopoulos said,[30] especially the right face. As Bresson put it: "Model: all face."[31] The long takes of Claude Laydu in *Diary of a Country Priest* suggest that Bresson had found not only his ideal priest but the model of the male protagonists in subsequent films. Having to work with the wrong face and personality in *Les Dames*, the actor Paul Bernard, convinced him of what he did not want. His feelings on the subject were apparent from the first, but it was only in the 1950s, with *Diary*, *A Man Escaped*, and *Pickpocket*, that they became a component of his aesthetic.

The three principal "models" in *Pickpocket* were amateurs with no ambitions to become otherwise. To hear them describe years later how they were directed to speak their lines, move their heads or arrange their bodies, and cast their looks off screen is to understand that Bresson thought of "performance" as something the *entire* film was doing, not just the "actors" in it.[32] The actor is one instrument, along with framing, lighting, editing, and sound, and it is usually these elements that displace the most dramatic "actorly" scenes. In place of facial expressions of tension and rage, for example, we see falling objects, toppling tables, a skimmer clattering across the floor, impeccably shot and cut, and piercing the sonic composure of the moment. We "hear" and "see" the emotion reverberating through space, often without the agent that sparked it.

It was not unusual for Bresson to shoot fifty takes of a single action to obtain the quality he sought. Martin La Salle recalls climbing the stairs to Michel's flat in *Pickpocket* dozens of times until, out of boredom and exhaustion, he did it with the requisite indifference. Marika Green describes how Bresson determined precisely how and when she should turn her head in a certain direction after delivering a line, itself rehearsed until it possessed a flatness of tone. She was discouraged from focusing on anything of relevance to her character; no advice was given about how she should feel; in short, no adopted or learned psychology, such as of the method school type, played a role in what she said or how she said it, how she tilted her head or glanced off screen.[33]

It is hard to imagine a professional actor tolerating such direction. And since only professionals could deliver dialogue convincingly, that feature would have to be minimized as well. Even a willing professional, in Bresson's judgment, could not suppress well-honed talents or resist internalizing and projecting a role without recourse to a repertoire of familiar facial, bodily, or vocal expressions. This ran counter to his conviction that we cannot know what goes on inside anyone except through inference. In the case of a film character, this is even more true since there is no inside, only what is inferred from externals. Bresson's aesthetic forbids actors to supply this "inside" through learned signs and mimesis, a limited range that converts the interior into a ready-made projection of overused codes, the falsity of which, in his eyes, is betrayed by the unerring, scrutinizing camera.

He insisted that each shot should resist the kind of closure that a professionally calculated expression or line delivery might produce: "If an image, looked at by itself, expresses something sharply, if it involves an interpretation, it will not be transformed on contact with other images."[34] As we have seen, the edict applies to Bresson's overall aesthetic. If an actor renders a vivid expression or interpretation, especially via a well-delivered line of dialogue, he or she insulates the shot in which this occurs from those before and after it. Keeping the shot open to the "response" of others precludes such insulation. The rhythm and movement of the film depends on how each shot anticipates and infects the next. Even, in fact *especially* brilliant acting halts, prolongs, or otherwise determines the rhythm of a film. This is deadly for Bresson's aesthetic, where what is important is how the *character*, not the performer, *acts*.

One remembers a Bresson film not for a performance but for the accumulated effect of the world created. This is beyond a theory of acting. He holds the cinema accountable to the same rigorous principle as he does the actor, cleansing it of rehearsed artifices and drawing from its "soul" whatever truth it is capable of revealing. No less than the body, face, and personality of the actor, the body, image, and personality of each film must serve this end. Bresson's answer, then, to the question How does one create a character in a film? is from the outside in, from the accumulation of actions and gestures that reveal the self.

Thus was born the idea of the "model," a word, no doubt, carried over from Bresson's early, abandoned interest in being a painter. The model is not just an eccentric by-product of Bresson's difficulty with temperamental stars.

Nor was it a perverse invention designed to punish his audience in the cause of spiritual severity. It is essential to the thematic and philosophic meaning of Bresson's work and speaks directly to his preoccupation with the relationship between free will and determinism. Given the predetermined logic of his narratives, the elliptical nature of his style, and his control over every frame, every cut, and every sound in a system in which the human figure is only one element among others, is it any wonder that Bresson required inexperienced and pliable individuals? Models, whom he often referred to as automatons, were critical to his project. They were forbidden to see daily rushes lest they form a premature concept of their characters. Only by living with the unknown, he claimed, could they maintain innocent, curious, virginal demeanors in front of the camera, eager to take the next step but ignorant of the overall design. Open to but unaware of the stratagems of their creator, the models are central to Bresson's scheme, at once automatons but, as Gilles Deleuze put it, "endowed with autonomy,"[35] which is to say that they believe they act freely, and to an extent, so do we.

As his directives to Marika Green suggest, Bresson rejected psychology as a constitutive component of how character is produced. Yet in preventing the closure that a performance might create and repudiating acting in order to leave open the image's capacity to be transformed by subsequent images, another, perhaps unanticipated opening seems unavoidable. The spectator's tendency is to fill in this void, to project motive and human need onto the character's mask-like demeanor, to apply a psychological reading to what we see. It is unlikely that this habit can be entirely vanquished. In fact, Bresson's intentions notwithstanding, I would argue that it plays an important, if subliminal, role in our comprehension, especially in those films that imply a last-minute transformation of the protagonist. Even a cynical viewer can unconsciously fantasize a *wished for* transformation, a desire to believe that some force *can* alter human behavior and effect change. If such projections were not inevitable habits of the human condition, for Bresson as well as viewers, what purpose would be served by seeking the "right" face, the "right" soul and "model"? Indeed, what could these terms mean? For this reason, I argue that Bresson's treatment of character provides more psychological credibility than is generally allowed, and more than once it plays a critical role in preparing us for the final transformations undergone by characters.

Bresson's Style as a Paradigm of Narrative Cinema

Bresson's practice goes beyond honing an individual style. His importance to film history lies in his efforts to create a paradigm of narrative cinema.

I believe this to be the real point of the distinction he made between cinema and cinematography. The former is "photographed theater," requiring acting and performance; the latter is "writing with images in movement and with sounds," an ambition akin to that of *la caméra stylo* ("writing with the camera"), the rallying cry of the auteurist polemic of the 1950s and 1960s.

Bresson's phrase, however, was not merely in sync with a contemporary polemic; it was borne out in his work as it moved further away from the dramatic accouterments of commercial cinema. Few, if any, narrative film-makers connected with *la Politique des Auteurs* were as interested in, much less steadfastly devoted to purging their work of extraneous narrative, bravura performances, and stylistic flourish. Bresson's declaration recalls the theoretical arguments of Rudolf Arnheim and Jean Epstein in the 1920s, which challenged filmmakers to sever connections with theater and literature and to exploit only those features considered inherent to the medium.

To examine Bresson's work closely is to confront the essence of what narrative cinema might be: a seizing of the phenomenologically visible and audible world of bodies and faces, actions and spaces, sounds and words, edited in an articulate order to suggest relationships and develop meaning. Moment by moment his narratives are driven by actions, gestures, sounds, and words that lead inexorably to successive actions, gestures, sounds, and words, the sum of which defines character and situation. We sense, in the art of this telling, the irrefutable logic of a life working itself through. That Bresson's style fuses that logic with the art and the character is a measure of his greatness. But he also crafted a cinema that represents a threshold in the advance of narrative filmmaking, arguably as critical as Griffith's or Eisenstein's. It is this dimension of his art that justifies a chronological focus on his work. In pursuing that approach, we encounter not simply the accumulation of themes and their resonances in style, the hallmarks of auteur studies, but the core and structural dynamics of narrative film itself.

Scene and Sequence

One way to differentiate Bresson's first three films from the later style, and traditional cinema from the paradigm of filmic narrative he strove to create, is to consider the distinction between scene and sequence, both commonly used in discussions of movies. In respect to Bresson, they should be as carefully segregated as cinema and cinematography.

The word *scene*, tied to the narrative film tradition since Griffith, the one Bresson labels "cinema," is a component of dramatic structure of the rising and falling action type. Scenes crystallize tensions in the story, bring emotions to the surface, and move toward a climax. They excel in expressive and expository dialogue and the clashing of conflicting wills. Acting is the primary vehicle of scenes, the motor of traditional theater and movies, which allows actors to do what they do best: to demonstrate an emotional depth appropriate to a situation and to reinforce the credibility of the scenario and the character's place within it. Such scenes proliferate throughout the history of narrative cinema. Most, if not all, famous performances in film history can be encapsulated by recalling key scenes, those moments often rewarded with prizes.

Considering how much rides on the impact of an individual scene, it is surprisingly difficult to pinpoint what is meant by the word and to support a definition of it by reference to the 2,500-year-old tradition of theater. A commendable scholarly source tells us:

> The division of the act of a drama into scenes is less logical or scientifically systematic even than the division of the play itself into acts. This is partly due to the lack of agreement as to what should constitute a scene. Sometimes the entrances and exits of important personages determine the beginning and ending of scenes, as in French drama. In some plays a scene is a logical unit in the development of the action. Many English dramatists consider the clearing of the stage as the sign of a change of scene.... Sir Edmond Chambers [Elizabethan stage] uses scene as a "continuous section of action in an unchanged locality." Theoretically, a well-managed scene should have a structure comparable with that of a play itself, with the five logical parts [i.e., exposition, rising action, climax, falling action, and catastrophe].... The most important principle in scene construction, perhaps, is that of climactic arrangement.[36]

If there is no unanimously endorsed definition of the term in theatrical history, the question is compounded by movies. Countless films not based on theatrical works are structured like well-made plays, and others have passages that resemble Thrall and Hibbard's catalogue of scene types: "transitional, expository, developmental, climactic," and so on. Movies have so multiplied the possibilities that any setting or spatial context for an action or a performance, however limited or extensive, might qualify as a scene. The longer the list, the less likely we are to determine whether all scenes have any features in common. Is a shot of an alleyway between houses in an Ozu film, without people or dialogue, a "scene" of the "transitional" type? Does an establishing shot in a film simply set the scene to follow, or is it a scene in itself? In many films objects and spaces lack a discernible function or outlive their function, although they might add connotative significance to the narrative. Such possibilities, according to André Bazin and Siegfried Kracauer, constitute film's unique provenance, its ability to restore a sense of mystery and presence to the world, to turn objects and spaces into protagonists on equal footing with characters.

How can we distinguish a scene in a movie from a sequence? Is a sequence, as some purists would have it, more cinematic? Bazin argues that some film versions of plays achieve an intensity not possible on the stage.[37] Furthermore, although a sequence may be filmically different from a stage-like scene, it too can increase tension and develop conflicts. But whereas a scene has a certain settling-in quality in which actors move about and speak freely as if the camera did not exist and the word *cut* were not an imminent threat, a sequence in almost any Bresson film after 1950 minimizes or dispenses with acting and expansive dialogue, neutralizes features essential to the dramatic thrust of a scene, and shifts the burden of carrying tensions, conflicts, and emotions to the cinematographic register: to framing, editing, and, even more tellingly, to off screen space and sound. The laws of theater and traditional narrative cinema are thus inverted: instead of using filmic means to serve the actor and the drama, acting and dialogue are made subservient to the precision and rhythm of framing and editing. A description of a "scene" from *Les Dames du bois de Boulogne* would stress different elements than a description of a "sequence" from *A Man Escaped* or *Pickpocket*. In *Les Dames* virtually everything critical to understanding the action is present before us; the narrative can be divided into self-contained scenes that achieve dramatic closure. In *A Man Escaped* or *Pickpocket* the connective fiber of the entire work is more prominent than its division into parts. The sequences that compose them are often so dependent on sound and off screen space that they sustain the link to the larger fabric of the film, precluding the impressions induced by self-enclosed units.

This distinction has critical consequence for Bresson's work. The less a film is broken down into scenes, the more momentum it is capable of building and the more inexorable seems its trajectory. Each film becomes an engine driven by a formal and moral imperative, the force of which is channeled through the rigor of its style. In this sense Bresson's determination to rid his films of digressions, distractions, and embellishments can be understood as clearing the way for seeing, in the fullest and most exacting sense, the line-through of the narrative's focus on the steady, inflexible progression of a character toward the ultimate goal.

The Artist in and through the Work, or The Question of Psychology

The greatest effort is to make films which have some meaning in one's

personal life without straying into the confessional.

—Michelangelo Antonioni, quoted in Fabio Rinaudo, "Foyer Antonioni,"

Croniche del Cinema e della Televisione, no. 7 (December 1955)

As indicated earlier, in this book I assign an important role to psychology in understanding character behavior in Bresson's films. This may seem incompatible with my assertion that the films affirm predisposition in human affairs. But even Freud recognized the paradoxical relationship between destiny and idiosyncrasy in human behavior, although he had a very different sense of destiny in mind. As a born Catholic, Bresson was undoubtedly exposed to the Church's doctrine that although God knows and sees everything in advance, sin is still a matter of individual responsibility. The one character trait shared by all his protagonists is pride, the deadliest of sins because it defies or denies the workings of divine will. Bresson's apparent ambivalence in respect to this paradox is reflected in the "splits" that I believe characterize his late work, along with that tendency toward what I call *sacred indirection*, which implies that he did not, and probably could not, wholly abandon the powerful appeal of the Christian perspective that drove his earlier work. *Lancelot of the Lake* is a strong reflection of the split, and *Mouchette*, *The Devil Probably*, and *L'Argent* manifest the operations of sacred indirection.

The transformations of character in Bresson's early films are not incompatible with the change that ensues in persons undergoing psychoanalysis when they discover aspects of themselves of which they had only a dim sense. To allow formerly blocked feelings to surface and become integrated with the rest of one's personality is a liberating experience. The sudden embrace of a different view of reality by several of Bresson's characters would hardly convince us if we had not internalized the human phenomenon of potential change that can follow a loosening of inhibitions and a conquering of fear, both of which are equally essential to the work of psychoanalysis.

Given Bresson's strict control over characters and the models who play them, it might be alleged that there is insufficient ground to analyze character. On the contrary, in stripping characters to essentials and isolating actions and gestures as central manifestations of the inner self, Bresson gives us an *objective* basis on which to understand character, reinforcing the idea that action *is* character. Any psychoanalyst could expostulate at length about how long it takes patients to acknowledge the gulf between what they do and what they say and to recognize that every action they perform, however involuntary, is an indication of who they are and what rules their lives. Not leaving this task entirely to the actor, Bresson's films, in their concentration on action and the revelatory powers of material reality, come closer to *embodying* the inner psychology of character than any narrative filmmaker I know.

In concentrating on the films and their cinematographic, imagistic, narrative, and thematic structures, I concede to Bresson's insistence that *they* are what matter. But, as I said earlier, the relationship between Bresson's themes and his style cannot be separated from Bresson himself. An underlying conviction in this book is that there is an autobiographical strain in the work that permits us to read Bresson's films, in part, as reflections of his ethos and character. I defer to an opinion on this matter that is hard to surpass: "All the things I have to say about the artist's nature, so strangely and mysteriously dazzling, have been more or less accurately suggested by the works in question; pure poetic hypothesis, conjecture, or imaginative reconstructions."[38] For one thing, there is the similarity of Bresson's protagonists: the inner force of their personalities, their spiritual struggles, and the balance they strike between pride and passionate conviction. These similarities are stressed not only by the situations of the films, but also by Bresson's concept of the model. By restricting the model to gestures directly tied to the core actions of each film, Bresson gives greater salience to the common ground his characters share and minimizes those idiosyncrasies that distinguish them from each other.

Then there is the look of the models: their youth, the angularity of their faces, the leanness of their bodies, the earnestness of their demeanors, as well as the innocence they project despite the range of experience their roles imply. Several of the men bear a striking physical resemblance to Bresson. Finally, all his protagonists struggle with the demands of the material world and an inner hunger for spiritual release, a constant preoccupation of the films, and therefore of the artist who made them. None of this implies that there is a literal identification between every character and situation and the filmmaker; it would clearly be a fallacy to suppose that because several of Bresson's characters committed suicide, we should have expected the filmmaker to do the same.[39]

Certain biographical details are useful in analyzing, possibly even in comprehending the work. Bresson can be seen in all three of his male protagonists of the 1950s. He shares with the country priest a missionary zeal to enhance both the life of the soul and the medium through which he worked.

His experience as a prisoner of the Germans for a year during the Second World War, which, according to his widow, scarred him for the rest of his life,[40] ties him to Fontaine and was undoubtedly essential to the authenticity and conviction that suffuse every frame of *A Man Escaped*. Bresson was as consumed with the precise design and details of his art as Fontaine is with his plans of escape. As for Michel's addiction, Bresson was guilty, as one critic cleverly put it, of "picking Dostoevsky's pocket" and borrowing from other sources without acknowledgment.[41] Perhaps most tellingly, when he was asked whether, like the prisoner in *A Man Escaped* and the thief in *Pickpocket*, he often felt alone, he responded without hesitation, "I feel very alone. But I receive no pleasure from this."[42]

That Bresson once aspired to be a painter who never exhibited his work and who gave it up, allegedly, because after Cézanne there was nothing more to do, is almost certainly the inspiration behind *Four Nights of a Dreamer*. His decision to abandon painting and pursue the cinema revealed his need to carve a unique place in the history of the arts. Following the artistic credo expressed by a secondary character in *Four Nights*, Bresson strove to expunge extraneous elements and forge the narrative cinema into an audio/visual engine of drive and precision—"an action painting," to appropriate a remark of a passing character in *Au hasard Balthazar*, or a "movement image," in Gilles Deleuze's terms.[43] In doing so, he brought the cinema, in the view of many, to a threshold after which one might wonder, as Bresson did of Cézanne, what there was left to do. There have been many good and great filmmakers before and after Bresson, but few have held the cinema to such exacting standards.

Despite their clarity and rigor, Bresson's films are not free of ambiguity, a quality that parallels his evasiveness in interviews concerning both his private life and aspects of the films. Blinded by the brilliance of the work and its often spiritual quality, as well as by Bresson's resistance to psychology, critics often avoid questions of a sexual or autobiographical nature as either beside the point or disrespectful. Yet it seems clear, for example, that Bresson's preoccupation with the virginity of several characters, male and female, as well as with what he called the "unspoiled quality" of his models, is rooted in personal obsessions that no doubt are deeply tied to his view of the world as fallen, but also, perhaps, reveal a yearning to be young again, to start life afresh. Up to the time of his death he was still interested in filming the Book of Genesis.[44] Yet innocence is a short-lived period for Bresson's characters and does not survive romantic or sexual attachment or marriage. *Four Nights of a Dreamer* is a cynical parody of romance, and *Une femme douce*, the only film to deal directly with marriage, is a bitter indictment of that state. However these preoccupations played out in his life, their omnipresence in the films is indisputable, coloring his views of humanity and the world. They are therefore no less germane to an understanding of his work than such elements would be to the study of any artist in any discipline.

A great work of art outlives any interpretive method, and psychoanalysis is no more reductive or threatening than any other approach. My hope is that there are sufficient rewards in the chapters that follow to interest readers without their having to fully endorse my interpretations. Bresson transposed his own feelings and experiences, as well as his unique take on literary works, into highly individual art. My aim is to trace how this was done in each case, creating a kind of aesthetic profile wherein a close examination of the films—their narratives and themes, the way they were conceived and executed, and the way they increasingly clarify a view of the world through a chastening and crystallizing of the medium—reveals the mind and personality of an artist of enormous seriousness, complexity, and self-discipline. If I fail to convince by a less than perfect argument, I remind the reader that what follows is an entirely personal reading of Bresson's art that no doubt reflects more contradictions in the author than it perceives in the works discussed.

Although I am a practicing psychoanalyst, I was a teacher of film and literature long before, and have been an admirer of Bresson's films for more than half of my life. No less than many people whose primary response to the work of great artists in any medium is one of unadulterated love, I often cringe when I detect the meddling hand and overanxious mind of those who apply psychoanalysis—or any other theoretical method—with a broad brush, particularly when they claim to speak for every viewer. As the reader goes through this book, I hope it becomes clear that I have tried to limit applying psychoanalytic principles to those instances and films that I believe benefit from such a reading. My intention is to deepen the implications of the films' aesthetic dimensions, not to diminish or displace them, and to enhance appreciation of how much they reveal about the artist who made them.

The Book

In light of the above, the chapter titles of the book were determined in the spirit of what I have called an *aesthetic biography*. With two exceptions, they draw attention not only to a specific aspect of each film, but to its place in Bresson's chronology and to the nature of his engagement with cinema. The title of chapter 1, "Rules of the Game," refers both to the conflict faced by the protagonist in *Les Anges du péché* and to the fact that Bresson's first two features—the second being *Les Dames du bois de Boulogne*—reflect the dominant cinema of the time, epitomized by Jean Renoir's great film of the same title, while they show signs of an emerging difference. "Author, Author," the title of chapter 2, announces his mastery over the medium, as well as the way the notion of the auteur, the director as God, has a special relevance to Bresson's concept of the model and how he educed the leading performance in *Diary of a Country Priest*. "Triumphs of the Will" (chapter 3) refers both to each protagonist's overcoming of great odds in the films *A Man Escaped* and *Pickpocket* and to Bresson's realization of his aesthetic aims in their quintessential forms, a realization that goes beyond mastery of what preexisted him and toward an original conception of the cinema.

Chapters 4 and 6 share the title "The Young Virgins of the Provinces" and are separated only to retain chronological order. The former is on *The Trial of Joan of Arc*, the latter, *Mouchette*. In both, the virginity of the protagonist is central; in *Joan* it is linked to glory and sanctity, in *Mouchette* to ignominy and despair. Both attest to the importance of virginity in Bresson's work as a sign of problematic innocence, marking an invisible line between the material and spiritual worlds. Chapter 5, "The Middle of the Road," is on *Au hasard Balthazar*, which has its own virgin and is the film between *Joan* and *Mouchette*. Also set in the provinces, the title alludes to a biblical tale about the spiritual vision of a donkey, but the discussion also links the animal's proverbial stubbornness to Bresson's adherence to a highly eccentric approach to his art. The chapter's title also marks the film's position in Bresson's career as parallel to that of *The Idiot*, one of its sources, in Dostoevsky's career. Bresson's absorption with this writer is further explored in chapter 7, "Dostoevsky in Paris," through his transposition of two novellas to post-1968 Paris in the films *Une femme douce* and *Four Nights of a Dreamer*.

Chapter 8, "The Ultimate *Geste*," is on *Lancelot of the Lake*, Bresson's parable of the collapse of values in the medieval world and its effects on the meaning of individual action. The chivalric code, compromised when torn from its founding faith, leads not to triumph but to death bordering on the absurd. That Bresson wanted to adapt the legend twenty-five years earlier makes the film an especially resonant barometer of his shifting convictions. Chapter 9, "Angels and Demons," links Bresson's two final, bitter meditations on the state of the contemporary world. In *The Devil Probably* a Parisian student arranges his suicide as a protest against society and the failure of its institutions. *L'Argent* is named after the value, money, called the "visible God" by one character, that seems, literally and figuratively, to rule the world. Set in Paris, both films reach beyond the insular worlds of the provinces, but

L'Argent evokes a more global phenomenon that threatens to erase all competing values.

The ruling assumptions behind this book are, first, that Bresson's aim was nothing less than the defining of cinematographic narrative; second, that he was one of the preeminent moralists of the cinema; third, that the rigor of his style is directly tied to that moral imperative, constituting one of the most effective fusions of theme and form in the history of film; fourth, that this fusion is marked by a unique strand of modernism, in which everything extraneous to the revelatory purpose of form is increasingly excised; fifth, that psychology plays an important, underrated role in his work; and last, that because Bresson's films compose an indelible portrait of their maker—as would the collected work of any idiosyncratic artist—they constitute an aesthetic biography, however incomplete, that can be richly illuminated through the diligent application of psychoanalytic investigation. My task in this book is to demonstrate the soundness of these convictions.

If you hear the word that ties you to another human being, do not listen to any others that follow—they are merely its echo.

—Catherine of Siena, quoted in *Les Anges du péché*

To set up a film is to bind persons to each other and to objects by looks.

—Robert Bresson, *Notes on Cinematography*

I

Rules of the Game

Les Anges du péché

What can we infer from the fact that Bresson's first feature is about the following and breaking of rules? Or rather, about unquestioned adherence to rules versus pushing them to their limits, testing their efficacy? No protagonist of Bresson's faces such a situation more literally than the novice Anne-Marie in *Les Anges du péché* (*Angels of Sin*, 1943).[1] Leaving the secular world to enter a world behind walls governed by strict codes of behavior, she soon reveals an impatience to enact her vocation more earnestly than those around her, much to their chagrin. As with all such protagonists, her pride must be curbed; but when it is, it becomes clear that her irrepressible fervor was but the sign of a deeper spirituality.

If Bresson can be said to have had a similarly impassioned novitiate, it would certainly comprise this film and *Les Dames du bois de Boulogne*, made the following year. Both abide by the conventions of mainstream narrative cinema, yet they are unmistakably fired with the genius of the true artist. One can clearly discern in *Les Anges* themes that resonate throughout Bresson's work and the emergence of the strong moral perspective that would come to define that work and that would tirelessly seek to discipline the form in which it is embodied. And, though it may be commonplace to observe that the coherence of a major artist's work is often discernible from the beginning, the evidence for this is often surprising. For example, if one can identify in *Les Anges* a catalyst for Bresson's subsequent preoccupation with form—his renunciation of acting, expository dialogue, and mandatory establishing shots; his attention to framing, editing, and the relationship of image and sound—it is apparent not so much in his handling of the conventions that he had inherited but in the film's subject and in the motto that determines its protagonist's raison d'être. In essence, the word that ties one person to another describes Bresson's vocation no less than it does Anne-Marie's. The pursuit of a purely cinematographic ideal through the chastening of the language of cinema is the cornerstone of his aesthetics and his filmmaking career.

He would hold filmic structure accountable to a particular scrutiny, curtailing its excesses, eliminating routine transitions, collapsing temporal relations. If editing became, increasingly, the most articulate implement of this ambition, it is because Bresson considered it the paradigm for all relationships in film, not only those between shots but those between actors and objects and the decor that surrounds them, and between action and the rhythm of images. Eventually, these relationships would be so impeccably conceived and executed that they would come to be called, whenever other filmmakers seemed to be striving to emulate them, Bressonian.

The Text

The credits on the screen attribute the scenario for *Les Anges du péché* to "R. L. Brückberger, *dominicain*, Robert Bresson, Jean Giraudoux," in that order, and the text to Giraudoux. This has not prevented some scholars from crediting Bresson alone for the scenario, "from an idea" of Brückberger's and attributing only the dialogue to Giraudoux. Jean Sémolué, for example, says that in 1943, although "the depth and extent of the subject was attributed to Father Brückberger...in reality, it was conceived by Bresson with the help of a book which Father Brückberger recommend he read: *The Dominicans of the Prisons* by Father Lelong," published in 1937.[2] Sémolué does not explain how he came to this conclusion, but some ambiguity in Brückberger's own account tends to support it. Brückberger affirms that he originally thought of making a film about the Bethany community of nuns in 1940, after seeing a film about the Salvation Army (*Les Visiteurs du Ciel*); in 1941, in a fortuitous meeting with Bresson, who was under contract to make a film but was looking for a subject, he suggested Bethany. According to Brückberger, "[Although]

Bresson knew nothing about the religious life and was ignorant of Bethany, he was immediately taken with the idea." Together, he and Bresson wrote the scenario "that remained intact until the completion of the film, and it was based on this scenario that Giraudoux agreed to do the dialogue."[3] Brückberger insists that because Giraudoux was equally ignorant of the religious life, he too appealed to the Dominican throughout the production.

If Bresson was "immediately taken by the idea," this strongly suggests that he was predisposed for personal, not only pragmatic, reasons. It is also unclear how the scenario could remain unchanged until the completion of the film while Giraudoux was writing the dialogue and "introducing the embellishments" that justified his being credited in third place.[4] Because correct attribution for a film's authorship is often a thorny, irresolvable issue, many scholars simply draw their conclusions with the benefit of hindsight, as is the case here. Sémolué, René Briot, and others argue—and their assumption is reflected in many filmographies—that as one came to know Bresson's work in later years, one could go back and identify those thematic and stylistic preoccupations that emerged more plainly in the later work. Although this tactic may bypass the extent to which early sources, inspirations, and working alliances profoundly affect even as singular a filmmaker as Bresson, it is also probably the only true test.

To be sure, the stronger and more integral the work becomes, the stronger the argument for attributing authorship by hindsight. In the case of *Les Anges du péché*, Father Brückberger's interest, as his allusion to the Salvation Army film indicates, seems to have been in the specific activities of the nuns of the Bethany community. It is hard to imagine, however, that anyone other than Bresson had conceived the idea of using this backdrop to tell the story of two lives coming together and forging a seemingly preordained course, ending in redemption for both. In its delineation of the roles of chance and destiny in such a story, *Les Anges du péché* establishes the narrative and thematic matrix of virtually every subsequent Bresson film. On the other hand, there is no reason to question Brückberger's knowledge of the religious life of the Dominican nuns; this undoubtedly contributed greatly to the film's convincing ambience. Indeed, it became Bresson's habit to research areas of relevance to his films in the interest of authenticity. In the case of *Les Anges*, the proof of this authenticity is on the screen, and for that neither Brückberger nor Giraudoux can claim credit.

As such knowledge is assimilated within the film's overall theme and style, so too, for the most part, is Giraudoux's dialogue, although it is far more expansive than would later suit Bresson. Even Sémolué, who admires the dialogue, affirms that since the playwright had already written dialogue for an earlier, unexceptional film (*La Duchesse de Langeais*), the distinguishing personality behind the success of *Les Anges* is really Bresson, since it was he who created the "very particular atmosphere" to which Giraudoux "generously subordinated" his contribution. Despite the affinity between the character Anne-Marie and Giraudoux's "fragile and inflexible heroines," the unabashed religiosity of the film is atypical of the writer's work, which usually hesitates between two ideas or beliefs rather than embrace a single-minded theme.[5] And though that religiosity was no doubt affected by Brückberger's influence, the treatment of convent life was controversial enough to generate some disapproval in the Catholic community at the time of its release.[6]

We should not underestimate Giraudoux's dialogue any more than we should Jean Cocteau's in *Les Dames du bois de Boulogne*. Both texts do their work efficiently, even eloquently, though clearly since both are authored by preeminent figures of the theater, there is a great deal more exposition and characterization than we find in Bresson's later films. Indeed the structure of *Les Anges* follows that of classical drama: a given order is challenged by a protagonist; the conflict develops through rising action, climax, falling action, and denouement; there is even catharsis. While the story and setting, therefore, are fertile grounds for Bresson's thematic interests to emerge, the dramatic structure and the dialogue that sustains it clearly posed a challenge to his ambitions as a filmmaker.

Narrative as Mandate

A prefatory note, the first of several in Bresson's work, informs us that the film will be about the "life of a French Dominican Community founded in 1867 by Father Lataste," and that the "images and details are close to the realistic atmosphere which rules in the convents and to the spirit which animates their mission." The mission of this particular convent is to rescue young women recently released from prison and offer them an alternative to the lives that led them to commit the crimes for which they were imprisoned. Some go on to begin new lives; others remain and become nuns. The dangers posed by this mission are established in the opening sequence, which details the routine by which the nuns, led by Mother Prioress, conduct their nighttime rescue operation.[7] That they do it comfortably and competently demonstrates their unanimity but also runs counter to the stereotypical image most films offer of convent life.[8] Their work done, the sisters return to the chapel with Agnès, the newest beneficiary of this practice, where the entire community has been assembled in prayer for the duration of the operation. All bow reverently before the altar as the hymn "Salve Regina" registers their solidarity and a fade-out marks closure to the sequence.

The fade-in to the next shot shows another young woman, Anne-Marie, arriving at the convent to join the order. In a touch familiar in classical cinema, we see a close-up of the door as her shadow falls across it, foreshadowing the clash that will ensue between the harmonious system we have just witnessed and, as will soon be evident, Anne-Marie's proud, independent spirit. Although from a bourgeois background, she is attracted to the work of this Order and eager to engage in it. Her manner charms the prioress, but it is apparent that Anne-Marie is ruled more by her impulses than by the convent's regimen. Though her pride blinds her to the wisdom and necessity of rules, she nevertheless poses a challenge to the spiritual integrity of the Order, urging an examination of how rules serve the essence of the religious life.

The first manifestation of this conflict is when Anne-Marie insists on accompanying Mother Prioress to the prison even though she has been told by Mother Saint-Jean that she is too new for the venture and that she should pray at their founder's grave to bring "peace" to her "troubled soul." A few moments later we see her arriving at the prison with Mother Prioress. Bresson registers this apparent exception to convent routine through one of two striking elliptic narrative tropes,[9] a strategy that will prove to be especially strong in his work. There is, to be sure, an important scene in the interim between Anne-Marie and her mother, who has come to persuade her to return home. Anne-Marie gently resists her mother's plea and, upon returning to her cell, throws the letters and photographs connecting her to the world into the fireplace (figure 1). A photo of her mother burns in close-up and the shot fades out on the image of its ashes.

In confirming Anne-Marie's resolve to reject all previous ties, this episode partly explains her eagerness to throw herself into her new life. Because both Anne-Marie's exchange with her mother and the scene in her cell are witnessed only by the viewer, he or she must presumably fill in the missing information, to wit, that these experiences have undoubtedly had an impact on Anne-Marie's subsequent, though unseen, behavior sufficient to move the prioress to reconsider the rules. Thus, when the camera fades in on the prioress and Anne-Marie at the prison in the next shot, following the fade-out on the burning photograph, we comprehend, without explanation, that Anne-Marie's previously denied request has apparently been granted.

At the prison they witness an incident in which a young woman, Thérèse, loses her temper when, while making her rounds with meals, she is mistreated by a guard. She thrusts the heavy wheeled food cart in her charge down a flight of stairs and runs off, but is caught and placed in solitary confinement.

Anne-Marie, who has already taken notice of Thérèse (figure 2), sneaks off to visit her when she hears her screaming. Thérèse complains that she is paying for a crime she did not commit. Anne-Marie's efforts to calm her are rebuffed, but back at the convent she remains haunted by Thérèse's predicament.

During the ceremony at which the sisters are given their "maxims"—randomly chosen quotes read to each of them and believed to "always fall right," that is, to miraculously suit the personality and nature of each sister—Anne-Marie is given the motto that prefaces this chapter (figure 3). Upon hearing it, she stands in deep thought, and when a sister asks if she is feeling well, replies, somewhat enigmatically, "I hear the word—The word of my maxim. I already heard it at the prison."

In the next shot she is desperately urging Mother Prioress to take her to the prison. Her abrupt manner startles both Mother Prioress and Mother Saint-Jean; the latter remarks, "Mischievous child!," to which Mother Prioress replies, "Which children should we listen to, the mischievous ones or the good ones?" The next shot fades in on a guard at the prison; it is only when he walks to the right and the camera follows that we see Mother Prioress and Anne-Marie awaiting Thérèse's release. Once again an elliptic cut marks the absence of exposition, suggesting perhaps that any explanation would be either inadequate or beside the point. It is clear that Anne-Marie's manner has won over Mother Prioress and that, mischievous or not, her spirit has once more triumphed over the rules.

Elliptic strategies of this kind can be found in many films, but their significance in Bresson, even at this stage, is that they bear directly on the moral and thematic foundations of his work. Here they appear to respond, as if by injunction, to the maxim that Anne-Marie is given, the "word that ties [her] to another human being," and to make inevitable the effectuation of its directive. In other words, the narrative structure itself, as executed through its editing strategies, is enjoined to fulfill the truth of the maxim. It is the moral conviction that underpins this connection between narrative trajectory and filmic form that, in my judgment, gives Bresson's work such undeniable force. For that reason, a subsequent parallel cut from Anne-Marie praying for Thérèse in the chapel to Thérèse, who has been released and is on her way to murder the man responsible for her imprisonment, transcends irony and implies a deeper bond as yet unclear to either character.

The next shot and scene further emphasize the tie between them. The fade-out on Thérèse standing in the hallway after shooting the man (off screen) segues into a fade-in on the nuns at work as Anne-Marie reads from the life of St. Francis. At one point she stops, insisting that she has heard the doorbell and knows it is Thérèse. Since no one else hears it, she is directed to continue reading, but she cannot suppress her excitement. The other nuns look at her somewhat critically while she exclaims, "The bell again. Why don't they open?," and finally, "I know it is Thérèse," as she closes the book, smiling radiantly, and as if by divination says, "The door is open." Her intuition is confirmed by the next long shot of the convent hall along which Thérèse is being conducted by one of the sisters to Mother Prioress.

Two striking details reinforce the structural implications of the bond motif. The first is how Thérèse's arrival is registered not simply as the next step of the story, but *indirectly*, by way of Anne-Marie's telepathic sense, as if Thérèse were being summoned, unwittingly, by the same word that rules Anne-Marie. The other detail is that although Thérèse *has* arrived, she has come ostensibly to hide from the law, and though this seems initially to mock Anne-Marie's naïve and presumptuous faith, it turns out otherwise.

Oblivious to Thérèse's real motives, Anne-Marie persists in treating her as her special project, irritating her superiors and generating conflicting opinion; many of the nuns think highly of her, yet others consider her a troublemaker. In a chorus-like scene set in the laundry, she is described by some as the closest to sainthood and by others as too proud to know her limits. The alternation of views is nicely mirrored in the mise-en-scène as the reflection of water from the large tubs wavers continually across the shots. In an exchange on the stairs, Thérèse warns Anne-Marie of the talk about her and tells her that even though Mother Saint-Jean has forbidden her to make any more prison visits, she remains Mother Prioress's favorite. Mother Saint-Jean reprimands Anne-Marie for devoting too much time to Thérèse and neglecting others, but Anne-Marie asserts that she would be betraying God and herself if she deserted Thérèse.

In keeping with the rule, Anne-Marie subjects herself to the community's judgment by going from cell to cell, asking each sister to assess her behavior. Predictably she receives conflicting responses: she is kind but stubborn; simple but conceited; clever but hot-headed; she is quick-tempered and partial but irascible; she lacks self-control but is true and simple-hearted; she is selfish, touchy, coquettish, ambitious, and obstinate and she doesn't understand people.

The situation reaches a climax during a communal gathering of work and readings when Anne-Marie disrupts the scene by protesting the presence of Mother Saint-Jean's cat, whom Anne-Marie calls Beelzebub, and the attention given it by the sisters, particularly Thérèse, who deliberately caresses it to antagonize Anne-Marie. The cat is a nice touch, allowing Bresson to connote a barely suppressed feline spitefulness between the two women, the toxic effects of which are suggested by the cat's unfettered roaming across the tables from sister to sister, an apt symbol of the spreading, unruly tension of the entire situation. On an impulse, Anne-Marie picks up the cat and hurls it from the room. In a meeting at which the nuns publicly identify each other's transgressions and accept punishment, Anne-Marie accuses several sisters of caressing an animal until an imperious Mother Prioress orders her to stop. Finally, at dinner, she defies her superiors by refusing to do her penance, after which the community decides she must leave.

But since the maxim must be fulfilled, the parallel destinies of Anne-Marie and Thérèse continue to operate. While the police conduct the investigation that eventually leads them to suspect Thérèse of murder, Mother Prioress learns that Anne-Marie has not returned home. Shortly after, we see that she has not even left the convent grounds but has lived outdoors, eating things from the garden. One night during a storm she prays by Father Lataste's grave and collapses; she is found unconscious the next morning and carried into the convent. Declared too ill to recover, she spends her last hours repenting her recalcitrant behavior and tries to convince Thérèse that though she may have behaved stubbornly, her motives were sincere. In the final scene Anne-Marie, near death, prepares to take her vows, surrounded by Mother Prioress, Thérèse, and others, as the entire community kneels in prayer. Too weak to continue speaking, she asks Thérèse to complete the words for her, a potent gesture of spiritual, and psychological, transference (figure 4). As Anne-Marie expires, Thérèse rises from her place without a word, a newfound peace and moral courage discernible on her face, wends her way through the mass of nuns, and delivers herself into the hands of the police (figure 5). The word that has tied these two together has finally been fulfilled. Their parallel destinies now fused into one, death and surrender are revealed as but two enactments of the same mandate.

The Filmic Text

The inevitability of this narrative structure, determined as it is by moral, philosophical, and thematic concerns, naturally affects the film *as a film*. Not having yet perfected the strategies that would eventually match the intensity, precision, and rigor of his thought, Bresson uses established conventions of film construction with varying results. For example, dialogue exerts a powerful effect not only on the atmosphere of the mise-en-scène but on the editing and rhythm of the film. Nowhere is this more pronounced than in the lengthy shot-countershot exchange between Anne-Marie and Thérèse near the end. Compared to the carefully balanced rhythm between dialogue and cinematographic features of the opening sequence of the film, this scene is heavily dependent on the verbal text. Thirty-six of its thirty-nine shots include dialogue, much of which verbalizes what has been more subtly implied in previous communications between these two characters.

The scene sets several tasks for itself. It must, first of all, show us a humbled Anne-Marie, fully aware of how her pride has led to her presumptuous behavior in regard to Thérèse. But although this confession redeems Anne-Marie, it begins to sound self-absorbed, inducing in Thérèse, its involuntary listener, both impatience and boredom. It is, in fact, ironic when Anne-Marie says that she now realizes that what Thérèse really needed was "someone who wouldn't talk, whose silence would dry [her] tears and calm [her] pain." The viewer might well sympathize and understand when Thérèse, in reaction to this, leaves the room, saying, "I can't stand one more minute with you.... You're lying, just trying another method. Prestige failed so you're trying friendship. You understood nothing!"

To the degree that this exchange is about contesting wills, it resembles the debates in Giraudoux's dramas between characters of opposing views. The difference lies in our awareness that despite Anne-Marie's awkward acknowledgment of her flaws, her aim is still consonant with that of the narrative, namely, to move Thérèse from moral turpitude and isolation to release and salvation. This of course is a Bressonian concern, echoed in other films.[10] As such, the scene, also burdened with this task, must continue. Perhaps because of an earlier hint from Anne-Marie that she suspects Thérèse may be hiding from something, Thérèse returns to the bedside. Anne-Marie temporarily shifts the subject to her illness, for which she also blames her stubborn nature. Thérèse appears to close off all avenues when she says that one might cure a "wounded heart" but not a "dead one," hers. To this Anne-Marie replies that the hope that such a cure could be accomplished would keep her alive, even if it took one hundred years. Startled and apparently moved by this, Thérèse tenderly places her hand in Anne-Marie's, a gesture that Bresson might not have resorted to later in his career and that even here seems a bit gratuitous. The moment's importance has already been marked by the fact that both the close-up of Thérèse reacting to Anne-Marie's remark and the following one of Anne-Marie closing her eyes are the only two in this entire sequence, except for the one that begins it, without dialogue. The scene ends with Anne-Marie's apt summation of the moment, the scene, and the narrative's aim; as the camera moves in to a close-up, she says, "Perhaps this is the first day of those one hundred years."

This scene, no less than the rest of the film, is beautifully lit, and as photographed by Philippe Agostini, who would also photograph *Les Dames du bois de Boulogne*, it achieves an ethereal quality, a luminosity to reflect its revelatory purpose. Its dramatic development, however—its emotional and thematic thrust, its stress on verbalized character interaction, its movement from distance to intimacy—is primarily carried by the dialogue. In a conventional film of the period, this would not be unusual, but typical of the French tradition of quality, which privileged writing over mise-en-scène and actors' expressions as the dominant feature of mise-en-scène. But knowing now what a Bresson film is, we naturally react with surprise at the copiousness of the text, its virtual tyranny over the scene, and its determinant effect on the editing. Given the length of the scene and Bresson's penchant, evident even in this first film, for cutting over long takes, it was perhaps inevitable that it would be broken down the way that it is. It is easy to imagine that it was precisely the dominance of language, exceeding its place as one element among others, which led Bresson eventually to deny it any such privilege. Indeed, Anne-Marie's remark, in that long bedside scene, that she understands that what Thérèse needed was "someone who wouldn't talk" might well be taken as the future motto of Bresson's leaner screenplays. That decision would affect all others: framing, camera angles, editing, narrative structure, and rhythm.

Contrast this scene with the film's opening sequence, a wonderfully assured and realized example of the Bressonian style in the making. In twenty-seven shots, twelve fewer than the scene just discussed, we are introduced to the convent's regimen and are apprised of the plans, preparation, and execution of the nuns' clandestine visit to the prison. In addition to Mother Prioress and other nuns, we see prison personnel, Agnès, the young woman being escorted safely away by the sisters, and the unidentified men they are trying to evade. All of this consumes six and a quarter minutes of screen time, one and a half minutes more than the time devoted to the scene at Anne-Marie's bedside.

Of the twenty seven shots of the opening sequence, fourteen employ camera movements. Although some of these are slight, all complement the mobilizing activity of the nuns: first, as the community is summoned to prayer, then as Mother Prioress, informed that the chauffeur is ready to take her to the prison, convenes a brisk strategy meeting before setting out. This momentum is sustained even in shots without camera movement, in which internal subject movement is framed to achieve a dynamic effect; for example, the car taking the nuns to the prison approaches quickly from background to foreground, its headlights stopping directly in front of the camera in close-up. The movement of the lights across an otherwise dark night scene on a deserted Paris street sustains the mood of danger and tension generated from the beginning. Movement is picked up and carried through in each shot. After they exit the car, Mother Prioress and her companion are seen approaching from background to middle ground in a shot again without camera movement; they appear as distant hooded figures in the night, their black habits fluttering from side to side in testimony to the hurried nature of their mission (figure 6). The whole thing has the air of an operation of the French underground, which, given the time of the film's production and release under German occupation, seems apropos. Indeed the rescue of the woman and the evasion of the menacing unidentified figures in the streets confirm this impression.

Dialogue is used in only nine shots, and much of it has that crisp, elliptical quality so distinctive of the filmmaker that it seems probable that Bresson insisted on tailoring it specifically in accord with the rhythm of the sequence as a whole. In the single shot of the strategy meeting, for example, Mother Prioress begins with a line—"I've drawn a sketch in order to avoid another failure"—that alludes to an unexplained prior event and provides only teasing suggestions of what is about to take place. Similar hints characterize subsequent lines in the same shot, such as "Don't forget to take a torch, Mother" and "We'll go right back to the taxi if all goes well." Although there is enough here and in a few other lines to spark curiosity and create suspense, it is not a full exposition of the plan. In keeping with the sense of urgency that the meeting evokes, the camera moves in at two points, animating the discussion even further.

In a further indication of the tightness of the sequence, the structure of the operation is framed by two brief scenes in the convent's chapel, one as the nuns set out for the prison and the other when they return. The nuns have been gathered and directed by the prioress, "[Pray] until we come back, for the success of our venture." As Mother Prioress leaves, we hear the assembly singing the "Salve Regina," and they are still singing it when she returns a short time later with another "angel of sin" from prison. Not only is the prayer hour a good cover for the militant activities of the convent but, in keeping with the spirit of the secret mission, it is something like the equivalent of synchronizing one's watches. The "Salve Regina" rings out and times the rescue operation, assimilating it within the province of the order's vocational aspirations. The actions of Mother Prioress and her assistants are simply another form of prayer, an equation Bresson affirms in many films and that imparts to the actions of his protagonists—such as the country priest and Fontaine, the prisoner who escapes—that quality of sacred ritual.

If the bedside sequence shows us Bresson not yet able to contend with a voluminous text in cinematographic terms, this opening sequence reveals

Bresson already in stride, with glimpses of what is to come. Perhaps unwittingly, the former sequence was, in effect a test of the conventions, in particular of the strength and limitations of shot-countershot as an effective strategy when it is prolonged *primarily* to serve the dialogue.[11] This is an important point, for there are certainly examples of extended crosscutting in Bresson's work, conceived wholly cinematographically. In *A Man Escaped* we witness what might be described as an ongoing dialogue between the prisoner and objects in his cell (e.g., the door as he works patiently to dismantle it) in a similarly restricted physical situation. But because of the way shots are framed and cut and the way we are sensitized to the man's precarious situation through the meticulous use of off screen sound, the experience of the film is total, one in which the mind and the senses are equally engaged in the act of perception. In the bedside scene in *Les Anges* the constant cutting between Anne-Marie and Thérèse is less subject to a cinematographic imperative, although one should not undervalue the beautifully lit faces of Renée Faure and Jany Holt, the actresses who play Anne-Marie and Thérèse, respectively. Nevertheless, just such an impression seems to have prompted Bresson to seek ways of rehabilitating the convention of shot-countershot editing and of freeing the cinema from, in his view, enslavement to the actor and the word.

Admittedly the bedside scene, by its very nature—requiring one character to be lying down throughout—would have taxed the efforts of any beginning filmmaker with serious ambitions. Other than trimming the dialogue, it is difficult to imagine what options would have been available to anyone working within the traditional narrative system. An earlier ten-shot exchange between the same two characters, set on a staircase, illustrates how setting and camera angle alone can enhance the shot-countershot structure when dialogue is paramount.

That the text in general presented a considerable challenge to Bresson is evident in the many camera movements he employs to offset static or stagy compositions. There are many sequences that a lesser filmmaker would have simply shot as written, treating them as pro-filmic scenes requiring no cinematic intervention. Countless examples of the practice can be cited from within the French cinema of the 1930s alone, the decade preceding Bresson's entry into feature filmmaking. One need only recall Marcel Carné and Marcel Pagnol, whose work, notwithstanding its charms, exemplified the notion that sound cinema *should be* canned theater. It was Jean Renoir who, in his films of the same period—notably, *Toni*, *Le Crime de Monsieur Lange*, *La Bête humaine*, and *La Règle du jeu*—liberated the camera from a fixed, contemplative stance and allowed it to be seized by the rhythm and dynamics of the action, catching behavior and events as if inadvertently.

Bresson's mature style clearly differs from Renoir's, yet it can be argued that the small but significant camera movements in *Les Anges du péché* owe something to Renoir, for by reframing shots and scenes in progress, often in conjunction with the movement of characters, they physically destabilize the sense of a pro-filmic space. As a constant force within the arena of action, the camera refuses to abandon the field to talking figures, thus helping to de-theatricalize the text. A noteworthy aspect of many of its moves is its peculiar consciousness of sites, the way it both responds to and exploits the architectural properties specific to the convent setting and, in the critical sequence of Thérèse's attempt to escape, to the prison setting as well. Indoors the convent is lined with corridors off of which are the individual cells of the sisters. When the camera is placed near the juncture of two such corridors, the image is framed initially to stress a diagonal recession of space. Two or more figures might pause momentarily at this juncture to converse and then move on, their exit marked by the camera's pivoting toward the adjacent, diagonally framed corridor. The effect, achieved even by a very slight move of the camera, is to authenticate the space in deep focus and to facilitate the recording of continuous movement toward and away from the camera.

Outdoors is a portico that runs along all four walls of the building, forming a square extension of the convent, surrounded by columns and enclosing an open-air garden in the center. The camera outdoors is often positioned as it is indoors or, as a variation, tracks straight back from approaching figures, pausing when they do to talk, then moving to the left or right when they move, only to reveal that it was momentarily poised once again at a dynamically pivotal juncture.

The Power of Grace

The iconography and thematic aspects of this first feature prefigure several of Bresson's later films. Not surprisingly, he found in the story and situations of this film a variety of characters that manifest the seven deadly sins. This palette is more comprehensively arrayed in *Diary of a Country Priest, Au hasard Balthazar*, and *Mouchette*, yet it is already apparent in *Les Anges du péché* that Bresson's cosmos—whether set in a convent, a provincial village, a medieval forest, or on the streets of Paris—is one in which human nature is inherently flawed, in which those characters who, in someone else's films, might embody a state of innocence corrupted by others are no less susceptible to the pettiness and weakness of the human condition than are their tormentors. That anyone in a Bresson narrative seems to transcend this condition is not confirmation of their having escaped it, but of their having come under the benign influence of what the country priest would call grace, "a gift [from God] bestowed on man's soul to enlighten and strengthen it above the measure of its natural light and strength."[12] Grace may be given or taken away and is not to be mistaken for an inherent virtue in the character. It can infuse a secular life as well as a religious one.

The concept must be understood in the light of hubris, the most serious of the deadly sins and the tragic flaw that brings down most protagonists of Greek tragedy. In action and dialogue *Les Anges du péché* expounds on the nature of pride more extensively and literally than do future works, firmly establishing this sin's centrality in Bresson's narratives. It is introduced almost immediately as the one negative feature of Anne-Marie's character. In a brief exchange she has with Agnès, a minor character who, like Anne-Marie, is a novice in her trial period, Agnès listens to Anne-Marie's assurance that she is ready for anything, insisting that she has chosen this convent because of its mission. She insists that she can handle any challenge; the more hardened the criminal, the better. In Anne-Marie's zealous anticipation Agnès discerns a potential flaw as she says, "One needs much pluck to kiss a leper—or much pride." Anne-Marie's mother cannot understand her daughter's aspirations when all she has known is comfort and luxury. And, as we have seen, at many critical points in the narrative, the conflict turns on the interaction between Anne-Marie's pride and the rule that requires humility and submission.

The concept of grace is designed to humble the prideful character, to make him or her aware that whatever is accomplished occurs through God's benevolence, not human willfulness. The concept therefore presumes the existence of God; it affirms that the intellect needs God to know anything, especially, says Aquinas, "truths that lie beyond its natural range." To grasp such truths requires the "light" of divine grace, which not only adds to the mind's "natural light" but is essential to its proper functioning. This does not preclude free will, although for nonbelievers this would be an unintelligible paradox. God's grace presumably "moves" man's mind and intellect to "accept grace freely," for "free will follows in its choice the ultimate practical judgment of the intellect."[13] There is a classification of graces specifically designed for certain ends and tasks. "Gratuitous grace…given to one person for the benefit and holiness of others," might describe Anne-Marie's effect on Thérèse and other members of the community. Anne-Marie's spiritual journey from restless novice to accepting nun can be viewed as a model illustration of the effects of grace, as described by Aquinas: "it heals the soul," "awakens the desire for good," helps one toward "actual achievement of good," "gives perseverance," and "conducts the soul to glory."[14] Are these not the stages of Anne-Marie's progress through the narrative? And does not the relationship between free will and divine grace, as articulated by Aquinas, speak to the paradox at the heart of the narrative—indeed, at the heart of most, if not all of Bresson's work?

That relationship is embodied in the motto that Anne-Marie is given and that she connects to her own instincts; when she hears the maxim, it merely confirms the word she has already heard internally. One can read here, quite legitimately, the apt convergence of individual psychology and spiritual inspiration that, in my judgment, is what makes Bresson's protagonists both compelling and credible. The elevation of the camera above the body of Sister Anne-Marie at the end of the film is a sign of this grace and its power of transmission, inspiring Thérèse, having at last been moved by Anne-Marie, to seize her own spiritual release. Descending the stairs of the convent, its walls lined with nuns kneeling in mourning for Anne-Marie—but also in unwitting tribute to the newly awakened Thérèse—she walks determinedly into the arms of the police, offering her hands to be cuffed. It is clear, from the radiant expression on the actress's face, the trajectory of the narrative, the spiritual nature of the transformation, and, not least, the surge of the march-like Grünenwald score, that an undeniable victory has been achieved, one shared by the living and the dead.

Not every film of Bresson's ends with such a pointed demonstration of the transmission of grace and the eleventh-hour transformations it engenders, but the concept is essential to understanding narrative design and characterization in his early films and should not be ruled out in the later ones. To ignore it is to devalue the moral convictions that impel the work. But since many admirers of Bresson cannot accept such an idea, clearly there must be other ways of coming to terms with the special nature of Bresson's narrative resolutions. As I suggested in the introduction, Bresson was a better psychologist than either he or any of his critics has been willing to allow. It is worth pausing, therefore, to consider what critics thought at the time of the film's release.

Since no one in 1943 would have been able to characterize the film's conclusion as Bressonian, how was the ending understood? Did Thérèse's surrender seem strained or unconvincing to contemporary viewers? Was it clear that Bresson was striving for something more than psychological truth to account for the effect of one character on another? Or is the subtle intersection between these two modes close enough to preclude confusion and disbelief? The screenplay was original, so no preexisting literary source could be used to dodge such questions, namely, by filling in relevant material left out of or only vaguely treated in the film.

In his review André Bazin suggested that the entire "subject of the film was fraught with danger," implying that the idea of a "dramatic" novitiate entering the Order of rehabilitating Dominicans and trying to "conquer the soul of a...lost woman" could easily have been botched in less secure hands. But then he simply summarizes the plot more or less at face value. Most of his attention is devoted to speculating on Father Brückberger's contribution, which he assumes was responsible for the film's "exactitude" and "the realism of the framework," elements that presumably worked against the "danger" of its being badly done. He also praises Giraudoux's dialogue, which, though "not the work of a believer... [is] an elegant synthesis of the spiritual life from the point of view of a dazzling intelligence and talent." In a brief penultimate paragraph, he says, "I have no space to expatiate as I should on the merits of director Robert Bresson and his cameraman Agostini."[15] As a French Catholic Bazin was certainly sensitive to the delicacy of the screenplay, but apparently saw no problem with the film's resolution and Thérèse's conversion, which he simply describes as the fulfillment of Anne-Marie's mission. But it is interesting, given what he says about Giraudoux and not knowing "in what measure Brückberger contributed to the scenario," that he gave no serious attention to how the film's coherent atmosphere and style could have been achieved.

Another critic, whose discussion of the film's theme and style is both detailed and sensitive, nevertheless says virtually nothing about its director, although he also fails to mention Father Brückberger.[16] The theater and film director and actor Sacha Guitry effuses over the film's perfection: "Not a lapse in taste from beginning to end...no sentimentality, no vulgarity, no pretensions....What a lesson to those who put on airs of genius....It is much better than cinema!"[17] Here too, only Giraudoux is singled out for mention, which, given Guitry's penchant for theater over cinema—he praises the film's "technique" precisely "because it is no more prominent than the beams of a beautiful abode"—is not surprising. One wonders how any critic could have ignored the fact that some unifying sensibility, other than the screenwriter's, had to be responsible for, in Guitry's own estimation, such unqualified artistic success.

In none of these considerations is there the slightest hint that the film is flawed either dramaturgically or psychologically. No one seems to have had a problem accepting the terms of the narrative, possibly because there was a natural cultural and religious affinity between the film's ethos and its critics. Yet consider what we are asked to believe: that a woman who has consorted with immoral men, has suffered for someone else's crimes, has spent time in prison harboring thoughts of revenge, has acted on these thoughts by murdering the man responsible for her situation, has lied to the nuns who have wished her nothing but good so that she can hide out in the convent, has played along hypocritically with convent rules the better to disguise the truth, has shown nothing but contempt for Anne-Marie's attentions—that such a woman could, suddenly, be so affected by Anne-Marie's persistent faith in her even at the moment of her own death that she would renounce her former rage and go willingly to face punishment. Moreover, though we too may be charmed by the spirited, irrepressible Anne-Marie, we can also understand Thérèse's exasperation with her endless efforts. All the more reason that the accent in the film's last scene is not exclusively on Anne-Marie, but on the binding force of what ties her to her mission. It is that which survives her in Thérèse, infusing Thérèse with the same moral courage that drove Anne-Marie.

If the film moves us to accept its given conditions, as any good work of art should, it must be because on some level it does not violate our understanding of human behavior, which embraces the possibility, the hope, that people can be stirred to change their lives under certain circumstances. This contravenes the view that many of Bresson's films are intelligible only to the already converted. But we engage in another kind of conversion—in life and certainly in response to artworks—that allows us to appreciate, understand, and even accept the beliefs, convictions, and perceptions of others, particularly when they are powerfully conveyed and touch common foundational aspects of human experience.

It is unlikely that this narrative would carry the conviction and force that it does if, as spectators, we could not comprehend the interaction between the characters, and between the characters and their circumstances, and believe the consequences of those interactions to be behaviorally and psychologically sound. Even if Bresson disavowed psychoanalysis, as he indicated more than once, and affirmed the bearing of other forces on human behavior, this does not preclude the spectator's applying his or her psychological understanding of how people behave and respond to worldly exigencies to characters in his films. Moreover to have such understanding does not mean that we always know exactly why anyone does anything. Neither does it rule out the inexplicable twists and turns that people are capable of, nor the existence of influences that may not be reducible to psychological or other specifiable categories. The latter are often the kinds of things some people consider, for lack of better terms, supernatural or spiritual. For one who espouses belief in God and the power of faith, life is filled with situations that take on moral gravity and spiritual meaning, and life itself is a transitory state and a testing ground to earn one's place after death in the kingdom of God. This is surely the principle behind every religious Order devoted to cleansing their members of worldly desires and fostering such virtues as charity, humility, and obedience.

I believe that the concept of divine grace was not only a religious conviction of Bresson's, at least at the time that he made *Les Anges du péché*, but that as a viewer I must *accept* this concept as a shaping principle of the film and as the explanation for Thérèse's rehabilitation at the end. I must accept it because it may be not only a private conviction of the filmmaker's but one that has suffused his treatment of narrative meaning and characterization; in short, I must accept it because it is inextricable from his aesthetic. But what *allows* me to accept it does not require a suspension of disbelief or a vacating of the rules of logic as I understand them. Nor is it exactly the same as accepting the rules of a genre, say, the horror film, by which logic a belief in supernatural events is often the norm.

In *Les Anges du péché* the premise of the narrative sets the world and its vanities against an ordered place within it, designed, however imperfectly, to cleanse the individual, whether "angel of sin" or well-meaning souls like Anne-Marie, of worldliness. It can nevertheless be seen as a microcosm of the world in which rules must be obeyed and pride conquered. However clear the contrast seems in this film, the moral contest with which the narrative is concerned is not restricted to the religious life. The camera that rises over Anne-Marie's deathbed at the end also rises above Agnès's bed at the end of *Les Dames du bois de Boulogne* after her husband's plea brings her back from her death-like swoon. It is the gesture that tells us that human love, however alloyed, remains the only reflection we have of the divine. Confessing her prideful excesses, Anne-Marie tells Thérèse that the only excuse for her stubborn behavior was that she loved her. The same words are uttered by Agnès to excuse her part in Hélène's nefarious scheme to ruin Jean, her former lover. "My only excuse," she tells Jean, now her husband, "is that I loved you." We are meant to see the first as spiritual since the love that inspires Anne-Marie leads another to renounce her hate and pride and change her life. But while the setting and the situation in *Les Dames* are secular, the effect is the same.

If art can both reflect and counter the way things are, Bresson's is among the closest to having done so. The epigraph to this chapter is included in his *Notes* dated 1950–1958,[18] yet *Les Anges du péché* demonstrates that "binding persons to each other and to objects by looks" was already the primary aesthetic stress for Bresson even though he had not yet refined his editing practice to infuse that aim with a moral force unlike any other filmmaker's. In *Les Anges du péché* the theme and moral imperative that drive all of Bresson's narratives are manifest. The task of Bresson's subsequent work would be to craft the form itself into an active agent whose trajectory would be as inevitable as that of the narrative. Form and style would thus become indistinguishable from meaning and morality. Whatever the world has done, Bresson, as *L'Argent*, his last film, clearly shows, remained strongly committed to the word that tied him to the singular pursuit of an essential, morally accountable cinema.

Les Dames du bois de Boulogne

Given its literary pedigree, a screenplay adapted from Denis Diderot's eighteenth-century picaresque novel *Jacques the Fatalist* and with dialogue by Jean Cocteau, *Les Dames du bois de Boulogne* (1945), like *Les Anges du péché*, appears to fit comfortably within the tradition of French "quality" cinema. But its affinity with the melodrama has also led some Bresson scholars to take it less seriously,[19] despite the fact that Bresson shared Diderot's interest in the conflict between free will and determinism. The Jacques of the book's title believes that "all is foreordained, 'written up above,' yet…constantly contradicts his own viewpoint by actions and feelings which are the behavior of a moral being. The novel can then be read as an elaboration in fictional form of [this] philosophical dilemma."[20] It would be hard to find a more succinct summary of the theme at the heart of Bresson's cinema.

In *Les Dames*, Hélène, a wronged woman, contrives an elaborate scheme to destroy Jean, the man who has fallen out of love with her, and a good part of the film is constructed to mirror her control over the plot. Yet although the scheme—to have Jean marry a woman with a disreputable past—succeeds, it turns out that Hélène was but the unwitting instrument of a larger design, and that, instead of disaster, she brings about a greater good than she was capable of imagining. That the narrative and cinematic design has such an aim is, in retrospect, clear from the first image: the waterfall at the Bois de Boulogne seen under the credits. The site where Hélène's plot is set in motion, it is also the place where, unsuspected by her, it comes unraveled. Hélène is trumped by something greater than herself, and the manner in which Bresson cast this struggle of moral forces takes the film beyond the aims of ordinary melodrama, in which the "apparent triumph of villainy" is dissipated with the "eventual victory of virtue."[21]

"Melodramatic good and evil are highly personalized," writes Peter Brooks; "they inhabit persons who indeed have no psychological complexity but who are strongly characterized."[22] For Brooks, Diderot's "drama of the ordinary" (not restricted to *Jacques the Fatalist*) in some ways prefigures melodrama, "itself a mode that exists to locate and articulate the moral occult," the "domain of operative spiritual values," essentially the "repository of the fragmentary and desacralized remnants of sacred myth.…Melodrama represents both the urge toward resacralization and the impossibility of conceiving sacralization other than in personal terms."[23] Watching *Les Dames* one has the sense that its melodramatic mode is indeed infused by an otherworldly residue of the mythic and the sacred. But if, on one level, the characters seem to embody good and evil, the denouement asks us to believe that people can change and that the source of that change lies in yet another kind of power beyond the world. Morality is not merely personal in Bresson but is rooted in a premodern spirituality. Indeed *Les Dames* can be viewed as a contest between the dark forces of a pre-Christian world and death and resurrection through love and faith.

Hélène evokes not only the femme fatale of film noir, before the latter term had any currency,[24] but a number of larger-than-life incarnations of the vengeful woman, from Medea and Clytemnestra to Racine's Phaedra and the title character of Keats's "La Belle Dame Sans Merci," who lures brave knights to their deaths. The darkness of the imagery associated with Hélène and the gravity with which Bresson treats her give her a near mythic aura, in no small measure reinforced by the Spanish actress Maria Casarés's hypnotic demeanor and Mona Lisa smile. Despite the problems Bresson had with her and she with him, she perfectly embodies the requisite qualities, as otherworldly as she would be in Cocteau's *Orpheus* films.[25] Though Hélène's scheme falls short of the ultimate fatalities brought about by her legendary sisters, in the context of the society to which she and Jean belong she certainly calculates his social death.[26]

The very polarities that the women of Bresson's first two films occupy (the only two with mature women in principal roles)[27]—namely, those devoted to the religious life and those of questionable morality—suggest the force of original sin in Bresson's universe. Each film has a secondary female character who must be rescued from her fallen condition. In *Les Anges* Thérèse kills the man responsible for her imprisonment and is saved by Anne-Marie; in *Les Dames* Agnès's disreputable past, Hélène's instrument of revenge, is ultimately redeemed by the power of love. To clinch the matter, at the moment of redemption Thérèse, in nun's habit, leaves Anne-Marie's deathbed a new person, just as Agnès, in bridal gown, lying as if on a saint's tomb, is roused from near death to a new, purified life. In a sense all three are novices who must die to their previous lives. Bresson's apparent disposition toward spiritual rebirth requires immoral characters in need of reformation, yet it is also true that he often links sin to sexuality and that most later characters, including the male protagonists of the three films of the 1950s and the female adolescents of the three in the 1960s, are either insulated from or corrupted through sexual initiation. To appreciate all of this is to realize that the generic frame of *Les Dames du bois de Boulogne* is largely skeletal and that Bresson had other things in mind.[28]

Just as he would qualify *Pickpocket*'s affinity with the police or crime thriller by asserting that his main concern was the strange journey of two "souls" toward each other, *Les Dames* also concerns the union of two individuals after a strange journey. The love that finally binds the unlikely couple, Jean and Agnès, is beyond Hélène's comprehension. Like Iago, whose evil schemes are underwritten by his envy of the love between Othello and Desdemona, Hélène cannot bear the thought that such a love can exist and that it can transform character. Where she miscalculates is to assume that Jean's capacities and values, sprung from the same class predispositions, are identical to her own. The denouement therefore marks the affinity this film has with its predecessor and its successors.

As determined to chasten cinematic form as his narratives are to redeem sinners, Bresson was not content simply to alter the objectives of melodrama in line with his spiritual preconceptions. He engineered the mechanics of conventional cinematic storytelling into the machinery of formal and narrative design, embedding the contest of wills directly within the connective tissue of the film's construction. Fades, dissolves, and cuts—those familiar, often redundant, tropes of sequential cinematic logic—are here loaded with moral and psychological weight, executing Hélène's calculated will even as they advance the narrative inexorably toward an end she cannot foresee. Just as Iago's designs propel nearly every move of *Othello*'s plot, Hélène's insidious plan becomes—until it is disrupted—the blueprint of the film's progression, its storyboard. The detailed analysis of the film's deployment of transitional devices (e.g., fades and dissolves) is intended to reinforce that idea, demonstrating how Bresson turned such structural conventions into instruments of narrative control. In this way the moral contest of wills that drives the narrative is mirrored directly by the alternating implications of fades and dissolves.

Diderot's Tale

The source of *Les Dames du bois de Boulogne* is an episode in Diderot's novel. The story is told by an innkeeper's wife to Jacques and his master in the course of their stay at the inn. Intended to illustrate the difference between men and women in matters of love, it is interspersed with exchanges between the innkeeper and his wife and Jacques's cynical remarks on male-female relations.

The heroine of the hostess's tale is Mme. de la Pommeraye, "a widow of high moral character, high birth, good breeding, wealth, and haughtiness," who reluctantly allows herself to be seduced by Monsieur des Arcis, who, but for his "unrestrained passion for love affairs was what one would call a man of honour." Suspecting his boredom, she sets a trap to determine whether he has fallen out of love with her. She so succeeds in convincing the marquis that she has fallen out of love with him that he immediately confesses that it is he who was "guilty" first. Mme. de la Pommeraye conceals her "fierce displeasure" while the marquis lauds the fact that by being honest with each other, they can remain friends. "Moralizing on the inconstancy of the human heart, the frivolity of oaths, of marriage vows," he boasts that they have spared themselves the reproaches, petty suspicions, and betrayals that accompany dying love affairs.

Overcome with grief, Madame vows revenge. She offers "a brilliant future" to Mme. d'Aisnon, an old friend reduced to running a bawdy house, and her daughter if they agree to change the family name to Duquenoi and follow her instructions. She sets them up in a respectable house, assumes their debts, and forces them to live a life above reproach. Feigning indifference to the marquis's affairs, she then arranges a "chance" encounter with the two women, confident that he will be charmed by the daughter's "simplicity" and "purity," qualities foreign to their own social circle. As expected, the marquis, finding Mlle. Duquenoi's face like that "of a Raphael virgin," becomes obsessed with her, and Mme. de la Pommeraye warns him that the young woman is beyond his reach.

In despair, the marquis engages in all the intrigues a man of his class would pursue to win the object of his desire, offering Mlle. Duquenoi half his fortune if she will be his mistress. Though mother and daughter are tempted, Mme. de la Pommeraye's scheme precludes any resolution short of marriage, to which, everything else having failed, the marquis finally accedes. While Mme. de la Pommeraye promises to investigate Mlle. Duquenoi's past to avoid scandal, the banns are published and the marriage takes place.

On the very next day, Mme. de la Pommeraye shamelessly confesses her scheme, telling the marquis that she has avenged his rejection by manipulating him into marrying a woman of tarnished virtue. Understandably distraught, the marquis, calling his wife an "unspeakable creature," leaves her and goes off to the country. Upon his return, his wife begs him to tolerate her presence until she can prove worthy, or else send her to a cloister. In a sudden reversal, the marquis forgives her and insists that as his wife she deserves both love and respect. "One cannot make one's spouse unhappy without becoming unhappy oneself....In all honesty I believe...that this Pommeraye woman, instead of avenging herself, has done me a great service." The marquis and marquise leave for the country, where "they spent nearly three years away from the capital."

Following this tale, Jacques's master complains that the hostess is not sufficiently "skilled in dramatic art," that since, in the course of the story, the young woman's behavior was as false as that of her mother and Mme. de la Pommeraye, we are not prepared for her sentiments at the end: "Not one moment's fear…not the slightest remorse.…Is the girl who plots with our two scoundrels the same imploring wife we have seen at her husband's feet? You have sinned against the rules of Aristotle, Horace, de Vida and Le Bossu."

The hostess's reply, though no attempt to compete with this educated assessment, merits our consideration. "I don't follow any rules," she says. "I told you the story as it happened.…Who knows what was going on at the bottom of this young girl's heart, and whether perhaps in the moments when she appeared to us to be acting in the most carefree manner she was not secretly consumed with sorrow."[29]

Either the Master's criticism was taken to heart by Bresson and Cocteau, or in order to register those moments when the young woman may be "secretly consumed by sorrow," the screenplay of *Les Dames* presents a more psychologically complex characterization of the young woman, called Agnès in the film. Far from the passive creature of the hostess's story, she is willful and suspicious throughout. She complains to her mother that she would prefer a fate of their own to one imposed by Hélène (the film's Mme. de la Pommeraye); she secures a job to free herself and her mother from Hélène's control; and when she finds herself falling in love with Jean (the film's marquis), she reveals her past in a letter that he refuses to read. As a result, the spectator is more prepared for her behavior in the final scenes.

Notwithstanding this bow to psychological verity, the hostess speaks to a question already posed in *Les Anges du péché:* how the sudden, inexplicable reversal of behavior can lift a character above narcissism to an acceptance of love and responsibility. In light of the changes in Agnès's character, *Les Dames* shifts the primary burden of transformation to Jean, which, though problematic because of the actor, is prepared for in the way Bresson shoots the scenes between Jean and Agnès.

Bresson provides more credible characterization through an accumulation of details that subtly prepare the spectator for the final scene, but not primarily through the dialogue. "I believe in dialogue not as a means of explaining the situation but as an integral part of the scene," Jean Renoir once remarked, a principle Bresson would take further. While screenplays in the "quality tradition" of French cinema provided extended exposition, Bresson had already imagined a different concept of the cinema, as the following remarks, made shortly after the release of *Les Dames*, indicate:

> It is the interior that governs. I know that may seem paradoxical in an art form that is entirely exterior. But I have seen slow films in which everyone is running about. And others, in which people do not move at all, that are fast. I have ascertained that the rhythm of images is powerless to correct any sluggish interior. All the intricacies tied and untied to the interior of the characters give the film its movement, its true movement. It is this movement that I strive to make apparent with something—or with a combination of things—that does not exist merely in the dialogue. A film is completely a matter of relationships [*en rapports*]. The subtlety…must be placed within these relationships [or exchanges]. The relationships of actors with actors, of actors with objects and the decor that surrounds them, of action with the rhythm of images.[30]

These convictions would be more fully realized in Bresson's later films, yet there are signs in *Les Dames*, despite its dependence on scenes in the melodramatic mold, of a calculated use of the language of film to create this "interior movement." This is evident in the way Hélène's pain is manifested when she learns that Jean no longer loves her and in the way her revenge plan requires a tireless disguise of her true feelings. The accent is on neither the melodramatics of the situation nor the histrionics of virtuosic performance. Casarés plays Hélène with a subtlety and intensity that interact effectively with aspects of the mise-en-scène—lighting, decor, and costume—those agents of *rapports*, as Bresson calls them.

Bresson's ability to find that thing or combination of things that evokes the immaterial was the mark of his genius. Like Diderot, he converted a cynical, social-minded tale into a morality play, but he went further by elevating it to a spiritual plane. And as we shall see, even the exterior conventions of fades, dissolves, cuts, and mise-en-scène are made the instruments of intensifying the film's interior movement.

The Engineer of Revenge

The film updates the story to 1940s Paris and the world of the upper crust. Bresson tells it straight, with none of the comic interruptions, narrative breaks, and intermittent commentary that mark the philosophically detached context of Diderot's work. The author's flavor is retained in Cocteau's dialogue, which incorporates many lines from the novel. There is even an allusion to the source in the first scene, in which Hélène's escort at the theater, a worldly cynic, or "fatalist," named Jacques, tells her that Jean does not love her. Jacques is himself a disappointed suitor, frustrated that he cannot "distract" Hélène, but though he is referred to later as a prospective mate, he never reappears. In sowing the seeds of doubt that lead to Hélène's plan, Jacques assumes a catalytic but metafictional role in the film, just as the Jacques of the novel is outside of the tale told by the innkeeper's wife.

The somberness of Bresson's approach is evident from this first scene. On leaving the theater, Jacques and Hélène converse in the car as medium close-ups of her face reveal her distress over his insinuations. The headlights of passing cars execute searchlight maneuvers over her face, capturing subtle changes in her pained expression. One of the few moments when we detect any quality to contradict our impression of her as conniving and deceitful, this is nevertheless the kind of chiaroscuro effect Bresson would largely avoid after *Diary of a Country Priest*.

The mood continues as Hélène ascends the elevator to her apartment. The medium shot of her standing alone highlights her illumined face surrounded by shadows, a map of unspoken thoughts. This concentrated effect is enhanced by the framing: Hélène stands against the elevator's glass exterior, so that the impression is less that of the elevator rising as of the succeeding floors noiselessly descending. Hélène seems the immoveable center of a deceptively manipulated environment, an appropriate visual metaphor for how she is poised within the strategies of her own design. In fact the elevator becomes a motif, suggestive of her control over the machinery of the plot. When she is in it, it rises as if in response to her will, but when it is occupied by Jean, Agnès, and her mother, it becomes a cage. In one scene the women are seen descending while Hélène remains immediately outside of its gate, closing them in; in another she actually interrupts its descent to prevent Jean from leaving.

Hélène's distress is more overt when she enters her apartment and calls out Jean's name. In the scene that follows, she tricks him into believing that she has lost interest in him. In an especially ironic touch, she describes, as evidence of her fading affection, how the elevator's rise no longer holds excitement, whereas we know from what we have seen that her feelings are quite the opposite. The scene is broken down in the conventional manner, with close-ups reserved for the climax: the moment Hélène realizes that Jean no longer loves her.

The final shot of this scene is a striking long take. It begins as a long shot of Hélène and Jean, having said goodnight, effectively ending their affair, walking silently at a funereal pace from the living room, preceded by a backward track of the camera, their arms akimbo. As they approach the foyer, Jean walks off left while the camera remains on Hélène, now in shadows, leaning against the wall. As we hear the door opening off screen, the light from the hallway falls across her face and throat in a dagger-shaped reflection, the tip of which is poised directly over her heart. As the door closes and the image darkens, the camera moves in to a medium close-up, Hélène's face in shadows but for her tear-filled eyes glistening in tiny specks of light (figure 7).

This is a quintessential scene in the tradition of film melodrama. The conversation between Hélène and Jean is executed in classic filmmaking terms: the dialogue governs both the rhythm of the cuts and the moves from medium shots to close-ups. From a dramatic point of view, the emphasis is, as Peter Brooks would have it, on the "right" material at the "right" moment. And the final image, the close-up of Hélène's teary cheeks, sums up the scene's point with a tableau effect achieved by a masterful use of mise-en-scène, within which acting is thoroughly integrated. Casarés's performance is doubly critical since her character is also acting in the scene; almost everything she says and does except, of course, for the subtle signs of emotional distress and her tears at the end of the sequence, is a lie. Not only are we made aware of how convincing she can be, ensuring her credibility in the rest of the film, but we are also unsettlingly drawn into Hélène's psychic landscape.

Other aspects of the scene, while serving the overall effect, draw attention to Bresson's preoccupation with form and how it might move past both melodrama and naturalism to what will ultimately constitute his signature style. Even the dialogue is somewhat subdued for melodrama, the focus more on Hélène's quiet absorption of a devastating revelation. Then, from the moment the characters rise and walk gloomily to the door, not another word is exchanged. Both are now figures within an elaborate long take in which camera and subject movement, lighting, cinematography, off screen space, and sound are orchestrated to reveal the emotional interior of the scene: the general hollowness of their lives and Hélène's narcissistic injury.

The silence enhances the self-conscious quality of the walk and of the camera's track. A similar but reverse movement at the end of the film, after the marriage ceremony, will reverberate with sinister symmetry. The silence makes all the more effective the only sound heard during the long take: the door opening and closing off screen. Although Bresson's use of sound at this stage generally follows standard practice, this moment hints at how critical it would become in conjunction with off screen space. And so, rather than echo what has been said through the dialogue and serve the dramatic pitch of the scene, the language of *film* imposes a somberness and a gravity that expose the lie underlying the relief both characters allegedly feel at the exhaustion of their love affair. The mood also anticipates the nefarious mind-set that will seize Hélène and threaten to destroy the lives of others.

A fade-out on Hélène's face ends the scene; the next shot fades in on the telephone in her bedroom ringing the next morning. The camera pans right to reveal a wide-eyed Hélène on her bed in the same clothes we saw her in the night before, denoting a sleepless night and a disturbed demeanor. Quietly, she says, "I'll have my revenge."

By separating this statement from the previous night, the vow of revenge and the feelings that have led to it register more strongly. Neither the termination of the affair nor Hélène's feelings of rejection are vitiated by a display of vindictiveness. Consequently her vow the next morning, delivered calmly with deliberation, carries greater moral culpability. The time elided between the fades is retroactively charged with meaning when we realize how it has been spent. It is the kind of transition that Bresson would later handle more elliptically. The gentleness with which Hélène strokes the dog on her lap, recalling the tender caresses of the malicious Thérèse in *Les Anges du péché*, is a wonderful counterpoint to the depth of her injury and the wrath that consumes her. It reveals how well she conceals her feelings and prefigures the adroit cunning with which she will execute her malignant plan. Our sense of her interior state therefore is strengthened by the temporal elision and affects our reading of her mood and her words. While Bresson's style became known for this ability to suggest much with the barest of means, Casarés's facial expression and understated body language should not go unacknowledged.

Hélène's vow is instantly converted into action, indeed, into the plot of the film itself, marked by a dissolve linking the shot of her seated on the bed to a shot of her dark-cloaked figure, made more ominous because it is seen from the back, taking a seat in the cabaret where Agnès is performing. The dissolve is almost undetectable because each image is dominated by a large black area on screen right, created first by the fade to black over Hélène in the bed and then by the black cloak, the garment of revenge, that visually displaces her figure on the bed. The impression conveyed is that of a dark, mysterious force descending, although the transition is so smooth that its effect is almost subliminal. During the dissolve we hear the sound of Agnès's dancing feet, another early indication of Bresson's astute use of overlapping sound. A contrast between the two women is soon suggested: Agnès dances in full shot and smiles in medium close-up while Hélène looks on, her head covered by the hood of her cloak, her face now fixed in the inscrutable smile that she will wear for the rest of the film.

When Agnès and her mother go off to their apartment, Hélène follows, and while Agnès dances with drunken men, Hélène learns of their sad plight from her mother, a friend from the past. To escape the men, Agnès locks herself in a room and in response to her mother's pleas cries, "I'm not your little girl, I'm a little tramp," prompting her mother to reveal the ugly truth: to survive they have been reduced to "entertaining" men. Hélène comforts her and promises to assume their debts and alter their circumstances. The speed with which her plans are implemented is marked by a fade-in to Agnès and her mother entering a new apartment. Agnès describes it as a "prison" and wonders what they are getting into.

No sooner are they settled than Hélène arranges a meeting with Agnès and her mother in the Bois de Boulogne, and then, while having lunch with Jean, casually suggests a walk there. As the phrase "*au Bois?*" leaves her lips, the scene dissolves to the waterfall where Agnès and her mother await this "chance" encounter. As Hélène had anticipated, Jean is impressed, remarking on Agnès's "country" qualities; later Hélène telephones Agnès's mother to tell them that she is pleased, to which the curious Agnès asks, "Pleased with what?"

As these descriptions suggest, the film makes cogent use of dissolves and fades. Both devices, standard practice since the silent era to denote spatial and temporal transitions, are here assigned an important structural role, articulating cause-and-effect relationships between moments of the action, that is, between an intention denoted or implied in one shot and its fulfillment in the next. For example, the dissolve from Hélène's vow of revenge to her arrival at the cabaret turns the "vengeful woman" into the "dark-hooded woman," indicating that her plan is in progress and that it will involve duplicity. Similarly her affected nonchalance concerning the walk to the Bois de Boulogne is belied by the dissolve that visually links her feigned inquisitive look with the women waiting at the prearranged rendezvous spot.

Thus, apart from eliding time, the dissolve seems tailor-made for the plot structure of the film, engineered by Hélène herself calling the shots, so to speak. Many of the film's dissolves and fades (about two dozen of the former and seventeen of the latter) underline her role in the propulsion of the action, and those that are less explicit reinforce it indirectly. Even character actions that appear autonomous strengthen Hélène's plan. When Jean asks her how he can see Agnès again, she warns him against it while allowing Agnès's address, Port Royal Square, to slip out.[31] After Jean rushes off, the camera stays on Hélène as she informs the maid that he will not be coming the next day. Hélène fades out, and the fade-in is to the water fountain in Port Royal Square, where

Jean wanders around in the rain awaiting Agnès's return. The new image furthers Hélène's plan and validates her ability to read Jean's character, at least for a time; her direction to the maid correctly predicts that his preoccupation with Agnès will preclude his visiting the next day. Thus, although Jean appears to act independently, his behavior predictably conforms to Hélène's plan.

When it becomes apparent later that Jean and Agnès have fallen in love, however, Hélène's control weakens even though her ultimate goal, to have them marry, is achieved. Agnès resolves to write a letter to Jean explaining everything. She leaves the apartment without divulging her intentions to her mother, who immediately shares this development with Hélène. Genuinely flustered for the first time, Hélène remarks, "I don't know where she is, but I'm sure she is doing something sublime, in short, ruining herself"—that is, ruining Hélène's plot. A dissolve from this to the Bois underscores the power shift. The earlier dissolve to the Bois involved the prearranged encounter between Agnès and Jean, whereas the later encounter has been arranged by Agnès without Hélène's knowledge. Despite this shift, the fateful nature of the Bois is reaffirmed, suggesting that even in their first encounter, more was going on than anyone had suspected.

Before that critical second scene in the Bois, however, Hélène arranges another of her "chance" meetings, a dinner party for Agnès and her mother, at which Jean will "coincidentally" appear. Since this was not prompted by her instincts, it backfires and moves Agnès closer to taking things into her own hands. When Jean arrives, to everyone's feigned surprise, her mother obsequiously thanks him for the flowers he has been sending, ignoring Agnès's complaint, "Behind every flower there was always a man's face and there still is." Her mother, however, is determined to sell her daughter, this time to a man of more impressive social standing. Stunned and mortified, Agnès drops a glass onto the floor, shattering the false composure of the moment.

The immediate response to this confirms her worst suspicions. Jean and Hélène smile conspiratorially and at Agnès's mother's prompt, "Make a wish," all three of them look meaningfully at Agnès off screen. The scene ends on a medium close-up of Agnès, dumbfounded by how her gesture, instead of disrupting the evening, has strengthened their solidarity. To clinch this impression, the shot of Agnès dissolves to a long shot of her and her mother caged in the elevator, descending quietly as Hélène returns to her apartment.

Agnès's dropping of the glass expresses what she cannot articulate and seems an apt displacement of her swoons. Immediately before, distracted by her mother's remarks, she looks off screen at her while extending her right hand with the glass until it is poised over the floor, as if she deliberately intended to drop it (figure 8). Only now does she fully realize how completely her mother has betrayed her and allowed Hélène to use them.[32] Agnès is thus severed from the full taint of the scheme, anticipating the honest remorse she expresses at the end. This renders her not only more credible and sympathetic than her counterpart in Diderot, but of far superior moral character to Hélène and her mother, as well as to the mother and daughter of the tale.

Whether by accident or design, and probably a combination of both, the act cues us to Agnès's rage and humiliation and is one of many tension-shattering moments in Bresson's films when the image and sound of an object breaking or reverberating—or, in the case of the soup cart in Les Anges, overturning—displace emotions that have reached an unbearable limit. As will be true of later films, this strategy conveys the extent of a character's anger and frustration not articulated through acting or dialogue.

The remarks following Agnès'action, as well as the conversation between Hélène and Jean afterward, indicate that though the dinner may have been disastrous, Hélène still believes her plan is intact. She thus misreads and misjudges Agnès, who tells her mother later that evening that she will never see Hélène again. What happens internally, therefore—not merely the surface action and dialogue—gradually undermines Hélène's design.

The turning point is directly tied to Hélène's narcissism. As Jean sits despondently in her apartment, she calmly plays the piano; the tears she hides testify that she knows she is not the object of his longing. Suddenly realizing that he has left, she runs after him. She pulls on the handle of the elevator and interrupts his descent long enough to run down the stairs, a frantic effort that underlines the mechanistic limits of her power. Jean presses the button and the elevator resumes its course. This blatant disruption of her composure reveals her miscalculation of the situation. Like the Marquise de Merteuil at the end of Les Liaisons dangereuses,[33] she recognizes that the rules of the game have changed and that the situation cannot return to what it was. Her plan will succeed, but not in the manner she had envisioned. The very thing she did not anticipate, a radical change in Jean's character, will wreck her scheme. The disparity between the surface achievement of her revenge, to have Jean marry a woman of low repute, and the profound internal transformation this event engenders is the essence of the Bressonian dialogue between the exterior and the interior, the world and the spirit.

The Engineer Outmaneuvered

When prior knowledge of events passes to Agnès, the shift that disorients Hélène is duly marked by the ironic replay, and reverse meaning, of a dissolve to the Bois. The strategy connotes that Hélène effectively operates only on the level of plot, reading everything in terms of how it fits her outward design. Because she believes that she knows Jean's character, she cannot anticipate or comprehend the possibility that he could experience genuine love or inner change. This deficiency, her inability to correctly assess what goes on inside of a person, is apparent early on, when she is shocked at both Jacques's allegation and Jean's confession. What blinds her, Pascal would say, are her passions, the all-consuming deadly sins of envy and pride. We glimpse, however, in the brief flashes of distress that Hélène underestimates, that Jean is more than she, or we, have suspected. It is even possible that Paul Bernard's flat and insipid performance helps to persuade us that he *is* the superficial hedonist that Hélène assumes.

When Agnès and Jean meet at the Bois for the second time, she has come to give him the letter that will clear her conscience. Refusing to read it, he leads her into a grotto as we hear him say, "I only have a moment to say everything. So let's make this moment endless.…Let's go far away." The rest is drowned out by the sound of the waterfall, and the camera, as if not entitled to intrude, does not follow them.[34] At this crucial juncture of the narrative, which will determine not just the outcome of events but the final transformation, Bresson, in the most calculated elision in the film, has followed the folk wisdom of the hostess in Diderot's tale, allowing whatever it is "at the bottom" of people's hearts to remain unarticulated. That he also views this "mystery" in terms of the Christian message that calls for change is suggested by the arch-like church entrance of the grotto itself and the waterfall, unseen during their first encounter, which here converts the second encounter into a ritual of purification. In other words, while the Bois is an indifferent backdrop in Hélène's plan, it now becomes a potent spiritual symbol for Agnès and Jean.

With this scene Bresson creates a perfect foil to Hélène's design. In a very real sense, Agnès and Jean's true marriage occurs in the grotto off screen, rendering the official marriage later a mere social event. The latter is a public display; the former is a private communion between the only two people who matter. Indeed, judging from what follows, we infer that a significant interior change has taken place in both of them, which will not be tested until the final scene. Appropriately, the dissolve that takes us from our view of them entering the grotto to their conversation in the car shortly after is an authorial gesture that excludes the viewer and supersedes Hélène's control by way of the very device that had been used to manifest it.

The import of what has transpired in the grotto is conveyed in the conversation right after. In the car we see only part of Jean's face reflected in the rearview mirror; it is Agnès's face, turned toward him in a long-held medium close-up, that commands our attention. As he declares his love and insists that there are no obstacles between them, she asks him one last time to read the letter. "We'll read it together some day…in the sunlight," he replies. The scene registers an inner change that has altered everything, as his earlier remark as they entered the grotto had already suggested.

Agnès's face registers her belief, perhaps for the first time, in Jean's words. Her familiarity with cads made her suspicious from the beginning, especially because of his link to Hélène, and we have seen that she has a talent for sensing ulterior motives. That she believes Jean's declarations of love to be real, therefore, is important both for her and the spectator. We know her true character as well as the contents of the letter. It is Jean's sincerity that we question but that we come to trust because it is reflected on Agnès's face.

One might argue that Paul Bernard's failure to incarnate Bresson's ideal "soul" accounts for the concentration on Agnès's face, just as his back is to the camera when he confesses that he no longer loves Hélène.[35] Yet on the way home from the Opera, the focus is also on Hélène's face and the faint flicker of her eyes as she denies Jacques's allegation that Jean no longer loves her. It is a stylistic trait, in which the emotional truth of a critical moment is to be found in the subtle reactions on the face of one character to the off screen words of another, seen elsewhere in Bresson's work, perhaps most powerfully in *Diary of a Country Priest*.

The official wedding day arrives as planned, the ceremony, an event not described in Diderot, executed in an abbreviated fashion. In a series of smoothly linked dissolves that seem to confirm Hélène's triumph, we see Agnès's entrance to the church; Agnès in a luminous white gown being led up the aisle, radiating an innocence all the more pronounced when she passes the dour-faced Hélène in her usual black; a close-up of Agnès kneeling at the altar; and finally the greeting of guests in the church vestibule afterward.

The mood resembles Hélène and Jean's funereal walk in the first scene. On the surface Hélène's plan appears a total success: Jean's life and happiness seem about to be shattered and her revenge complete. This is registered by a tracking shot that follows her, reversing the direction of the one in the breakup scene, as she walks with the same grave demeanor toward the vestibule and up to the couple greeting well-wishers. Hélène whispers the words into Jean's ear that will trigger the events of the final moments. She tells him that she was wrong about the girl and that he should make inquiries, then gives Agnès herself a cold Judas kiss on the cheek.

Assuming the worst, Agnès disappears. When Jean insists that she greet her guests, she faints and he leaves her in the care of servants. The character of the young woman in Diderot is also subject to sudden fainting swoons, but we learn very little about this condition except that it is serious enough to result in a death-like unconsciousness. In the film Agnès has an earlier collapse after dancing in her apartment, frightening her mother into thinking she might be dead. Inexplicably she revives, and we learn later that she has a weak heart. This instance may have been another effort to increase the credibility of the ending, yet the condition actually enhances the entire effect of the scene, quite unlike the way it figures in the tale.

Exasperated, Jean is about to drive off when his car literally runs into Hélène's. He asks for an explanation, and without batting an eye, she responds, "It's very simple. You've married a tramp." At her unabashed disclosure of her scheme, Jean is astonished, dismisses her behavior as abominable, and drives off. In uncut prints of the film, this gesture is prolonged. Jean has to maneuver his car to get around Hélène's, bringing her back into view three separate times before he can proceed.

As a result, the last image we have of Hélène carries greater weight. She is framed standing in place through the driver's side window of Jean's car so that when he finally moves off screen right, she is literally wiped off the screen, which then turns to black. It is a striking variation of the patterns composed by filmic devices. Here, the last view of Hélène, framed within the frame (figure 9), is erased, not by a cut, a fade, or a dissolve, that is, not by the mechanics of filmmaking, and certainly not by her own design, but by Jean's strenuous action framed to function as an optical wipe. In short, the filmic devices, of which Hélène was the mistress, have given way to an assertive human action, Jean's arduous efforts not only to tear her finally from his life, but to vanquish a heretofore unrecognized archenemy. Hélène's association with the film's mechanics is stressed in these three appearances by her frozen smile and stone face. Jean's gesture not only denotes his long overdue independence but speaks to that philosophical dilemma in both Diderot and Bresson. Here, as will be true of the final scene, he performs a moral action that contravenes the determinist forces represented by Hélène. And the fact that it is directly expressed through framing, tracking, and the resulting "wipe" confirms the way filmic devices, and their imitations, are linked in this film to the trajectory and meaning of the action.

The gesture leaves Hélène standing outside the narrative, indifferent to what will happen next, the reverse of the position she has occupied throughout the film. It is an appropriate final view of her that in one sense represents her insular, impenetrable narcissism and her inability to follow the film's interior movement. Yet more than any other shot in the movie, it also evokes her mythic role as a determinant, demonic force from which Jean must make repeated efforts to escape. It is as if the machinery of evil of which she was mistress has wound down, leaving her nothing to do. But like Medea, Hélène is not punished for her actions, as the villainess in a typical melodrama or film noir often is, because she represents the continued force of a shallow, mechanistic way of life. It is against this that the final scene must be understood.

A Marriage of True Souls

In Diderot, husband and wife spend the wedding night together and everything goes well. Not until the next day does the marquis learn the truth and confront his wife, prompting her to faint and him to leave for a fortnight. Their final conversation occurs upon his return, when she has more or less recovered. In other words, the illness is not a factor in the final scene, and the marquis, having had time to consider his situation, sees it somewhat pragmatically. He forgives her and respects her and insists that she assume her "proper place" as his wife, adding that he regrets nothing. He never says that he loves her.

Bresson compacts everything into the wedding day. The final scene has the burden of convincing us that Jean's love for Agnès can transcend everything. Despite what he has done to prepare us for it, Bresson has not aimed primarily for social, pragmatic, and psychological credibility, but for a transformative effect, deploying the full range of filmic strategies to achieve this.

Following the fade-out on the last view of Hélène, a fade-in shows Jean returning from his mad effort to get away. After brushing off Agnès's mother as the nuisance she is, he enters the room where Agnès lies, still weakened by her fainting spell. In a single take he walks dolefully to the bed and sits alongside it, his head lowered, not looking at Agnès lying across the lower half of the frame. The scene is beautifully lit, its background shadows matched by Jean in his groom's attire, but contrasting with the whiteness of his collar, his cuffs, his hands, and a lamp that illumines a large floral arrangement. Agnès, still in her bridal gown, lies in a bright area. Her appeal to Jean, many of the words directly out of Diderot, overlaps the crosscutting between close-ups of her, eyes alternately opening and closing, and medium shots of Jean:

> You're here. Maybe in time you'll forgive me...but there is no hurry...[she opens her eyes and looks off screen, but not at him]. Many good girls become bad girls. Maybe I'll be an example of the opposite [closes her eyes]. I don't deserve your approaching me yet...so wait...just let me keep hoping. You'll be the judge of my

conduct. Just tolerate my presence a little.... Tell me in which corner of your house I may live...and I'll stay there without a murmur. I'm not a bad person. I know myself. I was weak.... I loved you, that's my only excuse. I didn't dare open your eyes. Remember the letter...you wouldn't read?

[Jean turns his head toward her at this point] It wasn't a funny one [Agnès more visibly distressed now]. You can forget me...I won't trouble you any more...it'll be easy.

A contemporary audience no doubt would find these words both moralistic and patriarchal. Agnès's abjectness seems excessive, especially since her basic decency has already been established, as the line about the letter reminds us. But the words are not the only determining factor in the scene. Perhaps the best way to understand them is to place them within the connotations of the mise-en-scène and read the *entire* scene, not just the dialogue, in the Bressonian spirit. Agnès is lying on a bed, but the angle from which we see this, as well as the flower arrangements around it, suggests something far less mundane, something between the bier of a beloved and a medieval saint's tomb. Halfway between life and death, her speech is arduously delivered. This, along with the lighting, camera angle, and music, all seem designed to move us from the ordinary to an ethereal realm. In this context, her plea for forgiveness can be seen as directed not only to Jean but to a higher power, and so may constitute a last confession. This would render her humility perfectly logical, not unlike the humility Anne-Marie had to learn before taking her final vows on her deathbed in *Les Anges du péché*. Agnès too dies to her former life, an act that, in Bresson's world, restores her purity. It is not only Jean's declaration of love and ability to forgive that saves her, but her embrace of the good within her that releases the same in him. The love we are asked to believe they share is thus not exclusively of romantic origin, but a giving over of self, an expulsion of the narcissism embodied by Hélène. Unlike the film's *belle dame sans merci*, Agnès and Jean embrace both humility and forgiveness.

After speaking these last words, Agnès becomes silent and still, as if by merely letting herself go she could die. The soft music that accompanies her monologue suddenly stops, and the silence denotes a suspension of time in which life and death hang in the balance. Suddenly aware that she might actually die, Jean moves closer, the next shot framing them both: Agnès quite still, Jean leaning over and shaking her gently. A close-up of him follows as he tells her that he loves her, that she cannot leave him, that she must fight. In the next close-up of the two of them, Agnès whispers, "I'm fighting," as Jean addresses her as his wife and pleads with her, "*Reste! Reste!*" ("Stay with me. Stay.")

There is an appealing passage in a study of Lacan's contrasting of speech and language that, oddly enough, speaks aptly to this moment: "If language…appears timeless, the embodiment of the death of things, it is speech which introduces a human temporality, the temporality of action in time, of action in haste, to pre-empt the grim reaper. Archetypally, marriage is such an action, in which founding speech, 'You are my wife' ('I am your husband') is a Pascalian wager, the best bet under the circumstances, the circumstances of mortality in which speaking, human subjects find themselves."[36]

In the next close-up of Agnès and Jean, she opens her eyes and looks up, then half-closes them again as she faintly calls his name. The music softly returns when Agnès resolves to fight, then grows louder over the last two shots, its increasing force miming her gathering strength. The final shot, a marked departure in camera angle and framing, is a slightly high-angle view above the bed—Agnès lying on the left, Jean seated on the right—from which the camera ascends as Jean kisses her hand before the fade-out (figure 10). In the context of the film's syntax as described throughout, this movement, by virtue of its verticality, cancels Hélène's effects through dissolves as well as Jean's as he wipes her off the screen with his car. The camera lifts upward against the horizontal grain of these earlier gestures, displacing their mortal perspectives and the materiality in which they are grounded with the suggestion of a divinely bestowed blessing.[37]

To argue the credibility of this moment is to miss the point. Essentially this is the same ending as the one in *Les Anges du péché*. A young woman lies near death and in barely audible words speaks a truth that deeply affects the soul of one whose life, by chance or fate, has crossed her path. It is the second illustration of what becomes an abiding theme of Bresson's: the strange journey of two souls who come together despite seemingly impossible odds. Aside from the efforts made to give Agnès's character more substance, Jean's change, contradicting his mockery of marriage and sacred oaths in the breakup scene, must be understood not only according to the rules of Aristotle and psychological consistency, as the hostess's critics in Diderot's tale insists, but as a manifestation of that unseen interior movement, which Bresson's cinema avers, at least at this stage, is compelled by grace. To be sure, another Christian allusion here, as in the grotto scene, might be noted. In the Catholic Church's litany of saints, Agnès was one of the early martyrs persecuted for their refusal to worship or sacrifice to pagan idols. In cleansing herself, as well as Jean, the film's Agnès enacts a similar renunciation of the false values of the contemporary world represented by Hélène.

But as in *Les Anges*, what occurs here, though compatible with a spiritual reading—as this allusion, along with the orchestration of mise-en-scène, music, and atmosphere, enforces—is not foreign to a psychological reading. The human individual, as many philosophical and psychological theories attempt to explain, longs, however hopelessly, for an ideal, unconditional love. Celebrated in thousands of poems, novels, movies, operas, and songs, it is a desire and a condition no less improbable yet impossible to relinquish than the belief that a spiritual force operates in human affairs.

The endings of *Les Anges* and *Les Dames* affirm this fact by suggesting that the strength and sincerity of one person's love, particularly in the face of death, can ultimately stir the most recalcitrant heart and dislodge resistance. Grace gives this capacity a name. One might say that in Bresson's cinema, at least up to *The Trial of Joan of Arc*, every protagonist is a novice struggling to purge all signs of pride before taking his or her final vows. But if the ending of *Les Dames* celebrates a marriage based on genuine love and sincerity, it is noteworthy that such a thing never reappears in any other film of Bresson's. Married characters hardly behave as couples—certainly not the one in *Une femme douce*—expressing love and affection, regardless of age or class, as is exemplified in the three different marital situations in *L'Argent*.

Following *Les Dames* Bresson would leave the melodrama for more rigorous fare and would treat both subject and form in a more austere manner. The expressive cinematography of Philippe Agostini, in which the interplay of light and shadow shapes and intensifies dramatic moments attuned to the emotional highlights of the scenario, would soon vanish, as would the stars for whom such a cinema was designed. The use of nonprofessional actors would, in turn, require sparer scenarios and dialogue, since none but professionals could do justice to the screenplays of *Les Anges* and *Les Dames*, in which the contours of long sentences must be shaped into meaningful phrases through variances of inflection and emotional shadings. And the first-person narratives of his next three films would extend beyond the use of fades and dissolves to indicate character control.

If the reading offered here implies a certain segregation between structure and interior movement, it is because an experimental flair seems to characterize the aesthetic system of the film—a product perhaps of the challenges presented at this point in Bresson's career—namely, to employ the resources of traditional cinema as scrupulously as possible. My analysis of the film's dissolves and fades is based on the conviction that they are not used only to facilitate filmic continuity and viewer consumption. They signify the increasingly exacting efforts of the filmmaker to create a distinct narrative cinema in which every element of its construction is purposeful. Mise-en-scène, acting, and musical accompaniment—staples of melodrama—are permitted their full range of expressivity. It is the kind of cinema Bresson would move away from, following his conviction that images should not carry too much expressive power lest they fail to be affected by contact with other images. There is "no art without transformation."[38]

This is the essence of the distinction Bresson makes between cinema and cinematography: "cinematographic film, where the images, like the words in a dictionary, have no power and value except through their position and relation."[39] What we see in *Diary of a Country Priest* and subsequent works, therefore, is a gradual peeling away of those features used so brilliantly in *Les Dames du bois de Boulogne*. What takes their place is the refinement and intensification of the properties of what Bresson called cinematography itself.

A soul is a world. It is easier to undertake the political government of a

kingdom than the spiritual rule of a single soul.

—Saint Cyran, quoted in Marc Escholier,

Port Royal: The Drama of the Jansenists

2

Author, Author

Journal d'un curé de campagne

Diary of a Country Priest (1951), Bresson's first truly great work, is one of the peaks of postwar French cinema. If it is the last of his films to privilege key elements of traditional narrative cinema, it is no less an achievement for being so.[1] Possibly the least sentimental film ever made about a priest, *Diary* is a triumphant transposition of a serious work of literature into the poetics of cinema, all the more impressive since its screenplay was Bresson's first solo effort, without dialogue provided by someone else.[2] Poised at a juncture that augurs a formal breakthrough as much as it enshrines what was subsequently renounced, the film occupies a special place in Bresson's career. Its cinematographer, Léonce-Henri Burel, created magnificent atmospheric effects of the kind that would not be seen again in Bresson's work, even though he went on to photograph the next three films; Pierre Charbonnier, the film's art director, designed seven other films for Bresson. Dramatic scenes and dialogue are as crucial here as they are in *Les Dames du bois de Boulogne*, and the music of Jean-Jacques Grünenwald induces as somber a mood as it did in the preceding film.

For the first time, however, Bresson used nonprofessional actors. The most notable was Claude Laydu in the role of the priest, but no less bold a choice was Armand Guibert, pseudonymn for real psychoanalyst Adrien Borel, whose confident and paternal manner in the role of the curé of Torcy provides a fitting counterpoint to the curé's tormented nature.[3] Finally, there was Nicole Ladmiral as the disturbed adolescent Chantal. Though inexperienced, all three hold their own against such professionals as Marie-Monique Arkell, who plays the countess.[4] Finally, in keeping with his growing appreciation for authenticity, Bresson shot the film in "the small village d'Equirre, Pas-de-Calais" rather than in a studio.[5]

Although Bresson directed his largely unprofessional cast to speak and behave in a manner that would facilitate "consanguinity among his characters,"[6] some critics at the time were either insensitive to his intentions or unappreciative of the results. André Bazin praised the film but thought Bresson's handling of the actors "amateurish."[7] Bresson was moving toward abandoning trained actors altogether, and the performances and dialogue delivery in *Diary* no doubt reflect this fact. More than half a century later, the acting, professional and nonprofessional, seems neither dated nor amateurish, and the film rings with a conviction that surpasses most French films of the period.

If any one feature determined both the film's success and the future course of Bresson's career, it was the discovery of Claude Laydu. In him Bresson found the face and figure of the male protagonist that would become the prototype of those that would follow, especially Fontaine (*A Man Escaped*), Michel (*Pickpocket*), Gawain (*Lancelot of the Lake*), and Charles (*The Devil Probably*). Few male faces in the history of cinema come as close to embodying the virginal quality that, in Bresson's work, is the sign of innocence and access to genuine spirituality. Differences notwithstanding, Laydu's impact as the priest may rival Falconetti's as Joan in Dreyer's *La Passion de Jeanne d'Arc* in that both actors became inseparably linked to their roles.[8]

Laydu came from Belgium to Paris in 1948 to study acting and was introduced to Bresson by the filmmaker Jacques Becker, who knew of Bresson's project and thought the twenty-year-old Laydu would be perfect as the priest. But since there was no money for the production, Laydu was not tested and sought other work. Nevertheless he left a strong impression on Bresson, who invited him for a screen test two years later and convinced his wary producers to hire him despite his lack of experience.[9] An avowed Christian, though not a Catholic, Laydu agreed to Bresson's request to live for a few weeks with a group of priests serving the working class. There he not only learned the correct gestures but found the ragged cassock and shoes that he used in the film.[10]

In awe of Bresson and completely devoted to the project, Laydu carried the Georges Bernanos novel with him during the shooting and pursued an austere diet to lose weight so he would look more like the ailing priest. The very qualities this behavior manifests—obedience, obsessive concentration, a combination of fire and composure, and genuine dedication—were exactly those Bresson sought for his curé. His recognition of these features in Laydu no doubt explains the many close-ups and medium close-ups of the actor's face, some held for an unusually long time without voice-over or dialogue and moved into by the camera to isolate it from its surroundings. Carving a cinematic space that would never be duplicated to this degree, these shots are about more than performance. Bresson must have been enormously gratified to have found a face, an "exterior," that, as he said while making *Les Dames du bois de Boulogne*, would so successfully reveal the character's interior life and that gave instant validity to his conception of the "model: All face."[11]

Laydu's face is at the center of the film, the site at which its themes, its moral force, and the conflicts of its characters meet, and from which its intense visual style and spiritual power emanate. In its physiognomy we read sorrow and suffering, faith and doubt, pride and obedience, insight and innocence, and, not least, childish delight. But for the fleeting giggles of schoolgirls at one moment in the film, the priest's is the only face that hints at the possibility of joy, something of which neither of the more worldly young girls Séraphita and Chantal is capable.

But even as it radiates beauty and light, the face of the priest is the locus of the struggle between the spirit and the flesh, the theme that permeates the narrative and obsesses its characters no less than it seems to preoccupy Bresson. If Laydu's face gives radiant life to the country priest, it also embodied a personal ideal for the filmmaker: the unsullied fictional persona whose innocence must be preserved against the threat of corruption, even if it meant compromising the film's masterful use of first-person point of view. In its pivotal position within the gallery of portraits before and after, Laydu's face is emblematic of the film's position within Bresson's career, representing the summit of one kind of cinema while carrying the seeds of what was to come.

The Curbing of Pride

There is only one sadness; it is the sadness of NOT BEING SAINTS.

—Léon Bloy, quoted in Albert Béguin, *Léon Bloy, A Study in Impatience*

Diary picks up a theme introduced in *Les Anges du péché*, that of the spiritually obsessed being determined to save others. Like the priest's tendency to "burn" those around him with his fervor and directness—which an elderly canon quips, quite rightly, is exactly why people resist him—the novice Anne-Marie relentlessly pursues the sinner Thérèse, who is finally transformed at the novice's death. Redemption occurs in both films, but only at the cost of life itself, a pattern that replicates the Christian perspective on the meaning of history and that is manifest in *Diary*.

As with the scene near the end of *Les Anges* when the ailing Anne-Marie strives to rouse the resistant Thérèse, the longest and most dramatic scene in *Diary*, the priest's final encounter with the countess, confirms Bresson's preoccupation with hubris. Salvation in *Les Anges*, as well as in *Les Dames*, involves the breaking down of the character defenses that sustain hubris, something that, not so strangely, is also a goal of the secular art of psychoanalysis, where this degree of pride would be construed as an obstacle to progress. For Bresson, as for Bernanos, hubris is the greatest sin and its conquest the greatest victory. In *Diary* pride is manifest in many characters to different degrees, including the priest, whose zeal, as he is often warned, is dangerously confused with narcissistic gratification. His diary is as much a record of what occurs in the parish as it is an effort to monitor his interior spiritual journey.

From the first shot of the face of the priest wiping his brow to the last long-held image of him just before his death, the narrative is characterized as a chronicle of a life lived in imitation of Christ, replete with its falls, doubts, and temptations to despair. The parallel is illumined in the film, and the novel, by the curé of Torcy's remark that all priests are "called to the priesthood…but not in the same way." Each is fixated at the place and moment in the life of Christ that has sparked his vocation and defined its essence. For the country priest, that place and moment "has been Mount Olivet…in that very instant when [Jesus] set His hand on Peter's shoulder asking him the useless question, almost naive yet so tender, so deeply courteous: Why sleep ye?"[12] The revelation confirms that the priest's attachment to the passion and suffering of Christ deeply informs his ministry and shapes his life.

In the spirit of the question asked of Peter, the priest assumes the role of awakener, incapable of restraining militancy in the affairs of his parish but aware of the indifference of others to his mission. The narrative is not just the poignant chronicle of the life of a country priest, affecting as that is, but a record of a singular path followed by a genuinely spiritual human being, one that defines, in whatever terms it is humanly possible to comprehend, what it might mean to be a saint.

The Bernanos Text

Diary of a Country Priest, Georges Bernanos's most popular novel, was published in 1936, though had he followed his instincts it might not have been. "I don't like to talk about this book, because it is very dear to me. While writing it, more than once I thought of keeping it for myself....I wanted to put it in a drawer, and it would have been published after my death....I love this book as if it hadn't come from me."[13] The sentiment is no surprise, since the intimacy and sincerity that characterize this novel seem more than a little about Bernanos himself.

As with his other fictional works, "dramas of sin and degradation, of Christian love and divine grace,"[14] religion is not merely the presumed backdrop of the action, but its very substance. Given Bernanos's character and life, suffused as they were with deep, unflagging devotion to the Church, even while admonishing it, it could hardly have been otherwise. As one writer described it, "Everything he created is ecclesial existence that has been given form."[15]

Bresson was a young man during Bernanos's most productive writing years, yet it would be difficult to imagine a more congenial matching of artistic temperament and philosophic conviction. It is not only that both men were French Catholics of a particularly zealous stripe, but each brought an extraordinary rigor, determination, and intensity to his artistic calling. Bernanos more than once described his somewhat late coming to literature not as a result of an attraction, but as a duty imposed on him by God, as a vocation, not unlike the sense of supernatural appointment and degree of investment believed to constitute the call to the priesthood. There is no doubt that the portrait of the priest in the novel as vocationally driven and spiritually obsessed emanates from and directly reflects Bernanos's convictions; it is hardly less true of Bresson's posture in relation to his art.

Of course, there are differences. Bresson does not appear to have had the same political commitment as Bernanos.[16] From his early support of the conservative group L'Action française through his bitter reproofs of those Frenchmen who he believed had compromised their nationalism and their religion during the German occupation, Bernanos's activism is well documented. Although his politics was not a matter of adopting a particular program or endorsing one party over another, he did espouse a return to monarchism. He distrusted democratic as much as socialist and communist movements, for he had little trust in human nature and no faith in the ability of collective efforts to eliminate social injustices. Bernanos was a devout Catholic, attending mass virtually every day. But while he admitted that he "couldn't live five minutes outside of [the Church]," he continually spoke out against its all too worldly alliance with the rich and powerful and its failure to fulfill its true mission as the bearer of Christ's teachings. Rather than submit to the papal ban against L'Action française, he went without the sacraments for years. For him the Church was out of touch with social reality, especially with regard to conditions in France and the plight of the poor. Nevertheless he believed that it remained the only link between God and man, and the proof of its divinity was its saints.[17]

These issues and concerns are discussed in the novel in long, primarily monologic digressions, thinly veiled as conversations, in which the views and philosophies of several characters—the curé of Torcy, Dr. Delbende, the dean of Blangermont, and Dr. Laville (the last two of whom do not appear in the film)—on the relevance of Christianity and the Church in solving social ills are contrasted with the vocational constancy of the young priest. Although they clearly reflect attitudes toward the Church and the priesthood in 1930s France that affect the overall assessment of the priest's character, they are almost entirely absent from Bresson's film or, in the case of Torcy, are reduced to a few essential exchanges.[18] Their importance, however, should not be underestimated since it is against the backdrop of such views, most of them practical and worldly, that the priest's sanctity comes into focus, for if there is an uncelebrated, undeclared saint in Bresson's work, it is the young priest of Ambricourt, the protagonist of Bernanos's great novel.

The Narrative

The narrative traces the experiences of the priest, unnamed in both film and novel, at Ambricourt, his first and, as it happens, his last parish. These experiences, along with his reflections about them, are recorded in a diary, composed of a series of children's copybooks. The film is a chronicle of the priest's interior life and how it is affected by his duties and obligations, as well as his interactions with others. It is more overtly structured than the novel, which, true to the nature of a diary, is not as plot-conscious. And so, while the diary entries determine the course of the film, a dramatic structure is provided by two developmental lines. The first is the situation generated by the priest's arrival; though earnestly devoted to his vocation, he finds himself in an embattled position vis-à-vis his apathetic parishioners (figure 11). His determination to influence their lives is placed in perspective through several scenes with Torcy, a more seasoned and pragmatic clergyman, who tells him that the Church does not care if her priests are loved; it is more important to be respected and obeyed.

The second line is the priest's illness. Though young, he tires easily and speaks of a chronic stomach pain that is aggravated by his diet; he refrains from meat and vegetables and eats only hard bread soaked in bad wine. Both Torcy and Delbende, the doctor in Ambricourt who examines him, allude to the "alcohol in his background" and the fact that "we are all drunkards' children." In one of the film's final scenes, he visits Dufrety, a friend from the seminary, who left the priesthood because of illness resulting from the "lousy blood in their veins." The priest's condition eventually forces him to seek medical attention in Lille. Diagnosed as cancer, it proves fatal and leads to his death.[19]

The priest comes to know members of the community's different classes: the farmer, the professional, the clergy, and the local aristocracy. The first group is represented by Fabregard, an angry man who disputes the cost of his wife's funeral, and Séraphita, one of the young girls in catechism classes preparing for communion.[20] The second group is represented by Dr. Delbende, who makes such a strong impression on the priest in one scene that he is deeply affected by the doctor's suicide a short time later. Torcy and the canon give us two different perspectives on the clergy.

The bulk of the narrative centers on the priest's dealings with the count, the countess, their daughter, Chantal, and the governess, Mlle. Louise. It is his relations with this family and the situation that arises from the count's affair with the governess that accounts for most of the dramatic conflict that propels the narrative.[21] At first the count seems friendly, tolerating the priest's presence as long as he makes no attempt to "apply" any of his noble ideas. But the more the priest asks questions about Chantal's welfare and insists on visiting the countess, the more hostile the count's behavior becomes. It is clear from the priest's interview with the canon, the count's uncle, that the count wields the real authority in the community. Indeed, in her last scene with him, Chantal tells the priest that if he should return after his trip to Lille, her father would certainly have him transferred to another parish.

The priest's relationships with the three women in the count's life differ. Mlle. Louise, the sole attendant at daily mass, warns him that he has enemies. Her tears as she kneels in church suggest torment and helplessness. The countess, indifferent to her husband's infidelity, spends her days brooding over the death of her young son. The core of the scene between her and the priest is the struggle between his perseverance and her refusal to renounce her anger and accept her loss. In the end she acquiesces and receives his blessing and dies shortly after. It is his only unqualified victory in Ambricourt; not surprisingly, it also brings down the scorn of the count and the reproofs of the canon and Torcy himself.

Everyone concludes that it must have been his anguished scene with the countess, partially witnessed and misrepresented by Chantal, that induced her death. Only the priest and the viewer know that, on the contrary, the encounter brought the countess a longed-for peace. In the warm letter she sends the priest just before her death, she acknowledges that just as the death of her child plunged her into an abyss, another child, the priest, has taken her out of it. Though it may have helped to exculpate him, the priest does not mention this letter to Torcy, a decision that confirms his inner strength and the essence of his ministry, which, as the canon wryly remarks, probably does not concur with any two ideas of his own on how to run a parish. The canon concisely sums up the contest between the priest and the objects of his zeal when he tells him, "You're not the sort who can talk without saying anything, and unfortunately, that's what's wanted now."

The priest's relationship with Chantal is the most unsettling in both the film and the novel. Although this character has affinities with Bresson's later adolescent girls, Mouchette and Marie, she belongs to the privileged class and is more vindictive than either of her poorer, provincial likenesses, and less sympathetic as a result. Critics have objected to Nicole Ladmiral's performance as too melodramatic, but from the psychoanalytic point of view it perfectly captures the emotional confusion and sexual precociousness of the adolescent.[22] Her despair and loneliness are powerfully conveyed, particularly in the confessional scene, where she reveals her bitterness and hatred toward her mother, her father, and the governess, and what she is prepared to do to avenge herself for their indifference to her feelings.

In this scene, as well as the one with the countess, the priest reveals himself to be an astute psychologist. His ability to sear through the cold block of hate and resistance in which both characters are immured and perceive what they are hiding stuns Chantal into relinquishing the letter—in which, it is implied, she threatens to kill herself—that she had planned to send her father and which the priest intuits she holds in her pocket. This "supernatural charism of cardiognosis [sic] (or 'ability to read in men's hearts')" is a quality "possessed by both Bernanos's priests and his other saints."[23] In awe of such power, Chantal is convinced that the curé must be the devil (figure 12). In her last scene with him before his trip to Lille, amid her recriminations and acerbic remarks, she nevertheless cannot help wondering how he managed to move her mother, a woman who seemed completely withdrawn from the world and unyielding in her pride, to submit "gently" to the old faith. Chantal's curiosity hints at a potential for change, but there is no sentimental assurance of this possibility.

While these events shape the structure of the film, the narrative is also mobilized by the worsening of the priest's illness, which qualifies the role played by his clash with the count's family in the resolution of the story. Since he does not recover, the issue of whether he would have been able to return to Ambricourt is never tested. Indeed the illness is crucial; mere conflict between the priest and the count or criticism from the priest's superiors would hardly serve the film's Christological parallels. That is, the illness is not simply a fictional contrivance; it ensures the purgatorial trajectory of the narrative. It is the priest's dark night of the soul that the story relates, the painful progression of his sufferings and doubts, evoking the way of the cross in the life of Christ. The feeling he has that God has left him, reinforced by his inability to pray, is further intensified by Dr. Delbende's death, a probable suicide as a result of his loss of faith.

The final section of the film begins with the priest's trip to Lille. On the road to the train station he is surprised by Olivier, a young man who offers him a ride on his motorcycle. A nephew of the count's with little respect for his relatives, Olivier is a brave and forthright soldier in the Foreign Legion with cynical ideas about the modern world. It is a fleeting and ambiguous encounter; on the one hand, Olivier is the only character to promise genuine friendship and regrets that the priest is leaving. "Without that black robe, you'd look like one of us," he declares, buoying the priest's spirits and making him "feel young for the first time." Though somewhat cryptic, this remark can be understood in the spirit of "the quest for heroism" on the part of several writers, including Bernanos.[24] In that sense, the priest, as one who has fought in the trenches of provincial French life and faced the enemy— carnality, corruption, and despair—is no less a hero than the legionnaire, no less a soldier for being enlisted in the army of Christ.[25] However last minute, the sequence, possibly one that suffered from cutting, places the struggles of the priest into the larger context of the social war that led to such movements as worker priests in the 1940s.

On the other hand, one cannot help recalling other young men on motorcycles who turn up unexpectedly in French films, such as the black-shirted death figures in Cocteau's *Orphée*.[26] The association is not all that strange since much of Olivier's talk is about facing death, so that his appearance, immediately prior to the fatal news that awaits the priest in Lille, does not seem coincidental. In addition, the actor's manner borders on the seductive as he focuses on the bond between men facing death in what is, after all, a community without women, cues to which the priest seems entirely oblivious. Seeing Olivier as an angel of death may be, in part, a result of the film's compression; their meeting is considerably longer in the novel, covers many subjects, and is not directly linked to the priest's departure. Yet there is another aspect of the scene that deserves comment.

The motorcycle ride elicits an almost childlike glee from the priest, resulting in the broadest smile in the entire film, as he hangs on while Olivier speeds down the road. This glee is followed by the priest's surprise and plea-sure at Olivier's remark, a sense of having been accepted into a different community, one he may never have envisioned for himself: the community of men more fully engaged in traditional male pursuits. Earlier, Dr. Delbende, while examining the priest and remarking on his weak constitution, had expressed a similar sentiment, including the priest in the "race" to which he and Torcy belong, "the race that holds on," but there too we hear the priest's voice-over remark, "The idea that I belonged to the same race as these hefty men would never have occurred to me."

In the encounter with Olivier, the notion that the priest might belong to the community of men, living a more worldly and adventurous life, comes immediately before he learns he is about to die. The personal character of the priest, then, different from and notwithstanding his duties, is protected from the very associations with mature maleness and sexuality that would be incompatible with the virginal quality Bresson cultivates. At the moment he is symbolically embraced by a member of that male community, he faces death. Perhaps this is the way we should understand Bresson's religious protagonists, and, to some degree, the others as well: as those who have renounced both the world in which men and women go about their lives and perpetuate the race, as well as those who refuse that role in the name of trans-gressive sexual desires. Driven by neither heterosexual nor homosexual impulses, they are positioned at a precarious place in the middle and, if we consider their youth, a short-lived one at that, are cut off before their natural desires can emerge.

An even bigger cut from the novel, resulting in one of the film's most noticeable elisions, is the long scene with the specialist Dr. Laville.[27] Here, as in the cases of Torcy, Delbende, Olivier, and others, several subjects are discussed, including atheism, drug addiction, suicide, and the similarity between doctors and priests, both of whom, according to Dr. Laville, are forced to lie to their "patients." In the film, we do not even see the doctor, only the priest leaving his office downcast with the news of his stomach cancer, which he reveals soon after in voice-over as he sits in a café, writing in his diary. His last days are spent with his friend Louis Dufrety, a renegade priest living with a woman, and who also seems to be dying of a blood disease. His brief talk with the woman, prompts the priest's final act: to convince Dufrety to see Torcy and put his life in order.

Although there is no definite indication in the novel that Dufrety agrees to do this, the film's last scene begins with a close-up of the final diary entry: "He has agreed to see Torcy, my old master." Too weak to continue, the priest drops the pen, then the notebook onto the floor. He stands, moves toward the window, then sits and looks off screen until the fade-out. The screen fades in on a letter written by Dufrety to Torcy describing the priest's final moments and last words: "What does it matter? Grace is everywhere." The letter is read by Torcy's voice-over, during which the image changes to a gray backdrop against which the shadow of a cross, dividing the screen horizontally and vertically, is superimposed.

The Diary, Voice-over, and Other Strategies

Sanctity is constantly drawing from within itself what the artist borrows from

the world of forms.

—Georges Bernanos, *The Impostor*

The central character's consciousness dominates most of Bresson's narratives. As I argued in the preceding chapter, this was effected in *Les Dames du bois de Boulogne* through the use of technical conventions to underline Hélène's control over the plot. *Diary*, however, was Bresson's initial venture into first-person cinema, a form that he refined in his next two films. His preoccupation with it is easy to understand since first-person cinema would be fertile ground for the pursuit of two of Bresson's primary aims as a filmmaker: to intensify the means by which interiorization can be achieved through the external, and to reduce these means as much as possible to the essential, eliminating redundancy and minimizing the usual accouterments of the *cinema* in favor of the *cinematographic*. Restricting the narrative point of view justifies the delimiting of audio and visual material, which in turn makes the selection process both more exacting and more rigorous.

Frequently, the source of a first-person film is a literary work written in the first person. Because transposing such a work into a film often proves difficult, many conventional films employ the narrating character's voice-over now and then, but make little or no attempt to sustain the point of view by other means. Invariably, shots, even entire scenes, stretch, when they do not ignore, the legitimate parameters of the first person's knowledge or physical constraints.

The two films that follow *Diary, A Man Escaped* and *Pickpocket,* are exemplary in that virtually everything we see and hear is within the consciousness of the narrator, an effect reinforced by precise camera angles and movements that conform to the narrator's perspective. In *Diary* Bresson was faced with not just a first-person novel but one in the form of a diary, requiring an even more conscientious attempt to preserve the writer's intimate connection to the text and his private perspective. The challenge was not only to convey the perspective of the priest in the film's great scenes, such as the dramatic exchange with the countess and the confessional encounter with Chantal, nor even to sustain the sense that everything seen and heard is consistent with his point of view. The real challenge in converting this text to the externalized form of the cinema was to create various means to preserve the intimacy and deeply interior quality of the diary.

Bresson uses several strategies to enforce this quality; first, there are the shots of diary entries, many showing the hand of the priest as he writes, accompanied by his voice-over. This doubling effect indicates that the more than one hundred instances of voice-over apart from shots of the diary, several of these communicating things not elaborated cinematically,[28] are meant to evoke both. In other words, the spoken text is synonymous with the written text. Furthermore the action we witness is a virtual enactment of the words we hear and see, suggesting that the elaborated filmic text is, technically speaking, the equivalent of the spoken and written texts. To dismiss either of the latter as redundant would be to fall into the lulling comfort induced by the cinema's tendency to suggest a transparent reality. For whereas Bresson's cinema is among the most seductive in its commitment to the realistic, it is also exacting in positioning this "real" within an accountable framework and from a distinctly moral perspective. In place of an amorphous, illusionist realism, Bresson's method anchors everything within a specific consciousness.

Second, Bresson uses dolly shots, moving in to close-ups of the priest's face as he listens to and reacts to people and circumstances. Thus while the film offers expansive views of the village and atmospheric effects, we are repeatedly pulled back into the consciousness of the priest. The role of the dolly in this process is more extensive and purposeful than it was in his two previous films, another example of how Bresson invigorated the expressive potential of a convention. These moves of the dolly go beyond interactions between characters; they also imply "virtual interactions" between the priest and his inner self. His looks off screen in these cases are not to persons or things outside the frame but beyond the material world altogether. In both kinds of interaction Laydu's face is a critical factor. It is even likely that the frequent camera moves into long-held close-ups were a direct result of Bresson's discovery of Laydu. Finally, there are exceptions, those few instances when we see something outside the first-person perspective otherwise carefully sustained. These shed light on an important aspect of the priest's character and, arguably, on a preoccupation of the filmmaker as well.

The Diary Entries

Twenty-five close-ups of the diary do more than remind us of the point of view. Introducing scenes that flesh them out filmically, they sustain both the tenor and the tense, a mixture of the simple present and the indefinite past, of the priest's entries, countering the temptation to see the film as only a reconstruction of the past.[29] This is the impression one gets with the first shot of the hand that opens the diary and removes a blotter to reveal that the words heard on the soundtrack—"I don't think I shall be doing any harm if I note down, quite frankly, day by day, the humble and insignificant secrets of a life, which, in any case, contains no mystery"—have already been written (figure 13). When we learn at the end that the priest has died, we might think in retrospect that the diary in the first shot was opened by someone who knew him, either Torcy or Dufrety. This is contradicted, however, by the knowing and familiar gestures of the same hand as it handles the notebook, as well as by the priest's voice heard over the sentence. As has been alleged, the voice is equivalent to both the written and filmic text, a strategy underlined by several transitions from diary page to its filmic enactment, which are marked by dissolves that carry the act of writing over to the incoming image (figure 14), an inscription that equates writing with filmmaking. Thus all three modes occupy the same grammatical tense, permitting us to follow the priest's experiences as they occur in the present of the film's unfolding.

An early scene involving Séraphita demonstrates this interdependence of the diary's text and its filmic equivalent. In a shot of the diary the priest writes of the catechism class that prepares children for communion. The shot dissolves to the girls entering the building as the voice-over remarks, "The girls seemed so full of promise, especially Séraphita Dumouchel." This ends over a medium close-up of Séraphita, her hand eagerly raised in the class already in progress. The camera pulls back to reveal the other children facing front, one girl struggling to answer a question about Christ's establishing of the Eucharist. Finally the priest, smiling, nods to Séraphita, who stands and gives the perfect answer, her eyes glowing in close-up, as if in an ecstatic trance. The priest dismisses the class and calls her up for a "good mark." In a shot-countershot exchange between them, he asks if she is eager to receive communion, to which she replies, "No....It will come when it comes." His initial gratification somewhat dimmed by this response, the priest wonders why she has learned the lessons so well. Unabashedly Séraphita looks up at him and says, "It is because you have such beautiful eyes." Over this we hear the sound of giggling from outside. Séraphita leaves to join the others, and as they run off, the scene dissolves back to a shot of the diary, over which the priest's voice remarks, "They had arranged the whole thing between them. But why should these little ones be so against me? What have I done to them?"

The scene unfolds to place the viewer in the same frame of mind as the priest. His initial words prepare us to see the first shot of Séraphita in the same promising vein: her intent gaze, her extended arm unable to conceal her eagerness, the reverential way she responds—all of this underscored by Grünenwald's lyrical music and suggesting an amenable meeting of minds between her and the priest. Then comes the surprise exchange. The scene is thus set up cinematically and performed to mirror the priest's anticipation and subsequent disappointment; it is only at the end that the viewer senses the disparity between his perceptions and the facts. Had we detected the outcome beforehand, through a different treatment or acting style, the rendering would contravene the spirit of the diary and the perceptual process of the priest. Thus, even though the source of the scene is what is contained in the diary, its actualization allows us to experience what occurs *as* it takes place and *before* the priest actually recorded it in the diary.

Sometimes a diary entry and voice-over set up a scene that illustrates what has already been written and said. For example, the priest's remark that Séraphita "torments" him is followed by a brief scene in which, as he approaches her sitting on a fence by the road, she suddenly runs off, tossing her satchel behind her. Immediately after, he tells us that when he returned the satchel, he "got a cold welcome," and we see her mother taking the bag and pushing Séraphita into the house without exchanging words with the priest. Given the power of film and Bresson's penchant for realism, these scenes tend to validate the priest's subjective reactions, lending veracity to his perceptions.

The Face and the Dolly: Interactions with Others

Ah, the *other*—man, world, God—more ourselves in its secret avowals than we could ever be. You scrutinize its face. Meanwhile it models yours.

—Edmond Jabès, *The Book of Dialogue*

A typical example of how the dolly marks the move from an external, interactive space to the interior, private consciousness of the priest is the first scene with the curé of Torcy, following the priest's distressing encounter with the farmer Fabregard over the cost of his wife's funeral. As the tone and content of Torcy's speech becomes more admonishing, comparing the "church leaders" of his day with the "choirboys" of the present and warning the priest against wanting to be loved, the camera holds on the priest. As we hear Torcy, his voice slowly diminishing, say, "Create order all day long, knowing disorder will win tomorrow," the camera moves in to a close-up of the priest listening attentively to these words before the fade-out. As it does elsewhere, this movement literalizes the idea of the priest's taking in what others say. Further reflection is confirmed in the next scene, as he sits peeling potatoes in the kitchen, his voice-over repeating Torcy's advice.

The longest example of this tendency of the camera to remain on his face as another character speaks occurs near the end, when the priest, now dying, listens to his friend Louis Dufrety explain why he left the priesthood. Again Bresson binds the filmic experience to the first-person perspective as we perceive Dufrety's lengthy discourse via the transformations it educes on the priest's face: the furrowing of his brow and the intense gaze that implies concern for the spiritual condition of others. Penetrating his friend's defenses, the priest responds aggressively, contradicting the passivity that some critics believe these long takes imply.[30] Facing death, the priest continues to minister to the souls of others.[31]

Although these instances reinforce the film's subjectivity, Bresson was hardly a long-take director, nor was he inclined to indulge in prolonged attention to an actor's face. Yet here he is, this filmmaker for whom the marriage of actors and film was to lead quickly to divorce, displaying both traits. He must have known that such shots would be ineffective were it not for the earnestness registered on Laydu's face. That this film was the first and last occasion for such extended long takes of an actor's face—comparable perhaps to another one-of-a-kind cinematic encounter, that between Dreyer and Falconetti—suggests that Bresson's renunciation of such tendencies in the future may have been more than a matter of aesthetics, indeed may have been instrumental in the change in his style. As with Dreyer, a certain powerful seduction into a projective identification with this most ideal and obedient of filmic surrogates may have taken place. Laydu, whose commitment to the project was unstinting, is hardly just staring into space in such shots, but *performing* with every ounce of his being—emotionally, physically, and psychologically, a condition Bresson seems to have enthusiastically exploited to a degree he may not have wished to repeat. When he remarked of his models that they could offer their "virgin" personalities only once, he may well have been speaking of some part of his own character that was deeply affected by this experience.

Internal Interactions

Nowhere is Bresson's work with Laydu and the connotations suggested above more evident than in those moments when the priest is alone, consumed by doubt, trying desperately to commune with his God. Such moments must have posed a great challenge for actor and director. Here too Bresson chose the long take and the close-up. In a sense these moments constitute a subset of shots that embody not only the subjectivity of the narrative but the core relationship of the film, crystallizing the essence of the character, his moral dilemma and psychological conflict, and how he deals with them.

Relatively early in the film, for example, the priest feels abandoned and without faith, a state brought on by a series of perceived failures to be accepted by his parishioners. In three long takes we see him alone in his rooms trying, but failing, to pray. "Behind me, there was no longer the daily, familiar life from which one can escape. Behind me there was nothing. Before me, there was a wall, a blank wall." We hear this in voice-over as he looks so intently off screen with what Bresson aptly calls "the ejaculatory force of the eye," that the viewer anticipates, almost physically, a cut to the object of his glance that we feel certain is just beyond the frame. But of course nothing in the off screen space materializes to answer this shot, not even the cross hanging on the wall, which we see moments later behind the priest. In fact, its being behind him, where, in his words, "there was nothing," seems to accentuate the blankness "before" him, precluding the viewer's filling in the picture with the knowledge of the cross's presence in the off screen space to which he looks.

The sequence exemplifies the central relationship in the life of the priest, that between his God and himself, and the central conflict that he faces: sustaining his faith in the light of God's silence. While these themes weave throughout, the priest's interactions with others accord with his vocation and vows. His faith is manifested through actions and interactions, the directness and simplicity of which "burn people," as Torcy puts it. But when he is alone, he often suffers with doubt. These are the moments that expose his moral crisis and speak to the essence of the narrative, its core, and Bresson treats them with a subtle coordination of actor, mise-en-scène, and an extraordinary evocation of off screen space. On most, but not all occasions, voice-over also renders his monologue and the sense of void in the off screen space conjured by the intensity of his gazes directed there, so that when he finally says, "God has left me. Of this I am certain," we have already witnessed the filmic analogue to that thought.

Bresson's use of long takes at these moments, particularly when they are not accompanied by voice-over, as in the moving final shot of the priest following his last diary entry, was not, I would argue, to give his relatively inexperienced actor freer rein, as might be the case with more actor-friendly directors. The choice serves formal and thematic purposes. The long takes constitute the most convincing evidence that Bresson had found the ideal face and wanted to plumb every facet of its mysterious clarity. In addition they accentuate the absence at the heart of the sequences cited and often summon up a countershot that never materializes. I deliberately invoke the term shot-countershot, commonly used in conversations, because there is a conversation of sorts implied, albeit an inaudible one, between a believer and his unresponsive God. The very duration of these shots intensifies the silence of that hidden Being who *must* lie beyond the limits of the frame but whose immaterial existence is longingly sought in those unreciprocated gazes into off screen space.

In a sense these shots of the priest can be considered long takes by default; that is, they must do the work of an impossible shot-countershot structure. As such they become the filmic equivalent of the defining feature of the priest's torment, his need to sustain the faith that is both critical to his identity and valued only to the degree that it is *not* validated in material terms. In those intense looks beyond the frame, the priest confronts the core of his being, for it is only his faith that can fill the void. In terms of those *rapports* that define the cinema for Bresson, it is the *absence* of the countershot that matters here and that refers us back to the consciousness that looks while understanding that the truth of its vocation can only be confirmed by that absence.

These crucial shots might have failed in their objective without the unique qualities of this actor's face, its ability to reveal the character's interiority. Given the demands of this narrative, it seems inevitable that Bresson's camera would so privilege the face of the actor—hardly cause for surprise in the work of any other director. Bresson, though, was on his way toward repudiating professional actors precisely because he believed they were forced to exteriorize themselves from habit, and so could not convey genuine feelings. Yet his camera tracks in unhesitatingly, over and over, with utmost confidence, to the face of this neophyte. Clearly Bresson had made a crucial discovery: that the right face was more important than acting experience. The felicitous conjunction of the role of the country priest and Laydu's face produced a performance that can only be judged miraculous.

Laydu revealed that Bresson would read the Bernanos text aloud to the actor while the camera was running, to the understandable irritation of the sound man.[32] This would account for the alertness and intensity of his looks and the sense of conviction he radiates. Bresson was hardly aiming for a Kuleshov effect, in which the actor's expressions are intercut with a variety of objects of his or her gaze and the performance simply a product of the editing. Bresson's strategy stressed the primacy of the text and its determinant effect on every image, infusing shots of the priest with the very qualities that generated the diary's existence: self-examination and an inclination to solitude. But beyond that, it is clear that another kind of *rapport*, as binding as those within the film, was at work here: that between the action being filmed and what was occurring behind the camera. Bresson acknowledged Laydu's all-consuming dedication when he said that he could never use the actor again because, "I robbed him of what I needed to make the film. How could I rob him twice."[33]

So, as the priest gazes into off screen space in spiritual conversation with his God, the actor is engaged with the presence and the voice of *his* creator. What a fitting metaphor for the relationship between the fictional character of the priest and his God—no less effective for being hidden from the viewer, like that higher, equally hidden Being is to the priest. We might conclude, then, that the combination of the long takes of Laydu's face and Bresson's reciting of the Bernanos text allowed the dynamics of artistic creation to fuse—in the actor's mind and through the mysterious generative nature of performance itself—with the divine.

Exceptions

Given the care with which Bresson has shaped first-person consciousness in the film, what can be said of those occasions that seem to fall outside the priest's perspective? I do not mean the pictorial vistas typical of the classical tradition, like the one of a landscape at night, shot from a dramatic low angle, in which the priest in his black cloak is dwarfed by the silhouettes of huge tree trunks and branches against a moonlit sky. Such a shot expresses the formidable forces of nature against which the priest battles and is the kind of authorial commentary Bresson would avoid in the future.[34]

I mean those instances when the viewer learns something to which the priest does not seem to be privy. In the opening scene there is a medium-close shot of a couple, later identified as the count and Mlle. Louise, embracing on the grounds of the count's estate, looking off screen at, so the editing implies, the priest in extreme long shot standing outside the presbytery. Although there are several shots of the priest, who is on the far side of the iron fence of the estate, looking right and left, in no shot is his look directed toward the area where the couple stand; that is, no shot confirms that he sees or is aware of their presence.[35] Nor do his opening words or the voice-over remark that closes the sequence, "My first parish," imply as much. In fact, in later conversation with the count the priest is surprised that the count "seemed upset when [he] mentioned Mlle. Louise," when any foreknowledge of their relationship would preclude such surprise.[36]

Since this was Bresson's initial effort at first-person narrative cinema, prevailing conventions cannot be ruled out. In that tradition, shots not optically grounded from the narrator's perspective can nonetheless be accommodated if there are reasons for doing so. But the exceptions in the film are restricted to one group of characters: the count and his relations. In addition to the shots of the couple in the opening, there is another later as they watch the priest approaching the estate; a shot at an even later visit when the priest is seen by Chantal from behind a tree on the grounds; and two shots of Chantal standing outside and eavesdropping just below the window of the room during the tense scene between the priest and the countess. In all of these the priest is ostensibly unaware that he is observed.

Even in early Bresson, characters either see something or they do not. It is likely, therefore, that had he wanted unambiguously to imply that the priest sees the couple in the first sequence, he could easily have made this clear. If, for example, the iron fence were in the foreground of the shot of the couple, the shots before it and after it could be read as confirming reverse angles. The only things confirmed by those shots, however, are the proximity of the fenced-in area to the presbytery and that the priest is not looking in the couple's direction. Furthermore the final long shot of the couple is not from the priest's side of the fence, which might have pinpointed the relationship of the fence to both sides and implied that the long shot was from his perspective. It is possible that these connections were left deliberately indeterminate.

Although the film was subjected to extensive cuts, it is unlikely that they would have been at the expense of clarity.[37] It is possible that the producer or Bresson himself decided that the dramatic core on which the plot turns—namely, the adulterous couple, Chantal's distress, and the countess's death—should be signaled at an early stage of the narrative instead of halfway through, as it is in the novel. This still leaves the opening ambiguous.

It would appear that the behavior of these characters enjoys some immunity from the priest's narrative authority, compatible with their resistance to his discomfiting presence in their lives. Such shots inject a degree of suspense into the narrative and render the priest more vulnerable, which he only realizes when he learns that his exchange with the countess was, in fact, witnessed by Chantal. These exceptions qualify the notion that the diary is the equivalent of a master narrative in which everything exists only through its author's observation and perception. Unintended or not, these apparent punctures in the fabric of an integral point of view stress the impenetrable façades of characters who harbor secrets and object to the priest's presence in the village. In effect they represent the world itself as essentially impermeable to the spiritual fire of the priest.

However we explain the reason behind these shots, they effectively inoculate the priest from contamination, much like the way Bernanos's priest leaves "certain vexations" out of his diary, loath to name the "antagonist" that inspires them. In the novel we learn that he was forced early on "to see life as it really is" and is "terrified of lust...especially in children," who suffer and despair because of it. "The demon of agony is, essentially, the demon of lust...a mysterious wound in the side of humanity; or rather at the very source of its life!"[38] Chantal's pathology in both the novel and the film reflects the "madness" this "tumor" can generate in adolescence. As filtered through her psyche, the sexual activities between the count and the governess, no doubt acutely painful to the ears of a gifted eavesdropper, is deformed well beyond an illicit affair.

None of these obsessions with the crippling effects of lust, which the novel's priest wonders might be equivalent to madness, including his memories of witnessing drunken debaucheries, is recounted in the film. Even without the inevitable resistance of producers and censors to such material, it seems that Bresson opted to exclude anything that would tarnish the figure of the priest, as well as the actor who plays him. An unhealthy obsession with the fear of lust in children and the vexations it causes would more than likely have unbalanced his portrait, qualifying the legitimacy of the priest's insights and the genuine spirituality he inspires, for example, in the scene with the countess, as will be argued below.

Bresson's characters, male and female, as well as what he subsequently called the "models" who played them, came under this protective mantle. If his wish to keep the image of the priest as pure as possible was tied to the image of the actor, then Laydu was not only the perfect model of the country priest, but the model on which characters in subsequent films and the nonprofessionals who played them would be based. This suggests that the concept of the male model is as strongly bound to impressions of innocence and virginity as it is to theories about the difference between professional actors and amateurs. Neither Fontaine (*A Man Escaped*) nor Michel (*Pickpocket*) is a religious figure or a saint; nor is Charles (*The Devil Probably*) or Gawain (*Lancelot of the Lake*). Yet they share a family resemblance and, like the priest, seem poised at a juncture where innocence has not quite been overshadowed by experience and is not compromised by what they do, whether that be soldiering, thieving, or killing. Nor can it be a coincidence that with one exception (Charles), all find themselves in circumstances that, in one way or another, proscribe sexuality.

A Consummate Farewell

As the final scene with the countess demonstrates, this impression of the priest does not preclude his knowledge of the human heart or his ability to be effective. A "scene" in the most classical sense, it (a) occurs in its entirety within the same confined space; (b) involves at least two characters; (c) has a discernible beginning, middle, and end; and (d) is developed through a highly volatile verbal exchange. These features are enhanced filmically through a vigorous use of shot exchanges, camera angles, camera movement, and editing in sync with the rising and falling action of the situation. Running a full ten minutes, it is the longest, most poignant, and last scene of its kind in Bresson's career.

The first important aspect of the scene is that it highlights the difference between the professional actor and what Bresson would soon call the model. Marie-Monique Arkell is the epitome of the classically trained actor and the essence of nobility within the fiction. Claude Laydu is both an acting novice of fortuitous discovery and the embodiment of the inspired neophyte whose insights seem to spring from a source beyond him, much like the unexpected revelations Bresson believed he could draw from his models. Though one need not be aware of the difference in acting styles to feel the force of the scene, knowledge of it in conjunction with the fictional personae lends the scene greater resonance.

The second important aspect of the scene is that it exemplifies the inter-action between psychology and the spiritual, which, as I argued in the Intro-duction, is key to how character transformation is effected in Bresson's work. The scene's psychodynamics are dictated, initially, by the countess's declara-tion that the priest, who has come to warn her about her daughter's state of mind, hardly possesses the life experience to give advice so vehemently. Her remark that he is but a child himself suggests one way the scene can be read: not as an interaction between two adults with commensurate knowledge of the world, but as a struggle between one consumed by pride and one driven by ministerial vows. It is the priest's childlike directness and innocence, the outward sign of that "supernatural charism of cardiognosis," as von Balthasar puts it, that breaks through the wall of the countess's defenses and frees her from the deadly sin that consumes her. This scene puts in perspective the sexual questions cited earlier: it is not the sins of the flesh but the resistance of the spirit that keeps the individual from God. Though the priest's ability to reach the countess before her death is his only success in Ambricourt, the length and weight of this scene clearly attest that it is sufficient.

The scene occurs in the same room looking out onto the garden in which the countess received the priest on his first visit and where she spends her days reading and brooding over her dead son. Beginning on a close-up of the fireplace, the shot moves out to frame both figures. The countess is complacent, even haughty, as she dismisses the priest's concern that Chantal might kill herself. She mocks his theories as things "someone must have told [him]. "It's outside your personal experience," she says. But his remark that he fears his own death less than he does hers stirs her, a moment marked by a cut and a shift of ground. She walks to the window in the foreground and partly closes it, an ironic touch since this does not prevent Chantal from eavesdropping minutes later. Feigning indifference to her husband's infidelities, she asks why she should care after years of humiliation. She misconstrues pride as the strength to ignore the embarrassment a scandal would cause, whereas the priest implies something far graver.

The proof that he has touched a nerve is that as he is about to leave, she asks, "What have I done wrong?" It marks a tremor in the wall of her resistance; the priest seems to know something and perhaps has the means to heal her. "You're throwing a child out of her home forever," he says. When she concedes this to be true, he responds with a leap to the more provocative, "God will break you." Looking toward the photo of her dead son on the mantle, she says that he already has. A series of shot-countershot exchanges articulates the tug of war between his salvos and her "hardness," a word that so alarms her when he uses it that he knows he is at the core of her defense. Refusing to be silent, he warns her that the "coldness of her heart" will keep her from her son in the afterlife.

His voice-over registers the toll the heat of battle takes on him. His eyes close as we hear, "With my back against the wall before this imperious woman, I looked like a guilty man, trying in vain to justify himself." His sudden faintness arouses a motherly concern in the countess that momentarily equalizes the match and allows it to continue. She encourages him to gather his strength while insisting that nothing can separate her from her dead child, but he sees that her manner places her "beyond love's reach." When she asks why she should bear more guilt than her husband and her daughter, he responds, "No one knows what can come of an evil thought in the long run. Our hidden faults poison the air others breathe."

To purge her "hidden sin," he says that she must resign herself and open her heart. Again she misunderstands, or pretends to, by looking at the photo of the child and responding, "If I were not resigned, I'd be dead." "That's not the resignation I mean," he corrects. He cuts through her defense that she goes to mass and observes the rituals by calling it a "bargain" she dares to make with God. Up against it at last, she hurls at him, "God has ceased to matter to me. What will you gain by making me admit I hate Him, you fool?" As the camera moves in to the priest's face, there is the pause of a heartbeat or two before he asserts simply, defiantly, and confidently, "You don't hate Him now. Now at last you are face to face." Her utter silence confirms this to be true, as she walks slowly to a chair, her hand holding the medallion around her neck that contains a lock of her dead son's hair, and sits. For the first time she lacks a response.

In the final phase of their encounter, he speaks of the mercy of Christ until she says the words, "Thy kingdom come," that release her. At this moment there is a long shot of Chantal outside the window, the basis of her puzzlement later over her mother's demeanor. The countess admits that she "might have died with hatred in [her] heart," and as the camera closes in on her, she describes the state of her mind: "An hour ago my life seemed to me in order, each thing in its place. You have left nothing standing." She hurls the medallion into the fireplace, which the priest hastily retrieves, assuring her that God is no torturer. With that, she kneels to receive his blessing (figure 15). The letter she sends him later that evening, just before dying, affirms that she is at peace.

As the most extended illustration of how the priest works, this scene is a powerful demonstration of how Bresson weaves the psychological and the spiritual. If the priest's uncanny ability to discern the shifting fluctuations of the countess's feelings and the misery that oppresses her is, as he himself views it, the result of God's grace working through him, the instrument of its moment-by-moment progress and ultimate success is his mental astuteness, a combination of observation, intuition, and empathic identification that also marks a gifted psychoanalyst. From her initial efforts to demean him to her need to know what he knows, from her stubborn resistance via her assertion of innocence and compromises to her final letting go of the last bastions of defense, the countess enacts the necessary stages through which a person in analysis becomes aware of the psychic energy he or she has expended to sustain a lie at the cost of peace of mind. The priest's moves display a keen awareness of how far he can push at each stage, using silence as well as confrontation, serving as the safe "container" of the countess's emerging self as it slowly and warily sheds the armor in which it is encased. Like an analyst aware of the role counter-transference plays in his interactions with patients, the priest recognizes his own hubris when he says he felt like a guilty man trying to justify himself. And like an effective analyst, he understands the moment when the countess feels that he has "left nothing standing" not as psychic collapse but as the point at which new structures of the self can be installed. In his terms, yielding everything to God, pride and all, is an opening of the heart that can bring mental and spiritual health.

Though it resembles the bedside scene in *Les Anges*, in which another fervent individual struggles valiantly to save the soul of a hardened sinner while beset by a fatal illness, the interaction is more electric, the visual structure more dynamic. Bresson does not restrict it to a shot-countershot treatment. He makes more use of off screen space; sound, other than the voices of the characters; character mobility; and small but significant camera movements. Most of all there is the face of Laydu, with its intense gaze and radiant youthfulness. I said earlier that Bresson's dollies into this face literalize the sense of the priest's taking in the words of another, stressing interiority and therefore the diary. In the scene with the countess, this movement demonstrates how critical this feature is to the priest's ability to practice his ministry in the moment. This occurs at the turning point of the scene, when he grasps the true state of the countess's soul and her declared hatred of God. Just before the line "You don't hate him now," the camera moves in, underlining the pregnant pause and allowing us to see the inner glow that emanates from the priest before he speaks. This movement, in such a confined space, would seem to have no other purpose than to mark the complex nature of the encounter: the priest's acute attentiveness to the off screen countess, his openness to receive the "right" spiritual interpretation, and his ability to transmit to her the grace that comes through him. His next line, "Now you are face to face," refers as much to the countess's situation as it does to the interface between him and his God.

Bresson provides a wonderfully subtle touch that grounds this intensely spiritual moment in a naturalistic reality. Just as the film cuts from the priest to the countess absorbing his words, we hear the raking of leaves outside her window. It not only prepares us for the surprising shot of Chantal minutes later, but as a task that requires the patient and diligent gathering of dispersed material, the raking lends a workmanlike dignity to the priest's labor with the countess. Its allusion to the natural order goes further than any ethereal use of lighting or music that a more conventional film might deploy and confirms that even interior transformations are grounded in the physical world. This is the kind of genuine spirituality that characterizes Bresson and that speaks as well to the psychological acuity through which it works.

I remarked earlier that the exterior shots of Chantal compromise the integrity of the first person point of view. But here we sense Bresson's intuitive genius. For there is no better testament to the intense degree of intimacy achieved in this scene than the genuine shock produced by those shots, arousing in the viewer the sense of outrage and violation denied the unsuspecting priest and his confessor. In the countess's final surrender and request for the priest's blessing, we can also read Bresson's farewell to a grand acting tradition and the cinema of the scene. Just as the force emanating from the priest to move the countess to the transformation of her soul comes, he assures her, not from his own experience but through the power of grace, this model of future models enacts the mandate of *his* creator, illuminating the path along which Bresson's cinema would subsequently travel.

Passion and the Long Take

Considering that path, the final moments of *Diary of a Country Priest*, comprising four extraordinary long takes, exhibit such an unfaltering confidence in this filmic strategy as to make us wonder what happened to that Bresson. It is tempting to imagine that he understood and cherished the uniqueness of what he had achieved and by subsequently abolishing long takes of his models chose to keep this film and this performance distinct among his accomplishments, somewhat like Bernanos who was so deeply attached to his novel that he wanted to keep the manuscript in a drawer.

Because the formal characteristics of *Diary of a Country Priest* were virtually unrepeated and in the critical literature are given less weight than the style to follow, they warrant attention. The previous section analyzed a great scene in the classical tradition, making full use of shot-countershot. The four long takes that end the film are no less noteworthy. They should not be thought of simply as aspects of the more conventional kind of cinema that Bresson left behind. In the context of the time, they seem a response to the cinematographic style of Roberto Rossellini, as seen in his war trilogy, *Open City* (1945), *Paisà* (1946), and *Germany Year Zero* (1947), all released after Bresson's *Les Dames* and before he began *Diary*. It would be hard to find comparable uses of the static long take until the mature work of Antonioni or the avant-garde cinema of the 1960s (e.g., in the work of Warhol). Nor do Bresson's shots resemble prior effusions of the long take, such as those in

Welles's *Citizen Kane* (1941) and *The Magnificent Ambersons* (1942) or Cocteau's *Les Parents Terribles* (1948), all of which involve a greater sense of the theatrical and a more elaborate mise-en-scène. Though Bresson was undoubtedly influenced by the aesthetic shifts of the period, it is clear that he was equally concerned with how the long take served the needs of his scenario, especially the final stages of his protagonist's life.

The first such shot is noteworthy both for its minimalism and for its dialectic between on-screen and off screen space, neither, incidentally, primary motivations of the long takes in the films cited above. The priest, having been told that he is dying of cancer, has come to visit Dufrety, the friend from the seminary who has left the priesthood and is living with a woman. After their initial exchanges, we hear Dufrety's long rationale for the way he lives, along with the shuffling of his slippers against the floor, while the camera remains focused on a medium close-up of the priest's anguished, exhausted, but transfixed face, more concerned about his friend's state than his own illness. The shot, more than three minutes long, registers the changes on his face as he listens attentively, his eyes widening at times in response to the pain to which he ultimately succumbs, but not before he comments on his friend's skewed scale of values: "In your place, if I'd broken my ordination promises, I'd rather it had been for love of a woman than for what you call your intellectual life." Dufrety's disputatious response is interrupted when the priest seems about to faint, as the shot fades out.

The fade-in to the next long take begins on a close-up of the priest lying on a cot, suddenly sitting up and exclaiming that he doesn't want to die there. As the camera tilts up over the bed we see the couple in the background as Dufrety leaves for a pharmacy. The woman comes forward slowly, and as she sits to the right of the bed, the camera lowers to frame her and the priest in a two-shot for the bulk of this three-and-a-half-minute long take. Through her flat, almost uninflected speech, we learn that she is a cleaning lady and that she was against marrying Dufrety because of his ill health and alcoholism, but also because of the possibility of his returning to the priesthood. Through her manner and her discourse, she proves to be one of those who belong, as Dr. Delbende said of the priest, to the race that holds on. The priest is impressed by her simplicity and loyalty, with her "ageless voice that goes on through time…the voice which holds out against all the miseries of the world." It is a wrenching, subtly acted scene, more understated than almost any film of the time I can think of, including most Italian neorealist works. It is his exchange with this woman that moves the priest to his final act of ministry. When Dufrety returns and she leaves the shot, the camera moves in as the priest draws Dufrety closer and says, with all the energy he can muster, that he must speak to him about himself. The stillness of the shot during the exchange between the priest and the woman attests to Bresson's intuitions about models and shot duration, evidence of his mastery of the rhetoric of classical cinema. Given his aspirations, that fact is no doubt precisely what impelled him to move beyond it.

The second long take dissolves to a page from the diary, in which the priest makes his final entry, about Dufrety's agreeing to meet Torcy, "my old Master." There is a cut from this to the third long take, an almost two-minute medium shot of the priest, an old worn blanket over his shoulders, as loose sheets of the diary and then his pen slip from his feeble hands to the floor. He rises and walks to the window, then to a chair, where he sits staring into off screen space as the camera closes in on his face until the fade-out. It is our last view of him.

The sequence of the three long takes traces not only the priest's progression toward death but also his passion as he refuses to allow the faltering powers of his body to deter the work of his ministry. This is matched by the logic of the shots themselves: the first is a dialectic between him and the off screen object of his concern; the second an interaction contained within the frame; and the third a dialectic between the priest and the unknown that lies beyond the frame. In its extended duration in real time, the long take is the appropriate filmic gesture in all three instances, measuring both the suffering and the preciousness of the priest's final moments. In keeping with the analogies between his life and that of Christ, the final long take, quite rightly, is of the cross itself. It is preceded by a close-up of the letter Dufrety has sent to Torcy; as the voice-over, presumably Torcy's, reads its contents, the white page dissolves to the dark shadow of the cross on a wall, extending from the top to the bottom of the frame. Not coincidentally it is accompanied by a description of the dying priest's physical anguish, vomiting streams of blood, sweat covering his brow and cheeks, a rapidly weakening pulse. Holding a rosary to his chest, we are told, he asked for absolution from his renegade friend, whose hesitation to grant the request recalls Thérèse's being commandeered into completing the dying Anne-Marie's vows. Behind his final words—"What does it matter? All is grace"—is the confirmation of a life lived in faith, its mission, as the figure evoked by the cross said of his, "finished." The emphasis on suffering here and through much of the film is consistent with Bernanos, who was among the generation of Catholic writers deeply affected by the work of the nineteenth-century writer Léon Bloy, for whom the embrace of suffering was the only true way to approach and be worthy of Christ, something he not only expressed repeatedly in his own diaries, letters, and novels, but which he actively sought by living an impoverished existence.

The film's final long take, technically another exception from the ruling point of view, as are the shot and reading of the letter that precede it, can be viewed as an acknowledgment by the filmmaker of the veracity of the faith to which the priest has clung, a metafictional validation of his tenacity. Yet given the analogy implied between the priest's movement toward death and the passion and death of Christ, it is also possible to see the long take of the cross as the logical concluding image of the narrative, providing appropriate closure to everything that has preceded.

Beyond the symbolism of the iconography there is on the filmic level an intriguing variation of a key strategy of the film that bears on the reading of the final shot. The long take before it, of the priest staring out beyond the frame, is the final example of those core shots analyzed earlier that invoke the response of a countershot that never comes, that is precluded (figure 16). Within the parameters of that logic, the force of the outward gaze of the priest attests to the quality and degree of his faith. Its genuineness is mirrored by, indeed transposed into the repudiation of the fundamental structure of the syntax of narrative cinema, the shot-countershot. But with the final long take, this imaginary severing might be said to undergo belated repair through the visual evocation, after the priest's death, of the very thing he was denied in life. In a sense, the film seems to offer the viewer the cathartic release suspended throughout. That is, an ideal viewer might quite literally via the dissolve see *through* the Bernanos text—the mediating shot of the letter—to the image to which it yields. In doing so, the final long take of the cross (figure 17) would then be experienced not so much as an authorial statement as that long delayed countershot, indeed that "impossible" countershot denied throughout.

While making *The Gospel According to St. Matthew*, Pasolini, affirming his atheism, said that in order to be true to the source, he had to "plunge [himself] into the soul of someone who believed.... That is where you have free indirect discourse: on the one hand the narrative is seen through my own eyes; on the other, through those of a believer."[39] This idea, which he also called "free indirect subjectivity," is a useful way to understand the nature of many first-person cinematic narratives, as opposed to first-person literature, since it allows us to see things that are not necessarily seen by the apparent protagonist, but that are nevertheless a valid reflection of his or her view of the fictional world. In the case of *Diary of a Country Priest*, it might apply not only to those instances that are not technically from the point of view of the priest, but also to the reading of the final shot. This would suggest that the relevance of Bresson's faith to his work is as legitimate a question of his early films as it is of the later. What may be the more important difference is his view of the individual as a convincing carrier of this faith. Whether or not the final shot of *Diary of a Country Priest* confirms the religious beliefs of the artist who conceived it is something we can never know. But as the image that crystallizes the longing, the ministerial devotion, and the object of prayer for the film's protagonist, it validates—indeed it *defines*—his sanctity as that disposition which, despite his suffering, the anguish of doubt, and the pernicious torments of the body, remained devoted to the spiritual well-being of others.

I believe that one moves an audience only through rhythm, concentration,
and unity.

—Robert Bresson, in an interview by Charles Thomas Samuels (1970),

in Samuels, *Encountering Directors*

3

Triumphs of the Will

A Man Escaped (1956) and *Pickpocket* (1959) are among the few Bresson films
that do not end in either tragedy or death. The denouements of both are
triumphs, worldly as well as spiritual. In *Pickpocket* Michel awakens from his
nightmare and discovers the value of love; in *A Man Escaped* Fontaine escapes
from the German-held prison where he was condemned to death. As Bresson's most optimistic narratives, both films are preoccupied with freedom in
the literal and symbolic senses. Freedom is Fontaine's goal, the motivation of
every gesture, his raison d'être. Michel at first misunderstands it, believing,
after his first theft, that he is "master of the world." As with his prototype
Raskolnikov, the protagonist of Dostoevsky's *Crime and Punishment*, who
also thinks himself above moral and social laws, true freedom comes after he
is imprisoned and learns to accept his humanity.

As we have seen, freedom in a Bresson film is a paradoxical concept, like
the view of Diderot in which, though everything seems "written up above,"
one continues to perform moral or immoral actions. In *A Man Escaped* and
Pickpocket this contradiction is reinforced, even though both films are first-
person narratives and both protagonists are highly individualized. And

because the dynamic of each film springs from the tenacious behavior of each character, action determines the narrative, thematic, and formal impulses of both films. It is not unlikely that the refinement of Bresson's style, his honing of the craft of filmmaking, was a direct result of his decisive treatment of the physical activities with which both films are preoccupied. These actions are not just implied through voice-over narration; they consume a good deal of footage and screen time.[1]

In this sense, the triumph of the spirit each character experiences is matched by Bresson's leap forward in filmic form. Action becomes the narrating agent, the rationale for nearly every shot and the motive for nearly every cut. The efficiency and spareness—of shot material, shot duration, and editing—that we associate with Bresson's mature style are products of this concentration. Most shots either initiate an action or show one in progress, just as most cuts fall on an action, elide part of an action, or advance to a subsequent action. Consequently the imagery of both films privileges hands as well as faces. Even when the action is only a shot-countershot exchange of looks, it is marked by an exactness of framing and punctuation. There is in both films consanguinity between the diegetic action and the actions of the filmmaker.

This attention to action and detail and the stylistic shift to which it gave rise is tied to the concept of character, to the idea of character *as* action, and so to the fulfillment of Bresson's aim to create a more cinematographically oriented cinema. The filmic design of *A Man Escaped* is consonant with the aims, behavior, and character of Fontaine. We learn as much about him from observing what he does and the boldness and resourcefulness with which he does it as we do from his voice-over or his interactions with others. On the other hand, *Pickpocket* courts a fascinating disjunction between filmic design and the deluded behavior of its protagonist, embodying in this very dissonance the character's conflict and his tendency to displace his needs and desires. From a psychoanalytic point of view, Fontaine acts *on* his convictions and impulses, whereas Michel acts *out* his conflicts.

This tailoring of the cinematographic to instantiate the conscious, and unconscious, moves of these protagonists makes both films models of first-person narrative cinema. Against conventional Hollywood and European practice, which often violated first-person perspective by providing multiple angles of an action to ensure easy consumption, increase entertainment value, show off the budget, or give equal time to competing stars, Bresson's framing and editing were held to a strict standard. The camera's distance is determined by the need for coherence and lucidity. Most shots range from medium to what the French called *plan americain*, a shot of a figure from the knees up.

Close-ups are reserved for objects, parts of the body, or actions otherwise difficult to perceive: the physical tasks Fontaine performs in his cell, the thieving maneuvers in *Pickpocket*. They are almost never used for dramatic effect. Long shots are similarly restricted: in *A Man Escaped* by the physical limitations of the protagonist, in *Pickpocket* as a way of contrasting the social world around Michel with the pathologically insular nature of his obsession. Gone are atmospheric effects, elevations of the camera to suggest benediction, or shots invoking authorial or metaphorical commentary.

Angles are at the level of physical action, and framing never resorts to de-centering or distortion of spatial proportions. Expressionist shots and arbitrary camera angles are avoided. Lighting is generally devoid of chiaroscuro effects and heavy use of shadows. And although the camera moves frequently in Bresson, it does so in relation to figure movement or action, not as an omniscient independent agent. The look of *A Man Escaped* and *Pickpocket* reflects a concern for clarity and simplicity, an avoidance of theatrical or painterly effects; the same minimalist aesthetic governs the use of the model. This look draws attention not to itself but to the action that is central.

With these films Bresson's idea of the model is fully realized and, in the case of the male protagonists, is embodied in a very specific physical type. François Leterrier (Fontaine) and Martin La Salle (Michel) are as ascetic-looking and lean-bodied as the films themselves. They are natural heirs of Claude Laydu (the country priest), although their soulful eyes mirror a different interior. Because neither had had any professional acting experience, they were open to instruction on how to move and speak without resort to a repertory of conditioned responses.

Excluding physical features, there are two critical aspects of the model. The first is what the person does or does not do in a particular shot. The second is how what is or isn't done is integrated into the rhythm and texture of the film. The tighter the rhythm, the less the person can do, which means the shot may be limited to a single, quickly registered action, gesture, or move of the head or a single spoken word or phrase. The extended dolly shots into close-ups of the priest in *Diary* have no equivalent in either film, although the duration of many shots in *A Man Escaped* is longer than shots in *Pickpocket*. This may be why Fontaine's facial expressions seem more nuanced than Michel's. The pace of *A Man Escaped* tends to reflect the prison situation, which includes downtime and waiting.

Although these critical aspects obtain in all cases, there is no monolithic formula. Use of the model varies in each film, creating a different experience for the viewer. Both Fontaine and Michel are Bressonian in concept, action, look, and manner, yet Leterrier seems more natural than La Salle. This may have to do with Michel's behavior, ruled largely by what D. W. Winnicott calls the false self: all surface, bravado, and lies.[2] On the other hand, differences among models are of no less consequence than differences among professional actors: some are more credible than others in the situations in which we find them.

In both films sound emerges as a critical formal strategy, as discrete a channel in its own right as it is inextricably bound to the increasing efficiency of Bresson's visual language. Whereas image and audio tracks in conventional films frequently provide identical information simultaneously, in *A Man Escaped* and *Pickpocket* Bresson segregates them, articulating each track as a separate but equal component of the film's construction. The last twenty minutes of *A Man Escaped* and the train station and racetrack sequences in *Pickpocket* are breathtaking examples of Bresson's new mastery of sound.

Finally, consistent with my view that Bresson's filmography, like that of other deeply personal filmmakers, bears an autobiographical cast, each of these films, along with *Diary of a Country Priest,* can be said to flesh out a character that speaks to different sides and strengths of a single personality that is Bresson himself. The priest embodies the born Catholic and man of the spirit at war with a corrupt world, a fit description of Bresson; Fontaine is the man of action, no less inspired by faith, but focused on the material world. *A Man Escaped* exemplifies the fusion of materiality and spirituality in Bresson's work. The film's action, directed toward escape, becomes the means through which the filmmaker breaks through the constraints of the cinema to cinematographic freedom. If this freedom at first made Bresson feel "master of the world"—reflecting the success of both *A Man Escaped* and *Pickpocket*, for many critics the pinnacles of postwar French cinema—it may have been marked by a narcissistic denial, equal to Michel's, of the deepest influences: Bresson's failure to acknowledge the work of one of his great literary mentors, Dostoevsky, as the source of *Pickpocket*. Why should great filmmakers be any less prone than great poets to the anxiety of influence?[3]

And so, though many scholars group these films with *The Trial of Joan of Arc* as forming a prison cycle, I'm more inclined to view the three films of the 1950s—*Diary of a Country Priest, A Man Escaped*, and *Pickpocket*—as tracing the different profiles of the Bressonian protagonist, etched by those models whose physical deportments and countenances are not unlike their creator's, and whose aspirations, obsessions, and destinies reflect those of Bresson himself.

Un condamné à mort s'est échappé

Looking at oneself,…(*gnothi sauton*) [the "Know thyself" of the Delphic oracle], is always a vain and fruitless endeavor, since the essential does not lie in the self but in the task entrusted to one.

—Hans Urs von Balthasar, *Bernanos: An Ecclesial Existence*

Pastor: God will save you.

Fontaine: Only if he has help.

—*A Man Escaped*

With *A Man Escaped*, produced five years after *Diary of a Country Priest*, we see the full measure of how the *rapports* between character and objects, character and action—the essence of the cinematographic for Bresson—reveals the inner person. The screenplay and dialogue, both by Bresson, were inspired by a memoir by André Devigny, first published in *Figaro litteraire*, and then as a book entitled *Un condamné à mort s'est échappé* in 1956.[4] No doubt Bresson was attracted to the story in part because he had been a prisoner of the Germans in 1939.[5] Devigny was a factual advisor on the film, and a prefatory note assures us that the film does not embellish his account. Nevertheless there are important differences between the film and Devigny's work, and as Bresson's original title (*Aide-toi…*, part of a phrase meaning "Heaven [or God] helps those who help themselves") suggests, he stressed the spiritual significance of the story, to which the film's alternative title, *The Wind Blows Where It Will*, also attests. "I would like to show this miracle: an invisible hand over the prison, directing what happens and causing such and such a thing to succeed for one and not for another.…The film is a mystery.…The Spirit breathes where it will."[6] Miracles will indeed play a role in the film.

The film is set in German-occupied Lyon in 1943, its exteriors shot at Fort (formerly prison) Montluc in Lyon,[7] the site of the events, although a replica of the protagonist's cell was constructed in a film studio. The ropes and hooks Devigny made for his escape were preserved in Lyon and served as models for the ones used in the film.[8] Although it was made thirteen years after the events it depicts, the film has the fervor and intensity one might expect of a contemporary work about the French Resistance, an impression no doubt attributable in part to Bresson's prison experience.

Whatever his pedigree, Fontaine is a Bressonian character, sharing with the country priest a resolve against all odds and an extraordinary ability to focus on the essential, undeterred by pettiness. His determination to escape precludes the most primary emotions against his enemies. Fontaine may be Bresson's most normal character, ruled neither by superego (the country priest) nor id (Michel) but by a highly functioning ego balanced by duty and virtue. The antithesis of Sartre's characters in *No Exit*, for whom hell is other people, Fontaine wastes no energy, time, or words on self-pity or on vilifying the Germans and their French cohorts. He is a man without hate, and therefore without fear; thus his victory is the realization of one already manifest in his demeanor throughout.[9] In this he exemplifies an important feature of Bresson's aesthetic: as the protagonist seems above negative emotions, even when provoked, so the viewer is instructed not to seek sentimental forms of identification, but to look to the film's higher goal. Bresson uses his model as a vehicle in the exemplary sense of the word: not as a shortcut to the viewer's emotions, but as a means to carry him or her to a different plane on which to experience the film.

The Source

Devigny's original article impressed Bresson with its "very precise, even very technical account of the escape…a thing of great beauty…written in an extremely reserved, very cool tone."[10] What he says is true of the book as well, published in 1956,[11] which is as driven and as animate with details as Bresson's film, as free of cheap sentiment and false drama. In the work's focus on the routines of prison life, on the resolve to escape, and the attention given to the intricacies of his plan—all of which is virtually identical in the film—it had a profound influence on how Bresson shaped the film, and probably on his evolving aesthetic.

Devigny was a decorated lieutenant in the French Army who served in an infantry battalion during the Second World War, earned the Légion d'Honneur, and was awarded the Cross of the Liberation by de Gaulle following the war. He landed in Montluc Prison after being captured by the Gestapo on April 17, 1943, three days after killing a commandant of the Italian police in Nice. This episode haunted Devigny because it was the first time he had killed a man outside of combat, but it is not mentioned in the original memoir any more than the events that comprise the two and a half chapters in the book that follow the escape, in which Devigny and his fellow escapee Gimenez are recaptured in their efforts to elude the Gestapo. In a startling development Devigny, believing he had been betrayed, abandoned Gimenez to a worse fate. No doubt Bresson was aware of these circumstances since Devigny was technical advisor on the film, but he must have felt they would have soured the viewer of his film. In adapting the original memoir he could end the film on an uplifting note to the accompaniment of the "Kyrie" from Mozart's Mass.[12]

Nevertheless, because it was an authentic autobiographical account made public, one wonders why Bresson chose, or was compelled to change the names of the participants, as well as certain critical facts about his protagonist. Devigny was a married man with three children at the time of his imprisonment. His reputation as a Resistance fighter preceded him at the prison, as the enthusiastic greeting he received by a man named Bury (Terry in the film) indicates. Like Devigny, Fontaine is a lieutenant, but he receives no such greeting and seems younger, with a certain wide-eyed innocence that belies his experience as a soldier who has killed many men. In addition to eliminating any mention of a wife and children, the film further insulates Fontaine from the world of women by excluding the woman who occupied the adjacent cell, who deeply affected Devigny and about whom he wrote to his mother. She was a mother of three children (like his wife) and a wireless operator for the Resistance, arrested as she was trying to transmit a message. It is implied in the book that she was being raped and beaten regularly by the guards in the latrines. The only prisoner in an adjacent cell at this point in the film with whom Fontaine communicates by tapping on the wall is a man we never see and who is soon executed.

Clearly Bresson was more attracted to the inspirational nature of the story than to its autobiographical status and, as his remarks at Cannes indicate, to the detailed account of the escape itself. This is probably why we don't learn the specific crime for which Fontaine is arrested until later in the film, and then only that he is accused of treason. Yet the memoir obviously appealed to Bresson's fascination with first-person cinema.[13] Devigny's straightforward account no doubt lent itself more easily to Bresson's penchant for distilling the language, compressing narrative complexity, and eliminating psychology than, say, *Crime and Punishment*, the unacknowledged source of *Pickpocket*. Action could come to the foreground and cinematographic elements could dominate language, drama, and psychology.

Still, a Bressonian protagonist would have to surpass Devigny's achievement. The courageous soldier had to be invested with the same spiritual fervor to awaken others that possessed the country priest. This required the right personality, the right face, and as Bresson insisted in many interviews, the right voice—a model whose innocence of dramatic and theatrical artifice would transmit that virginal quality so dear to Bresson.

An Infectious Hero

Can anything be hoped for which is not an object of faith?

—St. Augustine, "Enchiridion on Faith, Hope, and Charity"

The title of the film contains its essence and structure. The contrast between *condamné à mort* (under sentence of death) and *s'est échappé* (has escaped) gives the plot away as it affirms the denouement, the man's victory over his death sentence. Furthermore, in the question it invites—*How* has one condemned to death managed to escape?—it predicts the film's preoccupation with the process of escape and its borderline miraculous events. Explanations for these events remain a mystery, but not in the sense that an unbeliever or an absurdist poet might contend. The film's alternative title, *The Wind Blows Where It Will*, a phrase from the Gospel of St. John 3:8, suggests that the mystery has to do with not knowing God's ways.[14] Characters manifest different responses to this ignorance: despair in the face of evil and thoughts of suicide (Blanchet); prayer and relying on God's help (the pastor); action, in the belief that one can affect circumstances (Fontaine). The film's ultimate point, incarnated in the character of Fontaine, is that we cannot know what is possible unless we hope and act even against impossible odds.

In this sense the film fairly represents Devigny's fusion of faith and action as described in his book. When he finally sets his mind on escape, he says, "There were two elements in the plan: mine and God's. Where, I wondered, was the dividing line set? Alas, I could not tell; but I felt that heaven would only aid my grimly resolute struggle insofar as I threw every physical and moral reserve I possessed into the balance."[15]

We hear the word *impossible*, and the sense of resignation and hopelessness that underlie it, many times regarding the chances of escape and of winning the war against the Germans. Yet almost every word and gesture of Fontaine's is a testament to hope, to its viability and its energizing power.[16] Because his unyielding spirit seems impelled by an inexplicable power, he is not just a Resistance fighter but a life force, a catalyst for change, an inspiration to those around him. Like the Jesus of Pasolini's *The Gospel According to St. Matthew*, Fontaine is a practical man on the move, spreading the "good news" through his actions and behavior. His manner is wittily contrasted to that of the pastor, who clings to his Bible and recommends trust in God. As the pastor proclaims his luck in finding a Bible, Fontaine says he too is lucky when he finds a second spoon by the sink to complete the dismantling of his door.

If the film is Bresson's most inspiring, it is because the character and actions of Fontaine convert such abstractions as hope and faith into instruments of liberation and change. When the pastor asks Fontaine if he ever prays, he admits that he does when things go wrong. Fontaine embodies a faith almost entirely transposed into self-reliance. Yet because his strength and convictions affect others, he unwittingly acts in the spirit of the gospels. He encourages a condemned prisoner in an adjacent cell by tapping the words of a Resistance song on the wall and makes repeated attempts to shake Blanchet's despair. Fontaine tells him that if for no other reason he should live for "all of us," meaning those fighting in the Resistance, and later reads him the story of Nicodemus to change his thinking. His success is marked in an exhilarating moment, when Blanchet contributes his blanket to help Fontaine complete his ropes.

Fontaine's rousing persistence keeps alive the flame of hope. The film even implies that this is why he has escaped execution. More than once we sense that his existence is blessed: he is not handcuffed in the car until he attempts to escape; he wonders, as we do, why he was not shot immediately afterward; roused by the guards, he shams weakness and imagines that this too has further delayed execution; a guard fails to see the spoon he conceals and uses to dismantle the door, and when it breaks he just happens across another one; he lies about having a pencil under threat of being shot and is not questioned; he is spared a cell search that would have uncovered his plan to escape.

There is a hint of recklessness in some of this to which even Fontaine admits; lying about the pencil, he tells us, was stupid. Devigny is more forthright when he says of the other prisoners' conviction that he is mad, "They could not understand that I needed danger as other people need drugs; it acted as a stimulant, counteracting the enormous nervous exhaustion which the strain and anxiety of the last few months had produced in me." Later he adds another credible piece to his behavior when he says that his worst fear was that he might "join the vast legion of the anonymous dead." "Death in itself I could accept; but I wanted my relatives to know that I had fought to the end, without relaxing or giving up."[17] Bresson excises these confessions, rendering Fontaine's motives less ambiguous and permitting a miraculous aura to hover over the film and sustain the sense of his being chosen.

In his symbolic role, then, Fontaine's inexhaustible efforts, embodied in the film's extraordinary attention to the means and instruments, inventions and process of escape, are manifestations of his faith and hope, repeatedly contradicting those who insist that escape is impossible. Fontaine's dedication is the more remarkable because he acts without a plan.[18] When Blanchet asks how he will escape, he replies that he hasn't the slightest idea. The remark may sound cavalier, yet it implies the greater importance of the *spirit* of freedom that drives him. As a man of action he cannot, like the pastor, simply wait for God's help, even if he cannot foresee every step in advance. On the contrary, the "plan" will be revealed only through an unflagging commitment to action, the seizing of each opportunity and believing it plays a role, however small, in the scheme of things. The so-called accidental occurrences that might discourage someone else are incorporated into the "plan," and in fact expedite the outcome. The fatal call to Hotel Terminus, the Gestapo's office, instead of obstructing escape, triggers its final stage; the arrival of Jost right after, arousing suspicions that the Germans may be on to him, turns out to be a stroke of amazing good luck, since, after Orsini's failure, Fontaine realizes that he needs a partner to make it over the prison wall.[19]

The ultimate test of Fontaine's beliefs is his decision to risk taking Jost with him, despite his suspicion that he might be a spy. This trust in one whose allegiance to the Resistance is questionable (we learn that Jost unknowingly collaborated with the enemy) is an act of courage that gives additional weight to Fontaine's enterprise. The irony, that his long-prepared-for escape ultimately succeeds because of a last-minute, unanticipated development, underlines an increasingly pronounced Bressonian theme: the intervention of providence in the guise of chance. In that sense we might recall Bresson's prefatory remark to *Pickpocket*—that it should not be taken as an ordinary *policier*—and say of *A Man Escaped* that it is not *just* a prison escape drama. As in *Pickpocket*, as well as *Les Anges du péché* and *Les Dames du bois de Boulogne*, two individuals who might otherwise never have met are brought together by "chance" to their mutual good fortune.

Point of View and Subjectivity

A Man Escaped is exemplary in its adherence to first-person narrative form. Fontaine does not keep a diary, as do the priest and Michel, which makes the role of the voice-over technique more critical. There are more than a hundred instances of Fontaine's voice speaking over the image, anchoring every action, event, and perception within his consciousness. Even when it is reflective it bears a direct relation to the action or reveals unspoken thoughts about an action, not always his own, that has just occurred or that he is contemplating. There is an immediate sense of the present in this text even though it was not composed until after the events had occurred. This play of three tenses in Bresson's first-person narratives, though not unique to his films, seems especially suited to the paradoxical tension in his work between free will and destiny, as if the "invisible hand over the prison," itself indifferent to past, present, and future, were too immense to be comprehended through the myopic temporal successions by which mere mortals live.

Cinematography in Action

The things one can express with the hand, with the head, with the

shoulders!...How many useless and encumbering words then disappear.

—Robert Bresson, *Notes on Cinematography*

Everything concrete is mystical.

—Pier Paolo Pasolini, in *Heretical Empiricism*

Everything that has been said concerning the theme of this film, its preoccupation with action, its focus on hands, its point of view, its use of sound, its way of establishing character, and the role of the model, is manifest in its first two shots. What could more conclusively demonstrate Bresson's new economy of form?

The first shot (following a prefatory note and the credits) encapsulates the impulse and imagery that structure the film. Two hands in close-up are held palms up (figure 18), then turned over and placed on the lap of their unidentified owner. A steady low grind of an automobile engine tells us he is in a moving car, and we realize that he is in the backseat when his left hand sidles toward the door's handle, the camera panning with it, to confirm that it is unlocked. The hand returns to his lap as the camera tilts up to the face of the prisoner Fontaine. A slight pan left reveals a second man seated beside him; as this second man's eyes briefly glance down, the camera tilts in the same direction to reveal that *his* right hand is handcuffed to the left hand of a third man who sits mostly off screen. The camera tilts up again to Fontaine's face looking steadily ahead, to the road off screen. This look prompts the cut to the second shot, a long shot of the road from Fontaine's point of view and our first view of a figure in the front seat.

The contrasting imagery of the first five-movement shot—hands uncuffed versus hands cuffed—is linked to the dominant action: the move to test the door. And though we do not yet comprehend the situation, why the other two men are handcuffed and Fontaine not, it is clear from Fontaine's stealthy moves that all are prisoners. The first thing we see, then, the palms-up gesture, is clearly signatory: it "speaks" the state of being unrestrained and therefore bound to act: that is, as long as one's hands are free, one is obliged to use them.

Moments later Fontaine tries to escape, following an assessment of the situation in nearly two dozen shots. Nine medium close-ups of his face show his alertness in response to two areas of attention: the changing road conditions ahead and the driver's gear-shifting rhythms. Six long shots of the road from Fontaine's point of view and three close-ups of the driver's hand are intercut with four close-ups of Fontaine's left hand, moving to and away from the door. Even the shots of the driver's hand, technically unfeasible as direct point-of-view shots, can be understood within Fontaine's consciousness since he is attuned to the shifts of the car's movements.

A horse-drawn wagon slowly enters from a side street directly in the path of the car. In anticipation Fontaine's left hand moves toward the door, where it remains until five shots later, after the car manages to swerve around the wagon. The tightness of this structure is further condensed when a second road condition is expounded exclusively through shots of Fontaine's face, the driver's hand, and Fontaine's hand moving to and away from the door. Though shots of the road are elided, we infer from the repetition of the others that a similar condition has occurred and been judged equally inopportune. In the last road condition, shots of a trolley cutting across the path of the car are crosscut with shots of Fontaine's face, without any close-ups of his hand on the door.

Finally the moment comes: the car swerves to avoid colliding with the trolley. This is followed by a long-held shot of the backseat focused on the middle prisoner as Fontaine rushes out the door. Through the rear window in extreme long shot we see a second car stopping and glimpse figures running from it in pursuit of Fontaine. We hear shouts of "Halt!" and gunfire as we continue to watch the impassive second man ("apathetic" in Devigny's memoir), suggesting the inevitability of Fontaine's failure. A moment later Fontaine is returned to the car amid a few outbursts in German from off screen and is handcuffed and struck on the head with a gun as a dissolve ends the sequence.

Compare this with the opening of *Les Dames du bois de Boulogne*: an establishing shot of people exiting a theater after a performance, a move in to a medium shot of a couple entering the back of a car, and then breaking down in the car into medium and close shots, dictated by dialogue and characters' reactions. An expository scene in the classical mode, the premise of the drama is presented through language and acting. *A Man Escaped* has no official establishing shot,[20] no dialogue, no acting of the traditional sort. The face and the voice are no longer the privileged means of expression nor the exclusive registers of what transpires. Facial expressions are primarily transitive, directing our attention not primarily to the character but to the conditions around him and to the objects of his interest in off screen space. Hands, no less than the face, are a crucial index of intention and the means of potential action. They do not complement the general expressiveness of the character; they function separately, conveying information and indicating specific actions or reactions. They do not duplicate but replace acting, facial expressions, and language. In *A Man Escaped* it is the prisoner's hands, the first thing we see on the screen after the credits, that announce the subject of the film as well as the nature of its subsequent action.

The equivalent of this scene in Devigny's memoir also begins with his hand testing the door, followed by a thought as to why he was "lucky enough not to be handcuffed," and the declaration, "Today, April 23, was to mark my first attempt at escape." But he also digresses with lengthy flashbacks to what led to this situation, and there is a more detailed account of what happens when he runs from the car. He notes that what made the escape attempt possible was that "the driver and the SS Sergeant were chatting away paying no attention to [the prisoners]." Given the voice-over that runs through the rest of the film, Bresson could have provided Fontaine's thoughts along these lines, yet he chose to avoid both the chatting of the Germans and voice-over commentary, which would have distracted from the action as constructed in cinematographic terms.

From Devigny's fuller narrative treatment—flashback exposition, description, the prisoner's internal monologue—Bresson distilled the core of the scene, that which reveals the protagonist's character and the theme, and projected this exclusively in the language of film. In so doing he raised the visual and audio tracks, as well as editing, to more articulate levels, fulfilling his doctrine that cinematography, the term he used to distinguish creative filmmaking from mere movies, "is a writing with images in movement and with sounds."[21] Independent of language and traditional acting, the situation is delineated through images framed and edited to render the action salient and through sounds strategically placed to heighten attention to the shifts in action. For example, consistent with Bresson's directive to "let the cause follow the effect,"[22] the sound of the car's motor precedes the fade-in to Fontaine's hands just as we hear the trolley seconds before its appearance. Bresson did not invent any of these strategies, nor is this the first time he consciously used them. But the opening of *A Man Escaped*, as well as the film as a whole, demonstrates his sharpened sense of how to make them fresh and meaningful by streamlining their relations and eliminating the unnecessary. In the process he moves the spectator into an active mode of perception analogous to that of the protagonist.

Those who continue to take issue with Bresson's concentration on the cinematographic with material of such historical specificity complain that he is more interested in formalism than social and political reality. There are echoes here of Stalinist criticism of Eisenstein's *Ivan the Terrible* and the same blindness to the truer radicalism of form over content. It might be said that Bresson's project to transform the art of film and habits of perception necessitated the stripping down not only of the stylistic excesses of conventional cinema but of the kind of narrative complexities and redundancies that try to rival what novels and historical works achieve more readily. But it would be wrong to suggest that Bresson's concentrated style ignores or neutralizes history and social reality; more accurately, it aims with precision to salvage the particularities of the human experience of both. Key to how this approach works is the model, a concept to which Bresson devoted more than sixty of his notes. It redefines the *actor* as not one whose expressions "force the spectator to look for talent on his face,"[23] but one who literally performs actions. His insistence on the model was not about eliminating expression but about isolating and privileging each nuance of it, in the same way that each image and each sound is designed to perform an individual task.

As I said in the introduction, Bresson was not the first filmmaker to use nonprofessionals or types. We find them in Eisenstein and others of the silent Soviet cinema, in De Sica, Rossellini, Visconti, and the Italian neorealists, and in the documentary tradition in the work of Robert Flaherty, among others. What distinguishes Bresson from these is the way the model is made integral to the film's compositional style, as malleable a constituent as the placement of an object, a camera angle, or the lighting. Yet the model is not a robot; he or she is the most moving element of the film's construction, the part that animates and gives purpose to the rest. In the opening sequence Fontaine may have only one basic look on his face, alertness, but it is that look which links the road to the hands, the hands to the door, and the man to the action he is about to perform. The look infuses every shot with the will of the prisoner and sustains the tension of the sequence moment by moment. And yet the model must adopt or allow a certain mechanical quality to affect the actions performed. Every emotion must remain within. Leterrier makes clear that the actor's behavior must reflect the character's, which is to say, to act without calculation or design, to focus entirely on the immediate task with no premeditation of its meaning or what it will lead to.[24]

It is the look that carries him through the film and the escape sequence, when we see at one point only the upper half of his face lit from below and surrounded by darkness as he leans over the edge of a roof, studying the routine of a guard before he can proceed. Technically, no acting is involved, nor does his expression change. Yet the small glowing area of his eyes and forehead is the focal point, embodying the poised and patient resolve that will see him through and hold the viewer within the controlled but intense rhythm of the sequence.

We see this in our first glimpse of Leterrier's face and throughout the film, the "spark caught in his eye's pupil [which] gives significance to his whole person."[25] The stress on the eye and the way light captures and is reflected in it is one of the film's subtlest and most expressive constants (figure 19). There are moments when the eye or eyes are the most important single communicative element on the screen. When Fontaine frees himself from the handcuffs, his success is registered not only by a slight smile but by the light that glitters in the pupils and whites of his eyes. This gleam, which reflected off the metal of the handcuffs as he removed them, has, through a tilt upward of the camera in the same shot, now moved to his eyes. Later, as he is about to crush the glass from the lantern under his blanket, he pauses, and it is the illumination of one eye that cues us to the keenness of his hearing, which then allows *us*, a moment later, to hear what he has *already* heard: the distant sound of boots on the staircase. Bresson uses cinematographer L.-H. Burel's mastery of light as a modeling feature to achieve the goal he sought as early as his first film, to animate the exterior as a means of revealing the alertness and glow of the interior. But because Bresson now eschews the pictorial, making one eye, the pupil of one eye, or both eyes, the focal point of an image—for example, as a motif of the mise-en-scène—is not an end in itself. In the spirit of *rapports* and the critical role of looks in general, it draws attention to off screen space, as when the sound of an approaching guard draws *our* eyes to the small peephole of Fontaine's door, waiting to see if the guard will pause to look into his cell (figure 20).

For example, at one point, having dropped the hook he is fashioning from the lantern frame, Fontaine quickly tucks it under his mattress and sits on the cot, awaiting the imminent arrival of a guard who he assumes has heard the noise. He tilts his head toward the door (off screen), the glint of light glancing off the whites of his eyes, making them the brightest points in the shot. The countershot of the door as we hear the guard approaching also has one bright spot of light, the peephole. If one superimposed the second shot over the first, the peephole would appear up and to the right, the point at which Fontaine's eyes are fixed. This optical transference of circles of light directs our gaze, focusing our attention to one point of the image by way of an invisible superimposition implied by the cut. In this way Fontaine's alertness triggers our own. We become so accustomed to this that even a long shot of the door of Orsini's cell across the hall draws us to the small peephole in the center of the frame, where the sudden darkening of the pinhole of light indicates that he is looking out at Fontaine and wants to communicate.

These three critical elements—the actor, sound, and off screen space—work together to define Bresson's mature style. In minimizing the first through the use of the model, Bresson maximizes the second and third. That is, because we are not focused on "looking for talent on the actor's face," we are more attuned, indeed made so, to the interaction of the filmic properties that come to the fore. To follow the model's look and eyes and the light that glances off them *while listening* for the sound that has prompted his look, and to transfer this attention to the next shot and the point in the image where the model was also focused in the previous shot, is to grasp how Bresson constructs his art and brings us into contact with both the external reality of the film and the internal reality of the character.

For Bresson, off screen space is as significant as, and often more significant than what we see and hear. When he was a prisoner of the Germans, he recalled, he was in a cell and heard someone being whipped through a door and then a body falling. "That," he says, "was ten times worse than if I had seen the whipping."[26] This may explain why we do not see Fontaine being beaten but only his bloodied face afterward. It also partly explains the powerful effects that sound and off screen space engender in his work. Consider the sequence in the film in which a condemned prisoner exchanges messages with Fontaine through tappings on the wall. This character is created exclusively through off screen space and sound. Never embodied in physical form or voice, he is entirely the product of Fontaine's attentive leaning against the wall and the faintest of reciprocated taps. Yet it is he who provides instructions on how to unlock the handcuffs with the pin, and the news of his death, conveyed by Terry sometime later, moves Fontaine to despair. Pure fabrication conjured from the most tenuous of formal gestures, the character's felt reality is a powerful testament to Bresson's aesthetic.

It is another instance of a tendency in Bresson to evoke the *concept* of the shot-countershot system without actually employing it, in order to suggest a realm beyond the world conjured by the film that interacts with the visible one before us. We saw this in what I called the core shots of *Diary of a Country Priest*, in which the priest's gaze beyond the frame evokes a countershot that never appears, that is in fact impossible because it involves an object of faith. In the sequence from *A Man Escaped*, the invisible prisoner off screen exists and responds to the appeal of his neighbor, who, as the instrument of faith, offers encouragement. This strategy is an important aspect of Bresson's aesthetic, which is largely concerned with the invisible, with what is not or cannot be shown, or what is replaced by sound. It is hard to think of a more fitting trope for an artist for whom the cinema is the art of *rapports* and who seeks to articulate the relationship between the concrete and the ineffable.

The deployment of off screen space is not limited to such purposes. As Bresson begins to use it in this film and after, it becomes more and more central to his style and to a greater appreciation of his ability to use a film convention to realize its potential as a component of a truly cinematographic art form. To illustrate the change, consider the way two critical dramatic moments are handled in his first two films.

In the prison where Anne-Marie first meets Thérèse in *Les Anges du péché*, we see Thérèse pushing from cell to cell a heavy hand truck holding a soup tureen. Prodded one too many times by the female guard, she angrily gives the cart a final shove, sending it tumbling down the stairs. We see her final gesture in one shot facilitated by a repositioning of the camera. While she goes from cell to cell, the camera follows close by, but with a cut it is suddenly positioned at the bottom of the stairs, the better to frame Thérèse's rebellious act in one visually comprehensive image. In a comparable moment from *Les Dames du bois de Boulogne* Agnès sits at the dinner table in Hélène's apartment when, in shock over a sudden awareness of the complicity between her mother, Hélène, and Jean, she suspends the glass in her hand directly over the floor and then drops it.

Both instances are examples of a motif in Bresson's work whereby a character reaches a breaking point. But the point here is not the thematic relevance of these moments; it is the way the actions are presented. In both cases a physical gesture is staged for the camera and shown in its entirety, the actor playing her part in accord with mimetic tradition. Despite the Bressonian touch that lies behind each, both fit comfortably in the filmmaking tradition tied to the aesthetic determinants of the proscenium arch. Each action occurs within a dramatic context; the role of off screen space and the visual field beyond the frame in our comprehension and registration of it is negligible.

Beginning with *A Man Escaped*, this is less and less the case. From the way the simplest actions are shown to the prominent use of sound, the greater visual field is constantly implied, rendering the image before us a fragment of or extract from that field, actively tied to it through the evocation of off screen space and through the editing. The action is no longer a self-enclosed staged event but a product of filmic construction. Even a minor example, such as the shot of a bloodied Fontaine deposited on the floor of a cell on his arrival at prison while his jacket is thrown from off screen and lands on top of him, is indicative of an overall shift in approach whereby the increasing importance of an off screen reality bears on the image before us.

Sometimes the model's off screen presence is evoked through the juxta-position of an image and the voice-over. In nearly three dozen shots, Fontaine's exchanges with Terry and other prisoners in the courtyard below his window are primarily about improving his morale (getting letters out, receiving invaluable objects, including a pin to unlock his handcuffs), reflected by his constricted view, stressed by high and low angles, his consistently downward look, and the repeated shot of the men approaching from a fixed position. But in the last shot of the courtyard before his transfer to another cell, he sees only the female prisoners crossing the yard and hears gunfire from the firing squad. As we watch this image, his voice-over tells us that his gaze is now on a "broader view" of the prison's structure, with an eye toward escape.

Of course instances such as these last two examples can be found in many other movies, but they generally coexist with more conventional approaches. Bresson's method is systematic, indicative of an overall reconception of film aesthetics. The irony of all this is that if he can be said to have realized his goal of moving narrative film from mere cinema to the art of the cinematographic, he achieved this by giving greater salience and expressive power to two noncinematographic properties: sound and off screen space. The result resembles neither the montage of the Soviet directors nor the Hollywood principle of invisible editing, avoiding both the often static, pictorial imagery of the former and the illusionist, actor-driven effects of the latter. The more Fontaine becomes involved in his escape plan in the isolation of his cell, the more we sense the uniqueness of Bresson's achievement.

The "Plan" Takes Shape

When one is in prison, the most important thing is the door.

—Robert Bresson, in an interview conducted by Ian Cameron in *Movie*,

reprinted in *Interviews with Film Directors*, edited by Andrew Sarris

As in *Diary*, the editing in *A Man Escaped* can be said to have its core relationships, the ones that best convey the nature of the character and his interactions with the environment. Weeks after his initial internment, Fontaine is moved from the condemned prisoners area to a cell on the top floor. Here he has daily contact with other prisoners through rituals at the washbasin and walks in the courtyard. Their general hopelessness contrasts with his determination to escape, which gradually becomes a source of inspiration for them. "Trapped in horrible solitude," his voice-over tells us, "one hundred of us waited to learn our fates. I had no illusions about mine. I had to escape, to get away." This is followed by a shot of him seated on his cot and staring at his cell door, which, he says, he's been doing for hours, observing the different grades of wood that will permit separation of its vertical panels. With a spoon he has purloined and sharpened against the stone floor into a chisel-like tool, he cuts into the joints and shaves away the wood until each panel is loose and removable.

This process takes over fifteen minutes of screen time and, excluding intervening shots of prison rituals, comprises close-ups of the door as Fontaine's hands work the spoon and of the wood shavings he brushes up afterward, crosscut with shots of his face (forty-six in all). He admits (as does Devigny) that the activity is as much about keeping busy and warding off despair as it is about reaching a goal. "It stopped me from thinking," he says. "My only plan was to open the door." By acting on his situation, he counters the regimented prison walks, the boundaries of which are marked by the repeated breaking off of Mozart's "Kyrie" just before its triumphant choral passage, which we hear at the beginning and end of the film. Fontaine's activity at the door becomes a dynamic *interaction:* two shots of him, as if from the door's point of view, show him leaning forward with the palpable excitement one might bring to an erotic encounter. The fade-out in the midst of this movement wittily recalls the use of that convention at such suggestive moments in many films.

This excitement is not derived from any calculated emotion on the actor's part. Leterrier quotes his character Fontaine, "This door must be opened; I foresaw nothing after." But when he adds, "This daily work did not lead to any known future; no plan or premeditation is implied. These gestures preclude all thinking," he describes not only the character's disposition, but the way he, the model, was instructed to perform the task.[27] In his total involvement with the door, he projects a passion directly tied to the immediate action, investing it with both inner and outer vitality, as if he had no more knowledge of the scenario's outcome than Fontaine does himself. Bresson's theory of the model seems especially germane to the character and situation of this film. It not

1. Anne-Marie burns traces of her secular life.

2. Anne-Marie meets Thérèse in prison.

3. Anne-Marie hears the word that binds her to Thérèse.

4. Thérèse completes the dying Anne-Marie's vows.

5. A regenerated Thérèse surrenders to the law.

6. A night mission to retrieve an angel of sin from prison.

7. Hélène in tears at the end of her affair.

8. An appalled Agnès about to drop a glass.

9. Jean's car wipes Hélène off the screen.

10. The camera elevates over Jean and a revived Agnès.

11. The priest at the outset of his first parish.

12. Chantal confesses hideous thoughts.

13. The priest's hand opens the diary.

14. The diary's inscription dissolves to catechism class.

15. The Countess yields to the priest's ministrations.

16. The final long take of the priest facing death.

17. The final image of the film.

18. Fontaine's hands free under custody.

19. Eyes alert to approaching guards.

20. The spyhole of Fontaine's cell.

21. Fontaine studies a spoon as a key turns in the lock.

22. Fontaine dismantles his bed to make ropes.

23. Fontaine and Jost on the roof during the escape.

24. Fontaine crosses the last span before freedom.

25. Michel's pleasure upon opening the woman's purse.

26. Michel and Jeanne at a café.

27. Michel's attention is arrested by a new target.

28. Michel's final and most extraordinary theft.

29. Michel sees Jeanne in a new light.

30. Joan's mother at Notre Dame.

31. Joan faces her judges.

32. Cauchon sits in judgment.

33. Cauchon spies on Joan in her cell.

34. Joan as seen through the spyhole.

35. Joan yields to pressure in the cemetery at Rouen.

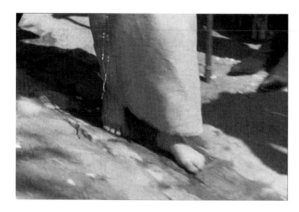

36. Joan walks briskly to her death.

37. The final image:
the smoking stake.

38. Marie and Balthazar
enact a transference rite.

39. Marie stripped and
beaten by Gerard and
his thugs.

40. Marie and her father embrace.

41. The image begins to dissolve.

42. Fading embrace gives way to Gerard on the road.

43. Gerard sets a trap for unwary drivers.

44. Gerard lets loose in the bar.

45. The wounded Balthazar surveys the valley.

46. The dead Balthazar.

47. A distracted Mouchette hears her name before school.

48. Arsène exits the bar, leaving the door ajar.

49. Mouchette tends her dying mother.

only concurs with Devigny's assertion that he acted without a plan; it adds appreciably to the quality of suspense we associate with a prison escape drama. This may be why the film seems the least withholding of Bresson's works. Leterrier's Fontaine is more naturalistically engaging than Bresson's aesthetic might suggest, not so far from actors in neorealist films of the 1940s.

The shots of Fontaine at the door, along with those of his fabricating ropes and hooks for scaling the prison walls, constitute the film's core relationships in that they materialize the character's demeanor, his refusal to concede defeat, and his conviction that action is a form of faith. The extended attention given these details confirms the value of persistent effort and the role of the smallest actions in determining the course of events. It is a lesson in the pragmatic form of faith that the film espouses. The shots also reveal, no less than what Fontaine says and how he relates to others, significant features of his character and personality. Through his actions we discern care, diligence, patience, persistence, precision, and thoroughness, as well as a striking attunement to the surrounding atmosphere.

This is where sound is crucial, lending a necessary tension to these shots, creating that suspense that might otherwise be precluded by the implication of the title. Fontaine performs his tasks while vigilantly keeping his progress hidden, in turn rousing the viewer's awareness of the risk of his being caught. Because the film adheres to the restrictions of the first person, we are confined in the cell with Fontaine, observing every gesture and cued to listening along with him for doors opening and closing and approaching footsteps on the stairs and in the corridors. The reality of the prison outside the cell at these moments is established almost exclusively by sound. But, consistent with what has been said about the greater field, sounds are not there simply to be identified and dismissed. Their heightened registration makes them as vital a presence as the image with which both character and viewer must contend. This is evident from the beginning, with the commands of the Germans delivered in amplified outbursts that require no translation. As do other sounds, they occupy the space in the absence of the bodies to which they belong.

An example of how creative and nuanced Bresson's use of audiovisual montage had become and how he linked it to his theme occurs at the very moment Fontaine is thinking about the door. As he hastens to finish his evening ration, we hear the guards approaching and unlocking each cell to retrieve the pot and spoon. At the precise moment that the key is turned in the lock of his cell, Fontaine finishes the last morsel of his food; suddenly he holds the spoon up for a second and gazes at it before dropping it into the pot (figure 21). A second later he removes it and places it on the floor between his shoes. As he gambled, the guard fails to notice it when he collects the pot and moves on. The moment in question, fleeting but memorable, is marked by the synchronicity between Fontaine's quick scrutiny of the spoon and the metallic sound of the key turning in the lock. Because this sound, accented from the beginning, is an audial sign of Fontaine's imprisonment, its juxtaposition with the image here represents a rupture in the routine. The sound does not simply contrast with the image or complement it; it is its codeterminant, linked, within the perceptual sphere of the filmic address, with the key object *in* the image, namely, the spoon. By a kind of phenomenological and magical transference effect, the spoon is identified with and then converted into the key—which is to say, Fontaine's way out. Bresson, who avoids metaphors, allows the amplified sound of unlocking to resonate over the image of the spoon in Fontaine's hand as his mind instantly conjures how he will use it. The spoon is not *like a* key; it *is* a key, just as, after he sharpens it on the floor, it *is* a chisel.

Watching and listening to this film therefore require alertness comparable to Fontaine's own. Attunement to the filmic dynamics becomes our task as the dismantling of the door is his. This foregrounding and intensification of the film's cinematographic register is not for its own sake, but is in the service of crafting the action as finely and clearly as possible, the material basis of Bresson's idiosyncratic modernism.

Despite Fontaine's success in removing three of the door's panels, which allows him to roam the corridors, he tells Blanchet that he still has no plan. It is the nature of his faith to act without knowing what lies ahead, believing that out of the smallest actions a plan will eventually reveal itself. He persists, taking apart forty yards of wire mesh from his bedstead one notch at a time to make the twelve yards of rope he needs to carry him over the walls (figure 22). In a half-dozen close-ups linked through dissolves we watch him removing the nails that hold the mesh in place; separating and unfurling a line of wire from the mesh; slicing his pillow into narrow slits; stuffing its horsehair innards into his mattress; folding the slits to make them stronger; placing a wire inside the folded strip; holding one end down with his foot and twisting the length of cloth and wire into a tightly woven cord. With one exception we see only his hands engaged in this activity. In a similar breakdown of shots, linked through dissolves, we follow the removal of his window, the breaking and disposal of the glass, his bending the iron frame into a hook by wedging it between a thick pipe and a steel door in the wall. As with the length of rope, he has determined the shape of the hook through careful scrutiny of the walls and ledges on his daily walks.

These episodes, in which everyday objects play a significant role in the narrative, and in the Devigny memoir from which they are drawn, also mirror Bresson's aesthetic. The film could be taken as an ode to the object, in the spirit perhaps of the poet Francois Ponge, one of whose works is "The Pleasures of the Door."[28] The inestimable value objects assume in the context of prison life as well as in the life of the spirit is expressed by the pastor, whose excitement over his Bible does not prevent him from responding to Fontaine's over the spoon: "It's enough," he says. The equation makes it clear how the sacredness of the film's themes suffuses every element in it: the spoon, no less than the Bible, keeps faith alive. Without a string to make a pouch, Fontaine would not have had the pin to unlock his handcuffs, or the razor to slit his sheets, blankets, and clothes to make ropes. Without the pencil he could not have communicated with his comrades; without the spoon he could not have left his cell; without the window frame he could not have scaled the walls. The same spirit of freedom that drives Fontaine and allows him to inspire others gives him the ability to see each object *and* to see something else *in* it, its unseen potential, to convert its everydayness into an instrument of that freedom. No less so has the filmmaker, confronted with the given tools of his craft, its optical and transitional devices, its audio and visual conventions, looked closely and seen greater potential beyond their familiarity.

While Fontaine reports his success to Blanchet, he still hesitates until the old man reminds him that he would not have known how to make the hooks if Orsini had not failed and shown him the way. "Strange," says Fontaine, "that you should say it," aware now that if his efforts have inspired even this old cynic, he owes it to all the prisoners to proceed. He attacks a package of clothes, slitting and shredding shirts, scarves, and a bathrobe, braiding them into another rope, a technique, he tells us, that he learned from watching his mother. This stage is punctuated the next morning with one of the film's simplest and most exhilarating moments: as the prisoners emerge from their cells, Blanchet turns to Fontaine and tosses him his blanket so he can complete the final rope. With this gesture—no less a turnaround than Thérèse's in *Les Anges* and Jean's in *Les Dames*—Blanchet renounces despair and weds his fate, emotionally and spiritually, to Fontaine's, marking the convergence of the two parallel lines in the narrative: the process of escape and Fontaine's efforts to sustain hope in his comrades. His role here as a triumphant Christ figure, as opposed to the Christ of the Agony with whom the country priest identifies, is clinched by his exchange with Blanchet. Fontaine reassures him that they will meet again. "In another world, perhaps," Blanchet responds. "No, in this one," says Fontaine. In a curiously inverted way, the exchange alludes to that between Christ on the cross and the good thief who he assures will be with him in paradise. That is, when Blanchet speaks of the other world, he does so cynically, whereas Fontaine's positive affirmation of faith refers to worldly freedom.

Just as Fontaine is encouraged to make his move, he is suddenly taken to Hotel Terminus and told he has been found guilty of treason and will be shot. To his great surprise, he is returned to his cell and falls onto his cot in relief. At his words sometime later, "I thought I was lost," spoken with his back to the camera, we hear again the pronounced turning of the key in the lock as Fontaine turns around slowly in response to another unexpected development. The manner in which this moment is handled—the sound of the key in synch with his gesture, followed by an unusually long held shot of Fontaine reacting to something off screen—is another instance of Bresson's tendency to show an effect before its cause. In this case it reinvigorates the dynamic interaction between on-screen and off-screen space. As he scrutinizes a new arrival, we hear Fontaine's voice-over description rather than see a reverse angle of the prisoner: "In French and German uniform, he looked repulsively filthy. He seemed barely sixteen." The paradox suggested by the uniform in fact suggests Fontaine's ambivalence about whether this is a dangerous or fortuitous arrival. Again it is the cinematographic synchronicity—the key in the lock in almost direct response to Fontaine's feeling lost—that cues us to the intervention of that "invisible hand over the prison directing what happens." In short, the arrival of Jost is another miracle, but as with all such, it must be believed to bear fruit. Fontaine has not yet seen that other potential in Jost. It is a test of faith for him and the viewer. Can Jost be trusted, or is he a spy?

Fontaine must decide whether to kill Jost or take him along. Once he reveals his plans, he makes it clear that Jost has no other choice. On the night of the escape, Bresson cuts directly from the cell to their emergence through the skylight, a striking elliptical edit that captures the decisiveness of their embarkation, something reiterated by subsequent shots that show us a site on the roof before they arrive at it. These shots register a simple fact: once begun, there is no turning back. It is another way of fusing individual will and design, the paradoxical understanding of human behavior that Bresson continues to assert.

The Sounds of Freedom

Never forget that our worst enemy is silence.

—Devigny to Gimenez just before they embark on their escape,

in André Devigny, *A Man Escaped*

The escape sequence runs eighteen minutes, excluding the black leader that ends the film, over which we hear the concluding passages of the "Kyrie." It displays cinematographic technique as inventive as the escape itself and once again confirms sound and off screen space as critical elements. *A Man Escaped* demonstrates what will be true of every subsequent Bresson film: that it was now of paramount importance to prevent sound from being swallowed up by the equivalent of illusionism. Whether it replaces an image or is heard seconds before the image that furnishes its cause, in each case it registers acutely on the listener.

As Fontaine and Jost proceed across the roof, we hear the soft crunch of the gravel as their stocking feet press gently down, making quicker advances only when the trains in the distance whistle and roll by (figure 23). The trains are a critical factor throughout the sequence, concealing the prisoners' moves and marking their progress, as does a clock tower that chimes first at midnight, then 1 A.M., and last at 4 A.M. If both sounds seem amplified in relation to the distance from their sources, this reminds us that the prison is in the midst of the city. Amplification also gives the sound a more palpable presence, the sonic equivalent of the close-ups and medium shots of the escapees and the camera's proximity to their every move. More local sounds are registered differently to stress their nearness or distance from the action. For example, we hear squeaking minutes before we see the bicycle that a guard rides around the perimeter of the prison between the inner and outer walls. Of more immediate relevance are the footsteps of a guard to and from his post, which Fontaine studies for several moments to gauge the man's regularity and his proximate distance at the moment he pauses and turns. Finally, under the cover of passing trains, Fontaine lunges into the darkness, "like a panther," writes Devigny, to silence the guard. The sound of the train piercing the darkness displaces the off screen act that Devigny describes in detail, stressing the persistence with which he throttled the man and then stabbed him in the back with his own bayonet—details Bresson excludes.[29] In all cases, the sound occupies the space of the image as if it were another character, entering and leaving the stage in a manner that neither the viewer nor the characters can ignore.

The most startling and unexpected sound is heard just before the final wall is breached. Fontaine hurls the last rope across the final enclosed space to the ledge of the prison's outer wall, which the hook grips along with a barbed wire that presumably encircles the entire prison. The rattling that reverberates as Fontaine tightens the hold—only the viewer actually sees the wire—is chilling, creating an acoustical tightrope matching the one he and Jost must negotiate, monkey-style, to cross the space and reach the outside (figure 24). I've always found it a subtle way of telegraphing both the boldness and the success of the escape throughout the prison. As stunning and tense as the moment is, it is over in seconds and treated no less modestly than any other of the film's ingenious touches.

In seconds both men have reached the outer wall and have leaped to the ground. The escape accomplished, Bresson's film ends as Fontaine and Jost walk off briskly in stocking feet into the streets of Lyon. Over the darkness into which they disappear the last passages of the "Kyrie" of Mozart's C-minor Mass close the film with a sense of release.

Conclusion

Despite his link to the other male protagonists of the fifties, Fontaine also resembles Anne-Marie in *Les Anges du péché*. Both manifest a combination of fervor and joy that no other Bresson protagonist can claim. The exuberance and persistence with which Anne-Marie pursues Thérèse and charms her way into the good graces of Mother Superior within a very different kind of contained environment provide an early model of Fontaine's less overt evangelism and his effect on his fellow prisoners. Anne-Marie is as determined to be admitted into the insulated world of the convent as Fontaine is to get out of prison.

The role of this exuberance in each, however, differs in respect to self-awareness and pride, that most serious of flaws with which all of Bresson's characters must contend. If Fontaine is the healthiest of Bresson's characters, it is partly because he is not obsessed with his influence on others and therefore not beset by the injurious effects of pride. Anne-Marie's battle involves the need to balance her drive to convert Thérèse with the pride that colors and can corrode this ambition. In the end, though Anne-Marie may not have fully conquered her pride, Thérèse responds to the intervention of that "invisible hand over the [convent]" of which Bresson speaks in relation to Montluc Prison, an intervention in the *form* of Anne-Marie's relentless efforts. It is this *use* of the other in the best sense, psychologically speaking, of taking in and growing through the life spirit that fires others, that both films display.

"Creativity [as] a whole attitude to external reality," D. W. Winnicott remarks, is essential to the healthy individual, to the feeling that life is worth living. Its opposite, "compliance, carries with it a sense of futility for the individual and is associated with the idea that nothing matters and that life is not worth living."[30] Anne-Marie must overcome hubris to comply with the rules of the religious life she has chosen and must accept. Fontaine's imprisonment was not of his choice and so compliance, as the resigned attitudes of other prisoners attest, equals death. Fontaine's persistent creative behavior confirms that his destruction of the objects of his imprisonment in order to convert them into the instruments of liberation is the testament to who he is—perhaps the only Bressonian character who acts *and* waits, acts *and* hopes, uncertain of success. In this Fontaine reflects the practice that Bresson himself describes in a later interview following the release of *L'Argent*. Asked about the relationship between calculation and spontaneity in his work, he says, "Basically, my film is a product of chance just as any work of art is a product of chance. When a writer sits at his desk…he writes one word. He cannot know how the sentence will turn out. He has a vague idea, but perhaps nothing more than that. His hand leads him on, helping him to continue and his state of grace, too, helps him continue. But you absolutely must not know in advance."[31]

The emphasis on spontaneity is inseparable from another kind of creativity, Bresson's use of the model, the end results of which are not known in advance. The model allows us to focus on the total filmic experience. We are not swept up with the personality, charm, looks, or skill of an actor, whose familiar persona would facilitate our *wish* to be engaged and convinced as if by an old friend. We are directed instead to the character's play with objects and others, the creativity of which is enhanced by his very lack of a plan, a situation, as Winnicott would have it, in which true discovery can take place. In the film this space of potential discovery is where insight and grace find entry.

Pickpocket

Few men have the terrible single-mindedness necessary to create their lie

from the inside.

—Georges Bernanos, *The Impostor*

Pickpocket continues Bresson's interest in first-person narrative and further refines the style he developed in *A Man Escaped*. The last of the male-centered films of the 1950s, it is, like its predecessor, propelled by a character obsessed with the activity identified in its title. However, whereas Fontaine's determination to escape is harmonious with both the narrative goal and filmic treatment, Michel's obsession in *Pickpocket* is at odds with the ultimate aim of the narrative, and this conflict is reflected in the filmic treatment. The forces against which Fontaine rebels are the depersonalized enemies of war; prison guards are rarely represented beyond off screen shouts, commands, and footsteps. Michel's behavior, on the other hand, is a prolonged acting-out of adolescent rebellion, characterized by a not untypical sexual ambiguity, and rationalized by a pseudo-philosophical theory. Counteracting forces are personalized and structured into the narrative via four characters: his mother, Jeanne, Jacques, and the inspector. Against Michel's antisocial behavior, these characters represent the compelling bonds of human society: family, romantic attachment, friendship, and the law.

Michel, like Fontaine, is present in every sequence and speaks in the same blend of confession, fact, and reflection that characterized Fontaine's voice-over, but his dominion over the film is undermined by the manner in which the counterforces act on him, exacerbating an inner conflict that eventually turns his life around. The tortured course of this conflict is the thrust of the narrative and its resolution the goal. Whereas Fontaine's freedom is both the culmination of his efforts and the crowning moment of the narrative, Michel's change seems the inverse of everything that has preceded it. Like Thérèse in *Les Anges du péché* and Jean in *Les Dames du bois de Boulogne*, both of whom experience last-minute transformations, Michel is moved ultimately by the power and persistence of another's love.

Pickpocket represents a challenging moment in Bresson's journey as a filmmaker. Perhaps because it goes further than its predecessor in narrative contraction and economy of means, its models seem more controlled than those in *A Man Escaped*, who, by comparison, have more affinity with nonprofessionals in the work of Rossellini, and de Sica. Some gestures of the models in *Pickpocket*, which they were asked to perform repeatedly until they had the necessary quality of indifference,[32] seem more stylized and self-conscious than those in *A Man Escaped*. The lowering and raising of a glance or a head at several points, presumably to denote a moment's thought before a response, something all three principal characters do, is almost divided into two segregated positions, recalling the biomechanic-like movements in Eisenstein's *Ivan the Terrible* (1943). Bresson may have hardened his position vis-à-vis the model against those who saw his method as simply another approach to training the inexperienced actor. There may even be a dynamic between this rote impression and more natural ones, which bears on the split in the main character between conscious action and unconscious impulses. This is especially true of Martin La Salle's Michel, less so of Marika Green's Jeanne and

Pierre Leymarie's Jacques, but is not discernible in Jean Pelegri's inspector or Dolly Scal, who plays Michel's mother. Although there is no hard evidence to prove that the distinction is calculated, it strikes me that the film's maternal and paternal figures, representing the norms of society that Michel resists, are more comfortably and naturalistically conceived and performed.

This phenomenon may in part be a result of the film's compression, the need to convey quickly the kind of information that usually requires more nuanced and subtle reflections, in which the actor runs the gamut of emotions in an effort to express the character's anxieties. I think Bresson was more preoccupied than he was in *A Man Escaped* with integrating the behavior of his models into the rhythm and design of his film not only because of his continued attention to streamlining filmic form but because of the particular nature of *Pickpocket*'s narrative. Where Devigny provided him with a text and a hero defined by action, the conflicted nature of the protagonist in *Pickpocket* was an acid test of whether Bresson's style was strong enough to minimize psychology. The challenge was to reconcile the reduction of means, in which every shot, every image, every cut, and every sound counts, with the need to reveal the conflict and register the change within his protagonist in credible terms. Could the style, in other words, displace the psychological onto the cinematographic?

This question has been a challenge for scholars. P. Adams Sitney sees the film as a Bildungsroman that leads to Michel's transformation via the illumined face of Jeanne, the woman he meets at the beginning but "sees" for the first time in the final sequence.[33] T. Jefferson Kline finds the notion of conversion at that moment implausible, which he attributes to a crisis of faith in Bresson himself.[34] Sitney's perception that Michel's words, "Something lit up her face," are not reinforced by a literal flood of light indicates a critical difference between Bresson and conventional cinema and confirms the importance of the interior for Bresson. Kline, who argues that such readings do not take account of the "evidence on the screen," seems less persuaded by the role of the invisible in Bresson and the signifying power of off screen space, both of which are key to an understanding of the filmmaker's prevailing interest in spirituality. Ultimately he characterizes Bresson in the negative, using the filmmaker's words against him to conclude that his films are only "fragments," as if this were synonymous with incoherence or meaninglessness. This said, I think Kline is correct in suggesting that Michel's behavior may reflect an internal crisis in Bresson and that the trajectory and conclusion of Michel's story may be a displacement or a working through of that crisis.

There are strong reasons for applying a psychoanalytic reading to this film. The first is that, intentionally or not, Bresson has constructed a provocative case study of a conflicted personality, all the more fascinating for being ambiguous. In the clinical terms of psychoanalysis, Michel is an obsessive-compulsive personality with an unresolved Oedipal complex that drives him toward sociopathic activity with homoerotic components. The film's conclusion affirms that Michel's conflicts obstructed his attraction to Jeanne, yet it remains unclear whether his dallying in criminal activity was a displacement of a repressed heterosexuality or homosexuality. The second reason, following and reinforcing this, is that the film's narrative structure, its distribution of scenes, and its framing of shots and editing manifest consistent traits that can be seen as formal reflections of Michel's acting out of the conflict that Bresson identifies in the preface. With that conviction, the following analysis breaks down the visual structure of the film to show how it mirrors the character's pathology. Though, as I have argued, psychoanalytic concepts can be fruitfully applied to Bresson's work in general, *Pickpocket* seems to demand such an approach, since every aspect of its narrative and visual design can be viewed as forms of cinematic acting-out, which is to say that much of what we see Michel doing is about something else.

Furthermore, because *how* we see what Michel is doing is so brilliantly executed, it is hard to believe that on some level Bresson was not aware that he was provoking a psychoanalytic response or that the film's scenario and imagery, as will be analyzed below, would not invite such a reading. As viewers we might feel like Michel, who pleads with the inspector to stop taunting him with his insights and arrest him, and begin to unravel Bresson's purpose by considering his pilfering of Dostoevsky. However one finally interprets *Pickpocket*, it is clear that the film's structure is concerned with tracking the conflict in the character stated in the preface—namely, that he is involved in an adventure for which he was not made—to the conclusion, in which Michel awakens from his "nightmare" and resolves the conflict. In other words, it is not the film's trajectory and resolution that are in question, but what we determine they mean.

Source as Inspiration

Not only do the credits of the film fail to acknowledge Dostoevsky's *Crime and Punishment* as the source, something nearly every scholar has taken for granted, but there is no credit for screenplay at all. The words "scenario and dialogues by," present in the credits of *A Man Escaped* following the reference to Devigny, are absent from *Pickpocket*'s credits. Immediately after the title we read "de Robert Bresson." The credits of *Diary* bear the words "un film de

Robert Bresson," but they follow the citation of the Bernanos source. Why just the word *de* in the case of *Pickpocket?* In suggesting both "by" and "of," does it imply a more complete authorial attribution that precludes a screenplay credit?

Like the pickpocket who walks jauntily from the racetrack, confident of his first success, Bresson's literary theft is soon detected and remains under suspicion throughout. And like Michel's acts, bolder and more intricate as the film proceeds, Bresson's tracks are hidden in plain sight. The self-obsessed character that justifies his criminal behavior with a half-baked theory, the efforts of others to affect his life, the cat-and-mouse game between the protagonist and the insightful detective, the sudden change of heart—all of this is in the novel.

It is possible that Bresson, an avowed admirer of Dostoevsky, did not wish to invite comparisons with *Crime and Punishment*, which the word *adaptation* would do, or that in draining the novel of its philosophical and psychological density he could not legitimately claim it as his source. At the same time, I would argue that it is *precisely* the psychological nature of Dostoevsky's text that attracted Bresson, since it provided the greatest challenge against which to demonstrate the efficacy of the cinematographic style he sought to perfect. This style could not be less like Dostoevsky's, and so, with the same audacity of his protagonist, he deliberately set out to contravene an example par excellence of the psychological novel. Nevertheless, although *Pickpocket* is not a thorough rendering of Dostoevsky, its theme, principal characters, specific interactions, and much of its dialogue are lifted directly from his novel. And, as I have already alleged, the film is, paradoxically, itself a model of a psychologically astute work of cinematographic art. Therein lies what may be the seeds of the *filmmaker's* conflict.

The name of Dostoevsky's protagonist contains the word *raskol*, the Russian for "split" or "schism."[35] The point of the novel seems to be that one cannot maintain a sane existence on the basis of actions presumably directed by intellect alone. When Raskolnikov surrenders and is sentenced to Siberia, his pride is wounded; he maintains that his error was not the murder but the form it took and his failure to exact any good from it. It is only his final surrender to his own humanity, in the last two pages, that leads to the possibility of salvation. This reconciliation of mind and heart is why he is more moved by the humble Sonya, as Michel is by Jeanne, than by the clever Porfiry, whose psychological acuity may remind him too much of himself.

In addition to the protagonist, the novel contains four other significant male characters, at least two of whom can be taken as foils for Raskolnikov, expanding and deepening the implications of his actions. One is his friend, the affable and forthright Razumikhin, to whom Raskolnikov entrusts his mother and sister Dunya. The other is Svidrigaylov, a tormented man, haunted by better instincts too weak to outweigh his inclinations to depravity and sexual predation. An intriguing aspect of the novel is the space—four chapters and more than fifty pages—that Dostoevsky devotes to the unraveling and ultimate suicide of this character at the very point, just before Raskolnikov's surrender, when we might expect such attention to be devoted to the tortured conscience of the protagonist. Itself an extraordinary displacement, it reveals another affinity Bresson has with Dostoevsky, like one he shares with Bernanos: a preoccupation with young virgins and childhood corruption. When Raskolnikov calls Svidrigaylov a "vile, disgusting, salacious creature," one supposes that we are to think of him as more of a monster than Raskolnikov himself, who murdered a "mere" old woman, as Porfiry says.

Bresson, like Dostoevsky, believed that evil exists and cannot be rationalized through political or social theories. For Dostoevsky, guilt is more than simply a bourgeois concept, and the only way to cleanse it is through Christian salvation. He therefore repudiated the philosophy of his proto-Marxist Raskolnikov, which allows that murder is permissible if it brings about social justice.[36] Dostoevsky was responding to philosophical and political ideas of his day, concerns that emerge in conversations in the novel. Bresson, at least on the basis of his films, showed less interest in how social conditions and psychological trauma affect human behavior. True, like Raskolnikov, Michel is poor and lives in a box-size room (alternatively called a "coffin" in the novel) about the size of Fontaine's cell and goes about in a suit only slightly less worn than Raskolnikov's rags, and that both his mother and Jeanne, like their literary counterparts, live in poor circumstances. Yet *Pickpocket* is a more concentrated fable of sin and redemption, in which the ills of the human condition do not excuse the sinner; repentance must precede redemption.

Psyche and Analysis

Any impulse carried out for its own sake assumes an erotic or sexual

connotation.

—Franz Alexander, *Our Age of Unreason: A Study of the Irrational Forces in Social Life*

The fact that Bresson, like many French intellectuals of his time, rejected psychoanalytic theory does not require the critic to follow suit.[37] For one thing, the crime in *Pickpocket* is not a single act of murder, but repeated acts of theft.[38] For another, the words of the preface—that the film traces "the nightmare of a young man whose weak nature drove him into an adventure of thievery for which he was not destined"—cues us to the split in the character's makeup, as the name Raskolnikov does, a situation no other protagonist of Bresson's faces so literally. These are not the words of an observing intradiegetic character, although they might easily belong to the inspector. They are the filmmaker's in a preface outside of the narrative, dictating, in the voice of a Hawthorne, the proper moral perspective from which we must judge what follows. We are directed to view the film, then, as one that will explore and heal the protagonist's divided personality.

My reading is prompted by a guideline in psychoanalytic practice: if a person's behavior is ego-syntonic, that is, not conflicted, securely integrated with the personality structure, and not disruptive of professional and social relationships, it need not be psychoanalyzed. If, on the other hand, a person's behavior or a significant part of it is conflicted, not comfortably integrated, the cause of constant anxiety and guilt, and an interference with social interactions, it is considered ego-dystonic and warrants analysis. From this perspective, Fontaine in *A Man Escaped* is an example of the ego-syntonic personality and Michel an example of the ego-dystonic personality. This is not an arbitrary determination but one that the preface to *Pickpocket* declares before the credits.

Following the credits, the first words we see Michel writing in his diary and hear through his voice-over indicate that he is at least vaguely aware of an internal contradiction: "I know that those who have done these things remain silent and those who speak have not done them. Yet I have done them." Behind the braggadocio is the sense that his compulsion to write about the things he does reflects a need to make them real as well as an unconscious need to understand what drives him to do them. The very generality of his statement suggests that "these things" might refer to anything and that the taboo of speaking about them has less to do with their literal nature (i.e., stealing) than with the unconscious erotic gratification they educe.

The narrative is composed of two kinds of sequences: those in which the protagonist acts on his compelling "unnatural" impulses, namely, his criminal activity; and those in which he interacts with other characters who either challenge or are puzzled about his behavior. Paris in the 1950s (as opposed to St. Petersburg in the nineteenth century) is constricted to those places directly related to Michel's activities. This insulated structure fleshes out the theme and contradiction stated in the preface and implicit in the first diary entry.[39]

It is the concentration of the film's apparatus brought to bear on the protagonist's internal conflict, along with the way Michel's compulsive behavior is mirrored by the film's implacable drive, that makes *Pickpocket* an irresistible case study. Unlike the world Dostoevsky creates, with its many digressions and character histories, there is nothing outside of *Pickpocket*'s central focus. It is as if one were hearing from the analytic couch the patient's own history of his pathology in which, true to the "colossal narcissism" of one with a "God complex," everything around him is a mirror of his delusional worldview.[40] The diary and voice-over reinforce this impression even when they merely clarify something we have not seen. At one point Michel returns to his room and wipes blood off his hands; just as we are wondering where it came from, the voice says, "I had run and fallen." The statement's conjunction with the image underlines the virtual present of the film experience, an impression Bresson also achieves in *A Man Escaped*, but here, owing to the difference between Fontaine and Michel, it reflects an aspect of the narcissistic personality that assumes the world is his audience.

The evocation of the diary, which we see in only three other shots, through the voice-over, reiterates Michel's loneliness and the anxiety that prevents him from doing anything about it. The loneliness links him to the priest of Ambricourt and to Fontaine, but the priest's devotion to his calling accounts for his isolation, and he is comforted by his faith in God, something Michel lacks. Fontaine fights against isolation by working to change his condition and he is part of a comradely community. Michel's diary reflects his need to commune with himself and others even though he denies this. From a psychological perspective, the distribution of the film's scenes (to be described later) represents a compromise between his socially acceptable needs and those that cannot be articulated, much less assimilated. Whatever else his thieving represents, the act itself, physically intimate without relational or emotional consequence, plays out this compromise as a fantasy of utter control, in which the "other" is not just passive, but utterly unaware that it has been violated.

Apart from the diary, we do not see Michel doing anything to substantiate his alleged literary ambitions. On a visit to his room, the inspector mocks these pretensions when he runs his finger along the cover of a notebook, collecting the dust it has gathered from disuse. Raskolnikov, on the other hand, has published an article expounding his theory, which is what places him under suspicion and makes for extensive verbal interaction. Consistent with the film's reduction of the novel's scope, the dozens of pages devoted to the psychologically attuned contest between Raskolnikov and Porfiry Petrovich (including florid digressions and details of the latter's idiosyncrasies), which drive Raskolnikov to distraction, are compressed in *Pickpocket* into several laconic exchanges between an anxious Michel and a composed inspector about Michel's theories. These reach a climax when the inspector visits Michel's room, adding to the latter's irritability, and Michel picks up a book and flings it down with the word "Enough!" Since the book is about George Barrington, *The Prince of Pickpockets*, whose life and methods fascinate Michel, the gesture carries a dual significance: it expresses his frustration over being suspected without being arrested, and it conveys unconscious rage over his inability to give up his obsessive activity. He is, in short, at the end of his rope because he links the inspector's delay to the prolonging of his sickness.

Bresson's focus on action matches the repetitive nature of Michel's obsession, inspiring another balletic cinematographic exhibition. But as there are differences between the protagonists of *Pickpocket* and *A Man Escaped*, a similar disparity exists between the actions engaged in by each character and their presentation in the film. Fontaine's actions, though stealthily performed in the seclusion of his cell, are visible and apprehensible to the character and the spectator. Michel's actions are not only surreptitious, despite their being performed in public, often in broad daylight, but are hidden even from their perpetrator. They depend more on touch and physical coordination.

With few exceptions, only the viewer sees the intricate, quick, and supple movements of each theft as only a carefully shot and edited film could show, capturing a process that could not be fully grasped by the naked eye. The filmic presentation of these actions, climaxing in the tour de force of the Gare de Lyon sequence, assumes a hyperreal quality. Time and narrative seem to stop in order to document a physical phenomenon that would otherwise escape the attention of both. This cinematographic exposition, beyond any character's point of view, effectively visualizes the dissociative status that the activity has in Michel's life. The variations in the treatment of the theft episodes trace the progressive degree of this dissociation, in which the intact self is increasingly detached from the act of stealing through the manipulations of framing and montage. Because this involves medium shots and close-ups of hands, it is almost as if Bresson had sought a cinematographic equivalent of the French language's use of the definite article (e.g., *les mains*) instead of the possessive adjective or pronoun to refer to parts of the body. Although these shots qualify, technically, as synecdoche, whereby the "picking of pockets" equals or stands for "theft," from the psychological standpoint of this reading, Michel's "true self" is not fully engaged in these activities. This does not mean that he is unaware of what he is doing or that he is not morally responsible for his actions, but that, no less than Raskolnikov, he does not comprehend the *nature* of what he is doing, its psychosexual etiology, or his guilt. It is because of this that I consider these actions and the cinematographic manner in which they are represented to be the core structures and relationships in *Pickpocket*. Significantly, the treatment of Michel's last act of theft is an important modification of the pattern.

The Lure of the False Self

In Michel's first theft at the racetrack, while there is already a disjunction between his face and his hands that becomes increasingly pronounced, he looks down at the woman's handbag (off screen) four different times in two shots before he actually opens it and removes the money. He is, of course, a novice. The shots that show us what his hand is doing, however, do not immediately follow these looks; that is, the cuts to hand and bag are not *on* the look, a delay that technically disqualifies them as subjective countershots. The only point-of-view exchanges occur prior to the theft, as a breakdown of the opening sequence shows.

It begins with a dissolve from the diary to a close-up of a woman's right arm and white-gloved hand, set off strikingly by an expensive-looking bracelet. She opens her handbag, removes some bills, and passes them to the left hand of a man standing screen center. As the man walks right, the camera tilts up and pans with him in medium shot as he approaches a ticket window to place a bet. Having done so, he turns toward the camera, pauses a moment to examine his purchase, and glances up quickly at something off screen. This look, of a figure who will never be seen again after the racetrack sequence, prompts the cut to a medium shot of Michel standing screen center and returning the look as the man enters the frame, passes in front of Michel into the background, rejoins the woman, and moves off with the crowd to watch the race. Michel, his eyes cast down for a moment as his voice-over tells us that, despite his anxiety, he has decided to proceed with the theft, turns and follows.

In the next two shots the crowd moves toward the stadium; Michel follows, the camera tracking behind him as he walks up to and stops directly behind the woman, who stands out in her all-white outfit. Sensing his presence, she turns and looks directly at him, prompting, like the man's look earlier, a cut to a reverse-angle medium close-up of Michel looking back. Eight shots, beginning with this one, constitute the theft portion of the sequence. In the fifth Michel stands behind and between the woman, on screen left, and the man, on screen right, holding a large pair of binoculars to his eyes. The woman turns her head again, then all three face front in the off screen direction of the race about to begin. Though the eye contact causes Michel to hesitate—"I had better quit," the voice-over says—he remains fixated and twice looks down. In a reverse-angle close-up, from behind the woman, we see the handbag hanging off her left shoulder and level with her hip, the front of it conveniently facing Michel as his left hand tries to undo the clasp. A reverse angle of his face shows him looking passively ahead. A close-up of the bag shows his hand releasing the buckle. Another reverse angle shows him closing his eyes for a moment in what clearly implies not just relief at his success, but gratification. He looks down and up twice. A close-up of his hand going into the bag is followed by a return to the set up of the fifth shot as the sound of the race grows louder. This indicates that the horses are passing off screen directly in front of them, a fact registered by the man's lowering the binoculars. In the last shot of the bag, Michel's hand removes a wad of bills, and just as the woman turns, quickly places them in his pocket.

In the final shots of the sequence, we watch the crowd turn back to the betting windows as an exhilarated Michel exits the park ("I felt I was mastering the world") only to be pursued by two plainclothesmen. As the shot of Michel walking dissolves to a medium shot of the interior of a car where he sits between the two, his voice-over remarks, "One minute later I was caught."

This sequence is critical in many ways. First, in its first two shots it stresses the difference between Michel and Fontaine and between the way subjectivity works in *Pickpocket* and *A Man Escaped*. In the first shot we assume that what we see is an objective view of the action, despite our awareness that Michel is telling the story. Only after the cut to him, motivated by the man's look, do we realize that everything in the first shot, from the woman opening her bag to the man turning away from the ticket window, has been witnessed by Michel, that unknown to the couple and the spectator, he has been eyeing them as potential targets.

This order of the point-of-view system differs from the opening of *A Man Escaped*, which introduces Fontaine's hands, face, eyes, and situation in an objective shot, and then proceeds to the action of the sequence upon his controlling look outward. Fontaine's point of view, as undisguised as his situation and intentions and without the need for reflection or voice-over, is forthrightly presented to the spectator (though not, of course, to his captors). We trust what we see and align ourselves unconditionally with this protagonist. In *Pickpocket* we recognize retroactively that we have been deceived by the camera and are unaware of Michel's presence and intentions until we see him and connect him to the off screen voice. The difference induces wariness rather than trust, although, as with Hitchcock, we are seduced into following every move of such a character.

Other subtle deceptions through camerawork occur periodically, in which Michel's point of view is either concealed or momentarily blurred. In this first instance the strategy gives a special edge to the look of the man leaving the ticket window, which registers surprise at Michel's pointed, off screen observation. The man, in other words, reacts as the viewer does, when he realizes that he is being watched. The directness of this look is not lost on Michel, whose determination to go through with his intention seems a direct affront to the parental *no*. The physical details suggest that these are people of means in a class above Michel's, but the psychological significance they connote is clear.

That both the man and the woman make eye contact with Michel not only makes his act more defiant, if riskier, but implies that he commits it against both. The ramifications of this are tantalizing, especially in the four frontal shots of all three facing the race, in which, while Michel steals from the woman behind their backs, the man wears blinders; he does not remove the binoculars until the race, and the deed, are nearly done. In psychoanalytic terms, the older man (husband and father figure) is rendered absent or symbolically impotent while the younger flagrantly violates the woman's person and steals the treasure. The pleasure registered on Michel's face when he unclasps the bag (figure 25) and his inflated sense of power as he leaves the track reinforce the erotic and psychological implications of the scene. Both his look and its fleetness confirm the depth of his repression and his distance from coming to terms with it. It is the first graphic evidence of the sexual nature of the activity he pursues. In this case, however, as there can be no Oedipal victory without great cost, the seizure by the law is inevitable.

Later in the film we learn that prior to his career as a pickpocket Michel had stolen from his mother and that she withdrew her complaint to the police when she realized, unknown to him, that he was the thief. His guilt over this prevents him from visiting her until she is about to die. The act repels Jeanne, whose response, "There's nothing lower," is nevertheless followed by a forgiving embrace, recalling the equivalent scene in *Crime and Punishment* when Raskolnikov "confesses" to Sonya by leading her on to guess the truth, as is the case in *Pickpocket*. In changing Raskolnikov's confession of the murder of the old moneylender and her sister into Michel's admitting that he stole from his mother, Bresson transfers the greater weight of the former onto the latter, and suggests that the real crime in *Pickpocket* is the violation of the mother, for which the racetrack theft, composed as the quintessential family romance, is both repetition and surrogate, a denial of the original crime, itself a displacement of Oedipal guilt, and a deluded attempt at reparation—in other words, both crime and punishment. The "blinded" father figure is, like Michel's father, absent, remiss as moral arbiter, a role later filled by the inspector. That the couple is wealthy, indicated by the dazzling bracelet on the woman's arm, allows Michel to rationalize his crime against his poor mother by transposing it onto those who "deserve" to be robbed, just as the old moneylender in *Crime and Punishment* "deserved" to be murdered. From this perspective, Michel's grandiosity is an attempt to displace his all-consuming shame, and his dalliance in the underworld a masochistic acting-out of repressed desires.

Michel is released for lack of evidence. We learn through his conversation with Jacques at a café that he is looking for work. Jacques has no idea how ironic he is being when he remarks that Michel "is good with his hands" before giving him a reference. Michel notices the inspector entering and greets him, "stupidly," as he says in voice-over, as though wearing his guilt on his sleeve. All three discuss the possibility that the law should ignore certain kinds of theft because of poverty, and Jacques mentions Michel's theory that "superior" individuals should be permitted to transgress the law. When Michel affirms that such people would stop after a single symbolic act, the inspector disagrees, highlighting the difference between the film and Dostoevsky's novel and making it clear that Michel is in denial over the obsessive nature of his activities.

On the subway the next day, presumably on his way to pursue Jacques's referral, his attention is drawn to a pickpocket. His voice-over remark, "Why were my eyes glued to that man?," not only underlines the unconscious nature of Michel's fascination but validates the inspector's skepticism over his theory. He is not a one-time transgressor of the law for symbolic reasons, but one consumed by a pathological obsession who must continue to act out. In addition, the self-questioning and general vagueness of the remark also invite, for the first time, the possibility that the obsession that compels him involves a fixation on men. Back in his room, he practices the man's moves, using a newspaper to conceal the act and to enfold a wallet after it's been lifted. The shot of the open newspaper in his room dissolves to one he holds on the train, prepared to imitate the pickpocket's method. These shots seem almost certainly inspired by Samuel Fuller's *Pickup on South Street*, a Hollywood film released in 1953.[41] Michel's first target exits before he has a chance to act, but a second soon materializes. His success prompts an exuberant reaction typical of the delusional mind. When Jacques asks if he has gotten a job, he says, "I need nothing," and runs off. Through the voice-over we learn that he has been picking pockets on subways for a week, changing routes to avoid suspicion, although he admits that the "pickings are poor and not worth the risk." The remarks are revealing: if the "pickings are poor," then money is not the primary object, whereas the sweeping compass of "need[ing] nothing" denotes that picking pockets satisfies a more primal, narcissistic need, the same one that made him feel "master of the world" at the racetrack.

The next attempt fails, but characteristic of Bresson's inventive approach, we learn this indirectly. A shot of Michel standing on the subway platform dissolves to a train arriving, but at another station and a later point; the ride itself has been elided. Michel exits and walks quickly up the stairs, but just as he reaches the top the camera, focused on the legs of a man passing him and then turning around to confront him, now pans up to the two of them as the man demands his wallet back and threatens to call the police. Michel stares at him, then relents, removes the wallet from his pocket, hands it over, and runs off. Leaving out the ride is an especially brilliant example of a Bressonian elision, surpassing the usual aims of this technique to avoid repetition and compress time. Apparently during the train ride we have not seen, Michel believed he had successfully lifted a wallet, only to be confronted afterward in public and exposed as a failure. In a similar fashion, the narrative gap assumed to be a mere convention turns out to be of utmost importance. Eliding what transpired on the train creates a fissure that parallels the shock to and instant deflation of Michel's ego, analogizing the psychic crisis into which he free-falls, consequent to a sudden wave of humiliation and shame. His subsequent decision to "stay in" strongly suggests his need to recover from a powerful narcissistic injury.

The Walk and the Stare: A Homoerotic Detour

Walking seems to cover time and space, but in reality we are always just

where we started.

—Agnes Martin, *Writings*

Two striking motifs in *Pickpocket* deserve mention. The first is the image of Michel walking or ascending and descending stairs. Given Bresson's tendency to concision and ellipses, as well as the seventy-five-minute running time of this film, it is extraordinary how much footage is devoted to these activities. Discounting moments when he is with others, we see Michel walking solo in more than thirty-five shots and negotiating staircases in more than a dozen.

Martin La Salle's complaint that Bresson made him walk up the stairs to Michel's room countless times until he did it with the appropriate indifference should indicate that these ambulatory movements were important to the filmmaker.[42] Michel walks with a determination and a sense of purpose completely at odds for a man without a job. He is no flâneur; he does not linger, meander, stroll, scan the sky, or window-shop. He hardly looks at other people unless they are targets. This man-about-town gait is another manifestation of the obsessive-compulsive personality who, of course, is convinced that he *is* going about important business.

As such, the deluded sense of freedom implied in this seemingly unrestricted activity is less real than the prison rituals imposed on Fontaine. Thus the counterimages of Michel's walks are those pauses and stops when he stares ahead at something, more usually someone who has caught his attention. This figure remains off screen long enough, a heartbeat or two before the reverse shot, to signify purpose. Here Bresson takes a principle that he extols in his notes, that one should put the effect before the cause, and applies it quite emphatically as yet another means of revealing Michel's character. He juxtaposes many of Michel's advances with sudden stops that freeze him in place, concretizing through these two gestures the two poles of his character: his conscious will, however deluded and misguided, to move forward, which is continually derailed and paralyzed by the pathology that rules his unconscious.

These alternating postures bear directly on his need to act out his conflicts. Directly following the subway encounter that deals such a blow to his ego, Michel is enticed into the underworld. Eventually he leaves his room and descends the stairs, slowing as he gets to the bottom, his attention caught by something off screen. His face in shadow as he pauses, he then descends the remaining steps, continuing to look off screen. The countershot is of a man standing in front of his building looking up, then directly into the foyer at Michel. He walks off, then returns and looks again at Michel. Michel returns to his room, leaves the door more open than usual, and sits on his bed. A moment later he hears footsteps and looks up; it is Jacques and Jeanne with news about Michel's mother. She is ill and wonders why he stays away.

Michel may have reason to suspect that he is being tailed by a plain-clothesman, but the man he sees is far more suggestive of a cruising homosexual. Indeed, when Michel returns to his room and leaves the door open, we have every reason to think it is an invitation to the stranger, and certainly the sounds of approaching footsteps seem to tease the viewer with this possibility. If there are already suggestions of repressed homoeroticism in the action of probing men's clothes and stealing something valuable from them, this provocative encounter takes the implications further. However confused or unconscious Michel's sexual inclinations may be, it is difficult not to read this sequence as a typical, and mutual, homosexual come-on. This does not mean we can conclude definitively that Michel's conflict is about repressed homosexual desire. Clinically speaking, an unresolved Oedipal crisis, which in orthodox psychoanalytic theory implies continued castration anxiety,[43] is frightening enough to induce pathological avoidance of heterosexual relations: Oedipus' first impulse on hearing the oracle about his fate is to run away. A flight to homosexuality is as viable a response as would be a flight to heterosexuality that results from pathological fear of homosexual desire.

Michel's anticipation that the stranger might enter his room is arrested by the surprise appearance of Jeanne and Jacques, who come to speak of his mother. His curt dismissal is an automatic response to the overdetermination of the moment. Not only is the visit a reminder of his original sin, of the shame and guilt over stealing from his mother and of his consequent need to avoid her. It is also about an emerging attraction for Jeanne that, because of her association with his mother, must be denied, since as I have indicated, the consequences of an unresolved Oedipal complex and castration anxiety include fear of heterosexuality as well as of sexual impotence. In the light of this abundance of failures, together with the recent humiliation at the subway, it is not surprising that Michel would seek any path that could restore narcis- sistic equilibrium, however delusionary. The ease with which he agrees to follow the stranger in the street is a step toward this goal. Without a word, the man leads him to a café and bar where they sit and, as Michel says in voice- over, "fifteen minutes later" become friends.[44]

No words pass between them—also a stereotypical feature of anonymous homosexual encounters—as is the case with all their dealings (with one exception, when a third accomplice is introduced). The stranger silently shows Michel the tricks of the trade in a series of seven shots linked through nearly undetectable dissolves. The fluidity of the effect, as opposed to that of a typical montage, accentuates the grace, elegance, and skill associated with a masterly performance, an impression confirmed by the stately musical passage from Lully that accompanies it. This quality suggests another effect of Michel's psychic compromise, in which the stylized gestures of thievery replace the role religious ceremonies and sacred rituals may once have played in his life. We sense this from his remark to Jeanne later that he once believed in God for three minutes. The seductive perfection of the stranger's moves elevates Michel's obsession from underground encounters to bravura displays in broad daylight. More than ever Michel, as Jeanne tells him later, leaves the real world and "shares no interests with others." The irony is that while he imagines that his immersion in this alternative lifestyle validates his self-image as an exceptional being, he has in fact submitted, like many narcissistically unstable young people, to a group psychology that flatters his false self and immature ego.

As this situation continues, Michel avoids Jeanne in order to pursue the titillating risks connected to his underworld associates. At one point he goads Jacques into courting her, after which we see him slightly smiling and caressing the watch he has just stolen from another man. His voice-over comment, "The watch was beautiful," is the only time he makes such an appreciative comment on a stolen object, confirming the thefts as erotic displacements. The pleasure Michel exhibits over these acts is sufficiently intense to suggest how easy it might be for him to surrender to homosexual behavior as a way to avoid solving his deeper conflicts, enforcing a psychic compromise between guilt and gratification. In this sense Michel's increasing expertise at thievery would be the sexual equivalent of flaunting forbidden desires while simultaneously hiding them, cinematographically speaking, in plain sight. As the description of the walk and the stare demonstrate, nearly all signs of homoerotic connotations are visual and silent; no diary entries or voice-overs clarify what is going on. Thus they not only play into a stereotype of anonymous sexual behavior but also capture how the psychic experience of such moments allows one to indulge in the infantile sexual wishes and gratifications undoubtedly revived.

As Michel becomes more accomplished, the thefts are so expertly recorded that it is difficult on a first or second viewing to comprehend the action. For example, on a street outside a bank, the victim is about to enter a taxi when Kassagi's character pretends to beat him to it as a ruse to force both distraction and a physical contact that allows the thief to reach behind him, unbutton the man's jacket, turn and lift his wallet with one hand, drop it into the other, and pass it to Michel, all in seconds. The actions are efficiently framed and edited in four shots, but the absence of point-of-view shots and the presence of two pickpockets momentarily obscure who is doing what to whom.

The next two jobs involve watches. In the first, five shots depict the action with the same speed and dexterity witnessed in the taxi scene, strengthening Michel's position among his accomplices. But the second only implies the theft through a characteristic use of elision and warrants comment. It is in the first shot of this sequence that Jeanne tells Michel that he does not live in the real world, after which she and Jacques go on an amusement ride while Michel sits at an outdoor table in a café (figure 26). As he waits for their return, he glances off screen. The countershot shows us the object of his look: a close-up of a man's left arm resting across a chair as he sits at a nearby table, a watch prominent on his wrist. The mere sight of this image at this point is enough to convey the obsessive compulsion that rules Michel's character and his inability to redirect it. It is the instantaneity of this perception that confirms the primal force behind his urge, and therefore the determinant role of sexuality in his behavior. Martin La Salle is especially good at such moments, conveying the sense of being suddenly seized while baring only the subtlest hints of unrest.

Momentarily he rises and leaves the scene. The third shot is of Michel at the table hesitating, looking down for a moment, then rising and walking out of the frame, as the camera lingers on the vacated table. A dissolve to the same table setup moments later shows Jeanne and Jacques returning and wondering what has happened to Michel. This dissolves to the staircase and landing in Michel's building as we see him returning to his room. It is only after he cleans the blood off his wrist and talks with Jacques, who arrives unexpectedly, that Michel removes the stolen watch from his pocket and grasps it with special pleasure. Eliding the actual theft in this case replaces dazzling expertise with a stress on the disturbing link between the thefts and Michel's crippling inability to cope with his loneliness through the pursuit of healthier social habits. This is the suffering that all obsessive compulsives endure and makes cures difficult: for them, it is more exciting to act out than to participate in a social outing.

Ecstasy and Deflation

In the elaborate twenty-shot Gare de Lyon sequence, involving five different thefts, two shots link Michel's point of view with the object of his attention, but only one of these is exclusively connected to a theft: Michel assists a man onto the train while holding his wrist and stealing his watch. The virtual absence of point of view throughout this sequence is revealing. It renders the action more impersonal, but it plays out a strategy that bears on the act in question and how it is perceived in the film. The brilliant orchestration of this sequence has been duly appreciated by others.[45] I wish to focus on a particular aspect of it.

At one point we see Michel looking off screen at a familiar figure he cannot identify and whom we see in the countershot; it is a detective seen earlier at the police station. The tracking movement of this subjective long shot follows the figure for a few seconds, but is then arrested as the camera's attention seizes on a new target: a man in a dark suit who puts down his suitcase, walks over to a merchant stand to make a purchase, replaces his wallet in his vest pocket, turns back to retrieve his bag, and walks off. The camera closes in as this occurs, then cuts to a close-up of the bag from an oblique angle as the man lines up at the gate to the trains. A quick tilt up shows his back as a hand enters the shot and taps his shoulder. A cut to a reverse medium-close shot shows him surrounded by Michel and his two accomplices. With the hand still on his shoulder and his distracted head turned left, another hand lifts his wallet and drops it behind, out of our view. The next shot shows us the wallet falling into Michel's hand, which then drops it into the pocket of an unwitting traveler, from which it is retrieved moments later on the train.

I want to consider the long shot in this series, technically from Michel's point of view, which yields information shared by his accomplices, as the succeeding shots indicate. Judging from their immediate convergence and expertly synchronized movements around the man with the bag a moment later, we must assume that they communicate with each other as surreptitiously as they thieve. Given the precision of Bresson's strategies, there seems to be more to that long shot than the ensuing action explains. First, there is the sense that what appears to be the object of one character's look shifts undetectably to a shared perspective at the point that the camera's track stops at the sight of the new victim. This would be consistent with an earlier theft in the sequence, in which the camera closes in on a potential target (the man with the billfold) and an action is performed without our knowing beforehand whose perspective the camera represents. Only an alert spectator would catch sight, on an initial viewing, of the newspaper and the coat over the arm that belong to the character played by Kassagi.

But there is another implication of the arrested motion of the camera: that it is a response to the arrested attention of Michel, away from his initial conscious focus—the detective about whom his voice-over tells us he is curious ("Where have I seen him?")—to an object that ignites his unconscious obsession (figure 27). In other words, his compulsion rules to such a degree that it has the power to effectively halt his investigatory impulse as embodied in the moving camera. That impulse surely reflected a real concern on Michel's part, justified, it turns out, when he later sees the detective and his partner conducting his accomplices to jail. From this perspective, the gray area in question—the moment when the long shot from Michel's point of view shifts focus from the initial object of his look—represents the force of his underlying conflict and the manner in which he presently deals with it. In essence, he is unconsciously compelled to reject an effort to recall the detective's identity, as it would clearly be tied to his guilt, and in defense merges his conscious perspective with the more general one shared by his associates in crime.

This fusion then allows the camera's comprehensive embrace of the visual field, one that seemed at first consonant with Michel's reflective, exploratory state ("Where have I seen him?"), to break up into the isolated components of the acts of theft. In effect, the social space, registered by the long shot–long take, is cut up, through montage, into the fragmentary, compartmentalized spaces of the sociopath's obsessional mind.

If Michel's initial efforts at picking pockets are displacements of forbidden sexual desires, it follows that his subsequent involvement with others, beginning with the homoerotically tinged encounter with the Kassagi figure, is a further substitute in this direction. The more forbidden and dangerous the activity, the more erotically charged and psychically irresistible it would be. This would account for the reading of the long shot at the Gare de Lyon in which Michel's initial point of view suddenly fuses with the ruling mind-set over which he has less control. Thus the progressive deftness of the thefts parallels an intensification of his involvement, climaxing in the flagrant, orgiastic display in the station. His inability to conduct a reasonable social life with anyone outside this circle is consistent with this mode of behavior. Yet his apparent reluctance to openly pursue a sexual object, heterosexual or homosexual, and balance it with a more evenly distributed social existence confirms that the internal conflict persists.

The last example that reflects the dissociation theme is also the only other such sequence in the film and occurs near the end at the racetrack, the setting of the first theft. The marked degree of its dissociative character matches the change in Michel's situation. Following the arrest of his partners at the Gare de Lyon, he leaves Paris for two years, a period elided entirely and described in a voice-over entry in his journal. We are told that he spent his time in various cities on gambling and women, something that often induces winces of incredulity if not outright laughter in viewers, who find it difficult to imagine this man of dubious sexuality and passive character living the high life in European capitals like some suave Lothario. It is this moment and Michel's subsequent behavior on his return that many critics have found unconvincing.

Returning to Paris, Michel discovers that Jeanne has had a child, has been abandoned by its father, Jacques, and ostracized by her own family. Michel vows to go straight, get a job, and help her, all of which he does. It is not surprising that at the threshold of going straight, he is tempted by his former weakness, or, let us say, irresolution, when he sees a man reading the racing pages in a café and goes to the track with him. The man flaunts the money he has allegedly won by opening his jacket and revealing it stuffed ostentatiously in his vest pocket. Michel remembers that the man had bet on a different horse, but despite his suspicion and what appears to be a setup, he pursues his aim.

The framing of the theft sequence reverses the physical positions occupied by Michel and his target in the opening sequence, in which Michel stood behind his victims. Now he stands in front of his target, which will require greater proficiency. The sequence comprises eight shots, the same number of the first theft, reinforcing, like the setting, its cyclical significance and compulsive nature. Four of them are medium shots of Michel, the man behind him, and others facing front as they watch the race, which, as was true of the first sequence, is off screen and suggested entirely by sound. These are crosscut with four close-ups of Michel's hand reaching behind his back and upward, going inside the man's jacket and removing the wad of bills (figure 28). As his hand descends in the last of these shots, we see the man's left hand come down as well and seize Michel's wrist while his right one clamps a handcuff around it. Without a reaction shot of either man, this image dissolves to Michel in prison.

We have here the most elaborate illustration of the way Michel's hands have assumed a life of their own, enacting a ritual that is otherwise indiscernible on either his face or in his body language when seen from the front. The perfect demeanor of the pickpocket, no doubt, but the effect is to perceive a gesture that seems physically improbable to perform. The twisting motion of his arm behind his back, its elongated stretch upward to reach the level of the vest pocket, the deftness and coordination required at this point of utmost muscular strain: the entire procedure, beyond dexterity, looks as if it would require the talents of a contortionist. Yet the very extremity of the act, smoothly performed and hidden from Michel's view, makes it an effective metaphor for the unconscious nature of its genesis, as if, indeed, it were powered by a force beyond the intentionality of its agent.

Is it mere irony that Michel is caught at his most daring and skillful performance? In prison he complains to Jeanne that what bothers him most is that he let down his guard, but surely he did so through an unconscious wish to put an end to his nightmare. He is suspicious of the man at the racetrack not once but twice, the first time concerning the money he has allegedly won, and the second while standing in front of him and looking over his shoulder while his voice-over says, "I read mischief in his eyes." What more would he need to deter him from proceeding unless he had reason to allow what happens to occur? In one sense Michel's resolve to go straight prompts him to allow capture by the law at the very peak of his game, a final display of grandiosity before punishment. Psychoanalytically this amounts to an acceptance of Oedipal guilt and a concession to the father.

From the standpoint of a homoerotic reading, however, the scene is an extreme, though unconscious effort to resolve, one way or another, the psychosexual conflict that underlies his nightmare. Consider the difference between the earlier face-to-face—more accurately, body-to-body—contact with the male targets and the final example. In the latter, Michel stands in front of his victim, a curious inversion that seems both a flagrant display of his prowess and an invitation to be taken by the man behind him, whose flashing of his wad of bills earlier is surely an exhibitionistic substitute for a different kind of bulge. The man is not only an authority figure, like Porfiry, but one who fills the role of the absent, longed-for father. This surrender and capture, then, might in this context be read as an acknowledgment not only of the original sin against the mother but also of the fantasized sin against the father and a desire to be punished in kind through the assumption of the passive posture in sexual congress.

It should be noted that any attempt to understand sexual etiology and identity must take into full account the *actual* behavior of the individual, both conscious and that labeled "acting out." Throughout the film, what we see Michel doing are not sexual overtures, but attempts to force a certain intimacy onto men, almost always older men, and to take something valuable from them. As Michel lacks a father, it is certainly reasonable to see such actions, quite apart from their sexual implications, as desperate, even vengeful attempts to recapture, relive, or more likely reinvent an early, less Oedipally charged tie with the father. In this sense the objects of his actions can be said to have the same "purely symbolic significance acquired at an extremely early age, usually during the period of the first three or four years of life," as is ascribed to actual sexual pursuits of such objects.[46]

However we interpret Michel's actions and behavior throughout and the imagery that elicits strong homoerotic connotations, the result of this final encounter, ambiguous as it is, can be understood symbolically as freeing Michel from his nightmare sufficiently enough to allow him to accept his need for a more stable human relationship, which, the film indicates, is what Jeanne offers. This move toward a heterosexual object is not incompatible with a psychoanalytic understanding of individuals who either act out or experiment with homosexual behavior. Of course there is a limit to how much one should speculate about a fictional character in a movie, especially a movie by a filmmaker as ambivalent and evasive on such matters as Bresson. To the degree, however, that the final racetrack sequence is charged with a real, if still unconscious homosexual desire, the embrace of Jeanne would be, at least initially, more of a "flight to health," an escape to a safer, more acceptable position from the point of view of the prevailing moral and social norms that Michel has resisted but to which he ultimately yields.

How Michel has reached this point, in which the forces that have sustained the stealing cycle give way to a slowly awakening conscious desire for a different life, can in part be accounted for by the film's structure, specifically its distribution of scenes and how it manifests the compartmentalization of his psychic life. Given his earlier resistance to the conventions of society that constrict "extraordinary" beings like himself, it should be noted that he may also see that the crime cycle, which his last theft threatened perhaps to revive, was itself imprisoning and not the existentially free condition he had imagined. The cycle cannot be maintained without great effort and expense to character structure, especially if it is repeatedly challenged by counterforces in the form of natural human ties. The loneliness only partly assuaged by keeping the diary reflects an interiority that must either self-destruct or ultimately succumb to the appeal of those ties.

Michel's curt response to Jeanne that he once believed in God for three minutes reveals an almost childlike disappointment in the power of faith to give meaning to his life. Nevertheless, in the judgment of this writer, his change at the end does not require the leap of faith on the spectator's part that certain writers have assumed.[47] As I continue to assert, even if one accepts the intervention of a spiritual force at the end of a Bresson film, two things would still obtain. First, the subject who changes must be open to receive the effects of divine grace: "It is impossible for God to will the absolutely impossible."[48] Second, this openness results either from an underlying disposition that unconsciously seeks such a thing, or a conflicted nature that wants to be extricated from its misery and brought into serenity. Neither of these preconditions is inconsistent with the way psychoanalysis sees the individual, who, says Freud, can be relieved of the destructive effects of repression and learn to live as a relatively happy neurotic. Throughout the narrative Michel is pushed and prodded by the faces, words, and circumstances around him and by those who refuse to give up on him: his mother's death and his learning that she knew he had stolen from her; the inspector's keen understanding and fatherly concern; Jeanne's love for him and the courage she displays in her own situation. The accumulation of these features as they are assimilated and reflected upon eventually assume a weight and value that overcome Michel's resistance and arouse his natural needs.

Les Places des discordes

You know what the trouble is, like Pascal says, all the *malheurs* in the world

come from a man's inability to sit alone in a small room.

—William Gaddis, *The Recognitions*

The brevity of *Pickpocket* is in part a result of the efficient way it distributes its "scenes," by which I literally mean the sites of its actions. There are thirteen basic settings. Four of them—Michel's mother's room, a church, a bank, and a payroll office—appear only once. Three others—the racetrack, the police station, and Jeanne's room—appear twice. There are three scenes on the subway and at the Gare de Lyon, four in the prison, five on the street, seven in a café, and eleven in Michel's room. The distribution of narrative action in these various locations reveals interesting correlations.

All four of the locations seen only once are associated with avoidance or failure on Michel's part. He initially flubs a robbery attempt in the bank, and the payroll office represents the straight life he has resisted. Both the church and his mother's apartment embody the guilt he feels over having stolen from her. If, as he claims, he loves his mother more than himself, he may long for the spiritual peace that she found in religion. Fittingly, therefore, the one scene in church is the occasion of his mother's funeral. The three locations seen twice support these impressions. They represent stages of the "crime and punishment" cycle, from the racetrack, the scene of his first and last theft; to the police station, where the inspector taunts his conscience; to Jeanne's room, where he vows to go straight and care for her and her child.

The psychological relevance of these correlations is even more pronounced in regard to the Gare de Lyon. Unlike the subway and the street, whose functions remain constant, but somewhat akin to the racetrack, the Gare de Lyon shifts meaning in the course of three appearances. At first it is a playground for thieves and an apt metaphor for Michel's contempt for the life of ordinary people. He goes there not as a participant in the social fluxus of the city, nor as a traveler, any more than he is a mere passenger on the subway, a sojourner on the street, or a spectator at the racetrack. But if at first the Gare de Lyon is a theater of grandiose fantasies of mastery, an orgy of acting-out, it soon deflates such illusions when his accomplices are arrested. As a sign of a turn toward reality, Michel's third visit is to use the station for its designated purpose: he embarks on a train and leaves Paris to escape arrest.

Of the remaining settings, the prison is only the literal embodiment of what the subway, the street, and the café, typical public spaces in any large city, eventually represent: places where he is compelled to pursue his compulsion ("Why did fate force me to watch that man?") or obsess about it theoretically to Jacques and the inspector. These spaces are linked with Michel's cell-like room and the prison; they confirm that alone or in public, he is a man driven and obsessed.

This structure sustains the dynamic of conflict, eventually creating the possibility of change. If we take as a focal point Michel's returns to his room as representing many of his characteristics—his insularity, his loneliness, his disconnectedness from others—in short, as symptomatic of the state of mind in conflict with the forces around him, an intriguing rhythmic structure emerges. For most of the film, alternations between the room and other settings chart a clear pattern, somewhat like a musical composition or metrical lines of verse:

a. —— —— / —— —— / —— —— —— —— /
b. —— —— / —— —— / —— —— —— /
c. —— —— —— / —— —— / —— / —— / —— / ——

    Each diagonal line marks a scene in Michel's room and each horizontal line one of the other scenes. A break in the pattern of line c immediately precedes Michel's departure from Paris. Upon his return, there are no scenes of him alone in his room. The alternation in the film's last section is between Jeanne's apartment and Michel at office, café, and racetrack, followed by the four last passages in prison. Prior to Michel's departure, the conflict is reflected by alternations in which at least one outside situation challenges his conduct. When this is not the case, the conflict enters his room directly through unexpected visits by friends (Jeanne and Jacques) or by the letter Jeanne leaves for him urging him to visit his mother.

    After his activities are disrupted by his mother's death and the funeral in the church, there is an upsurge in criminal activity, followed by an upsurge in outside conflict (a café meeting with the inspector, a scene at the police station). The rhythm repeats as the triumphant Gare de Lyon sequence is followed by the disastrous one, which leads to retrenchment and two scenes in his room, the first when the inspector tells him that he knows he is guilty, and the second when he prepares to leave. In between is the scene in Jeanne's room when he confesses. When Michel returns to Paris, the signs of change are indicated by his resolve to help Jeanne and by his acceptance of her love while in prison. There is a subtle reflection of this change in his voice-over question when he enters her apartment; looking downward and off screen, he asks, "Why was I watching that child?," just as the camera tilts to reveal Jeanne's baby sitting on the floor. In paralleling the voice-over question we heard earlier, when he wondered what drew him to the pickpocket on the subway, Bresson suggests that Michel is now on the verge of an equally strong attraction. Just as the earlier question led him into a life of crime, the one in Jeanne's apartment draws him to a life of responsibility. That the child is seen in the same shot by way of a camera movement rather than through a countershot is another mark of the difference between the two moments. The former connotes a natural link, whereas the latter, consistent with the argument made throughout this reading, suggested Michel's unnatural appetite for an underground, criminal life. From this perspective, the lapse at the racetrack is a necessary, if strange move to make reparation.

This distribution of scenes orchestrates the manner in which counter-forces bear upon Michel, first from the outside and then in his room. Except for two occasions, the door to this room is ajar, in part because the lock is broken. Outwardly this implies that he has nothing worth stealing, but unconsciously it can be read in at least one instance as a sexual invitation, as when he seems to wait for the Kassagi figure, and certainly as a wish to be caught and pulled out of his moral turpitude. This motif comes directly from *Crime and Punishment*. Not only is Raskolnikov's room never locked, but even when he murders the old woman he neglects to close the door to her apartment, which is why he fails to hear the arrival of the innocent Lizaveta, his second, unintended victim.

Each visit of a character to Michel's room brings the conflict he tries to keep outside into his only refuge, inadequate and suffocating as it is. Raskol-nikov says, "You've been in my wretched little hole, of course, you've seen it....Do you know, Sonya, that low ceilings and cramped rooms crush the mind and the spirit? Oh, how I hated that hole. But all the same I would not leave it."[49] The inspector in *Pickpocket* echoes this sentiment on his visit to the room when he tells Michel, "It's unhealthy to be shut up in here." The visits result in either a heightening of criminal activity or an exacerbation of the conflict. For example, instead of going with Jeanne and Jacques to his moth-er's, he follows the man cruising his building and becomes a better thief, as the two subsequent scenes develop. But after he discovers Jeanne's letter, the next two scenes (his mother's bedside and the funeral) are dominated by conflict.

As the merger with his accomplices proceeds, the conflict intensifies through a visit by Jacques, found reading the book on Barrington, and in discussions with the inspector at a café and the police station. With the scene at the outdoor café, when his social outing is disrupted by his pursuit of the man with the watch, it becomes harder to segregate his two lives. Following his confrontation with Jacques over Jeanne, the tour de force at the Gare de Lyon functions as an orgiastic reaction to and displacement of his confusing erotic interests as well as his avoidance of Jeanne. But after his accomplices are arrested, conflict increases when Michel learns from the inspector that his mother knew all along about his theft. This knowledge jolts Michel out of his slump, prompting his confession to Jeanne and prefiguring a resolution, since the shame attached to the crime against his mother and his ability to expose it to another woman relieves him of further need to act out.

One can see in this structure how Michel's insular existence is increas-ingly encroached upon and ultimately broken down, creating the rupture in the precarious balance and artificial barriers between forces, which he believes he has maintained as one of life's extraordinary beings. Although this breakdown of the film's tightly conceived structure appears implacable, it is less the structure of fate than the structure of conflict that *Pickpocket* manifests. A key image that reiterates Michel's conflict is the staircase landing itself, a threshold that reflects the one that continually poses the moral challenge to his behavior. "In Raskolnikov's dream," says Bakhtin, "*space* assumes additional significance. . . . *Up*, *down*, the *stairway*, the *threshold*, the *foyer*, the *landing* take on the meaning of a 'point' where *crisis*, radical change, an unexpected turn of fate takes place, where decisions are made, where the forbidden line is overstepped, where one is renewed or perishes."[50]

Personal interactions bring about shifts and force the conflict into the open, where it interferes with Michel's activity and ultimately forces him to change. It is not the schema but the persistence of human intercourse that eventually moves him from the course on which he is bent and "for which he was not made." The narrative therefore demonstrates that conflict is the driving force of moral growth and that temptation to deviant behavior or despair is never fully averted. The test of one's will is always the sign of life, an idea perhaps underappreciated in Bresson's work. Fontaine could have fallen into despair, like Blanchet. Michel could have remained a criminal, indeed become a more accomplished one, but only at the expense of severing his connections to the human community, of precluding the realization of his other, all too ordinary desires.

To detail and analyze *Pickpocket*'s structure is to see how everything matters in a Bresson film. Nothing is without meaning, no setting a mere backdrop. It is this stylistic scrupulosity that makes his films seem to many closed and unyielding. I have tried to show how the manner in which the thefts are rendered and in which spaces are distributed and the way the narrative is structured illuminate Michel's character. The physical action in this film, no less than that in *A Man Escaped*, is revelatory, tracing the path by which each protagonist, one forthrightly, one deviously, finds his way to allying his heart with his will.

Conclusion

For when true love awakens, dies the self, that despot dark and vain.

—Jalal al-Din Rumi, in Theodor Reik, *Listening with the Third Ear*

In the final sequence in prison, Michel seems to let go of his resistances, which allows him to *see* for the first time. It is not only Jeanne whose face is illumined but his own inner being and what his recalcitrance has cost him (figure 29). The question is whether the viewer is convinced of this change and whether he or she believes it to be a consequence of actual grace.[51] It is not conclusive that Michel believes in God, any more than Raskolnikov does at the end of *Crime and Punishment*, although this is not precluded.

Some critics who find this ending problematic (e.g., Samuels and Kline) attribute it in part to La Salle's performance, which would be the conventional way of judging credibility of human behavior in movies.[52] Does the actor make us believe? But it is just as true that many contrived situations have been rendered credible by good performances. Convincing actors allow us to accept the improbable. Is this any less an illusion or willful suspension of disbelief than what Bresson asks us to accept through other means?

Pickpocket is a critical test of using the actor as raw material ("*precious raw material*," Bresson qualifies), like other elements of the film's construction, which means our habits of assessing the credible or accepting the incredible are turned upside down. Bresson exposes the greater illusion to which virtually all narrative cinema subscribes, even that of great directors like Jean Renoir, who frame images in what has been called a more "democratic" manner: namely, our belief that characters are free to be and do what they choose, that they operate as independent agents beyond the confines of the author's or director's control and narrative dictates. This is the supreme illusion of most narrative art, especially that in which flesh-and-blood actors embody fictional beings.

Bresson's more concentrated, controlled, confining narrative and image structures, in which the freedom of the actor is limited to the way he or she translates the filmmaker's directives into humanly recognizable gestures, is arguably more honest. This may be the greatest difficulty people have with Bresson. It not only precludes the game of pretending we revert to in order to explain how and why we accept and believe what we do, but it denies us the pleasure of watching great actors. The rigor in Bresson is the distillation of this finer-tuned, less muddled version of whatever truth underlies the power of film narrative. It is his truth, his view of human action that we must judge through the means he insists we use to judge it.

Pickpocket epitomizes this question, speaks to the heart of Bresson's cinema up to this point. If, as I claim, it lends itself to a psychoanalytic reading of its protagonist's behavior, even overdetermines the case, it also seems to leap over all clues and implications to that effect, over what has been delineated here as the symptomatology of the character, over his neurotic fixations and obsessive behavior, and pulls the rug out from any reductive explanation a viewer might construct. Nevertheless I would argue that the ending is less a sudden reversal of the character's behavior than a result of the kind of reading provided in this chapter. A psychoanalytic understanding of how and why a character changes is not intrinsically any more reductive than spiritual transformation or, for that matter, narrative closure. "How long it takes to recognize something you always knew unconsciously," says Theodor Reik, a truth that, though hardly original, is always revolutionary in terms of its effect on each individual.[53]

As I indicated in the introduction, the change we are asked to accept at the end of several Bresson films would not work if it were not prepared for through an underlying psychological truth. In this sense, the difficulty some critics have with the leap in the final scene of *Pickpocket* might have to do with the sexual ambiguity that hangs over the character throughout, and which is neither sufficiently explicated nor sufficiently dissolved by the end. It may well be that, in presenting such a provocative case of a character in deep conflict over his emotional, psychological, and sexual life, Bresson opened, perhaps not intentionally, a Pandora's box of possibilities that his conclusion does not entirely close.

And yet that conclusion, which presumes that love from and for another human being is the preeminent healing factor in life, is not the problem. It is in fact consistent with virtually every psychoanalytic theory from Freud on, which posits that the real achievement of psychological health is the ability to enjoy real intimacy based on a reciprocal attachment. Michel's longing to be free of his conflict, however we characterize it, and to embrace a better and healthier way to live is also the goal of any psychoanalytic undertaking. A powerful, thorough, and lasting change through a wrenching confrontation with inner demons is no less transformative than spiritual rebirth. In fact the genuineness of the latter presumes the existence of just such a confrontation. This is what I believe occurs in *Pickpocket*. Michel's ability to embrace a healthier life and the love of another presumes recognition and relaxation of the guilt and shame with which he was living, a process "in which the superego forgives the person who is aware of his misdeeds or sinfulness.... We call this self-forgiveness. Religion calls it grace."[54]

Bresson did not deny the underlying psychology of people's behavior. He was against interpretations that reduce all possibilities to a single perspective. Yet I believe his strategy in this film to be as deft and as intricate as any of Michel's crafty maneuvers or Kassagi's prestidigitations. From the perspective employed in this reading, *Pickpocket* is a viable psychological model of how human behavior can be understood. Those who are persuaded by this should have no difficulty reconciling it with Bresson's convictions that there are hidden movements of the interior—something of which he spoke often and on which he claimed his entire aesthetic system was based—that are not reducible to explanatory systems. We need not conclude that the sudden change in Michel is only the compromising flight to safety suggested earlier. Another, deeper desire that motivates humanity as a counterpoint to destructive instincts is the desire for life, embodied, as Freud instructs us in one of his most complex and inadequately understood works, in the union with another human being, "introducing fresh 'vital differences' [into one's life] which must be lived off."[55] This desire, if strong enough, can mitigate or control the compulsion to repeat, which, he hypothesized, ultimately and unconsciously served the death instinct. Freud's atheism notwithstanding, this view is not incompatible with a belief in God or spiritual awakening. Michel's flight is not just a running away from sexual desires, Oedipal, homosexual, or otherwise, but a path to embracing the life force embodied in Jeanne. After her first visit to him in prison, he remarks that he had forgotten to add, "Why go on living?" That he is despondent during the three weeks she stays away we infer from the expression of pleasure on his face when she returns, and from his admission, as he is about to see her, that his heart begins to pound.

Perhaps Bresson had a twofold mission: to display his ability to make a psychologically challenging narrative film as good as those of any great filmmaker, and to assert the privacy of the artist about whose personal life we must adopt that perspective he maintained in respect to many of his characters: that there is much we don't know about the human heart and its promptings. At the end of *Pickpocket*, then, as with other Bresson films, we are brought into a space where we come to *see*, as Michel does Jeanne's face, what is, and has been, before us for the first time. For Freud, this prompting toward life provides perhaps only a temporary respite from the eternal call of an older urge to return to the quiescence of death. But that long detour, with which all art in some way must come to terms, is called living.

The originality of the Pucelle, the secret of her success, was not her courage or her visions, but her good sense. Amidst all her enthusiasm the girl of the people clearly saw the question and knew how to resolve it.

—Jules Michelet, *The Life of Joan of Arc (1844),* in *History of France*

The roots of historical truth are therefore the documents as voices, not as witnesses.... The closer the document comes to a voice, the less it departs from the warmth which has produced it, and the more it is the true foundation of historical credibility. This is why the oral document is ultimately superior to the written document, the Legend to the texts.

—Roland Barthes, *Michelet*

4

The Young Virgins of the Provinces I

Procès de Jeanne d'Arc

Following the male-dominated narratives of the 1950s, Bresson launched a decade devoted to young female protagonists with a film about a teenage girl of the fifteenth century who esteemed private revelation above Church authority, claimed to have been sent by God to revive the spirit of France, managed to persuade hardened soldiers, cynical courtiers, and scholarly churchmen to make her general of the French forces, and made good her promise to lead the dauphin Charles to Reims, where he was crowned king. In less than thirteen months, she reversed the course of the Hundred Years War and spent the final months of her short life imprisoned, tried as a heretic, and burned at the stake by the faction of the Church sympathetic to the English, in whose vital political interest it was necessary to prove she was sent by Satan. Proclaiming herself a virgin, she insisted on wearing male clothing in prison as she had while living with soldiers, two facts that came to obsess her judges and plague her case.

Bresson could not have found a more apposite figure in French history to resemble his previous three male protagonists than Joan of Arc, whom he considered the "most interesting" historical personage, "an inexhaustible treasure trove."[1] As isolated and lonely as the country priest, whose capacity to burn people with his intense spirituality also proved unwelcome, she is as determined to persevere in her cause as Fontaine (who, like Joan, was imprisoned at a time of foreign occupation and national disunity) and like him believed, as she answered many times when questioned, that God helps those who help themselves. In her lack of trust in her judges, she reveals, like Michel, suspicion of prevailing authority. Joan is also the last of Bresson's protagonists to overcome despair and achieve spiritual triumph. The very points that emerged repeatedly in the trial that condemned her—the source of her voices, her resistance to Church authority, her refusal to put off male clothing, the question of her virginity and its bearing on her claims—are issues not unrelated to Bresson's preoccupations before and after *The Trial of Joan of Arc* (1962).

Like Carl Dreyer's *La Passion de Jeanne d'Arc* (1928), Bresson's film focuses only on Joan's trial, relying, as did Dreyer, on the official records. At sixty-five minutes, it is also his shortest film, completing the brief run from 1956 to 1962, when he sought increasing narrative succinctness. In part this was because he felt that a film composed almost entirely of questions and answers might tax the audience's patience. Although the film falls barely midway in his career, it defined for many the nature of the Bressonian experience and is the boldest up to that point in that its final image, a smoking stake from which Joan's body has disappeared, leaps over realism and psychology to a declaration of her sanctity. From a naturalistic point of view, this leap is as inexplicable as the representation of the events that precede it is a model of clarity. In that sense the film is the essence of Bresson's style, which lies in the elusive link between these two extremes. By 1962 many aspects of that style were tailor-made to the documentary-like nature of the film: its soberness, the use of nonprofessionals, the directness and simplicity of framing and editing, the eschewing of cinematic and theatrical flourish. Though just as this style effectively complements the trial record, that record in turn serves as the looming shadow of fate in Bresson's world, in which the ending is already written and the action is the crucible in which the individual is sorely tested.

The film raises a question about how Bresson dealt with a historical subject. In the case of *A Man Escaped*, he had not only the memoirs of the protagonist but the man himself as advisor, to both of which he was true, this truth having nothing necessarily to do with the real or complete truth of the events depicted. But the central figure of *Joan* is haunted by many conflicting stories, legends, myths, documents, witnesses, and historical accounts, none of which may be said, in the end, to constitute *the* truth. And so relying on trial records and revisions of those records is only a nod to the way official history is handed down.

What may escape us, then, in assessing Bresson's film, is how strikingly its felicitous marriage of form and content—the way his style, in avoiding dramatic and cinematic embellishment, fits the subject—illuminates a theory of history averred by Tolstoy, to wit, that the truest history lies not only, or even primarily, in documents, official records, statistics, political and social analyses, and biographies, however authentic, but in what it is impossible to chart: the inner lives of the individuals who live it, the promptings and stirrings of inexplicable feelings, in short, the spiritual core of the personality.[2] In Joan's case the idea of a hidden interior has a special relevance and poignancy because it is the part of her that was directly challenged by the Church, which considered itself the final authority in matters of spiritual revelation.

The paradox of Bresson's film is that although it is probably the closest a film can be to documenting the events and circumstances of Joan's trial, it affirms that she continues to elude us as effectively as she did her judges. Reaching for the hidden interior in an art form enchained to the exterior is the challenge Bresson made the crux of his aesthetic since *Les Anges du péché*. By adhering to Joan's words, as recorded in the Trial of Condemnation, and her outward demeanor, as described by witnesses at the Trial of Rehabilitation, his film is a testimony to the rule of the external. But by virtue of this very restriction and by force of his commitment to the model, Bresson points the way to the means by which we may glimpse a sign of the interior, a manifestation of its presence and power.

Toward this end he made the film look more contemporary rather than like a recreation of the fifteenth-century setting, convinced that "the more we remove historical figures from their epoch, the closer they are to us and the more true."[3] He further grounded this principle by using a nonprofessional whose look and demeanor, more than one observer has remarked, was that of a French female student of the 1960s, alert, focused, and more than a little insolent in the face of authority.[4] The description is apt, capturing the spirit exuded by Bresson's Joan, informed neither by abject deference nor self-pity, as well as making it clear why she enraged ecclesiastical authorities. In recalling, therefore, not only the male protagonists of the 1950s but also the prideful Anne-Marie (*Les Anges*) and the resilient Agnès (*Les Dames*), she is yet another powerful surrogate of her maker: stubborn keeper of a singular, personal vision, in search of its purest manifestation. *The Trial of Joan of Arc* may be Bresson's most underrated film.[5]

A Multitude of Joans

With the exception of Christ, few religious figures have received as much attention in historical accounts, literature, and the arts as Joan of Arc. After her death she was the subject of many paintings and folkloric pageants. She was reviled as a witch in Shakespeare's *Henry VI, Part I*; satirized in Voltaire's epic poem *The Maid of Orleans*; eulogized as the "soul of France" by the English writers Robert Southey and Thomas de Quincey; the subject of a dramatic play by Schiller; the heroine of operas by Tchaikovsky and Verdi; and the object of sympathetic works by Charles Péguy and Mark Twain. Following her canonization in 1920, an eclectic range of cynics and believers—including Anatole France, Bernard Shaw, Bertolt Brecht, Jean Anouilh, Paul Claudel, Joseph Delteil, Maxwell Anderson, Arthur Honegger, and Georges Bernanos—made her the subject of plays, novels, operas, and essays.[6] In France she was appropriated by ideologues of the Right and the Left during the controversies of the Dreyfus case at the turn of the twentieth century and during World War II.[7] That no other canonized saint has prompted such varied attention has largely to do with Joan's age and sex, as well as the inexplicable effect she had, despite both of these, on clerical, military, political, and royal authorities.

Of the features and short films made in the silent era devoted to Joan, the most famous are Cecil B. De Mille's spectacle *Joan the Woman* (1917), Marco De Gastyne's *La Merveilleuse Vie de Jeanne d'Arc* (France, 1928), and Carl Dreyer's avant-garde masterpiece *La Passion de Jeanne d'Arc* (1928). In the sound era Victor Fleming's *Joan of Arc* (1948), a Hollywood vehicle for Ingrid Bergman, took the spectacle approach, in contrast to Otto Preminger's literate version of Shaw's *Saint Joan* (1957), Roberto Rossellini's *Joan of Arc at the Stake* (1954), and Bresson's sober treatment of 1962. More recently two overwrought productions, Luc Besson's *The Messenger* and Christian Duguay's *Joan of Arc* (both 1999), were outclassed by Jacques Rivette's luminous and intelligent *Joan the Maid* (1997).[8]

In using the trial, Bresson echoed Pierre Champion's insight that but for the official record, calculated and crafted to destroy this young woman and published to prove its legitimacy, we would never have known Joan at all, never heard her in her own voice.[9] With the exception of Dreyer, Rossellini, Rivette, and of course Bresson, most other filmmakers, either through pious sentimentality or shrill melodramatics, have failed to come to terms with the perplexing nature of this historical figure who clearly had one of the most incredible, if not preposterous careers in any nation's history.

The Two Trials

Pierre, by divine mercy Bishop of Beauvais, to the venerable father master

Jean Graverent, doctor of theology, Inquisitor of Heretical Error, greeting and

sincere love in Christ. Our lord the King, burning with zeal for the orthodox

faith and the Christian religion, has surrendered to us as ordinary judge a

certain woman named Jeanne, commonly called *The Maid*, who, notoriously

accused of many crimes against the Christian faith and religion, suspected of

Heresy, was captured and apprehended in our diocese of Beauvais. The

chapter of the cathedral of Rouen, in the vacancy of the archiepiscopal see,

having granted and assigned us territory in this city and diocese in which to

hold this trial, we, desiring to drive out all unholy errors disseminated among

the people of God, to establish the integrity of the wounded Catholic faith,

and to instruct the Christian people, teaching them salvation, particularly in

this diocese and other parts of this most Christian realm, resolve to examine

the case of this woman with all diligence and zeal, to inquire into her acts and

ways concerning the Catholic faith, and, after assembling a certain number of

doctors of theology and canon law, with other experienced persons, did,

after great and mature consultation, begin her legal trial in this town.

—"Letter of the Bishop of Beauvais to the Lord Inquisitor of Heretical

Error," in *The Trial of Jeanne d'Arc*, a compilation of the original Latin and

French documents

This statement immediately precedes the account of the first public session of Joan's trial at Rouen on February 21, 1431, following the gathering of documents attesting to the need for such an event. As the language denotes, the record of this trial, known as the Trial of Condemnation, was an official document of the Catholic Church. It was edited some years after Joan's death primarily as "the apology of her judges…instructing posterity [that they] acted righteously, tenderly, justly…according to the immutable doctrine of the Church, in accordance with all forms of law, after having exhausted the aid of all lights of reason."[10] It is supplemented by dozens of official documents signed by numerous French and English Church officials endorsing both the need for the trial owing to the "irreparable damage" Joan had done to the tenets of Catholic teaching, and the conclusion reached that Joan was a "relapsed heretic" who had to be severed from the Church's arms like a "diseased limb," on which basis she was surrendered to English civil authorities and certain death. This document, "a masterpiece of partiality under the appearance of the most regular of procedures,"[11] is to be distinguished from the Trial of Rehabilitation, which was officially begun on November 7, 1455, at Notre Dame in Paris, following initial inquiries for more than three years prior. The second trial included many lay witnesses and was designed to redress the wrongs of the first trial, including the perception that Charles VII, whom Joan had crowned, made no attempt to save her.

The first trial was designed for calculated ends. For the English occupying forces as well as their French allies who did not accept Charles VII as the rightful king even after he was crowned at Reims, the trial was a fait accompli. Many military and political careers tied to the eventual crowning of a very young Henry VI of England hung in the balance. Condemning and burning Joan as a witch, and when that proved untenable, as a relapsed heretic, was necessary to discredit Charles's legitimacy among the people, to attribute his rule not to the grace of God but to the evil machinations of Satan. The trial is not a literal transcript of the proceedings in which questions and answers are recorded in the first person. Both are paraphrased in a routine manner, beginning with the phrase "Asked how" or "what" or "whether" or "why" Joan did or did not say or do such a thing, and followed by "She answered" thus. Many questions were repeated at each session, both to confuse the witness and to elicit a more incriminating response concerning such key issues as her refusal to submit to Church authority in matters of faith and revelation over her private voices, and her insistence on wearing male clothing. To avoid falling into traps of inconsistency, Joan often referred to her previous answers.

Without a transcript format, the identity of the interrogator is sometimes unclear, as it is in the film. In most sessions it is Pierre Cauchon, bishop of Beauvais, the territory being within his jurisdiction. Other sessions are led by Jean de la Fontaine, "Our Commissary and Deputy," and Jean d'Estivet, who was especially charged "to act extra-judicially and to give, send, administer, produce and exhibit articles, examinations, testimonies, letters, instruments, and all other forms of proof, to accuse and denounce this Jeanne, to cause and require her to be examined and interrogated."[12]

Reading through the trial, one gets the impression that the assembled body of prestigious Church authorities, especially those from the University of Paris, the final judge of all theological matters, above whom not even the pope held sway,[13] were models of patience, exasperated by Joan's clinging to her beliefs and behavior. Because she refused to embellish her accounts with more detail, she was asked to swear an oath each day to tell the whole truth, something she repeatedly qualified by saying she would do so in all matters unless what was asked required that she betray her voices and God's wishes.

The Trial of Rehabilitation was similarly impelled by political motives, namely, to reaffirm Charles's legitimacy by proving Joan was not a heretic and that she was tried illegitimately by the enemies of the king and France. In other words, it was not purely a matter of the Church's desiring to undo a great wrong. But, political or not, "as the case develop[ed]…the inquirers [were] overwhelmed by their inquiry and themselves astonished at what it brought to their eyes."[14] Among the conclusive findings of the Rehabilitation Trial that led to the unmitigated judgment against every procedural move of the first trial and ultimately to its nullification were the following: (1) that Joan was not tried in the province of her birth according to law, thereby giving the bishop of Beauvais and the English authorities unwarranted control over the proceedings; (2) that though she was being tried by ecclesiastical authorities on religious matters, she was nevertheless held in irons in a secular prison; (3) that she was not permitted legal counsel at any time; (4) that the court threatened any clerics and judges who made an attempt to advise her; (5) that no witnesses from her childhood, or from among the soldiers with whom she fought, or from the French court were called to testify; (6) that official notaries were continually directed to alter the language of Joan's responses, especially when the original French was translated into Latin for the official record, as well as not to record disputations from those judges who protested the proceedings; (7) that she did not fully understand the phrase "Church Militant" (which meant the Church on Earth as distinguished from the Church Triumphant, or Church in Heaven, to which Joan believed she had a direct line), and wrongfully assumed that submission to the Church meant unequivocal submission to the judges present before her, whom she considered her enemies; (8) that she was allowed to remain in ignorance of this distinction, despite her dismissed appeals to the pope and the Council at Basel, so as to reinforce the general impression of her pride and willfulness; (9) that she never saw, much less signed, the final, forged document listing the "agreements" of abjuration that was used as a basis to prove that she forswore her promises; (10) that, after agreeing not to do so, she was tricked into resuming male garb through threats of molestation and rape, and so was deemed relapsed; (11) that despite being condemned as a relapsed heretic who flouted the authority of Church and religious doctrine, she was nevertheless, contrary to Church law, allowed to receive the Holy Eucharist before her death; (12) that despite the clerical and popular belief at the time, established by a clerical court at Poitiers prior to her victory at Orléans, and during the trial itself, that her proved virginity was a "confirmation of the truth of her mission," Cauchon refused to allow any discussion or evidence of this in the trial record.

All of these details are reflected in Bresson's film, an amazing achievement, given its breathtaking brevity.

Bresson's Text

In a prefatory note Bresson tells us that his film is based on the "authentic text and minutes of the Trial of Condemnation," using Joan's words before the judges, relying only "in its last instances" on the depositions and witnesses of the Trial of Rehabilitation. In light of the film's incorporation of the findings of the Rehabilitation Trial as listed above, this is somewhat misleading. The very tenor of the film and the manner in which oral and visual exchanges are presented reflect the thrust of the official record of the first trial *as seen through* the perspective and findings of the second, giving us a fuller, richer, more complex picture than even a witness to the first trial might have perceived. This strategy is implied in the pre-credits sequence,[15] in which "Joan's mother, in mourning dress and supported by her two sons, advances toward the chancel where the archbishop, envoys of the Pope, and prelates await her. She kneels before them. She carries a petition in her hands" (figure 30).[16] This moment accurately follows the record prior to the Rehabilitation Trial, which required that a reopening and investigation of the original trial be formally requested by a relative. After Pope Calixtus granted Isabeau Romée, Joan's mother, the right to open the suit, the scene took place at Notre Dame Cathedral in Paris in 1455.[17]

This scene raises an important question, for although the woman's speech makes it clear who she is, the viewer unfamiliar either with the history or the published screenplay (only in French and not easily available) would have no idea that the two male figures who accompany and support her are Joan's brothers. This is the manner of the entire film. Except for Joan, no other figure is identified by name within the film, not even Cauchon, whom we would likely identify because he is described in the prefatory note. The screenplay, on the other hand, makes it clear at every point who is interrogating Joan and identifies Warwick's interjections and those of the friars who act as her spiritual guides. It is hardly likely that Bresson presumed that his audience would know the names of all the important figures of the trial. Two conclusions seem reasonable: that he did not want the players in Joan's "drama" to be reduced to "characters" and risk their seeming fictional constructs, and that he was imitating the published record, which also at times withholds this information. It seems he may have wanted the film to be perceived as a legitimate "document" in its own right, mirroring its sources.

In beginning the film with the mother's appeal, Bresson implicitly confirms that his screenplay is based on both trials. By holding the opening shot of the mother in black, seen from the back as she makes her appeal, and held by her two sons, under the ensuing credits, he establishes that what follows will be not a plain reconstruction of the original trial but a fusion of both trials, in which the sentiments and statements of the witnesses at the Rehabilitation Trial have been incorporated within the film's structure, affecting the overall atmosphere as well as specific situations throughout.

For example, at a number of critical points, Joan looks briefly in the direction of the Augustine Brother Isambart, one of her spiritual advisors, who, from Joan's perspective, sits to the right of the tribunal, facing her inter-rogators, as she does. With a quick, barely detectable gesture of his right hand, Isambart often cautions Joan before she answers a risky question. There are several cuts to the notary's book as his pen records the exchanges. At one point Joan declares that she wants to submit to the Holy Council in Basel, where she might receive a fairer hearing. Aware that this idea could not have occurred to her unprompted, the furious Cauchon threatens anyone who has been advising her, then quickly turns to the notary. A close-up of the notary's pen hovering above his book indicates that he has heeded the bishop's glance as a directive to censor the transcript. In such instances Bresson makes it clear that however official the record, it is also both incomplete and at times distorted, an impression immediately confirmed by Joan's curt remark in the next shot that the court records only things against her. These instances reflect ongoing circumstances, but are not part of the official trial record. They evince the testimonies of Martin Ladvenu, Joan's confessor, and two of the notaries heard in the Rehabilitation Trial. Still other testimony of clergy that opposed the proceedings and, in the case of Nicolas de Houppeville, left the court under Cauchon's threats, finds its way into the film although these disputations were also struck from the official record.

Then there are occasions when we hear whispered exchanges of the authorities as they peer into Joan's cell through a spy hole and no witness is present. In one case, Warwick, the English governor, warns Cauchon that unless he accelerates Joan's condemnation, thousands will be clamoring for his death. Cauchon's response, that he is guided by his conscience, reflects some historical accounts attesting to his nitpicking theological prowess. But it takes on a different connotation in light of his later remark, after he declares Joan a "relapsed heretic" and exclaims publicly to Warwick, "It is done! She is caught!" Unlike the first example, this moment was witnessed by Martin Ladvenu, who testified that the bishop laughed as he delivered the words, having finally achieved the end that was the aim of the trial all along.

And so the film is a composite of the two trials, the second occurring more than twenty years after Joan's death. The spirit of the trial as represented in the film springs from the way the Trial of Condemnation has subsequently been understood in light of the Trial of Rehabilitation. Neither the pregnant pauses and striking nuances nor the momentum that shapes the film is an enactment of the official text. Of necessity, Bresson condenses the trial, and by eliminating many repeated questions creates a propulsive rhythm, which, in turn, determines the rhythm of the editing.[18] The accumulative impression one has reading the text is of a sometimes hesitant and confused defendant, whereas the rhythmic exchanges of questions and answers in the film have a dynamic quality, already seen in *A Man Escaped* and *Pickpocket*, that manifests Joan's confidence and intelligence.

Cinematography and Language

She said that when she entered her king's room she recognized him among

many others by the counsel of her voice, which revealed him to

her....Asked whether when the voice showed her her king, there was no

light, she answered: "Pass on to the next question." Asked if she saw no

angel above the king, she answered, "Spare me that. Continue."

—*The Trial of Jeanne d'Arc*

No illustration of Bresson's forthright and unadorned treatment of the trial could improve on these words, though they were probably recorded as proof of Joan's insolence. Although later in the trial she remarks that her voices were accompanied by light, it is this early moment, its clipped manner and eschewing of special effects, that captures the Bressonian spirit. Joan often answered thus not just to avoid the implications of a question but because she was impatient with the repetition and, to her, the irrelevance of certain questions. The film's style respects the privacy of Joan's revelations and her choice of direct and simple language. This simplicity is not to be equated with simple-mindedness. Bresson did not see Joan as "a simple peasant girl," but as "very elegant…as a modern young girl."[19] As Pierre Champion puts it, "On the judgment of these men, whose eyes are constantly on their superiors or staring at the floor, Jeanne expiates the crime of plain-speaking and of looking straight into the eyes of her adversaries."[20] This is how Bresson presents her. Differences aside, it is also how Shaw saw her and what attracted many actresses to the role in his play. "There's no self-pity in Joan. She's like a clean arrow. I do find it, on the whole, wonderful if you meet someone who can speak from a still center.…Joan is saying what she means. There's nothing underneath, she's not being crafty; what she says is what she means."[21] Bresson's Joan frequently casts her eyes downward, presumably to reflect or to gather her thoughts, but her answers are accompanied by direct glances at her interrogators, often very forceful ones. In fact, this twofold aspect of the model's behavior repeatedly enacts the distinction Bresson makes between the unseen interior and its external transmission. The approach echoes the assessment of Joan's most ardent nineteenth-century chronicler: "The singular originality of this girl was…good sense in the midst of exaltation, and this, as we shall see, was what rendered her judges implacable."[22]

Such remarks should alert us to another aspect of Joan that Bresson, more than any previous filmmaker, underlines. An orthodox psychoanalyst might consider Joan's claim that she hears voices that direct her behavior to be a symptom of hysteria as several modern skeptics have. Yet if Joan was a victim of hysteria, we would have to similarly characterize the entire society of which she was a member, since no one, least of all the Church clerics who judged her, seems to have doubted that she heard voices. The question was whether they came from God or the devil. Images of Joan as primarily emotionally driven or mentally deranged do not take these facts into consideration. Bresson's Joan is a model of deportment, keeping her emotions in check and her mind focused on the challenge before her. As all evidence and testimony, including the trial records, demonstrate, her replies to her judges were too clear and intelligent to be the products of a disordered, irrational mind.

As an exemplary match of subject matter, source, and style, the absence of the theatrical and the spareness of language is the common ground on which Joan and her filmic creator stand. I have suggested that Bresson's cinema had been evolving into an aesthetics of action. In tailoring language to its essence, *The Trial of Joan of Arc* does not contradict this. Words and their power to generate tension, arouse hostility, and endanger the person who uses them constitute the primal element of the film, the means by which Joan and her accusers are revealed and their parries and thrusts are executed.

The language is primarily neither expositional nor descriptive, neither narrative nor reflective, the variable modes of *Diary of a Country Priest*, *A Man Escaped*, and *Pickpocket*. The interrogations in *Joan* are also marked by a frequent lack of continuity, when there is little or no developmental probing, and serious questions compete with what Michelet called "out-of-the-way" questions.[23] Questions often go from one point to another, often unrelated point in an effort to disrupt Joan's focus and uncover an area of weakness. Given this practice and the political engineering behind the scenes, the language is hardly dialogical either. Of the slightly more than four hundred shots in the film, 294 of them are devoted to Joan's interrogations. Every question is fraught with potential entrapment; every answer risks incrimination. Nothing is random; every exchange confirms what is at stake.

These conditions give the language a combative quality, tantamount to, if not the equivalent of action. Bresson treats the words accordingly, allowing them to assume a solid, material reality, filling not just the time but the space of the film.[24] Indeed he instructs us concerning the active principle of language, its capacity to exert as forceful an effect as physical gesture. Language is certainly important in his previous films, but the relentless thrust of questions and answers in *Joan*, revealing the terrible consequentiality of words, is paramount. Bresson shows us how the spectacle of exchange can pervert the true function of speech, replacing communication with provocation. Working without sound and with the questions and answers relegated to intertitles, Dreyer conveyed this perversion through eccentric camera angles and disorienting compositions in which Joan nearly falls out of the frame. Bresson lets the language speak for itself, allowing us to contrast the attack mode adopted by her judges with Joan's forthrightness.

The effect of this language is enhanced by the use of shot-countershot, which often assumes a metronomic effect. This not only makes the language, its bluntness and simplicity, the primary instrument of revelation and tension; it empowers it with the force of the cut. Though not every cut is determined by a question or a response, this is often the case. The relationship between statements and cuts varies. At times a series of questions from off screen are heard over a shot of Joan as she answers each one. At other times the beginnings or endings of questions and answers overlap the cut, so that one or the other might begin over an image of Joan or one of the judges and continue through the cut to the next shot. This variation tends to thwart efforts to look for patterns that might be read metaphorically and so sustains a neutral quality suited to the shifting rhythms of trial procedure. Because of the insistent nature of shot-countershot controlled by questions and answers, what the practice demonstrates, perhaps more pointedly than previous films of Bresson, is the principle repeatedly affirmed by him: that no individual shot should be self-enclosed, that its meaning is dependent on the shot before and after it, and that it is precisely this interrelationship of the chain of images that distinguishes film from theater.[25]

As we would expect, Joan's character is established as much by framing and editing as it is by the aggressive nature of the dialogue or anything the model does. During the first interrogation, Joan is centered in medium shot, from the top of her head to just below the bust line, positioned at a slightly acute angle to the camera so that her gaze is to just right of center toward the judges off screen (figure 31). Her gaze is firm and steady, except when she lowers her head to think before she speaks or to listen when the charges against her are read, or looks in the direction of her counsel. Dressed in a plain gray tunic, her hair falls to her upper neck, away from her perfectly oval, Modigliani face. The ensemble conveys both youthful feminine beauty and stoic, military demeanor. The repetition of this framing in all the public sessions creates a portrait of a constant, stalwart Joan who has little in common with the suffering figure in Dreyer, frequently dislodged from her position in the frame, whose borders are porous, vulnerable at any moment to outside threats.

Nor does Bresson isolate Joan in the frame, as Dreyer did, during the interrogations.[26] Though there is never a true establishing shot, every shot of her during the public sessions of the trial, as opposed to those in her cell, is placed in context, the background peopled with clerical and court figures arranged against the stone walls of the public hall on either side of Joan along a diagonal extending backward. This allusion to depth, however, is more illusory than usual since the images have a flattened effect, reinforced by Joan's immediate backdrop: the robes of those behind her and the outer wall. This tends to stress the foreground along with the fact that the gazes of those figures are either vacant or directed nowhere. They barely register beyond their prop-like function. There is little movement or shifting of position, reflecting the controlled and frozen atmosphere induced by Cauchon, as verified by the witnesses at the Trial of Rehabilitation. Against the immobile impression of this backdrop, which seems to belong to the tradition of tableaux, Joan's looks, vibrant, alert and reactive to the machinations around her, and animated by language, bring her into the present of the cinema. Cauchon and those around him are framed more frontally at a similar distance (figure 32). Hardly anyone gets up and walks about once each session begins. Nor does the camera move to compensate for this by imposing an artificial energy onto the situation.

The shift from this approach occurs during the interrogations in Joan's cell, a development, the film implies, necessitated by the shouts of "Death to the Witch" by the unruly English outside the Rouen castle, but that, according to many historians, had nefarious motives as well. By permitting only a few court officials into the cell, Cauchon exerted even greater control over the proceedings. Bresson reflects this deviation from the court's formality not only by shooting the space of the cell and Joan's relationship to her interrogators with more flexibility, but through his extensive use of the spy hole—in the French screenplay called a *trou-judas*, that is, Judas's hole—on one wall of the cell, a small, jagged opening that allows guards and others to spy on Joan and listen in on the proceedings. This produces a striking new effect in Bresson's work: the paralleling of simultaneous moments, achieved not through a conventional form of crosscutting but by shooting Joan through the spyhole, that is, from the point of view of the bishop or the English governor, as she is questioned. The technique visually illustrates that two conflicting perspectives are at work, whereby the public face of the trial as fair and impartial is undermined by this off-stage display of the secret compact between the bishop and Warwick, which reiterates that no matter what the outcome of the trial, Joan must burn. The significance of the spy hole and its connotations will be further explored in a later section of this chapter.

A Minimalist Joan

Since every Bresson film after *Joan* ranges from eighty to ninety-five minutes, it is likely that its brevity has as much to do with the subject as it does with Bresson's streamlining of his narratives throughout the 1950s. As a result of its economy and documentary-like style, there is no tour de force sequence in *Joan*, nothing like the montages of escape preparations or the escape itself in *A Man Escaped*, or the Gare de Lyon sequence in *Pickpocket*.

There is also the specter of Dreyer's film, the only previous treatment worthy of serious attention. Though Bresson acknowledged Dreyer's achievement, he found repulsive such elements as the stress on the facial grimaces of Joan's judges, and he objected to Dreyer's expressionist-like angles and camera movements and the prolonging of Joan's responses through multiple cuts to her judges, stressing their perverse pleasure in torturing her.[27] Indicative of Bresson's subtler approach is a moment in Dreyer's film that he found beautiful, when at the stake Joan lifts the rope her executioner has dropped and hands it back to him so he can continue to tie her firmly to the stake.[28] Bresson composes his shots simply, consistently privileging the trial's text over the filmic text and allowing the language to command our attention. Though Dreyer's is a silent film, it is the only other film strictly devoted to and based on the text of the trial, and so provides a useful backdrop. Among the most glaring differences between them is their choice of players. Dreyer took well-known stage actors and created a theater of grotesques, emphasizing in huge close-ups the pockmarked faces and muscular contortions of the judges. Bresson used no professional actors at all.

The composure of the formal sessions in *Joan* is never disrupted, not even during contentious moments. For example, one of the most dangerous questions Joan is asked, a "hideous and base question," Michelet remarks,[29] concerns whether or not she is in a state of grace. In Church doctrine, this would mean that she is free of mortal sin and certain of salvation.[30] Since she is accused of valuing her private revelations over ecclesiastical authority, the question clearly insinuates that, from the Church's point of view, she is quite probably *not* in a state of grace. For Joan to flatly declare otherwise would confirm the extent of her pride and justify the trial. Her response to the question—"If I am not, may God place me there; if I am, may He keep me in it"—was one of her more brilliant evasions of efforts to trap her, confounding her accusers, "Pharisees," Michelet calls them, who "were struck speechless."[31] According to some reports, the clerk could not resist adding the words "*Superba risponsio!*" (Proud or magnificent response) in the margins of the original trial record.

In Dreyer's film this moment is distended by more than a dozen shots, crosscutting between Joan and various wide-eyed judges eagerly anticipating her falling into the trap and concluded by a rapturous Joan looking heaven-ward, as if her answer had been divinely inspired on the spot. The elaborate prolongation of time stresses the emotional, psychological, political, and spiritual resonances of the question. Not surprisingly Bresson is both more economical and elliptical. Cauchon asks the question, then quickly turns to his right (i.e., off screen left). A shot of the notary's table implies that he should take care not to miss Joan's response. In the next shot, Joan too looks toward the notary before facing forward to give her answer. This is followed by a brief cut to Isambart, looking down and then in the direction of the tribunal, an indication that he recognized the seriousness of the question but concluded that Joan handled it well. The gravity of the moment is registered without visual or dramatic flourish and nary a change in Joan's deport-ment, reinforcing both her confidence and her astute assessment of her enemies.

The episode is characteristic of how Bresson's style works in the film. First, it acknowledges how he used the testimony of the Rehabilitation Trial to flesh out the scene of the Trial of Condemnation. The words spoken are from the latter, but the looks in different directions, the pauses, and their implications are *ways of interpreting* the testimonies of the former. Second, by precluding expressive acting, Bresson avoids reading Joan's thoughts, conveying the necessary information through the externals, integrating the image of the model within the framing and editing of the sequence. We are not directed to observe the performances of the models, but the performance of the film: its orchestration of actions, the shift in the usual rhythm via the shot of the clerk's hand, and Joan's look in that direction. Here is an illustration of Bresson's claim that the greatest challenge for a filmmaker is to uncover interior truth in a medium enchained to the external.

Bresson's unvarying visual perspective in these sessions parallels Joan's unwavering position vis-à-vis her judges, but also reinforces his resolve not to let filmic manipulation distract from her words and the text of the trial. He uses the same straightforward approach throughout. Following the first interrogation, Joan is escorted to her cell and chained; after the guards leave, she breaks down and cries,the only time we see her doing so. It is a privileged moment that registers her vulnerability while underlining the control and strength she displays throughout.

Similarly, Bresson avoids elaboration of the torture scene, an occasion for some of Dreyer's most eccentrically framed and horrific imagery, rapidly intercut with wild-eyed judges and a swooning Joan, who faints and slips to the floor. Before she does, she manages to tell the judges that even if they separate her soul from her body she will not give in, and if she does, she will later declare that it was forced out of her. Bresson's Joan says the same as she lies quietly fastened to a rack in a scene free of unusual camera angles and with only two countershots of her judges. This approach accords with the record, since whether Joan was actually placed in this situation, as opposed to being threatened with it, has never been established, not even by the Rehabilitation Trial.

Dreyer also elaborates the incident of the judge Nicolas de Houppeville rising to protest the illegitimacy of the trial and leaving the hall, unleashing Cauchon's wrath and Warwick's orders to have him escorted by soldiers. More than seventy shots stress the dramatic upset caused and the fear it instills that Cauchon will not tolerate contradiction. In Bresson the moment occurs during a private session among the judges; de Houppeville gets up, says his piece, and leaves, Cauchon's objection notwithstanding, and is followed unceremoniously by two other clerics. Brief though it is, it is enhanced by the framing: as de Houppeville protests, "None of us here is free to speak," he stands in the very space Joan occupies during the interrogations, framed against the same backdrop of clerics and stone walls.

As we have seen, through the use of understatement and ellipses Bresson resists reading Joan's mind. In the scene at the cemetery of Saint-Ouen, the theologian Erard warns Joan that unless she recants and throws herself on the mercy of the Church, she will be burned immediately. At first refusing as she has all along, Joan, head cast down and eyes closed, suddenly and quietly says, "I will do whatever you want." No cuts to the stake, skulls, worms, gravediggers, or other images of death—all of which are among the seventy-two shots of the sequence in Dreyer—are inserted to suggest the chain of thought that prompts her decision. Bresson's treatment echoes Michelet's description in which, following the false promise that if she recants she will be "taken out of the hands of the English and placed in those of the Church," Joan replies, "Well, then, I will sign."[32]

Another example immediately follows this moment, which ends as Joan learns that she will remain in prison to atone for her sins. The next shot fades in on Cauchon and others entering her cell to demand why she has resumed male garb. The ellipsis eschews any presumption to know what has transpired in the interim to account for Joan's change of heart. According to Michelet and others, the circumstances were complicated and involved a trick by her guards to deprive her of the female garments she had agreed to wear so that she would be forced to resume male clothing and incur retribution. Nevertheless when Cauchon asked her why, "she made no excuse."[33] Bresson's ellipsis mirrors this position, cutting through the many reasons to the heart of the matter. He presents only the recorded evidence of what Joan said to the bishop; in addition to a threat of attack by a soldier when she was in female dress, she says that she betrayed her voices when she recanted.

Bresson's minimalism displays respect for the historical record as much as it is a tribute to Joan herself, a way of aligning the film with her point of view, to capture the simplicity of her nature. Because Bresson was proscribed from adopting the first person he employed in his three preceding narratives, it is fitting that his formal choices be dictated by the personality of his protagonist as historical accounts and witnesses have described her. Even when Joan is being watched through the spy hole, she indicates by way of slight nods and gestures in the direction of the wall that she is alert to what is happening. Despite her awareness, however, Bresson is able, by way of this spy hole, to introduce elements into the film not entirely foreign to Joan but beyond what the record reveals about the nature of the feelings she aroused in the men around her.

The Maiden

Her eyes shone with the brilliance and malice of virgins.

—Joseph Delteil, *Joan of Arc*

The issue of Joan's virginity, ignored in Dreyer, is not surprisingly a salient aspect of Bresson's film, as it was in the trial, in most historical, and some literary accounts.[34] This is so even when the topic is parodied, as it is by Voltaire, who makes it the very first question the dauphin asks of Joan when they meet.[35] In the film, Joan is questioned as to whether her voices would have come to her if she were not a virgin. Although she vowed to keep her virginity at age thirteen, her response to the implication of the question, in both trial and film, is that no such connection had been revealed to her.[36] Because there is doubt, supporting the judge d'Estivet's allegation that she is an instrument of the devil, yet another physical examination is conducted, finding her to be intact.[37] Bresson alludes to this in his typically elliptical manner by way of a brief shot of the women as they leave after having conducted the examination and a shot of Joan on her bed, a sheet drawn up to her neck. This proof too is turned against her. In the list of articles that condemn her on the basis of unwarranted assertions she was supposed to have made, she is wrongly accused of claiming that her virginity guaranteed her salvation.

The film includes two moments outside the compass of the official trial record. The first is a brief exchange between Cauchon and Warwick standing at the spy hole as Joan is questioned in her cell. Warwick finds it "grotesque" that she could be a virgin after having lived among soldiers. Cauchon is not at all doubtful and in fact asserts that Joan's virginity is the source of her strength, echoing a popular sentiment of the time.[38] Later Warwick threatens to have an English soldier rape her precisely to test the theory. Though willing, the soldier shrinks from the task, loath to remove the male garments that protect her. His sentiment echoes those of soldiers at the Rehabilitation Trial who testified that lustful thoughts never entered their minds when they were around her.

In other words, the virginity issue comes up while Joan is questioned in her cell, not in the public hall seen earlier, and is related to the repeated use of the spy hole. Although this device appears in Dreyer's film, where it is also called a *judas*, we see it in only one scene and the context is entirely different. There are three shots of Cauchon's eye as he observes the cleric Nicolas Loiseleur winning Joan's trust, the better to deceive her; these are a character and situation absent from Bresson's film. In Bresson the spy hole plays a greater role, evoking voyeuristic and sadomasochistic connotations. There are twenty shots at nine different points, twelve of the eyes of different figures and eight reverse shots of Joan seen through the hole by the person spying.[39] In addition to Cauchon, we see Warwick's eye at the spy hole or hear his voice behind it or over the reverse shot of Joan on all occasions except two, one when Cauchon alone spies on her, and one of the young soldier doing the same. In general the device embodies the not-so-secret alliance between Cauchon and Warwick, rendering them virtually interchangeable through the momentary difficulty we have identifying whose eye we see at any given moment looking through the hole. More than once Cauchon's eye is accompanied by the voice of the off screen Warwick, fusing, by way of audiovisual montage, Cauchon's mind-set with that of the English, in accord with historical evidence (figure 33).

It is while they are at the spy hole that Joan is questioned about her virginity for the first time, prompting the exchange between Cauchon and Warwick cited earlier. But there are two instances when Warwick stands at the spy hole alone,[40] silent, in juxtaposition to certain remarks of Joan's. This is noteworthy because, as far as I can tell, no historian places Warwick at the spy hole at all. In addition to Cauchon or d'Estivet, it was used regularly by the English bishop of Winchester. That Joan is aware of being watched is indicated by the tilts of her head over her left shoulder, for example, while remarking that the English will be driven out of France, which we see in a reverse angle. These reverse angles, though not the only isolated images of Joan in the film, have an uncanny effect: she is framed by a jagged shape in the wall, seated and in chains, as if she were a dangerous animal. In fact, whereas Joan is framed in the public sessions as the filmic equivalent of a sculptured bust, the spy hole affords a view of her entire body. She is no longer the formally positioned figure fixed safely in place, but the mysterious creature about whom rumors of witchcraft had long been circulating.

We see Warwick at the spy hole just before the voice of a judge (Lemaître, off screen) asks Joan whether in her visions St. Michael is naked, and then moments later just after the same judge reads a text from the scriptures to condemn Joan's male dress. A shot of Warwick's eye is seen, then moves off just as we hear, "'Women will not dress as men or men as women,' says the Holy Scripture," spoken over the shot before it cuts to Lemaître completing the phrase, "for it is an abomination to do so." A moment later, in the published screenplay but not in the film,[41] Warwick's eye appears a third time, in juxtaposition to Joan's response to Lemaître's quote on the sexes that she "make[s] no distinction between the two." These links are enough to suggest that

Bresson implies that Joan's virginity and her wearing of male clothing were objects of fear, loathing, and perverse fascination, that both conjure the specter of gender confusion, a mysterious incarnation that speaks not only of her otherness but of an otherworldliness, the very nature of her claim that must be repudiated. The issue of Joan's dress is stressed in the film as it is in the trial, but the placing of specific words and exchanges in conjunction with the shots at the spy hole are Bresson's invention.

The three men who look at Joan through the spy hole provide an interesting range to characterize this in erotic terms. As a Churchman, Cauchon is, technically, forbidden to see Joan as a sexual object; the young man enlisted to rape her bluntly declares his willingness but is put off, apparently superstitiously, by her male garb; Warwick, in contrast to his bullying military stance and far from his beast-like counterpart in Dreyer's film, is portrayed as somewhat less than virile, even a bit effeminate, contrary to descriptions of him in the scholarship and suggesting a paradoxical fusion of gender characteristics similar to Joan herself. (One might recall that other sexually disturbed voyeur who peered through a spy hole at young women in the Hitchcock film made two years earlier.) These male images differ from those of the French soldiers, and even the brigands, who lived and fought with Joan and who testified at the Trial of Rehabilitation, all of whom convey a more convincing, if stereotypical impression of masculinity while acknowledging the respect that contained their desires.

The array of connotations suggests more than "a hint of voyeurism…and sadism."[42] They turn the spy hole into a minitheater of speculations on the closeted psychosexual ramifications of Joan's trial, the aspects of it that could not be displayed openly or placed in the record. In this context the size and shape of the hole become relevant. When we see it from inside Joan's cell, its shape is nearly indiscernible, the focus primarily on the eye behind it. In reverse angles of Joan, however (i.e., from the point of view of the male figures mentioned earlier), the aperture is large, marked off at the top and bottom by the edges of the film's frame, and evoking either a jagged, misshapen phallus or a damaged vagina, reshaping the screen itself as if through the deformed lens of a perverse eye (figure 34).[43]

Not coincidentally this suggests an inverted view of the question of virginity. For the faithful, it is a sign of unassailable virtue, linking Joan to the Virgin Mary, the worship of whom was more prominent in this period than that of Christ. For others, it is a repudiation of male prowess, an evocation of the Amazon warriors of ancient myth, and a suggestion of lesbianism,[44] all of which can be perceived as threats to the male ego. From all the evidence, the English were both enraged by and terrified of Joan, who had dealt a humiliating blow to their masculine as well as military pride. Having heard the rumors of her supernatural powers, the English soldiers cowered or fled when she made her first charge at Orléans. To be defeated in battle by a mere girl could be borne only if one believed her to be an instrument of the devil. At several points in the film we hear English voices (off screen) shouting, "Burn the witch!" Bresson sustains these imprecations by placing Warwick at the spy hole instead of Winchester. From all accounts, Warwick, who had fought with Henry V, was considered one of England's best and bravest warriors. Bresson could have chosen no better figure as a conduit of the hatred and fear English soldiers felt toward Joan, yet his choice of the model to impersonate him evokes a less than convincing embodiment of masculinity. It would seem, then, that Joan's attested virginity and persistent wearing of male clothing confused and complicated the feelings she aroused, which can be discerned in Warwick's combination of fascination, rage, and disgust and by his need to destroy all material evidence of her existence.

Although we can only speculate on what role these connotations may have played in how Joan was perceived and why she was destroyed, it is my contention that Bresson's use of the spy hole, in conjunction with the central themes of male clothing and Joan's virginity, is another way of insinuating that the official history of these events is incomplete. That is, just as we do not know enough about Joan's inner self, we do not know enough about the secret psychosexual dynamics that drove her enemies. In the words of the woman who played Joan, "The spirit of evil and conspiracy, an unhealthy spirit, filmed in the folds of the ecclesiastical cassocks, spreads indistinctly between the men in women's dress and this girl in man's dress."[45]

As if to counter the impressions of the militaristic Joan, Bresson provides images that stress the youthful beauty and delicacy of her features. We see her lying in bed in a plain white nightgown, the first time awakened by noises made by the guards who sleep nearby and who have apparently been creeping toward her. These images have a softer glow about them that contrasts with the way Joan appears in the rest of the film, reminding us of her origins, of the life she has left behind, and the many country girls whose relatively normal lives she will never share. They validate the public reasons for Joan's adoption of male dress. Seeing her as a vulnerable young woman, which no doubt compelled her curious guards to take a closer look, we understand why she chose to shield herself.

Beyond its importance at the time, what is the significance of Joan's virginity for Bresson? She is distinguished from his other female characters not only by the fact that her virginity is sustained, but by what it implies. The others, with the exception of Anne-Marie, lose their virginity, at least

The Young Virgins of the Provinces | **173**

two—Marie (*Balthazar*) and Mouchette—as we shall see, under ugly circumstances, or, in the case of Chantal (*Diary*), are beset by mental torments associated with it. Bresson's Joan, like the legendary figure attested to by witnesses at the Trial of Rehabilitation, dies intact and, by virtue of the final shot of the film, is presumably elevated to sainthood. But as a soldier fired with a spiritual mission, Joan is also kin to Fontaine and the country priest.

Like the medieval believers in his film, Bresson seems to link virginity to superior spiritual strength and view its loss as a reminder of weakness and the fallen nature of humanity. This film moves to center stage the aura of virginity that envelops many Bresson characters, and Joan herself comes to embody the purity and sign of the divine potential visited upon mere mortals and glimpsed in the youthful, still innocent faces that grace his films. Perhaps this is why the questioning of Joan's virginity and the brutish associations it generates are consigned to the sequences at the spy hole. The camera, unmoored from the niche it occupies in the public sessions, where it records Joan's forthright deportment, is, at the spy hole, enshrouded by the jagged orifice in the stone through which she is ogled. In thus mediating these images of Joan, Bresson perhaps disavows any unwelcome aspects of his own interest in her virginity, deflecting them onto the perspectives of the perverse eyes of her enemies.

The Model

As he did in his two previous films, Bresson avoided professional actors in *The Trial of Joan of Arc*. Cauchon is played by Jean-Claude Fourneau, a well-known painter, and the judges and clerics are played by doctors, lawyers, and lecturers,[46] professions that no doubt facilitated the sense of authority they exude in the film. Joan is played by Florence Carrez (later Delay), who was chosen because of her gentleness, a quality Bresson felt needed to be conveyed along with courage.[47] Seated years later in an area of the Rouen castle believed to be Joan's cell, Delay says that she had no sense of Joan as a saint when she made the film but thought of her as an intrepid individual with a mission to perform. She related to her as a young woman of the 1960s facing enormous odds. She speaks persuasively of the effect her experience had, of the way it inspired her to think and learn more about Joan over the years, sentiments that echo those of the three actors in *Pickpocket* whose experience working with Bresson was memorable.[48]

Delay describes Joan's cell as her only refuge, the place where Joan could communicate with her inner life. Whereas the public chamber was associated with interrogation and inflexibility, the cell was where she could relax, pray, and worry. Delay's remarks are affecting, but do not entirely correlate with what we see in the film. The repeated shots of the staircase leading to and from the cell, which seem excessive in a film of such economy, reiterate the distance between the spaces, but Joan is never really alone. Guards sleep in her cell to prevent her from escaping, and the spy hole is evidence that she is always being watched. Neither of these renders the atmosphere "relaxing." Except for the moment when she weeps, there are hardly any shots of an intimate nature or of her praying in private.

This absence prompted criticism by Susan Sontag, who judged the film a failure because Bresson's "experiment" had reached the "limit of the unexpressive" both with his choice of Delay and because the film lacked a "dialectical" structure in that "Jeanne is not portrayed for us in her solitude, alone in her cell." Sontag acknowledges Bresson's focus on the interior of his characters, but she affirms that in *Joan* "conflict has been virtually suppressed....However interior the drama, there must be drama." This is a curious importunity, a weakness in Sontag's otherwise impressive appraisal, and possibly an assessment she might have revised upon further viewings. While her complaint was not unusual—the film was initially judged Bresson's least successful critically and commercially—it flies in the face of Bresson's aesthetic and his declared intentions for this film. It also contradicts Sontag's own perception that Joan's trial was "the perfect story for Bresson...in that the plot is... foreordained...and the words of the actors not invented" and that Bresson's aesthetic was moving in the direction of documentary.[49]

The kind of scenes Sontag misses would not only have been precluded by Bresson's decision to adhere to the official records, but would have contradicted his resolve not to read Joan's mind. That is, lacking corroborating evidence, he does not provide her with a "revealing" project in her cell, like Fontaine's, or like Dreyer's Joan, who weaves a straw crown when she is alone. Furthermore, because this was the first sound film to make extensive use of the words of Joan's trial, it is clear that the interrogation scenes would have precedence over everything, that all conflict would stem from the dialectic produced by the language used by Joan and her judges. Bresson provides more than adequate conflict and dialectic in these encounters, in which the very rhythm of questions and answers creates tension and suggests the persistent danger of Joan's falling into the traps laid by her interrogators. Given the restrictions of Bresson's aesthetic and the specific requirements of this project, Delay's performance seems perfect, an unsentimental embodiment of a singular historical figure that bears out Bresson's concession, when pressed, that his models *were* actors, but only of "a particular role."[50]

Beyond these considerations there are more personal ones. Many of Bresson's characters and the models who play them exhibit the desirable, if romanticized virtues of youth, that period of earnestness and innocence, of almost pathological fervor to do something great, admirable, and enduring before they are defeated by age, authority, and cynicism. I think that for Bresson, Joan is the apotheosis of adolescence at its most promising, fired by arrogance, enthusiasm, irrational aspirations, and feverish imagination. No less than the country priest and Fontaine, she embodies the human figure not just as a noble creation, fictional or nonfictional, but as the projection of the filmmaker's elusive idealized self.

To create such a personally resonant phenomenon, the model who played her not only had to possess whatever features Bresson imagined belonged to the historical Joan, including at least the illusion of virginal presence, but she had to be pliable and autonomous at the same time. She had to be a medium, in both the natural and supernatural sense, through whom he could summon the fantasized Joan, but she also had to be empowered by what Bresson called an unknown interior truth that can be glimpsed but not plumbed to its core. She had to retain this mystery before the camera, something Bresson believed only a nonprofessional actor could do, which would fuse with the inaccessible mystery of Joan herself. The image of Joan, then, is not just a cinematographic fact or a painterly portrait, but a mirror through which the artist could fall, Cocteau-like, into endless imaginings of the possibility of locating somewhere *in* the human a verification of the divine.

The Saint

It is far more dangerous to be a saint than to be a conqueror.

—George Bernard Shaw, preface to *Saint Joan*

"If we could learn the secret of that strange moment, we should have the key to all the rest; but the secret is well kept.... The unknown child took her secret with her."[51] Bernanos is referring to the moment in the cemetery when Joan, under threat of immediate burning, changed her mind and recanted the claims she stubbornly held to throughout the trial. His remarks concern the critical, underappreciated role of Joan's innermost thoughts, a point that equally applies to the period after her recantation, when she had to dwell on what she had done. In Shaw's play there is no mystery. As soon as Joan hears that the Church condemns her to perpetual imprisonment, she seizes the document she has signed and tears it up, speaking the words, "Light your fires," that begin her strongest speech in the play. In other words, Shaw conflates the recantation scene with Joan's abjuration, rendering her immediate judgment both practical and courageous.

Bresson's handling of both moments respects the given evidence. Her recantation is brief and ambiguous, reflecting the historical record; we know that Joan recanted, but there remains doubt as to why (figure 35). As Bernanos sees it, it is not until that moment in the cemetery when Erard and Cauchon speak of the Church's imminent severance that she feels completely isolated. Being wrenched from the bosom of Mother Church would be no less irreparable and terrible an abandonment than the utter rejection of a parent. And so she relents. Lacking any solid evidence or witnesses, we are even less certain of her state of mind preceding the second critical moment, whether that comprises one night or several. It is marked by the most important use of ellipsis in the film; indeed, the situation is tailor-made to Bresson's style, the antithesis of the need for dramatic coherence and climax that motivated Shaw.

Bridging perhaps the most significant juncture in her story, about which neither official records nor the testimony of witnesses can provide a definitive account, Bresson's ellipsis speaks directly to the question of that core aspect of internal truth that remains private and that underlies the principle of Bresson's theory of acting. Nevertheless, though he does not violate the mystery, the elided period in question can be illuminated by reference to an abiding theme in his work, cited more than once in this book. This concerns pride, the one deadly sin shared by all of his characters, before and after Joan.

Joan's sense of righteousness, her strong belief in her private visions and voices, both attitudes further entrenched by the impact she had on the historic moment, were her driving inspiration and the basis of the Church's impatience. Her insolent manner, however justified by the calculated situation with which she had to contend, is exactly what irritated her judges. But it was not only her personal affront and seeming disdain for the Church Militant to which they objected. More crucial was the fact that her refusal to yield to their judgment meant, despite her assertions to the contrary, that she did not recognize the authority of the Church, thus blatantly courting heresy. Joan's hubris was virtually hidden from her, disguised by her certainty that she enjoyed a privileged position as God's emissary. It also blinded her to the gravity of her situation, worsened by her failure to fully grasp the distinction between the Church Militant and the Church Triumphant.

Hubris is the grave dilemma of all those divinely inspired. We see it in Anne-Marie's compulsion to convert Thérèse (in *Les Anges*) and in the priest's unrelenting efforts on behalf of his parishioners (in *Diary*). In both cases, the divine spark induces behavior exceeding the demands of their office in the view of their spiritual mentors. Both must experience a dark night of doubt to cleanse them of the pride attached to religious fervor. Anne-Marie is sent away as unfit for convent life and spends a rainy night on the grounds before she is welcomed back. As she lies on her deathbed, her final vows are completed by Thérèse, enacting the transmission of the spirit that drove Anne-Marie. Though she achieves her fondest wish, Thérèse's salvation, it is not a personal victory but the result of her newfound humility and the recognition that she was but the instrument of divine grace.

Bresson's Joan too appears to have her dark night, though it is represented not by a scene of muted anguish, but by its absence through the ellipsis. Among the things Joan must have contemplated alone in her cell following her recantation was the Church's reversal of its promise and its judgment of perpetual imprisonment. In light of that, she recognized not only that she had been betrayed, but, even worse, that she had betrayed herself. In retrospect her recantation must have been a humiliating experience, a startling come-down from the brave, uncompromising figure we see throughout the trial, confident in the truth of her mission and her eventual triumph.

What must this Joan have experienced upon realizing that to save her life she had succumbed to the very authority that condemned her, only to realize that it had no intention or power to save her? Pride would surely have yielded to shame and recognition of her mortality. She had been too trusting that in the end the Church would reclaim her from the English. For Bernanos, Joan was a child, as accustomed and confident from her early years of being a child of the Church as she was an infant at her mother's breast. In light of this, the period following her recantation can be understood as the utter collapse of that grandiosity that blinds all children to reality. Joan's awakening is accompanied by a greater humility and an awareness that the predicted martyrdom will in fact be her death. In accepting her error, she blames no one, asserting only that her voices were real. By the time she faces her judges again and hears the words, "Joan, go in peace. The Church abandons you to the secular arm," she has prepared herself and embraced the death to which she was destined. To view Joan simply as a maverick opposing an authoritarian Catholic Church, or as the first Protestant, as Shaw portrays her, is to miss the resonance of these connections. Both Joan's recantation and the unknown nature of her dark night can be said to "belong to the topos of a last flinching before a willed, accepted self-sacrifice….Without this flinching, there would not be the self-knowledge which gives to self-sacrifice its lucidity and meaning."[52]

No shot of her better encapsulates both the child and the martyr than the tracking shot that leads her, in penitent's gown, carrying a small wooden cross, shorn of male clothing and the career it symbolized, running barefoot with quick tiny steps to the stake (figure 36).[53] This shot parallels the tracking shot that opens the film, in which her mother approaches the prelates to appeal her daughter's trial. In both cases, the camera aims at the ground and the feet of each character, Joan as she moves diagonally from left to right, her mother as she moves diagonally from right to left, as if they might meet at the convergence of the invisible V line thus formed on the imaginary screen of history. These are the only real tracking shots in the film,[54] and the one of Joan is the only shot in which an extended camera movement of any kind is aligned with an action of hers.

If the track of Joan to the stake prefigures the one in the future by virtue of the film's past, it is because with this movement Joan enacts the final destiny that even she hoped she would elude. In so conflating chronology, Bresson collapses history and erases the strictures of time, a trope we may take as seeing both the beginning and the end of the narrative at once—which is to say, from the viewpoint of an omniscient God.

The tracking shot that leads her to the stake separates the formality of the language-driven trial scenes from the final twenty-five shots, two of which contain Joan's last words reaffirming the truth of her voices. The change in tenor is introduced by a single shot of a dog that seems to have wandered onto the path just traveled by Joan. It walks tentatively forward, looks up and off screen, presumably at Joan being chained and tied to the stake, and then turns away, its presence and demeanor instinctively sensing, said Bresson, that something unnatural was occurring.[55]

This affecting image initiates a quashing of naturalistic detail and a shift to a more symbolic register. Immediately the shouts and grumblings of the crowd off screen cease, soon to be replaced by the amplified sounds of roaring flames. We see only two shots of the wooden pyre as it is torched along with her shoes and garments, and only one other shot of the flames as they surge upward into the foreground of the final image of Joan as she expires. Other-wise sound alone describes the growing, but brief, intensity of the fire throughout eleven shots and its diminishing to a bare crackling over the last five. The visual track is distributed proportionately: there are seven shots of Joan at the stake; five of the two friars below holding a cross up to her; four of the cross against the sky, enshrouded by smoke; two of the observing judges and Warwick under a canopy; and two of doves alighting on the roof of that canopy, seen from below, and then flying off. The gentle fluttering of their wings is an especially apt counterpoint to the roar of the fire.

The final shot caps this movement toward the symbolic. Following the second shot of the doves and while we can still hear the fluttering of their wings as they fly off, we see a smoke-filled screen, through which the stake is barely discernible. As the smoke clears, the stake comes fully into view, the charred wood still emitting faint smoky threads, the chains hanging loosely, but with no sign of the body that has just expired. The drumroll heard over the opening credits returns, an extradiegetic filmic imposition that signals this shot as an authorial statement.

If Joan's career lacked the miracle required to prove that she was God's emissary, the empty stake supplies the missing evidence (figure 37). Beyond attesting to her virginity, it implies that her body was incorruptible, as Joan herself declared, even immortal. Warwick had ordered that all her belongings burn with her to avoid the possibility of their becoming relics; the film takes his directive to the extreme and, by removing Joan's body, raises the very specter of her sanctity he thought to extinguish.

Because of the power of the final image, it is easy to forget the *way* it comes into focus, slowly, through a screen literally filled with smoke. More than a delaying tactic, the smoke acts as a medium separating every image that precedes it from the one revealed when it clears, as if the viewer were being prepared for admission not so much to a different world as to a different way of looking at the world—a world in which signs of immanence often go unnoticed.

What Bresson's portrait—and in the end, it is *his* portrait—shows us, notwithstanding his efforts to create an accurate representation of the trial record, is that historical documents, however official and revised, do not tell the whole story. To be thorough they would have to trace the untraceable: the inner lives, motivations, beliefs, and passions of the individuals who live history. In this case, it is an extraordinary individual who aroused a nation, disturbed the body politic, flouted the rules of the religious establishment, denied biological destiny, and died to remain loyal to her convictions—all of this before she was twenty years old. Her history was initially composed of the records amassed by those very national, political, social, and religious authorities with whom she had to contend. Bresson acknowledges these sources, but in the end he is on the side of the inner life. This not only prompts his reservations about history and reality; it is what fuels his aesthetic and his theory of the model: that only the person who has not been trained how to react, how to determine which emotions are appropriate, and how to erase the self can allow something of the inner life to break through and reveal a psychological truth.

His portrait of Joan rests on three critical points: that, ultimately, as the hostess in Diderot's *Jacques the Fatalist* insisted, we cannot know the true nature of what lies in the human heart; that nevertheless Joan's every action and word testified to the conviction and strength of this unknown core even to her death; and that, in having a young woman, an acting novice, embody this Joan, Bresson allows her to escape the predictable and preserve her secret, thereby confirming this principle as a truth worth weighing in our explorations of history, art, and character. What better model exists in Bresson's oeuvre to mirror the three key aims that drove his professional life: to perfect his craft, to be perceived as God's emissary, and to remain a mystery!

And so, while the final image of the stake vacated by Joan's body seems to be a declaration of her sanctity, avoiding both the garish spectacle of her body slumping through the flames (Dreyer) and the terror and doubt evoked by her shrieking the name of Jesus (Rivette), the perhaps more significant meaning of that image, consistent with Bresson's aesthetics and morality, is that it confirms her mystery, renders the truth of her inner life inaccessible to the means and procedures, legal and filmic, used to investigate or explain her away.

Let it not be said that I have said nothing new; the arrangement of the material is new.

—Blaise Pascal

Observe the ass... his character is about perfect, he is the choicest spirit among all the humbler animals.

—Mark Twain, *Pudd'nhead Wilson*

5

The Middle of the Road

Au hasard Balthazar

Judging from initial critical response, the originality of *Au hasard Balthazar* (1966) confused and disturbed those who thought they had Bresson neatly categorized.[1] The film adheres neither to the singular focus nor the apparently redemptive conclusions of its predecessors, and its narrative, leaving many ambiguities unresolved, even less the model of clarity one had come to expect. *Balthazar* complicates the givens of Bresson's earlier work and compounds its difference by making its protagonist an animal whose passive nature precludes the very notion of narrative drive.

The perception that Bresson's work had become darker seems tied to this point. The sense that human lives are preordained, manifest in every film from *Les Anges du péché* to *The Trial of Joan of Arc*, is balanced by narratives driven by strongly motivated characters compelled toward specific ends. The sheer willfulness of Anne-Marie and Thérèse, Hélène and Agnès, the country priest, Fontaine, Michel, and Joan, however deluded, allows us to speculate on the role of psychology in the narrative's logic.

In *Balthazar* the sense that lives are ruled by design is more forcibly, if paradoxically, conveyed through a narrative not only free of the intention and will of a single protagonist, but one in which, despite the fortuitousness of appearances, things occur with "the unswerving punctuality of chance."[2] All the more devastating, then, that despite its episodic nature, the narrative is generated by iniquitous character behavior, or, in theological terms, by sin. What more conclusive way for Bresson to stress the fallen nature of the world.

Such an interwoven network of characters and situations required a narrative perspective different from preceding ones. In Bresson's first two films the dominance of one personality is poised against a ruling thematic line. In *Les Dames*, while Hélène's schemes are converted into actions directly linked through dissolves, suggesting her apparent control over the narrative, they ultimately serve the story's higher moral purpose. In the three films of the 1950s, Bresson mastered the subtleties of first-person cinema in which the protagonist's voice-over either is aligned with the thematic thrust of the narrative (*Diary of a Country Priest* and *A Man Escaped*) or reflects the character's resistance to its moral trajectory (*Pickpocket*), in which the *seeming* disjunction between the character's obdurateness and narrative design reveals internal conflict.

By contrast, the narrative mechanics in *Balthazar*, especially its use of foreshadowing, reveal a pronounced use of the omniscient mode. No other film of Bresson's contrasts the lives of its characters over an extended period of time in order to stress what has been lost. The final image of the opening sequence, the young Marie and the young Balthazar as seen by the young Jacques, barely registers before it dissolves to shots of a man cracking a whip and of a protesting donkey, just as Jacques's parting words, "Until next year," yield to the authority of a superimposed title: "The years pass." In the time elided, the playful Balthazar has become a beast of burden, and a thematic idea—the defeat of hope and the triumph of drudgery—is conveyed.

Both the condensing of time and the meaningful juxtaposition of past and present are the marks of the omniscient narrator, whose sovereignty the film's subsequent transitions and ramifications demonstrate. Whereas character motives in the earlier films are ultimately subsumed by an emergent overarching design, in *Balthazar* the sense of doom glimpsed at the outset seems even more inevitable. The darkness that jarred critics, then, has less to do with a radical shift in Bresson's worldview than with its first unmediated articulation.

The tenacity with which Bresson proclaims so bleak a vision is what set him apart from his contemporaries. The omniscient narrator may be incompatible with a modernist sensibility, yet it is precisely this "anachronistic modernity" that characterizes Bresson.[3] This is perhaps what Balthazar himself embodies. The jokes about his being modern, the embarrassment he causes his owners, his refusal to move, his stubborn but noble wisdom: what are these but reflections of his creator? Balthazar not only suffers for the sins of his various masters; he embodies the filmmaker's own anachronisms. The very idea of paralleling an animal's life, suffering, and death to the story of Christ is both thematically bold and, as we shall see, an extraordinary test of Bresson's aesthetic.

And why a donkey, we might ask?

Sources and Inspiration

Chrestos ei.

—Pontius Pilate addressing Jesus on the morning of the crucifixion

In citing the story of the prophet Balaam who beat his donkey when, upon seeing an angel, it refused to budge from the middle of the road, Bresson could not have found a better metaphor for his own adherence to a vision few, if any, of his contemporaries could sustain.[4] Nor could he have chosen a more biblically inscribed animal to illuminate the tone and theme of *Balthazar*. In use in the Middle East ca. 4,000 BC, long before the horse, and frequently mentioned in the Old and New Testaments, the donkey is the animal on which Jesus rode into Jerusalem on Palm Sunday,[5] and its associations with the baby Jesus led to superstitious beliefs over the centuries, including one held among the poorer classes in Europe in the late eighteenth and nineteenth centuries that the animal had healing properties. At the Feast of Fools in the Middle Ages, a ceremony in which the donkey celebrated mass was held at the Cathedral of Notre Dame. In Voltaire's poem *The Maid of Orleans* the ass performs miraculous feats. Even in the tradition of Islam there is a legend that the animal transported Mahomet to heaven.

As the Balaam anecdote confirms, the donkey's proverbial characteristics include patience and stubbornness, but upon seeing the angel, it was also granted the power of speech. Bresson's Balthazar does not speak, but he does manifest remarkable intelligence, as when a circus performer, training him to calculate numbers, remarks, "His kind understands everything." Balthazar was also the name of one of the magi from the East who followed a star to the infant Jesus.[6] While Bresson's Balthazar is ennobled through this association with royalty, sagacity, and spiritual revelation, his sojourn, unlike that of his namesake, who was rewarded with a joyous epiphany, bears witness only to human cruelty and the harshness of life.

In a passage in a sixteenth-century work by Cornelius Agrippa, which, among other things, condemns scientists and theologians as the men least "prepared to receive Christ's doctrine," Agrippa praises the simpler qualities embodied in the donkey, who "in the eyes of Hebrew scholars was a symbol of strength and courage" and had "all the qualities essential to the disciple of truth; he is satisfied with little and endures hunger and blows…was useful in the triumph of Christ…able to perceive the angel as Balaam had not done.…No animal had ever the honor to rise from the dead except the donkey, the donkey alone, to whom St. Germanus gave back life; and that suffices to prove that after this life the donkey will have his share of immortality."[7] Although the overall quality of asininity described here was later condemned as representing too passive a form of grace, this tradition seems to distinguish the donkey by granting it, above all animals, a soul.

These ties with ancient history, literature, and religion underline Balthazar's symbolic value. But the probable source of the film's structure, specific characters, and narrative elements is Apuleius' *The Golden Ass*, the only Latin "novel" to have survived (published ca. AD 160) in its entirety. An "unprecedented synthesis of entertainment, fable, and testament,"[8] its influence extends from St. Augustine to Cervantes and Shakespeare. In a series of random adventures, Lucius, the first-person protagonist, accidentally transformed into an ass, encounters a number of characters: a skinflint, a wretched boy, robbers, a baker's wife, and a virtuous young girl who dies tragically, all of whom abuse him and to whose follies and vices he bears witness. The style of the work is often graphic, moving easily between comic and tragic situations, and ending with a spiritual transformation when Lucius, returned to human form, resolves to devote his life to the worship of the goddess Isis.[9]

Au hasard Balthazar bears extraordinary resemblance to this work, which, like the film, parallels the fate of the young girl (Charite) with that of the ass and assigns Fortune an important role in human affairs. Bresson, however, performs a metamorphosis of his own, converting Lucius' abuses and torments while in animal form, as well as his final transformation, into the terms of Christian allegory. In the film characters mock Balthazar's archaism, but it is what he represents—forbearance, humility, saintliness—that appears anachronistic in a morally corrupt world.

Balthazar marks a transition from the six films before it, in which the power of faith overcomes despair, to the films after it, in which the apparent absence of that power tends to render the view of the human condition much bleaker. A formidable narrative achievement and a tour de force of characterization, the film is more than the charming fable some early commentators took it for. It seems fitting, in fact, that in this pivotal work Bresson chose for his innocent protagonist not a person but the animal whose braying roused Prince Myshkin, the Christ figure of Dostoevsky's *The Idiot*, from depression and clarified his vision. In the interview conducted just before production, Bresson expresses tender feelings about donkeys and reads a passage from the novel in which Prince Myshkin recounts his stay in Switzerland to Mrs. Yepanchin and her daughters: "I completely recovered from this depression, I remember, one evening at Basel, in reaching Switzerland, and the thing that roused me was the braying of a donkey in the market place. I was quite extraordinarily struck with the donkey, and for some reason very pleased with it, and at once everything in my head seemed to clear up.... And because of that donkey I suddenly acquired a liking for the whole of Switzerland, so that my former feeling of sadness was gone completely."[10] A similar role is ascribed to Balthazar, whose braying during the credits interrupts the second movement of the Schubert piano sonata (A major, op. 959) during a passage described as "the wildest outburst of fantasy Schubert ever committed to paper... [with its] torrential scales, pulse-threatening rhythms, trills, shock harmonies, writhing chromaticism,...stabbed chords," and as the most "irrational" piece of music the composer ever wrote.[11] The movement is the only one in all of Schubert's sonatas labeled *andantino*, a determination that may also differentiate the film's pace from the *allegro* of the three that precede it. The donkey's braying halts the frenetic buildup of this movement, shifting the perceptual mode of the listener, and spectator, from the entangled web of Romantic discord to the clarity and simplicity of a single voice. Indeed the primary musical theme heard intermittently has a slow, ambling, but persistent rhythm that parallels the way Balthazar moves.

The braying may at first amuse, but as the tragic dimension of the tale unfolds, it takes on a mournful quality. The more Balthazar experiences and witnesses, the more his plaintive cries, as well as his existence, reiterate the simple perspective from which everything throughout the film must be judged. Bresson therefore magnified the role of the donkey. Whereas it took Dostoevsky eight versions of his novel to realize his "main idea," namely, "the representation of a perfect man,"[12] Bresson, in creating *his* Christ figure, eschewed the human altogether.

In the spirit of Dostoevsky's novel and the metamorphosis in Apuleius,[13] Bresson fused Myshkin with the donkey, bestowing on the latter a nobility to join those qualities—hardworking, strong, patient, and long suffering—that Myshkin attributes to the animal. Like Myshkin, Balthazar enters the narrative arbitrarily and lacks a permanent home; Myshkin's idiocy parallels Balthazar's stubbornness. Each is a catalyst, provoking reactions that expose vices and weaknesses. Each is used capriciously: although Myshkin is everyone's confidante whose forgiveness is sought, he is also resented for being such; Balthazar, an even more neutral witness, is similarly used and abused. Each is the only constant figure, yet each recedes when others occupy the foreground, a tactic that, in relation to Dostoevsky's work, has been described as "polyphonic discourse."[14] Last, but certainly not least, each is the natural target of displacement. In *The Idiot*, when Ganya rages at his sister Varya, "mad with fury, he [gives] the prince a resounding slap in the face."[15] Myshkin, like Balthazar, receives the blows intended for the real objects of frustration and rage.

Bresson created a protagonist suffused with the human but beyond its taint, free not only of original sin but also of motive and psychology. As he is the purest of vessels, Balthazar is also Bresson's most plastic, least self-conscious cinematographic model. Far from the Christ figure as "another devaluation of Christianity…expressive of the broad secularization of Christian concepts…[a] levelling down…[in which] any man can take on the marks of Christ,"[16] Balthazar reaffirms the otherness and uniqueness of Christ, his mysterious, unattainable perfection. And yet it is the nature of this most complete of fictional constructs that its parabolic function can be sustained only precariously, a fact to which the film's final shot attests.[17]

Balthazar as Character

Beyond cultural, literary, and religious associations, what kind of character is Balthazar? Can we relate to his experience? Does he have an interior life and understand what happens to him—the basis of Greek and Elizabethan tragedy? Or does his baptism, the sacrament that "leaves on the soul an indelible mark called a character…a spiritual quality which gives to him who receives it a special power to serve God,"[18] preclude those features fictional characters usually have? Before baptism, according to Catholic doctrine, every individual born into the world is in the state of original sin, the only exceptions being the Virgin Mary and Jesus Christ. As an animal, Balthazar is clearly another exception. This is the point of his role and of the baptism scene, which, though presented as a charming childhood ritual, is really an initiation into the world of suffering shared by all humanity.

In fact, though, Balthazar is no more of a problem than filmic incarnations of Jesus in countless biblical epics,[19] where the challenge is how to evoke the divine through the corporeal (especially when the corporeal is in the form of a movie star) and bypass any psychology. Can a film about Christ convincingly render an inner life when, despite *The Idiot*'s six hundred pages, we learn little about Prince Myshkin's? By rooting Balthazar in blunt physicality, giving new meaning to the idea of word made flesh, Bresson avoids the problem altogether as well as such clichés as images bathed in ethereal light and off screen evocations of the divine presence. In short, there is a built-in constraint faced by all writers and filmmakers who approach divine or saint-like figures: the more one strives to humanize the character, the less believably perfect the figure will be. As the narrator of Graham Greene's *End of the Affair* remarks, "Goodness has so little fictional value."

In narrative films a character's conflict and inner life are conveyed through the actor's performance, a route that Bresson's aesthetic denies us. *Balthazar* takes that aesthetic even further, for not only is the protagonist an animal, but we have no way of knowing if it is the *same* animal throughout.[20] The three films immediately preceding *Balthazar* have prepared us for this development, having shifted the focus from the actor's repertory of expressive looks and gestures to the entire cinematographic system of *rapports*, of which the actor's face, body, and voice are only three signs among many. From this perspective, Balthazar's character is formed both directly—through framing, editing, and mise-en-scène—and indirectly, through the associations and feelings that come to rest on him as the only constant object before us. In the absence of any central human consciousness, the spectator uses Balthazar, somewhat analogously to the way the film's characters do, as a repository of the emotions aroused in the course of the story. It is the accumulation of displacements and projections rather than sentimental anthropomorphism that creates the character Balthazar and induces the catharsis of the final scene.

An early example of how this works is the scene in which Balthazar, running from the farmer whose cart has overturned, finds his way to the manor where he passed his first years. He ambles about the yard and appears to deliberately circle the bench on which young Jacques had carved his and Marie's initials, allowing us to transfer their loss of youth and dreams to him, before entering his old stall, where he brays disconsolately. This return to the place that held such hope and joy suggests not only that Balthazar remembers but also that he may be capable of longing for happier times.

Even more suggestive, if mysterious, is the wonderful passage of Balthazar's point-of-view exchanges with the circus animals as he hauls hay from cage to cage. Each view of his head, centered in medium and close shots and framed to emphasize one eye, is followed by a shot of one of the others: a tiger, a polar bear, a chimpanzee, and an elephant. No dialogue or music distracts; the only sounds are of Balthazar's moving the wagon and those made by the animals: the bear growls a bit, the chimp is the noisiest.

How can we read such a passage? Do these looks import some arcane wisdom about the world? In denoting eye contact, the framing and editing suggest a significance that we cannot decipher, and perhaps that is the point. By structuring the passage in terms of shot-countershot, the cinema convention that binds elements, Bresson implies that there are privileged communications among animals that lie beyond our capacity to decode them and that are therefore outside the discourse of the narrative. Yet the strategy also implies, in the aesthetic and rhetorical terms of the film's fictional world, that Balthazar not only suffers at the hands of men but understands that he does so—in other words, that he may have a consciousness and interior life.[21] As the circus passage clearly indicates, point-of-view shots play an important role in establishing this.

Point of View

In *Diary of a Country Priest*, his first venture into first-person narrative, Bresson revealed an acute sensitivity to the implications and limits of the shot-countershot system. The most powerful exchanges are not between the priest and other characters but between the priest and his unseen God. The force of the priest's faith as he stares into off screen space charges that absence with the traces of an internal dialogue so strong that we expect a countershot that never comes.

The broader spectrum of characters and narrative situations precludes the first-person perspective in *Balthazar*, and Balthazar himself, though the only constant figure throughout, no more tells the story than Prince Myshkin does his. Nor is the donkey present at every moment in every scene. Nevertheless *Balthazar* is yet another refinement of Bresson's increasingly rigorous attunement of point-of-view strategies, which in this case gives the animal a privileged perspective suited to his role as true witness. Owing to the physical structure of a donkey's head, which, like that of a horse (or the elephant in the circus sequence), apportions one eye to each side, a shot that implies a gaze outward toward an object off screen (i.e., a point-of-view shot) must be of one side of the head showing one eye in close-up. A frontal shot would not do since the prominent slope of the head and nose would effectively block the protuberance of the eyes and create an effect distracting to the purpose.[22] Point-of-view shots, after all, generally imply intent, or at the very least some other conscious process, such as awareness or curiosity, and the eyes play a central role in what may be inferred.

But what of the unseen eye? The implications of this for *Balthazar* are striking, for while one eye suffices to implement the point-of-view exchange and all that it connotes, the other is cast upon an off screen space and a scene to which we have no access. While that space is contiguous to the one before us, it is, for the duration of each shot that blocks it, a privileged domain, one that only the donkey can see at the same time. Can we not view this dual vision of the donkey as an expression of his being in two worlds simultaneously? Is this privileged vision perhaps what allows Balaam's ass to see an angel in the middle of the road? Is it why the donkey is stubborn, unwilling to move because it can already see what surrounds it on both sides?

To say that the shot-countershot system at such moments articulates a tension between a *here* and a *there*, between presence and absence, a dynamic *unified* in the figure of the donkey, is to say that Balthazar fuses the earthly and the otherworldly, the corporeal and the spiritual, the two ways, in fact, that we are asked to perceive him. He is an elastic character, now an animal in the real world, now a symbol of innocence and purity, and indeed, this is the uniqueness of his conception. For although in the course of the film we are cognizant of both roles, it is not until the end, in the stillness of its final moments, that they come together to resonate so unexpectedly and elicit such powerful emotions. By then any resemblances either to Apuleius' ass or to the conventionally comic features associated with donkeys have been profoundly displaced.

Narrative and Structure

Because coincidence gives us a sense of "what it must be like to live in an ordered, God-run universe," it should be "permitted [only] in the picaresque." True fiction attests "that things are chaotic, free-wheeling, permanently as well as temporarily crazy … [with] the certainty of human ignorance, brutality, and folly."[23] *Balthazar*, filled with seeming coincidences, borders on the picaresque and the parabolic, fusing the accidental and the deterministic. But the question it poses, more problematically than any prior film of Bresson's, is how one can believe in a God-run universe in face of the triumphs of ignorance, brutality, and folly. This is a question that will haunt his subsequent work.

Exactly what kind of narrative is *Au hasard Balthazar*? Certainly it resembles the allegory, like *The Golden Ass*, in which characters personify abstract qualities in a work with moral, religious, or political meaning, and the fable, like those of Aesop and La Fontaine and the medieval *Roman de Renart*, in which animals personify or caricature human vices. But it inverts the fable by having its animal protagonist assume virtues and its human characters embody the seven deadly sins: Marie's father is guilty of pride; the corn merchant of covetousness; Gérard of both anger and lust; the baker's wife envies Gérard's relationship with Marie; when he drinks, Arnold is guilty of gluttony; at other times, he is an image of sloth, although the more pernicious effects of that "most amiable of weaknesses," as Evelyn Waugh has described it, may characterize Jacques, whose seeming indifference to the ugly aspects of Marie's affair with Gérard borders on what Waugh, searching for a modern equivalent of the "spiritual torpor" connoted by the original Latin *accidia* and *pigritia*, calls "plain slackness."[24] Two of these characters, the baker's wife and the corn merchant, seem introduced primarily to complete the palette.

Balthazar assumes attributes and virtues generally absent from the human community. His passage through the film links the actions and lives of these characters, all of them illumined by the manner in which they use him. He is subject to a number of cruelties at the hands of each new owner: he is abused, beaten, exploited, kicked, overworked, starved, and whipped. Although the film's iconography and structure demand that we read his journey figuratively, he is also, like Prince Myshkin, both catalyst and foil. Unlike a prototypical fable, however, *Balthazar* cannot be reduced to anything as simplistic as a moral. And unlike the animals of fables, Balthazar is a cinematographic fact, a physical presence whose sufferings are all too real.

> It was precisely these issues that led Bresson to note the narrative difficulty he was forced to address: It was hard…from the point of view of composition. For I did not want to make a film of sketches, but I wanted, too, for the donkey to pass through a certain number of human groups—which represent the vices of humanity—and that these groups would overlap. It was also necessary—given that the life of a donkey is a very even life, very serene—to find a movement, a dramatic rise. So it was necessary to find a character who would be parallel to the donkey, and who would have that movement; who would give the film that dramatic rise that was necessary for it. It was just then that I thought of a girl. Of the lost girl. Or rather—of the girl who loses herself.[25]

The overlapping that Bresson cites links transient characters to primary ones. Gérard is introduced while Balthazar is with Marie's family and is further developed during his employment with the baker and in the Arnold section. The baker and his wife, however, are dropped altogether after Balthazar is taken by Arnold. The film's most eccentric character, Arnold is first seen at the police station in connection with the same unsolved murder for which Gérard is summoned. Later he shows up inexplicably just as Balthazar is about to be killed. Marie's parents are present at the beginning and end and appear intermittently: her father emerges from a notary office and literally crosses paths with Arnold; her mother appears in the middle of Arnold's wild celebration at the bar to persuade Marie to leave Gérard. In the same scene, we see the corn merchant for the first time, at whose house Marie will later seek refuge.

This episodic quality is countered by the "movement" of which Bresson speaks. Everything that happens to Balthazar has its parallel in Marie's life. Following the childhood sequence in which she, Jacques, and Balthazar cavort unsuspectingly, the passing years trace Balthazar's transition from pet to working animal as they do the dismal fortunes of Marie's family. The commonality of their fate is underlined in two critical sequences. The first, their encounter with their nemesis, Gérard, on the road, will be analyzed later.

The second, in which Marie places flowers on Balthazar's head and gently kisses him, has the air of a mysterious ritual (figure 38). Set at night with the sounds of insects on the soundtrack, it evokes from Gérard, hiding in the brush with one of his cronies, a crude suggestion that there is something unnatural between the girl and the animal, "as in mythology." The vulgarity and cryptic nature of his remark notwithstanding, the sequence does suggest a ceremony of sorts, marking a union, not lacking a certain eroticism,[26] that joins Marie and Balthazar in terms of the fictive axis on which the narrative turns, a bond stressed by an exchange of point-of-view shots as haunting as those between Balthazar and the circus animals. What occurs immediately after clinches the significance of the scene when Balthazar is physically abused by Gérard in frustration over Marie's rejection. Thus a rite of transference is enacted through which Balthazar assumes the role that the narrative has bestowed on him and Marie is made the dramatic catalyst that will propel his fate.

As such, her behavior is critical, embodying the vacillation of the narrative's moral center. She manifests contradictory attitudes in respect to both Jacques and Gérard: though pleased with Jacques's renewed marriage proposal, she is bored by his bland submission to bourgeois values; she lashes out at Gérard's cowardice at one moment and melts at his bravado the next. Though of a different social position, her mercurial behavior is almost certainly modeled on Nastasya Filippovna in *The Idiot*, whose life is also ruined through seduction. Like Nastasya, who tells Myshkin, "You're the first human being I've seen," Marie's only completely unsullied relationship is with Balthazar. All other love bonds—parental, sexual, and romantic—are contaminated by comparison.

The ensuing parallels delineate this pact with increasing force. During Balthazar's sojourn with the baker, his presence on the road prompts Marie to stop her car, which leads to her seduction by Gérard. The parallel is bolstered by specific shots and gestures; for example, in an earlier scene on the road, Gérard sets fire to Balthazar's tail to make him move, then gathers the subdued animal's chain from the grass. This is drawn directly from Apuleius, where Lucius, while transformed into the donkey, finds himself in the charge of the "most abominable youth in creation, who savagely beats [him] by repeated blows" and at one point ties bundles of thorns to his tail, then places a "glowing coal" in it, which "bursts into flames."[27] Moments after Balthazar's submission to the abominable Gérard, Marie runs from Gérard and falls in the same grass before she submits, while he cowardly waits for a car to pass before pursuing his intentions, as he had before setting fire to Balthazar's tail. Gérard blows his horn twice, the first time to announce the bread delivery, the second after his conquest of Marie, underlining the callous equation. Through part of the seduction Gérard literally chases Marie around Balthazar.

In the course of her affair with Gérard, Marie moves toward shame and despair while Balthazar is ignored, left out in the cold, and almost dies from neglect. Rescued by Arnold, he wanders off into a circus during one of Arnold's drunken sprees, just as Marie seems to lose herself, rejecting her mother's pleas to return home. Following the bar sequence, both Balthazar and Marie become homeless, he, when Arnold suddenly dies, and she, when Gérard becomes bored, impelling her to run off. Both are then taken in and exploited by the corn merchant, who abuses Balthazar, deprives him of food, and works him almost to death, while Marie is forced to have sex in exchange for food and lodging.[28] In a feeble attempt to make amends, the merchant returns Balthazar to his original owners, Marie's parents, just as Marie herself returns.[29] The fleeting sense that Balthazar is now safe is matched by Jacques's surprise visit and renewed marriage proposal. Hope is quickly dashed, however, when Marie, breaking off with Gérard, is stripped and beaten, an experience that leaves her broken and, presumably, leads directly to her "going away." This is followed by her father's death and Balthazar's final journey with Gérard. Carrying contraband to the border, he falters and is beaten three times as he climbs the hill where he will be left to die, not only evoking Jesus' falls while carrying the cross to Calvary, but paralleling Marie's on the way to her own undoing at the hands of Gérard's gang.

As schematic as this might appear, neither Balthazar nor Marie is a mere figuration of the other, and this balance reflects another on which the narrative is critically poised, with its appropriation of Christian analogy on the one hand and its accommodation of ambiguities on the other. These include the murky facts surrounding the allegations against Marie's father; the unsolved murder for which both Gérard and Arnold are questioned;[30] the inexplicable arrival of Arnold at the moment Balthazar is about to be killed; Balthazar's sudden recovery; his arithmetic performance at the circus; Arnold's inheritance out of the blue; and Marie's mysterious disappearance at the end. One or two of these are compatible with a religious reading of the film; for example, Arnold's fortuitous intervention can be said to prolong Balthazar's life for some as yet unfulfilled purpose. But in these instances and others, the verbal text compounds rather than clarifies the mystery. Words between Gérard and Arnold about the alleged murder, for example, are brief, elliptical, and teasing, as are Gérard's reference to "mythology" as he spies on Marie and Balthazar and the mother's remark that Marie has gone. The text therefore courts ambiguity. By refusing to resolve such lacunae within the parameters of the parabolic model, the film escapes reduction to the strictures of allegory, biblical or otherwise.

Marie's exit is the most disconcerting. We cannot dismiss her as a fictional contrivance even if she was brought into the narrative to give it a necessary dramatic rise. Perhaps Bresson felt that her shame and humiliation were sufficient and that her death would unbalance the parallel and render the final scene anticlimactic. In a sense Balthazar's death stands for both and in a way that Marie's could not, since it is he who fuses the corporeal and the spiritual.

Marie is another of Bresson's virgins, poorer cousin of Chantal in *Diary of a Country Priest*. But unlike Chantal and, of course, Joan, she does not remain one, any more than Mouchette. Marie, however, is the first instance in which Bresson's preoccupation with virginity, from *Les Anges du péché* to *The Trial of Joan of Arc*, seems more emphatically tied to his view of the world. All of the characters' sins in *Balthazar* may be equally deadly, yet Marie's loss of virginity, an event approached with morose resignation and preceded by a literal fall in the grass, seems to carry more weight because it is tied to the original sin, the sexual knowledge that marks humanity as a fallen species. In the context of the film's allegorical ambitions, Marie's fall is therefore of greater consequence, a foil for Balthazar's innocence that marks the limits of their parallelism.

It is worth noting, however, the effects of the stripping and beating scene, which remains vague as to whether it includes sexual violation. The shot of Marie's nude body kneeling and facing into a corner of the floor in the cottage where she and Gérard had their trysts comes as a shock (figure 39). It is as if her earlier surrender to Gérard has been erased, replaced in our imaginations and made more immediately concrete by this violent and sexually ambiguous encounter, insinuating a fantasized rape scenario that may not have occurred. The scene would almost be gratuitous were it not that, in effect, it restores

Marie's virginity and underlines once more the way sexuality in Bresson is made to represent the violent event that marks human experience.

Very likely the scene was inspired by a story Myshkin tells in Dostoevsky's novel of a young idiot girl, also called Marie, who was seduced and abandoned by an older man and made a public spectacle by her mother.[31] In the comparable cottage scene in *Balthazar* strangers arrive to look at Marie, who we see for the last time riding home with her father and Jacques. Ambiguous as her subsequent disappearance is, it takes on more potent implications in the light of Myshkin's tale, which recounts a life destroyed by shame.

While the parallels between Marie and Balthazar are characterized by passivity, the dramatic movement is also generated by actions taken by characters as a direct result of their particular flaws or vices. That is, the narrative, the linking of episodes, is moved along by a series of displacements whereby a character's behavior generates, by way of Balthazar, subsequent action and the next episode. This usually appears casual—*au hasard*, so to speak—but it is precisely this repeated combination of character indifference and iniquitous consequence that assumes such unbearable weight by the end.

The pattern ranges from the comic to the tragic. We are amused when the farmer, whose dozing causes his cart to overturn, blames Balthazar rather than himself, forcing the animal to run away. We are less amused when Gérard, frustrated over Marie's rejection, takes it out on Balthazar. Balthazar's expulsion from Marie's home follows her father's failure to mend relations with his employer. Here and elsewhere, as both his wife and Marie note, his pride has devastating consequences, but rather than admit it, he renders an incongruous judgment about Balthazar, insisting that *he* is the embarrassment they must be rid of. This convergence of events catapults both Balthazar and Marie into the hands of the thuggish Gérard, precipitating a relationship that will destroy them both.

When Balthazar becomes ill through Gérard's neglect, the bakers have no use for him. Only Arnold's intervention saves him from death, but depending on Arnold's state of inebriation, the donkey's fortunes are up or down. At one point, to escape mistreatment he wanders off into the circus only to be discovered soon after by the drunken Arnold. Arnold's glutinous consumption of alcohol finally brings on his death, depriving Balthazar of another master. He is then taken in and overworked by the corn merchant, whose unconscious guilt over his treatment of Marie and unregenerate miserliness impel him to return the animal to Marie's parents. Finally, when Gérard borrows Balthazar for his trip to the border, he abandons the animal on the hilltop to receive the bullets meant for him. In effect, Balthazar does not just change hands arbitrarily; his moves from one episode to the next are the results of the baseness or vice of each owner. It is, I would argue, this fact—that the narrative is never impelled by virtuous action or positive behavior but entirely mobilized by moral infirmity—that convinced many commentators that Bresson's universe had taken a turn for the worse.

The film's structure thus exhibits aspects of several narrative traditions. If its trajectory does not resemble that of Bresson's previous work, it nonetheless includes characters and behavior we have seen before. *Diary of a Country Priest*, also set in the provinces, features characters who manifest a similar array of vices and, like *Balthazar*, structures the protagonist's journey as a via dolorosa. Unlike the donkey, however, the priest must struggle, like his parishioners, against pride and weakness and between flesh and spirit, doubt and faith.

In *Balthazar* the "arrangement of the material is new" and the accent more widely distributed, yet whatever role Bresson assigns to chance, human behavior is still the most unflinching reality of the narrative. This is largely the basis of his attachments to Bernanos and Dostoevsky, both of whose works are deeply cynical about the human condition, obsessed with the fallen nature of human beings, while holding on to the barest hope of spiritual redemption. It is noteworthy that just as Bernanos and Bresson do not link this hope to the Catholic Church, but, as Bernanos once put it, to its saints, the only extended passionate sentiments expostulated by Prince Myshkin in *The Idiot* are his attacks on Roman Catholicism as the Antichrist, clearly a reflection of Dostoevsky's own deep suspicions. All three artists turn instead, in one form or another, to Christ as the model of spiritual perfection that enlists the sinner to change, but from which the world has consistently and repeatedly moved away.

And so, to see the structure of *Balthazar* as a tour of a "certain number of human groups representing the vices of humanity," as Bresson described it, is both accurate and deceptive. For though its characters may blindly indulge in their vices, there is nothing isolated or random about the consequences of their behavior. The truth that underlies this impression is that every human action affects others, and that no single vice is necessarily less destructive than any other. Some might see Gérard, for example, as the devil, yet the family he destroys lives in no Eden. The effects of Marie's father's pride are just as lethal and, as we have seen, lead to equally negative circumstances. Thus, as the analysis below will try to show, the dissolve from the father's remark about the land to Gérard pouring oil on the road does not simply register the introduction of evil into a happy family's life, but illustrates two skewed visions of the world, each based on a lapse from virtue: the father's hubris on the one hand, Gérard's sociopathic malice on the other.

The interconnectedness of these clashing yet complementary lines and perspectives led Bresson, understandably, to a more complex narrative and cinematographic approach.

Cinematographic Omniscience

The dragon is by the side of the road, watching those who pass. Beware

lest he devour you. We go to the father of souls, but it is necessary to pass

by the dragon.

—St. Cyril of Jerusalem

Compared to the increasingly close-knit structures of *A Man Escaped, Pickpocket*, and *The Trial of Joan of Arc, Au hasard Balthazar* at first seems rather diffuse. But its apparent looseness, so unlike Bresson's previous work, is integral to the philosophy and vision of the film, in which seemingly random actions are linked, through omniscient narration and cinematographic choices, to an ever-widening design. We see this in the childhood sequence through the way the sick child, excluded from play with Balthazar and the others, is strategically placed in the frame of five different shots. Whether a blurry figure on a stretcher in the corner of the shot in which her sister climbs up to a hayloft to join Jacques, Marie, and Balthazar, or asleep and carried to the car for the family's return to Paris, her presence is felt. We learn soon after that she has died.

In the context of an otherwise joyous evocation of childhood, the dying child darkens the atmosphere, anticipating the tone that governs the rest of the film and the narrative situation that will affect the lives of the principal characters. Her death is the reason that her father fails to return to the country, keeping Marie and Jacques apart for many years. Their chance to renew their vows years later is also aborted thanks to the contention between their fathers. But for these circumstances, Marie's family might have escaped the decline into which they are led and Marie herself avoided the fatal relationship with Gérard.

The marginal presence of this minor character, overshadowed by the engaging aspects of the opening sequence—the baptism of Balthazar and the bond between Marie and Jacques—turns out to be of the utmost consequence, casting a shadow over the lives of the others. The sick child's position in the shots in which she appears, interacting, however mutedly, with those around her, barely hints at the unforeseen impact she will have. The setup of the shot of her in bed is striking since as an unknown entity she seems both conspicuous and arbitrarily placed in the frame, blocking the alleged primary action of the shot: Marie passing behind her to join the others in Balthazar's baptism ritual, an unusual composition for Bresson. This shot and the manner in which the sick child is structured into the opening sequence prefigure the narrative strategy, cinematographic design, and underlying viewpoint of the film.

A far more elaborate demonstration of how Bresson's narrative economy achieves a new complexity in this film is the road sequence—composed of eight shots, virtually without dialogue, and less than two minutes long—that brings together for the first time four principal characters: Balthazar, Marie, her father, and Gérard. At the same time the scene anticipates how the fortunes of the first three will be determined by the fourth. It begins with a close-up of oil being poured onto the road by a crouching figure in denim and leather jacket (Gérard), who empties the can and tosses it off screen, after which he and his gang drive off on motorbikes. The third, most complex shot begins with a tracking close-up of Balthazar as a shadow, followed by a hand entering from off screen right and grabbing his harness. A track back reveals Gérard and his cronies on opposite sides of Balthazar, and Marie and her father seated in the cart. Following the remarks of Gérard and his gang ("Smart animal that....It's fast...and modern"), the only words uttered in the sequence, and a close-up of Gérard smiling snidely, presumably at Marie off screen, her father in the fifth and six shots strikes Balthazar and the cart moves off left.

As it does so, the bikers remain to watch the effects of their earlier handiwork. We hear a car approaching from off screen left, then see it pass the boys and move off right. A cut to a medium shot shows it skidding on the oil slick and spinning out of control onto the grass. In a reverse angle, Gérard and his gang watch indifferently as a second car comes from off screen left, passes before them, and moves off screen right. The final shot is the capper: a medium close-up of Gérard looking off screen right, awaiting the anticipated crash. As expected, we hear the second car crashing into the first, but even before the sounds of collision end, a bored Gérard moves off screen left, followed by his gang.

In a noteworthy departure from his usual method, Bresson suspends one line of action while a second, ostensibly unrelated, is introduced and concluded. In the longest take (shot five) both lines are fused, the resolution of the second overlapping with the resumption of the first. If the initial encounter of the principal characters is the primary action, why, we may wonder, is it nested within the framework of the oil slick stunt? On the one hand, it tends to render the encounter less inevitable than coincidental—*au hasard*—and the gang's behavior as just another manifestation of its randomly expressed cruelty, like the trap it has set in motion. On the other hand, one can see the initial action as a narrative decoy analogous to the trap itself, and the unsuspecting drivers who fall into it as foreshadowers of what will happen to Marie, her father, and Balthazar.

In fact, Gérard's later seduction of Marie will also evolve out of an unforeseen trap on the road: she stops because she sees Balthazar, only to find Gérard in her car when she tries to leave. The overlap of shot five, then, suggests that the encounter shares not only the same filmic space as the stunt but its nefarious calculation as well. The effects of the malicious stunt spill over with ramifications for the fortunes that lie ahead for Marie, her father, and Balthazar. Gérard's interest in Marie as more tempting prey clearly displaces the thrill of the stunt to which he then shows complete indifference—the same behavioral sequence with which he will subsequently treat her and the very quality embodied by the nesting structure.

Gérard successfully masks his true character not only in his seductive manner with Marie but with the baker's wife, old enough to be his mother, who spoils him with presents, ignores his criminal tendencies, and envies his relationship with Marie. His duplicitous nature is chillingly conveyed in the shot of him in the choir loft, his angelic voice luring Marie below while sending shivers through the spectator, who must match the Gérard he or she knows with that voice, an apt, if unwitting analogue for the demonic fusion in his character.

The road sequence is a realistic unfolding of aspects of the narrative, which demonstrates how Bresson avoids reducing action, character, or gesture to a purely metaphorical or symbolic function, allowing, through association, one thing to be seen in terms of another. In this sense *Balthazar* is more complex than those forms—fables, parables, allegories—that it most resembles. In that tradition, Gérard would be simply the embodiment of evil. But just as Balthazar is both real animal and symbol of innocence, Gérard is both human and symbol of evil. In making him an orphan, Bresson even suggests a basis for his pathology, just as his representing one or two of the deadly sins confirms his place in the human community. Yet although he may be no less human than his victims, Gérard, particularly as he is introduced in the road sequence, also embodies that "other meaning" contained in many allegories.[32]

A clue to how he may have been conceived, and how the road sequence might be understood, is the allusion Bresson makes, in that interview conducted three months before he began shooting *Balthazar*, to Uccello's first version of *St. George and the Dragon* (1455).[33] As he speaks, Bresson stands by a reproduction of the painting, in which three figures appear. The dragon in the center, rearing up on its hind legs, faces St. George, mounted on a powerful gray on the right, whose spear has pierced the monster's lower jaw. On the left, a graceful female figure stands in prayer against a recessed expanse of land. The composition might well have prompted Eisenstein to dissect its various areas according to the montage principle,[34] as indeed Bresson's remarks themselves tend to do. During the interview, the camera, following Bresson's description, focuses first on the dragon, then pans left to the lady as he describes her "unexpectedly beautiful presence" against this vast backdrop of plowed land with a faraway perspective, "an area of quietness before the horror of this dragon."[35] The sense of a dynamic contrast within the same pictorial frame is clearly suggested, and the distinction between the material on the left and that on the right enhances this impression. In cinematic terms, one might see these halves as successive shots, or as what Eisenstein called montage within the shot, rather than as one panoramic long shot.

The painting, executed during Uccello's narrative phase, has at least two distinct areas of attention that suggest temporal succession—Bresson's "before"—as easily as simultaneity. In fact, Uccello painted a second version of the subject, readable as a further *stage* of the action.[36] In that one, the lady is a more integral part of the central action and no longer seen against the backdrop of the land, which is absent altogether. But it is the first version's evocation of temporality and the praying lady against the land that seem to have struck Bresson and to have inspired the sequence immediately prior to the road sequence in *Balthazar* and the dissolve that links the former to the latter.

That prior sequence of five shots begins with a close-up of Marie caressing Balthazar as she awaits her father and ends with a shot of her father embracing her on the cart, the image that dissolves into the shot of Gérard pouring oil on the road. In the second shot Marie's father approaches on the tractor; the third shows her waiting; and in the fourth her father dismounts and walks toward the cart. In both, he is seen against a vast receding landscape of the five hundred acres he has plowed, which not only provides evidence of his accomplishment, but in its "faraway perspective," a rare instance of a shot of almost infinite perspective in a Bresson film, also mirrors his grandiosity. As he walks forward exuding pride, his first word, *"Regard!"* invokes both meanings: it directs Marie, and the spectator, to "look," that is, to admire what lies behind him, and it expresses his satisfaction at having learned from books how to "plow and ready the land," an achievement he expects will impress his daughter. Marie's reminder that the land does not belong to them balances the picture, so to speak, but has little effect on his demeanor. "It doesn't matter," he says, "we'll be happy anyway." With these words, he puts his arm around her, draws her close, and kisses her on the cheek. It is this gesture that dissolves to Gérard's hand holding the can of oil directly over the embracing figures of Marie and her father. As the incoming image becomes stronger, we can see (in good-quality prints) the reflection of Marie's arms being replaced by Gérard's reflection in the oil, itself resembling the spill of the dragon's blood in the second painting (figures 40–43). Together with what follows in the road sequence, it is a sinister suggestion that in the real contemporary world the dragon has taken on human form.

Bresson's alterations mark the difference between the culture and world-view from which the painting springs and that which informs his film. In the painting, the dragon, a figure that appears many times in the book of the Apocalypse as symbol of the devil, is flanked by two embodiments of the spiritual: the lady praying on the left and St. George on the right. The possibility and means of destroying evil therefore lies in the critical role of the spiritual, in its metaphysical and pragmatic manifestations, in the world reflected. From this perspective, the image of the lady praying against the plowed land depicts a harmonious blend of nature and civilization founded on an acknowledgment of and faith in God.[37]

In the spirit of *Balthazar*'s bleaker view of human nature and the contemporary world as godless, Bresson complicates these readings. The image of the father against the land replaces the spiritual with the worldly, the humility of prayer with the sin of pride. The "quiet area" is compromised, more compatible with the father's vaguely idyllic attitude than with reality. As for St. George, neither the father's pseudo-heroic bluster and protective embrace nor Jacques's vapid amorality qualifies. In keeping with Bresson's revisionist transformation of the painting, St. George is not only missing; it is inconceivable that he should be present. Yet however delusory, this moment between father and daughter *is* the last "quiet area" of their life together before the entrance of the "terrible dragon." And in the same spirit of inversion, the blood that will be spilled will not be Gérard's but Balthazar's at the end of the film.

Chaos and Epiphany

The God who beheld everything and also man, that God had to die! Man

cannot endure that such a witness should live.

—Nietzsche, *Thus Spake Zarathustra*

The shift in narrative and cinematographic style in *Balthazar* has to do with its more ambitious scope. The film seems more concerned, as will *Lancelot of the Lake*, *The Devil Probably* and *L'Argent*, with a general collapse of values than with the fate of individuals, a theme crystallized in the bar sequence in its last quarter. Encompassing a number of minidramas involving all of the major characters—with the exception of Marie's father, who is the subject of the dialogue between Marie and her mother—it is the most intricately designed (sixty-three shots) sequence, narratively, thematically, and cinematographically, of any Bresson film to this point. Purportedly a celebration of a fortuitous event (Arnold's inheritance), the sequence ends in destruction, death, and abandonment, with no discernible change in mood or rhythm. Framed by the swift rise and fall of Arnold's fortunes, somewhat like the oil slick stunt framed the road sequence, it begins with a close-up of a firecracker sputtering and exploding on cobblestones and ends with a close-up of Arnold's dead body lying on the road at Balthazar's feet.

Though the sequence is filled with exploding firecrackers, loud music, and shattering glass, the only reaction shots to the general ruckus are Balthazar's. Over the first of these we hear Gérard off screen shouting and inviting everyone into the bar because Arnold is buying the drinks. In the bar a notary confirms that a deceased uncle has left Arnold everything. Amid the chaos, Arnold, virtually speechless throughout, literally drinks himself to death. His silence irritates Gérard, whose questions ("Not breaking anything? You're not angry?") and taunting remarks ("Drink, you halfwit...You social parasite") prompt only moronic smiles. In forcing Arnold to drink, Gérard indirectly causes his death, as he does those of Marie, her father, and Balthazar. It is he who sets the tone of the sequence, smashing mirrors, sweeping bottles and glasses onto the floor, and toppling tables.

Outside Marie's mother pleads with her to return home. By crosscutting between them, Bresson keeps in view both areas of action, bar and street, stressing the futility of the mother's appeal and the coarseness of Marie's attachment. The entrance to the bar acts as a border zone between interior and exterior. Her mother expresses concern; Marie accuses her of spying. Her mother mentions the father's despair; Marie says he is more attached to his pride. To her mother's question of what Marie sees in Gérard, Marie says that she would kill herself for him.

Their exchanges are interrupted by shots sustaining the party motif: two of Gérard's buddies throwing firecrackers off screen; an overhead shot of a firecracker exploding; a medium shot of Balthazar reacting to a second one exploding off screen. Marie's comment about killing herself is almost eclipsed by the shot of the mother turning away in sync with the sounds of firecrackers exploding. Each passage of dialogue is punctuated by explosions—their proximity as well as their intrusion a constant reminder of Gérard himself—and by shots of Balthazar, whose reactions are the true barometers of the underlying tension of the sequence. Constructed in this manner, the gang's behavior accentuating the dissonance between mother and daughter, the sequence seems a replay in a more explicit register of the road sequence.

Its destructive edge erupts more openly when Gérard lets loose inside the bar, his actions virtually unnoticed as the music continues uninterruptedly and couples dance on the debris-strewn floor. Marking the end of the passage between Marie and her mother is a close-up of a juke box, its 1960s style music setting the tone of the next dozen shots and articulating a disturbingly harmonious commingling of teenage rituals and social violence moving comfortably to the same beat. The sequence more closely resembles Hollywood movies of the 1950s (e.g., *The Wild One,* 1954) than student protests of the 1960s. Gérard's gang embodies an aimless, nihilistic rage, more primitive than rebellious, with perhaps a tinge of the death figures from Cocteau's *Orphée.* An image that succinctly captures the genesis of their particular animus is the one of Gérard, leaping, crouching ape-like onto the bar, and then sweeping a row of bottles off a shelf in one continuous motion.

These shots have an extraordinary physical acuteness. In only two do we see Gérard's face, in another his arm as it sweeps along the length of the bar, sending dozens of glasses and bottles onto the floor. As the camera pans up to reframe the mirror reflecting the room full of dancers, a bottle suddenly flies into the shot from off screen left, hits the mirror and shatters it, leaving a small fragment intact long enough to observe that the dancers remain undisturbed. A close-up of a corner shelf behind the bar is visible for only a second before another bottle, hurled from off screen, enters from the right, smashing those on the shelf. In the final shot of this passage, a table covered with glasses is seen tilting over and toppling onto the floor.

Some of this can be read psychologically: both Gérard's flinging a bottle directly into the mirror reflecting the dancers and himself (figure 44) and the blank stare with which Arnold faces him like another mirror imply unconscious self-loathing. But such notions are overwhelmed by the extent of the destruction and its cinematographic registration. The framing and cutting of these shots, the use of off screen space, and the sound accentuate the immediacy and assaultive nature of the action. In the absence of Gérard's face and body, we are directed less to the personality and motive of the perpetrator than to a sense of chaos and mindlessness. Terms like *barroom brawl* and *drunken rampage* are inadequate. Gérard's actions seem global and impersonal and the destruction he wreaks the triumph of barbarism.

The connotations of image and sound are especially resonant in the context of Bresson's work. The piercing sounds of the mirror shattering, preceded and continued by sounds of other broken glass, carry a familiar motif to an excessive level. Previous audiovisual renderings of shattering objects, from Thérèse's overturning of the soup cart in *Les Anges* and Agnès's deliberate dropping of a wine glass in *Les Dames* to the book Michel slams down in *Pickpocket*,[38] are single, unrepeated gestures that mark the moment when a character has been pushed too far. But the serial crashing of multiple objects in the bar sequence of *Balthazar* suggests an inchoate, boundless force beyond the emotional parameters of a single character. As an audiovisual evocation of physical violence, it prefigures the opening of *Lancelot of the Lake*, with its clashing armor, thundering hooves, severed limbs, and jets of spouting blood.

If the scene projects a sinister view of youth, however, the unperturbed presence of the notary and the grain merchant, the latter calmly paying for the damage, suggests it is not an aberration. In containing what would otherwise pass for unacceptable behavior, the bar is a microcosm of this society, just as in bringing together the main characters, the sequence counteracts the episodic quality of the narrative with a view of a unified, if perverse, social order. "A dreadful vision of the world and the evil in it," as Godard described the film.[39]

It is against this view and the sensorial overload to which it gives rise that the final sequence should be understood. Like the relationship of the donkey's braying to the accelerated passage of the Schubert sonata over the credits, it provides a calming, clarifying counterpoint to the disruptive violence of the bar scene. The sequence is preceded by Balthazar's last journey, his back packed with contraband, climbing uphill to the mountainous border, where he is left behind by the fleeing Gérard and one of his cronies when a guard shouts for them to halt. The close-up of Balthazar, standing in place while sounds of gunfire echo around him, seems interminable as we wait for the bullet that will surely find its mark. When it does, his reaction, like those in response to the firecrackers, is a mere spasm of the body.

The final scene fades in on Balthazar standing at the edge of the wood on a serenely quiet morning, the sounds of birds distantly audible. A cut to a close-up of his right foreleg reveals the still-bleeding wound. He walks a few paces to the crest of a hill and looks out to the horizon (figure 45). The grandeur of this image of Balthazar, back to the camera, set against a backdrop of mountains and sky, both implies and excludes us from the animal's perspective.[40] We hear the faint sounds of sheep bells, like those in the opening sequence in a similar, if not the identical setting, then see in the valley below a flock slowly making its way up the hill, shots of barking dogs intercut with its progress.

As the sheep approach, the camera tilts down from the sky and comes to rest on perhaps the most eloquent image in the film: the now recumbent Balthazar, surrounded by the sheep in what appears to be both a gesture of comfort that recalls his visit to the caged animals and, in the context of the film's Christological iconography, a recognition, one no human character can make, of his symbolic role in the narrative. As Balthazar's head lowers and his eyes begin to close, the sheep begin to move away and we hear the slow section of the second movement of the Schubert sonata for the last time. It ends as the sheep exit the frame and Balthazar, breathing his last, lies prone.

Had Bresson been aiming exclusively for that transcendence thought to characterize his work, this might have been the final shot.[41] But it is followed by one more, a decidedly unpretty picture of the donkey's dead body, its prominently displayed abdomen still bound by the leather pouches, lying on the ground in random fashion, a freeze frame a news photographer might seize on the run (figure 46). No empathic Schubert or tolling sheep bells soften the effect. Like Holbein's *Dead Christ*, a copy of which appears in Rogozhin's rooms in *The Idiot*, "an image of Christ after the Crucifixion as a bruised, bloody, and broken man, without a trace of supernatural or spiritual transcendence,"[42] this stark, impersonal image of Balthazar's body tends to qualify the narrative and religious associations delineated throughout this reading.

There is no precedent for this emphasis on the dead body in Bresson's work, which had previously linked death, implied but not represented, to the spiritual transfiguration of his protagonists. The deaths of Anne-Marie, the priest, and Joan are passages to another realm, symbolized by the images that replace the body on the screen: a transformed Thérèse, a cross, an empty stake. However convincing a Christ figure, Balthazar will not rise from the dead, Agrippa's sentiments notwithstanding, any more than he gathered disciples or taught beatitudes. He cannot be the carrier of the concept of Christian redemption, if only because, as an animal, he is not a fallen creature. If the final scene approaches transcendence, the final shot seems to expose this for the fiction it is, prompting the realization that everything that has preceded was illusory, *mere* allegory.

Is it possible to reconcile the film's Christological parallels with this reading of the final shot? Does the shot erase the connotations of the image of the bleeding Balthazar taking his final steps to the crest of the hill, as moving an emblem of suffering innocence as any work of art has produced and an image that almost repairs the link between the natural and spiritual worlds suggested in the Uccello? That final image is shattering in that two signature moments of the Christian parable are conflated and emptied of their original meanings: as Balthazar reaches his Calvary, he still carries the bags containing the contraband gold and perfume, which, here, drained of the value they possess in the biblical allusion, attest not to the coming of a savior but to the confirmation that the world remains enslaved to corruption and that it will always persecute the innocent.[43] On the other hand, the juxtaposition of the last sequence and the final shot constitutes the essence of the film's vision. In having only the sheep bear witness to Balthazar's death and returning him to his animal nature, Bresson underlines the distance between the Christian message and the world's indifference. Like Prince Myshkin's innocence, Balthazar's innocence is an affront to those mired in sin; like Myshkin, he is an easy target for abuse. Indeed, in his use of the donkey, Bresson implies the essence of Agrippa's characterization that the quality of asininity, as inherently humble and passive, is not likely to be noticed, much less appreciated, by a world increasingly governed by materialism.

"Just before Myshkin falls into an epileptic seizure, suddenly amid the sadness, spiritual darkness and depression, his brain seemed to catch fire...and [his] mind and heart were flooded by a dazzling light. All his agitation, all his doubts and worries, seemed composed in a twinkling, culminating in a great calm, full of serene and harmonious joy and hope, full of understanding and the knowledge of the final cause."[44] We cannot know whether Balthazar has a comparable vision, any more than we can decipher his point-of-view exchanges with the animals. But in a move both aesthetically daring and supremely right, it seems to be the vision, that of Myshkin in his pre-epileptic state, offered to the spectator. But if so, what exactly is being clarified? For one thing, to see Balthazar only as a Christ figure is to erase his suffering by rendering it purely symbolic. The final image not only places that reading in question, but it restores to Balthazar his animal nature and by doing so gives him that soul otherwise denied by acknowledging that his suffering simply *is*—it's purpose is not to redeem anyone, but to give evidence of the world as it is. This may be his true affinity with Christ: "Even he who ended on the cross—it is not because he suffered *for us* that he still counts for something in our eyes, but because he *suffered* and uttered several lamentations as profound as they were gratuitous."[45]

In the last scene of *The Idiot*, the best Myshkin can do when he finds Rogozhin nearly mad with grief after having murdered Nastasya Filippovna is to wait with him through the dark and dreary night. He makes no judgments and preaches no religious pieties. He is, but for a moment, calm and serene, unsurprised at the tragic outcome of the couple's tempestuous affair but helpless to be anything more than its merciful witness. Joseph Frank argues that Myshkin is "inevitably doomed to catastrophe because the unearthly light of love and universal reconciliation cannot illuminate the fallen world of man for more than a dazzling and self-destructive instant."[46] He "cannot resolve the conflict between his apocalyptic aspirations and his earthly limitations.... [The] eschatological ideal, incarnated by the Prince, could do no more than provide a beacon to light up this world with the unearthly illumination of a higher one."[47] In recognizing the prince's role as spiritual witness, Rogozhin manifests the only form of redemption of which he is capable: an awareness of the good that he cannot embrace himself. In acknowledging this recognition, Myshkin enacts, as unwittingly as Balthazar, a form of forgiveness that only the truly good have the power to bestow. Having completed the sojourn in the tempestuous world, we last see him convalescing in Switzerland, drained of all energy and as mute as Balthazar, who has made it only to the border.

Because Balthazar is removed from the human condition, it is the spectator who must judge the behavior of characters and assess their capacity, or not, to recognize goodness, to yearn for it as a balm to the tormented soul. Marie seems intuitively to be one such character, though her mother is the only one in the film to verbalize the point, when she tells the immune Gérard that Balthazar is a saint.

It is this uncomplicated, uncorrupt nature of the animal, as opposed to the fallen state of the human, that allows the final sequence to resonate with such power. As the donkey's braying cut through Myshkin's cloudy mental anguish, so the final moments of Balthazar's life clarify the tortuous journey that has brought him, full circle, to this place, burdened with everything he has experienced along the way. Like certain powerful images in poetry, the one of the dying Balthazar—for the first time since the first shot in complete harmony with his surroundings—has a culminating effect, drawing all within it and dispelling ambiguities in the name of a greater, all-encompassing truth. The intuitive grasp of this truth, the "final cause" as Myshkin understood it when he heard the donkey's braying, is both convulsive and pacifying.

In discussing *The Idiot* Bresson remarked, "Absolutely admirable, to have an idiot informed by an animal, to have him see life through an animal, who passes for an idiot but is of an intelligence....And to compare this idiot...to an animal that passes for an idiot...that is the subtlest and the most intelligent of all. That is magnificent."[48] Although this is praise of Dostoevsky's achievement, it describes Bresson's no less remarkable conception of a protagonist fusing these two beings, risking the absurd in pursuit of the sublime. In doing so, Bresson has given us his most God-like performance, miracles and all, conflating species as easily as fictional modes, creating and dropping characters, lifting our hearts to glimpse the divine, only to return it to ashes and dust. It is an unmitigated vision of human existence, teetering on the edge of the abyss, yet capable of hoping—not necessarily believing—that the fall might be averted. It is this vision that is embodied in the juxtaposition of the transcendent final scene and the final shot that qualifies, if not denies, its resonances.

6

The Young Virgins of the Provinces II

Mouchette

With *Mouchette* (1967), Bresson's second adaptation of a work by Georges Bernanos, the balance between the bleak depiction of the world and the faith by which some characters transcend it becomes increasingly tenuous. Earlier protagonists might be said to unconsciously bring about their deaths prematurely by the way they live. The priest in *Diary of a Country Priest* accelerates his death through fasting and the consumption of bad alcohol. Mouchette, however, whose life holds not a glimmer of hope and who takes no comfort in faith, is the first of Bresson's protagonists to commit suicide. The film might be entitled *La misérable*.

Made immediately after *Au hasard Balthazar*, *Mouchette* has strong links to that film. Both are set in the provinces and focus on female protagonists who lose their virginity by force and are overcome by shame. But whereas Marie's family can be described as working class, Mouchette lives an impoverished existence in every sense, making her situation much gloomier. At home she sleeps and dresses, along with her father and brother, in the same room where her mother lies dying and a baby wails. The false pride of Marie's father is completely foreign to Mouchette's, who transports bootleg liquor and often arrives home drunk.

Compared with any previous Bresson protagonist, Mouchette lacks every essential for mobilizing the narrative. She has neither Anne-Marie's fervor nor Hélène's insidious determination. She utterly lacks the spiritual strength of the country priest and resembles neither the infectiously courageous Fontaine nor the warrior saint Joan. Her fleeting signs of rebelliousness pale next to Michel's; Marie manifests more spunk and willfulness. In short, whereas the usual thrust of Bresson's work springs from the charged tension between a character's inherent drive and the film's design, *Mouchette*'s design, as the opening and closing scenes in the woods demonstrate, has no countering force.

In a sense Mouchette's precursor is Balthazar, for whom life is also a series of mistreatments that must be borne and whose complaints barely register on anyone. The imagery that pervades the film and the novella, in which she is described as "half-animal," suggests as much. Like the birds and rabbits hunted and ensnared in the woods on the edge of the village, Mouchette is prey to the cruelty of the townspeople, and like Balthazar is subject to the use and abuse of nearly everyone she encounters. As Balthazar ambles from one owner to another, Mouchette walks through her village, circumscribing its physical and moral smallness. In her ill-fitting clogs, the noise she makes on roads and wooden floors—"like a pair of castanets," says Bernanos—announces her presence along with her poverty, inviting the disdain that her very name, "Little Fly," provokes. Her walk describes the crisscrossing of paths, typical of a provincial village, at once *au hasard* and unavoidable—casual passings that prove to be anything but.

Yet Mouchette is not quite as passive as Balthazar, and her characterization is no more sentimental than it is in Bernanos, although one can easily imagine how mawkish it could have been in the hands of a lesser filmmaker. The way she is treated by others has its effect, turning her against everyone except her mother and the poacher Arsène, who she imagines is an outcast like her. Snubbed by her classmates, she looks down on her elders, has contempt for her father, and on occasion displays a meanness that rivals Chantal's cruelty and Marie's pride except that it lacks any pretense of surface manners. Unlike Chantal or Marie, Mouchette is verbally inarticulate, and in fact speaks fewer words than any other leading character of Bresson's. Her scorn is largely physical: throwing mud at her classmates, stomping her feet in a puddle before entering a church, grinding mud into an old lady's carpet, flinging a croissant behind her in disdain.

Although *Mouchette* has affinities with *Balthazar*, it is less allegorical, more rooted in genetic and social realities. Arguably it comes closer than any other film of Bresson's to a naturalistic view of the world—not in Words-worth's sense of the shared mystical link between humanity and nature, but in terms of the "mechanistic and deterministic assumptions developed by late 19th c. science," in which nature is the agent of "rapacious destiny," a corro-sive, determinant force that impedes "virtuous self-fulfillment."[1] This is far more pronounced in Bernanos. Whereas Bresson conferred on Balthazar the noblest of human qualities, in *Mouchette* he shows people driven by preda-tory, animal instincts without an ideal foil. While *Balthazar* is a "dreadful vision of the world," as Godard described it, *Mouchette* is a dismal, more localized picture of provincial existence, less a narrative characterized by movement than a slowly constructed mosaic of a way of life virtually defined by stasis. Even Bresson's elaboration of the triangle involving the poacher, the gamekeeper, and the barmaid is stillborn, exposing it as a pathetic stab at passion that seems to go nowhere.

Bernanos knew this environment well, and his novella bears out his remark that "it takes centuries to change the rhythm of life in a French village."[2] The film effectively captures this ambience and conviction in the formal construction of its sequences and their link through cinematographic gestures. The interconnections of places, times, actions, habits, and charac-ters are more emphatic than usual. Some transitions of sounds and shots are so pronounced that it is as if they carried the weight of those previous centu-ries, suturing not just images and moments but the ruling mind-set of the provincial. Bresson weaves Bernanos's sentiment into the very interstices of the film's cinematographic fabric.

A Naturalistic Tale

To Georges Bernanos, "the feeling of God's absence was the only sign left of his existence." His despair was tempered by his commitment to writing. "The Catholic novel is not the novel which only nourishes us with nice sentiments; it is the novel where the life of faith is at grips with the passions. Everything possible must be done to make the reader feel the tragic mystery of salvation." The Catholic novelist, he averred, was more capable of "descending into the abyss" and shedding light on the human condition, for "he carries a torch [i.e., his faith] in his hand."[3]

For Bernanos, nowhere is the human tragedy more evident than in the contemplation of childhood and the loss of innocence. The sins committed by adults against children are without remission. Evil is attributed to the machinations of Satan rather than to a flawed human nature. He wonders about its origins, its "arbitrary," "sudden," and somewhat mysterious eruption, and its destruction of the "innocent" state of childhood: "Here you have this child in its cradle, all grace and innocence, fresh and clear as a running brook, new like the spring, and sincere as the light of morning.…Who is it then…that works away inside it with so sinister a care and clairvoyance, with the precision of a surgeon who knows where to put his scissors and forceps in order to reach the most delicate nerves, day by day and hour by hour, until twenty or thirty years later you find this radiant little creature transformed into an anxious and solitary animal—envious, jealous, or avaricious—eaten up alive by the absurd hatred of itself."[4]

At age fourteen Mouchette already manifests malice and defensiveness, although it is hard to imagine, given the psychological and sociological deprivations of her life as Bernanos delineates them, that she was once "a radiant little creature." She is impoverished in almost every way and rejected by her peers; her home life consists of caring for a dying mother and infant brother. Unaware of her emotional vulnerability, she misplaces her affections onto a man who rapes her. Confused and ashamed, she returns home to see her mother die and, believing herself completely alone, drowns herself. As if to preserve her inner world, Bernanos adopts a Jamesian fusion of third-person narration and first-person experience.[5] An omniscient assessment, he seems to imply, psychological or otherwise, would deprive Mouchette of her loneliness and pain, the only real signs of her existence.

There are four chapters in Bernanos's novella. The first and longest begins with a brief scene of Mouchette at school, but the bulk of it takes place in the woods where she takes shelter from a storm on her way home and encounters Arsène. It is clear that Mouchette knows Arsène, half expects to find him in the woods, and is attracted to him, in part because he seems "familiar" and is an outsider like herself. Their encounter is tinged with erotic suggestion, and Mouchette wonders if what she feels is love. It is also touching; when Arsène has an epileptic fit, she supports his head and sings to him on key, something she is unable or unwilling to do at school. Arsène's mysterious altercation with Mathieu, the gamekeeper, recounted later and leaving Mouchette confused, forms the basis of her bond with him. Believing he may have killed Mathieu, she vows to keep his "secret." But when she tries to leave, Arsène, inebriated and aware of her feelings for him, prevents her, becomes half-mad, and then rapes her. Later Mouchette hides and makes her way home in the wee hours.

The second chapter describes life at home: her mother's illness, her father's indifference and habitual drunkenness, her caring for a new baby, the sense of poverty everywhere. Considering how long Mouchette has been gone, her mother seems only moderately concerned. Mouchette feeds the baby, then lies on her mattress, but is racked with anxiety. At daybreak, she tries to speak to her mother, but having worsened during the night, the woman is distracted, warns Mouchette about idlers and drunkards, then, just as Mouchette is about to unburden herself, dies. Moments later her father and brother return and react to the death as they do to every misfortune: "It is only another unavoidable burden they [the poor] have to bear." Mouchette curses her father and leaves the house.

In chapter 3 she wanders through the village, encountering a series of humiliations. A grocer, initially sympathetic over her mother's death, offers Mouchette coffee and croissants, only to revile her as a "little slut" when she sees scratches on her chest. Shamed and frightened, Mouchette "accidentally" drops and breaks the bowl of coffee. On the street she is addressed as "rat face" by the brewer's boys, who expose themselves when she passes. She wanders to Mathieu's house, as if to verify Arsène's fears, and discovers that Mathieu is alive. Under questioning she confesses her night with Arsène, and in feeble defense brags that Arsène is her lover. Her last stop is the old woman who cares for the dead. While the woman calls her a witch under her breath, Mouchette is fascinated by the woman's talk about the dead; when she leaves with her mother's shroud and the dress, her purpose is clear. The final chapter is set at an old sand quarry, now filled with water. Mouchette muses on death as a "dear familiar face." She meditates on the lack of human warmth and caress in her life, and then slips quietly into the water.

For Bernanos, Mouchette's life is essentially Godless. She does not encounter a single "true Christian." God and the Church are merely habits of mind that have not infiltrated the lives of the villagers. They are not unlike the venal characters in *Diary of a Country Priest*, indifferent to the efforts of the curé to save them from their hypocrisy and wretchedness. In *Mouchette* the only allusions to the local priest are negative.[6]

True to the naturalistic tradition, *Mouchette* is rife with animal imagery, which, though consonant with the surrounding woods, extends to the actions, movements, and feelings of Mouchette and other characters, from Mouchette's ambivalent feelings about Arsène's attack, which seems like the weight of "an invisible animal attached to her body," to the description of the old woman sitting curled up in her chair, "her fingers [moving] so restlessly and quickly along her black dress, that her hands were like two small gray animals hunting an invisible prey." In the final scene at the sand quarry, where Mouchette often "returned each evening like an exhausted animal... [the] deep, secret impulse towards death [seizes] her again...so violently that she was almost dancing with anguish, like an animal caught in a trap."

As they do in Bresson's film, hands reveal character and behavior. In the novella they convey the estrangement between the body and the soul, record the effects of poverty and toil, and symbolize internal conflicts between self-love and self-loathing. Like the body in general, hands have memories and often act independently or rebelliously. With her hands Madame, impatient with Mouchette's musical ineptness, drags her to the piano and pushes her head onto the keyboard, an image captured with physical bluntness in the film. At the moment of Arsène's rape, "he seized her with his hands, to which his fit of lust had lent an unnatural strength." At home afterward, Mouchette's "hands, with no forgiveness in them, lay clenched on the mattress and refused to touch her hated body." In the end she runs her hands over the shroud, but is suddenly repulsed because they remind her of "countless humiliations." In the pond Mouchette holds "herself up in shallow water by the pressure of one hand on the bottom" until she twists over, looks up into the sky, and feels "the insidious flow of the water along her head and neck, filling her ears with its joyful sound"—a description that implies, but elides, the final gesture of "letting go" with both hands that makes death possible.

In the twenty-four hours of the action, Mouchette thinks of death more than once, but it is the old woman's speech that conjures it as an option. Reverence for the dead is the true religion, the woman says; she understands them. If so, and if talking to the dead is comforting, then being with the dead, a community that now includes Mouchette's mother, would be desirable. Mouchette seems to come under the spell of what psychoanalysts call magical thinking, motivated by "the wish to gain support and strength through joining the powerful lost loved object."[7] Giving Mouchette the dress and shroud for her dead mother, the woman evokes the image of Mary Magdalene or Veronica ministering to Christ,[8] unwittingly performing an act of obeisance before one about to die. After she leaves the woman's house, Mouchette wraps herself in the dress, converting it into the "garment of the dead," her actual immersion in the water merely the final gesture of an already introjected state of mind.

An earlier figuration of this end might be seen in the song Mouchette's classmates sing in the beginning. It recounts Christopher Columbus's efforts to keep his crew from despair before sighting land. He asks them not to give up hope, promising that in "three days" he will "give them a world." In less than three days from that song, which Mouchette fails to sing on key with her classmates, she will die of hopelessness, though given the frame of mind just outlined, perhaps believing that she will find a new world of forgiveness and peace.

Suicide is the ultimate sin in the eyes of the Catholic Church, a surrender to despair. Traditionally, the confirmed suicide was denied burial in consecrated (Church-blessed) ground. Bernanos describes it as an "inexplicable and frighteningly sudden event," an impulse that seizes Mouchette violently and is not fully understood. He does not judge it as an act of lost faith because there is no evidence of faith in the story. "She did not want to die. All she felt was a strange shame, an inexplicable timidity." In light of the associations aroused by the old woman's behavior and the song that promises hope, Bernanos seems bent on lending Mouchette's sufferings a sacral quality that tenuously compensates for the lack of faith and hope that has marked her existence.

Bresson's Sacred Indirections

The cumulative structure of the novella, building in intensity without unbalancing the weight of each experience, is not unlike Bresson's approach. But Bresson fleshes out incidents to which Bernanos only alludes, expands the social setting, and breaks up the one scene with the mother in the novella into five different segments, reinforcing her critical role in Mouchette's life. He also expands the duration of the story from twenty-four hours to nearly five days and frames the narrative between two hunting scenes in the woods, neither of which is in the original. In the hunting scenes he transposes the animal imagery and its connotations, so pronounced in the novella, to a setting integral to the milieu.

Mouchette has two opening sequences, neither of which is in the novella and neither of which, atypically, includes the protagonist. In the first one, Mouchette's mother, in the only shot of her not lying in bed, is seated in a church with her hand over the "stone in her chest," wondering aloud how her family will manage after her death. Placed before the credits and the woods sequence, it may recall a previous pre-credits sequence, in which another mother enters another church to request that the Catholic Church reopen the trial that condemned her daughter to death twenty-five years earlier. This perhaps unconscious allusion to *The Trial of Joan of Arc* suggests a way to consider the critical question of Mouchette's suicide, a context further embroidered in the woods sequence following the credits. Though not directly, both sequences prefigure the end of the film and anticipate the sentiments Mouchette's final act evokes concerning its meaning and intentionality. In recalling *Joan of Arc*, the shot of Mouchette's mother points the way, for it is in the light of that film, about a far more celebrated and revered virgin, that we can assess the ignominious course of Mouchette's life and the act that ends it.

The sequence that follows the credits is set in the woods bordering the village. Its point of view is established through close-ups of a man's face and eyes, but it is not until later that we identify him as the gamekeeper Mathieu. The situation begins in media res, compounding the already disjunctive nature of the framing and editing, which delineate isolated actions of spying, of the poacher setting the wire traps, and of the quails that approach, become ensnared, and struggle to get free. The poacher, later identified as Arsène, is also presented in fragments: the lower part of his body, his arms and hands as he sets the traps, and one eye as he watches the gamekeeper freeing a quail from a trap. That gesture too is presented as pure action, framing only the gamekeeper's hands removing the wire, holding the bird, and then releasing it.

The sequence is constructed through what have become familiar hallmarks of Bresson's style: isolation through synecdoche and point of view, zero-degree acting, the importance of hands, a singular focus on purposeful gesture and action, a critical rhythm dictated by editing, and a selective but pronounced use of sound. Although the sequence introduces two of the three men who have a bearing on Mouchette's life, the style accentuates their actions and the woods. Anticipating two other such sequences, the first one introduces the theme of entrapment, as a number of unwary quails walk into the wire nooses placed by Arsène and thrash about helplessly. In the last hunting sequence rabbits run about as gunshots ring out from all sides. In the middle sequence Mouchette is unwittingly ensnared in the encounter with Arsène that leads to her rape. In this way the woods and the struggle for survival that rules them become the model of existence against which Mouchette's story unfolds.

Unlike the second woods sequence, however, the first one also carries the theme of release, when Mathieu frees a quail and sends it aloft, a shot that may recall another image from *The Trial of Joan of Arc*: the doves resting briefly on the canopy after Joan's immolation and then flying off just before the empty stake comes into view. If in that film the soaring doves suggest that Joan's martyrdom is complete and that her soul has been released, in *Mouchette* another kind of release is suggested by the image of the quail that, like Mouchette, is set free from the trap into which it has stepped unwittingly. Unlike her predecessor, Mouchette is no *confidente* of God and has achieved no glory; hers is a friendless, unbearable existence, and her escape from it an act that can be said, paradoxically, to preserve her soul. Like Joan, Mouchette is also enfolded in a white garment of death after having worn gray throughout. And as the shot of Joan's mother reaches across time to reclaim her daughter, Mouchette dies in the hope that she will rejoin her mother. Bresson stresses the link between the pre-credits shot of Mouchette's mother and the final shot in the film by reintroducing Monteverdi's *Magnificat*, first heard over the credits just after the mother leaves the shot, and now heard over the image of the pond just after Mouchette has disappeared from view.

I discern in these first two sequences the initial signs of a tendency in Bresson to veil or obliquely allude to, through a variety of cinematographic gestures, Christian iconography and ideas within a narrative from which they are ostensibly absent. These are the kinds of things presented directly in *Les Anges du péché*, *Diary of a Country Priest*, *A Man Escaped*, and *The Trial of Joan of Arc*, even *Au hasard Balthazar*, the film immediately preceding *Mouchette*, given its Christological parallels. It is a tendency, I will argue, that accounts for the liturgical and biblical connotations of certain moments in *The Devil Probably* and that lends a similar cast to the narrative trajectory and audiovisual montage of *L'Argent*. As those referrals indicate, the instances of the tendency vary from specific iconographic or rhetorical material to the general structure of a film. For this reason, terms such as *figura* or *schema* would be limiting and misleading. It is the tendency itself that matters, allowing the possibility that it may not always be conscious and deliberate on the part of Bresson. Wherever the phenomenon seems present, in *Mouchette* and subsequently, I will refer to the relevant material as manifestations of an indirect strain in Bresson's discourse, more precisely, given the particular quality that marks it, as instances of *sacred indirection*, a phrase denoting that a religious aspect is being cited or alluded to but in an elusive, implicit manner.

In *Mouchette* the allusions to *Joan* that I have alleged can be detected in the pre- and post-credits sequences, both of them Bresson's invention. As examples of this sacred indirection, they are not immediately obvious on the denotative level, though they can reasonably be understood as the filmmaker's way of insinuating religious associations within a secular context, pointing to a meaning beyond what is apparent or given. In the case of *Mouchette*, the instances are allusions to the artist's own work, but this is not a precondition of the phenomenon. I consider the concept of sacred indirection to be a useful and justifiable means to characterize a tendency in Bresson's later work, but it is an interpretive strategy like any other and must ultimately be judged on the basis of its ability to illuminate the work.

To interpret the pre-credits shot of Mouchette's mother in terms of the pre-credits shot of Joan's mother is to superimpose on the former the gravity and religious significance of the latter and to seal the connection by way of such parallels as the mother-daughter bond, the virginity of both protagonists, the new garment with which they go to their death, and the symmetry of the beginning and ending of both films. In this way Joan's death, which she welcomes in lieu of total capitulation to authority and betrayal of what she believes, bestows a spiritual complexion on Mouchette's, which can be seen as the only means by which she can escape an equally oppressive milieu. The reading of the woods sequence is designed to reinforce this way of looking at the suicide: if the entrapment of the quail can be seen as analogous to Mouchette's situation, then its release, evoking the other allusion to *Joan*, can be seen as analogous to the aim and meaning of her act.

Although at the time he made *The Trial of Joan of Arc* Bresson could say, "I see her with the eyes of a believer,"[9] we cannot be certain what this belief imports about his faith or attachment to Catholicism, either in 1962 or at the time he made *Mouchette*. It must be stressed, therefore, that the impact, resonance, and usefulness of the tendency of sacred indirection and the associations it provokes depend entirely on their tantalizing elusiveness. To pursue them with the aim of pinning them down definitively would serve neither the aesthetic nor the thematic dimensions of this film, or any of the others where the phenomenon may be discerned. Indeed if, as I believe, such powerful chains of associations can be attributed to certain abiding convictions from the filmmaker's past, the residue, perhaps, of periods of faith—they must remain among the glancing though telling signs of a not entirely abandoned point of view. In response to an interviewer who made a distinction between Christian subjects and secular ones, Bresson said quite clearly, "For me, the entire universe is Christian. I do not see one subject as appearing less Christian than another."[10]

In the case of *Mouchette*, the associations linked to death, entrapment, and release allow such themes to resonate freely throughout the narrative and, in the end, to offer a framework, in the absence of the expository and qualifying prose available to Bernanos, for grasping Bresson's treatment of her suicide.[11] And as we shall see, the introduction of Mouchette herself in the next sequence speaks silently but eloquently to the general thrust of these readings.

Sound and Light: Ties That Bind

To weld the implications of the woods sequence to the life of the village, Bresson strengthens the filmic connections as well. Increasingly he uses sound not only to bridge sequences, but often to bind them closely. The transition from the woods to what follows is achieved through two succeeding shots of the gamekeeper: in the first, he emerges from the woods and climbs the embankment onto the road, a site subsequently associated with Mouchette as she hurls dirt at her classmates; in the second, he passes Mouchette on her way to school. The sound of Mathieu's boots as they first hit the pavement is startling, aurally marking the line between the woods and the town, and its continuance over the image after he exits frame right, reemerges in the following shot, and passes Mouchette establishes the school's proximity to the embankment. We do not yet know what, if any, link there will be between Mathieu and Mouchette—neither acknowledges the other—yet the succinctness of this narrative transition, the pronounced overlapping of sound and its precise establishment of place, register a calculation of consequence.

As if to mark both the *au hasard* quality of the brush with Mathieu and the aesthetic aspect of the moment, Mouchette's name is called out, presumably by one of the girls as she enters the schoolyard. The word itself, the first one spoken in the film, apart from the mother's pre-credits monologue, is less a greeting than a declaration, announcing the arrival of the main character. It is the first of many such calls that never seem quite forthright, that is, a simple mode of address with a single purpose, friendly or otherwise. In fact, it often begins as the former only to revert to the latter. Mouchette pauses, barely turning her head in the direction of the girl, and then looks off screen right, her head cast down (figure 47). Her distracted demeanor suggests that she is not as anxious to get to school as the others. But there is also in it a faraway, enigmatic quality, reinforced by the absence of a countershot to her off screen look, directed not toward the school, nor toward the woods from which Mathieu has just emerged.

Yet though we now see the film's title character, no connection is made between her and the preceding sequence or, for that matter, between her and the woman in church. Nor is this point clarified by what follows, for immediately after this shot, which leaves Mouchette standing outside the school, the film cuts to Mathieu arriving home, putting down his rifle, removing the wire traps from his bag, and remarking to his wife, "It's him again." Just before the fade-out, the camera closes in on the traps as Mathieu's wife, the only figure to manifest genuine concern for Mouchette later, picks them up as if she had some prescient sense of their link to the girl's fate. The shot fades in to yet another intricately designed sequence, set in the local bar, that also excludes Mouchette.

The delaying of the connection between the nominal protagonist and the narrative action is unique in Bresson's oeuvre. Mouchette is introduced between two important sequences, both of Bresson's invention, that on the surface appear to have nothing to do with her. Moreover, though her presence is fleeting, it immediately suggests a number of things. Contrary to the action in the woods and the social interaction in the bar, Mouchette's entrance connotes inaction and isolation. Unlike the active figures in the sequences before and after or the dutiful classmates who move past her, Mouchette neither moves with purpose nor engages with those around her. Her looks left and right hardly suggest an active or restless mind, although her demeanor instantly conjures pathos. Barely raising her head, she seems frozen to the spot where the film leaves her.

Her introduction not only raises the question of how and where she fits in—the very subject of the narrative—but it permits this single shot to stand out as paradigmatic of her difference, her misery, and her confusion. Standing on the sidewalk, passed on the left by a schoolmate and on the right by Mathieu, each purposefully pursuing opposing directions, she is caught between the world of adolescence and the unknown that beckons. Moreover her look tells us what the subsequent narrative will substantiate: that she has already experienced more than her share of the world's misery. And so, although the calling out of her name is what we hear, Mouchette's state and her sidelong look in Mathieu's direction as he passes suggests that there is another call that she alone hears, a vague sense of, and longing for, something that will free her from the life she knows. "The voice which Mouchette had just heard hovered in the air a long time, like a dead leaf floating interminably," Bernanos tells us in his first paragraph. That she does, in the end, heed that call, and that the confusing series of circumstances that will lead her to do so will involve the woods themselves and the man who has just passed, is both the moral and aesthetic rationale for this shot.

On a first viewing, the shot may be as easily overlooked as Mouchette herself, who we do not see again until after the bar sequence. As thematically focused as the woods sequence, this one brings together all of the adult male characters who affect Mouchette's life. It also stresses the leveling role that alcohol plays in their lives, a generalizing strategy reinforced by the repetitive style of framing and editing in the sequence. In short, although differences among the characters are noted, symmetry of design dominates. The fade-in is to a medium shot of Arsène standing at the bar, finishing a drink. Louisa, the barmaid, pours him another and tells him to go home. He drinks the second and then a third, after which he turns and leaves. In a reverse shot, Louisa says, "But come back again." As Arsène exits, he leaves the door slightly ajar (figure 48). The composition of this shot is repeated with the arrivals and departures of the next three men. The sound of footsteps precedes the arrival of Mathieu, who enters the bar from the same angle we saw Arsène exit and leaves the door ajar in the same position. He walks up to the bar just as Louisa removes Arsène's glass, seizes her wrist, looks intently at her, still off screen, and greets her by name. In a reverse shot, Louisa greets him more formally as "Monsieur Mathieu." He continues to stare at her as she fills his glass. As he drinks, we hear behind him and outside the sound of an engine. Mathieu's turn to look over his shoulder toward the door prompts a cut to the exterior.

A passage of seven shots develops a second line of action, connected to the first through the sound of the motor and the headlights of a truck. We see an exchange of shots between two men who have just arrived. About to remove something from the back of the truck, they are interrupted by two gendarmes in a police van, who pause momentarily, glance at the truck, then drive off. The men remove the canvas to reveal cases of liquor, which they carry into the bar. On their way out, they stop for a drink, are paid, then exit. As they do, they leave the door ajar in the same manner for the third time.

So uniform is the composition of that shot, seeming to follow the rules of framing and editing, that the viewer may fail to notice that Bresson has elided what has happened to Mathieu and Louisa, both of whom disappear from the scene. The proprietor's wife, whom we glimpsed at the edge of the frame in an earlier shot of Louisa, serves the last two men, and her husband pays them. The use of synecdoche makes it momentarily unclear who is filling the glasses, just as in a later scene the same technique makes us mistake Mouchette for Louisa behind the bar. Bresson aborts the first line of action in order to follow the second. We assume that during the visual exchange between the truck and the gendarmes outside, Mathieu has left, as Arsène did before him, and that, possibly, Louisa has gone with him. Such an aporia is not inconsistent with other phenomena in the film that are either confusing or mysteriously explained. This may be Bresson's way of placing the viewer in a position frequently occupied by Mouchette, who puts two and two together and gets five. The ultimate example of this is the sequence in the woods and the distorted account of what happens between Arsène and Mathieu that Mouchette comes to believe.

When the men who deliver the liquor drive off, the film follows the truck's headlights beaming and reappearing in the next shot as the truck, moving in a contiguous direction, turns into a driveway, illuminating the blackness of the night and the interior of a house, where we see Mouchette. She looks out of a window, then resumes tending to her mother (figure 49). A series of brief shots captures the family living situation. It is only when the two men enter the house that we realize they are Mouchette's father and brother. The former immediately collapses onto a mattress on the floor as Mouchette tucks in her mother's blankets, picks up the baby to calm him down, then assumes her own spot on the floor. As her father's hands and mutterings drunkenly mime the act of driving, Mouchette, who has still not uttered a word, stares ahead until the image fades out.

When this film was released in 1967, the narrative construction just delineated would have appeared far more unusual than it does today. But though we may be more accustomed to the delaying tactics of filmmakers, the economy and precision with which so many connections are made still warrant attention. From the moment Mathieu passes Mouchette on the road to the fade-out on Mouchette just cited, we hear only seven lines of dialogue, totaling, in the English translation, twenty-one words. Bresson has constructed the action and linked characters through his usual deft handling of cinematic properties: framing, editing, ellipsis, synecdoche, off screen sound, and light, the last functioning, in the form of the truck's headlights, as both an identifier and a transitional motif. This tightly woven interdependence of cinemato-graphic elements mirrors that of the action, so that a repeated composition, such as the one of the open door in the bar, becomes not only a form of linkage in space and time but one that erases the differences among the four male characters and renders their functions in the life of the village, and more immediately in that of Mouchette, virtually interchangeable. That the repeated shot should involve an open door in the local bar further emphasizes the common bond of alcohol in the lives of these characters. Mouchette's mother, dying of cancer like the country priest, uses gin to deaden the pain. Mouchette too is given a drink by her father after her Sunday shift behind the same bar.

Transitions in the movement from the opening woods sequence to the first view of Mouchette's house are more emphatic than usual. Both sound (Mathieu's boots on the pavement) and light (the headlights that take us from bar to house) are pronounced audio and visual signs that underline the unavoidable, fateful encounters between people and circumstances typical of small provincial towns. They stress the endurance of routine and the improb-ability of escape. With the prominent sounds of his footsteps, Mathieu carries into the town the rule of nature that prevails in the woods, a fusion Mouchette too reflects when she crouches by the same embankment and throws dirt at her classmates. Such contiguities are less metaphoric or metonymic than they are paratactic. It is as if Bresson had invested these particular transitions with a quality sufficiently intense to affect the way we perceive even the film's more conventional editing strategies, such as montage and shot-countershot, lending to all of them an adhesion both contained and enforced by the habitual undulations of provincial life.

Humiliations

The second day is relatively compressed but includes the only sequence in Mouchette's classroom. It is so strongly etched as to confirm her school expe-rience as a constant source of humiliation and the motive for her daily mud attacks on her classmates. As the other girls rush to get to the classroom on time, Mouchette lags behind. She stands out in her drab, sack-like dress and long black stockings. With his usual economy, Bresson conveys both the terrifying specter of a sadistic authority figure and Mouchette's rebellious reaction in a brief tracking shot and a single shot-countershot exchange between them. Because Mouchette is the last to enter the classroom, the sound of her clogs against the floor is especially loud, the camera tilting down to focus on them as she approaches her desk. A match cut follows as she maneuvers into her seat and looks up at the teacher off screen. She folds her arms like the two girls seated behind her on either side, but whereas they are clean and well groomed, Mouchette's hair is unkempt and her face barely washed. Nor can she disguise her frown. The cut is to a long shot of the matronly teacher behind her desk at the front of the room, her eyes fixed on Mouchette with a stare that could kill.

If Mouchette gets any satisfaction from turning her tardy entrance into a small racket that "drives the mistress wild," she soon pays a high price.[12] The face of the teacher dissolves to a medium shot of several girls standing to sing. Though Mouchette stands with them in the center foreground, she does not join in. The song is about Christopher Columbus encouraging his crew not to give up the prospect of finding land. "Have faith in hope; in three days, Columbus told them, pointing to the vast heavens on the horizon, three days and I shall give you a world." As they sing, the teacher enters from frame left, slowly walks between the girls, and stops directly behind Mouchette. As she leans over and notices she is not singing, the song continues, "You who have no hope. His eyes opened to see it." The teacher, now standing behind Mouchette to the right, grabs her neck and turns her head to face her, then with both hands violently pushes her forward and off screen left. As the girls, open-mouthed and undeterred, sing the lyrics "in the empty vastness," the teacher stands tight-lipped and scowling.

In a match cut, Mouchette in medium shot stumbles in from frame right toward the piano as the teacher comes in behind her, her left hand pushing Mouchette's head down over the piano while her right forcefully pounds the notes of the melody. "*Chante!*" she commands. Mouchette sings the melody solo, the words clearly known to her, but hits the last note of the phrase off-key.

Some tittering accompanies a reaction shot of the girls, standing as before, an empty place in the center where Mouchette had stood. At the piano, the teacher hits the key in question several times; Mouchette tries again, once more singing the final note off-key. More titters are heard off screen as the teacher relaxes her grip and Mouchette moves off and back to her position.

She resumes her place and sings with the group, her eyes cast down, and a third time misses the note. As the girls on either side look at her, a cut to the piano shows the teacher's hand impatiently hitting the right key amid random giggling. In the next shot Mouchette raises her hands to cover her tear-stained face and muffle her sobs.

As a demonstration of Mouchette's failure to fit in, the music lesson succeeds, even as the lyrics of the song itself, stressing loss of hope and perseverance, provide ironic counterpoint to her efforts. But though there are titters among the girls, the girls we actually see in the same shots as Mouchette are not reduced to stereotype. Some of them are similarly, though more carefully attired and even seem sympathetic, though reluctant to show it. Nevertheless when school lets out, Mouchette walks to the embankment and assumes her usual position, crouched in readiness to attack her classmates. However pathetic, her contempt is her only weapon; she uses it again moments later when one of the brewer's boys calls her and drops his pants, eliciting from Mouchette a disdainful snub that lends her a momentary air of dignity. When she finally arrives home, eagerly runs to her mother's bedside, and kisses her hand, we realize what a haven from the gauntlet of humiliation her mother and the hovel the family lives in represent.

When the film dissolves from the mother's bedside to the next morning, Sunday, Mouchette is singing cheerily to herself as she prepares coffee. Few moments so aptly and touchingly capture both her rudeness and her grace as her continuous movements over the four cups, first with the pot of coffee and then with a bottle of milk, deft and agile on the one hand, a bit clumsy on the other as the milk spills. In the same spirit of the child-woman, she proudly flips the top of the pot upward and it lands in place, a gesture she repeats later in the bar, when she throws a sponge behind her as she finishes work, and again near the end when she tosses the croissant the grocer has given her onto the counter behind her. These gestures, though performed with calculated "ease," awkward sallies into adulthood, also suggest, along with her stomping her Sunday shoes in the mud before climbing the stairs to church, the limits of Mouchette's protest. The futility of her actions is confirmed by her father's response to the last one, coming up behind her as he is prone to do and shoving her violently, much like her teacher, into the vestibule of the church.

All of the characters, except Mouchette's mother, are present in the Sunday sequence. The rivalry between Mathieu and Arsène over Louisa is further developed, setting the ground for the confrontation between the two men in the woods the next day. Mouchette witnesses enough of this to fill in the gaps of Arsène's story during their night together in the hut. The most affecting episode of the Sunday sequence is Mouchette's brief, aborted

50. A moment of joy before the slap.

51. The humiliating scratch exposed to the shopkeeper.

52. Mouchette hails a farmer in the distance.

53. Mouchette rolls down the slope to her death.

54. The marriage proposal at the zoo.

55. The husband places the wedding ring at dinner.

56. The husband watches his wife as she watches *Hamlet*.

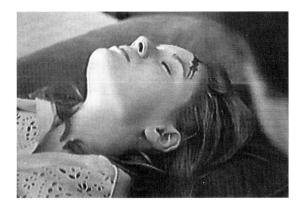

57. The pale body and the single red wound.

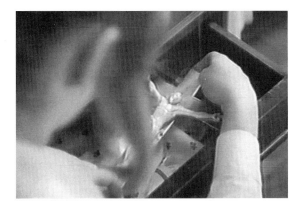

58. The wife gazes at the crucifix in a drawer.

59. The gentle woman's gaze in the mirror.

60. The wife just before she leaps to her death.

61. The wife's shawl descends after her leap.

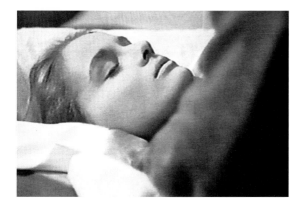

62. The husband bestows one last kiss.

63. Jacques hitchhikes back to Paris.

64. The first night along the Seine.

65. Marthe tells her story
to Jacques.

66. Jacques's "tears"
through the windowpane

67. Marthe sees her first
lover as Jacques gazes at
the moon.

68. An unidentified
knight receives a mortal
wound.

69. Lancelot greets
Guinevere in the loft.

70. Guinevere reminds
Lancelot of his vow.

71. Arthur, Lancelot, Gawain, and the fractured round table.

72. Gawain lights the way for Lancelot's return.

73. Lancelot approaches a cross out of focus.

74. Guinevere prepares for her lover.

75. Gawain, visor down, en route to the tournament.

76. A knight about to be unseated by Lancelot.

77. Arthur, Gawain, and crowd stunned by Lancelot's performance.

78. The dying Gawain forgives Lancelot.

79. The armored detritus of Medieval chivalry.

80. Alberte embraces Charles.

81. Charles muffles the sounds of falling trees.

82. Charles and Michel on the "devil-driven" bus.

83. The chaos of traffic in imaginary collision.

84. The psychoanalyst questions Charles.

85. Charles tampers with the doctor's art objects.

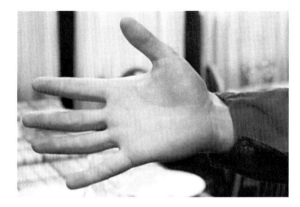

86. Yvon's hand after
shoving the waiter.

87. The first exchange:
Norbert receives his
allowance.

88. Elise visits Yvon in
prison.

89. Yvon raises the skimmer in anger.

90. Yvon meets Lucien in the prison chapel.

91. Yvon walks by a toystore.

92. Yvon's shadowy reflection amidst the toys.

93. The widow confronts imminent death.

94. Yvon surrenders to the police.

95. The unquenchable
curiosity of the mob.

96. The widow and Yvon
share a garden rite before
the murders.

flirtation with an older boy in the bumper cars. The ride is vigorously edited to suggest both erotic attraction and youthful exuberance, feelings of which we hardly imagined Mouchette capable. It is one of the occasional revelations that make us aware of the spirit of life that has been crushed. The sequence gives that impulse an especially poignant and hopeful cast before sweeping it away in a single harsh gesture. Several shot-countershot exchanges between Mouchette and the boy amid the furiously friendly collisions of the cars elicit enough smiles to warrant her following him like a puppy after the ride as he walks to a concession stand, encouraging her with a few over-the-shoulder looks. At the moment Mouchette walks up behind him and the boy turns, a reverse angle frames her in the middle ground as the boy, his back to the camera, stands facing her. No sooner does a smile begin to break on her face than her father appears out of nowhere, spins her around, and slaps her violently, instantly squelching her short-lived excitement (figure 50). The girl we mistook for a woman moments earlier in the shot of her tending bar until the camera tilted up to reveal her identity is once again reduced to a child, humiliated and punished for any gesture toward independence.

Rape, Shame, and Death

The episode in the woods on the next day is as extensive as it is in the novella, though not for the same reason. Bresson adds the fight between Arsène and Mathieu, but the erotic implications and ruminations of what's going on in Mouchette's mind leading up to the rape are gone. In the novella, even before she enters the woods, Mouchette wonders about Arsène's whereabouts and a short time later sees him "walking softly and carefully towards her, like some wary nocturnal animal." Arsène is a younger man to whose physical nature Mouchette is drawn, even to the way he walks and breathes. When they take refuge from the storm, he removes his shirt, and for a good portion of the scene "his naked chest gleamed like copper." When he "clumsily caresses her back and thighs" to see if she is dry, she is not alarmed. When he paces in the hut as he tells her what he thinks has happened between him and Mathieu, he has "all the ease of the wild animals in their cages."

Their encounter is characterized by furtive glances, tremors, and a confusion of feelings on her part. She is fascinated by his account of the details of his fight with Mathieu and how he may have killed him with the iron trap. His "seemed to be the first human face she had ever really looked at. Her attention was so absorbed and so tender that it seemed to be an extension of her own life. It did not occur to her to find Arsène's face handsome. It was simply that it seemed made for her." During his epileptic fit, she holds his head on her lap, caressing his face, and wiping foam from his lips as she sings. "If it had occurred to her then to kiss the forehead that her tumbled hair was gently touching, she would have done so. But the idea did not come to her. Her desire, like the warmth of her living body itself, was spread throughout her veins and not concentrated in any one precise image."

Bernanos makes it clear that Mouchette is lost in a reverie, overcome by feelings she thinks may be love, joy over her own voice, and recognition of her blossoming youth. It is when Arsène recovers and seems not to have remembered anything that she panics, fearing that the very confidence, intimacy, and trust that awakened her feelings are now endangered. When she reassures him that she will lie to protect him—"I'd sooner kill myself than do anything to harm you"—Arsène, with animal acuity, senses her vulnerability. "Why are you so scared of harming me?" he asks. She immediately detects a change in his demeanor, signaled by his "disembodied" voice, a "falseness" that she associates with callous youths. Animal instinct has taken over and he is driven by lust, but though "a word would probably have been enough to recall Arsène to his senses, no sound escaped her tight throat." He seizes her violently and throws her against the wall. She groans "for a moment," then "there was nothing to be heard in the shadows but Arsène's panting breath."

Bresson's treatment of this episode implies nothing of an earlier attraction between Arsène and Mouchette. He converts what is going on in Mouchette's mind into concrete physical gestures, among which the most articulate and expressive are, not surprisingly, her hands. Two instances in particular, not in the novella, condense the implications of Bernanos's prose. The first occurs when Arsène asks why Mouchette is so afraid of harming him. She stares dumbfounded as her schoolbag slips from her hand and falls to the ground. An example of how "hands show so much more than the eyes and cannot lie,"[13] the easy, involuntary release of the bag immediately exposes her emotional and physical pregnability. Instantly her face registers alarm that Arsène has detected her feelings, as well as fear of what she now sees has been aroused in him. As in the novella, she is speechless, helpless to say anything to abate the force that has been unleashed.

The second gesture occurs after Mouchette has fallen and Arsène overcomes her. At first she brings her arms up to shield her face, as if she were more afraid of being beaten, something Bernanos tells us her father did often. As her body is completely covered by Arsène's, her hands flail on either side of his back, the clenching of her palms more expressive of her childlike nature than any other gesture in the film. Then her two arms, inexperienced and hardly long enough, close over his back and cling to him. Each phase of the movement conveys both the helpless child and the desperate, needy adolescent. The evocative face of Nadine Nortier that has so compelled our attention throughout the film is here replaced by her hands. As if looking at them for the first time, we may be surprised to see how small and fragile they are.

Despite these images, Bresson underplays the way Arsène pervades Mouchette's thoughts and, but for one shot, virtually eliminates the erotic component of their interaction before the rape. That shot occurs when Arsène first stumbles on Mouchette in the woods and points his flashlight on her legs as she is putting on her wet stockings. But this implies an erotic interest on his part, not hers. This may be why the later shot of Mouchette clasping Arsène may surprise some viewers. His treatment stresses how utterly bereft Mouchette's life is of intimacy and companionship.

Given Mouchette's confused state of mind, her fantasized bond with Arsène, and her emotional and physical vulnerability, she does not experience the ill effects of the rape itself until later. Bernanos makes it clear that she did not feel any anger or hatred against Arsène because "in her child's mind the memory of that violence was somehow mixed with that of many others, and her reason could scarcely distinguish it from her father's savage beatings." She also has no illusions about losing her virginity, "the value of its surrender…unimportant to her." She does not tell her mother about it right away, and her sleep is restless. The most pernicious effects of the experience are an all-consuming shame barely concealed in her anger toward others. In the film Mouchette's late return home is noted by her mother but is quickly displaced by the woman's worsening condition and the need to tend the baby. Only later does Mouchette approach her mother desperate to unburden herself, but it is too late. In the morning, her father addresses her in his usual rude fashion, prompting her to rush out the door with her milk pail, directing a long overdue "*Merde!*" at him. As he does with similar provocations, Bresson allows Mouchette's anger to surface while the deeper blows she has been dealt remain unarticulated. Interestingly enough, this is not only in keeping with the limits of the model's expressivity, but is also an accurate rendering of how the adolescent experiences the death of a parent. Thus, the impact of losing the only person to whom she could confide her confusion and shame has barely registered when Mouchette has the encounter with the grocer, compounding the devastating experiences that already overwhelm her with one that could hardly be matched for its lethal effects on every front.

Bresson marks the encounter with the gravity it warrants through the most dramatic use of shot-countershot between characters in the film. (The bumper car sequence is more extended but has a lyrical quality.) If any sequence reveals the core of Mouchette's experience, it is this one, reflecting her fundamental situation and exposing both her vulnerability and the community's attitude toward her. It begins, innocently enough, with the grocer's inviting Mouchette in for coffee and croissants. She alludes sympathetically to her mother's death: "Don't worry. We all die someday." While Mouchette calmly enjoys what will be her last breakfast, the woman comes up behind her and places an extra croissant in her dress pocket. Startled, Mouchette turns briskly, undoing a button on her dress and revealing a large scratch on her chest (figure 51).

The intense shot-countershot passage at the heart of the sequence, sixteen of its twenty-six shots—eight of them of Mouchette, five of them of the grocer—begins with this shot. There is one shot of a customer, the object of Mouchette's glance off screen, and two of the cup of coffee as it teeters at the edge of the counter at Mouchette's sudden turn and then falls to the floor and shatters. The looks on each face in the passage in question could not be more explicit. The grocer's contempt is thinly veiled under the faintest of smiles, reminiscent of Hélène's in *Les Dames*. Mouchette's shame is converted instantly into a series of physical gestures: her quick clutching of her dress to hide the incriminating mark; her effort to button her dress; the disturbance of the cup that crashes to the floor. It is at this point that the grocer's initial kindness is revealed for what it was: a trap. Her cruelly rhetorical "What's the matter?" is followed by "Little slut!" Mouchette grabs her pail, turns to go, flings the croissant from her pocket onto the counter behind her, mocking the woman's charity, then exits the way she entered. Our last view of her in the street before she passes out of frame suggests that she has resumed her original path, as if only momentarily interrupted.

The scene condenses Mouchette's experience of life in the village. Whereas the rape is converted into a comforting lie in the scene that will follow with Mathieu and his wife, there is no appeal to the irreparable damage done at the grocer's. The structure of the sequence, moving from seductive compassion to sadistic rejection, subverts the maternal resonance it evokes, replacing the dead mother with the bad mother. This is reinforced by the milk pail Mouchette carries but that she never gets to fill, its emptiness a signifier of her mother's absence. The sequence is the human equivalent of the opening woods sequence. Mouchette enters the trap as unsuspectingly as the quail that walks into Arsène's wires. And like that sequence, this one, in the context of Bresson's economy, is an unusually extensive elaboration of a moment through a prolonged use of shot-countershot. It seems literally to clock the time required for Mouchette to take in the significance of what has happened, to fully discern in the face of the grocer the scorn and repulsion of the world and its merciless judgment at a moment when her defenses are at their weakest.

Apart from words, the sounds that accompany the whole sequence are those of Mouchette's clogs, the rattling of the milk pail, the bell that tolls every few moments—four times in all—and the shattering of the cup that replaces its solemn regularity. Like Thérèse's overturning of the soup wagon and Agnès's dropping of her wine glass, it shatters the false composure of the moment, displacing and expressing Mouchette's inner rage. The bell tolls again later, when Mouchette accepts the dress from the old woman, and again as she approaches the wood.

Back on the street she exchanges looks with the older women entering the church. Are they going to pray for her mother's soul, or are they exchanging vicious gossip about her? Is the bell that tolls just the summons to mass, or does it toll symbolically for one about to die? Her humiliation continues when the brewer's boys shout "rat face" as she passes by, and the visit to Mathieu and his wife further confuses her. There, realizing that her shame has been exposed, she tries to escape its effects by defiantly declaring Arsène her lover. At her last stop, the old woman's line that the dead are the only ones past inflicting unkindness is more than timely. In her discourse on the dead, she asks Mouchette whether she has ever thought about death herself, strengthening the appeal it seems to have for her. In the earlier woods sequence, Mathieu had disentangled the quail from the wire and sent it flying into the air. Mouchette's release will come only with death.

She pauses near a group of trees as she hears shots ringing out and sees rabbits scurrying in all directions. The next twenty-nine shots are crosscut between several hunters firing rifles, rabbits running through the clearing, some getting hit, and two of Mouchette standing in place. One rabbit struggles to get up in two shots, then dies to another tolling of the bell just as Mouchette, who has run to see it, looks down at its body. What is also striking about this sequence, which surely recalls the hunting sequence in Renoir's *Rules of the Game* (1939), is the presence of unidentified men who play no part in the narrative but allude to the existence of a different class from what we have seen throughout the film, a species entirely remote from Mouchette's world that nevertheless uses the same woods to hunt.

As she turns and walks off screen, there is a cut to the place where she herself will die, a lovely slope with a tree on the left and a body of water below, a scene dappled with sunlight and suffused with tranquility. Mouchette unwraps the package from the old woman and holds up the dress, which immediately catches on a branch and tears. As she looks to the right, there is a cut to a closer view of the embankment nearer the water with a small bush at its edge, an image accompanied by another tolling of the bell.

Wrapping the dress around her clumsily, she slides down the slope, then rolls and comes to a stop as we hear the sound of a tractor. She stands, walks forward, and raises one arm as if to call out (figure 52). In a reverse shot we see the tractor passing in the distance, its driver looking back briefly in her direction. As she turns to walk back up the slope, the bell tolls again. She lies down, clutching the dress in one hand, and rolls to the left in three shots (figure 53), landing just at the edge of the pond against a bush, its fragile branches a sign of the thin line that exists between life and death. We hear another tolling of the bell. She walks up and repeats the action almost identically, this time rolling down in two shots, after which we hear the plunge of her body, now off screen. The final shot shows us the splash still in progress and the dress clinging to the bush as Monteverdi's *Magnificat* returns and continues over the fade-out. The shot has a curious optical quality whereby the continuous flow of the water is arrested, gently surging back and forth in a loop-like fashion. Though death has claimed Mouchette, the cinematographic immortalizes her, replaying her final moment as if to enlist nature in the sacral ritual invoked by the *Magnificat*.

True to the novella, the manner in which Mouchette's final act is presented leaves room for ambiguity about her frame of mind. But whereas Bernanos elaborates on this and conveys the confusions and intricacies of her thoughts even up to the moment she lowers herself into the water, Bresson, lacking the luxury of the novelist, creates a more abrupt effect in his elliptical treatment. If the actions of his characters in general are a fusion of fate, will, and chance, Mouchette's cannot be viewed as a suicide in any other but the technical sense, especially since, as an adolescent, she has an immature concept of death. Her acts of rolling down the slope might even be construed as a game, an expression of these ambivalences suggesting both conscious aim and a plea to contingency. Maybe she'll make it, maybe not, and maybe another distraction, such as the farmer passing on a tractor, will deter her. One critic cites the end of Rossellini's *Flowers of St. Francis*, when the brothers "spin round and round to make themselves giddy," resigned to go out to preach the gospel in whatever direction they face when they stop. Mouchette's rolling down the hill is also a submission "to the world or fate...a similar physical, accepting act," which "though suicide...is also life-enhancing," like the scene in Rossellini.[14]

But game or not, and notwithstanding her bragging about being Arsène's lover, we cannot underestimate the annihilating effect of shame that ensues from the rape, an experience aptly described by Dostoevsky in *Demons*. The character Stavrogin is haunted by his violation of Matryosha, another fourteen-year-old girl, who hangs herself in a chicken coop afterward, an act he fails to prevent from fear of exposure. Her shame for having given in to the sudden desires aroused in her by his inappropriate caresses is so great that she believes she has "killed God." Stavrogin cannot erase the image of her waving a disapproving finger at him moments before she kills herself, accompanied by a look of "despair such as was impossible to see in the face of a child."[15] Like Mouchette, Matryosha is so regularly abused by adults, physically and otherwise, that she seizes on the intimate attentions of a less threatening individual, mistaking them for affection. The projection of unbearable guilt into a grandiose fantasy of deicide expresses the utter abjection that leads to the need to annihilate the self.

Somewhat differently Melanie Klein suggested that the person who commits suicide aims not only to murder his or her bad internalized objects but also to preserve his or her "loved objects, internal and external."[16] From this perspective, in destroying the part of her overwhelmed by shame, Mouchette also protects the part of her capable of love and compassion—as we saw in her caring for her mother and her cradling of Arsène during his fit—and of course her desire to be reunited with her mother, before these too are destroyed by exposure to the cruelty of others. It is perhaps the fusion of inner, incomprehensible states that drives Mouchette and removes from her act any taint of sin. Indeed since the text of the *Magnificat* is the canticle of the Virgin Mary in the Gospel according to Luke (1:46–55), it lends both dignity and salvation to Mouchette, particularly since the passage we hear is relevant to her situation: "He hath put down the mighty from their seats, and exalted them of low degree."[17]

In expanding the story, Bresson increased its duration from twenty-four hours to ninety-six—Mouchette dies on the morning of the fifth day—so that it does not correspond to the three days of the song sung in class or to the passage from Good Friday to Easter Sunday in the Christian analogy. In the spirit of sacred indirection, however, the associations such a congruence would have with the Passion, death, and resurrection of Christ do not seem entirely unrelated to the Trinitarian cast of Mouchette's far more modest via dolorosa, particularly the three visits she makes before entering the woods and the three times she rolls down the slope. Both of these are Bresson's invention, as are the earlier instances of the three shots of the door in the bar, stressing the commonality of the three men in Mouchette's life, and the three gestures of flipping things behind her.

It is difficult not to see the sequence from the moment Mouchette enters the woods as a replay of the final sequence in *Au hasard Balthazar*. As

Mouchette stands under the trees watching the hunt, we may recall Balthazar onthe morning after he is shot, just before he climbs the hill to gaze at the horizon before his death. The shots ringing out around Mouchette multiply those of the customs guards as Balthazar stands awaiting the bullet that will hit him. But whereas the earlier film stresses the distance between a crippled and petty human nature and the presence of the divine, *Mouchette*, lacking any such redeeming figure, seems to confirm the rule of the animal in human nature, an impression one has reading the novels of Zola. In *Balthazar* Bresson gives us a powerful, moving allegory of Christian redemption, only to withdraw it, one might argue, at the last moment, somewhat like the Eucharist offered and then denied Joan. In *Mouchette*, where the more explicit signs of the sacred are aural—Monteverdi's music and the church bell that tolls for the living and the dead—it seems no one is capable of recognizing the value of such an offering.

7

Dostoevsky in Paris

Bresson's next two films are adaptations of Dostoevsky novellas. Although these are the first to acknowledge his debt to the writer, it should be evident by now that Dostoevsky is an abiding presence in Bresson's work, discernible well before any official adaptation.[1] The narratives of both artists are crisis-driven, with characters on the threshold of some grave situation that tests their mettle and requires a difficult choice. Death is rarely the natural end of a normal life cycle in either Dostoevsky or Bresson; it is usually premature, often violent, sometimes the result of suicide.

But whereas Dostoevsky expounds at length on the inner conflicts of his characters and the contradictions that can erupt at any moment, Bresson, through the juxtaposition of shots and gestures or through the use of ellipses, projects a moment of sudden reversal without warning. At such points his models give physical form to the mercurial nature of character; on a dime, Marie (in *Balthazar*) turns from fondness to contempt in response to Jacques's renewal of his marriage proposal. The abrupt shift of the interior expressed outwardly has great force largely because it elides the kind of acting that in conventional approaches would register the nuances of anguish and turmoil that would lead to outward expression. The viewer's familiarity with that kind of acting (e.g., of the Stanislavsky school or the method), closer to Dostoevsky's style,[2] is why many people find it hard to appreciate Bresson's approach.

I would argue that the insight into human psychology that lies behind Dostoevsky's work is also key to Bresson's aesthetic, and that Bresson's reading of Dostoevsky is itself about getting to the core, to that extraordinary *volte-face* of the soul that can change everything. Dostoevsky's psychological leaps resemble the formal jolts in Bresson. Certainly this is true of characters who manifest internal conflict, like Michel in *Pickpocket*, or who seem oblivious to their own flaws and limitations as they narrate, like the husband in Bresson's adaptation of Dostoevsky's "A Gentle Creature." A similar trait in a less dramatic, more satirical mode is discernible in both Jacques and Marthe, the leading characters in *Four Nights of a Dreamer* (1971), Bresson's adaptation of Dostoevsky's "White Nights."

The two films discussed in this chapter are the only ones of Bresson's to give extended attention to the subjects of marriage and romance. *Une femme douce* (1969) is a cynical view of the former, and *Four Nights of a Dreamer* a parodic treatment of the latter. Made back to back, the former is a tragedy, the latter an amusing gloss on the fickleness of romantic love. Bresson compounds these impressions by setting both tales in late 1960s and early 1970s Paris, *the* stereotypical romantic city and the one often likened to St. Petersburg, the setting of Dostoevsky's stories.

The presence of St. Petersburg in "A Gentle Creature" is reflected in the quasi-desperate circumstances of the young girl that lead her to marry the narrator, mirroring the atmosphere of impoverishment and oppression that Dostoevsky evokes in his novels and diary entries. It could not be more different from the image of Paris in the films, a ravishing counterpoint to the misbegotten nature of the characters' lives. Specific sites bring the city into play with the action—the Champs Elysées, the popular Left Bank café Les Deux Magots, and the zoo in *Une femme douce*; and the glittering *bateaux mouches* that move languidly down the Seine in *Four Nights of a Dreamer*.

Une femme douce

For the first time, in *Une femme douce* (*A Gentle Woman*) color introduces an interesting counterforce to the increasing darkness of Bresson's films. The tracking shots of nighttime Paris under the credits pulsate with the lights of restaurants, bars, theaters, and traffic along the Champs Elysées. At least two images in the film—a pan of the Paramount Elysées marquee, a spiral sculpture in the Museum of Modern Art—seem shot solely to indulge in the rapturous glow of golds, reds, and yellows. Paris looks as vivid as it does today, an impression that underlines the classic nature of Bresson's world. But dazzling as it is, color lends a more melancholy aspect to the story.

Une femme douce is his last film of the 1960s, the decade of the female adolescent in Bresson's work, all of whom die tragically, two explicitly and one perhaps through suicide. As it is also Bresson's only sustained narrative about a marriage, it may tempt us, in retrospect, to read the endings of *Les Dames du bois de Boulogne* and *Pickpocket* more cynically, although the couples in those films have already survived a crisis of trust, whereas the one in *Une femme douce* embarks prematurely on the wrong foot. In fact, the wife's situation in the film might have been the fate of Marie (in *Balthazar*) had she left the provinces and married Jacques, whose proposal disgusted her. The husband's banal view of marriage in *Une femme douce* is no better, completely at odds with his wife's needs, which he fails to understand. Marriage for the "gentle woman" is little more than a bourgeois trap, no less killing to the soul than the traps laid by Arsène were to the bodies of unsuspecting creatures in the woods in *Mouchette*.

Unlike the first-person narratives of the 1950s, the film makes use of flashback reconstruction, although Bresson refutes this. Even *A Man Escaped*, which recounts events that have already occurred, unfolds and is experienced in the present tense. The narrator of *Une femme douce*, however, is not the title character, and though scenes alternate between a present and a past, they do so in a manner that blurs the line between the two. The reasons for this will be elaborated further on. For now, I note that they involve a major change in Bresson's style as a result of color. Previously transitions between sequences were achieved through fades and dissolves, so that even when the sound of a subsequent sequence was heard over the present one, as in some of the transitions in *A Man Escaped*, *Pickpocket*, *Au hasard Balthazar*, and *Mouchette*, it was brief and usually accompanied by one of these optical devices. They are abandoned beginning with *Une femme douce*, primarily because the visual tonalities of fades and dissolves are difficult, if not impossible, to control in a color film. Along with them, Bresson also stopped using extradiegetic music, like that of Mozart, Lully, Schubert, or Monteverdi, to bridge sequences.

In place of these staples of his previous films, overlapping sound becomes the dominant transitional device between sequences and in many instances assumes a critical structural role. Like the films before it, *Une femme douce* continues to strike a balance between continuity editing and elliptical passages. It would be hard to exaggerate the effect of its stunning opening sequence, the most Bressonian to date. Comprised of four shots, it "depicts" the suicide of the young woman of the title with neither the model's enactment nor a representation of the action itself, but in purely cinematographic and elliptical terms, making the most of sound and off screen space, the two features that continue to rise to prominence in Bresson's aesthetic.

"A Gentle Creature"

The whole trouble is that I am a dreamer: I was quite satisfied to have

enough material for my dreams. As for her, she, I thought, could wait.

—Feodor Dostoevsky, "A Gentle Creature"

The inspiration for Dostoevsky's story was a newspaper account of "a young woman who jumped to her death while holding a holy icon of the Virgin Mary."[3] Dostoevsky sought for a way to include the incident in a narrative and found in his notes a "long standing fascination with the figure of a 'usurer'—the base epitome of an egoistic selfishness excluding any concern for others."[4] Initially he published it in his *Diary* and subtitled it "A Fantastic Story," an allusion to its form, "neither fiction nor biography." "Imagine a husband whose wife only a few hours earlier has killed herself by jumping out a window; her body now lies on the table before him. He is in a state of bewilderment and still has not managed to collect his thoughts. He paces through the apartment, trying to make sense of what has happened, to 'focus his thoughts.' He is, as well, an out-and-out hypochondriac, the sort who talks to himself." And so he is talking to himself, telling the story, and trying to *make it clear* to himself.[5]

The fantastic element of the story, says the author, is that it seems as if a stenographer were taking everything down in shorthand and he were just editing it. Technically, the story is a prolonged soliloquy, although one can imagine the narrator's discourse transposed into one of those ensemble scenes typical of Dostoevsky's big novels, in which characters expose their basest transgressions to a horde of listeners, transforming a social gathering into a scandalous event. There is always a listener in Dostoevsky, real or imagined, whom the narrator assumes is judging him. Since the reader is addressed as the listener in the case of "A Gentle Creature," it reads more like a dramatic monologue, as astute and ironic in the creation of its narrator's character as Robert Browning's "My Last Duchess" or "Fra Lippo Lippi."

The situation, as well as the voice of the husband, though, is quintessential Dostoevsky. The narrator's irresistible urge to probe his psyche and confess to the world is matched only by a narcissism that qualifies, if not precludes, any genuine insight. He tells us at the outset that he already "understands everything," but it's not long before the reader realizes that all his wrangling self-examination amounts to a desperate effort to ward off the loneliness to which his last line attests: "When they take her away, what's to become of me?" In other words, it is debatable whether his ruminations really produce a true epiphany. The "gentle creature" remains as much a mystery to him as she was at the beginning, although the reader may have more reason to conclude that her suicide was, at least in part, a response to living with such a self-absorbed man. The narrator is an example of a type, found in many of Dostoevsky's writings, that struggles, in this case unsuccessfully, with the dialectic of love and egoism.

He is a forty-year-old pawnbroker with a checkered military past when he marries a young female customer, fifteen years old when they meet,[6] in part to "rescue" her from a "filthy" arrangement her aunts are about to make with a fifty-year-old widower with children to rear. He is struck at first by the minor items that she pawns and her shy, awkward manner. "She was so delicate and blonde, a little taller than average," but the "main impression, the synthesis of everything [was] that she seemed terribly young," a fact he repeats frequently yet fails to appreciate when he assesses her behavior. There are hints even before the marriage of his teasing and defensive manner, as when he tells her he is "part of that Power which still doeth good, though scheming ill," words used by Mephistopheles to introduce himself to Faust. And when he confesses himself a "cheap egoist" with "highly unpleasant qualities," he does so with pride, presenting himself as her deliverer. Though she agrees to marry him, he imagines her hesitation to be about choosing the lesser of two evils.

From the start he is willfully immune to her "sweet chatter of innocence" and "delight" in speaking of her childhood, "pouring cold water on all her raptures," responding with silence to her "transports." He imagines this sternness makes him an "enigma," declaring it his "trump card." It soon becomes clear that silence is his weapon of choice. "I have spent all my life speaking without words. I have lived through whole tragedies without uttering a word." He wants her to "discover him by herself," expecting the "fullest possible respect." Nowhere do we sense that he is overcome with love or passion. While he acknowledges the generous spirit of her youth, he attributes it to "inexperience," suggesting that among other things such innocence and promise is a reminder of his own failures. And so they do not speak, even while going to or returning from the theater. To her furtive glances he becomes even more withdrawn. And to her "outbursts of affection" he is cold, characterizing them as "morbid and hysterical." Yet he is surprised when her "gentle face" seems insolent and he becomes "loathsome" to her. This blindness reflects another, more insidious one in that the sadomasochism inherent in his use of silence is never overcome or replaced by genuine love.

The husband attributes most of his differences with her to his being a pawnbroker, a demeaning profession in Dostoevsky's work, and though he refuses to defend it to his wife, he feels compelled to do so at length to the reader: "I had a right to open the pawnshop. You have rejected me, you—the people, I mean—have cast me out with contemptuous silence. For my passionate desire to love you, you have repaid me with a wrong from the consequences of which I shall suffer all my life. Now I have a right to erect a wall against you, to save up the 30,000 roubles and spend the rest of my life somewhere in the Crimea, on the south coast, among the mountains and vineyards, on my own estate... far away from you all, with malice against none, with the woman I love at my side, with a family if God will send me one."

The contradictions and blindness in the character, typical of the "genuine underground type" described by Dostoevsky in his *Diary*, are apparent in many such outpourings. That a man bent on putting a wall between himself and "the people" should be capable of living in peace with anyone without bearing malice is a grand delusion. And of course the irony of his having constructed this wall in his own home and enacted the very same punitive silence against the woman he allegedly loves escapes him. He justifies his behavior by concluding that *she*, in her "ignorance of life and the cheap convictions of youth," is the "pitiless tyrant and torturer" for being blind to his "noble soul."

The Self Psychology View

Desire which refuses the Other is only a simulacrum of itself; it is not itself if it is not Other.

—R. A. Shoaf, *Dante, Chaucer, and the Currency of the Word*

Although many of Dostoevsky's narrators give the impression that they are fully aware of the psychodynamics of their relationships, to which a psycho-analytic reading might add very little, in fact, the opposite is often the case.

The portrait of the husband in the story is a compelling example of a specific type of narcissistic disorder that continually needs affirmation and that *uses* people, in the phrase first conceived by Heinz Kohut, as "self-objects."[7] From the self psychology perspective, a person afflicted with this disorder suffers from an early emotional and psychological deficit, caused, it is theorized, by inadequate mirroring from parents or other caregiving figures. This failure of interpersonal recognition during the critical years, when emotional and psychological structures are formed, impedes the development of a stable ego, often freezing it at a certain stage. Such a person grows up lacking an adequate sense of self and is compelled to look to others around him or her as potential suppliers of what is missing. These others, imagined extensions of the earliest caregivers who failed to provide what was needed, are experienced not as separate beings with identities of their own, but as missing parts, or objects, of the impaired self. Since this is a doomed project, the self, in constant need of replenishment, is always in search of others—as opposed to the Other—not for their individual qualities but for how they can fill up internal psychic and emotional emptiness. Rather than fully recognizing the otherness of people in the manner required for genuine relationships, such a person seeks people—or objects or forces—only to the degree that they can buttress or validate aspects of the inadequate self.

In Dostoevsky's novella, and in Bresson's film, a typical sign of a person ruled by this need is the husband's astonishment at any manifestation of his wife's independent reactions to his behavior. After he castigates her for issuing large loans to customers and insists it is his money, he describes her response: "All of a sudden—what do you think?—she stamped her foot at me. She was a wild beast. She was in a rage.... I was petrified with amazement." His shock is less about whether her behavior was appropriate than that she manifests a willfulness that suggests she is a separate being and therefore indifferent to her "real" role to fulfill his needs. The very fact that he married such a young, unworldly girl speaks to his need for someone he can mold to conform to his requirements and endorse his delusive self-image. He "saw clearly that he had to train [her]...to add the final touches to her, even to conquer her." He acknowledges, "She was the only human being whom I was developing for myself."[8]

Both the novella and the film provide evidence of the husband's past narcissistic injuries. In the novella he was dismissed from his military regiment; in the film he was fired from a bank. In both cases, he claims he left voluntarily, innocent of all accusations, after which he fell into poverty for a number of years. "No one anywhere ever liked me," he remarks.[9] In the novella, becoming a pawnbroker after such a fall is the height of humiliation, although he must inflate his occupation above such reproach since it must repair the injury to his pride. In the film there is more than a little sarcasm in the wife's declaration that as a pawnbroker, he has become a "financier" all the same.[10] These blows to his ego reveal a weakness of character consistent with the passage cited earlier in which he wails about how the world's rejection will force him to live in isolation. Such wounded egoism is consistent with his sadomasochistic character.

These insecure features in turn lead to his tendency to control everything, forbidding his wife to go anywhere without him. In retaliation she tries to humiliate him by meeting with a former regiment colleague who reveals that her husband was dismissed from the regiment for refusing to fight a duel and then spent several years begging in the streets. Suspecting infidelity, the husband takes a gun and spies on his wife but learns that she is faithful even though she does not return to his bed. In a characteristically fantastical scene, she picks up the gun herself and holds it to his temple while he feigns sleep even though they have fleeting eye contact. He concludes that in proving that he was not a coward, he has "conquered her" forever. From here the marriage deteriorates and the wife falls ill for many months until one day, he says, "the scales" fall from his eyes and in a sudden ecstasy he rushes to her, falls at her feet, and kisses her. She is reduced to tears when he vows to sell the pawnshop and take her away.

Her reaction prompts him to realize that he has completely misunderstood the situation. "She believed that she'd always be sitting at her table and I at mine, and that the two of us would go on like that till we were old. All of a sudden I came up to her as a husband and a husband wants love. Oh, how blind I was! Oh, what a frightful misunderstanding!" When she vows to be a faithful wife, he kisses her passionately, "like a husband for the first time after a long separation." Almost immediately after this, the housekeeper enters the room just in time to see her standing on the windowsill, then leaping, holding the icon of the Virgin.

In the last two pages the husband reveals that he would do anything to bring her back, even if it means renouncing his privileges as a husband and allowing her to take on a lover. Some literary critics find this a genuine turnaround in the husband's character, and it is supported in part by the sweeping nature of his decision to confess all to her, to admit that his motive for marrying her was to stave off the loneliness that consumed him. Yet such behavior is not inconsistent with the narcissistic personality from the self psychology point of view, which in desperation can assume a masochistic and servile posture. One can read his sentiments at the end as no less selfish than they were earlier, and that what he really mourns (not unlike the character of

Charles Foster Kane, who pleads with his wife not to leave him) is the loss of the person he needs to replenish the deficits of his flawed personality. And so although the story is a moving, eloquent discourse on how one deals with the suicide of someone close, is haunted by it, reliving, regretting, and revisiting every moment in search of understanding, there is also evidence that the narrator's erratic behavior and isolation from others made his sudden, extreme declaration of love and worship, as he himself intimates, frightening and overbearing to her.

Marriage and the Self: Objects in Conflict

Dostoevsky's story gave Bresson the opportunity to explore marriage and its effects on the integrity of the individual, a subject virtually absent from his other work. As the few prior examples of married people in his work—in *Diary*, *Balthazar*, and *Mouchette*—indicate, his view of the marital state was skeptical, an attitude unlikely to have softened by turning to Dostoevsky for inspiration. Marriage, as several of Ingmar Bergman's films demonstrate, is the severest testing ground of the relationship of self and other, its success possible only if a measure of selflessness and sacrifice—not idolization, not martyrdom—continually negotiates the two.

Bresson saw the story as an example of how a marriage disintegrates when two people understand each other too well.[11] Yet the situation he creates not only differs in a fundamental way from that in the story but is also loaded to begin with. The husband in the film resembles Dostoevsky's controlling narcissist, but the wife is not identical to the young girl of the story. She lives in impoverished circumstances from which the husband, like the one in the story, wants to free her, but she also expresses serious doubts about marriage as an institution, compatible with views of contemporary women in the late 1960s. In addition, by casting actors (Dominique Sanda and Guy Frangin) who seem compatible in age, level of maturity, and physical attractiveness, Bresson has made the young woman more susceptible to seduction. Her behavior on their wedding night is anything but inhibited.

As far as understanding goes, the husband comes to certain realizations only after her death. Just before it, when he resolves to close his business, take her away, and worship her, she responds, "I want something else." This is not clarified and, as in the story, seems incompatible with her promise the next morning, the day of her death, that she will be a faithful wife. When he embraces her, he seems oblivious to her emotional distance. So the understanding

Bresson alludes to is more of a misunderstanding; the wife knows that he will never quite grasp her doubts and fears, and the husband is convinced that as long as he worships her, everything will be fine. It is a tragedy of misunderstanding, made even less necessary because Bresson collapses the distance between their ages: the wife, when she first arrives at the pawnshop, is "about" sixteen and the husband in his mid- or late thirties.

For all the woman's mysterious air and failure to expound on that "something else," we assume that it would contradict the conventions and expectations of middle-class marriage—something she had warned him about when he proposed—especially his need to idolize her as pure and virginal. Bresson appears to share her fears, staging the proposal at the zoo, where a monkey leaps about freely but within the confines of a cage, a metaphor for the woman's sentiments. Her suitor in turn swings from bullying pleas to shallow idolization.

For example, against her wishes, he follows her into her apartment building, and on the staircase reiterates the proposal in the tone of a spoiled, tyrannical child. In his *"Dites oui. Dites! dites!,"* one can hear Erard in the cemetery at Rouen badgering Joan with his relentless, *"Révoque, révoque!."* The tone and delivery have the same effect on both women: they give in only to regret it. On the other hand, when the husband apologizes for the night he followed her and found her with another man, he concludes that he was wrong to suspect her, that she is innocent, an assessment that makes her sob uncontrollably. In other words, he ranges from demanding compliance at one extreme to obsequious deference at the other.

At the zoo she says that marriage bores her, that she wants something more. Yet as soon as she closes her apartment door in the staircase scene, we hear the first words of the justice of the peace, "You have given your vows," and the remainder, "I now pronounce you man and wife," over the subsequent shot of the woman, now wife, standing in place looking off screen right in the direction of the speaker. Behind her stands Anna, the housekeeper. Only when the camera pans left as the wife walks to a desk do we catch a glimpse of the husband's suit as he takes a pen and signs the marriage document, then hands it to her. From the beginning the marriage is presented as a legal agreement entered into by a young, acquiescent woman and a very insistent man whose presence at the ceremony is linked to its off screen and official apparatus, validating what she tells him at the zoo: "You don't want love. You want me to agree to marry you" (figure 54).

This sense of the couple as an arrangement is reinforced in the next sequence. As soft piano music begins over the shot of her signing the marriage contract, the cut is to a close-up of a table in a restaurant set with wine glasses and bread. From frame left the husband's right hand reaches in to the center to meet the wife's left hand, entering from frame right (figure 55). After he places a ring on her finger, each hand withdraws, followed by the husband's placing a ring on his left hand by himself. As he picks up a glass of wine, a match cut shows him facing her and is followed by a reverse angle of her. Without words or smiles, each holds a glass and looks into the other's eyes. Then a waiter blocks the foreground, concealing the cut to their arrival at the building where they will live above the pawnshop.

After a wordless embrace, she runs up the stairs into the apartment, into the bathroom, and then to turn on the television; she runs back to the bathroom, draped in a towel, then to the husband on the bed, then back to turn off the television—at which point, the towel falls and we see her nude back briefly—and finally she climbs into the bed. The whole time she runs with brisk little steps, humorously echoed by the black-and-white images of racing cars on the television, the entire effect suggesting that she is capable of joy and excitement. In the bed she giggles and bounces under the sheets. Bresson takes the husband's line in the story that he "poured cold water upon all her raptures," which referred to her "chatty" enthusiastic way of talking about her childhood *before* their marriage, and places it over the shot immediately following this uninhibited delight on the wedding night, a scene that does not exist in the story. The image of their cavorting under the sheets cuts directly to a shot of their apartment door as his voice-over says, "I quenched this elation," a line reminiscent of the duke's words—"I gave commands. Then all smiles stopped together"—in response to his wife's overfriendly manner with other men in Browning's "My Last Duchess." In the shot of the husband in the present that follows, he adds, "Why did we take to silence from the first?"

His question corroborates what we have seen, but he does not connect it to his prior remark, which suggests that the problem between them turns on this very dissonance: her youthful excitement versus his Old World reserve. Their attendance a bit later at a screening of *Benjamin* (1968), a banal French period movie, speaks to the point. The scene is a view of bourgeois society sprawled across a lawn as the young libertine, Benjamin, approaches, gazing at the spectacle as an endless prospect for sexual and social conquest, the opposite of the wife's image of marriage as a cage. The threat is immediately transferred from the movie to the couple in the audience as we discover that a young man is about to make knee contact with the wife, forcing her to change seats with her husband.

Outside she embraces her husband, perhaps out of fear of the temptation the stranger embodies. As they enter their car, we hear the husband's voice-over in the present say, "I was sure then that she loved me, or wanted to love me, or wanted to love," his search for the right phrase indicative of his insecurity and failure to understand how she thinks. He admits he suffers from incessant jealousy, wondering constantly where she is and what she is doing. In the meantime, when she is not working in the pawnshop, we see her looking at books, listening to records, and eating pastries, occupations that seem more about her desperation to fill the time than a passion for any one thing. Yet her perusal of natural history and art books, followed by their visits to museums devoted to both, imply that she brings a broader interest in culture to the marriage. On the other hand, her abrupt shift of moods, randomly replacing a pop record with a classical piano piece, suggests restlessness and an inability to concentrate, although her attention during a performance of *Hamlet* seems to contradict such an impression.

Bresson places the viewer in a position similar to the husband's, making the prospect of understanding "the gentle woman" the question posed by the narrative. For example, although we grasp her theoretical resistance to marriage, there are few clues to her true nature. During a jaunt in the country, she picks a bouquet of daisies, but after spotting an affectionate couple in another car with the same bouquet, she cries, "We make a pair, too, all built into a pattern," flinging the flowers out the car window. Being a couple, in other words, even, perhaps especially, a couple in love, means to conform, a distinct threat to the freedom and uniqueness of the self. The film's way of countering that threat is to render the woman mysterious. Even in the final scene, when we see her apart from her husband's memories, Bresson sustains the impression of an almost impenetrable personality through a provocative juxtaposition of contrasting images, which I will discuss later.

In a sense the woman's behavior could be construed as typical of young people of the time, rebellious against social norms but uncertain about what they want in their place. She discloses no definite ideas or plans, nor are her actions driven by idealistic aims. Most of her assertive gestures are stereotypical. She overpays customers for pawned objects because she feels sorry for them, and when her husband confronts her, she rebels at his attempt to control her with money. At best these are the sentimental gestures of an immature personality, just as the opposition between culture and money to define them is reductive. Yet the husband in the present is shocked that her "gentleness was replaced by defiance, revolt." Calling him a coward, she runs off for the day, returning just in time to make it to the theater, where they have tickets for a performance of *Hamlet*. When he asks where she's been, she is evasive, leaving a cloud over the entire evening.

The excerpt from *Hamlet*, like the one from *Benjamin*, contrasts dramatically with Bresson's aesthetic, and no doubt both are included to highlight this difference, exemplifying the kind of acting and the kind of cinema alien to his own. It is the final scene, in which the king's sinister plan to kill Hamlet via Laertes' envenomed foil goes awry, resulting in the stage full of dead bodies that usually closes Shakespeare's tragedies. Shot primarily in long take with a few cut-ins that barely disturb the continuity of the action, the excerpt consumes a dozen shots, interrupted by six cuts to the wife apparently absorbed in the performance. The most obvious point of difference is that between the stage acting and Bresson's radical ideas about film actors. To stress the point, he has the wife run to the bookcase at home and open a copy of the play to the passage of Hamlet's instructions to the players not to overact, a scene cut from the performance, she complains, to allow the actors to "bellow." It is clear that she voices Bresson's ideas about acting, although watching her during the play we would never guess that she was unimpressed.

But the scene goes on too long for it not to have further relevance. I take my cue from Bresson by citing another key scene from the play not included in the film. Consumed by dark thoughts, Hamlet knows that the king and queen have set the naïve Rosencrantz and Guildenstern on him to observe and report on his moods. To convey the futility and insult of their efforts, he offers Guildenstern a recorder and insists that he play it. Guildenstern refuses, admitting that he knows not "the touch of it" and "has not the skill." "Why, look you now, how unworthy a thing you make of me," says Hamlet. "You would play upon me, you would seem to know my stops, you would pluck out the heart of my mystery, you would sound me from my lowest note to the top of my compass; and there is much music, excellent voice, in this little organ, yet cannot you make it speak. 'Sblood, do you think I am easier to be played on than a pipe?"[12]

The wife is no Hamlet, yet the sentiment captures the dilemma her character poses to both husband and viewer. While he sits behind her during the play, unable to see her reactions, we can see her face plainly, though it remains inscrutable, her expression unchanging. In all six cuts to her during the performance, her reactions might be read as intense involvement or as disinterest. Only her failure to applaud at the end is telling.

On the one hand, the sequence is a miniature demonstration of the automaton-like demeanor of Bresson's models, intensified through its juxtaposition to the conventions of theatrical acting. On the other, the wife's lack of expression suggests a deep, inner reaction to the situation in the play, in which she locates some aspect of her own situation. The play, among other things, is about male potency at its extremes: the king's brutish resort to murder and Hamlet's righteous course of revenge. The classic conundrum for scholars trying to understand Hamlet's procrastination has often revolved around what lies between, that is, his cultured, reflective, ultracivilized nature, which proves too thoughtful in the clinch. Forced to resort to the way life's game is played by those who make the rules, his crisis may seem familiar to *la femme douce*, just as his final plea to Horatio to "draw thy breath in pain to tell [his] story" might appeal to the paradoxical need of the willfully mysterious person to be, in the final analysis, understood.

Perhaps her reaction to the "bellowing" of the actors, then, is also a reflection of her "gentle," oversensitive nature and her resistance to overbearing men. It would seem that Bresson has nicely ensconced the wife's vulnerable psyche within a general observation of the difference between theatrical acting and what he demanded of his models, concealing her psychology within the question of aesthetics. Since this speaks as much to her as it does to Bresson, who chose to cite the quintessential text about Oedipal rivalry and the struggle of conscience to determine the course of moral action, it raises another question concerning the possible conflation between the character of the gentle woman and the artwork Bresson has made around her.

After the theater she continues her silence about her whereabouts earlier in the day, behaving, the husband's voice-over remarks, "as if nothing had happened." Nevertheless following an exchange of erotically charged glances as she lies in her bath, they make love. In fact, the husband's remark that he "sought only the possession of her body" implies that he makes no effort to understand her feelings and thoughts, that any real intimate knowledge of her was beyond him. This drives him to intensify his sense of ownership. Jealous of her attentions to a man who has made three visits to the shop, he suspects infidelity. Everything becomes an excuse to quarrel. When he grabs her and demands to know who sent her flowers, she pushes him away and leaves with the words, "It is not possible now." With a gun in his pocket, he waits until dusk at a rendezvous spot and sees her talking with someone in a car. Although the few words he hears are "to her credit," he demands she come home. This is the first night she does not sleep beside him; it is climaxed by the incident in which she takes the gun he has left on an end table and aims it at his face as he pretends to be asleep.

This is a turning point. He purchases another bed: "[It was proof] that I had seen, that I knew." He imagines this gives him more power over her, and that his refusal to act to protect himself counters her suspicion that he has done something cowardly in the past. Perversely he leaves the gun on the table to torment her; then, when she becomes feverish, he reassures her that he is alive. Thereafter they sleep separately. Soon she falls ill; for weeks she is nursed by the housekeeper and reduced, in his eyes, to a "beaten, humiliated" creature for whom he feels pity along with a "certain satisfaction." "I enjoyed our inequality," he admits.

It is clear from such remarks that the husband's deluded sense of self depends on the wife's humiliation. Like the man in Dostoevsky's tale, he can thrive only at her expense. Any attempt she makes toward independence must be squelched. As it does in the story, this pattern changes when he is astonished to hear her singing to herself. "In my house? Has she forgotten I exist?" He runs upstairs to verify what he has heard, then rushes out of the building and has a moment of revelation, covering his face with his hands. "I did not pity her. It was something else," his voice-over says. "No one would understand my feelings of rapture." The viewer may well ask, What is it that has so transformed him? Does he see in her the pitiable gentle creature whose rebellious streak has been crushed? Is this a moment of genuine sudden reversal, like the one at the end of *Les Dames du bois de Boulogne*, when the husband brings his wife back from the brink of death?

On his return he pours out his heart in words no less about himself than about what preceded his revelation. He blames his behavior on "a man's foolish image of a woman. I wanted to take, not give.... But I shall give you all, make a paradise for you." It is difficult to know from her stare whether she is relieved, confused, or startled, although like the viewer she may be all three. "I want to believe in you," he continues, "to be proud of you through utter faith. I love you. I want you." With this, he goes to his knees and embraces her legs, then picks her up and carries her to the bed. "Don't torment me," she cries, as he reassures her that he will sell the shop and they will go away wherever she likes. "And I was thinking you'd leave me," she says, words that his voice-over in the present says "pierced [his] heart." When he insists that contrary to her fears they can change completely, that their quarrels and unhappiness will disappear, and that he will adore and worship her, she merely responds, "I want something else." He cannot fathom this nor comprehend why his love is not enough, adding that he misjudged her innocence when he suspected her with the other man. He seems to miss her visible wince before she cries.

No doubt the overbearing nature of the husband's "good" intentions and irrational expectations lead to her resolve the next morning that she will be "a faithful wife," that she will respect him. He embraces her "like a husband after a long absence," then goes off to a travel agent, as his voice-over questions his decision to leave her at that moment. Why? Did he, in fact, hear the clear tone of unhappiness in her words? He certainly does not seem to realize that his newfound love is no less controlling and suffocating than the proud and punitive attitude he assumed following the gun incident. Typical of one in need of a self-object, he hears only what soothes his wounded narcissism: that she has promised to respect him and be a good wife.

That she cannot live with the compromise she has made becomes clear in the final sequence, in which Bresson offers us, contrary to Dostoevsky, tantalizing suggestions of the thoughts that preoccupy the woman's mind immediately before she leaps to her death. Before this sequence is discussed, however, the film's aesthetic dimension will be considered since it has a direct bearing on the husband's concept of the wife and the role it plays in the last scene.

A Bridge of Sound

Not surprisingly, in his first extended use of a flashback structure, Bresson reinvigorated this convention just as he had all others, no doubt prompted by the nature of the narrative. Present and past seem to bleed into each other, creating a continuity of gestures, spaces, and moods knitted together by voice-over narration and a pronounced overlapping of sound between sequences, most frequently that of the husband's footsteps as he paces back and forth near the body of his wife. We experience a sustained *filmic reality* that qualifies the separation between present and past by creating a dialogue between them that stresses continuity over disjunction. Figuratively speaking, every cut to the past revives the wife in a manner that both grants and mocks the husband's wish to reverse time and bring her back. This is consistent with his reverie in the last few pages of the story, in which he says he would promise anything—to whom, we might ask, since he is alone—if only she were alive again.

In response to an interviewer, Bresson denied that there are any flashbacks in the film.[13] Trying to explain such a "perverse" assertion, one scholar suggests that he must have meant that "the images of the marriage are not being filtered through the husband's subjectivity,"[14] which, given Bresson's aesthetic, must be necessarily true. Whereas we are trapped at every moment in the Dostoevsky by the consciousness and language of the narrator, Bresson avoids such an impression in two principal ways. The first is the use of overlapping sound between sequences and time periods, a strategy he employs here really for the first time. The second is the physical presence of the wife, both ethereal and sensual as incarnated by the exquisite Dominique Sanda, which exerts a power of its own consistent with our impression of her in the sequence just before her suicide.

The significance of this moment, not witnessed by the husband, is in direct contrast to the many instances of the husband's staring at her. For example, there is an elaborate ten-shot sequence of exchanges between her image in the rearview mirror of the car and his as he gazes at her. We also see him looking at her at the performance of *Hamlet*, during which, in one of those reaction shots, he is seated behind her, watching her as she watches the play, a notable example of his need to keep the self-object constantly in view (figure 56). In the car she asks if it is not dangerous to drive so fast and so close to the car in front, and just as he dismisses this, he is forced to come to a screeching halt to avoid ramming the car in front. It prefigures the final scene by suggesting that the real danger is how obsessive idolization leads to disaster. This sequence strikes me as a perhaps unconscious allusion to the more literal "look that kills" sequence in Cocteau's *Orphée*—also, in part, a study of narcissistic love—where the protagonist's allegedly accidental gaze meets his wife's (Eurydice) in the rearview mirror of a car, thereby causing her death. Perhaps Bresson had his friend and former collaborator in mind and was paying homage.

But there is more to the questions raised by the flashbacks and subjectivity. The difficulties of transposing into cinema a work of literature in the first person are compounded in a case like "A Gentle Creature," in which the reader has every reason to question the reliability of the narrator. As his films of the 1950s demonstrate, Bresson was acutely sensitive to the challenges film poses to the restrictions of the first person. Filming a story with an unreliable narrator would constitute a dichotomy for Bresson because it would require creating an ambiguous filmic reality, in which the integrity and truth of the image would be in question, a phenomenon entirely incompatible with his approach to the medium and his concept of the model. So when he says there are no flashbacks, we must examine what he has done, cinematographically, to reconcile the narrative with his aesthetic.

The first and most obvious strategy is that he provides a listener for the narrator, eliminating the "fantastic" element alluded to by Dostoevsky, whose narrator speaks to himself. Unlike the story's Lukeria, Anna, the housekeeper, kneels or stands by her late mistress's body for most of the nineteen sequences in the present, speaking barely a word until near the end, as the husband ruminates, often addressing her ("you") rhetorically to verify a particular memory. There are moments when the nearly blank expression on Anna's face suggests volumes about whether his recollection or impression of a certain point is accurate.

Second, the past is immediate, not only because the evidence of it, the wife's suicide, has just occurred, but also because her inert body is actually before us in the present. She is as vivid a part of the mise-en-scène as she was while alive, dressed in the same familiar way and, not coincidentally, an ironic "listener" to her husband's efforts to understand her, less a contrast to than a continuation of the silence that prevailed between them. And because he speaks in the frame of mind he has only recently assumed, with renewed hope for the marriage, his efforts to comprehend an action that has confounded his expectations belie a continuation of that mind-set as it directly confronts a negating reality. It is this intradialogical continuity that the film's structure mimes.

The sounds of the husband's footsteps as he paces around the body mark the dividing line between temporal zones, while his narrating voice exhibits a tonal continuity that blurs that line. It is more immediately involved in what we see, as opposed to the more detached, quasi-omniscient timbre of a conventional flashback voice, and helps to sustain the material impression of the filmic present. When we hear his voice over an image of the past, it seems as much an interior monologue *belonging to* the past as it does a reflection about it after the fact.

His footsteps are what we hear most often to alert us that we are with the husband as he paces the room, as if softly returning after an excursion into the past. But there are also instances in which the same sound from a past scene begins early and overlaps into the present, as when the steps of the "gentle woman" and her classmates leave the university. And there are instances when sounds other than the husband's steps alone continue into the present, as when the sound of the couple walking through a museum carry over into the space of the room where the dead body lies. By not employing the overlapping sound of footsteps exclusively as a return to and therefore a sign of the narrator's present, the film refuses to concede narrative dominance to those moments or to that narrator. Past and present fall under the law of the film's narrator, Bresson. The overlapping sound helps to sustain a sense of continuity that mirrors the narrator's frame of mind and figuratively mimes his traveling back and forth between past and present, itself a powerful analogue for how the past is often a vivid, ongoing aspect of the present.

This continuity is not limited to the use of sound. As events move closer to the end, that is, to the present, Bresson uses the simple rules of spatial continuity to enforce temporal continuity. For example, in the present, the husband, addressing Anna, recalls that during his wife's recovery from an illness Anna "put her in that chair." As he speaks, he walks out of frame left, and the next shot, framed as a match cut, is of the wife entering from the left into the identical space and being placed in the chair. Continuity is more easily evoked when the past involves an action that occurred in the same room.

Another way of sustaining temporal fusion while evoking enough of a distinction to suggest a dialogical relationship is the way passages from the past seem directly responded to in the present. As she lies ill, the husband tells his wife that he will sell the shop and they will go away, at which point she averts her eyes with what seems a feeling of guilt or shame. Almost simultaneously, and consonant with the viewer's perception, the husband's voice-over in the present says, "I didn't realize then that she was ashamed." As this implies that the preceding image of the wife is an objective one, it confirms that the narrative is not mediated by the husband's subjectivity. It also reinforces what we already know, namely, that the husband missed many clues to his wife's personality, which the viewer discerns over and above his narration.

A more elaborate example of this interaction is the sequence in which he finds her in the car with another man. As they drive home, he mulls over her behavior: Was the "redeeming" dialogue he overheard motivated by her having seen him in the rearview mirror, or was she honestly rebuffing the other man's attentions? His doubt induces an interruption of the sequence, a twenty-second return to the present, in which he looks directly at her body as if to seek conclusive evidence, comparing what he felt at the time with what he feels now. As the sequence resumes and the ride home is completed, he decides that indeed she was faithful to him. While this seems to underline the self-probing dimension of the husband's discourse, consistent with Dostoevsky's method, it has an uncanny and dual effect in the film. On the surface, it places the husband on the same plane as the viewer in relation to the construction of the past: neither is in a superior position to assess what is on the screen. But by looking to his wife's dead body for reassurance concerning a possible act of past conjugal betrayal, he not only lends further credence to the blurring of past and present, but he enacts the most extreme example of the narcissistic personality for whom the other is a self-object. It is as if he can draw even from her mute dead body the response he needs without fear of contradiction or humiliation.

As these examples indicate, Bresson used a variety of means to undercut the kind of rigid boundary that often characterizes a flashback. In doing so, he found a way to solve the credibility problems that ensue from such a narrative. By validating the images of the past, to which the husband must look, along with the viewer, for an explanation of what has happened, he escapes the problem of the unreliable narrator and the more serious ontological problem of having the viewer question the veracity of the filmic world.

A Gentle Palette

If the young wife is a self-object for the narrator in both Dostoevsky's tale and the film, Bresson also makes her an aesthetic object, translating the "otherness" of the one being used as a self-object into cinematographic terms, thereby analogizing the husband's suffocating idolization. In doing so, however, he also brings her vividly to life. She even governs the color scheme, the soft pastels of the decor—greens, grays, yellows, browns, tans—that complement her fair complexion and the way she dresses. We might be tempted to call such a palette bloodless but that it has a beauty and vibrancy that is easily over-looked, much like she whose raptures have all been quashed. This palette has been meticulously orchestrated with the color of blood in mind, since red is used in a very calculated way. It is not seen in most of the decor, on walls or furniture, or in the clothes people wear, with the exception of the vivid royal garments worn by Claudius and Gertrude in the scene from *Hamlet*. Yet red appears throughout, usually as a relatively small patch on the left or the right or in the corner of the frame, or in something passing in the street beyond the pawnshop: a jewel box, the edge of a book, a lamp, a pattern in the carpet, the panels of an Oriental screen, the lining of a raincoat, a passing car or truck, the taillights of a vehicle, the edge of a blanket, a traffic sign, a corner of a painting. Rarely more than a fleeting swatch or an oval or square of vividness, it nevertheless stands out against an otherwise harmonious blend of recessive hues and pastels. This design takes its cue from the recurring image of the wife's dead body lying on the bed, paler than usual and dressed to match, but with a single, small blood-red wound on her forehead (figure 57). In fact this captures the sense of the last pages of the story: "How thin she looks in her coffin! How sharp her little nose has grown! Her eyelashes lie as straight as arrows. And nothing was crushed in her fall. Not a bone was broken. Just that 'handful of blood.' A dessert spoonful, I suppose. Internal hemorrhage."

The spots of red throughout the film echo this handful of blood on the sidewalk after her fall. Bresson keeps alive the image of an intactness barely but fatally bruised, as if she were not only a physical body but an objet d'art like so many others in the mise-en-scène. As we shall see, it is not the only stylistic touch that seems designed to lend "the gentle creature" an aesthetic aura.

The Question

No one likes to recognize himself as a stranger in a mirror where what he

sees is not his own double but someone whom he would have liked to have

been.

—Maurice Blanchot, "Michel Foucault as I Imagine Him"

In the final sequence of the film, Bresson offers to the character of the wife, and to the viewer, something Dostoevsky does not: a privileged moment during which she seems to weigh, internally and silently, her feelings, her situation, and, as it turns out, her options, before she steps onto the balcony and leaps to her death. The sequence is free of the narrating voice-over heard throughout and, except for Anna's two brief intrusions, is without dialogue or an eyewitness. It is the only sequence in which the wife's presence is unmediated by the voice or observation of another, although, as implied earlier, the shots of her at the performance of *Hamlet*, unseen by the husband who sits behind, seem equally private. Like those shots, the final sequence may be ultimately unreadable, despite the fact that Bresson marks its significance with several images, intrascenic and filmic, that seem to vie for prominence in any speculation on what determines the wife's decision. Entirely of his devising, the sequence both enlightens and confounds, suggesting clues to what goes on in the wife's mind, but in so doing, rendering her character and her decision more ambiguous.

The images that produce this paradoxical effect include a mirror reflection, the first in Bresson's oeuvre that can be said to actually impute conscious awareness on the part of the one who looks,[15] and what must be the most extreme close-up of a face in any Bresson film. Both gestures place the very notion of image front and center. In addition there is the image of the crucifix that the wife fondles before quickly hiding it away in a drawer when Anna makes one of her appearances. Against these three actual images, we should place the figurative image of the husband's suffocating, idealized view of his wife, in which, as argued earlier, she can be understood as his self-object. As such, she would remain not only unknown but also, in effect, unseen.

Before analyzing these images, let us consider how the wife's situation might reflect Bresson's viewpoint. Judging from the virtual absence of a positive image of marriage in his work (the couple at the end of *Les Dames* have barely embarked on it), the "something else" the wife wants in *Une femme douce* would seem to convey Bresson's disenchantment with the marital state, at least at the time he made this film. If marriage is a cage, as the proposal at the zoo would suggest, in which one is required to fulfill the fantasies or ideals of the other, there is little chance for the self to grow, to learn in fact what constitutes the self. In Bergman's work, the agonistic engagement with the other is dissected through language, at times even physical combat. No such confrontation seems possible in *Une femme douce*; neither the wife nor the husband is secure enough to understand their differences, much less thrash them out. The husband's solution to their dilemma is simply to move from calculated distance to a no less controlling adulation. Indeed the most cynical sign of Bresson's judgment is that the transformative meaning of the last-minute changes that characterized earlier films has here been inverted. In *Les Dames* Jean recognizes the hollowness of social sanctioning as a direct, if ironic result of Hélène's monstrous scheme. The genuineness of his feelings is measured by his ability to call Agnès back from the brink of death. At the end of *Pickpocket* it is Michel's renunciation of his insulated, narcissistic posture and acceptance of his need for love that allows him to see Jeanne for the first time. By contrast, the husband's presumed change in *Une femme douce* does not result in greater self-awareness or genuine recognition of his wife's needs. Without considering for a moment what they might be, he immediately reverts to his former strategy of deciding for the both of them what they must do to save the marriage: go away. His behavior does not move outward to invite her in from her isolation, but exactly the opposite: by making her ungrateful, it reinforces her sense that obedience is required, setting the stage for what will be her only way out.

I have suggested that the husband's image of her as a self-object is what she had to escape. His approach in the penultimate scene complicates and compounds this. Like the punishing parent who suddenly forgives and showers love on the errant child, he puts her into a terrible quandary. A characteristic theme of Dostoevsky's is that nothing exerts greater antipathy than not being able to repay with equal fervor and sincerity those who presumably do everything for us, those who would love us to death. It is an unbearable weight that, for a young and inexperienced person, is compounded by ambivalent feelings of gratitude and guilt. Despite her vow to be faithful, therefore, the wife cannot tolerate the thought of the endless project of sustaining her husband's idolization. Perhaps for her, as for Antigone, according to one scholar, "Freely chosen death is a primordially feminine reply to the loquacious inhumanity or imperception of men."[16]

How do the images noted above bear on these conditions? Let us begin with the first of the actual images that we see: the crucifix she caresses at the beginning (the fourth shot) of the final sequence. In Dostoevsky's story, the religious icon the girl pawns and later takes to her death is a small statue of the Virgin Mary holding the baby Jesus. In light of the husband's remarks about her naïveté, it is unclear whether they have actually consummated the marriage, a possibility that would give the icon a special relevance. In fact, the husband's sudden insistence on asserting his matrimonial rights may be one motive for the girl's suicide. In changing the object to a crucifix, Bresson eliminates the virginal association, perhaps in light of his couple's unambiguous embrace of sexuality. But in the context of the final sequence, the crucifix may be more relevant in that, in addition to casting over the sequence the shadow of Catholicism, the teachings of which proscribe suicide, it also carries associations of sacrifice, suffering, and redemption more readily at odds with the action the wife contemplates. Since at the time the woman pawned the crucifix, before the marriage, she showed no interest in keeping the Christ figure when offered, as opposed to the gold on which it is mounted, it is unclear not only why the figure is once again affixed to the gold cross, but also why, at this critical moment, she should be gazing at it and then hiding it as if it were an object of shame. This is especially curious as there is no clear evidence in the film of religious faith on the part of either character; the marriage, for example, is a civil ceremony.

How should we understand the woman's handling of the crucifix, the shot of which is from a slightly high angle, over her shoulder as she sits at a desk against the wall (figure 58)? The angle is telling for two reasons: first, it is one of several shots in the sequence that stresses intimacy purely by virtue of the physical closeness of the camera, nestled up to the right side of the model's head, cheek, neck, and shoulder; second, the angle and closeness serve to preserve the wife's need for privacy as she strokes the crucifix in the drawer. In the medium shot that precedes this, she is seated at the desk looking down into the drawer; in the medium shot after Anna enters the room, the wife quickly closes the drawer, rises from the chair, and stands against the desk as if guarding a treasure. Unlike the shots around it, then, the over-the-shoulder shot has a self-consolidating quality, in direct contrast to her intuitive sense of being a self-object. This feeling characterizes several shots in the final sequence, in which the camera seems almost attached to the wife, all but fusing with her body and point of view.

We can only speculate about her state of mind. Does her caressing of the crucifix imply a skewed embrace of its connotations of selfless love and sacrifice? This would be compatible with her recent resolve to be a "good wife" and her renunciation, presumably, of that "something else" she said she wanted. More cruelly and perversely, does she imagine herself a martyr whose death will haunt and therefore punish the husband forever? Is this her version of Hamlet's revenge? Is the crucifix a last-minute appeal to a faith she may have had and lost? Is it perhaps a family heirloom? And is her need to hide it out of fear that Anna would intuit her intentions, or embarrassment to admit such a nostalgic longing? That all of these may apply suggests that Bresson believed that a person contemplating suicide is beset by conflicting thoughts and ambivalent emotions. Yet that the woman also seems to have come to terms with a self that insulates her and eludes us is strongly indicated by the way Bresson presents the other key images.

Before we see those images, the wife assures Anna that she is "happy" and "reconciled" with her husband. Anna, however, is no more convinced than the viewer as she reluctantly leaves the room and reappears at the French doors moments later for another check. In the interim, the wife goes to a bureau and removes a white shawl and throws it over her shoulders, white on white. She walks over to the bed and sits, holding to the brass railing, her head resting on her hands. When she rises and walks off frame left, the cut is to a close-up of the middle of the balcony door from the outside, which we see her approaching, mid-body, from inside the room. At the doors, her right hand turns the knob from inside, partly opening the doors, only to close them immediately and stand with her back against them. She walks back to the bed, the camera following as it did before, but this time she leans over the railing, then turns and looks off screen left. Recalling the film's opening, we realize that these movements measure her hesitation to end her life.

In contrast to the movements is the cut from her walking off screen in the shot just cited to another extremely close shot of her mid-body as she enters the frame and sits, it seems, directly against the camera, as if joining an invisible companion that has been awaiting her. The closer she comes to the final act, in other words, the more elliptical is the cutting. Her head is at three-quarters in close-up within the frame and seen from a slightly high angle. She looks off left and up, and then smiles faintly and enigmatically. The cut is to her mirror reflection, a medium shot of her framed like a portrait within the borders of the mirror, and at another slightly tilted high angle so that the floor of the room and the bed behind her are visible (figure 59). This is followed by a return to the close-up, her head up but with her eyes cast down. In effect, this is a shot-countershot exchange, not between the woman and someone else, but between her and her mirror image. As such, her smile before the reflection, though brief and slight, connotes a number of things: a friendly greeting to a stranger she has only begun to know, or reacquaintance with a self she has had to hide from view. There is no hint of the kind of internal division mirrors are often used to imply in the classical cinema, and no sign of self-loathing or despair. If, in contrast to the sacrificial love connoted by the crucifix, the mirror reflection evokes the self-love of the narcissist, this too is difficult to affirm.

Her exit from this shot cuts immediately to the extreme close-up of her face as it emerges from the French doors onto the balcony, eliminating the short passage from the chair just occupied to the doors. The doors open, as if automatically, the one white vertical border we see moving across her face like an optical wipe, allowing the outdoor light to fall slowly and fully onto her face (figure 60). This has a presentational effect that enhances its uniqueness as a filmic image. In this last view we have of her alive, her face is framed to isolate her from the appurtenances of the life she leaves; her mouth is close to the edge of the lower frame and her forehead extended to the upper frame, her hair framing both sides. Her gaze is steady and direct, forbidding rather than inviting scrutiny of her serenely composed face. Like the intactness of her body, her face conceals an equally intact mystery, an "internal hemorrhage," perhaps, in Dostoevsky's phrase, that neither the husband nor the viewer can fathom. The sense of the camera's increasing closeness to the woman, first in the over-the-shoulder shot as she touches the crucifix and then in the shots in front of the mirror, culminates in this startling image that nearly fills the frame, as if to hypostatize the state of mental exclusion that the determined suicide is thought to inhabit. The shot might even be said to contradict Bresson's insistence that an image not dominate at the expense of the ones before and after it. But if any situation suggests an absence of *rapport* with what comes next, it would be the act of suicide, for which the extreme close-up would be an appropriate filmic analogue.

We should not assume that in giving the woman and the viewer this privileged final sequence, Bresson intended to explain her action any more fully than did Dostoevsky. If anything, he renders it more ambiguous by providing conflicting clues to her state of mind. In other words, despite what we know about the husband, and even if my reading of the way he used his wife is correct, he is not wholly responsible for her suicide, and she is not simply a victim. But because this is the fourth film in a row that ends with the death of the female protagonist, in this decade devoted to female protagonists, and because at least two, arguably three of them are suicides, it behooves us to examine the treatment in that context.

As opposed to the earlier films, the suicide in *Une femme douce* "occurs" not once, but twice—another unique gesture of Bresson's—since it opens and closes the narrative. And although we do not actually see the act, its filmic conjuring is more emphatic than the suicide in *Mouchette*, which was clearcut compared to the vague allusion to Marie's fate in *Balthazar*. It would seem that the less ambiguous the act, the more pronounced is Bresson's aesthetic treatment. In *Une femme douce* the suicide is the occasion of two of the most memorable passages in his work: brilliant fusions of editing, ellipsis, sound, color, and off screen space. In the beginning, as Anna opens the French doors, we see an action painting in progress: the balcony's table and objects in midcollapse, the chair on which the wife stood still rocking, and the white shawl floating against the sky and the building (figure 61), suggesting both the solidity of the body and the weightlessness of the spirit that has just left it; screeching brakes are heard, after which cars and people, and the body itself, appear on the pavement. In its replay at the end, again there is the toppling furniture, the sound of off screen braking cars, and the shawl, this time floating against the sky only, its shifting curvature resonant of the shoulders on which it has recently lain, followed by the cut that instantly transfers its descending whiteness to that of the inner lining of the coffin (figure 62). If the *Magnificat* heard over the image of the pool in which Mouchette drowns bestows an empathic blessing on her life, if not her act, the wife's action in *Une femme douce* is redeemed by Bresson's art—a suicide by virtue of the cinematographic, through which, in effect, he steals her from the husband, removes her from the demeaning status of self-object, and saves her from a bourgeois marriage.

The three positions of the wife's movements (the dresser, the bed, and the balcony) as well as her hesitant gestures (the first attempt onto the balcony, her two brief passages to and from the bed), parallel Mouchette's three rolls down the slope. But a more significant link between the two characters, and between them and Marie, is the sense of shame that afflicts them. Marie is overcome by shame following her final humiliation at the hands of Gérard and his thugs and disappears from the narrative without explanation. Mouchette brags that she is Arsène's lover in order to obliterate her mortifying exposure at the grocer's. The wife's shame is more subtle: it is not only the result of her near infidelity and the gun episode, but the fact that she consented to marry in the first place, betraying her desire for independence. This suggests another, less conventional reading of the crucifix, or more precisely, of the figure of Christ, whose significance for Dostoevsky was that he represented moral freedom.[17] In replacing the statue of the Virgin and Child with that of the crucified Jesus, Bresson invokes the unorthodox implications of Dostoevsky's Christ in the service of his own embrace of Christ's significance. Redemption begins to assume a darker hue in Bresson's world, for however disturbing the notion and despite the general prohibition against suicide in Western cultural and religious tradition, we cannot rule out its apparent symbolic importance for Bresson, for whom it becomes an increasingly viable option for a character who believes he or she cannot achieve moral freedom in any other way. The idea will be more forthrightly presented in *The Devil Probably* eight years later. From this perspective, the presentational effect of the huge close-up of the wife as she steps onto the balcony can be read as the first, and last, display of a newfound self.

These teasing ambiguities are well served by Bresson's aesthetic, in which the preservation of the mystery of the human personality is assured by the profound, inscrutable blankness of the model. For him, "An actor is someone who continually hides behind his acting, behind his art, as if he was hiding himself behind a screen." That is to say, the actor hides the self *on* the screen. On the other hand, the method of keeping models "totally unaware of what they are doing…draws from them the deepest things that you could not draw from an actor.… Rather than being a form of photographed theater, then, the cinema can be a means of psychological discovery."[18] Whatever inexpressive quality is inherent in the Bressonian model, it is compounded by the enigmatic character of the wife. The question is whether the final sequence, in bypassing the husband, is designed to illuminate her character. If not, what purpose does it serve?

It is altogether possible that Bresson is affirming here, as I have suggested he did of Joan, that the human heart is, in the end, unknowable. This would seem to complicate, if not contradict the obsessive control he exerts over his characters and the models who play them. It is also possible that he is affirming that women are unfathomable and that by definition all marriage is doomed because it attempts to fix and channel this unfathomability and so deny its discomfiting reality. I suggested earlier that the *Hamlet* performance touches on this very question by way of the wife's complaint about the "bellowing" of the actors. Her deeper resentment, reflected in Hamlet's resistance to being "sounded out," may be that it reflects the patriarchal norm that assumes it is only men whose minds are too complex to decipher. I concluded that Bresson may have slyly interposed a subtle hint about the wife's character in the guise of her role as spokesperson of his aesthetic views on acting. Is it possible that something similar is at work in the final sequence?

Consider the three images: the crucifix, the mirror reflection, and the extreme close-up. Apart from their roles in the film, they can be taken as indicators of the three planes on which, I have been arguing, Bresson's work functions: the religious, the psychological, and the filmic. If so, the final sequence would seem to be posing the arenas in which the woman's conflicting feelings are played out while simultaneously suggesting Bresson's ambivalence concerning the roles religion and psychology continued to play—or are thought by his critics to play—in his narratives. The wife's ambiguous caress of the crucifix and her enigmatic smile in the mirror would therefore speak to Bresson's reluctance to reduce character motivation to religious or psychological terms. The crucifix is quickly hidden away, possibly as an object of shame. The mirror reflection, a film convention used to denote a split between a character's internal and external selves, here sheds no light on the wife's psyche. It comes as no surprise, then, that the most triumphant of the three images is the filmic: the blazingly forthright and luminous close-up that speaks eloquently through the miracle of the cinema. The truth it declares is that only the one who has made her choice and confronts death could know how to read such an image. But the carrier of this truth is not the character, but the model, who, in this instance, literalizes one of Bresson's "Notes," speaking through, and of, the frame itself as "all face."

Quatre Nuits d'un rêveur

Not since his first cinematic undertaking, *Les Affaires publiques*,[19] has a Bresson film ventured to amuse its audience. As its brief pre-credits series of shots—a young man hitchhiking in no particular direction, somersaulting in a sunlit meadow, and singing to himself in the country—immediately establishes, *Four Nights of a Dreamer* (1971) is true to the youthful, spring-like mood of Dostoevsky's novella, an unexpectedly bright interval between the three somber films that precede it and the trio of martial violence, suicide, and serial murder that follows. As such, it maintains a more leisurely pace, holding on shots of lyrical prettiness to an almost indulgent degree. Less taut than the editing structures of the films of the 1960s, not to mention those of *A Man Escaped*, *Pickpocket*, and *The Trial of Joan of Arc*, *Four Nights* has a more relaxed rhythm, largely because its main character, Jacques, is, with the exceptions of Balthazar and Mouchette, the least driven, most feckless of Bresson's protagonists. The film's long takes run between thirty seconds and one and a half minutes, reflecting not only the slackness of the narrative but the flâneur-like behavior of the protagonist.

As he did in *Une femme douce*, Bresson uses the film as an occasion to comment on contemporary art, cinema, and culture. After *Une femme douce*, it is the second of three films to portray the manners and mores of Parisian youth of the late 1960s and early 1970s as a backdrop to the story. *Four Nights* is set in the heart of the Left Bank, less in its traditional accent on bookshops and café life than in the 1960s-style hippie culture reflected in American folk songs sung in English. *The Devil Probably*, made seven years later, presents a more cynical youth with a hopeless view of society and its institutions.

Four Nights also alludes to specific moments in Bresson's previous work and prefigures one in his subsequent film, *Lancelot of the Lake*. Beyond its relationship to its source, the film is something of a gloss on Bresson's career, an autobiographical commentary on his early interest in painting and the possible reasons he abandoned it to become a filmmaker. There is even, dare I suggest, the gentlest ribbing of his preoccupations with virgins and models. Given Bresson's evasiveness in interviews about anything personal, it should come as no surprise that whatever tantalizing affinities with his life and allusions to his art one can discern in this film are cleverly masked by a lightness of tone and an irony untypical of his work. More overtly, if wryly, romantic than any other film of his, it is worth noting that the glittering apparitions of the *bateaux mouches* that cast such a spell over the protagonists would have been visible on a daily basis to Bresson as they moved up and down the Seine on both coasts of and a stone's throw away from the Ile St. Louis, where he lived for many years.

"White Nights"

Dostoevsky's novella is subtitled "A Sentimental Love Story (From the Memoirs of a Dreamer)" and is told in the first person by a protagonist who remains nameless.[20] Though it reads like a reflection of a past experience, it also feels as if it is occurring in the present. Indeed the first sentence suggests a more mature man than the one who experiences the events: "It was a lovely night, one of those nights, dear reader, which can only happen when you are young." He then refers to himself in the third person as a "young man," as if he were speaking of someone else. He tells us that although he has lived in St. Petersburg for eight years, he has no real acquaintances. Lonely and peevish, he cannot sit quietly in his room and resents the fact that everyone has gone off to the country and left him behind. This mood changes suddenly, when after walking for hours to the edge of the city, he comes upon cornfields and meadows of lush grass and immediately feels cheerful, as if "a heavy weight had lifted from [his] heart." He attributes this to contact with nature and St. Petersburg's spring.

On his return to the city, he notices a young girl leaning and weeping against the railing of one of the canals that weave throughout the city. When a strange gentleman seems about to threaten her, he intervenes, thus initiating the encounter that spans four nights. He is twenty-six and extremely shy, having "never spoken to any woman." He calls himself a dreamer who continually falls in love with an ideal. She is touched by his shyness and agrees to see him the following night at the same spot, but for her own, as yet undisclosed reasons. He immediately thinks that she has helped him "to reconcile with himself," a phrase, used more than once, suggesting that the story is really about the symbolic effect of their encounter.

On the second night, despite her request, he insists that he has no story to tell, that he is, in fact, "a queer chap, a kind of freak" who lives in those parts of the city made up of "a mixture of something purely fantastic, fervently ideal, and at the same time frighteningly prosaic and ordinary, not to say incredibly vulgar." These places are "inhabited by dreamers," not men but "creatures of the neuter gender." Such a man he counts himself, who cannot even have a normal social exchange as a man of the world about normal things. So distracted is he as he walks along the street that he barely notices other people, yet at home he feels empty and forlorn. His is a "humdrum" existence and lackluster personality; both abject and proud, he resembles other Dostoevsky characters, such as the underground man. With nothing in his past, even regrets, he "wanders about like a shadow, aimlessly, and without purpose, sad and dejected, through the alleys and streets of Petersburg." He is heartened that the young woman, Nastenka, like "a good angel," has listened to all of this with fascination instead of laughing at him: "[For] at least two evenings in my life, I have really lived."

In one long passage, the narrator recounts what he dreams of in place of all the "dull and insipid" existence around him. The list evokes numerous characters in nineteenth-century Romantic fiction, from the works of Walter Scott, George Sand, Prosper Merimée, E. T. A. Hoffmann, and Alexander Pushkin. His daydream of being in love with an inaccessible woman fettered to an older man in an ancestral castle, besides being a nod to the Romantic trappings of such writers, suggests an Oedipal fantasy of the first order, which might also be a way of understanding his initial interference with the older man who approaches Nastenka.

At the end of this second night, Nastenka tells her story. She lives with her overprotective grandmother. One year earlier she fell in love with a young lodger who vowed to return and marry her as soon as he improved his financial situation. The year has passed and he is back in St. Petersburg but has not yet contacted her. For this reason she waits by the canal at the place where they parted.

On the third night, the narrator agrees to help Nastenka communicate with her long-absent beau by delivering a letter to friends they had in common, all the while conceding to the reader that he is in love with her. She, on the other hand, is happy because she believes that he has *not* fallen in love with her so that they can remain friends. Nevertheless she begins to compare the two men and admits that though she still loves the lodger, the narrator is a better man. Concluding that the former lodger is not coming, they part at eleven o'clock.

When they meet on the fourth night, she is despondent, complains of the man's cruelty and negligence, and vows to forget him. This inspires the narrator to confess his love, while accusing himself of egoism. She admits she has been foolish to expect anything less, suggests that after all, perhaps her love was only self-deception, and agrees that even though it will take her time to forget, she will grow to love the narrator. Just as they embrace and begin to make plans for the future, the other man shows up. She rushes to him and throws herself into his arms, returns to embrace the narrator with a goodbye kiss, and vanishes into the crowd with her former love.

In the dreary, rainy morning that follows, the narrator receives a letter from her announcing her marriage and asking for forgiveness, hoping that he can still love her like a brother. In the final paragraphs of the story, he says he cannot harbor any resentment that would cast a shadow over her happiness and ends with a not unexpected sentiment: "Good Lord, only a moment of bliss? Isn't such a moment sufficient for the whole of a man's life?"

The narrator resembles many of Dostoevsky's characters in mood and demeanor, a combination of submissiveness, aloofness, and melancholy lone-liness, yet the story has a lightness of tone and tends to characterize both figures as young and impulsive idealists who have been overly affected by ideas and stories typical of Romantic fiction. Nastenka too has read a great deal of Walter Scott. An indication of Dostoevsky's intention to gently satirize their emotional immaturity is the reference to Rossini's comic opera *The Barber of Seville*, to a performance of which the lodger invites Nastenka and her grandmother, and which the narrator mentions later as something they should see together.

The Visconti Touch

One way to appreciate Bresson's take on this story is to consider it in relation to *White Nights* (1957), a film that occupies a position in director Luchino Visconti's career similar to that of *Four Nights* in Bresson's, namely, as an interlude between more serious neorealist projects. Unlike the Bresson, however, Visconti's film exudes the charisma of two actors on the cusp of becoming international stars, Marcello Mastroianni and Maria Schell, as well as Cocteau's favorite actor, Jean Marais, in the smaller role of the lodger. All three were older than the characters in Dostoevsky. Marais especially seems less a romantic hero than a father figure with a mysterious past, which may have been Visconti's way of interpreting the irrational fixation of the girl, Natalia, who has lost her actual father. But it changes the entire nature of the story and its accent on inexperienced youth. That the Marais character's absence for a year is left dark and ambiguous casts a certain gloom over the already somber tone of the film. Something about it feels like old Europe, and the fact that both the Schell and Marais characters are described as foreigners gives them a displaced quality, as if they were refugees of the Second World War.

In contrast to this, Mario (Mastroianni), unlike the dreamer of the story, is more worldly, full of life and joy, and psychologically grounded. From the beginning he finds absurd Natalia's rationale for waiting every night for the return of the lodger, telling her that as a man he knows that this lover will never keep his word and show up. He tells her she is crazy and should forget the ghosts of the past. And because he is in love with her, he tears up the letter he had promised to deliver, in contrast both to Dostoevsky's character and to Bresson's protagonist. In other words, Natalia, not Mario, seems to be the real dreamer in this version. Visconti ups the ante by including a strangely exhilarating cabaret scene, where the two dance happily together to the music of Bill Haley and the Comets until the clock strikes ten and she runs off, Cinderella-like, to the waiting place. There is more sense of doom and fate in this film than in the Dostoevsky and Bresson combined.

Compounding all of this is the studio set Visconti chose in place of a natural setting, clearly aiming for an artificial look and a poetic, timeless atmosphere rather than a real time and place. It is neither St. Petersburg nor Paris, nor, despite canals, an Italian equivalent, although it was apparently modeled on Livorno.[21] The effect is of an abstract theatrical arena where competing views of life seem to battle. The dialogue echoes distractingly in this set, the static quality of which is stressed by Visconti's penchant for very long takes and slow camera movements. The strength of the actors' personalities tends less to overcome the static nature of the production than to overwhelm the fragility of the characters that Dostoevsky created.

A Dreamy Ambience

From the start Bresson sets an entirely different tone, much closer to Dostoevsky's although without first-person narration. Jacques, his protagonist, hitchhikes with the most lackadaisical hand signals one can imagine (figure 63). This is followed by an animated shrug of indifference, shoulders heaving, arms flailing about, in response to a driver's question, "Where to?" "Anywhere" seems to be the answer. We next see him somersaulting down a slope and humming while strolling through the grass, capturing the mood of Dostoevsky's hero when he visits the country. The film eliminates the complaints of loneliness and isolation that precede this mood in the novella. In place of the grim social commentary that the narrator makes on St. Petersburg and that speaks to his psychological makeup, Bresson gives us a Paris of glittering colors and lights—all the more prominent since a third of the film takes place at night—and populated exclusively, it would appear, by young people and lovers. This may be the only film of Bresson's in which there is not a single old person in sight. He even replaced the heroine's grandmother with a younger, sophisticated mother. Bresson's lean and pretty models of both sexes aptly reflect this atmosphere, itself symbolized by the luminous *bateaux mouches* that glide gracefully down the Seine, a floating sound and light show that, in one critic's description, is as unreal and spectacular an apparition as the spaceship in *Close Encounters of the Third Kind* (1977).[22]

However, when Jacques eyes a young woman leaning against the Pont Neuf suspiciously focused on the river below, we may be reminded of Bresson's previous few films. Unlike the young woman in the Dostoevsky story, Bresson's Marthe is about to jump into the Seine, the pretext for Jacques's intervention and his escorting her home, which comprises the content of their first night, a mere three and a half minutes of screen time (figure 64). On the second night we hear their stories. While Marthe is motivated by the same disappointment, her counterpart declares in the novella—namely, that the lodger who promised to return in a year to marry her has not materialized—the potential suicide tends to lend more gravity to her story than to Jacques's. By eliminating most of the unnamed narrator's discourse on dreamers, St. Petersburg, and his wasted life, a consequence of not retaining the story's first-person perspective, Bresson lightens the tone.

Points of View

As with *Une femme douce*, Bresson again seems determined to avoid the consequences of a first-person narrative, the implication that all things be interpreted as products of the speaker's subjectivity. Even the three masterful first-person narratives of the 1950s do not require that we view everything with reservation. We do not question the veracity of what the priest or Michel write in their diaries or what they and Fontaine say in voice-over, wondering if these conflict with what each film shows us. This is not to say there is no subjectivity, but that it is integrated into the world that unfolds, is not a divisive element that requires constant adjustment between what the first-person character says and what the viewer sees. This is one reason Bresson doubled the level of narration in those films, having the protagonist say or write something that we then see, reinforcing the objective reality of the filmic world and the narrator's place within it. The genius of Bresson's method was to establish this framework while not allowing it to detract from the interiority of the character. For example, the internal monologues of the country priest often reveal his feelings about what is happening directly outside of him at the moment. In *Pickpocket* the disjunction alleged in the discussion of that film in chapter 3 is not between the narrator's diary or voice-over and the world, but between Michel's resistance to the moral impulses of his interior nature and his failure to see where his actions are leading him.

The Dostoevsky stories that are the subject of this chapter pose a special problem vis-à-vis this aim of Bresson's to avoid compromising the integrity of the filmic world. Largely this is because the narrators of *Une femme douce* and *Four Nights of a Dreamer* are sufficiently neurotic for the reader to suspect that their realities are skewed products of their imaginations. This in turn points to another, perhaps overlooked factor that bears on Bresson's aesthetic, particularly his conception of the model. It can be sensed by listening closely to the voice-over of *Diary of a Country Priest*—preferably while not looking at the image—and comparing it to the voice-over in any subsequent Bresson film. The warmth, tenderness, and tonal shifts, in short, the feelings conveyed by the voice in the former exceed everything Bresson sought to subdue by using models rather than actors. The eccentric, wilder ravings of Dostoevsky's possessed do not lend themselves easily to the neutral, impassive locutions that Bresson's models were encouraged to master.

As we saw, Bresson found a clever way around these dilemmas in *Une femme douce*, first by placing the housekeeper Anna in the mise-en-scène as a direct audience for the husband's ruminations, and by keeping the voice-over narrations to a minimum. These strategies serve to reduce, if not eliminate, the insular, indulgent hysterics of Dostoevsky's character. In addition, Bresson brilliantly orchestrated the image and sound tracks, permitting a fluid exchange between past and present that enfolds the husband's narration within the film's more balanced omniscient reality.

In *Four Nights of a Dreamer* he devised other ways of freeing the narrative from the constrictions of the novella's first person, first by literally not making the male protagonist the singular, overriding voice. When Jacques tells his story, he speaks only an initial sentence, identifying where he lives—"I live at 6 Rue Antoine Dubois, a loft on the third floor"—as we see the street plaque and watch him enter the building with groceries and walk into his apartment. Everything after that is not only rendered visually but in keeping with the diffident nature of his character, Jacques never utters a word during the first brief sketch we get of his life. The only other times we hear his disembodied voice is via the tape recorder, itself a whimsical device that reveals the nature of his reveries and when played back at different points serves to wittily, and poignantly, counteract the poker face he adopts. This will take on more importance on the third day. Moreover when Marthe begins her story, she also speaks a few voice-over sentences—"I live with my mother. We barely exist on my father's alimony. Every year we rent out the room next to mine"— before it is taken over by audiovisual elaboration (figure 65). And so, even though the film begins and ends with Jacques, he is never made the official narrating voice in the film, although it can certainly be argued that the hues and colors that characterize Paris in almost exclusively romantic terms is a direct reflection of Jacques's personality. Still, even more emphatically than he did in *Une femme douce*, Bresson has transposed the story into the third person.

A perhaps unintended but wonderfully ironic consequence of this approach, in conjunction with the particular nature of the male character, is that the emphasis on the seemingly passive face of the model Guillaume des Forêts so perfectly suits this character that one tends to react, at least in the first third of the film, as we would to the performance of a brilliant comic actor whose forte is a blank face and understatement (e.g., Buster Keaton). We may not appreciate des Forêts's "performance" on a first viewing, but I have since come to see it as a greatly underestimated coup, not least because it throws unexpected light on the concept of the model, exposing an unforeseen comedic potential underlying its austere regimen, while allowing us to admire Bresson's masterful way of containing and redirecting that potential here and in his other films when necessary.

Incurable Romantics

The brevity and thrust of the stories Jacques and Marthe relate on the second night are enough to telegraph immediately that they are both victims of idealistic and sentimental views of life, the quality Dostoevsky imputes to his characters when he writes that they read the fiction of Hoffman, Merimée, Pushkin, Sand, and Scott. The lodger in the film lends books to Marthe and her mother, but the only one we get to see when Marthe picks it up and skims through it is *Irène*, an erotic work of fiction that will be discussed later. Both Jacques's and Marthe's stories are exclusively about romantic delusions, apparently the image Bresson sought to capture of the sensations that rule young people's lives. Jacques begins, in fact, by saying that he has no story, but then sketches an account of how he spends his day following young women around, though he is too shy to approach them. We see him pursuing a woman in one direction only to hesitate when another going the opposite direction catches his eye. At one point Bresson parodies his wandering attention when he has him stand on the sidewalk, undecided which way to move after his latest target has gotten on a bus. Next to him is a poster advertising the Opéra-Comique, an indirect allusion to *The Barber of Seville*, the opera to which the lodger takes the woman and her grandmother in the story and itself a satirical view of the frivolities of love. At such moments des Forêts's deadpan gaze with just a whiff of a smile is incomparable, a look no voice-over could match.

As the film cuts back to Jacques and Marthe sitting on the embankment of the Pont Neuf, he remarks, "How many times I was in love!" "With whom?" asks Marthe. "With no one, an ideal, the woman in my dreams." To which Marthe replies, "That's stupid." The implication that both are more self-aware than we might have thought is contradicted by subsequent events. Jacques may be shy, since several of the women return his glances with equal curiosity without prompting a response from him. It is more likely, however, at least in the film's first third, that he is more interested in having fantasies than in acting on them. Making him an artist rather than a clerk might suggest that the fantasies serve his art and that art is an erotic displacement, but this too is an aborted path since he hardly manifests enough passion for the viewer to conclude this. Yet we cannot wholly dismiss Jacques's remark to Marthe just after she tells him that his pursuit of an ideal is "stupid" and just before he continues his story: "God has sent me an angel to reconcile me with myself." Straight from Dostoevsky, the line refers to Marthe's intervention in his life, suggesting at least the possibility of change. She is, after all, not only presumably the first woman that he has approached but the one to whom he entrusts his fantasies.

These intensify as he tells her of a woman he saw going into a building with an older man who became a source of wild invention. In the story he speaks into his tape recorder, she lives with the man in an ancestral castle but loves Jacques with a "pure" and "innocent" love. After recording this in his flat, he rewinds it and listens to it as he paints, applying a stroke or two, in black and red, to each of two paintings "in progress." It's hard to take either the story or his painting seriously. Like his inability to control his fluctuating attention to women, it seems he cannot concentrate on one painting at a time. A dabbler in art, as he is a mere ogler of women, he seems doomed to see nothing through to the end.

Although Jacques's encounter with Marthe involves an actual rescue, his hesitancy to approach women and the story of the woman bound to an older man have the hallmarks of Oedipal arrest, as does Jacques's line: "The husband scares us a little, but our love is pure and innocent." The words "pure and innocent" are repeated five times in one scene, twice from Jacques directly as he applies color to his canvas, further hints that his art is a kind of erotic displacement, as stealing was for Michel the pickpocket. Possibly it is about a misguided need to keep his encounters free of carnality, as pure as his art. From what we see, the paintings are composed only of rich primary colors—red, blue, green, yellow, and black—without shadings or tonal transitions, applied to round and oval shapes that resemble human figures but lack facial definition. This suggests Jacques's inability to see life in terms other than those of blunt, shadow-free oppositions. When he concludes his story, Marthe asks incredulously, "Is that your life?" Although the tone remains light, we should not miss the underlying despair in his reply that there are days when he feels he has nothing to live for and that if he died, he would lose "zero."

Despite the year Marthe has been faithful to a man she hardly knows and awaits like a child who has been promised to be taken to the circus, her story is also tinged with irreality. Bresson accentuates the illusory and fickle nature of her love by having her not lay eyes on the lodger until the night she goes to his room and gives herself to him (at least we assume so, since one cannot always be certain of this in Bresson). What could more clearly indicate that she loves a phantom of her own conjuring, fueled by his teasing efforts to date her, by their just missing each other on the elevator or in the apartment, by the books he lends to her and her mother, and finally by the night they tap on each other's wall and hover just outside each other's room.

Before getting to that night, let us consider the book Marthe peruses since it not only arouses her interest in the lodger but also possibly alludes to Bresson's reflections on his treatment of eroticism. The book is *Irène*, the scandalous central image of which is that of an elderly man who spies on his granddaughter's sexual couplings with a series of men.[23] Marthe pauses on two pages long enough for us to read the text. The first is the old man's recollection of observing the "affairs, deceptions, and vices" of the young girls and boys who come every spring to work on the farm where he stays. "From my corner I saw couples made and unmade, and sometimes curious triangles and complex arrangements.... There were even some who were amused by my presence."[24] The second page warrants consideration in full:

> Thus I greatly envy erotics, whose eroticism is their expression. A
> magnificent language. It is really not mine. Notwithstanding what I
> think of the limitations of erotic experience, of the inescapable,
> unavoidable repetition of an elementary theme that is perfectly
> reducible to any other indifferent action, I have the deepest respect
> for those to whom this limitation seems to be freedom itself. They

are the true masters of the physical world, the perfect executioners of a kind of meta-physic of annihilation in which, for me, the spectator, all morality is summed up.[25]

Marthe returns the book to the pile, careful to place it under several others rather than on top, where she found it. Like other indirect communications between them, this one increases her curiosity about the lodger and his sexual interest in her. Yet it is hard not to see both passages as also revealing of Bresson's thoughts, as a man approaching seventy when he made this film, on the subject of the sexual behavior of the young, "of couples made and unmade," and of his own distance from the "magnificent language" of erotic expression. Whereas the first passage strongly suggests a voyeuristic interest in the sexual abandon of youth, the second might be read as an apology for lacking the *filmic* language to do justice to that phenomenon and to the "true masters of the physical world." Without applying this too literally, one might reasonably consider that, like Jacques, Bresson may have felt that he could not quite bridge the gap he perceived between a "pure" and "innocent" art and an explicit embrace of carnality. As I have tried to show in earlier chapters, this tension is present throughout his work and no doubt has to do with his insistence on segregating the virginal and the erotic. It might be argued, however, that increasingly in his later work, the preoccupation with the virginal becomes the basis of the erotic.

All the more intriguing, then, is the beautiful rendering of Marthe's sexual awakening and the narcissistic core that attends such an event in a scene unique in Bresson's work. As she listens to music in her room, Marthe removes a transparent nightgown and gazes at her body, softly lit and photographed at oblique angles in a montage of eight shots. Close-ups of her nude back, waist, breasts, and legs are crosscut with shots of her face as she looks with a sidelong glance over her shoulder and moves as if assessing herself as an object of desire for the first time. Here, as in *Une femme douce*, Bresson gives us a young female openly sensual and appreciative of her body, without the humiliation and shame associated with Marie's nudity in *Balthazar*.

A comparison with Marie is signaled by an inescapable allusion to that film. When Marthe learns the next morning that the lodger is leaving, she enters his room and pleads to go with him. He first says it is impossible, then begins to undress her. They stand caressing each other as we hear her mother walking through the apartment calling her name. In *Balthazar* Marie and Gérard copulate in an abandoned farm building as her father passes by, calling out to her. In both cases, the proximity of the parent marks the threshold at which the adolescent moves from presumed virginal child of the family nest to the world of sexuality and adulthood. The plaintive tone of Marie's father as he wanders across the fields is a wistful commentary on his own falling off in her world, but it also speaks more ominously of Marie's surrender to the sadistic Gérard and the loss of innocence in general, a central subject of that film.

While the calls of Marthe's mother make more immediate sense as she enters the apartment, the sequence is still charged and prolonged enough to warrant comment. We first hear her calls as she walks up and down the hallway outside the bedroom just as Marthe and the lodger are engaged in the only extended kiss of any Bresson film; as he unbuttons her dress, there is a cut to the hall and the mother; we hear her pacing loudly over a shot of the lodger removing Marthe's bra and tossing it on the bed, along with his glasses, followed by a cut to the mother still walking about; finally, over a panning shot up Marthe's nude body as they embrace, we hear her mother calling out, "Marthe, my dear." Earlier Marthe accused her mother quite bluntly that the reason she takes in young lodgers is that she wants Marthe to get married. Since the lodger rents the room adjacent to Marthe's, and since Marthe was upset just a short while earlier that her mother did not tell her that he was leaving, it is hard to believe that her mother does not suspect that Marthe is in the room with the lodger. The extended treatment Bresson gives the sequence would suggest, then, despite the difference in the circumstances, that here too we have a parent who bears some responsibility for throwing her child into the arms of her first lover and then reacting with surprise, even denial of, the inevitable consequences. Thus, the lovely shots of Marthe's nudity and the attachment of Marthe and the lodger notwithstanding, the crossover from virginity is again of paramount interest to Bresson.

Given Bresson's comments in various interviews over the years concerning the virginal qualities he sought in his young models, his reluctance to use them again after having taken something precious and irreplaceable from them, and the overprotective manner he apparently exercised over some of them during production,[26] it would not be a stretch to read into these scenes of parental concern Bresson's ambivalence about the role he played in hiring young people in whom he glimpsed a reminder of lost "purity" and "innocence" and pushing them by way of his art across that critical line. Perhaps that is what Jacques unconsciously avoids and why at the end he remains a virgin, content to have had a few nights of imaginary contact with the angel God sent him.

Despite all this, Bresson follows the sequence of Marthe in front of the mirror with an equally charming sequence that precedes the one in the lodger's bedroom and that qualifies as a kind of foreplay to the morning's lovemaking. After Marthe's anatomical study, she sits on her bed, turns off her radio, and hears the lodger tapping on the other side of her wall. When she leans against it, there is a cut to the lodger tapping, then slowly removing his tie and jacket. In the next shot of Marthe, still leaning against the wall, she puts on her nightgown. Hearing no sound, she walks over to her door and opens it. The cut is to the dark hallway, as she peeks out and to the left, then stealthily tiptoes to his room; the camera tilts down just as the light under his door is extinguished. Marthe runs back to her room and closes her door, but continues to lean against it. A cut to the lodger shows him now in the hall, moving up to her door. When he arrives, there is a shot-countershot of the two of them on either side of her door, each waiting for the other to make a move. Suddenly he walks away as the camera stays on the door handle of her room that he has just released. In the next shot Marthe moves away from the door and goes to bed, covering herself with pillows. This cuts to the next morning, when she confronts her mother for not telling her that the lodger is leaving.

Clearly the night business is prompted at least on the lodger's part by its being the last opportunity to see Marthe before leaving. Somehow, the fact that neither has yet really seen the other is key to their attraction, and the back-and-forth bit in the bedrooms and hallway in the dead of night only serves to heighten it, preparing us for her sudden appearance in his room the next morning. Are we to assume that Marthe is aroused by his choice of reading material, the scatological novel *Irène?* Or is it what she later admits to Jacques, that she was bored and needed to get away, an accurate picture of the impulsive decisions many young people make? If we judge the lodger to be one of those men Marthe's mother warns her about, interested only in a one-night fling before leaving (in this case, for America and a fellowship at Yale), this is contradicted by his return. In short, we know next to nothing about what motivates these two except for the teasing dance of youthful romance and the desire for new and exciting adventures. The lodger promises that he will return in a year and that if she still loves him, he'll meet her "day for day, same time." After Marthe sees him off in a taxi, the film cuts back to her and Jacques at the end of this second night. "It has been a year," she says.

A Messenger Despite Himself

Like those characters in Shakespeare's comedies who must hide their strongest feelings while disguised as a member of the opposite sex, Jacques's behavior on the third day and night is marked by what we might call the archetypal Bressonian malady, which is to say, suffering inside while presenting a sober front. When, at the end of Marthe's story, he learns finally why she was ready to leap into the Seine, that the lodger has in fact returned to Paris but not kept his promise, he immediately offers his assistance. He suggests that she write a letter to the lodger's friends, which he will deliver the next day. No sooner does he convince her of this plan than she produces a letter already written. The fusion of guile and helplessness this reveals may elude Jacques, but the viewer notes it by way of the song "Mystery Lady" that some strolling minstrels sing as they pass.

On the morning of the third day we see the first signs of Jacques's conflict as he looks out of the window of his flat, his face lined by the streams of rain coursing down the window pane (figure 66). In a conventional love story this would be a cliché, but here it works as one of those outward signs that counteract the mask the Bressonian model wears. Yet not until moments later do we sense just how strong his feelings have become. On the bus ride to the destination where he will deliver the critical letter, we hear "Marthe! Marthe! Marthe!" coming from the tape recorder he has tucked into the left side of his jacket, the sound literally emitting from the region of his heart. What could be more Bressonian than this expression of a character's emotions through the juxtaposition of image and sound: a man assertively on his way to help the woman he loves to reconnect with his rival as his inner voice screams in protest. In keeping with the film's subtly humorous tone, the poignant effect of this is mitigated by the barely suppressed reaction of two women sitting opposite Jacques on the bus. The insistent repetition of the name approaches incantation as it continues into the building where he will complete his mission. The closer he gets to fulfilling *his* promise, the more his suppressed feelings cry out for release.

Unlike the earlier recordings of Jacques's elaborate fantasies, the present ones speak nothing but the name of the object of his affection, a difference that more persuasively conveys the force and immediacy of his emotions. Bresson's use of ellipsis adds to the affect and surprise of this development because only in retrospect do we realize that Jacques, after agreeing to deliver the letter, must have spent the previous night speaking Marthe's name repeatedly and with regret into the tape recorder. That we did not witness his doing this makes the sequence just described much stronger. Over the next few minutes we hear "Marthe!" called out more than forty times as Jacques walks about the city where, typical of the adolescent in love, he also sees her name in various places: on a glamorous shop window and on a barge going down the Seine, the latter's dinginess in such contrast to the nighttime vision of the *bateau mouche* as to dispel the romantic aura the name conjures. That Jacques is not alone in this characterization of the vagaries of adolescent love is reflected in a scene where he is seated on a bench ogling lovers in the park and spots a young woman staring distractedly at him over the shoulder of the young man embracing her.

The possibility that Jacques may really be in love and that the encounter with Marthe has helped him turn his life around is compounded by the events of the third night, the most lyrically romantic section of the film. Marthe begins to see that her hopes for the lodger's return are unrealistic and that Jacques has proved the better man. She voices what the viewer may have already intuited, that the brief hour she spent with the lodger does not match the two nights of shared intimacy she has had with Jacques. Although Jacques is stirred by these sentiments, he holds back when they both agree that the letter may not yet have reached the lodger. They linger along the embankment, at one point leaning over to watch the *bateau mouche*, shot from above as it glows and glides slowly down the Seine, its rhythm in sync with that of the mellow love song performed by a small group of Latin singers on the boat. Nine shots of the boat are crosscut with Jacques and Marthe as they follow its course and run to the other side of a bridge to watch it as it emerges. The most affecting of these registers the wavering glimmers of light emanating from the boat and moving across their faces as they lean over the bridge. Touched in passing by the god of romance, they seem, as Marthe tells Jacques at the end of this evening, "bound forever." But this has a hollow ring since it echoes the title of the schlocky gangster movie *Bonds of Love*, tickets to which the lodger had given Marthe and her mother a year earlier, an equivalent of the opera tickets in the story. The last shot of this imaginary film is of a man riddled with bullets kissing a photo of his girlfriend for the last time before he dies, which is not only a caricature of the "bonds" that Marthe presumably feels tie her to Jacques and the lodger, but a parody of the kind of commercial cinema that purveys cheap sentiment in the guise of love. On her urging, Marthe and her mother leave, ostensibly because she feels the lodger has tricked them into attending a worthless event in revenge for her not agreeing to date him. As he did in *Une femme douce*, however, Bresson conveys his own feelings by way of his character's disgust.

The events of the fourth night bring an abrupt end to any romantic possibility for Jacques and Marthe. After her despondent recognition that the man she trusted will never show up and that she has deceived herself, Jacques declares his love, probably the most momentous advance he has made in his young life. At first he hesitates to follow up on it, and Marthe now becomes the pursuer, assuring him that she will eventually forget the lodger if Jacques will only be patient. They embrace, stop at a café, then stroll along the busy street like so many lovers, arm in arm. But no sooner do they speak of plans for Jacques to move in as the new lodger than the unexpected expected happens. Bresson registers it in perhaps the film's most heartbreaking image, capturing the difference between the two characters. As they stand clasped together, Jacques, the dreamer, his head tilted upward, gazes at the moon, while Marthe gazes straight ahead, transfixed on something off screen (figure 67). "It's him," she says, running to the man who has just emerged from the crowd calling her name. As in the Dostoevsky, she embraces and kisses the lodger, runs back and does the same with Jacques, then returns to her lover and walks off arm in arm, vanishing into the crowd. This shot of Marthe and her lover merging into the crowd is the clincher of several throughout the film of characters walking into the distance and disappearing from view. It also speaks poignantly to the portrait the narrator paints of his life in St. Petersburg in Dostoevsky's story, isolated and disconnected from the social web of the city.

But if he is once again alone, Jacques is not drowning in tears. We see him again speaking into the tape recorder, distorting and embellishing his latest experience and rewriting the ending.

> She sees me from afar. She flies toward me. The night is luminous, marvelous, the only such night in a lifetime. An enthusiastic cry! All is forgotten: separation, pain, tears, in "Jacques, forgive me for being wrong. I was blind. I hurt you as I hurt myself. I have suffered for you a thousand deaths…but it's you I love." I am astounded, elated. Oh, Marthe. What strength makes your eyes shine with such a flame, lights your face with such a smile? Thank you for your love. And be blessed for the happiness you bring me.

We hear this again, as is his wont, over the image, the final one, of Jacques kneeling on the floor between the two canvases we saw him working on earlier. But it is not the last thing we hear. When the tape ends, the film continues for thirty seconds as he paints, the only sound that of the brush-strokes against the canvas. Should we conclude there has been growth? Does the last sentence imply that he has gained something lasting from his encounter with Marthe? Or does the fact that his imagination has turned experience into fiction merely to provide dubious inspiration suggest that he remains closed off from a fuller life? This ending differs from the one in an earlier Bresson film, in which a young man also wanders about Paris. Michel suddenly sees, as if for the first time, the illumined face of his beloved on the other side of the prison bars, but it transforms him. Jacques may see his beloved only in his imagination, but it is the imagination of an artist.

Or perhaps it would be more accurate to say, a future artist, since, after all, this is a portrait of an artist as a young man, which means concluding on a somber note would be inappropriate. If, as I have suggested throughout, the film bears an important connection to Bresson's development, Jacques's turning his experience into fiction is a foreshadowing of the future artist who will abandon painting and turn to narrative filmmaking.

An Allusionary Film

Four Nights of a Dreamer is one of Bresson's most allusion-conscious films. In addition to the ending that indirectly recalls *Pickpocket* and the sequence of Marthe in the lodger's room that resembles one in *Balthazar*, there is the lodger's stopping of the elevator to command Marthe's attention, as Hélène does to prevent Jean from leaving in *Les Dames du bois de Boulogne*, and the lodger's tapping on the wall that recalls the tapping of the condemned prisoner with whom Fontaine communicates in *A Man Escaped*. Like *Mouchette* and *The Trial of Joan of Arc*, *Four Nights* has a pre-credits sequence, and like *Une femme douce*, it begins with a young woman about to kill herself.

It is worth considering these allusions in light of a sequence that is an invention of Bresson's, involves a character we never see again, and would seem to have no narrative relevance. This is the visit that Jacques receives from a young man who claims to know him from art school. It is one of the funniest in the film. At first, as Jacques lies on his bed listening to his tape, he ignores the doorbell. On the second ring he decides to answer it, although not before cleaning up the dishes and bottles strewn about and turning all of his paintings to the wall. When he finally answers the door, the actor gives another of his wonderfully ambivalent gestures. As the visitor asks, "Jacques, remember me?," Jacques moves his head from side to side, miming a decisive "no" while he says, "Oui." If the quintessential paradox of Bresson's work is the coexistence of affirmation and negation, this moment should stand as evidence that he was capable of being amused by his own seriousness.

Trying to be social, Jacques brings out a bottle of whiskey and glasses, which the young man refuses, having come, it seems, only to pronounce a barrage of sweeping theoretical statements about contemporary art. He is no sooner through the door than, without any small talk, he launches into this:

> Craftsmanship is dead. Chardin's *brioche*, Manet's *pivoines* [peonies],
> Van Gogh's chair and *godillots* [hobnailed boots]. It's over. I'm for

mature art that does not burn in contact with nature, but is simply a meeting of the painter and a concept. What's crucial is not the object, not the painter, but the gesture that lifts the presence from the object and is suspended in a space which delimits it, and, in fact, supports it. Not the object there, not the painter there, but the object and the painter which are not there. Their visible disappearance makes the canvas so sensually structured as to form a whole light source which is specifically solid.

This monologue is punctuated at three points with an insistent "*Comprends?*" to which Jacques does not respond.

On one level, the scene confirms Jacques's general lack of sociability in the student art world to which he presumably belongs. The amusing tenor of the scene as well as the visitor's out-of-the-blue harangue tends to mask its further relevance. For one thing, his remark about craftsmanship being dead, along with his examples, though pompously delivered, echo Bresson's interests. He greatly admired Chardin and implied that one reason he abandoned painting, was that there was "nothing left to do after Cézanne." And yet, when an interviewer asked him, "You were a painter before becoming a filmmaker?," he responded, "I am a painter. One cannot have been a painter and be one no longer."[27] Indeed, Bresson transferred his painter's sensibility to a different art form, as confirmed by his subsequent statements on the art of cinematography, those collected in *Notes on Cinematography* as well as those in his many interviews. They presupposed that craftsmanship was still possible in the cinema, an art he believed was still in its infancy and capable of unimagined possibilities. But Jacques's behavior, first by noisily searching for a bottle of whiskey to serve his guest while the latter rattles on, and then by an utter lack of response to anything he has to say, including a blank look to the repeated question "Understand?," emphatically denotes not only lack of understanding but complete indifference.

Because the art and craft of the cinematographic were of primary importance to Bresson, Jacques's imperviousness to what amounts to a cryptic allusion to the Bressonian aesthetic invites a fictionalized autobiographical reading whereby Jacques is the aspiring painter whose frustrated daydreams contain more imagination than his painting, and his visitor is the distant voice that only the later artist would be able to hear. Jacques's earlier repetition of the refrain "pure and innocent," which in context was a reference to the love he fantasized about, is also a way, albeit simplistic, of describing Bresson's mature art, freed from the contamination of the vulgarities of cinematic tradition. The visitor's remarks on the importance of absence and minimalism in art speak directly to Bresson's increasing use of off screen space and spareness. But Jacques has no clue about any of this since Bresson has cleverly couched it in the guise of parody, mocking both the visitor's preachy theorizing and Jacques's simplistic use of imaginary encounters to inspire his art. Bresson was also once a painter who invented stories who later resolved his dilemma by becoming a filmmaker. The fact that no one, at least on record, has seen any of Bresson's paintings is also reflected in the sequence when Jacques turns all of his paintings to the wall, including the ones on the floor that he was working on before admitting his visitor.

In light of that, we can now perhaps understand why Jacques appears to be an unserious painter, a realization that would most certainly have driven Bresson to abandon the practice and pursue another path. Given that fact, along with the allusions to his previous films, of the revealing excerpt from the erotic novel, and of the seemingly gratuitous speech about contemporary art by a character with no other place in the narrative, *Four Nights of a Dreamer* emerges as Bresson's most self-conscious exercise, a caesura in his career, a look back at what he might have become. In that context, one should note that there is a relaxation of certain formal characteristics we came to expect in his work. There is already in *Une femme douce*, made two years after *Mouchette*, a sense of a difference, marked by the embrace of color and the elimination of nondiegetic music. In *Four Nights* such formal givens as the use of ellipses and the strong sense of the cut with overlapping sound are minimized, softened to attune the connective tissue of the film to the casual demeanor of the dreamer. Consistent with that is more frequent use of the long take. Although Bresson was not among those directors known for their long takes, there are powerful examples of it in his early work.

The final shot of *Diary of a Country Priest*, which runs eighty-five seconds, is the longest final shot until *Four Nights of a Dreamer*, and shares with its closest competitors—*The Trial of Joan of Arc* and *Mouchette*, at forty and forty-five seconds, respectively—a marking of the death of the protagonist and his or her replacement by a symbolic image and sound. All three are among Bresson's most spiritually infused endings and involve an abstract quality that requires more time for the viewer to absorb. All other final shots, from *Les Anges du péché* to *Une femme douce*, range between twelve and twenty seconds. As an Average Shot Length (ASL) analysis of each film reveals, however, it is certainly not only the duration of the shot that prompts our readings, since in the three cases noted above, final shots fall within the range of shot lengths in the films as a whole. *Diary*, for example, includes several takes that are longer than its final shot.

Within the overall context of Bresson's oeuvre, then, it is noteworthy that the final shot of *Four Nights* is longer than the one in *Diary*. It is true that like *Diary* it includes a voice-over, but the shot continues well after this concludes. My feeling is that it is not only a melancholy commentary on the lonely life of the protagonist but a mirror of the life and art of its creator, both reflective and reflexive. Looking at this charming and shy young man as he labors on, it is hard not to sense the special resonances this long take must have had for Bresson, the man behind the camera looking back at the young, aspiring painter, unaware of his future path. In the final thirty seconds of the film, one feels that beyond the gentle parody of adolescent dreams, there is a lingering farewell. Yet the sounds of those brushstrokes as Jacques applies color to his canvas also register the story of the many days and nights in which the lone artist behind the camera tirelessly practiced *his* craft against the grain of many who believed him to be a dreamer of dark, hieratic visions, out of touch with the contemporary world.

It was not the Grail, but God you all wanted....

God is no trophy to bear home.

—Guinevere to Lancelot in *Lancelot of the Lake*

8

The Ultimate *Geste*

Lancelot du Lac

Lancelot of the Lake (1974) is surely the darkest film anyone has made of the
Arthurian romances. The film takes up the saga at the point *between* the spiritual revelations at the heart of the quest for the Holy Grail and the repentance
and redemption of Lancelot and Guinevere that conclude the epic.[1] Bresson
focuses on the nadir of the Arthurian chronicle, the moment of the disinte-
gration of the Round Table, the erosion of the chivalric ideal, the decline of
faith in what sustained it and of the values it represented. Although the quest,
the highpoint of the legends on which the film is based, chronologically
precedes the events of the film, it haunts the narrative as yet another reminder
of a crisis of faith and loss of innocence, two of Bresson's abiding themes. In
light of his treatment, a question arises. Bresson wanted to film the story in
the 1950s. Without an original screenplay in hand or clear evidence—oral or
written—of his intentions, we cannot be certain whether an earlier film
would have resembled the one we have or whether it would have been more
compatible with his work of the 1940s and 1950s. From the perspective
adopted in this book, which views the changes in narrative and spiritual tone
in Bresson's films as reflections of shifts in his convictions and worldview, a

280

reasonable supposition is that this imaginary *Lancelot* might have been less bleak. That Bresson remained drawn to the subject over the years suggests that of all his films, *Lancelot of the Lake* may bear the traces of early and late Bresson and is therefore a reasonable barometer of the filmmaker's own spiritual journey.[2]

The subject is certainly compatible with Bresson's preoccupation with destiny and the concept of a divine plan. Both ideas can be seen in the magician Merlin's predictions as well as in the symbolism of the Grail itself. Nevertheless the key in which these themes are played in his later films and how characters fare in relation to them undergoes a tonal change. The question is whether this change, as registered in the film, displaced an original design or is the product of two different Bressonian modes. I would argue for the latter. On the one hand, the film teeters on the edge of metaphysical despair in denying its titular protagonist the final redemption one thought might ensue from his having undergone a spiritual awakening during the quest for the Grail. On the other hand, it appears to grant something like redemption to a secondary character. In other words, unlike any other narrative of Bresson's, *Lancelot* seems to split its male hero in two. Lancelot belongs to late Bresson whereas Gawain, the most congenial and compassionate of the knights in the film, has more in common with earlier protagonists, as his behavior throughout and his deathbed scene demonstrate. This can be felt even in the choice of models. Luc Simon's Lancelot has a dark, swarthy look and rough-hewn facial features untypical of Bresson's male protagonists, whereas Humbert Balsan's Gawain has the bright, youthful, innocent look—not to be equated with inexperience—closer to that of the country priest, Fontaine, Michel, and Charles.

This split mirrors the one in Lancelot himself, who reveals a troubling weakness in respect to two conflicting promises: the vow of love he made to Guinevere and the vow he made to God during the quest, requiring renunciation of the former. In the end he fails to honor either one. After yielding to Guinevere, he is forced to return her to King Arthur, having achieved neither the sexual renewal of their affair nor the reparation of his knightly bond in time to prevent the collapse of the Round Table and the destruction of Arthur's court. As he dies on a heap of armor in the forest, he speaks Guinevere's name for the last time, an ambiguous utterance that seems to slight his vow to God and shows no hint of remorse. As the film's title suggests, it is Lancelot's dilemma and failure that Bresson wished to illustrate as a reflection of the diminishing hold of Christian thought on the modern world.

Gawain, on the other hand, is from the beginning a nobler figure, defending both Lancelot and Guinevere against the worst accusations made against them while remaining loyal to the king. He also proves the better man when he forgives Lancelot for having mortally wounded him and begs Arthur not to seek revenge. Gawain is not a Christ figure, but he fights the good fight and manifests the virtues of charity, humility, and mercy despite his violent career. In the wake of the failure of the quest and the moral ennui that pervades Arthur's court, he is the only knight who pleads with the king to give them a purpose. This portrait of Gawain as a man of courage and virtue is at odds with the one in much of the literature, but it shares a strong family resemblance with Bresson's most admirable protagonists. His presence in so late a film suggests a compromise between early and late Bresson; Gawain carries the torch, so to speak, which is literally what we see him doing in his first appearance in the film.

The split I have alleged characterizes other aspects of the film, which harkens back to the earliest Bresson, *Les Anges du péché*. Although characters seem destined to live out the course of events according to a divine plan, which much of the film's iconography reinforces, they nevertheless reveal greater complexity—Guinevere in particular—than one finds in their literary counterparts. Although this opens the way to a psychological understanding of behavior that seems to resist the concept of a divine plan, in fact it reinforces the conundrum that Bresson's cinema reiterates emphatically and literally: that a sense of destiny appears to operate beneath the proud affirmations of independent will characteristic of the godless modern world, wherein people only imagine they determine their lives and so misrecognize the signs that cross their paths.

In this regard, once again Bresson stresses the role of hubris, down to the way a knight is quick to reach for his sword at the slightest insult. And by having Lancelot die in the final battle between Arthur and Mordred, a battle in which he does not participate in the literary sources, Bresson structures the legend with the sense of finality in Athenian tragedy. Yet unlike classical tragedy as Aristotle viewed it, the film does not aim for catharsis and gives no sense that the world's order has been restored. Does Lancelot's final utterance, "Guinevere," evoke the passion and tragic flaw that were the catalysts of the action? Or does it imply the futility of all that has happened? Indeed the split I have suggested is further complicated by the pivotal and morally ambiguous role of the queen in the unfolding of events.

The film moves from the unraveling of a preexistent order to the realization that no reconstruction is possible. The decimation of the Round Table, a "symbol of the wholeness of virtue," as conceived by Merlin, reflects the collapse of the world. Thus, although the film has the force and trajectory of tragedy, it ultimately evokes a modern sense of absurdist void. The terrain of the film during this descent is a *between* state, bordered by two conclusive failures: the quest for spiritual perfection and the attempt to recuperate the previous order. In this fictional construct neither the spiritual nor the material realm is secure. Suspended between heaven and earth, every character wriggles in a limbo of purposelessness. On both the personal and the social level, lack is the ruling sentiment. That all of this may nevertheless be a matter of design is the film's ultimate paradox.

The knights, returned depleted from the unfulfilled quest, want for something to do. The tournament, the centerpiece of their present lives as well as of the film, comes as welcome relief, but is also a reminder of a former, more assured time when such activities carried greater meaning. The same frustration is echoed in Lancelot and Guinevere's affair. For this perfect knight, not only has the quest revealed his spiritual limitations, but after valiant efforts to resist the queen, his surrender also falls short of gratification. There is no evidence from what we see or hear that the affair, technically speaking, is ever resumed. The film is riddled with impossible strivings and unfulfilled desires, in which the moral vacuum following the quest can be neither denied nor displaced through rededication to physical or sexual pursuits.

Lancelot of the Lake is also one of Bresson's most aggressively filmic works, perhaps his most exhilarating artistic expression of religious doubt. Its bravura use of editing, sound, color, ellipsis, and synecdoche rivals the propulsive physicality of its tournament sequence. The film epitomizes many of Bresson's strongest stylistic tendencies, as well as such thematic preoccupations as grace, virginity, and the search for God. That a film can be such a brilliant carrier of an artist's ideas and strengths yet convey so bleak a message is a question raised by Bresson's late work, although it is hardly less relevant to the relationship of character behavior and destiny in *all* of his work. In the exquisite creation of dark flowers, Bresson is not alone. But the situation that *Lancelot* recounts is especially resonant since the image of the Grail conveys both the absence or unattainability of God and of the perfectibility of Art.[3] The quest for an ideal filmic achievement, as Bresson more than once remarked, is unending, every film merely a venture in that direction. For the filmmaker, no less than the characters in *Lancelot,* the quest may represent the inadequacies of the past, but it continues to haunt and shape the present.

Characteristic of Bresson's minimalist approach, physical action, a staple of the genre *Lancelot* evokes, is limited, rendering indelible its images of graphic violence.[4] Had Bresson made the film earlier, it is unlikely he would have allowed the violence and despair to unseat, almost, such motifs of the legend as honor, virtue, and reverence for the good. And if such earlier films as *A Man Escaped* and *Pickpocket* illustrate two poles of individual psychology, *Lancelot* reflects the destructive power of group psychology as incarnated in what Freud called the primal horde and the instinct to make war. This is explicitly realized in the way the film presents the knight, who, once mounted on his horse with visor down, is an indomitable war machine—not just a man on a horse but a fusion of two beings, likened to the centaur. This was the result of the invention of the stirrup, which changed the nature of combat by making it possible to wear heavier armor while remaining mobile.[5] Bresson's penchant for synecdoche brilliantly suits this effect, in which preparations for mounting and jousting for tournament or battle are generally filmed to stress the partial nature of objects, particularly the lower halves of the knights and of horses' bodies to which armored legs cling. The prevalence of the tendency in this film, as opposed to its limited use in the two that immediately precede it, is worth noting since it conjures a number of important connotations.

Pars pro toto, the rhetorical device of having a part stand for a whole (or vice versa), is rarely just a stylistic strategy in Bresson, as the previous analysis of *Pickpocket* argued. In *Lancelot* it seems to encode the overall moral and psychological crisis at the heart of the narrative, namely, the disintegrating social world it depicts and the personal breakdowns it generates. For example, in an early sequence, Arthur, Lancelot, and Gawain walk around the Round Table, which we see, through the framing and editing, only in sections, as the king laments the loss of so many knights and wonders if God has punished the fellowship for having provoked him. It seems insufficient to observe that each piece of the table stands for the whole and leave it at that. In context the synecdoche stresses fragmentation and loss, a broken, irreparable unity, and the dissolution of the virtue that it symbolized. As he has elsewhere, Bresson demonstrates not only that established conventions of the cinema can be put to original use but that his own stylistic hallmarks are not fixed in their implications. Unlike the knights after the quest, Bresson's return to vigorous form in *Lancelot* is a triumphant display of cinematographic eloquence.

The Legend

Although the figure of Arthur and the events of the fifth century whereby he was made king are chronicled in Geoffrey of Monmouth's *History of the Kings of Britain* (ca. 1138), there is no hard evidence that he ever existed. Of the numerous works about him, the various knights of the fellowship known as the Round Table, and the events that brought about their dissolution, the multivolume French romance of the thirteenth century, known as the Vulgate cycle,[6] was the most important. Its authorship is unknown, but its structural unity suggests that even if written by several authors, it conformed to the imagination of a single architect.[7] In the same century, the French writer Chrétien de Troyes composed several romances based on the legends and was presumably the first to introduce the figure of Lancelot into literature.[8] Among the best-known works in English, Thomas Malory's *Le Morte D'Arthur* comes closest to the scope of the Vulgate, tracing the genesis of Arthur's illegitimate birth, his conquest of the rival kings of Britain, his confrontation with Rome, and the founding of the Round Table. It also provides a thorough account of the knights' adventures. Many events are prophesied by the magician Merlin, including the adulterous affair of Queen Guinevere with Lancelot, Arthur's favorite knight; the quest of the Grail and its outcome; and Arthur's destruction through the revolt of his bastard son, Mordred.

The subsequent discussion of Bresson's *Lancelot* relies on English translations of the last two books of the French cycle, *The Quest of the Holy Grail* and *The Death of King Arthur;* a more recent translation of the latter titled *From Camelot to Joyous Guard;* the romances of Chrétien de Troyes; and Malory's work.[9] The events of the film follow the narrative line of *The Death of King Arthur,* which, of all the medieval Arthurian romances, is the least dependent on fantasy and supernatural events—no dragons, dwarfs, or giants—and the most psychological.[10] But since the quest of the Grail immediately precedes the film's events and is alluded to in the pre-credits scroll, its significance must be noted.

Depending on the source, the Grail is the cup, chalice, dish, or caldron believed to have been used by Jesus at the last supper and to contain drops of blood and sweat from his wounds when he was crucified. As legend has it, these were collected by Joseph of Arimathea, a follower of Christ according to the four canonical gospels, who, granted permission by Pontius Pilate, took down and buried Jesus' body.[11] In some legends drinking from this cup had miraculous healing powers. According to one legend, Joseph carried the Grail, along with the lance with which Jesus was pierced while on the cross, to Glastonbury, where he founded the first Christian church in Britain, under Roman rule at the time. "Once these precious relics had come to Britain, their custody devolved upon a line of Grail-keepers, known as the Fisher Kings, descendants of Joseph of Arimathea. The Grail was preserved in their Castle of Corbenic, enveloped in mystery and hidden from the sight of such adventurous knights as went in search of it."[12]

Because the legend incorporates ancient fertility cults and Celtic myths, the relevance of the Grail story to Arthurian legend is complicated in that "the relics of the Last Supper and the Passion are made to appear responsible for the malefic enchantments and perils afflicting King Arthur's kingdom." Étienne Gilson believed that the book of the *Quest* illustrated the "doctrine of grace and mystical union with God [and that the] Grail itself is the symbol of God's grace." According to that doctrine, grace is available to everyone, but only to the degree each person is capable of receiving it. Thus it is somewhat misleading to speak of the failure to find the Grail since those of complete purity, Galahad and Percival, not only find it, but are judged worthy to perceive its mysteries and live in its service. Galahad (illegitimate son of Lancelot), his name derived from Gilead in the Song of Songs, one of the mystical designations of Christ, is himself a second Christ, so that when he arrives at Arthur's court on the feast of the Pentecost to inspire the quest, he fuses the themes of the Descent of the Holy Ghost and the Resurrected Christ. Because of his perfection, however, he is elusive and vanishes without a trace, frustrating the knights who seek him as the exemplary manifestation of God's grace.[13]

The quest therefore is a kind of religious awakening, in which the spiritual strength of each knight is tested and the state of his soul revealed. And so to the concrete images of the Grail—cup, chalice, caldron, dish—we might add another: the mirror, in which is reflected the true state of the soul of those who pursue it and, by extension, the general unworthiness of a fallen mankind. We learn only in this part of the Arthurian saga that the endless, often arbitrary bloody combats to which most other parts of the work are devoted under the rubric "adventures" are what prevent the knights from being worthy of "achieving" the Grail, of experiencing the mystery of Christ and being healed. For example, both Galahad and Gawain encounter the same seven knights (representing the seven deadly sins) blocking their paths. Galahad overcomes them without killing them, whereas Gawain slaughters them all. He is then told by a holy man that he misunderstands the quest, that it is not like his former adventures, "consisting in the murder of men or slaying of knights [but] of a spiritual order higher in every way."[14] Because he has killed unnecessarily, Gawain follows the path of sin and, like most of his fellow knights, is unworthy of the Grail. More ominously, he is told that in the state of mortal sin nothing he does in Camelot thereafter is likely to bring any honor. The two knights who succeed, Galahad and Percival, do not return to the materialistic life of the court. Even the most remorseful among the others resort to their previous ways. Lancelot, having renounced his carnal desires for the queen that prevented him from succeeding in the quest, resumes the affair with increased ardor immediately upon return. The book of the *Quest,* therefore, "reveals the inadequacies and the dangers of the courtly ideal."[15]

It is the atmosphere of the fallout of this experience that Bresson's film absorbs and in which the characters of Arthur's court attempt to breathe. In the film, when Lancelot first arrives after two years on the quest, he is greeted by Gawain with the words "The first is last," which, in the context just provided, has a double meaning. On the surface it means that the best of all knights is the last to return, but in the spirit of the author of the *Quest,* no doubt following the New Testament, in which the celebrated attributes of the knights are strongly indicted and shown to be spiritually impoverished, the first is indeed, the last. Which is to say that, Lancelot, the object of undiluted fame and respect in the eyes of the king and most of the knights, proves to be spiritually weak and the cause of the destruction that will follow.

Thanatos and the Queen

It is no surprise therefore that Bresson begins his tale not with an act of chivalry, romance, or religious zeal, but with bloody violence and manslaughter. The shock of the pre-credits sequence is unprecedented in his work, its imagery not only a faithful rendition of what one finds in the literature, but an overture of the themes that will govern the film. A series of five graphic passages comprises the sequence, each followed by a long shot of a group of five knights riding from left to right through a dense forest and disappearing into the distance. The visual and rhythmic similarity of these rides conveys the implacability and normality of their activities. In the first of the brutal scenes, two knights in combat wield heavy swords with great effort until one, shorn of his weapon, is beheaded by the other. The deliberateness of the act is matched by the deliberateness of the camera's gesture, focused on the heaviness of the wielded sword as it is lifted upward from the ground and, in a brilliantly matched cut, makes a sweeping strike at the juncture of helmeted head and neck, stressing the labor and deadly precision of the act. The victim falls to the ground, blood gushing copiously from the gaping wound.

In the second scene, a knight, visor raised with eyes peering out, is surprised by his opponent; as he reaches for his sword, the other's plunges into his groin; he clutches his body and groans (figure 68). Nearby a knight stands over another knight seated on the ground; he swings his sword and smashes the other's helmeted skull; the latter falls back as blood spouts from his head. The riding knights pass two armored skeletons hanging from trees; immediately after, we see them leaving an area of scorched earth, strewn with burned bodies. In the last of the series, the rump of a horse in close-up enters a chapel, its rider's arm sweeping his sword across the altar, overturning candles, the tabernacle, and holy cards. As the knights ride off, a drumroll and bagpipes begin on the soundtrack; a silver cup, the Grail, is centered against an otherwise all-black screen, and a scroll recounting the recent activities of the knights of the Round Table and their failed quest unrolls.

The initial imagery is familiar to anyone raised either on the legends themselves or on movies of medieval lore,[16] but we should not overlook their specificity within the film's design. For one thing, the images are graphic, but their context is ambiguous. Since nothing precedes them and they are followed by the scroll, they could represent actions performed by the knights during the quest. By not contextualizing the violence, Bresson allows the imagery to represent the behavior of the knights before, during, and after the quest and makes it a central concern. This is further suggested by the use of sound. The galloping of horses and the clanging of armor that belong to the repeated shots of the knights riding through the forest are heard for several seconds over each image of the bloody action that precedes them.[17] This overlapping technique, most often the sound of horses or armor, not only sustains the driving force of the film's action but reinforces the ritual behavior of the knights throughout the film and indicates the enduring presence of these elements in the world evoked.

The only other explicit action sequence, the tournament contest, involves clashing armored bodies and horses but nothing as deadly as the opening. Even the battle that ends the film is treated elliptically. In typical fashion, Bresson provides minimal but memorable evidence of the brutality typical of Arthur's knights, not as an ongoing naturalistic part of the narrative, as a conventional costume epic would treat it, but as a singular articulation of the excessive violence inherent in the legend. It is against this backdrop that the film's more critical concerns, arising from the struggles of conscience that besiege Arthur, Guinevere, Lancelot, Gawain, and their cohorts, are set. The vividness of the initial imagery prefigures these conflicts: heads (the seats of conscience, pride, and reason) are lopped off; groins (the source of lust and desire) are penetrated; and sacred objects (symbolic of the values on which the society is based) are desecrated. No image more potently speaks to Bresson's underlying theme than that of the armored skeletons, a macabre reminder of last things, the corruptibility of the body, and the unknown fate of the soul. The image haunts the film via the pronounced metallic rattling that we hear throughout, suggesting an uncanny affinity between armored limbs and joints and the skeletal structures they are designed to protect. Imagine the two hanging figures as the demythologized bones of Lancelot and Gawain, and the film's preoccupation with the death of individuals and cultures rings clear.

These associations lend the imagery the force of what Freud called the component instincts of early development, those elements tied to a source (e.g., the oral or anal instinct) and an aim (e.g., the scopophilic or mastering instinct). In the Freudian system these are presumed to fuse eventually in variously organized psychic structures, yet their persistence as segregated drives in adult life results in regressive or perverse behavior.[18] The behavior of the knights—"angels who kill all they meet," as a character in Chrétien de Troyes's tale calls them—exhibits the tendencies of group psychology, those "manifestations of the unconscious impulses" that often "deman[d] of its heroes…strength, or even violence."[19] As illustrated in the film's initial, noncontextualized imagery, the knights' actions suggest wanton aggression, such that the entire film might be read as a manifesto of the death instinct. In his essay on that subject, Freud links it to the "component instincts whose function it is to assure that the organism shall follow its own path to death."[20] The film's soundtrack, dominated by thundering hooves and the relentless clamor of armor, sustains the mood of the imagery of the preface with its twin surges of propulsive movement and clashing combat.

Given the thrust of these associations, the situation of the Round Table and the affair between Lancelot and Guinevere have all the hallmarks of the family romance, as Arthur contends with three "sons"—Lancelot, Gawain, and Mordred—and the developing contentions become matters of sibling and Oedipal rivalry over the throne as well as the queen. Guinevere incurs guilt by insisting that her affair with Lancelot has nothing to do with the destruction that looms over the court. That the film avoids the incestuous relationships in the literature and any hint that Mordred is Arthur's bastard son might reflect Bresson's reluctance to invite such a reading.[21] Then again, he introduces disturbing elements that reinforce it and that are not in the literature. In their last conversation, Guinevere resolves to return to Arthur, but not without declaring how much she loathes him and mocking Lancelot's vow to keep her and fight the king with the curt reply, "You didn't kill him yesterday," that is, when he had the chance.

Nevertheless, the characterization of the queen also seems to undergo a split, for by the end it is she who seems the voice of reason and determines to return to Arthur to atone for and put a stop to the bloodshed. Initially, though, she represents eros against the thanatos-dominated mind-set and resists Lancelot's determination to end their affair. Bresson complicates the issue of her guilt and selfishness by having her question, rather persuasively, the reasoning that attributes the mood at court to her love for Lancelot. In doing so, he seems to be asking which behavior has the more deleterious effects on human events. In giving Guinevere the soundest judgment in the film, he challenges the morality and wisdom of the arguments often given to justify aggression and war. In fact, he goes further by implying that Lancelot and Guinevere never resume their affair. In their first two scenes together, their exchange is explicitly about *not* continuing the affair. In the third, Lancelot appears to give in when Guinevere advises that they wait until the king and the knights have left for the tournament. But Lancelot changes his mind and goes to the tournament, and the wound he incurs keeps him from returning until much later. In two subsequent scenes between them after he rescues her from prison, Guinevere seems to share the same space in the castle as the knights; not even the final exchange she has with Lancelot occurs in private, as knights continually walk in the background; and in their final moment together, Lancelot leads her back to the king.

In sum, no shot or scene or off screen suggestion implies that they have reconsummated their affair. Nor is there a line of dialogue that establishes or suggests that it has occurred. When Arthur offers to take her back, it is because there is no proof of adultery. This is contrary to Malory, and presumably the Vulgate on which it is based, which includes a scene of Lancelot and Guinevere trapped in her bedchamber, where they have made love all night and are discovered by Mordred, a situation from which Lancelot cleverly escapes but which leads to the condemnation of the queen.[22] So although the film clearly alludes to the preexistent affair between Lancelot and Guinevere, no evidence of an ongoing affair is provided. Indeed the amount of time and dialogue devoted to the *delay* of the affair's resumption would seem to confirm its permanent suspension. This delay, like Hamlet's procrastination, becomes as important as the action.

According to the medieval code, actual sexual congress is irrelevant since intention and display of unlawful affection would be sufficient to confirm the couple's treason and justify the king's retaliation. By creating ambiguity about its literal status, Bresson, like Guinevere, questions the affair's centrality to the larger issues at stake and complicates the simpler morality of posing adultery against such qualities as loyalty and honor and the value of life. Lancelot's initial resistance and Guinevere's later decision to leave him alter the logistics of the original story, making both characters far more complex.

The progression and shifts of the interactions between Lancelot and Guinevere are registered effectively in the filmic treatment. In their first meeting upon Lancelot's return, the formality observed in their initial greeting—she entering their secret rendezvous spot and standing in place as he approaches, kneels, and lifts her dress gently to his face, as befits her rank—continues in the twenty shots of their subsequent conversation in the loft. Each is alone in medium shot, Lancelot facing off screen right, Guinevere facing off screen left (figures 69, 70). Consistent with the tenor of their exchanges, in which Lancelot asks to be released from his vow to her so that he can be true to the one he made to God, the sequence, unfolding in sequential profile shots, sustains a sense of ceremonious reserve in sync with their bodily restraint, proscribing the comfort level of the over-the-shoulder shot-countershot conversation between Guinevere and Gawain much later. The effect resembles that of many two-paneled tableaux of the Annunciation scene, the Archangel Gabriel on the left and the Virgin Mary on the right receiving the divine message. Lancelot is no angel and Guinevere no virgin, yet this impression suits Lancelot's earnestness as he tells her that he has "seen the Grail." Though the greater connotation of the allusion will not become clear until later, when Guinevere changes her point of view, Lancelot, in this first exchange, transmits the divine message that, unknown to both of them, will ultimately bear fruit in her.

The second meeting in the loft is more varied in treatment, at first suggesting Lancelot's torment, then a loosening of rigidity. Its most striking passage is a single take of Lancelot walking from right to left and back again three times while Guinevere remains off screen until he shifts direction and joins her on a bench. The contrast is between wavering mobility and immoveable certitude, aptly expressed by her first response to his plea to free him from his vow. "You have changed, but I am the same," she says. He insists, "[At stake is] the salvation of us all," to which Guinevere responds by drawing attention to the arrogant pride implicit in such a notion, and saying, "God does not ask us to forswear love." She objects to the idea that the moral decline at court was instigated by their affair. "You were all implacable. You killed, pillaged, burned [the very images we saw in the preface]. Then you turned blindly on each other like maniacs. Now you blame our love for this disaster." Perhaps because her logic seems unassailable, Lancelot cannot respond.[23]

The third meeting begins with similar restraint but quickly dissolves the distance between them when Lancelot removes his armor, putting aside his knightly loyalty along with his physical and moral resistance, and embraces her. This occurs despite his knowledge that Mordred and other knights are waiting and watching for exactly such an incriminating moment. The queen, aware that someone has taken the scarf she left behind from the last meeting, is more cautious; just as they are about to make love, she suggests that they wait until everyone has left for the tournament the next day.

In sum, Bresson's treatment of the relationship is more intricate than it is in the literature, where reference to the affair's resumption is directly stated early on in *The Death of King Arthur* and in the second paragraph of "The Book of Sir Launcelot and Queen Gwynevere" in Malory's work. Rather than take it for granted as the premise for the contention among the knights and the basis of the breakdown of morale, Bresson offers us a set of challenging ideas about individual responsibility, group psychology, conscience, and moral courage. Instead of a simpering Guinevere, he gives us a strong, thinking young woman, who, unlike her literary model, loathes her husband (for reasons that are unclear) even while resolving to return to him. When she leaves Lancelot, the man she loves "more than anyone has loved anyone," and says that "she will suffer instead," this astounding act makes her Bresson's strongest heroine after Joan.

The Course of Fate

As the contrast between the queen and the violent lives of the knights implies, the film is a streamlined treatment of the saga. Unfamiliarity with the literary sources would make it difficult to appreciate the extraordinary economy of the plot. In the literature Mordred comes into the foreground only in the late stages of the epic, when he tries to seize power from Arthur to seduce Guinevere, precipitating the final war in which both he and the king are killed. In the film he is the primary antagonist from the beginning, accusing the queen of adultery, setting traps to catch the couple in action, and instigating the internecine war that results in Arthur's and Lancelot's deaths and ends the film. Many incidents from the literature are eliminated, and except for acknowledging Gawain and Agrivain as Arthur's nephews, Bresson ignores the implications of significant blood ties, especially the blunt Oedipal cast to Mordred's behavior as Arthur's bastard son.

By tailoring the scope, narrowing the focus, and eliding many details, Bresson molds the tale into a post-quest world in which the purest, virginal characters (Galahad, Percival) are absent and the forces of aggression, betrayal, and despair are dominant. In the literature Merlin conceived the Round Table as "the symbol of the wholeness of virtue." By filming the actual table only in sections, Bresson evokes not only the diminution of its power and the sadness of the losses bemoaned by Arthur, but the fracturing of virtue and its capacity for instilling spiritual meaning. "Give us a purpose," cries Gawain, to which Arthur replies, "Pray," presumably to appease the God he fears they have provoked.

The course of fate is more contracted in the film. In the pre-credits sequence following the scroll, an old peasant woman living in the forest with her family, the same one who later tends Lancelot's wound, delivers the film's most ominous line. As we hear the sound of an approaching horse, she says, "He whose footfalls precede him will not outlive the year." "Even if the footfalls are those of his horse?" asks the young girl with her, to which she replies in the affirmative. A moment later Lancelot arrives and utters his first line, "I've lost my way," a phrase that resonates within the context of the legend as well as Bresson's universe. As surrogate for Merlin and the filmmaker, the woman not only predicts the future but heralds the prescient significance of sound and off screen space and the identification of the knight with his horse—all without a hint of the supernatural. Her serene, unsentimental wisdom, like that of other noble maternal figures in Bresson, from the Mother Superior in *Les Anges du péché* to the widow in *L'Argent,* comes from life and observations of human nature. She does indeed set Lancelot on course, directing him to the very destiny she foresees. This woman may have been inspired by the widowed mother at the beginning of Chrétien de Troyes's *Story of the Grail,* whose husband and sons were all knights slain in combat and who strives to keep her only surviving son (Percival, as it happens) ignorant of the existence of knights.[24] The mother's manner and experience closely resemble the way the old woman in the film behaves, especially later, when she tries to prevent the recovering Lancelot from returning to combat. Her exchanges with him as he lies awkwardly in what looks like a child's bed seem far more intimate than their relationship would indicate, as if they were mother and son.

That moment is in striking contrast to the way the knights usually appear, just as the horses seem to be different creatures when not saddled and mounted for combat or contest. For example, in the first sequence after the credits when Lancelot kneels before the king to apologize for not having brought the Grail, their exchange is interrupted by an extreme close-up of Lancelot's horse, specifically of one eye that seems to register agitation. Over this image we hear Arthur's words, "The Grail eludes us," after which the previous shot is resumed. There are two previous close-ups of this horse, most recently one showing his excitement perhaps induced by the whinnying of others in their stalls. But the first occasion is in the forest encounter with the woman. The close-up shows us a much calmer creature, over whose image we hear her say, "I'll show you the way," a conjunction of image and text too calculated to ignore. So is the one under discussion, which is as uncanny as certain shots of the donkey in *Balthazar.* Does the shot qualify Lancelot's gesture by drawing attention away from it? Does it imply some irony concerning Arthur's remark?

As Bresson said of the dog that turns away from the sight of Joan at the stake and as his treatment of Balthazar implies, animals are so grounded in the natural world that they have an unerring sense for detecting any disturbance in it. By superimposing Arthur's remark over the eye of the horse, the notion of a mystery that must remain unsolvable may be equated with the quest for something that must remain unattainable. When this horse is felled in battle, it is the side of his head, pierced with an arrow near an ever-alert eye, that we see. Beyond the implication that horses are innocent casualties of war, there is the sense that the consciousness of Lancelot's horse, whatever that may be, is no less subject to death than that of his rider. Perhaps the horses represent a collective alternative point of view outside that of any of the characters. If so, they are more than the bottom halves of the war machines invented by men, and the persistent whinnying on the soundtrack is a reminder not only of their presence but of voices that go unheard.

The order of events following Lancelot's arrival is divided between his meetings with the queen and his attempts to mediate between the contentious knights. Both lines of action are brought to a head in the tournament sequence, a climax in the classical sense, but thereafter deteriorate in rapid fashion toward the denouement. Lines are drawn between Lancelot's advocates and those allied to Mordred. That Mordred is the immediate agent that destroys the Round Table is implied in the scene in which Arthur, Lancelot, and Gawain circle the table as the king painfully recalls the many who have died. In every shot of this sequence, but for the entrance and exit to the room, a segment of the table is always visible, linking all three as integral to the fellowship (figure 71). That the table is not shown entire, that is, as simply a prop in the room, stresses that it is constituted *as a whole* only through the identification of each knight with one of its parts. And so it is significant when Mordred stealthily opens the door to the room and remains at its threshold while he exchanges words with the king. As his remark about how unwise the quest was and Gawain's response confirm, Mordred is outside the circle in every way. And yet though he is the antagonist that catalyzes the action, he is not a cardboard villain. What Mordred suspects and says, however malicious and damaging, is true, and he is more realistic than idealistic, compared, for example, to Gawain, who seems his natural foil. Gawain's flaw may be that he believes in the perpetuation of the dream, of Camelot, while incapable of devising any means to realize it. Mordred's flaw is that he speaks the truth out of poisonous jealousy, wants only revenge, and has no plan or desire to preserve order.

There is a striking use of light and color that contrasts the roles of these two figures in two separate scenes. Lancelot's arrival at nightfall seems calculated to pose a sense of hope to counter the calm declaration of fate voiced by the old woman in the forest. As he crosses the drawbridge and rides into the courtyard, the tents in the foreground are suddenly set aglow, a deep orange filling the screen, as if animated by his arrival, the first almost magically. Then we see the figure of a knight, Gawain, carrying a lantern and walking from left to right in the foreground on the near side of the tents, illuminating them in turn (figure 72). Gawain's walk parallels Lancelot's ride on the far side of the tents in the same direction, their movements brought to a halt with a cut when Lancelot lifts his visor and Gawain lifts the lantern to illumine his face. It is fitting that Gawain should be the lantern carrier who greets the yet to be identified Lancelot since the two are deeply bonded throughout. We soon learn that Lancelot does indeed represent hope to Arthur and the community in general, and that his arrival promises to be the much needed balm, as the king puts it, to counter the poisonous air.

This nightly orange glow of the tents becomes familiar, but there is one other striking instance when it reverberates with equal intensity while reversing the meaning of the earlier scene. We see the shadow and outline of a lantern in large close-up inside of a tent, its size lending it an infernal look. Upon Lancelot's entrance, it becomes clear that it is Mordred's tent and that it is he who carries the lantern, deliberately directing its light away from the queen's scarf that he has confiscated from the loft and leaving Lancelot in the dark. Lancelot holds out his hand in friendship, hoping to dissolve the enmity between them, but the reverse shot shows Mordred, unmoving against the fiery glow that fills the space behind him, refusing it. As the presence of the scarf implies, his rejection is linked to his intention to destroy Lancelot by exposing the affair. In the light of Gawain's remark that all of the knights, including Mordred, have been seen looking up at the queen's window, it seems that Mordred is as envious of Lancelot's position as the queen's knight and lover as he is of his being the king's favorite. In this scene the positive symbolism of the earlier sequence with Gawain is reversed, casting a visual and moral shadow, not only on Lancelot's character but over any possibility of knightly comradeship overcoming envy and of Lancelot's being the instrument of change.

What is noteworthy about the contrast between Gawain and Mordred is that each tells the truth as far as he knows it, whereas Lancelot, the film's titular protagonist, lies. This is not Bresson's invention. The literary Lancelot consistently lies about his relationship with the queen to the king and to the knights closest to him, declaring nevertheless that "a true knight is neither adulterous or lecherous."[25] When, in the film, he attends a chapel to pray for strength to resist Guinevere, we are given an appropriate visual expression of this contradiction. The shot displays a large out-of-focus gold cross on the altar in the foreground as Lancelot, in the far background, opens the door of the chapel and walks forward. As he comes nearer and finally reaches the cross, we might naturally expect it to come into sharp focus; instead it remains noticeably out of focus (figure 73). This is another of Bresson's singular filmic gestures designed to produce a specific effect. It seems that the same moral imperfections that kept Lancelot from finding the Grail prevent him from fully approaching Christ. The internal contradiction and ultimate frustration of his prayer to resist the queen—he will, in fact, succumb to her the next time they meet—is mirrored in the illusion of the shot, framed to suggest a collapse of deep space but in the end withholding optical gratification by not coming into full focus. For Lancelot, God, it seems, is still at a vague remove.

His prayer is barely finished when we hear the sound of galloping horses from the next shot, which is something of an echo of the one just described, showing two knights approaching from the distant background into the foreground and to the entrance of the castle. They come to invite Arthur's knights to a tournament. While this is an occasion to improve morale, as Gawain observes, it is also an ironic answer to Lancelot's prayer, since, as yet unknown to him, it will be his fateful decision to go to the tournament that will, in the words of his prayer, "deliver [him] from a temptation [he] can hardly resist." We see the knights preparing themselves for the contest while the antagonism between factions persists. Mordred, having found the queen's scarf in the loft and believing that Lancelot intends to remain behind, now moves more brazenly toward open hostility, lying in wait by the queen's quarters with his cohorts to assault Lancelot, whose last-minute change of heart denies Mordred that pleasure. Thus, unwittingly, Lancelot's prayer is the catalyst for the rest of the film. Like Fontaine and Michel, he is an instrument of a design beyond his control, and his subsequent actions are an unconscious working out of fate. That this plan does not preclude the destruction of Arthur's court does not invalidate it as such; indeed it concurs with the perspective we are given of the courtly ideal in the book of the *Quest*, where it is found to be morally inadequate and dangerous. Even Lancelot's unintended frustration of Mordred's scheme and his later decision to fight for Arthur against Mordred work toward this end. Although Arthur no doubt had the preservation of the kingdom and the restoration of unity in mind when he advised Gawain to pray, it may be the ultimate irony that Lancelot, for completely different reasons, is the one who enacts this directive, bringing about disunity and the downfall of the kingdom.

Tournament *Des Forces Du Cinéma*

The tournament sequence, like the Gare de Lyon sequence in *Pickpocket*, is an exhilarating tour de force and one of the most spectacular passages of editing in film history, no less stunning an illustration of the inherent powers of the medium than the Odessa steps sequence in *Battleship Potemkin* (1925). As was his wont, Bresson turns the spectacle inherent in the genre into a filmic one, a dazzling display of how the arsenal of cinema—framing, editing, sound, color, off screen space, synecdoche, and ellipsis—can depict and suggest action. When Gawain, recognizing the disguised Lancelot by his style of combat, exclaims his name over and over, the spectator, recognizing the incomparable style of the filmmaker, is tempted to shout "Bresson! Bresson!"

Although there are several tournaments in the literature, Bresson gives us only one, making it both the centerpiece of the film and a determinant event in the fates of his characters. This is clear from what happens before and after. Lancelot's decision to go, after having agreed to be with the queen, has important narrative and psychological implications. He goes, ostensibly, to defend not so much his own honor as that of Gawain and Lionel for supporting him against Mordred's accusations. But surely guilt plays a key role in his decision since he knows that the accusations are valid. As he is mulling over these thoughts, alone in his tent and hours after the others have departed, there are cuts to the film's most sensual images of the queen, her nude body in the bathtub being scrubbed by her attendants, shot in the warm glow of flesh tones (figure 74). The crosscut captures the thematic contrast the film develops between erotic love and knightly loyalty. Although Lancelot promises, as he gazes at the queen's window, to return the next day to be with her, his decision to leave is another instance of the film's thwarting all paths to the sexual commingling of this couple. But there is another, more menacing crosscut here, to Mordred's men lying in wait for Lancelot just outside the queen's chambers, drawing their swords when the door opens and a mere hand-maiden appears. Their presence reflects the degree of Mordred's envy and how he has managed to find allies willing to kill the favored knight. The proximity of drawn swords to the queen's flesh gives the scene an erotic charge that has several connotations. First, it expresses Mordred's desire for the queen, masked by his hatred of and overly righteous spying on Lancelot; second, it situates the queen's sexuality more bluntly as an inducement to violence; and third, it marks the anticipation of sexual release, suspended during Lancelot's long recovery after the tournament and perversely achieved when, bloodied sword in hand, he rescues the queen from prison much later.

As we hear him riding off into the night over the image of the queen's window, the sound of his galloping horse fades and is displaced by the sound of the armor and horses of the knights on the way to the tournament in the next shot. Arthur, raising his visor, asks why Lancelot is not with them. After a pause, Mordred, raising his visor, says, "Love, sire. Lancelot loves." Off screen Arthur asks, "Who?" Following an awkward pause, Mordred, in the same shot, answers, "The queen." In the ensuing exchanges of medium shots, Mordred swears to Lancelot's betrayal as Gawain swears that his insinuation is false, until Arthur orders Mordred to be silent. Arthur's seeming naïveté here serves his determination not to hear any evidence that would require him to act. This is true of his demeanor in the literature when he acknowledges having known all along of Lancelot's affair with the queen, since it was predicted by Merlin, but did nothing about it out of love for both of them. The sequence ends over a shot of Gawain explaining the rules of the tournament—"choice of adversaries, sharpened points, weakened lances"— then lowering his visor as the sounds of the crowd are heard in anticipation of the event.

By now it is obvious that overlapping sound is one of this film's most prominent techniques, although it seems as underappreciated as the constant clamor of the armor, which some writers believe should have been muffled or eliminated, as though Bresson had not deliberately intended the effect. This is to underestimate the importance of material reality in his films. The sound of the armor is a critical element in Chrétien de Troyes's tales.[26] It is no less so for Bresson, whose treatment of the sound here surpasses the importance of the husband's footsteps in *Une femme douce,* those of the guards on the stairways in *A Man Escaped,* and those produced by Mouchette's ill-fitting clogs. It lends weight to the physicality of the film, as does the sound of the bird that marks the area just outside the loft and as do the various latches on wooden doors that vibrate during a storm. To mute the prominence of these sounds would be the aural equivalent of making the editing invisible, in short, to denaturing Bresson's modernist approach to the medium.

Of equal note in the sequence just recounted is the stress on the raising and lowering of the visor in order to facilitate conversation. A conventional film might have avoided this detail as an awkward distraction. The raising and lowering of the visor speaks to a constant motif in the literature, whereby knights meet and clash, often without knowing each other's identity until afterward. In the tournament sequence, the visor clinches Lancelot's disguise from all but his closest allies. The sequence just discussed begins with a shot of the king with visor down and ends with a shot of Gawain lowering his, rendering the visor a kind of cinematic trope, opening and closing the sequence (figure 75). It also provides a striking contrast between the knights as individuals and as figures of the cultural landscape. The knights' faces, like the unprotected backs of their leggings, reveal the vulnerable flesh beneath the armor. To judge from the more than fifteen shots of Gawain as he walks away, Bresson seems to stress this quality as a counterpoint to the armored shell. On the way to the tournament, Gawain's lowering of his visor creates a poignant contrast between the noble and vulnerable youth and the impassive warrior.

Typically Bresson, eschewing a conventional approach to the tournament, focuses on its quintessential features to illuminate the milieu of the medieval court. The cinematographic display of the action is therefore both revealing of and synchronous with its appeal to that culture, both physically brutal and aesthetically mesmerizing. As the only such sequence in the film, it represents all that remains of the fellowship of the knights, the only outward sign of its relevance. At the heart of the sequence is Lancelot's matchless jousting, performed, like a true Bressonian character, with accuracy and directness, and resulting in his unseating of nine knights. It is "his manner of strength and style," as Malory expresses it, that reveals him to Gawain and Arthur.

At no point in the sequence do we see an establishing shot of the setting or the field of combat. The closest we get is the glimpse of a crowd clustered in a small rectangle of the background in one shot of the piper. The setting is constructed through the repetition and variation of a series of images, sounds, and motifs, some of which are elided after the pattern becomes familiar. This in turn accelerates the action as it reaches its peak, generating a filmic excitement to match the one experienced by the spectators of the tournament. Not counting the rides of the knights to and from the event, the sequence runs nearly five and a half minutes and, by one scholar's count, contains ninety-three shots.[27] In other words, though it is about one-sixteenth of the film's running time, it totals a little more than one-sixth of the 644 shots in the film. A full one-third of them (thirty-one) include horses, seen mostly from their flanks down as they are positioned before the charge and gallop toward the opposing knights. Such framing enhances the action-driven thrust of the sequence, focusing on the musculature of the horse's body and the centrifugal force of its legs as it is ridden into the contest. Peripheral to these images are shots of the dusty ground and of the wooden railing along which the contesting knights ride in opposing directions.

Two slightly registered clashes occur before the arrival of an unidentified knight (Lancelot) sparks curiosity. We see him in thirteen shots as he exchanges lances after each tilt and raises them in deference to the king before each match. Once he is in the ready position and during the charge, however, the focus is on the galloping horse as the camera tracks it left to right on the screen, followed by a shot of the opponent's ride in the opposite direction. Our ability to identify Lancelot is facilitated by the patch of his orange saddle-cloth, seen fleetingly at the top of the frame. The actual moment of contact between Lancelot's lance and his opponent's shield is registered, at first, only through the sound of the clash heard over reaction shots of Gawain and Arthur and other onlookers in the stands, confirming Bresson's remark that "the tournament sequence was staged for the ear."[28] In each case the clash is quickly followed by a shot of the defeated knight in the midst of falling off his charger, an image we see eight times. Because the object of the contest is to unseat the opponent, this pattern isolates that moment as the heart of the action. As the sequence develops, however, we see five instances of the moment of impact between lance and shield in sync with its sound, framed and edited to effect an optical and aural impact on the viewer analogous to the physical clash on the field. That is, each cut to the impact is the visceral equivalent of the jolting collision of lance and shield (figure 76). In one instance the camera seems actually mounted on the charger as Lancelot's lance, the only object on the screen, diagonally penetrates the space before it toward the yet unseen opponent, as if it had a life of its own. Soon the pattern shifts again, elimi-nating the intervening images of the ceremony we saw earlier, to give us four impacts in quick succession, separated only by brief reaction shots of Gawain and Arthur exclaiming the name of the victorious rider (figure 77). The sheer physicality of this design, in which both represented and implied action are paralleled and then made increasingly synchronous with their filmic rendi-tion, is unmatched in any film of medieval combat I can recall.

Before the jousting takes over the experience, the ceremonial routine is carefully established. In seven shots, framed almost identically, we see the piper—from the neck down, focused, typically, only on what he *does*—playing the same melody, the first three bars of which are heard over his image, and the remainder over the image of a white pole on which the flag of each knight's colors is hoisted, an image shown eight times. Medium shots of the spectators constitute the second greatest number of shots: seventeen of Arthur and Gawain surrounded by others, six medium close-ups of Gawain alone, as befits his curiosity about and recognition of the mysterious knight.

As the sequence proceeds, specific elements of the ceremony are elided, such as the expected shots of the piper, of the flag, and of Lancelot throwing down his used lance and seizing a new one. As the action approaches its peak, elisions multiply, collapsing the core aspects of the sequence into pure moments of attack, impact, and reaction, accompanied by the sounds of galloping horses, the thuds of lances against shields and of falling bodies, and roars of the crowd. In the last twenty shots of the sequence, for example, there are no shots of the piper or the pole with the flag, and then none of the intervening steps. As if this were not sufficiently condensed, the succession of impacts followed by reactions is more radically streamlined when we hear the sound of the charging horses of the *next* impact in sync with the reaction shots to the previous one. In other words, as with the imagery, time collapses, so that reactions can now be read simultaneously as anticipations.

Moving and galloping horses, impacts, knights riding into combat, and falling knights total approximately fifty shots devoted to physical movement around the jousting itself. The total of reaction shots is almost half that number. The great majority of shots in the sequence therefore are divided between action and spectatorship. By segregating these, that is, by not displaying the action and spectator reactions, along with the ceremony, in any combinations of overall scenic or social wholes,[29] each activity occupies its own filmic space, achieving its own weight and thrusting itself on the viewer as individual emotive and psychic forces.

In psychoanalytic terms, the distribution is between the aggressive or mastering instincts and the voyeuristic, mediated by the images of ceremony that demonstrate how these separate elements, like the component instincts, are sustained by the structure of ritual. If the sequence is the most viscerally exciting in the film, this confirms, for Lancelot as well as the knights in general, the dominance of aggression over eros, or the displacement of the latter onto the former.. Indeed the love affair, dominated by dialogue about tortured doubts, guilt, and God, is wholly cerebral, whereas the tournament sequence, in its breathtaking appeal to the aural, visual, and tactile senses, approaches the orgasmic. This is consistent with the film's overall dynamic, contrasting the lure of violence and knightly adventure with the more docile pleasures of romantic love, a phenomenon that would appear to turn on its head the raison d'être of chivalry as the knights' championing of damsels in distress. The many shots of the queen's window high up and out of reach, which, Gawain remarks, many of the knights, including himself, are caught staring at, allude to this notion as well as render it abstract. As the only, but unavailable female erotic object in the film, it would appear that the queen represents more than just the "sun," as Gawain ideally expresses it. Yet the very fact that she is the *only* such object and *unavailable* speaks to the absence, even impossibility, of erotic fulfillment for any of the knights—an impression that is at odds with the literature.

If Lancelot's performance at the tournament is a displacement of his erotic longing for Guinevere, it is also an exhibitionistic celebration of what he, and the fellowship, do best; it is a critical reminder of the prowess and cultural viability of the knightly ethic. Lancelot does his duty to the king and as a member of that group, in particular to his closest comrades, Gawain and Lionel. But he also appeases two more urgent, unconscious demands: the need to deny the crime of which Mordred has accused him and the need to defer the act that would give the lie to his denial and seal his guilt. Considering the number and scope of emotional, psychological, and morally complex forces at work, it is no wonder that the tournament sequence is so richly and exhilaratingly constructed. In this reading it is a spectacular acting-out of primal, egoistic, and superegoistic drives, the compelling forces of which are mirrored by the increasing intensity and focusing of the filmic components.

What Lancelot cannot imagine is the grander scheme that he has helped to set in motion, one that will destroy the very things his performance was designed to preserve. And so, following the tournament, the contrast between eros and the fellowship is sustained and complicated, for now his inability to be with the queen is because of the wound he has incurred. We see him riding alone into the forest, where he collapses. The wound itself is from the tip of a lance that has lodged in or near his groin after the joust with Lionel, one of the two knights most loyal to him. Recalling an image from the pre-credits sequence in which a knight is mortally stabbed in the same area, the wound is likely to preclude any intercourse with the queen, and so is yet another sign of the impossibility of this occurring. Because it is the tip of a lance by a fellow and beloved knight, it also carries homoerotic implications, as a concrete reminder of the bond among the knights and the king, which, it would appear, is stronger than the one Lancelot has with the queen. The wound not only signifies the effects of the combats and his decision but is a sign of his unending loyalty to the Round Table.

Things Fall Apart

The film cuts from Lancelot's fall in the forest to the return ride of the knights, a mirror image of the earlier scene in which several knights identify Lancelot as the mysterious champion of the tournament. "It was his horse," says one; "Only one lance is a thunderbolt," says another; "Only one knight charges with his visor down," says a third. They conclude that Lancelot did not remain behind, as Mordred implied, in order to be with the queen. Lionel then reveals that he delivered Lancelot a grave injury. On their return, Gawain reports all of this to the queen, who refuses to believe it and insists that Lancelot must have gone away. Shots of Arthur and the knights looking warily at her alert her to a dangerous turn of events. Two knights are sent in search of Lancelot but return without success. The morning after a storm, all the flags on the knights' pavilions are blowing in the wind except Lancelot's, a sure sign to Mordred that he is dead. That Gawain and the others immediately agree indicates that, despite their rivalries, when it comes to the significance of omens the knights share a common psychology, something we saw earlier in relation to the way they interpreted the moon and a passing cloud. In disbelief, Guinevere awaits Lancelot in the loft, which Gawain warns her is a sign of her guilt. Against his advice she boldly confesses her love for Lancelot and seems oblivious to the consequences. Gawain declares that he would die to save her honor, but fears it is too late.

While all this develops, Lancelot has been recovering in the old woman's house in the forest where the very sight of him sitting up in a bed too small for his hulk evokes the image of an overgrown child. To prevent his leaving, she lies to the knights searching for him, but to no avail. Insisting that he hears "someone calling" him, Lancelot is determined to go. Angrily she gives him his armor and tells him, "Go and get killed," both a sigh of complaint and a knowing nod to the fate she foresaw in the beginning. As we hear Lancelot riding off, the young girl kisses the ground he has just left. It is a curious and touching gesture that recalls her undisguised child-like crush the first time she saw him and may be a veiled allusion to the story of the young woman in the literature who literally dies of unrequited love for Lancelot. The girl looks up and in the direction he has taken, then lowers her head to the ground again. What she and the old couple represent is the family life that is just as out of reach for Lancelot and his cohorts as the Grail. Thus, although he tells the old woman that he rides off to life, the images confirm that he has left it behind.

The close-up of the girl hovering over the ground cuts to a long shot of several unidentified figures running through the forest at night with torches, seen through the bars of the prison holding the queen. It is one of the most stunning narrative ellipses in Bresson's work and the first of several in the final quarter of the film bent on collapsing events with breakneck speed. As we take in the image and recognize what it imports, we hear a crash of something just out of sight and then Guinevere, off screen, crying out Lancelot's name at the very moment he enters, his hand and sword covered in blood. It is the most potent and sexually displaced moment in the film, confirming that the only consummation they will achieve is tinged with blood and death. How and when Guinevere was placed in the prison is elided; the fate that awaited her is never explained, although Gawain hints at what is clearly stated in the literature: that if judged guilty of adultery she would have been burned at the stake as a traitor.[30]

To grasp the effect of this elision, consider what has been left out. We know neither when nor why the king has moved from compassionate concern to judgment; we know nothing of the dispositions of the various knights, nor how judgment was determined. Had her death already been decided before the rescue? How did Lancelot learn of the events? How did he so quickly muster enough support to storm the prison? Bresson, in short, has allowed a startling break in narrative continuity to parallel the sudden rupture of events, jolting the viewer into the realization that everything has fallen apart.

After the queen is rescued, she is taken to an unidentified castle (called Joyous Guard in the literature), where Lancelot and his followers prepare to withstand any attacks from Arthur. He learns from Lionel that during the rescue, he has inadvertently killed Agrivain, Gawain's brother, which provokes another battle, also elided, in which Lancelot mortally wounds Gawain. We are again shocked at the rapidity with which this occurs. Just as Lancelot was absent from the narrative while he lay wounded in the forest, Gawain is suddenly missing from the scene. In a way his absence is the most telling sign of the breakdown of unity and another parallel that supports the idea that he and Lancelot share the spotlight as male protagonists. The temporary absences of both register as critical ruptures in the narrative's structure. As we wonder what has happened to Gawain, we are suddenly confronted with his body, swathed like a newborn in bloodied white bandages and comforted by Arthur—the culminating image of the many shots exposing his vulnerability (figure 78). It is one of the most affecting moments in the film, confirming the portrait of Gawain throughout. It is he, not Lancelot, who is the "saint," forgiving all and, like the country priest, devoting his dwindling energies to the welfare of others. His dying words are efforts to urge the king to prevent more bloodshed.

The Last Judgment

Le geste = gesture, action, sign

La geste = deed, heroic achievement, exploit

There is no such thing as sin; rather, you yourselves are what produces sin when you act according to the nature of adultery, which is called "sin."

—Lines spoken by Jesus in "The Gospel of Mary," in *The Complete Gospels*

The editor's note for the quote from this gnostic text explains that what Jesus means is that "*sin* is not a matter of wrong acts, but rather has the *nature of adultery*. It means joining things that do not belong together, specifically the spiritual nature of the Good, with material nature."[31] It is in the spirit of this idea that the final section of the film can be seen as another kind of contest. Whose final actions might be said to avoid "adultery" in the sense given here and rise above the materialistic?

Gawain's deathbed counsel shows him to have at last found a purpose, namely, to advise the king and save lives. In conceiving his character, Bresson seems to have been influenced by those alternative literary portraits in which Gawain, not Lancelot, is the knightly ideal. Of all the characters in the film, it is Gawain who longs for spiritual revival even though, like Fontaine, he doesn't use such phrases. More than Lancelot or the others, he represents the balance between following the chivalric code and innate goodness. If there is a moral point of view among the knights, it is certainly Gawain's, which may be why he seems much closer to the Bressonian hero than Lancelot and why the models who play these characters differ so markedly. Bresson presents this difference as if he could have it both ways. Gawain evokes the ideals and qualities of the country priest and Fontaine, content that God has made him the way he is, as he tells the queen, and dying in good faith despite the disastrous turn of events. Indeed when he tells Guinevere early in the film that he would be much cheerier except for "the baleful faces around [him]," he all but literalizes the idea suggested at the beginning of this chapter, that he is indeed an early Bressonian protagonist who has found himself in a late Bresson film. By contrast Lancelot continues on the path of violence and revenge and dies on the junk heap of an annihilated medievalism.

It is to Arthur's credit that he follows Gawain's advice and offers to take Guinevere back and call a truce. This is the subject of the last conversation between Lancelot and Guinevere, the occasion that defines the difference between them. Nearly everything Lancelot says at first—"I won't capitulate.... I shall not give you up to him.... I'll rid you of Arthur.... Right is not justice.... I crave the impossible.... If I lose you, what is left for me?"—reeks of selfishness and stubborn adherence to a childish grandiosity. It is the queen's persistent appeal to human decency and common sense—"This is our last night, let us accept.... We must atone for so much bloodshed.... Your duty now is to return me to Arthur.... Right is on his side.... I have nothing more to give you.... Leave this woman while there is still time of your own free will"—that finally moves him to accept the inevitable. And she does this without appealing to God and without denying what it costs her: "[My heart] bleeds and is torn."

This last dialogue between them, like the others, is marked by its formal handling. The first nine shots follow the shot-countershot pattern, with three instances of one character's speaking from off screen. The tenth shot, however, is a long take of the queen, comprising twenty-three lines of dialogue, eleven of which belong to Lancelot, speaking from off screen. It all ends with a shot of him refusing to give in just as Lionel, interrupting, tells them, "It is time." The long take is an appropriate closure to the thoughts of the queen as they have evolved from the beginning and confirms the credence Bresson gives to the firmness and correctness of her resolve. Lancelot, on the other hand, is as adamant now about holding on to Guinevere as he was earlier about giving her up. In a manner unanticipated by either of them, the queen enacts what she said at their second meeting in response to Lancelot's question, "Are you then the enemy?" "I am the one created to help you," she had answered earlier, "who will go with you through the void, the darkness." As another instrument of destiny, her words now take on a different meaning, since the continual delay of the affair has led to this moment.

The scene of Lancelot leading her to Arthur's camp is capped by a shot that confirms this and seems an inverted replay of the one of Lancelot's prayer in the chapel. After he lets her go, we see an extreme long shot of Arthur waiting, standing against his tent and surrounded by knights. The queen enters into the foreground of this shot, at first out of focus, like the cross in the chapel, but as she walks into the distance and arrives at Arthur's side, everything comes into sharp relief. The sign of her having made the morally correct choice, this image is in stark contrast to that of the cross in the foreground to which Lancelot prayed but that remained blurry.

In the literature both Lancelot and the queen live beyond this moment, atoning for their sins and dying peacefully in religious establishments. But in the film, no sooner has Lancelot walked back to the castle than he is told that Mordred is preparing to launch an assault and seize power. Without breaking his stride, he orders everyone to horse, "for Arthur, against Mordred." For the last time we see the preparations for battle: repeated shots, rapidly edited, of saddlecloths hurled into place, swords plunged into scabbards, knights mounting, visors lowered. From the shot of the abandoned ground, over which we hear the rumbling of thundering hooves, the cut is to a long-distance shot of the forest, smoke rising out of the trees and bells tolling.

Yet another battle has been elided. Its casualties are exhibited by way of one of the most poignant, if not surprising vehicles Bresson could have devised: the galloping of a single, riderless horse. Though not a literal point-of-view character, the horse leads the camera through the maze of the forest to the sites that mark the final moments of the collapse of what the Round Table has symbolized. Unlike Lancelot, who earlier lost his way in the forest, the horse appears to know exactly where it is going. A long shot shows us a relatively quiet area of the forest; we hear, then see emerging from the dense green background this horse, moving quickly into the foreground and out of frame right. What follows is almost a replay of the opening. Like the five knights riding through the prologue, this horse runs a similar path five more times—indeed, at first we might think we see five different horses—interspersed by violent images and clashing sounds: a knight on his knees bleeding from under his helmet; the ground strewn with dead and dying knights; the corpse of the king, sword still in hand, identifiable by the crown on his helmet; a group of knights disappearing into a thicket of trees from which a clashing of swords is heard. At three different points, rapidly edited shots of archers crouched in trees are followed by arrows flying in all directions. We see a close-up of a horse with an arrow in its head, its rider struggling out from under it. Though not immediately recognizable, he is soon revealed to be Lancelot. In subsequent shots he stumbles, sword in hand, over to a tree, then to a pile of dead knights, upon which he falls after his last utterance, "Guinevere." This cuts to a shot of a bird flying high overhead, presumably scanning the ground for prey. Then the final image: a long shot of the immobile, indistinguishable pile of armor. Suddenly an armored leg and a head, Lancelot's, settle noisily into place, the last metallic rattle we hear (figure 79).

The image of a heap is not inconsequential: the sense of waste that it conveys, of the discarding of the vestiges of an entire way of life, is overpowering. But Bresson was not a polemicist. He did not make a film to trash chivalry or its legends. More likely he bemoaned the failure of a culture that allegedly aspired to maintain harmony between earthly and religious goals and had as its motto, as Arthur says, "Perfect yourselves." The film captures the essence of that aspiration and what has been lost in acutely felt details as only someone who understands and appreciates their meaning could impart. But as I have argued, the structure of the film is composed of violent images or inclinations on the one hand and the stumbling course of a love affair on the other. In problematizing the love affair—which, let us remember, is post-Grail—the film suggests the consequences of knowledge in the post-Edenic sense. Once one *knows* that God disapproves of one's behavior, one cannot resume it with the same gusto and indifference. But another reading is hard to dismiss: once one believes that God is silent, loss of faith and everything it sustained is imminent. Lancelot's problem is that he knows what he should do but is unable to do it. Guinevere, who does not reject God, nevertheless does not appeal to divine judgment; she acts, like the peasant woman, in accordance with what she has learned from experience. As she sees it, the knights behave badly and think illogically. She speaks with the directness and insight of a modern-day character with the hindsight of history, as if she had found herself removed to the Middle Ages. She knows that something must be done, sacrifice must be made, and suffering must be endured. But though she acts rightly, she cannot prevent disaster. And in this paradoxical situation, she seems closer to Bresson's thinking about God, the world, and his engagement with his art than any of the male characters in the film.

Gawain's last gesture is forgiveness and counsel; Arthur's is morally inflected political compromise; Lancelot's is heroic futility. None can be dismissed, for these are the actions, however flawed, of negotiation between the material and the spiritual. Guinevere, because she chooses life over death, even if it must be suffered and lived in an absurd world to which God no longer seems connected, makes the most difficult but the only possible moral choice. Bresson has created perhaps the clearest paradigm of how knowledge and choice function in a world we cannot understand. If characters in his films up to *The Trial of Joan of Arc* appear to know why things happen the way they do—even if we question their confidence—characters after that appear to lack that certainty. The forest in *Lancelot* embodies the maze of possible directions and the dilemma of choices; the place where battles occur and where Lancelot loses his way, it is also where the old woman predicts his fate and tries to keep him from destruction.

Perhaps more than in any other film, Bresson has given us a comparison of compelling choices, which may well reflect his own fluctuating convictions about how life must be lived in the face of existential doubt. Given his early interest in this story and his long-postponed filming of it—perhaps every bit as charged with frustration as Lancelot's and Guinevere's delayed affair—it seems both a likely narrative strategy and a moving testament to the persistent appeal of the idea of redemption even while contemplating the triumph of waste. This is why Guinevere's voice rings so powerfully. But if she firmly chooses life in the face of such absurdity, Bresson's next protagonist, in *The Devil Probably*, will assume a different attitude. Together they form the poles of what may be the most philosophically inclined positions of Bresson's late work.

There is but one truly philosophical problem, and that is suicide.

—Albert Camus, "An Absurd Reasoning," in *The Myth of Sisyphus*

and Other Essays

Angels and Demons

Le Diable probablement

Suicide, an action taken by at least two previous Bresson characters and attempted in *L'Argent,* his final film, is the subject of discourse in *The Devil Probably* (1977). Neither Mouchette nor the wife in *Une femme douce* mention it as an option, nor do we know whether either gives it much forethought, and it remains only a possible explanation of Marie's mysterious disappearance in *Balthazar*. But Charles, the protagonist of *Devil,* speaks of it openly and argues it as a reasonable response to an unbearable world. Neither reclusive nor celibate, he shows few of the classic signs of depression, has a strong appetite for food and sex, and is loved by his friends. In the film's longest sequence, he tells a psychoanalyst, cynically named Dr. Mime, that he doesn't really want to die, that he hates death even more than life, and having already tried to kill himself, is convinced he could never go through with it. Charles relates all of this, as he does almost everything else, in a forthright manner, with charm and understated wit, as laid back as Jacques in *Four Nights of a Dreamer* but far more intellectual and with a good deal more verbal flair. Nevertheless, thanks to perhaps the biggest faux pas ever committed by a movie psychoanalyst, Charles solves his dilemma by way of the doctor's ill-considered, badly timed allusion to the method used by the ancient Romans, and bribes a friend to do it for him.

Both *Mouchette* and *Une femme douce* are literary adaptations; thus *The Devil Probably* is the only original screenplay of Bresson's in which the protagonist commits suicide. As we saw, Bresson complicated the wife's suicide in *Une femme douce* by adding a sequence comprised of images suggestive of her thought process. The situation in *Devil,* made eight years later, suggests that he believed the subject warranted more attention. Citing an alleged actual event as his premise, Bresson again follows Dostoevsky, who seized on the murder of a student of the Moscow Agricultural Academy in 1869 as a key element of the plot of his political novel, *Demons.* In that novel the character Kirillov, a member of an underground revolutionary circle, conducts a study of suicides in Russia and, though he loves life, agrees to shoot himself as a gesture of protest for "the cause." A significant difference in Charles's case is that he more or less renounces all political causes, so that his act not only is more sweeping in its implications, but has a far more personal cast.

We learn of Charles's fate through two newspaper headlines following the credits, after which the film flashes back six months. Yet the narrative is less driven by the need to account for the reasons behind what happened than is the husband's narrative in *Une femme douce.* The elusive nature of the woman, prompting both her husband and the viewer to look closely for clues to her apparent despair, gives the film a mysterious and tragic tone. Though we may not know Charles's ultimate motive for arranging to end his life— something perhaps only psychoanalysis, that bugaboo of Bresson's, might unravel—neither his situation nor his act, to this viewer at least, induces the same feeling. Nearly everything that Charles says is wrong with the world is convincing, as is his confidence, narcissism notwithstanding, that he is blessed with a superior mind and clarity of vision. Yet none of this seems especially urgent or tragic. Like Charles himself, the film is preoccupied with serious thoughts but is in no special hurry to reach its conclusion.

This pace allows time for what seem to be digressions about the disastrous conditions of the natural environment and the global greed behind them, concerns that give heft to Charles's cynicism but are not directly tied to the course of his behavior. At first this seems simply a clever strategy, whereby the stock footage that establishes these conditions creates a backdrop of negativity that objectifies Charles's sense of malaise and justifies his disgust. But as the film progresses, there seems to be more to this structure. In fact, the reason suicide is not *a* but *the* subject of discourse is that the film focuses not only on the fate of the protagonist but also on that of the self-destructive society in which he lives. Plagued by an increasingly vacuous materialism and, as one character puts it, "an earth ever more populated and ever less habitable," the careers of both civilization and the planet, the film asserts, are equally bent on suicide. One might think that Bresson was responding to those critics who found him isolationist, disengaged from issues of social and political importance. But though environmental issues were becoming more publicized at the time the film was made and young people were actively engaged with them, Bresson seems less interested in addressing them as immediate realities to be dealt with than as conclusive evidence of how bad the world has become.

This contextualizes Charles's state of mind, renders it parallel to what we learn and see about societal and world conditions, and allows us to view his act as one of several positions one might take in response. No doubt because of this the film was banned in France as an "incitement to suicide."[1] But Charles's suicide seems less an act of despair or emotional breakdown than a gesture of protest, even, perhaps, an empathic identification with an ailing world. If the film immediately prior, *Lancelot of the Lake,* is about the collapse of a culture based on belief in God and the quest for spiritual perfection, *Devil* indicts a modern society bereft of comparable values, even as failed aspirations. In the analysis of *Lancelot* I suggested that Bresson had split his hero in two. In dividing attention in *Devil* between Charles's story and the greater concerns of society, Bresson seems to split the narrative itself in two.

Charles's decision to end his life is at once destructive and symbolic. In the same spirit, Bresson made an unprecedented choice that might be similarly characterized.[2] In deploying faded stock footage to document environmental ills, he both compromises and reinforces the rigorous aesthetics that distinguish his art: on the one hand risking contamination of the look of his film, on the other, highlighting, by contrast, the beauty and purity of his art against the possibility of its corruption. As objective material lying outside the fictional parameters of the film, this footage is not an abetment of Charles's actions. But to the extent that we agree with the dire message it delivers, we can understand, if not endorse, his choice as a disturbing rather than a disturbed reaction. This distinction would appear to be the point of Charles's interaction with the psychoanalyst, the occasion of Bresson's strongest critique of the failure of professional intervention to provide adequate solace to the troubled soul. We might wonder whether Charles senses that there is something superior to human intervention, even though he may not know what it is. Despite the world Bresson has painted since *Balthazar,* Charles is not exactly a casualty of godlessness or loss of faith. When the analyst asks him if he believes in God, he replies, "As far as possible, I believe in eternal life. But if I commit suicide, I can't think I'll be condemned for not comprehending the incomprehensible." The only place he seems to find comfort is in a church. With his gentle looks, long hair, and searching demeanor, he could even pass for one of Jesus' wayward disciples, too far removed to heed the call. Though not a Christ figure, Charles descries the means that, within the film's context, have brought about the death of the soul in contemporary life. In that sense he represents, for the viewer if not anyone in the film, one whose final action calls for regeneration.

The Devil Probably, then, walks a thin line between two equally power-ful urges, which perhaps is the unconscious thrust of the opening scene. Someone—it turns out to be Valentin, who Charles later designates as his enabler—is examining the soles of shoes of random characters on the embank-ment of the Seine. He determines that only by leaning one's weight equally to the left and the right does one preserve the sole of the shoe, and on this basis declares who knows how to walk and who does not. The film then takes a discursive path, skirting both the Left and the Right, the nature of which dis-guises the seriousness of what is at stake, at once questioning the value of living in a world that one finds irredeemable, while insisting, as Charles's friend Michel does, that one must live, if only for the sake of the "life force."

A Deviant Narrative

The film opens with a juxtaposition that declares both an affinity with and a difference from Four Nights of a Dreamer, Bresson's other late film about contemporary Parisian youth. The first image, over which the credits appear, is that of a bateau mouche emerging out of the darkness in the distance and glowing colorfully along the Seine, as it did in the earlier film. But this image, which epitomized the atmosphere of Four Nights, could not be more misleading. No magical, sardonic fairy tale unfolds in Devil; Paris is neither bathed in sunlight by day nor aglow with romantic hues by night. The general color scheme throughout is dominated by muted grays and browns, with hardly a trace of bright blues, greens, or reds (all of which return in L'Argent). Charles and company exhibit desperate hedonism, which he pursues to ward off despair. The river embankment where post-sixties folksingers made a wistful chorus in Four Nights, is in Devil a darker place where drugs and guns are easily purchased; the social and political issues excluded from Jacques's fantasy world in that film are now pushed into the foreground.

The initial glimpse of the bateau mouche is both fleeting and remote, never to be seen again. It is followed by a shot of a newspaper announcing Charles's suicide in Père Lachaise, one of Paris's most famous cemeteries, and a second headline suggesting that he may have been murdered. At once we have a juxtaposition that raises the first of several conflicting, or coexistent, truths. Allegedly in love with two different women, Charles contemplates marriage to one while carrying on with a third. Claiming devotion to licentious pleasure, he considers nude photos of his ex-girlfriend distributed in church to be disgraceful. Mocking the conventions of bourgeois life, he also objects to left-wing calls for their destruction.

Charles is the embodiment of a certain kind of young adult, gifted, intelligent, and sensitive, whose detachment from society is more than matched by society's own estrangement from any abiding ethical values. Although the film is rooted in the dispiriting atmosphere of post-1968, mid-1970s Paris, its image of what many young people experience in the contemporary world resonates beyond a specific time and place. Unlike Gawain in *Lancelot,* Charles cannot imagine anyone, or anything, to whom he might appeal to give him a purpose. So vapid is the atmosphere he breathes that even his suicidal thoughts are listless. His friends are more concerned than he is. In most of the interactions between Michel and Alberte and between Alberte and Edwige, it is Charles's state of mind and behavior they discuss. That all the models who play these people are physically attractive, though none of their characters is any happier than Charles, supports François Truffaut's impression that the subject of the film is "the doomed beauty of adolescence."[3] With *Four Nights of a Dreamer* and *The Devil Probably,* Bresson has characterized the Parisian youth of his day as either hopelessly romantic or insufferably cynical. Facing similar circumstances, Camus's "absurd man" would make a leap neither toward faith nor suicide; even a sense of disillusionment would be improbable because he would have had no illusions to be shattered. For Camus, suicide is a nostalgic, romantic act, a complaint that the world has let one down and that life has not lived up to whatever one thought it should. But the absurd man accepts everything for what it is, understands that it can never be anything more than what it is, and moves on.

In the course of the narrative we see extensions of the four principal characters engaged in other, equally dead-end pursuits. They attend noisy political rallies that appear to lead nowhere. They participate in discussions about the Catholic Church's attempt to adapt to the modern age, but exhibit neither faith nor interest. They attend scientific lectures on the consequences of the atomic bomb and the arms race, only to have their fears dismissed. Charles also attends these events, but he speaks out only once, against the pointlessness of those calling for destruction, and is quickly shouted down. And so Charles is not an isolated case of adolescent angst. His difference is that he sees nothing productive either in the world or in an activist stance.

The adult society that beckons promises only the perpetuation of phony comforts and allegiance to false values.

Amid these concerns there are lighter, even amusing moments in the film. A curious episode of young people cavorting in a park and hiding in the weeds from the police hints that perhaps not every member of Charles's generation is preoccupied with gloomy thoughts. Nor do those who frequent the river embankments to hear folk music dwell much on the dismal fate of a society from which they are already removed. Yet romantic entanglements continue to reflect Bresson's skepticism. As we see also in *Four Nights* and even *Une femme douce*, sexual liberation seems to have made relationships less, not more satisfying, not to mention less durable. Thinking he is in love with Alberte, Charles leaves his former girlfriend, Edwige. Alberte moves in with him while reassuring Michel that it is really he she loves (figure 80). Edwige carries on with a rather sleazy bookshop owner who later makes a play for Alberte as well. It might be *La Ronde*, divested of any hint of romanticism.

These sequences ground the film in a certain quotidian reality, but they also counter any drive linked to Charles's move toward death, despite the well-placed cues throughout that keep the subject alive. Shortly after Alberte moves in with Charles, she finds cyanide among his things, along with a note he has scribbled amid his mathematical formulations: "When will I kill myself, if not now?" Following his affair with a third woman, he tries to drown himself in her bathtub, only to joke about it afterward; he borrows a gun from one of the embankment slackers to take potshots in the river; he discusses suicide with the psychoanalyst; and finally he buys the gun that Valentin will use to shoot him. The quiet way all of this is woven into the film's fabric, alternating with unrelated material, is a convincing simulation of the nebulous air and behavioral mode that the film implies is characteristic of Charles and his generation. The ease with which Valentin agrees to and goes about killing his friend is more disturbing for how aptly it conveys the emotional paralysis of an indifferent world. The film's rhythm bears little resemblance to that of the two films before it that feature suicides or to that of *L'Argent*.

To further complicate the already discursive nature of the narrative, there is a highly ambiguous sequence, structurally unprecedented in Bresson's work, that speaks directly to the relationship between Charles's story and the objective realities alluded to in the footage. Not long into the film, Charles and Michel drive back to Paris after a stop in the country, where trees are being felled to make room for roads. As Michel drives, Charles sees books on the backseat, picks up one titled *Mission: Survival*, and turns the pages, remarking, "The growth of what? Of happiness? Happiness on credit? The credit card? Or the happiness of walking in the country and diving in a river?" On the word *river* there is a cut to a shot of discolored water from an industrial plant being poured into a larger body of water, initiating a series of seventeen images of stock footage. The first eight images trace the course of toxic waste being dumped into water supplies and eventually into the Mediterranean Sea, and then to a small fishing boat alongside an abandoned Japanese submarine and the long-delayed effects of this process on human life: a Japanese woman and a young man with deformed limbs. Interspersed with this footage is a shot of the projector running it and four shots of Michel and his colleagues—the same ones we saw earlier looking at similar footage— whose voices also overlap the footage at three points.

It is natural to conclude that Bresson's film has cut directly from Charles's remark in the car to a meeting of the environmental group attended by Michel sometime later, or even that Michel has taken Charles to a meeting of his group to show him the footage, an assumption of many viewers. But these impressions are contradicted by the absence of Charles from any of the crosscuts of onlookers while the footage is being projected, as well as by the first shot that follows the footage sequence, which is of Charles standing directly outside of Michel's car, having just been dropped off somewhere in the city, that is, at the end of the same drive initiated earlier. His quasi-facetious remark, "It's up to science to save us! We'll only be able to wave our limbs about, eat cakes, and go completely nuts," picks up not only on the discussion in the car *before* the passage of the footage, but also alludes to the deformities of the Japanese woman and the man waving his hand and finger *within* the footage. In other words, the drive has been interrupted by the footage with no indication of how it fits into the logical continuity before and after it. And it would appear, all logic to the contrary, that Charles, not present at the environmental meeting, has nevertheless seen the same footage that we have.

In a film by a lesser director we might think this was a careless editing mistake. If the footage is simply a motion picture illustration of the book Charles is perusing, it doesn't explain Michel's presence and narration as it is being projected. Perhaps it is Bresson's way of fusing Charles, after all and despite himself, with the larger concerns to which Michel and the film are devoted. Still, he has chosen a curious way to do so. As it involves the two parallel strands of the film's progress, it seems Bresson wished to leave the issues of narrative continuity and point of view ambiguous, perhaps in the vein of reflexive gestures familiar in the films of Godard and others in the two decades prior to Bresson's film. The stock footage would not be out of place in those works. Perhaps Bresson's gesture is a belated nod to the cinéma vérité and reflexivity that informed the work of other directors of the new wave. But if so, he casts this footage in a light very much in keeping with the overall despondent tone of the film, using it to buttress, not contradict, the theme of suicide.

Requiem for a Dying Planet

We sense this despondency in the voice-over narrations of the stock footage sequences. The first such sequence that appears in the film's first five minutes, immediately after the political rally, is introduced with the title "The Society for the Conservation of Man and His Environment." This refers to the ownership or producers of the footage, not, as far as we can tell, to the group watching it. Besides Michel, this includes an unidentified man and woman, who we see in the more ambiguous sequence just discussed. They sit in a darkened room at a table as a projector screens images of various environmental crises, and read from a book they have before them, presumably designed to accompany the footage and probably the one Charles picks up later in Michel's car. Michel is an author of politically concerned books, but it is not clear whether the people with whom he views the footage are part of an activist group.

Some of the narration simply identifies the footage, as when, following shots of cityscapes with toxic emissions wafting across them, Michel mentions an X-ray of the legs of a bull affected by the contamination of the air just before we see the X-ray on the screen. Other phrases seem more like commentary, as when we hear over images of various farm vehicles spraying crops, "Destruction of birds and insects beneficent to agriculture," or over images of jets taking off and leaving trails of fuel, "There'll be no more blue skies." A series of shots of garbage dumps elicits, "An earth ever more populated and ever less habitable." This is followed by several shots of gutted and rusty automobiles piled up, an image that recalls the metallic heap of armored knights at the end of *Lancelot*. Both are signs of a culture that has used up its defining features. The sequence ends as the narration speaks of the "destruction of entire species for profit," calculating the numbers of elephants, rhinos, and baby seals that have been destroyed. The film emphatically shifts from the passive nature of most of the footage to more disturbing images: shots of a baby seal and what appears to be its mother lounging on the snow, followed by a close-up of the mother moaning, an image of a trail of blood across the snow, and a long shot of a baby seal being bludgeoned to death.

The accumulated impression of the narration is not that of outraged citizens bent on doing something about what they see, but of a group sitting in judgment over ongoing activities that spell doom and show no sign of interruption or change. The lines are delivered in a tone both rueful and admonishing, a litany of grievances that are beyond repair. The three narrators might be Olympian gods looking down on Earth and pointing to evidence of the abuses of nature and the terrible waste of which humans are guilty. Even the way the sequence begins in media res with the words "And all around thousands of dead trees" has this tenor, as does the resigned tone implied by the choice of tenses in the lines "The risk of death still wouldn't stop them" and "Don't they see any risk?" It is as if Zeus, Demeter, and Poseidon, preparing to punish the human race, were reciting their rationales: See how man acts! See how he disregards the gifts of nature!

This reinforces the sense of gloom that hangs over Charles. Though he refuses to do anything, we do not see that those presumably more engaged are any more effective. And so the stock footage serves Bresson's efforts to incorporate documentary reality not only within the fiction—for example, as evidence of Michel's interests—but outside the fiction and therefore not subject to the rules of narrative or point of view. Once again the effect is to segregate allusions to external reality, to allow them neither to be subsumed by Charles's perspective nor to contradict it. In what follows we see that apart from the stock footage, the film's structure as a whole maintains this distinction. In the first three passages discussed below, Charles is part of a greater social whole, whereas in the three discussed after that, he is the central figure.

The Church, the Trees, and the Bus

And the fifth angel sounded the trumpet.... And out of the smoke there came forth locusts upon the earth. And there was given to them power, as the scorpions of the earth have power. And they were told not to hurt the grass of the earth or any green thing or any tree; but only the men who do not have God's seal upon their foreheads.

—Apocalypse 9:1, 3–5

Perhaps the richest passages in the film, cinematographically speaking, are the first sequence in St. Remy's church, the one of trees being cut down, and the ride on the bus. Charles is present in all three, along with friends in the first and with Michel in the other two. Although all three allude to serious subjects, the first and the last, notwithstanding those who deny that Bresson has a sense of humor, are quite amusing. The scene in the church comes early. Charles, Edwige, Valentin, and two other friends enter and take seats amid a throng already gathered. They are engaged in a discussion on the status of the Catholic Church in contemporary society. Several people ask questions of the leader and voice criticism; Charles does neither, in contrast to his instant negative reaction to the calls for sweeping destruction at the political rally in a previous scene. The church topics range from specific theological questions (e.g., Luther's position on the sacredness of the host) to the relevance of the Church in contemporary society. But as the sequence progresses, it seems another voice insists on being heard.

Bresson sets up the sequence with a shot of the organ in the choir loft as a technician prepares to clean and tune its pipes. We are reminded of this in subsequent shots inserted during the discussion. As the sequence develops, we hear sharp, pronounced chords resonating throughout the church's space, timed to the remarks below in what can only be construed as an intrusive and comical manner. For example, the discussion leader's line "preparing the Church of tomorrow, to build a more logical Christianity" is punctuated by a single loud chord. The next line, "But all religions are illogical! That's why, like it or not, the Christianity of the future will be without religion," is followed by two even louder chords, which prompts everyone to suddenly look up, as if in response to a rude, off screen presence. Another chord follows the line "To hell with the times," and when a young girl remarks that the church's music is dull and the hymns trite, an abrupt, piercing shriek of the organ makes her wince.

These moments are too cleverly synched to be dismissed as mere annoyances, like the vacuum cleaner. On the one hand, a simple analogy seems to be at work: just as the organ needs tuning, the Church needs updating to be in tune with modern life. The negative reference to Protestantism, however, implies that such changes result in a watering down of Catholicism, a lukewarm version of Christianity. But the forceful and timely sounds of the organ, especially when synched with a cut to the majestic and lofty sweep of the system above the altar, suggests more: the voice of an angry, disapproving God, perhaps, reacting to the irreverent remarks of a callous and indifferent humanity. This fits Charles's later allusion to Victor Hugo's remarks on cathedrals as "holy places" in which "God is present."

At one point Michel takes Charles along on his visit to an area where land is being cleared to make roads. The sequence begins with a slow

creaking sound we may not immediately recognize until we see a tree beginning to topple over. Before it hits the ground there is a cut to Charles waiting
in Michel's car, both hands covering his ears (figure 81). A similar image
occurs four more times, interspersed with thirteen shots of trees and
branches falling in different directions. At one point we see four big upper
branches falling in succession and then three huge trees in a row hitting the
ground with a thud, interrupted by a shot of Charles. The effect is that of
great, majestic beasts felled by an unseen power. Although we do not see the
men with the buzz saws, the rate at which the trees fall is clearly faster than
that of their being cut. In fact, they fall cued to the film's cutting, which is to
say, each cut to a different shot is to a tree or section of a tree beginning to
fall, just after the moment it has been severed, as if by the editor's splice. In
other words, the sequence is designed less naturalistically than, like the last
stages of the tournament sequence in *Lancelot,* as a montage spectacle of
aural and visual acuity. Charles's sensitivity to this is singular since neither
Michel nor the workers seem affected. That it might be more than sound
that Charles shuts out is suggested later, when he tells the psychoanalyst
that he is "not sure," but he thinks his father is a contractor who pulls up
trees.

The bus ride consists of twenty-five shots and is the most craftily
designed sequence in the film. Charles and Michel are returning from a
lecture on the consequences of nuclear power on the environment and speak
of responsibility. Their first exchange sets the tone. Charles remarks that all
evidence of nuclear dangers is denied in order to reassure people, and Michel
says, "Evidence? It's all supernatural." When a man sitting two seats forward
volunteers an opinion—"Don't accuse governments.... It's the masses who
determine events"—other voices chime in with similar remarks: "Obscure
forces whose laws are unfathomable," "Something drives us against our will."
At the questions, "So who is it that makes a mockery of humanity? Who's
leading us by the nose?," the first man responds, "The devil probably,"
prompting Charles to nudge Michel (figure 82). The phrase is yet another
reference to Dostoevsky, this time from an exchange between Ivan and his
father Fyodor in *The Brothers Karamazov.* A cut to the bus driver shows that
he is distracted and is not looking at the road. As he quickly faces front, there
is a cut to a close-up of his foot on the brake, followed by sounds of screeching
and a crash. Everyone is jolted forward. After the driver exits the bus, we
hear more and more horns honking, indicating that traffic has been
stopped.

In the course of the scene, we see shots of the apparatus of the bus itself:
a low-angle close-up of the hand straps, close-ups of the "stop requested" sign

in red and of the button the driver pushes to open the doors; a high-angle shot of the exit door and steps and of the ticket machine as people get on. Close-ups of the driver's side-view mirror create a disorienting effect as we see oncoming traffic in the filmic space adjacent to the mirror, in which the traffic moves in the opposite direction, that is, the same direction the bus takes; although the spaces are segregated, their juxtaposition within the whole image creates the illusion that cars are careening recklessly toward each other (figure 83). This image is held while the remarks about "obscure forces" and "something is driving us" are heard, and is repeated a moment later as the questions about who is mocking humanity and leading it astray come from off screen passengers. Most of these shots confirm the technical proficiency of the bus, and the images of the traffic in opposing directions are accompanied by the buildup of the discussion. When we see that even the driver has been affected, the notion that things are out of control is clear. However brief and seemingly random, the sequence is a lesson in the paradox of Bresson's view of how things work. The bus runs smoothly as long as the person in charge is alert and presses the right buttons, but, unavoidably, human motives—anger? curiosity? frustration?—intervene, distract us from our focus, and bring about catastrophe. In brief, we have an illustration of the larger question raised by Bresson's work: the relationship between human will and design.

Though Charles is present in these sequences, they really belong to the film's other focus: the ills of society and the unraveling of Western culture. This combination of sequences may seem arbitrary, even in view of the striking filmic values they have in common, but collectively they lend a particularly biblical slant to the film's other theme. Consider the connotations of the imagery and sounds of each sequence as described. The notion that the loud cries of the organ timed to provocative statements about Catholicism suggest the voice of an angry God might be a stretch in respect to someone else's film. But such precise audiovisual juxtapositions are hardly coincidental in a Bresson film, especially given the setting and the nature of the remarks. In addition, when considered in relation to the bus episode, which suggests that humanity's chaotic drive toward self-destruction is the work of the devil, it is hard to resist seeing the sequences as opposing sides of a metaphysical debate. In the wake of the "failure" or "irrelevance" of Catholicism in the modern world, as the remarks in the church allege, has faith in a benevolent divinity been replaced by the belief that an evil supernatural force directs human affairs? Perhaps to reflect the unlikelihood that anyone in the film could seriously entertain such a question, Bresson constructs both sequences in a disarming manner.

How does the trees sequence fit into this context? Its subject belongs to the environmental concerns of the stock footage, which addresses the destruction of animal and plant life and the pollution of bodies of water and skies. As the only such passage shot for the film (by cinematographer Pasqualino de Santis) and edited into an audiovisual tour de force, it lends a gravity and sympathy to the fall of these living creatures. It thus stands apart from the washed-out images of the stock footage while extending the focus of that footage into the narrative context of the film. This is emphasized by the five crosscuts to Charles protecting his ears against the cracking and imminent crashing around him, a mute witness to what seems a massive destruction of nature's majestic powers. Even Charles's assertion later, in response to the analyst, that his father's occupation is pulling up or tearing down trees, does not overshadow this moment of silent communion between the toppling of these ancient giants and the protagonist's meditation on ultimate extinction. Quite probably, the pain Charles seems to suffer was inspired by Bresson's impassioned denouncement, years earlier, of the destruction of trees in Paris, particularly on the Ile St. Louis where he lived.[4] In the spirit of the notion of sacred indirection, then, we have an angry God, the widespread destruction of his creation, and the image of society as a bus, powered by the devil, en route to disaster—a vision that, for all its naturalistic and sociological ambience, borders on the apocalyptic. Not even the sensitive Charles, an unsung prophet, is fully attuned to the implications of what he hears and sees. And yet in three later sequences there are just enough hints of Christological import to lend his death a sacrificial quality divested of redemptive value.

The Church II, the Police, and the Analyst

Notwithstanding the collective significance assigned to the three passages just described, they are relatively self-enclosed, each introducing different thematic material relevant to the social parameters of the film. The three discussed below have a sequential narrative connection bearing directly on the last stages of Charles's story. The contrast between the two groups attests to the unique position this film occupies in Bresson's oeuvre. We saw that although Charles is present in all three of the first group, he is more of a peripheral witness, and in the church and bus passages is eclipsed by more vocal participants. In the three sequences of this section, however, Charles is the primary focus, and what occurs happens directly to him. The probable precedent for this construction is *Au hasard Balthazar,* in which Balthazar is sometimes the main character in a sequence and sometimes just a witness on the periphery. Indeed, Charles and Balthazar may have more than a little in common.

The second church sequence is preceded by a scene in which Charles and Valentin are gathering things to spend the night there. Charles stuffs everything into a huge sack, including a phonograph and a Monteverdi recording, and then before leaving takes a book from the shelf and reads the Hugo passage on cathedrals: "'Such places are really holy!' But somewhere else he says, 'A church is divine. God is present. But if a priest appears, God is no longer present.'" Looking at Valentin, he asks, "He goes too far, don't you think?" To which the blank Valentin shrugs and responds, "Oh, me and God, you know." Valentin agrees to join Charles only if Charles allows him a dose of heroin. A close-up of Valentin's arm as he shoots up is accompanied by the serene sounds of the Monteverdi, which continue over the following image in the church of Charles and Valentin already in their sleeping bags. The audiovisual bridge is provocative, in effect suggesting that the music and the drug share not only a soothing effect but that for Charles's generation, religion too may be no more than a drug, that the Church offers little more than the artificial aura of God via Gothic architecture and sacred music—an impression that would not contradict the first church scene, in which young people sit in judgment on the failings of Catholicism. But although this might apply to Valentin and others, Charles's sentiments remain ambiguous, as both his remark about the Hugo quote and the statement he makes later to the analyst imply.

The sequence barely begins when Valentin gets up and breaks open two poor boxes while Charles sleeps. Coins pour noisily onto the floor as he fills his pockets and leaves. The music stops as we hear the sound of distant sirens, followed by the police entering the darkened church and standing over Charles, who sits up in surprise. Another sound bridge, of a typewriter, links this shot to the police station, where he is questioned about what happened. He pretends he doesn't know Valentin's name, but is also questioned about crumpled-up leaflets in his pocket, presumably from the political rally. Ruling out robbery and the distribution of leftist leaflets, the police ask Charles what he was doing in the church playing music. He does not refuse to answer, but when he says they would not believe him, the cop standing behind knees him violently in the back, eliciting a groan and forcing Charles to double over in pain. The cut from this is to Charles lying in bed in Edwige's apartment, refusing attention and asking to be left alone—the first time he reacts in such a manner. In an exchange with Michel and Alberte, Edwige explains that he has been like this for days and that the police incident really shook him up. She remarks that only a great analyst like Dr. Mime can help him.

Both sequences are striking for the indirect way they allude to the stations in the Passion of Christ as recounted in the Gospel of St. Matthew, particularly Judas' betrayal in the garden of Gethsemane, the thirty pieces of silver, and the arrest by the authorities who fear Jesus as a political threat and whose real purpose is beyond their ken. Though Charles is not a Christ figure, these allusions are difficult to ignore and hint at a Christ-like presence by virtue of its absence in a contemporary world too cynical to recognize, much less embrace, the real thing. Charles is neither saintly nor godly, but he is suspended between the material and spiritual worlds, an angel, not of sin or virtue so much as confusion, who is nevertheless willing to take his chance at the possibility of eternal life rather than surrender his soul to the devil's playground.

Two very brief passages, four shots in all, follow Edwige's remark as Charles lies in bed. The first establishes that Alberte and Michel are now a couple. The second shows both of them arriving at Edwige's apartment, only to learn that Charles has "escaped" from his bed. As they go off in search, we see him on the street approaching the psychoanalyst's office, which, given the state he is in, suggests that he does not go just to appease his friends.

The first image in the office is a medium shot of the analyst, a stern-looking, middle-aged man with glasses, seated behind his desk against bookshelves, intently facing forward at Charles off screen (figure 84). His first question, "How did this clash with society arise?," implies one of three things: a preceding exchange between them; Edwige's description of Charles's state to the doctor beforehand; or a premature assumption of the analyst. Charles, still off screen and unsurprised at the question, answers directly: "It's my normal state.…I kept it quiet for a long time." Subsequent exchanges proceed more or less in the same manner. The analyst gathers information about Charles's family history and asks him whether the pleasure he derives from refusing to participate in life and his confidence that his views are correct do not compensate. None of this is unorthodox or distorted, and neither Charles's behavior nor anything he says suggests that he is uncomfortable. Quite the contrary: he feels free to get up, take a cigarette from the desk, and tamper with objects on the mantle over the fireplace (figure 85). No question unnerves him or reduces him to mumbling. It is hard to imagine Michel (*Pickpocket*) or Jacques (*Four Nights*) or the husband in *Une femme douce,* or anyone in *Balthazar* or *Mouchette* holding his own with a psychoanalyst and not missing a beat or succumbing to internal pressure. Charles may brag about his superior ability to see things clearly, but he also exposes his insecurities without embarrassment.

The problem comes at the end of the session, when, after rising to leave, he resumes his seat, a sign that something has affected him. Apparently stirred by the doctor's insistence that, despite his denial, he *does* have a death wish, Charles says that he could never actually kill himself, that he hates death more than life and cannot bear the thought of suddenly losing consciousness. Shockingly the analyst misses the cue to shore up these hopeful signs. Partly to flaunt the accuracy of his diagnosis and partly to get Charles out of the office, he tells him about the ancient Romans assigning the task to a friend, thus providing Charles with the method to go through with his "wish." Not unlike the embittered pastor in Ingmar Bergman's *Winter Light,* who imposes his own religious doubts on a despairing parishioner and drives him to kill himself, the analyst, in an almost offhand manner, crosses a line and gives Charles too much information. It is a tragic mistake, but it is also difficult to believe that the methodical analyst we have heard throughout the session would have made such a grievous error in judgment. One might argue that it is irrelevant how and where Charles received the information since the *manner* in which he dies does not invalidate the analyst's perception. To pursue this further would get into hair-splitting arguments over the subtleties and theoretical fine points of psychoanalytic technique, which would take us far afield of Bresson's own predispositions. These warrant more extended comment in light of the fact that before the moment described, Charles has proved a good match for the analyst, and was very likely groomed for this purpose by his creator.

A Voluble Spokesman

The cravings of youth are too good for the world. The best in us is buried

alive.

—Bernd Alois Zimmermann, from the opera *Die Soldaten*

The analysis session is more ambiguous in conception and execution than a first impression might suggest. Viewers who seize on the severe demeanor of the analyst as proof of Bresson's desire to lambaste the profession may be measuring the image against the cuddly bear stereotypes familiar from Hollywood movies.[5] They also ignore two factors germane to the impression: first, that by profession a psychoanalyst must assume a neutral stance from the start, which can seem aloof and cold to the uninitiated; second, that a psychoanalyst in a Bresson movie, enacted by a model, is performing double, if not triple duty in this department.

The sequence is the most extended confrontation Charles has with anyone in the film, composed almost exclusively of shot-countershot editing that recalls the interrogation sequences in *The Trial of Joan of Arc*. There is only one exception to this. When Charles stands up and plays with an object on the mantle over the fireplace, we see his reflection in the mirror above it, along with that of an abstract white sculpture of a human figure, and the analyst entering the shot to take the object from him and placing it back where it was. For the brief moment they are in the same shot, the analyst, resorting to type, suggests that the spanking Charles received as a child might be responsible for his problems with society.

The exchanges fill in aspects of Charles's life that we knew nothing about (e.g., that his father, presumably an engineer, pulls up trees; that his mother is impressed by the amount of money his father makes) and link the social connections that we have witnessed in the film. As a summary of Charles's life and point of view laid out with greater exposition than we have seen in a Bresson film, the approach alone should give us pause. On the one hand, it is clear that Bresson wished to render the analytic encounter authentically, perhaps to critique it more convincingly. And indeed it is among the most accurate and thorough representations of an initial, information-gathering session to be found in a narrative film. But it also seems he had another purpose in mind, particularly since the sequence is the last and the longest encounter—running seven and a half minutes and at fifty-four shots, twenty-six more than the second longest sequence—Charles has before he buys the gun and arranges his death. This places an emphasis on the scene out of proportion to the political, religious, and social failures noted throughout. One way to read this is that psychoanalysis is not just another failed institution but is possibly more flawed than the others because its aim, in the eyes of many, is to help people adapt to or at least learn to tolerate the very conditions to which they attribute their alienation.

As a protagonist who rejects every aspiration and institution of modern life and thinks of dying not in terms of the pleasures he will leave behind but of the pointless future he will avoid, it is fitting that Charles's final dialogue should be with one whose expertise is designed to ferret out the unconscious reasons underlying such negativism. Yet Bresson uses the encounter not primarily to reveal the personal reasons for Charles's despair—a case that, incidentally, he does make—but as an opportunity to conduct a debate of sorts on the ultimate question the film raises. In that respect, the analysis session ups the ante by virtue of its assumed purpose, for the solution to *this* patient's problem would involve his surrender to the forces he believes to be at the root of *society's* problem, which the film has gone to great pains to document. For Charles, an alternative to suicide can be only one of two things: complete acquiescence to the world and its values, however meaningless, or blithe indifference to social and political disasters.

Just as the stock footage shows the utter contamination and destruction of the environment, Charles points to other horrors, the promises of the "good life." He reads a list of these to the analyst from a crumpled-up ad in a magazine, summarizing what he would miss if he died. As a thorough account of cultural banalities, from "family planning" and "package holidays" to the "cultivated man's library" and "preparations for marriage," it is a damning indictment of contemporary Western civilization in the spirit of the ninety-five theses against papal corruption that Martin Luther nailed to a church door in the fifteenth century. As one side of the debate, the list rivals and mocks the analyst's comprehensive interrogation, exposing the very ways the familial, social, romantic, sexual, political, and religious aspects of one's life—the thrust of the analyst's information gathering—have been co-opted and trivialized by the reigning culture.

Charles may be the most verbal of Bresson's protagonists since Joan, but of a different order from the first-person narrators of the 1950s, who are revealed by their actions. In deliberately refusing to be "useful in a world that disgusts [him]," he is something of an anomaly in Bresson's work. By comparison, Michel's misguided activities in *Pickpocket* are impassioned displacements of a desire to become involved in life. Charles's manner of speaking exhibits none of Michel's anxiety or the husband's in *Une femme douce,* nor the nonchalant self-absorption of Jacques in *Four Nights.* He does not suffer from a tortured conscience like the country priest or burn with infectious zeal like Fontaine, and unlike the wife in *Une femme douce,* he hardly shuts up. This may seem beside the point since he neither espouses a creed nor acts in accordance with an ultimate purpose. He sees no point in social or political causes, yet, as a product of the middle class, neither does he fit in with the slackers who frequent the embankments of the Seine. He looks askance at his friend Michel's concern with environmental destruction, yet in his conviction that the world is plagued with the detritus of materialism and its mindless pursuits, he seems to be Bresson's spokesman.

But in differentiating him in characterization and behavior from every other protagonist, Bresson distances himself from Charles's ultimate decision, providing instead two conflicting ways of understanding the film's denouement. The first is to view the analyst's final gesture and remark as the catalyst for Charles's action, all the more devastating because it follows an otherwise authentic representation of the psychoanalytic encounter. In acting on it, Charles not only finds a way out, but he can claim further evidence of the failure of cultural interventions. From this perspective, psychoanalysis emerges as the most arrogant and potentially dangerous of all such efforts.

On the other hand, should we not view the exchange with the analyst within the context of a persistent theme of Bresson's, to wit: If everything contributes to a working out of one's destiny, is not the analyst's remark, no less than the many apparent coincidences throughout Bresson's films, purposefully instrumental in Charles's fate? Unless the Bresson of every film from *Les Anges du péché* to *Lancelot of the Lake* changed his thinking considerably, the psychoanalyst, whether blundering narcissist or the devil in disguise, merely plays his role in the divine scheme of things. As a figure conditioned to hear everything without prejudice, he is potentially the ideal listener, unlike a spiritual confessor who dispenses judgment and forgiveness. On the other hand, the very neutrality required of his profession can be too easily confused with the indifference of the world to the unspeakable acts done in the name of progress. This puts Charles in the position, not of one who can be helped by what the doctor has to offer, but of one whose problem, regardless of its biological and psychological roots, cannot be extracted from the larger question of massive societal breakdown.

In this context, it is worth considering whether we should view the analyst's allusion to the way the Romans committed suicide solely as the final straw that drives Charles to death. Or whether through this ploy, Bresson found a way to insinuate his own conviction that there is something noble about Charles's decision, akin to such heroic figures of Roman history as Cato, who chose to die by his own hand rather than compromise his principles and live under tyranny. In Plutarch and most accounts of Cato, his suicide was judged entirely consistent with his unimpeachably virtuous life as "the most uncompromising of all men,"[6] as well as with the practice of ancient Romans, for whom it was neither cowardly nor immoral nor a transgression against religious law. The prohibition against suicide in Catholic doctrine is a much later development. Bresson's strategy allowed him to have it both ways: he could critique the irresponsibility of the psychoanalyst for planting the idea in Charles's mind, while planting in the viewer's mind an association that places Charles in admirable company.

If we are to take seriously everything he does and says throughout the film, Charles is a symbol of those values, independence and freedom, that society purports to hold up as most important while making it impossible to put them into practice. His litany of social absurdities is a cry against the ways society enforces compromise and moral vacuity. If he speaks for Bresson in so indicting the banality and blinding materialism of the world—and everything in the film tends to support this, as well as the views of the world expressed in the films Bresson made before (*Lancelot of the Lake*) and after (*L'Argent*) this one—then his choice to die is also a reflection, however mediated, of the artist. This does not mean that the filmmaker would have made the same choice, but that within the context of Bresson's art and concerns, Charles's decision symbolizes the severity of his creator's judgment against the contemporary world.

The End

In *The Devil Probably,* as in *Four Nights of a Dreamer,* characters stroll about quite a bit. This suits the ambling nature of the narrative as well as the seemingly aimless lives of its young characters; the effect is that nothing is urgent enough to require rushing, nor does anything warrant sustained attention. This pace does not change in the light of Charles's resolve. Upon leaving the analyst's office, he returns to Edwige's apartment to get some money, not his own as it happens, goes to the embankment to purchase a gun, wakes Valentin, and lures him with the prospect of earning money so he can buy more drugs. Together they take the metro to the Invalides station, stop for a moment at a café, then walk to Père Lachaise and scale the wall—all of this with an elaboration and tempo quite unlike the sense of implacability engendered by ellipses to which we are accustomed in Bresson and which returns with vigor in *L'Argent.* The difference in approach makes one wonder whether it serves as yet another distancing technique for Bresson, a way to achieve the narrative goal but without enforcing it through his preferred stylistic execution. In a sense the subtle difference in rhythm tends to stress the freedom of Charles's act, as opposed to its being inevitably dictated from elsewhere.

The final sequence has the same monotonic pulse as the rest, but it carries a more sour note in the form of Valentin, whose muted impatience to be done with the affair has to stand as the bitterest commentary on a character's death in all of Bresson, despite the fact that he, too, must be part of the design. That Charles has chosen Valentin for this very quality confirms his assessment of humanity. Valentin watches impassively as Charles sips a small drink, then eagerly tries to wrest the gun from Charles's pocket. As they walk toward the cemetery, Charles lingers a moment before an open window of a ground-floor apartment where a television plays what looks like a solo ballet performance keyed to a soft, classical melody. On a first viewing this seems an ironic touch, a lovely image that cannot compete with the overpowering force of the stock footage seen earlier, and so perhaps a farewell to the fragile and remote capacity of art to redeem such a world. Yet the moment may also be a figuration of Charles's act: lonely, isolated, tuned to a singular melody but no less touching.

Once over the cemetery walls, Charles walks forward, then stops, cocks the pistol and hands it to Valentin. Charles tells him he can do it "here or there," wherever he likes. Three brief tracking shots follow, the first of Charles walking left to right, the second of Valentin walking behind, then stopping to check the gun. The third is of Charles continuing on and saying, "I thought at a time like this, I'd have sublime thoughts," turning to look back, then resuming. A shot of Valentin shows him raising the pistol and aiming off screen right. We see Charles's back in medium shot as he utters his last words, "Shall I tell you what I'm th——," interrupted by the sound of the shot. As with his remark in the first scene at the rally, "Our only strength…," we don't get to hear the rest of the thought. In both cases, the words are certainly tantalizing, the beginning of a formation with an assertive thrust. Valentin walks forward, aims the pistol down, and shoots again, then crouches and clumsily places the gun in Charles's right hand. The camera pans over Charles's body, his left hand resting calmly over his stomach, as Valentin reaches into his pockets for the money. We see his legs walk off, then the camera rises to watch him run off into the dark, his footsteps audible long after he is out of view. This shot reverses the opening shot of the *bateau mouche* brightly emerging out of the darkness.

The drab ordinariness of the scene seems designed to dispel any romantic or heroic notions one might have about Charles's act, as if in raising the specter of Roman nobility Bresson had to undermine its implications. For Charles to ask Valentin, a pathetic drug addict, to pull the trigger is a mercenary gesture far removed from such nobility. In fact, since he must realize that Valentin will be held accountable, Charles has destroyed not one life, but two. In this way Bresson seems to further distance himself from the act, which seems distinct from the suicides of Mouchette and the wife in *Une femme douce*. And yet, if a continuing focus of his work has been the line between adolescence and adulthood, or more generally the threshold at which whatever remains of childhood innocence must shatter before the truth of the world, then Charles is notable for refusing to cross over. Unlike Mouchette, however, whose life promises nothing but further misery, his reasons may strike us as abstract, seeing things all too clearly, as he tells the analyst. Like Balthazar, he is a witness to human temerity and venality, but too tarnished an angel to be altogether innocent.

And yet there is ambiguity, for his belief in an eternal life would seem to contradict the notion of suicide as "an explosion of the will," a supreme gesture of metaphysical defiance that Dostoevsky embodies in the character of Kirillov.[7] In a way, Charles's act might even be seen as we view those of certain characters in classical tragedy. Whatever else may be true about them, they achieve a certain dignity and nobility from a sheer refusal to compromise. Charles occupies a world bereft of the moral absolutes of classical tragedy, and this renders his action all the more extraordinary. He is neither mad nor angry, and he refuses to lose whatever is unique about him and live out his days enslaved to a society defined by nothing higher than compromise. Perhaps that is why, suicide or not, the film struck many commentators at the time as far less despairing than *Au hasard Balthazar* or *Lancelot of the Lake,* in which individuals are overwhelmed and crushed by a culture that itself appears doomed.

L'Argent

We have art in order not to die of the truth.

—Friedrich Nietzsche

There is not a kingdom of death and a kingdom of life. There is the kingdom

of God and we are in it.

—Robert Bresson, quoting Georges Bernanos in the interview, "Ni vu, ni connu."

If the suicide that ends *The Devil Probably* troubled many viewers, *L'Argent* (*Money*, 1983) proved even more disturbing. A much angrier work, it convinced many of what they had suspected for years, that Bresson had lost any remaining faith in human nature or in something beyond it capable of redeeming mankind. The belief that he had succumbed to a nihilist vision was reinforced by his decision to exclude the conversion and rehabilitation theme of part two of *The Forged Coupon*, the Tolstoy novella on which the film is based. The crux of the issue is the behavior of the character of Yvon in the last section of the film. Few earlier Bresson characters practice what we might call genuine evil, perhaps Hélène in *Les Dames du bois de Boulogne* or Gérard in *Au hasard Balthazar*. Although Yvon is the victim of the mendacity of others and assumes an almost passive demeanor in three-quarters of the film, the murderous course on which he embarks in the final quarter casts a pall over the whole.

Unlike other Bresson protagonists, Yvon does not appear to engage in a struggle of conscience. He moves from working-class man whose life is ruined to accomplice in a bank robbery and serial murderer. Even Tolstoy explains that Stepan, Yvon's counterpart in the novella, kills easily because he did it in the army. However justified one might deem Yvon's anger and desire for revenge for the injustices done to him, the murders he commits, especially of the woman who befriends him, enact the most shocking ellipses in Bresson's work. In their leaps over moral and psychological reflection, they exceed the effects of the formal use of this trope. Such leaps suggest that the real struggle the film presents, and with which the viewer must come to terms, is between the image of a materialistic, unjust, and violent world on the one hand, and the viability of any moral principle on the other. As the denouement implies, it is a struggle to the death.

Nevertheless it can be argued that the film's final moments imply that a change of direction is not precluded. First, despite its secular subject, the narrative manifests at critical junctures the tendency toward sacred indirection introduced in the discussion of *Mouchette*. For example, Bresson's use of parallel structure in *L'Argent* leads to genre expectations that are disrupted by a turn of events with supernatural implications. In addition, Yvon's encounter with the widow is expanded beyond its fleeting treatment in the novella, deepening her character as a figure of Christian principles whose behavior genuinely, if belatedly, affects him. This ending recalls the theme of *Les Anges du péché:* the awakening of a dead soul from self-righteous victimization to moral choice. To ignore these cues would be to suggest that Bresson developed the relationship between these characters solely to compound the evil of Yvon's acts and confirm the futility of charitable behavior, a strategy utterly uncharacteristic of this artist and cynical in the extreme.

This is not to underestimate the harshness of the film, all the more pronounced because it is Bresson's last word. Unlike Tolstoy, whose eccentric spiritualism late in life would qualify him as a character in Dostoevsky, Bresson was not a polemicist. And yet, as he said more than once, the presence or existence of God is not contingent on whether characters have faith or undergo transformation. One way to read the final section of *L'Argent* is to see it as a contest between the Old and New Testaments: between the rule of an eye for an eye that drives Yvon and the widow's sentiment that if she were God, she would forgive everybody. Given the dark, boyishly handsome figure of Yvon, however, fusing the angelic and the demonic, this contest may be unfairly matched, in that his murderous rampage has the aura of divine wrath from which no one can claim immunity. For if the circuit of lies and evil, begun with the passing of a forged bill, implies a common humanity, then everyone shares the guilt, even the ostensibly innocent. Consistent with the view Bresson manifests from his first film, the real currency in *L'Argent* is original sin.

L'Argent pursues an implacable logic, working its way through many characters, incarnated and propelled by a style by now so aurally and cinematographically meticulous that it is impossible to separate it from the subject. Arguably more compressed than any film since *The Trial of Joan of Arc*, with the exception of *Lancelot of the Lake*, *L'Argent* establishes the situations of eight characters in its first twelve minutes. Though driven neither by a strong main character or an overtly spiritual subject, the sense of underlying purpose and foreseen end is as resolute as ever. Because of this, the film once again declares the operation of a theo-rhetoric in Bresson's work, in which a ruling design is imposed not only on its theme, but also on its form and structure. Yet although God may be an insinuating, though distant force in the mechanics of the plot and in certain cinematographic details, the driving principle of the film's first three quarters is underwritten by an opposing value. Indeed, as I hope to show, the core images of *L'Argent*—namely, the close-ups of money changing hands—do more than exemplify a theme. Unlike the core images identified in *Diary of a Country Priest, A Man Escaped*, and *Pickpocket*, the ones in *L'Argent* are not confined to an individual but constitute a communal rite, enacting transactions between and among all characters. As such, they symbolize the more general material nature of exchange that pervades the film, affecting relationships between characters and situations in the narrative as well as relationships between shots, spaces, and cinematographic tropes. Given the complexity of this execution, it is all the more intriguing that in interviews Bresson said that although he used a storyboard as always, he felt himself working more freely, more intuitively on *L'Argent*.[8]

"The Forged Coupon"

Embracing twenty-four characters in its first fifty pages, Tolstoy's *The Forged Coupon* is marked by the moral compulsion and concise execution we associate with Bresson. It was published posthumously in 1911, along with several other short works. Like most of Tolstoy's late pieces, it reflects the author's promotion of Christian principles, a process begun during a spiritual crisis in the late 1870s that led to his denunciation of *War and Peace* and *Anna Karenina* as "bad art."[9] Written when Tolstoy was in his seventies and had long since renounced money, private property, and the pleasures of the flesh, the story reflects a near child-like belief in the power of the gospels to transform human lives.

The novella consists of two parts. Part one traces the domino-like effect of a series of criminal acts involving multiple characters. It begins when Mitya, son of a government official, is denied sufficient allowance to pay off a debt. His father warns that he will become a "swindler," and in revenge the son fulfills the prophecy, persuaded by a friend to forge a government coupon and cash it at a photography shop. The cycle of fraud thus begins in the bosom of the family and extends to members of every social class—government officials, landowners, merchants, peasants, clergy, educators, and revolutionaries—ending with the brutal murder of Maria Semyonovna, virtually the only good character in the story. Except for her, everyone rationalizes the wronging of others as compensation for perceived injuries.

Tolstoy's ultimate purpose emerges in part two, beginning with the transformation of Stepan Pelageyushkin, Maria Semyonovna's murderer. Stepan is so haunted by her final words that while in prison he inspires several characters to believe in the message of the gospels. Other characters from part one who show up in the prison are affected by this message until the plot comes full circle ten years later, when Mitya, forger of the original coupon, working as an engineer in Siberia, is accompanied by the convict Stepan on his explorations. The encounter "turns [Mitya's] soul upside down"; he resolves to abandon his life as a gambler and philanderer to marry and use his money and advantages to "serve the common people as best he could."[10]

In its use of character types, its cyclical structure, its sharp contrasts—between the city and the country, the rich and the poor, the educated and the peasant class—and its overt Christian message, the novella is an elaborate parable of good and evil. Tolstoy implies that just as evil begets evil, foul deeds and injuries arousing people's basest instincts, good can be equally infectious; acts of kindness bring out the best in people and can even change their lives. Unlike evil, however, good does not always work its influence immediately, as the central encounter in the narrative between Stepan and the old woman illustrates. The farmhand Stepan is the victim of theft, but so lacks normal inhibitions that he kills on impulse. In the military he was part of a firing squad and sees no difference between that and his killing of the peasant Ivan, who has turned horse thief. When he is released from prison, he has nowhere to go, having lost his family, and falls quite naturally into thievery and more killing. And so, before he meets the old woman, he kills a worker at a wayside inn and a potential employer's wife and children, acts that fail to arouse compunction.

From any rational perspective, Stepan in part one is a sociopath, without the barest trace of conscience and seemingly incapable of change. Tolstoy follows the description of his mindless propensity to violence with a single-page encounter with Maria Semyonovna, in which three short sentences uttered by the woman just before Stepan slashes her throat have the power to turn his life around. The difference in approach is inseparable from the message. The requirements of that literary art Tolstoy renounced are irreconcilable with the aims of a didactic work. Tolstoy explicitly wrote that the essence of "true" literary art, as practiced by one convinced of the Christian message, is opposed to those qualities that would be appreciated by the educated classes: "Good Christian art of our time may be unintelligible to people because of imperfections in its form…but…it must be the art, not of some one group of people, nor of one class, nor of one nationality, nor of one religious cult.…It must transmit feelings accessible to everyone."[11] Conceivably a rationalization of weakened literary powers, there is logic to Tolstoy's choice of the simpler literary form if one sees it as a modern version of a New Testament story, in which spiritual transformation would occur, as it does in the gospels, suddenly and inexplicably.

Maria Semyonovna's sentences—"What are you doing? Have mercy on yourself. You think you're harming others, but it's your own soul you're ruining."—haunt Stepan because of their directness and simplicity. Her life exemplifies goodness and Christian behavior, in contrast to the novella's negative image of the clergy, in particular the figure of Father Vvedensky, a hypocrite who takes revenge on those who oppose him and forces others to accept official teachings of the Church in order to reinforce his own faith. Later, in the guise of Father Misail, Vvedensky fails to quell a sectarian movement begun by peasants (under the influence of a crippled tailor who in turn was influenced by the same Maria Semyonovna) that rejects the Church and its icons in favor of following the principles of Christian brotherhood.

Tolstoy's point is clear: the good person is not the one who studies theology or goes to church while violating Christian principles in everyday life; it is the person who lives a good life, sacrificing for others, not in the hope of eternal reward but, as Maria Semyonovna says, because "it is better to live that way." The genuine nature of her beliefs, compatible with her actions, is reflected in her gaze, the very thing Stepan cannot withstand and murders her to erase.

The message of the gospels—of brotherhood, charity, and forgiveness—is held as the only salvation for the human propensity toward vileness and weakness. Social and revolutionary action, the novella implies, are ineffective, as the fates of the characters Katya Turchaninova and Tyurin indicate. But this message cannot be entrusted to the officials of organized religion; it must be lived and disseminated, from individual to individual, through charitable behavior and good works.

L'Argent generally follows the organization of part one of Tolstoy's tale, but eliminates many characters and situations. From part two Bresson draws several circumstances and dialogue, including the scene of the murderer's surrender, the model for the film's final sequence. Bresson excludes the action, sermonizing, and upbeat religious and socialist denouement of the story. But his extension of the encounter between Yvon (his Stepan) and the widow (Maria Semyonovna's counterpart) in the last quarter of the film is surely the substitute, an elaboration of Tolstoy's idea that it is the life of humility and sacrifice that disseminates the Christian message from individual to individual. Despite the brutal image of the world in his last film, then, Bresson, contrary to the views of many on *L'Argent*'s release, does not appear to have rejected the possibility of moral regeneration.

Au Hasard un Protagoniste

The lie is the specific evil which man has introduced into nature.

—Martin Buber, *Right and Wrong: An Interpretation of Some Psalms in*

Good and Evil

Like *Au hasard Balthazar*, *L'Argent* has an affinity with the parabolic mode and at first does not establish a main character. But whereas the characters in the former are differentiated across a varied palette, *L'Argent*'s title implies that everyone is driven by material values, even though no character is especially pathological about money, as is the niggardly grain merchant in *Balthazar*. Money in *L'Argent* symbolizes a more pernicious and pervasive falsification of values, blurring the difference between classes, destroying lives indifferently, obscuring the meaning of justice, and perverting the nature of desire.

In its first quarter the focus is on three young men of different classes and the people around them: Norbert (Tolstoy's Mitya), a high school student, and his bourgeois parents; Lucien, employed at the photo shop owned by a middle-class couple; and the working-class Yvon, with a wife and young daughter. The film's second and third quarters follow the fortunes of Yvon and Lucien, and the final quarter concentrates on Yvon. How they are connected is delineated in the film's first twelve minutes. Whereas *Balthazar* follows its characters via the changing ownership of the donkey, *L'Argent* is preoccupied with the aftereffects of the acts that link the characters, cutting back and forth to keep us abreast of what is happening to one as we follow another, an unusual structure for Bresson, which highlights how class difference affects the fate of each character. The consequences for Norbert evaporate when his mother buys the shop owner's silence, ending his story in the first quarter; because neither Lucien nor Yvon are so privileged, they are compelled on a parallel course toward prison in the second and third quarters of the film.

Who, then, is the real protagonist of *L'Argent?* Does the film have a protagonist at all in the Bressonian sense? Yvon, the only one with any reasonable claim, bears little resemblance to his predecessors, from Anne-Marie (*Les Anges*) to Charles (*Devil*). In contrast to his phlegmatic surface, Charles is an impassioned lover of life, despite, or perhaps because of, his choice to end it; his actions and thoughts are the conduits of the film's themes. But as the initial sequences of *L'Argent* imply, it is by pure "chance" that Yvon becomes the focus and that the course of his life, after falling victim to the chicanery of others, determines the narrative's trajectory. In passing on forged 500-franc notes, the photo shop owner has no one in mind; Yvon just happens to deliver oil on the wrong day. This random manner in which anyone's life can be ruined by an indifferent, unethical act is central to the widening structure that is rooted in the film's core exchanges. Even after Yvon is made the focus, there is little to dispel our impression of him as passive when he first enters the photo shop to be paid, head lowered, barely uttering a word.

Yvon's emergence as the main character implies that even a relative nobody can be wrested from obscurity and impelled toward ruin through unavoidable interactions with the social community. These interactions are developed through the elliptical structure of the opening sequences. From the moment Norbert leaves his home in pursuit of extra cash, his request for a larger allowance having been refused by his father, to the photo shop where the husband berates his wife for accepting a fake 500-franc note, the cutting sustains the theme of money as the driving force behind people's false dealings with each other. The shot of the husband resolving to "pass on" several forged notes cuts to a medium shot of Yvon delivering oil to the shop. After he is paid with the phony bills, we see him parking his truck and entering a restaurant. This cuts to the waiter refusing the notes in payment for his lunch. When the waiter calls him a crook, he rises in anger and shoves him violently across the room.

This action establishes Yvon as both the victim of a circuit of lies and a man capable of violence, the obverse of his passivity. The cuts leading to this point become increasingly elliptical. The meal at the restaurant is elided; Yvon's action is broken up into two brief shots: the first, a close-up of the waiter's arm as Yvon seizes it and thrusts him off screen, his open hand suspended as we hear crashing sounds (figure 86); the second, of tables overturning and dishes falling from the impact of the waiter's body. Before the cut to the arrival of a police car, we hear the sound of its motor and assume they have come to the restaurant. But we soon see that they are at the photo shop, with Yvon already in custody. On the shop owner's advice, Lucien, with a shrug and a shake of his head, denies having seen Yvon, after which the detective takes him away. And so Yvon, an unwitting victim, becomes the protagonist by default.

As Bresson never fails to remind us, such chance occurrences have the force of inevitability. His elliptical style is never only about narrative economy, but also about the binding links between actions and people and their moral consequences. Eliding what lies between intensifies the narrative's advance, converting the course of action from the possible to the necessary. This is stressed with the cut from the waiter's fall to the police car at the photo shop. Left out are the call to the police, the accusation, the explanation, and the decision to check Yvon's story. Typical of Bresson's method, this series of elisions is retroactively endowed with an unforeseen purpose by way of a more extreme example that consolidates the others and reveals the imperative underlying all of them.

Yvon's recessive nature is further indicated when Lucien denies seeing him. Without complaint, he mutters almost indifferently, "They're mad." When at court the judge releases him and admonishes him not to make false accusations against honest people, not a glimmer of righteous anger passes over his face. When he agrees to drive the getaway car for a bank heist, both his easy slide into crime and the way the sequence is constructed minimize assertive agency on his part. He sits in the car while the sequence ingeniously and wittily unfolds by way of an unidentified man strolling through the streets reading a newspaper, oblivious to his surroundings, until he comes upon the police crouched across from the bank. As gunfire rings out, Yvon starts the engine, but when the police become suspicious, he pulls out impatiently and engages in a chase that ends in a crash. A cut to his wife, Elise, shows her waiting at the police station for news of his arrest. Not surprisingly, then, Yvon is overshadowed by the film's dynamic form, just as he will be by what ensues. The shot of Elise cuts abruptly to the trial, the transition given extra force by the words "The Court!," followed by a frame saturated in the red of the judges' robes as they pass in the foreground. Unlike the first trial, the audiovisual juxtaposition carries the weight of the sentence that will alter their lives. Yvon is found guilty by a majority of eight, with mitigating circumstances, and is sentenced to three years in prison.

Despite his apparent passivity, Yvon has something no other Bressonian protagonist has: a last name, or more accurately a first and last name. We hear it in court and at the prison and see it written on letters from his wife. Is it a coincidence that the name Targe, but that it lacks an *n*, is an anagram for the film's title? And could the missing *n* denote negation, the French *non*, a way of stressing that the character lacks the very thing his name evokes? Then again, to the question Who is the protagonist of *L'Argent*? might this negative imply *not Targe*?

Perhaps the protagonist, as the title suggests, is money, the force that sets everything in motion and that, like the devil alluded to in Bresson's previous film, is driving humanity to destruction. Money would then be the devil's instrument, a means of spreading deceit and lies and of poisoning the well of human communication. Indeed, the original poster for the film on its French release depicts two large rectangles one atop the other, forming a metallic-looking face. The top rectangle has two eyes, the bottom the image of a ten (or twenty) franc note, and the edges of both are lined with teeth. We might conclude that, in turning his back on a world enslaved by this monster cash machine, Charles in *The Devil Probably* is Bresson's last genuine protagonist, and that in *L'Argent* we are faced with the infernal culprit behind that list of banalities that Charles reads to the psychoanalyst.

The Aesthetics of Exchange

Money is the more or less temporary disappearance of difference; it is the

reduction of the random to quantifiable system.

—R. A. Shoaf, *Dante, Chaucer, and the Currency of the Word: Money, Images, and*

Reference in Late Medieval Poetry

Because the film is about money, the strategy of exchange, manifest especially in these initial sequences, is more calculated and resonant than usual. The exchange of shots and looks are at the heart of Bresson's filmmaking; in *L'Argent* the concept extends to a wider array of elements and relationships. Although the film's characters belong to different classes, in terms of how their lives are affected by a single act they are almost interchangeable. The principle also characterizes the film's themes: freedom is exchanged for imprisonment, truth for lies, love for hate, forgiveness for judgment.[12] Bresson's work often involves the delayed or unknown consequences of change in a situation. In those narratives in which a character is imprisoned or about to be, loss of physical freedom eventually produces an unforeseen gain in which the character (Thérèse, Fontaine, Michel, Joan) undergoes a transformation.

In such circumstances, the reciprocal aspect of exchange is initially hidden, subject to future revelation. *L'Argent* pushes this notion to an extreme since we cannot know for certain whether Yvon's confession at the end will result in a substantive change.

The variety of exchanges ranges from the immediately apparent to the abstract. Virtually every exchange of money is in close-up, framing each person's hand: the allowance Norbert's father gives to his son; Martial's showing the forged bill to Norbert; the shopkeeper's holding the bill against the light to test its legitimacy; her handing over the change for the bill; the forged bills the shopkeeper's husband uses to pay Yvon; the change Lucien gives to the customer he has cheated; and the bribe Norbert's mother offers to the shopkeeper. All of these exchanges are tainted, either because they involve the forged bill (or bills) itself or because the money is being used for an inappropriate purpose: Norbert's father gives him an allowance in exchange for being left alone; his mother buys the shopkeeper's silence to protect her son. The close-ups draw attention not only to the exchange of money but to the duplicity underlying these exchanges, the dubious purposes facilitated by its use. The exception to the pattern is when Yvon pays for his lunch and the waiter declares his money "no good." Instead of a close-up of hands engaged, Yvon is seated as the waiter stands over him rejecting bill after bill. Ironically, it is the only honest exchange in the series since Yvon is unaware that the bills are phony until the waiter exposes this fact.

The initial use of the forged bill is revealing: Norbert seeks help from his schoolmate Martial, who gives him the forged bill; though Norbert resists, Martial insists he take it and at the shop pretends that Norbert received it from his father. Later, when Norbert is confronted at school, he flees from his class out of guilt while Martial sits "innocently" in his seat. So if the first sign of the corrosive effect of money is its capacity to displace a proper parent-child relationship, the second is its capacity not only to be falsified but to counterfeit friendship as well. A similar hypocritical betrayal characterizes the shopkeeper's behavior: after bribing Lucien to deny recognizing Yvon and to lie in court, he then righteously fires him when he catches him embezzling.

Here we have a clue to Bresson's method in the film. In his detailed study of particular cantos in Dante's *Divine Comedy*, R. A. Shoaf speaks of the analogies between money, language, and faith in the Middle Ages as three forms of exchange equally susceptible to falsification. Dante places a figure called Master Adam in Hell because he introduced an alloy into the coin known as the florin, thus corrupting its gold base. And he speaks of the need for the poet to rise above narcissism, an even greater form of fraudulence, in order to properly reflect humanity and the divine Being that created him. Bresson is not present in the bodies and texts of his films, as Dante is in his poem, but he was no less earnest in applying a rigorous moral standard to the behavior of his characters and in drawing attention to the destructive nature of pride and narcissism. The analogy that Shoaf delineates can apply to the way *L'Argent* links the exchange of money to deceitful, narcissistic behavior, which, in a variation on Shoaf, is further reflected in verbal exchanges: Martial mocks the shopkeeper's test of the legitimacy of the forged coupon, compounding the initial false dealing by perverting the proper use of language. A major theme in *L'Argent* might be thus characterized: "Fraud is a falsification of the Image of God in man."[13]

These monetary, immoral, and linguistic exchanges are flanked in turn by exchanges of physical spaces: between interiors and exteriors and between shots dominated by internal frames and those with open-ended views. An unfolding series of images extends outward, rooted in the transactions at their core, an architectural design analogous to Tolstoy's structure, in which the initial exchange within the family moves beyond to encompass all social classes. The implication is that the very nature of corrupt forms of exchange is infectious and widespread. Certain shots tend to literalize this; a shot of Norbert riding his motorbike down a street and of an unidentified prisoner walking down a corridor, held until each is entirely out of view and exceeding any discernible narrative purpose, seem to merge with an extradiegetic social fabric. It is a real Paris and a real prison that we see.

The way money relates to this dynamic is suggested by the film's first image: a medium shot of an automatic cash machine on the sidewalk, its door closing just after a transaction not witnessed, over which the credits are superimposed. Such a machine figures in the narrative, its armed, forbidding look connoting both privileged access and imprisonment. Its relation to the flow of Paris's street traffic, heard on the soundtrack, embodies the film's image of how money rules social reality: a fixed symbol determining the restless currents of lives buzzing around it. Sounds of cars, buses, vans, and traffic are the most frequently heard throughout the film; traffic is also a frequent visual backdrop, not just linking spaces and people, but as the literal conveyor of an endless circuit of which the characters and situations seem but particle phenomena, all subject to viral contagion.

As the noise of the traffic fades, the first shot of the narrative proper comes into view, marked by a frequent style of composition. The image, framed at a slightly acute angle, is divided into a number of vertical panels: a door on the left, a strip of wall, and a pair of French doors, themselves segmented into rectangles. Norbert approaches, opens the door, looks off screen, and reminds his father (off screen) that it is allowance day. Their dialogue comprises several shot-countershots; the only shot in which they both appear is the close-up of their hands and the exchange of money (figure 87), an interaction that seems to constitute the extent, if not the essence, of their relationship.

While the elegance of these shots, especially those of Norbert against the panoply of rich decor, denote privilege, the overdetermination of frames has a confining effect, thus bringing into the domestic sphere both connotations of the cash machine. Despite differences in class, this dynamic is universal. Characters are often framed vertically in the center of an image marked by internal dividers. When Yvon arrives home and is about to unlock the door to his apartment, it suddenly opens, the light from inside contrasting sharply with the dark hall. In the illumined vertical space, compressed by the angle, a small child appears looking up happily. Yvon steps inside and opens another door, revealing a glimpse of a kitchen, immediately adjacent and aligned vertically with the space. This simultaneous opening and constricting of spaces is confined to a narrow strip in the center of the frame, as if the lives within were similarly cramped. The effect is not unlike that of the shot of Yvon entering the Hotel Moderne much later, and to the shot of the widow opening doors within doors. As it happens, the fates of those within all three spaces are linked: the destruction of Yvon's family leads to his murdering the people in the hotel and at the widow's house.

Virtually all of the film's interior spaces—bourgeois and working-class apartments, school, photo shop, restaurant, courtroom, prison, hotel, country home, tavern—are marked by a pronounced sense of framing, often frontally or acutely angled to a pinched effect, emphasizing windows, doors, and doors opening onto other doors, a design subtly offset by the camera's occasional tendency to reframe by way of a pan, a track, or a tilt upward or downward. There are seventy-seven shots in *L'Argent* with such movements, about one-sixth of the film's 449 shots, although, like most camera movements in Bresson, they usually go unnoticed, perhaps because they are always actuated by a move or gesture of a character. It is as if the mobility of characters in relation to such calculated framings was in direct proportion to the role of human will in relation to predetermined design.

The contraction and expansion of physical spaces is the rhythm of the film's breathing, so to speak, either in conjunction with or balanced by its temporal ellipses. An organic system in more ways than one, the body of the film assumes a life and energy of its own, governed by the principles of economy and exchange. A pronounced directive drives its movement as surely as Anne-Marie's determination to affect Thérèse drove *Les Anges du péché*.

But whereas God explicitly imbues the latter, *L'Argent* is driven by the idea of a theo-rhetoric, a concept rooted in medieval culture. The stress on the particular nature of exchange that operates in the film, rooted in false transactions, confirms that money, the "visible god," as one character calls it, and the deleterious effects it has on human relations, has assumed the place in Western culture once occupied by the moral and religious principles grounded in belief in the invisible God.

This theme might seem obvious, yet Bresson's embodiment of it in aesthetic terms is not. If money has the power to reduce all relations and displace all other values, then money underwrites and determines all relationships between individuals and between individuals and society. As Shoaf suggests, in the Middle Ages Christianity and its teachings formed the basis of social structures, determining how people should look upon each other and treat each other as equals, at least in the eyes of God. In such a system individual behavior within a community is directed by a moral-religious standard, whether adhered to or not, so that to treat someone not in accordance with this rule was to violate God's and man's law. As such values became increasingly irrelevant and as the structure of human relations no longer depended on a higher spiritual standard, the notion of the dignity of the individual, always tenuously sustained, disappears. In consequence, all exchanges in a godless society are affected, from the simplest transaction between merchant and buyer to the bonds between lovers.

It is my contention that the first three-quarters of *L'Argent* depicts this state of affairs while its last quarter is an urgent plea against it. Bresson gives us a picture of contemporary society ruled by money and the devaluation of life and human exchange that it has brought about. He presents this not only as a theme that slowly emerges but through the framing and editing of the film, in which all relations extend and mirror the commercial exchanges at its core, perpetuating that falseness which such transactions both mask and permit. It is worth noting that the filmic exchange essential to Bresson's cinema is of course a determinant element of all cinema, its communal language, so to speak. But montage, the instrument of this exchange, can be used both poetically and falsely: as a means of fruitful investigation of internal and external reality on the one hand, or to sell cheap sentiment and manufactured products on the other. It is precisely this potential for corruption that Bresson's insistence on a rigorously moral, accountable cinema aims to correct. Perhaps then, to the list of the elements of exchange in the Middle Ages subject to narcissistic or instrumental falsification that Shoaf illuminates—money, language, and faith—we should add the invention of the cinema.

The Unseen Path

He neither reveals, nor hides but rather he shows.

—Heraclitus, "Fragments," cited by Martin Heidegger, *Sojourns:*

The Journey to Greece

Although not evident in its first half, the principle of sacred indirection plays a strong role in *L'Argent*'s construction. Not until the film's midsection, where Bresson makes more use of the convention of parallel structure than ever before, do we discern signs of it. The alternations between Yvon's worsening situation in prison and Lucien's "good-intentioned" thievery that lands him in the same prison seem to follow the pattern of a typical crime thriller, in which everything points to the eventual confrontation between the two characters. But when Yvon and Lucien finally meet, this outcome quickly dissolves to reveal that a different design is at work, both sacred and indirect. This is not immediately apparent either to the viewer or to Yvon, who, having lost his child, his wife, and his freedom, is on a downward spiral toward self-destruction.

Yvon's arrival at the prison is announced by the color blue, as striking as the red of the judges' robes in the court, both colors filling the screen and associated with authority, and together with the white van sometime later, completing the palette of the French flag. A blue van pulls into the prison yard with new arrivals; blue is the color of the guards' uniforms, and its return later, when the police arrive in the village where Yvon takes refuge after his release, comes as a shock against the lush green world of the widow's surroundings. The shot of the van and unloading of prisoners is one of the film's longest takes, its importance made clearer when it is repeated upon Lucien's arrival. This open shot gives way to an interior shot of an iron gate stretching across the screen, through which prisoners pass to their cells.

A cut to the shopkeepers running into the photo shop to discover that their safe has been robbed is followed by a shot of Lucien and his cronies running into a subway with a suitcase filled with its contents. Bookended by shots of Yvon at the prison, the elliptical nature of these passages expedites Lucien's fate. As if to telegraph what lies in store for him, the long shot of the empty subway platform after his escape cuts to a close-up of the door of Yvon's cell, another open view of freedom giving way to a confined one. The link is reinforced by the sound of footsteps of people exiting the subway, fusing undetectably with those of a guard in the next shot. He comes to escort Yvon to the visiting area. Seven shots through the constricted passageways of doors, gates, and stairwells contrast with effects generated by elliptical cutting. By distending instead of collapsing time, they articulate the protracted experience of prison life. Separated by a glass partition, Yvon assures Elise that he will work hard when he is released, but she leaves abruptly, unable to tell him what she does later by letter: that their daughter, Yvette, has died (figure 88).

Between her visit and the letter, Lucien tampers with the cash machine, from which he robs random accounts. The shot of the machine's door closing, similar to the shot under the credits, cuts to the prison yard as a white van arrives with the mail. As Elise's letter is opened, it appears on the screen, followed by a cut to Yvon lying face down on his cot, his head buried in a pillow as his cellmates read the devastating news. This cuts to the shop owners, who have been forced out of business, learning from a friend about Lucien's donations to the poor. The scene ends as the husband opens the mail and finds a letter from Lucien alluding to the "mean trick" played on him, accompanied by a check for what he stole. "Incredible," exclaims the husband, wiping a single tear from his face, a mask of affected sentiment that contrasts with the genuine misery suffered by Yvon in response to *his* letter.

Bresson treats the Robin Hood theme in Tolstoy's novella rather skeptically, rendering hypocritical Lucien's pretentious claims in court about helping the poor when a judge wryly remarks on Lucien's taste for expensive suits. Bresson implies that attacks on the system, whether bank heists or narcissistic acts of conscience, are futile. Money, "the visible god," as Yvon's philosophical cellmate calls it, rules. It accommodates both ethical and unethical norms of business practice as part of the smoothly run commercial system that sustains capitalist societies.

Word has gotten around that Yvon's letters have been returned, prompting inmates in the dining hall to taunt him about his wife's infidelity. Seizing a skimmer from a food trolley, he raises it threateningly over a guard and then drops it with such force that it slides for several seconds along the floor (figure 89). Followed by the camera at ground level, it hits the cement wall in a wobbling clatter. It is the final instance in Bresson's work of a favored motif: an object reverberating with the inchoate rage that consumes the character. Yvon is sentenced to solitary. A prison official remarks, "A man who hasn't killed can be worse than a mass murderer," predicting the consequences of Yvon's barely controlled inhibitions.

The model Christian Patey's understated impersonation not only conveys Yvon's recessive manner but effectively conceals his thinly suppressed anger. Yvon is a synthesis of two characters in Tolstoy: before Stepan, there is the peasant Ivan, who makes his living selling firewood but later becomes a horse thief. It is he who is cheated, tries to use the forged coupon at a restaurant, and has a tussle with a waiter. In the film Yvon's reaction to the waiter is more like Stepan's, the farmhand whose indifference to killing prompts him to beat Ivan to death. It is fitting that Yvon should be a fusion of these two, the first of whom is killed by and then replaced in the novella by the second, as if each embodied one side of his character. Bresson cleverly collapses Tolstoy's inventions with one of his own. Yvon's suicide attempt is against the Ivan part of his character, the victim who tries to use forged notes and is arrested, and then turns criminal by agreeing to drive the getaway car for bank robbers. Though Yvon survives, he returns to prison as the murderous Stepan, now bent on revenge.

Before that, we sense his mix of rage and calm in solitary confinement as he scrapes a metal cup repeatedly against the cement floor. The irritating sound is interrupted only when an intern arrives with his sleeping pills. Unlike Tolstoy's Stepan, whose wife has gone begging and dies while he is in prison, Yvon turns his violence against himself, exposing a vulnerability that makes him more human. Instead of swallowing the pills, he has hidden them in his mattress. In the film's most unusual elision, the sound of a motor is heard over a close-up of the pills, which cuts to an almost indecipherable close-up of someone's feet standing on tiptoe. The next two shots reveal that they belong to Yvon's cellmates, straining at the window to look down into the courtyard below. A high-angle shot reveals an ambulance into which two attendants carry Yvon on a stretcher. The cellmates exchange looks; one closes the window as the other kneels. "I always pray for suicides," he says, as we hear beeping sounds from a life support machine at the infirmary.

While Yvon lies there, the film cuts to Lucien in court, where, despite his plea, he is sentenced, assuring the court that he will escape to resume his "good works." On the day he arrives at prison, Yvon returns from the infirmary. Bresson underscores the conjunction by an identically framed long take of the blue van with prisoners, followed by a pan right to the white ambulance from the infirmary. As the logical end point to the paralleling of their fortunes, Lucien and Yvon are brought together again, this time in a socially equalizing space.

On his bed Yvon listens as his cellmate paces the floor, musing on justice, natural rights, and the world's absurdity—allusions perhaps to Tolstoy's didacticism. He ends with the phrase, "Oh, money, visible God, what wouldn't we do for you?," delivered in a somewhat offhand, whimsical manner. Yvon's indifference would suggest that he is preoccupied with other things. Just then he receives a message that Lucien wants to meet him at mass. Though his cellmate cautions him not to go, two shots later Yvon sits beside Lucien in the chapel while prisoners exchange items behind their backs (figure 90). The guileful nature of their activities lends a similarly underhanded cast to Lucien's offer to take Yvon with him when he escapes, which is nothing less than another attempt at false exchange; consistent with his fraudulent socialist aspirations, his real aim is to placate his conscience. Unpersuaded, Yvon vows to kill him. At almost one and a half minutes, their exchange is the longest take in the film, yet on the surface it appears to lead nowhere. The meeting effectively dissolves any anticipation aroused from the parallel structure that brought these two together.

Over the next shot in the cell we hear sirens. Awakened by activity in the corridor, Yvon sits up and exclaims, "That's him. That's Lucien." His cellmate assures him that Lucien will be moved to a higher security prison and that Yvon should be relieved: he has gotten revenge without lifting a finger. "Someone fond of you protects you from afar. A relative, or a friend, say." Yvon tells him he has no relatives or friends and shows him the farewell letter from his wife. "Never mind," says the other. "Toe the line. You'll leave soon in good health." To this advice Yvon is deaf, pounding the door in rage that his opportunity for revenge has been taken away.

Although Yvon misses the implications of the remark, "Someone fond of you protects you from afar," the viewer should not. In the spare aesthetics of Bresson's world, fewer and less explicit words are of consequence. The cellmate does not necessarily mean God, but the phrase invokes the possibility. The idea of being protected from afar suggests that unknown forces intervene in our lives and that we do well to heed them, however obscure. In essence this is the point of sacred indirection, made more compelling when the brief exchange between Yvon and his cellmate is linked to the preceding scene. Together they provide a key to the film's move in a new direction and the idea of design.

The Unheard Word

Bresson's scrupulous attention to sound is nowhere more evident than in transitions between sequences, where its overlapping does not just propel the narrative but turns the bridge itself into an acutely realized audiovisual montage. Sound almost never overlaps from a preceding shot unless it belongs to the material of the one that follows, and in bridging instances it is always introduced just before the cut from one to the other. In the early example in *L'Argent*, the sound of the police car heard over the toppled table in the restaurant does not just drive the action forward; it accentuates its advance to its prescribed end. This might be described as a form of stitching the film,[14] a strategy to strengthen the sense of its predetermined course. In Bresson's early films the same goal was accomplished via the use of fades and dissolves, but since *Une femme douce*, sound has assumed this role more emphatically.

As the previous section tried to show, Bresson increased the tension in *L'Argent* by paralleling Yvon's worsening fortunes in prison with Lucien's activities until these characters meet again, and then short-circuits the payoff one would expect from such a generic structure. But just as *Pickpocket* is not an ordinary *policier*, *L'Argent* is not a conventional prison drama. An important sign of the difference is cued at the very end of the chapel scene through another revealing use of audiovisual montage. Just as Yvon and Lucien finish talking in the chapel, and all other sounds cease, we hear one last phrase, spoken not by either of them, but by the priest saying mass off screen. The words "per Christum Dominum nostrum" (through Christ our Lord) conclude several prayers in the traditional Catholic mass asking God to cleanse the devout of their sins and make them "clean of heart." Given the context, these words, isolated and articulated so strongly from an off screen source, along with their significance in Catholic ritual, attest, perhaps not so indirectly, to the notion of design. They imply that both Yvon and Lucien could be forgiven their wrongs and go on with their lives *if* each were willing to renounce the deadly sins that consume them: Yvon's anger and desire for revenge; Lucien's hubris and false sympathy. That the words are instantly followed by a dark screen, pierced by the prison alarm going off seconds before the next shot seems an immediate response to their utterance, as if to exclaim the very intervention they imply and to which the cellmate will allude moments later. In short, Lucien's failed escape attempt is an opportunity for him to curb his pride and for Yvon to renounce his anger. The audio montage announces the significance of the moment, preparing the way for the cellmate's unwitting articulation of its meaning, that "someone fond of [Yvon] protects [him] from afar." In terms of the logic by which one connects narrative material and filmic execution, the priest's words, the alarm, and the cellmate's remark constitute three parts of this instance of sacred indirection.

But although the audiovisual montage and dialogue are linked, Yvon is blind to their meaning. Still consumed by the desire for revenge, he cannot intuit any connection between the priest's words, Lucien's escape attempt, and his cellmate's remarks. In fact it is unlikely that the priest's words have even registered. It will take something far more concrete to shake Yvon's morbid self-absorption. He is not ready to heed the cellmate's appeals to calm down and renounce his rage, anymore than he is capable of seeing any link between the priest's words and those of the cellmate.

And so we might ask: For whom does Bresson offer these tantalizing clues to the looming possibility of design, to yet another instance of a hand over a prison directing events, as Bresson said of *A Man Escaped*? If, as I believe, they are aimed at the viewer, it is likely that Bresson's purpose differs from what it was in, for example, *Les Anges du péché*, in which the protagonist "hears the word" that directs her life. Here is yet another way Yvon differs from all other Bressonian characters. He does not hear the word that would allow him to relinquish his rage, and because of that he moves on, in his Stepan mode, to the horrors of the film's final quarter, compounding an already problematic moral question for the viewer as to Bresson's intentions. Bresson allows the viewer to hear the word and to recognize Yvon's indifference to its ramifications. If anything finally moves Yvon beyond his wretched state of mind, it will not be a moment of transcendent realization, but in Tolstoy's terms, what is transmitted individual to individual. Under the circumstances it is fitting that yet another elliptical cut and audiovisual montage will take Yvon from the prison into the final section of the film.

The cut elides the remaining time of his sentence and takes us to his release. The footsteps of a guard, heard over the shot of the cellmate complaining about Yvon's pounding on the door, continue into the next shot as the guard approaches the outer gate of the prison. Another guard hands Yvon his release papers and opens the gate. In a departure from the numerous shots of doors opening and closing, the gate is not closed all the way until moments later, when we hear it locking into place over a shot of Yvon walking away and reading the documents. Notwithstanding the sheer formal beauty of Bresson's audiovisual articulations, meanings still impose themselves. This audiovisual montage, synchronizing the sound of the gate's locking over his release documents, appears to cement the idea that prison is behind Yvon, a closed chapter. Yet because he leaves with his anger in tow, the truth is that prison awaits him in the future. Thus the suspension of the sound of the gate's locking, delayed until Yvon walks away and then superimposed directly over the release document, enforces yet again his inability to read the signs; just as he failed to make the connection between Lucien's escape and his cellmate's remarks, here he misreads the freedom document not as a new lease on life, but as an opportunity for revenge.

A Fateful Encounter

Happiness is the deferred fulfillment of a prehistoric wish. That is why wealth brings so little happiness; money is not an infantile wish.

—Sigmund Freud, letter of January 16, 1898, to Wilhelm Fliess, in *The Origins of Psychoanalysis: Letters to Wilhelm Fliess, Drafts and Notes*

The last quarter of the film (111 of its 449 shots), excluding the brief final sequence in the café, concerns Yvon's encounter with the woman in the country, a more elaborate affair than Tolstoy's and a moral corrective to the deformed nature of exchange that dominates earlier sections of the film. Like Stepan in the story, Yvon notices the widow emerging from the paymaster's office, where she collects her pension, and follows her home. But whereas Stepan runs off and returns the same night to commit the murders, Yvon lingers for what seems a day and a half. Unlike Maria Semyonovna, the widow in the film says nothing before she is murdered, nor does Yvon rob the house after killing her. And when he asks earlier whether she expects an eternal reward for her hard life, she does not say, as Semyonovna does, that it "is simply better to live that way." Bresson replaces those words with the actions that define the woman's life and character and that affect Yvon. By expanding their relationship, Bresson embellishes the implications of the words. Everything that happens between them before the murders is his invention.

Following his release from prison, Yvon stops at a hotel. Through one of those tightly framed vertical compositions, we see the people who run it when the door opens to admit him. The inner glow from a lamp introduces a warmth that contrasts dramatically with what follows. A shot of the sign, "Hotel Moderne," cuts to a constricted interior view of a staircase. Quietly Yvon descends, bag in hand. Not until he washes his hands in a sink, which fills with blood, do we realize what he has done. He changes his bloodied slacks, walks behind the reception desk, opens draws, and fills his pockets with cash. Just as quietly, he opens the door and leaves, the sound of traffic once again absorbing everything in its flux. The sequence is a marvel of understatement, not least for the way it balances shock and recognition. Though we sensed that Yvon was capable of murder, this elliptic treatment and his unhurried demeanor render the actuality chilling.

In a startling juxtaposition, the film cuts from his exit to a shop window displaying children's dolls, toy clocks and boats, and musical instruments (figure 91). Amid the bright reds, pinks, blues, greens, and yellows is the dusky reflection of Yvon in the glass (figure 92). The most immediate association is to the death of his daughter, but the shot is also relevant to what follows. Footsteps are heard off screen; a cut to a long shot shows him standing in front of the store window as a woman enters the shot from frame right and walks past him. She looks back briefly and they exchange glances. Though he follows her off frame left, their reflections remain visible in the window for a few seconds.

This second shot is a variation of a tendency mentioned earlier, whereby shots are held until figures or vehicles disappear from view. Here the usual depth of field of such views is replaced by a diaphanous image of the two departing figures in a flattened space. Though it is unusual for Bresson to stress an image for its symbolic value, it is hard to ignore the connotations of this shot and the preceding one in terms of the subsequent relationship between Yvon and the woman: the lost boy and the archetypal mother. As if to place the encounter within an imaginary realm, the shot, unlike those long-held ones cited, registers a ghostlike recession vanishing into the objects of childhood.

At first the woman, emerging moments later from the post office tucking bills into her pocketbook, seems only to be Yvon's next target. As their exchange of glances predicted, he follows her home like a stray dog. In a country green setting with wild grass and bushes, Yvon is seen in the distance as she crosses a small footbridge over a brook in the foreground. Before entering her house, she looks back briefly. Later, as she dries dishes, the dog growls and Yvon enters the house as if he has always lived there. She tells him to sit down and feeds him.

After a direct look at him, she walks off screen. In the next shot she walks through one door, then another, recedes into a long shot, disappears, and reappears in the next shot near another door, beyond which we see an elderly man in a bedroom, the door of which she closes before moving off right. In the next shot, from inside a bedroom, another door opens, the woman peers in, moves to the bed, pulls the covers over a young boy, then leaves, closing the door. This multiplication of doors and rooms, overdetermining an aspect of the film's design, suggests efforts to protect her family from a stranger as well as Yvon from being overheard, but as we will see, she succeeds in doing neither. Effectively sealing off the rest of the house, she returns to the kitchen. From her question—"Why did you kill?"—we realize there has been an elision and that Yvon has already confessed to the murders. And yet the effect implies prescience, as if, with the same intuition as the woman who greets Lancelot in the woods and predicts his death, this woman suspects the extremity of his situation. "I enjoyed it," he says, sipping his soup. "I took very little and spent it all....I remember every detail.... Their appearance sickened me."

His remarks confirm that money was less important than gratification, for which his repulsion is both a displacement of self-disgust and a denial of the otherness of his victims. In acting on his desire for revenge, Yvon yields to the old law of an eye for an eye, but the way he entered the Hotel Moderne and left death in his wake also evokes the image of an avenging angel. More shocking than his remarks perhaps is the woman's response. First she asks, strangely, whether he went back to revive them. Then she reassures him that he'll be forgiven. "If I were God, I'd forgive everybody."[15] She exchanges the old law for the new. Yet her response is puzzling, almost disturbing in that it exhibits not even a shiver of surprise.

A widow lacking a child of her own, she plays a maternal role in the household, tending an aging father, her sister and brother-in-law, and their crippled son, as well as doing the cooking, cleaning, and shopping. She does all this without complaint. Just as Yvon expresses confidence that she will not denounce him, the sound of motors overlaps as the image cuts to a shot of police vehicles passing on the highway. The police have come to town looking for the killer of the hotel owners.

The next morning as she walks to the shed where Yvon has spent the night, holding a cup of hot coffee, she is confronted by her father. His manner suggests that this is not the first time she has taken in strangers. When she objects to his demand to send Yvon away, he calls her a mad fool. We barely see his hand move to slap her when it is displaced by a close-up of her hands, shaken by the blow, the hot coffee spilling over them. The image embodies her life and character: standing her ground and enduring abuse without losing composure, her devotion to service undeflected. Far from passive, she defies her father, whose suspicions of Yvon and objection to her misguided intentions are, admittedly, eminently reasonable. It was clever of Bresson to characterize the father as a brute while making him the surrogate for the viewer, who, knowing Yvon is a murderer, is no doubt even more stupefied by the woman's reckless solicitation of this stranger. The shocking paradox of this strategy, as I hope to show, is at the heart of this final section.

Later we see how attuned the widow is to every contingency when, as her father plays the piano, the glass of wine he has placed precariously at the edge of the keyboard falls to the floor. The sound reaching her in the kitchen, she immediately grabs a dustpan and cloth to clean up the mess. By contrast, her interactions with Yvon are calm, as if she were recounting events that trans- pired in the absence of the prodigal son. She blames herself for her father's behavior and drinking, which began after she was widowed. In the garden she turns up potatoes and Yvon carries them to the house. Yet when she goes to town, he runs about looking for money.

In town she emerges from a bakery as two gendarmes enter, a fleeting look of concern on her face. During the next exchange with Yvon, she scrubs clothes in an outdoor tub as he wonders, being so taken advantage of, why she does not drown herself. Is she expecting a miracle? "I expect nothing," she responds. Of course his question is a projection: it is Yvon who tried to kill himself and cannot imagine any course but revenge for the injustices done him. The last eight shots of this final exchange between them before the murders are without dialogue. Set amid the vibrant lushness of grass and trees, they comprise a beautiful passage all the more poignant in light of what follows. As the woman moves the wheelbarrow of laundry along the clothesline, Yvon plucks nuts from the trees and hands her the wash. In one shot they face each other as they each take a nut into their mouths. The moment seems to mark an implicit but ambiguous understanding between them. More pointedly, it is in striking contrast to the film's earlier impersonal exchanges of money changing hands, as restorative of human contact as it is emblematic of a sacrificial rite.

The camera follows their movement until the screen is nearly filled with the whiteness of the linens hanging on the line, recalling the red that dominated the shot of the judges entering the court and the blue of the prison yard. This whiteness cuts to a dark image of the door to the house. It is night; a glow from off screen falls onto the door as a pair of hands approaches, carrying a lantern. Placing it down, Yvon pries open the door with the axe he spotted earlier. What follows in the next twenty shots is the most extraordinary use of light in all of Bresson. Together with sound, ellipses, and off screen space, this penultimate sequence is one of the most remarkable passages of purely cinematographic narration in his work.

The manifest action is Yvon's slaughter of everyone in the household,[16] but of course we do not actually see it happen. The sequence is sculpted out of darkness by the light cast by the lantern from off screen. Each elided action is discovered after the fact by the dog running through doors and passageways, up and down stairs, following the trail of blood. In his course, we see the father dead on the floor, the sister and husband sprawled on the stairs. An innocent surrogate for the viewer's frustrated voyeurism, the dog appears in fourteen of the twenty shots. Doors and corridors appear in eleven, the lantern in five, its light cast from off screen in another five. The only sounds are those of the animal's feet scrambling furiously against the wooden floors, up and down the stairs, and its helpless, unrelenting whine.

The pattern changes with the final murder. The dog appears at the threshold of the woman's room, staring off. This cuts to a shot of her sitting up in bed, a lamp lit to the right (figure 93). She looks up at Yvon (off screen), who asks, "*Où est l'argent?*" The question barely registers before the cut to a one-second shot of his arms swinging the axe from left to right. Another shot of the dog barking is followed by a split-second shot of the axe as before, then swinging back left. The next shot shows the side of the bed and the lamp as the axe sweeps across the frame, knocking over the lamp and splattering blood across the wallpaper, having struck the woman (off screen) in its passage. This is held as the sound of water comes in, continuing into the next shot of the stream outside as the axe comes hurtling from off screen and sinks into its depths.

Though the action could not be clearer, questions remain. That Yvon acts before the woman has a chance to reply to his question makes it unlikely that money is what motivates him. His question is Tolstoy's: automatic, literalizing the film's alleged theme, but unlike the Tolstoy, it is not followed by a search for money. Killing "an entire family," mother figure and all, is something else, not only an act of displaced rage against Lucien and the shop owners, but an attempt to destroy the very symbol of what he has lost—his wife and child certainly, but also the idea of the family as the cornerstone of society, the film's initial example of which is a denatured model.

Yet something of the woman's life and how she has treated him stirs Yvon. After the murder, the frame is filled with the green darkness of the stream, followed by the film's most mournful shot: standing where he had watched the woman scrubbing, Yvon is flanked by the vertical columns of a structure both contained and open, his head cast down. It is hard not to infer that despair, if not the stirring of remorse, has descended upon him. While Tolstoy's Stepan is haunted by the woman's words, Yvon may be even more haunted by the fact that she said nothing, that her look in the face of death was neither afraid nor judgmental. "You kill for a reason," she had remarked earlier. That this crime was motivated by neither the repulsion he felt for the hotel keepers nor the prospect of getting money would seem to make it impossible for him to continue, thoughts compatible with the shot of him standing alone shrouded in darkness.

The sounds of footsteps begin over that image and continue into the next shot of yet another door. It is opened by a figure entering from the left, revealing the interior of a café. Three men enter, one of them a gendarme; as they move into the space, Yvon enters as well. He takes a seat in the rear, has a drink, then rises and walks into the other room. The next shot shows a proliferation of gendarmes: one stands in the right foreground, back to the camera, as Yvon approaches from the rear; on either side of him wall mirrors reflect clusters of other gendarmes standing off screen (figure 94). Yvon walks to the foreground and speaks his final line: "I killed the hotel owners to rob them and I've just killed a whole family." Six gendarmes pass behind him, and in the next shot all the waiters and customers move into the room to see what has happened.

The final shot, the reverse of the one that began the sequence, is the exterior of the café as the door opens and five gendarmes, escorting a handcuffed Yvon, exit from the interior and move off screen. A crowd huddles at the left of the door, every head straining in unison to peer into the café. No one turns toward Yvon or the police as they emerge. All remain fixated on the interior, even after Yvon and the gendarmes have passed off screen (figure 95). Whereas Lucien's seeming failure to recognize Yvon when the police bring him to the photo shop is a lie, here Yvon is truly invisible to the thrill-seeking crowd. In surrendering voluntarily, Yvon has enacted the film's final exchange, choosing imprisonment over freedom, punishment over crime. In doing so he passes beyond the material economics of exchange that dominate a godless society, a spectacle the crowd frozen at the border between inside and outside is incapable of understanding.

The Spirit in Action

Just as language is a kind of coin, a medium of exchange, so is faith.

—R. A. Shoaf, *Dante, Chaucer, and the Currency of the Word: Money, Images, and*

Reference in Late Medieval Poetry

One of my arguments in this book is that two seemingly irreconcilable impressions characterize late Bresson. The first is that, beginning with *Balthazar*, he abandoned explicit acknowledgment of redemption or salvation for his characters. The other is that he did not, or could not fully expunge vestiges of those concepts from his art. In the chapter on *Mouchette* I introduced the term *sacred indirection* to describe how those vestiges found their way into the films and alleged that a sustained but not necessarily conscious tendency toward this practice could be discerned in subsequent films. This implies that a spiritual reading can be wrested even from Bresson's bleakest works. *L'Argent* is the toughest challenge to that idea, first because Yvon's behavior at the end seems to preclude remorse, and second, because even if he were capable of it, it is unclear whether it would outweigh the horror of his actions. Yet although multiple viewings do not diminish the impact of the murders, neither do they eliminate ambiguity or quash the notion that a parallel, if not alternative reading of the film is viable.

For one thing, Yvon's surrendering to the police actually interrupts his bloody rampage, presumably because of his encounter with the widow, but for whose charity, however misplaced, he might have continued down that path. The surrender itself recalls the final scene of *Les Anges du péché*. In both cases, a murderer has reached a point where his or her behavior is too much to bear. To be sure, Yvon's face and demeanor lack the radiant sense of resolution and inner peace that infuse Thérèse, not only because of the radical changes in Bresson's style between the first film and the last, but because he raises a disturbing question without resolving it: Even if there is goodness in the world, what chance does it have against the perpetuation of evil? This is not a new question, but in *L'Argent* it seems rhetorical. If Yvon cannot be moved sufficiently by the woman's introduction of charity and forgiveness into his life, and into the film, to forgo acting on his violent impulses, how can belief in redemption be anything but folly?

Yet Bresson has gone beyond Tolstoy to develop the character of this woman and her relationship with Yvon. And although, just before she is about to be murdered, she does not speak the words that haunt Tolstoy's Stepan, she does project a look like the one that torments that character. If Bresson has resisted Tolstoy's polemics, it can be argued that he has retained his message, conveyed through the widow's embrace of a life of sacrifice and service. In the absence of the literal evidence of remorse and conversion that Tolstoy provides, therefore, the question Bresson's film poses is whether signs of sacred *indirection* are strong enough to counter Yvon's barbarism.

Consider the widow's affinity with other Bresson characters. Whereas the hotel owners evoke disgust in Yvon, the woman conjures something more primal. She recalls other maternal figures: the Mother Superior in *Les Anges*, Michel's mother in *Pickpocket*, Joan's, Marie's, and Mouchette's mother, the old lady in the forest who greets Lancelot—all of whom, however flawed, fuse charitable demeanor and worldly wisdom. The actions the widow performs, for Yvon as well as her family—tending the sick, feeding the hungry, giving drink to the thirsty, and sheltering the homeless—are consistent with what are called corporal works of mercy in Catholic theology. And the very things Yvon believes are reasons for her to drown herself—comforting the sorrowful, bearing wrongs patiently, and forgiving all injuries—are among the spiritual works of mercy. It is unlikely that Bresson was unaware of these concepts of Catholic teaching when he created a character who would not only "forgive everyone if [she] were God," but whose actions exemplify the spiritual *and* practical value of living a life of service. This was his way of incorporating the tenor and theme of the last part of the novella.

Given her behavior and her affinity with earlier maternal figures, how can we respond to the hypothesis that the primary purpose of her character, as Bresson has expanded it, is to welcome violent death for herself and her family?[17] This is not to dismiss psychological motives for her behavior, at which the shot of the first encounter between Yvon and the widow hints. The image of the toy store and Yvon's reflection in the glass certainly allude to the daughter he has lost, but that the woman passes him at this moment and is also reflected in the glass suggests further childhood connotations. It would seem that mutual need is conjured here: as Yvon is desperate for more humane contact than he has encountered since he entered the photo shop, so the widow, who, as her father implies, has a weakness for taking in strangers, is drawn to him out of desire for a child of her own. The risk she takes exposing herself and her family to a confessed murderer, then, may be a result of displaced maternal instincts. These impressions, along with her defiance of her father, make her more human and place her charitable nature in a credible domestic context.

This does not invalidate her goodness and the effect of her behavior, which, unlike that of the other characters, reflects values opposed to those of a world ruled by the "visible God" and that would be dismissed as ludicrous in such a world. This is the meaning, I believe, of the garden rite before the murders and the widow's composed silence in response to Yvon's question, "Where is the money?" In the garden scene, they look into each other's eyes and quietly share the nuts from the trees, a ritual act that restores the "human" in human interaction and is shot in direct contrast to the impersonal monetary exchanges in the film by framing the heads *and* hands of each character (figure 96).

The final interaction is even more emphatic. Because Bresson has established the woman's character more fully than Tolstoy, the silent look in response to Yvon's question is charged with what he and we know of her life of service, kindness, and beliefs—that is, with the meaning of her life and the strength of her faith. Her look authenticates the integrity and reality of these qualities, which is why its penetrative power haunts Yvon, challenging, if not overturning, the value of the visible god and its law of false exchange. In addition, the look rhymes with but inverts the meaning of the first silent look he gets instead of words when he asks Lucien in the photo shop if he remembers him, and Lucien shrugs his shoulders in denial. If that indifferent gesture placed Yvon on the path to ruination, the woman's gestures sear him to the core and provoke his embarking on a new path. The bleakness of the film implies not that there is no evidence of a "better way to live," in the spirit of Tolstoy's Maria Semyonovna, but that the contemporary world, like nearly everyone in the film and like Yvon while in prison, is largely indifferent to the signs.

If Bresson could not follow Tolstoy to the end of his tale, it may be because he was closer to Dostoevsky at heart. In the bloody penultimate sequence of *L'Argent* and its redemptive potential, one senses that he aimed not to spread the "good news," as Tolstoy did, but to evoke the tension, paradox, and sacrificial dimension of the Christian fable. Harsh as it is, this perspective is neither Dostoevsky's nor Bresson's invention and is not limited to brooding European artists. Readers familiar with the writer Flannery O'Connor would have no trouble recognizing the troubling marriage of Christian charity and violence as well as the characters in *L'Argent*. Work for work, O'Connor's vision of the American South is even more merciless and driven to shocking resolutions than Bresson's. Like Bresson, her fiction is free of sentimentality and sermonizing; unlike him, her commitment to Catholicism until her death was anything but ambivalent. In her stories, her essays, and her letters she is wholly convinced of the divinity of Christ, the mission of the Church, and the mysteries of salvation. The recklessness of the widow's behavior in *L'Argent* and her unconscious knowledge of what lies inside Yvon recall the grandmother in O'Connor's story "A Good Man Is Hard to Find," whose attempt to comfort the murderer of her family with the words, "Why you're one of my babies," prompts him to "[spring] back as if a snake had bitten him and [shoot] her three times."[18] No sentimental proselytizer of the "Jesus Saves" variety, those who seek, as E. M. Cioran puts it, the "*orgasm* of repentance,"[19] O'Connor describes a world infused with the same harsh, unforgiving view of human nature and violence that we find in Bresson.

Like Anne-Marie in *Les Anges*, whose pride does not preclude the effect she has on Thérèse, the widow's impulsive charity and naïve, all-forgiving embrace affect Yvon, as first indicated by that mournful shot of him after he has killed her. Like Anne-Marie and Tolstoy's Maria Semyonovna, she functions as the figure who, unwittingly, brings Yvon back from the deadness into which his soul was cast and in which he has wallowed to justify his thirst for revenge. Recall that the ultimate change Anne-Marie effects in *Les Anges* is not immediate. In one instance, her prayers for Thérèse cut to a shot of the latter as she confronts her ex-lover and shoots him. We do not conclude that the prayer was useless or caused this anymore than we should that the widow's behavior has no beneficent impact on Yvon. That she herself is a victim of his unsated rage, far from qualifying this, confirms it. As Yvon was repulsed by the hotel owners, he is moved by the woman's charity, and so, killing her triggers the opposite of the pleasure he claims he felt earlier. Like the character of the grandmother in O'Connor's parable, she is the blood sacrifice necessary to change his course. Whatever psychology is played out between them serves this other purpose, the one hinted at by way of the communion rite they enact in the garden. The mother-son image endows their encounter with something beyond the family romance, an impression reinforced by her surrogate role in the household: neither a mother to the crippled boy, nor a wife to a dead husband. The fact that there is no hard evidence beyond what he tells the gendarmes that Yvon kills this boy suggests that the child evokes not only his daughter but his own lost childhood.

These allusions may help us to see that neither the violent resolution of *L'Argent* nor the brutal slaying of a good woman precludes the film's adherence to Bresson's overall vision. The director of *L'Argent* is the same Bresson whose country priest is admonished by Torcy for wanting to be loved, whose Joan resists the easy slide into religious conformity, and whose Fontaine refuses to rely on faith alone to be either saved or martyred. All reflect the anxious, restless embrace of the Christian God that hangs on a cross.

Bresson did not radically alter the essence of the literary works he adopted. Yet polemics never suited him, and he must have known they would not persuade the contemporary viewer. And so he has not so much rejected Tolstoy's message as he has brought it into tension with a more cynical view of the modern world, converted it into the physical actions and demeanor of the woman and their internalized aftereffects on the broken soul of Yvon. His chosen method of cinematographic writing reaches a level in this film almost wholly unalloyed, purified of the literal, declamatory ways of making meaning. Morality is channeled through aesthetics, leaving an open and silent space in which the interior of the characters and that of the viewer can find common ground. That space is initiated by the woman's wordless look at Yvon in the face of death and is evoked in the shot of Yvon standing in the dark after he has murdered the only person who has offered him shelter rather than imprisonment, compassion rather than punishment, forgiveness rather than judgment. That neither he nor the woman could know beforehand how this would affect him is both the essence of the mystery of the human heart alluded to by Diderot's innkeeper and that of the negative route to God traversed by many a Bressonian character.[20]

I alleged at the outset of this study that Bresson's vocation as a filmmaker was no less prescribed than Anne-Marie's in *Les Anges du péché*, and that with each film he came closer to embodying the force that directs his characters' lives within the form and structure of the film itself. If *L'Argent* lacks a recognizable Bressonian protagonist, if we can no longer discern glimpses of the emotional, psychological, and spiritual life of the artist in Yvon's murderous rage, it is perhaps because the filmmaker, working more intuitively than ever, has in his last film imposed his will without mediation, transforming his art into the instrument of that supreme will only indirectly alluded to within the world of the narrative. In *L'Argent* the sense of a predesigned order is embedded in the art itself. However intuitive its procedure, it carries in every atom of its craft the aesthetic and moral logic of implacability.

Afterword

As I have argued throughout this book, Bresson's cinema manifests no diminishing of interest in the subject of faith, although the concept is made the fundamental dilemma at the core of existence rather than a given truth that invests life with meaning. To the end, the tenor and effect of the films rehearse the drama of a soul racked with conflict and confronted with the absence of a faith that once gave value to experience. Like the country priest, we are denied definitive signs, left to see or not see the traces of faith and redemption in Bresson's films by choosing to weigh indirect signs against the image of a dreadful world. I believe that such things can be inferred, however obliquely, from the work, even at its cruelest. But to read Bresson's cinematographic signs as proof of an unambiguous embrace of Christian redemption would be to deny the existential challenge that his films pose.

A striking aspect of how this paradox is played out is the presence of strong mother figures in the films. That these are not idealized any more than other characters was perhaps Bresson's way of disguising their importance and leaving their impact indirect. Yet mothers or mother figures are frequently tied to the concept of faith and are the least morally ambivalent of all Bresson characters. There are exceptions, of course. In *Les Anges du péché* Anne-Marie's mother represents the world her daughter leaves behind, a point stressed when Anne-Marie burns a photograph of her in the fireplace at the beginning of her novitiate. She is supplanted by the tough-minded but genial Mother Superior, the first to sense the genuineness of Anne-Marie's fervor, an exemplary mother figure fusing psychological acumen and spiritual guidance with the disciplinarian of loving disposition.

This figure never returns in quite so complete a form, but her qualities can be discerned in subsequent characters. Not in *Les Dames du bois de Boulogne,* where Agnès's clueless mother throws her into the clutches of the pernicious Hélène. In brusquely dismissing her at the door of his wife's chamber at the end, Jean passes judgment on her perversely intuited maternal instincts. The significance of mothers who fail and need redemption can be seen in the long exchange between the priest and the countess in *Diary of a Country Priest,* in which another flawed mother is so consumed with grief over a dead child that she ignores the tormented, morally twisted child in her midst. Although her conversion is a genuine personal triumph, it leaves a shadow over Chantal's future.

In contrast, the mothers in *Pickpocket* and *The Trial of Joan of Arc,* though marginal, are significant moral forces. Michel's avoidance of his mother is directly tied to his theft against her and the shame that drives him to crime; her deathbed forgiveness has the delayed effect of helping him turn his life around. Joan's mother, whose appeal to the Church to have her daughter's reputation as a heretic expunged, leads to Joan's rehabilitation. If these mothers indirectly invoke the image of the biblical Mary, there is a more explicit example in *Au hasard Balthazar,* in which Marie's mother sits near the ground and weeps when Balthazar is taken away, eventually to meet his death. Marie disappears and her father dies of despair. Only the mother has a deep sense of this tragic parable at work and lives through the suffering while bearing witness to the sanctity in the midst of her grief-torn world.

In later films the mother figure is the only character whose constancy, linked either to uncanny wisdom or Christian faith, provides a counterpoint to more skeptical protagonists, even when she herself is weak. Mouchette's dying mother is the first character we see before the credits, as she prays in church for the family she will soon leave. Her words, "What will they do without me?," convey the importance of her role, and it is her death that compounds the already miserable state that leads Mouchette to suicide. The old woman in the forest who tends Lancelot and predicts his death is empowered with prognostication. No scene more tellingly reveals her motherly function than the one of Lancelot sitting up in bed like an overgrown child as she tries to deter him from going back to fight. Though technically not a mother, the widow in *L'Argent* performs overtly Catholic works of mercy and refrains from judging Yvon's murderous behavior. Her death can be construed as the sacrifice that intercedes between a stern God and the recalcitrant Yvon, even though its moral effects, like the mother's forgiveness of Michel in *Pickpocket*, are delayed.

These positive mother figures are linked to the concept of sacred indirection, the strategy that I have argued characterizes Bresson's later work through which the director's feelings and convictions about how saving grace operates in human affairs is discernible. Mothers embody this notion by adopting roles attributed to Mary in Catholic tradition, specifically as a figure of intercession, succor, limitless mercy, perpetual help, and perhaps most apropos Bresson's world, of incessant mourning. Although certain paternal figures share similar qualities (e.g., Torcy in *Diary of a Country Priest,* the inspector in *Pickpocket,* and King Arthur), others (the fathers of Chantal, Marie, Mouchette, Norbert, and the widow in *L'Argent,* as well as the psychoanalyst in *The Devil Probably*) are either morally nebulous or aloof and judgmental. Common sense, if not the approach of this book, suggests that such patterns can be read in psychological terms as a reflection of Bresson's relationship with his own parents, of perhaps a need to alternately reenact it or, as we all do but artists have greater opportunities to do, reinvent it.

Although a biographical basis for developing this maternal theme is lacking, at least presently, the family resemblance among the filmic configurations makes the temptation to speculate irresistible. If mothers are, as they often appear to be, compassionate and wise and fathers are often inaccessible, totally absent (as in *Une femme douce, Four Nights of a Dreamer,* and *The Devil Probably*), or harsh dispensers of judgment, the family romance of psychoanalytic theory, manifest in several of the narratives, must be an underlying impulse in all of Bresson's work. More than once, he acknowledged that he put himself into his films and that this was facilitated by his use of the model.[1] In this light, his predisposition toward young protagonists, many of whom, male and female, seem projections of himself, as well as his insistence that they be played by unspoiled, inexperienced young people, is especially poignant and revealing. Each narrative, however different from each other, becomes a replay of a critical conflict at a significant threshold of life, a moment in which faith and hope are tested and often overwhelmed by forces against which they can barely be sustained. That this scenario results so often in the defeat of the promise we associate with the young may be the cruelest, most heartbreaking effect of Bresson's films. In the end the harsh view of human nature and the world to which his films subject us may be less distressing than the fact that such bleak visions are filtered through and ultimately destroy the young, made even more vulnerable through the beautiful, illumined, clear-eyed faces of his models.

I cannot think of a sadder visage of the effects of poverty and human vindictiveness than Nadine Nortier's Mouchette; a stronger image of the enigmatic suicide than Dominique Sanda's gentle woman; a more unnerving example of the disturbed and tyrannous adolescent than Nicole Ladmiral's Chantal (in *Diary*); more compelling proof of the foolhardy and staggering courage of the fired adolescent than Florence Delay's Joan; a more penetrating gaze of the spiritually driven than Claude Laydu's country priest; a more inspiring embodiment of the determined freedom fighter than François Letterier's Fontaine; or a purer, more gallant knight eager to serve a cause that has lost its meaning than Humbert Balsan's Gawain. Bresson's films allow us not just to experience these characters but also to grasp the essence and vigor of youth behind them through a gallery of unknowns burning with unrehearsed, unpremeditated zeal.

That so many viewers were, and still are, unmoved by Bresson's models, mystified by the style of nonacting and monotonic line delivery unique to this filmmaker, is, I confess, a sentiment with which I can no longer sympathize. For me, the perfection of these faces is so deeply tied to the filmic experience that it is impossible to grasp the art without what many consider Bresson's eccentricities.

Those who ask, But couldn't he have told the same stories with the same effect and used "real" actors? overlook not only the entire thrust of his aesthetic, but another, not so minor effect of the model's demeanor: those moments of madness that suddenly erupt into the even-toned atmosphere, actions or words that seem to come out of the blue and expose the raw vitality of an emotion or psychic distress otherwise suppressed. Without a word, the serenely composed Michel (in *The Devil Probably*) takes the box of candy Charles had given to Alberte and tosses it out the window. *"Explique!"* Alberte demands. But of course he does not and cannot, and if he did, it would destroy the absurdist beauty of the gesture. When *Pickpocket*'s Michel suddenly picks up a book, slams it down, and shouts "Enough!" at the inspector; when Marie (in *Balthazar*) turns with unsuspected, comprehensive loathing and tells Jacques, her blandly tolerant childhood sweetheart, that he disgusts her; when the gentle woman holds a gun against the face of her "sleeping" husband; when the widow in *L'Argent* asks Yvon without a hint of shock or fear, "Why did you kill?" and he answers, "I enjoyed it"—these are precious, incomparable, unforeseen moments precisely because they are not anticipated by the intelligent architecture that "real" actors erect to prepare us for them. It is not with mise-en-scène, a moody change in cinematography, or an emotionally charged musical score that Bresson signals the emergence of madness into the everyday, but with unrehearsed, momentarily shocking departures from placidity or social decorum. His models, floating along an underlying river of conflicting impulses, sporadically eject missiles of misbehavior, disturbances of "model" conduct.

And so Bresson's is not only a meticulous cinema, a filmic career of the first order, but a mysterious and evasive cinema that courts faith and doubt in equal measure; a primal cinema in which mother and father figures do more maneuvering backstage than anyone might have suspected; a cruel cinema that celebrates but often frustrates the aspirations of the young and the beautiful; a mad cinema that refuses to normalize the explosive nature of psychic disturbance through naturalistic containment. In seizing on and privileging the physical agencies of unfamiliar hands and faces, Bresson's films restore, with impeccable cinematographic grace, the sense of wonder at those fleeting glimpses of the divine within the human—in short, a model cinema.

Notes

Introduction

1. Jacques Rivette, André Bazin, Jacques Doniol-Valcroze, Pierre Kast, Roger Leen-hardt, and Eric Rohmer, "Six Characters in Search of Auteurs: A Discussion about the French Cinema," *Cahiers du Cinéma,* 71 (May 1957), extracts translated by Liz Heron, reprinted in Jim Hillier, ed., *Cahiers du Cinéma: The 1950s, Neo-Realism, Hollywood, New Wave* (Cambridge, Mass.: Harvard University Press, 1985), p. 36.
2. Jean Cocteau, in André Fraigneau, *Cocteau on Film: Conversations with Jean Cocteau,* 1951, trans. Vera Traill (New York: Dover, 1972), p. 77. Of course, one can make such an assumption only about filmmakers who have exerted absolute control over virtually every aspect of their work, as was the case with all three filmmakers cited here.
3. Susan Sontag, "Spiritual Style in the Films of Robert Bresson," in *Against Interpre-tation* (New York: Dell Laurel Books, 1969), p. 182.
4. In such films as *Stromboli* (1949), *Europa 51* (1951), *Viaggio in Italia* (1953), *Joan of Arc at the Stake* and *Fear* (both 1954).
5. Peter Brooks, *Reading for the Plot: Design and Intention in Narrative* (New York: Vintage Books, 1985), p. 192.
6. The Gospel According to St. Luke, 2:2, 42–43, in *The New Testament,* trans. from the Latin Vulgate (Paterson, N.J.: St. Anthony Guild Press, 1947), p. 230.

7. Bresson interviewed by Roger Stephane on May 11, 1966, for the television series *Pour le plaisir* (included on the Criterion DVD of *Au hasard Balthazar*). While filming *Four Nights of a Dreamer* in 1970, Bresson told an interviewer that there is "no such thing as an atheist," and spoke openly about his Christian point of view. (Charles Thomas Samuels, *Encountering Directors*, New York: G.P. Putnam & Sons, 1972. Interview available at Masters of Cinema.com

8. Georges Bernanos, writing to a friend in 1918 just before the end of World War I, quoted in Robert Speaight, *Georges Bernanos: A Study of the Man and the Writer* (New York: Liveright, 1974), p. 57.

9. Keith Reader in *Robert Bresson* (New York: St. Martin's Press, 2000) says that his "readings of the films will try to take their Catholic dimensions into account without rendering them inaccessible to those with no interest in, knowledge of or sympathy for Catholicism." It would be foolhardy to deny other ways to appreciate Bresson's work, yet I believe that Catholicism pervades his films and cannot be put aside so easily. I am also unpersuaded that Bresson's "faith" can be explained with reference to Pascal's wager, the notion, conceived by the seventeenth-century philosopher Blaise Pascal, that it is more reasonable to believe in God than not, so that if it turns out God exists, we will have taken the safer course, and if not, we will not have suffered any loss. That Bresson may have been ambivalent about the existence of God must be weighed against the powerful images of faith and transformation even in his darkest films.

10. Comte de Lautreamont [pseudonym for Isidore Ducasse], *Maldoror,* trans. Alexis Lykiard (New York: Thomas Y. Crowell, 1973).

11. Anna Balakian, *Literary Origins of Surrealism* (New York: New York University Press, 1947), p. 71.

12. Paolo Valesio, foreword to Erich Auerbach, *Scenes from the Drama of European Literature* (Minneapolis: University of Minnesota Press, 1984), p. xvi, italics mine.

13. Bresson quoted in "Entretien avec Christian Defaye," Television Suisse Romande, 1983, included on the DVD of *L'Argent.*

14. Jean-Claude Biette, Jacques Bontemps, and Jean-Louis Comolli, "L'Ancien et le nouveau: Entretien avec Eric Rohmer," *Cahiers du Cinéma* 172 (November 1965), reprinted in Hillier, *Cahiers du Cinéma,* p. 87.

15. Sontag, "Spiritual Style," pp. 181, 184, 195.

16. Among those whose work has been indisputably influenced by Bresson are Chantal Akerman, Olivier Assayas, Laurent Cantet, the Dardenne brothers, Claire Denis, Bruno Dumont, Eugene Green, Michael Haneke, Benoit Jacquot, Aki Kaurismaki, Gaspar Noé, and Andre Techiné. Even before the period in question, Bresson had an indisputable influence on the aesthetic of Jean-Luc Godard, who, as early as *Le Petit Soldat* (1960), "set out to make a film in which he would seek a Bressonian spiritual depth and intensity of inner experience without reference to God or religion," and as late as *Hail Mary* (1985) shot many takes of an actor to "remov[e] any trace of theatrical expression" in the performance. Richard Brody, *Everything Is Cinema: The Working Life of Jean-Luc Godard* (New York: Metropolitan Books, 2008), pp. 97–98, 461.

17. André Bazin, "The Stylistics of Robert Bresson," in *What Is Cinema?*, vol. 1, trans. Hugh Gray (Berkeley: University of California Press, 1967).

18. Paul Schrader, *Transcendental Style in Film: Ozu, Bresson, Dreyer* (Berkeley: University of California Press, 1972).

19. Despite the title of his book, Joseph Cuneen in *Robert Bresson: A Spiritual Style in Film* (New York: Continuum, 2003) cautions against "any airy discussion of 'spirituality' in Bresson's work."

20. Clement Greenberg, "Modernist Painting," *Arts Yearbook* 4 (1961): 103.

21. Robert Bresson, *Notes on Cinematography,* trans. Jonathan Griffin (New York: Urizen Books, 1975), p. 14.

22. Pier Paolo Pasolini, "The Written Language of Reality," in *Heretical Empiricism,* trans. Ben Lawton and Louise K. Barnett (Bloomington: Indiana University Press, 1988), p. 205.

23. P. Adams Sitney, "Cinematography vs. the Cinema: Bresson's Figures," in *Modernist Montage* (New York: Columbia University Press, 1990).

24. Bresson, *Notes on Cinematography,* p. 6.

25. Bresson, *Notes on Cinematography,* p. 28.

26. Gilles Deleuze, *Cinema 2: The Time Image,* trans. Hugh Tomlinson and Robert Galeta (Minneapolis: University of Minnesota Press, 1989), p. 242.

27. Bresson, *Notes on Cinematography,* p. 3

28. In a poll published in the magazine *Sight and Sound* in 1952. These films were directed by David Lean, Vittorio De Sica, and Robert Flaherty, respectively.

29. Exceptions to this include Jean-Claude Guilbert, who appears in both *Balthazar* (Arnold) and *Mouchette* (Arsène). Several unfamiliar faces became internationally recognized through the work of other filmmakers. Anne Wiazemsky, who plays Marie in *Au hasard Balthazar,* appeared in Godard's *La Chinoise* the following year and in subsequent works of Godard's; Dominique Sanda, the young wife in *Une femme douce* appeared in Bernardo Bertolucci's *The Conformist* and Vittorio De Sica's *The Garden of the Finzi-Continis,* both released in 1971, bringing her much acclaim.

30. Markopoulos's remarks, made in 1962, are reprinted in James Quandt's anthology, *Robert Bresson* (1998; Toronto: Toronto International Film Festival Group, 2000), pp. 574–76.

31. Bresson, *Notes on Cinematography,* p. 16.

32. All three leads—Martin La Salle, Marika Green, and Pierre Leymarie—are interviewed at length on the subject in Babette Mangolte's film *Les Modèles de Pickpocket* (2003), an eminently useful document.

33. The memories of these models, as recorded by Mangolte, are consistent with those of other models.

34. Bresson, *Notes on Cinematography,* p. 5.

35. Deleuze, *Cinema 2,* p. 178.

36. William Flint Thrall and Addison Hibbard, *A Handbook to Literature,* revised and abridged by C. Hugh Holman (New York: Odyssey Press, 1960), pp. 440–41, 156–57.

37. See Bazin's discussions of Jean Cocteau's *Les Parents terribles,* Orson Welles's *Macbeth,* and Laurence Olivier's *Henry V* in his two-part essay, "Theater and Cinema," in *What Is Cinema?,* pp. 76–124.

38. Charles Baudelaire, "The Painter of Modern Life," in *Baudelaire: Selected Writings on Art and Artists,* trans. P. E. Charvet (Cambridge: Cambridge University Press, 1972), p. 395.

39. This was the position espoused by Marvin Zeman in "The Suicide of Robert Bresson," *Cinema*, no. 6 (spring 1971), 37–42.

40. Mylène Bresson in conversation with the author.

41. T. Jefferson Kline, "Picking Dostoevsky's Pocket: Bresson's Sl(e)ight of Screen," reprinted in Quandt, *Robert Bresson*, pp. 235–73.

42. France Roche and Francois Chalais, "Entretien avec Robert Bresson," *Cinépanorama* (1960), extract included on the DVD of *Pickpocket* (Criterion).

43. Gilles Deleuze, *Cinema I: The Movement Image*, trans. Hugh Tomlinson and Barbara Habberjam (Minneapolis,: University of Minnesota Press, 1986).

44. Mylène Bresson confirmed that Bresson wrote a treatment for this unfilmed project, which she plans to publish. (Conversation with author)

Chapter 1

1. This film has been translated as *Angels of the Streets* in Bert Cardullo, ed., *Bazin at Work: Major Essays and Reviews from the Forties and Fifties* (New York: Routledge, 1997), a reasonable alternative to *Angels of Sin*. The practice I follow in this book is to identify each film by its original title in French at the heading of each chapter and afterward by the title by which it is commonly known to English speakers. *Les Anges du péché, Les Dames du bois de Boulogne, Au hasard Balthazar, Une femme douce,* and *L'Argent* are generally referred to by their French titles, often abbreviated, whereas English titles are used for *Diary of a Country Priest, A Man Escaped, The Trial of Joan of Arc, Four Nights of a Dreamer, Lancelot of the Lake,* and *The Devil Probably. Pickpocket* and *Mouchette* are the same in both languages.

2. Jean Sémolué, *Bresson* (Paris: Flammarion, 1993), p. 31.

3. Cited in René Briot, *Robert Bresson*, Collection 7th Art (Paris: Les Éditions du Cerf, 1957), pp. 15–16. The original title for the film was *Béthanie;* according to Briot, the producers preferred the more "melodramatic" *Les Anges du péché.*

4. Ibid.

5. See Jacques Guicharnaud, *Modern French Theatre from Giraudoux to Genet,* Yale Romantic Studies, revised ed. (New Haven: Yale University Press, 1967).

6. René Briot reports that it was not unusual for people attending screenings to complain about the film's showing of quarrels and jealousies within convents (*Robert Bresson,* p. 25).

7. According to René Briot, because of the terrible conditions imposed by the war, the entire film had to be shot at night (*Robert Bresson,* p. 15).

8. This sequence will be analyzed later.

9. Writers commonly use the rhetorical device *ellipsis* as a short-cut to describe the economy of Bresson's style. But it is worth distinguishing instances in his films that more closely resemble the linguistic model from less compacted examples. In the tournament sequence in *Lancelot of the Lake* rapidly edited shots composing a single action might be considered an elliptical syntactical unit equivalent to a line in verse. Such passages are akin to the shots of the Cossack slashing the face of the woman in *Potemkin* (1925), where the actual contact between saber and face is omitted. In less compacted instances, however, we sense that the logic

governing a narrative sequence has been disrupted by a strategic leap from one point to another that appears to omit something we have reason to expect should have been included. Although the immediate comprehension that obtains in the first instance is not what occurs in *Les Anges du péché,* a form of elliptic construction does seem to be at work. I would suggest that at least four conditions must be met to assert this. The first is that one must be able to cut off the segment of the narrative in question and see it as a unit of some kind in order to recognize that a key part of it has been omitted. Second, the omitted element should be as specific and as easily supplied by the viewer as the missing word or term in verse. Third, the recognition that we are dealing with an elliptic filmic trope rather than a carelessly constructed scenario must be established by context, pattern, and purpose. Fourth, in order for the effect to register, there must be some element of surprise, even shock, and perhaps momentary confusion, a sense that some prior knowledge of things has been altered, if not contradicted. All four of these, I believe, are evident in *Les Anges du péché.*

10. At its most succinct, in *Pickpocket,* a critical exchange between Michel the protagonist and the police inspector is reduced to a handful of words and a single gesture, condensing dozens of pages from Dostoevsky's *Crime and Punishment.*

11. One might cite *The Trial of Joan of Arc* (1962) as an example of this very thing, but I would argue that the results are quite different. First, the trial situation renders the context more dynamic; its interrogative nature is set against a very charged, though largely off-screen backdrop that bears on the shot-countershot exchanges in unpredictable ways. Second, because of this context, the use of off-screen space and sound is far more complex than anything in the bedside sequence in *Les Anges du péché.* Third, the framing and editing of the exchanges are far more pointed and assertive, every shot and cut as crisp and as tensely balanced as the dangerous questions posed by the judges and Joan's answers. In short, the text is integrated within the cinematographic whole.

12. As defined by Thomas Aquinas, adapted by Paul J. Glenn, *A Tour of the Summa* (St. Louis: B. Herder, 1960), p. 180.

13. Ibid., pp. 178–82.

14. Ibid., p. 180.

15. André Bazin, "Marcel Carné's *Les Visiteurs du soir* and Robert Bresson's *Les Anges du péché,*" *Revue Jeux et Poésie,* end of 1943, reprinted in André Bazin, *French Cinema of the Occupation and Resistance: The Birth of a Critical Esthetic,* trans. Stanley Hochman, collected and introduced by François Truffaut (New York: Frederick Ungar, 1981), pp. 48–50.

16. Jacques Audiberti, "*Les Anges du péché,*" *Comoedia,* no. 105, July 3, 1943.

17. Sacha Guitry, in *Panorama,* July 22, 1943, reprinted in *Le Cinéma et Moi* (Paris: Ramsay, 1977).

18. Robert Bresson, *Notes on Cinematography,* trans. Jonathan Griffin (New York: Urizen Books, 1975), p. 6.

19. Paul Schrader gives no attention to the film in *Transcendental Style in Film: Ozu, Bresson, Dreyer* (Berkeley: University of California Press, 1972), despite the many cues in its final scene that invite speculation along the lines of the thesis of his book.

20. Martin Hall, introduction to Denis Diderot, *Jacques the Fatalist,* trans. Michael Henry (London: Penguin Books, 1986), pp. 16–17.
21. Peter Brooks, *The Melodramatic Imagination* (1976; New Haven: Yale University Press, 1995), p. 20.
22. Ibid., p. 16.
23. Ibid., pp. 5, 13, 16.
24. The film was in production the same year that Billy Wilder's *Double Indemnity* (1944)—perhaps the first recognized example of film noir in Hollywood—was released.
25. In her autobiography Casarés devotes barely a sentence to her experience on the film, which nevertheless reveals the difficulties professional actors might have had with Bresson and exactly the kind of disposition he wanted to avoid: "[There were] very long days spent submitting to the continuous paring down we suffered at the hand of the implacable Robert Bresson during the shooting of *Les Dames du bois de Boulogne* ... [and] during long nights, interrupted only by failures of electricity, during which Bresson, by candlelight, paraded his slim and elegant silhouette in front of me, using the 'break' to find, for me, the precise intonation I was to give to the most spontaneous of lines: 'Oh! Jean! You frightened me.'" Maria Casarés, *Résidente privilégiée* (Paris: Fayard, 1980), pp. 231, 235. This translation, quoted in note 33 of Mirella Affron's essay, "Bresson and Pascal: Rhetorical Affinities," is presumably Affron's own. Reprinted in James Quandt, ed., *Robert Bresson* (1998; Toronto: Toronto International Film Festival Group, 2000), p. 186.

    Maria Casarés appeared in Cocteau's *Orpheus* (1950) and *The Testament of Orpheus* (1960). Since no one remotely like Hélène appears in any other Bresson film, it is tempting to think that Cocteau had something to do with her characterization. This is implied by François Truffaut in his remarks on the film, translated by Leonard Mayhew and reprinted in Quandt, *Robert Bresson,* pp. 582–83. On the other hand, René Gilson reports, that Cocteau avoided all disagreement with Bresson by simply providing the words for the scenes Bresson gave him along with instructions as to the number of lines he should write. *Jean Cocteau: An Investigation into His Films and Philosophy,* trans. Ciba Vaughan, Éditions Seghers' Cinéma d'Aujourd'hui (New York: Crown, 1969).
26. This is confirmed by the original title, "Public Opinion," contemplated when production began. René Briot, *Robert Bresson* (Paris: Les Éditions du Cerf, 1957), p. 26.
27. Mature women appear throughout Bresson's work, but not as prime motivators of the action. Female characters do not assume central importance again until *Pickpocket* (1959), but there, as in the four films of the 1960s—*The Trial of Joan of Arc, Au hasard Balthazar, Mouchette,* and *Une femme douce*—the characters are either adolescents bordering on womanhood or very young women.
28. Largely because it was a melodrama, the film was deemed a safe project during the Occupation. The production, begun in April 1944, when even inferior film stock was hard to get, was distracted by the constant noise of airplanes overhead and, interrupted during the Liberation, resumed several months later with a changed crew. A lively account of the difficulties with cast and crew is chronicled in Paul Guth's *Autour des Dames du bois de Boulogne* (Paris: Julliard, Ramsay Poche Cinema series, 1945).

29. Diderot, *Jacques the Fatalist,* pp. 108–13, 131–45, 148–49.

30. Bresson, in an interview with Jean Queval, *L'Écran française,* Nov. 12, 1946, my translation.

31. The section of Paris where Hélène has set up Agnès and her mother may ironi-cally allude to the convent of nuns at Port Royal in the seventeenth century. In Diderot's novel and in the film, the lover believes that the young woman is as virtuous as a nun, and at the end of the novel she vows to enter a convent rather than shame her husband. Hélène's calculated slip also draws attention to the paradox between accident and design in human events, a theme of relevance to both Diderot and Bresson.

32. Agnès's mother is the antithesis of other mothers in Bresson's films: she manifests neither the noble bearing of the countess in *Diary of a Country Priest* nor the basic decency of Michel's mother in *Pickpocket* or Mouchette's, and bears no affinity with Marie's in *Au hasard Balthazar.* Nor has she anything in common with such symbols of Christian charity as the woman in *L'Argent* and the mother superior in *Les Anges du péché.*

33. *Les Liaisons dangereuses,* an epistolary novel by Pierre-Ambroise-François Choderlos de Laclos, was published in 1782, shortly after parts of *Jacques le fatal-iste* had been published in *Literary Correspondence.* Although Diderot's work was written earlier, it was not published in its entirety until 1796. *Les Liaisons dangere-uses,* an immediate *succès de scandale,* is also an exploration of morality and the upper classes, written by an ex-aristocrat who took part in a plot to dethrone Louis XVI and Marie Antoinette.

34. In reality, it was no doubt impossible for the camera to follow, as the entrance to the waterfall grotto in the Bois is narrow and approached by way of a rocky, sinuous path.

35. Bresson preferred Alain Cuny for the part, an actor whose lean, angular physique and sensitive demeanor suggest that Bresson already had his ideal in mind. Cuny was unavailable, as was Cocteau's favorite actor, Jean Marais, who apparently refused the role because he was preparing to do *Beauty and the Beast.* Gilson, *Jean Cocteau,* p. 31.

36. John Forrester, *The Seductions of Psychoanalysis: Freud, Lacan, and Derrida* (Cambridge: Cambridge University Press, 1990), pp. 188–89.

37. A similar use of the camera can be seen in *Three Comrades* (1938), directed by Frank Borzage, whose style has also been described as spiritual. At the end of the film, as Margaret Sullivan struggles to rise from her sickbed, the camera assumes an angle just above her, somehow lightening her effort as if she were assisted by an otherworldly force.

38. Robert Bresson, *Notes on Cinematography,* p. 5.

39. Ibid.

Chapter 2

1. The film was the first of several of Bresson's to garner many awards, including the Grand Prix of French Cinema, 1951; the Prix Louis Delluc, 1950; the Grand Prix at the Venice Film Festival, 1951; the International Catholic Office of the Cinema

Award, 1951; the Italian Critics Prize, 1951; and the Prize for Best French Film by Film Critics, 1951.

2. John Ford's *The Fugitive* (1947), made three years earlier, is similarly austere, an offbeat portrait of a priest hunted by the Mexican Army and trying to flee his destiny. He is redeemed by chance, when he is betrayed by his "Judas" and tricked into giving the last rites to a criminal. A screenplay of *Diary*, written by Jean Aurenche and Pierre Bost, collaborators of many French film classics, was rejected by Georges Bernanos, no doubt because of the tendency of these writers to reduce the eclecticism of their sources to formulaic film treatments.

3. Elisabeth Roudinesco, *La bataille de cent ans: Histoire de la psychanalyse en France, vol. 1: 1885–1939* (Paris: Seuil, Éditions Ramsay, 1982)

4. In his filmography of Bresson's work, *Bresson* (Paris: Flammarion, 1993), Jean Sémolué mentions that Arkell was a well-known theater actress before the war under the name of Rachel Berendt. Sémolué distinguishes the cast listing of *Diary* from its two predecessors using the word *modèles* instead of *interprès*, but given the features of the acting that are difficult to ignore, I think this nod to Bresson's later style is premature.

5. Ibid., p. 69.

6. Robert Bresson, in *Supplements Lettres et arts de Recherches et Debats*, no 15 (March 1951), cited in Philippe Arnaud, *Robert Bresson* (Paris: *Cahiers du Cinéma* Collection "Auteurs," 1986), p. 177, my translation.

7. André Bazin, "*Le Journal d'un curé de campagne* and the Stylistics of Robert Bresson," in *What Is Cinema?, vol. 1*, trans. Hugh Gray (Berkeley: University of California Press, 1967), p. 132.

8. Falconetti apparently made at least one other film, which remains obscure, but French audiences would know Laydu from other films (e.g., *Le voyage en Amerique* [*Voyage to America*], 1951; *Nous sommes tous des assassins* [*We Are All Murderers*], 1952; *Dialogues des Carmelites* [*Dialogue of the Carmelites*], 1960), as well as from a popular television program for children, *Bonne Nuit les Petits,* in the early 1960s, which was rebroadcast periodically as late as 1995.

9. Laydu had never made a film before *Diary*, but had appeared on stage with the great Jean-Louis Barrault.

10. These details of Laydu's encounter and work with Bresson were provided in a question-and-answer exchange between Laydu and Babette Mangolte at a retrospective of Bresson's work in Paris in spring 2000. Some of the answers were in direct response to questions submitted by the author of this book.

11. Robert Bresson, *Notes on Cinematography*, trans. Jonathan Griffin (New York: Urizen Books, 1977), p. 16.

12. From the text of the film.

13. Georges Bernanos, *Le Cahier*, November 1936, quoted in *Bernanos par lui-même*, ed. Albert Beguin (Paris: Seuil, 1954), p. 173.

14. H. Stuart Hughes, *The Obstructed Path: French Social Thought in the Years of Desperation 1930–1960* (New York: Harper and Row, 1966), p. 123.

15. Hans Urs von Balthasar, *Bernanos: An Ecclesial Existence*, translated from German and French by Erasmo Leiva-Merikakis (San Francisco: Ignatius Press, 1996), p. 19. To label von Balthasar's book either biography or critical study would be misleading; more of a delineation of the interior mindscape of the writer as the

quintessential Catholic novelist, at least a quarter of the book's six hundred large pages is in Bernanos's voice, sometimes almost indistinguishable from von Balthasar's own.

16. One cannot be definitive about this, since, in the absence of any biography, little is known about Bresson's activities before or during the Second World War, including why he was imprisoned by the Germans for a year at the beginning of the war.

17. Robert Speaight, *Georges Bernanos* (New York: Liveright, 1974), p. 239.

18. Much in the way that Bresson, in *Pickpocket,* condenses to a few terse exchanges dozens of pages of philosophical speculations on crime in the conversations between Raskolnikov and the inspector in Dostoevsky's *Crime and Punishment.*

19. Among the aspects of the novel that are autobiographical is the priest's cancer of the liver, the condition that killed Bernanos's father, became for Bernanos "a palpable image of evil," and eventually killed him. von Balthasar, *Bernanos,* p. 68.

20. Séraphita is the only child character in this group that we get to know in the film, whereas there are several boys as well as girls in the novel.

21. This is not true of the novel to the same degree since neither the priest nor the reader is apprised of the affair between the count and the governess until halfway through, when Chantal visits the priest and confesses her hatred and despair over the situation. That Bresson introduces this information in the very beginning has repercussions for the film's narrative point of view as well as the characterization of the priest and will be analyzed later.

22. For example, describing the atmosphere in which the adolescent lives, Anna Freud speaks of the "anxieties, the height of elation or depth of despair, the quickly rising enthusiasms, the utter hopelessness, the burning—or at other times sterile—intellectual and philosophical preoccupations, the yearnings for freedom, the sense of loneliness, the feeling of oppression by the parents, the impotent rages or active hates directed against the adult world, the erotic crushes—whether homosexually or heterosexually directed—the suicidal fantasies." "Adolescence," in *The Psychoanalytic Study of the Child* (New York: International Universities Press, 1958), 13:255–78.

23. von Balthasar, *Bernanos,* p. 142.

24. Hughes, *The Obstructed Path,* chap. 4.

25. von Balthasar sees the relationship between the priest and Olivier as a complementary one that in fictional terms plays out the two fronts of Bernanos as writer: novelist and cultural critic. In other words, as the priest is the model of the true Christian saint, Olivier is the "exponent of [Bernanos's] whole culture-critical aspect....Both can extend their hand to one another in a deep and indispensable pact of friendship: in this handshake they are creating the Catholic balance." *Bernanos,* p. 35.

26. Released in 1950 but filmed in the fall of 1949. Cocteau, who had written the dialogue for *Les Dames du bois de Boulogne,* remained a friend of Bresson. That the most productive years of Cocteau's film career, between 1945 and 1950, were also the years in which Bresson was inactive may suggest that Bresson was especially prone to creative influence during this time, particularly by artists he respected.

27. Judging from stills in some French studies of Bresson, some of this material was shot and later cut from the released version. As it is, *Diary* is longer than most French releases at the time.

28. It is possible that some of these voice-overs allude to material shot and later cut from the released version.

29. Reading the novel, we must adjust one-third of the way when we come across a "N.B." in italics and parentheses, informing us that "the next few pages of the exercise book in which this diary is written have been torn out." This might be a notation by Louis Dufrety, the priest's friend in Lille, who would have discovered the diary after the priest's death and whose letter to Torcy ends the novel, but it also asserts the presence of the author. Both facts qualify the experience of *being with* the priest in the present. None of these parenthetical notes are acknowledged in the film, which renders the intimacy of that experience more immediate, that is, until the end, when a new voice informs us how the priest died.

30. See Nick Browne's essay, "Film Form/Voice-Over: Bresson's *The Diary of a Country Priest*," in *Robert Bresson*, ed. James Quandt (Toronto: International Film Festival Group, 1998).

31. This image of the devoted priest can be found in another Bernanos novel, in which a humble priest strives in his dying moments to save another priest who has lost his faith. *The Impostor*, trans. J. C. Whitehouse (Lincoln: University of Nebraska Press, 1999).

32. Laydu-Mangolte Q&A.

33. Marjorie Greene, "Robert Bresson," *Film Quarterly* 13, no. 2 (Winter 1959): p. 7.

34. A passage in the novel links a similar setting with the diary: "At the top of the hill, whether it be raining or blowing, I sit down on the trunk of a poplar, forgotten these many winters ago, nobody knows why, and rotting with age....It is here that the idea of this diary first occurred to me, and I don't feel I could have thought of it anywhere else. In this country of woods and pastures, streaked with the quickset hedges and all grown over by apple-trees, it would be hard to find such another place from which to overlook the whole village, gathered together, as it were, in the palm of a hand. I look down, but it never seems to look back at me. Rather does it turn away, cat-like, watching me askance with half-shut eyes." Bernanos, *Diary of a Country Priest*, trans. Pamela Morris (New York: Doubleday, 1954), p. 31. The sense of isolation and the perspective it provides are integral to the setting, the entire ensemble evocative of the image of Jesus sitting alone on a hill overlooking Jerusalem, which has been the subject of many popular religious paintings.

35. Nevertheless some critics have taken it for granted that the priest does see them. Raymond Durgnat writes, "The opening shot of the Count and his mistress embracing behind the grille, and abruptly separating as the priest catches sight of them, make any elaborate explanation unnecessary." An article originally published in *Films and Feeling* and adapted as "Le Journal d'un Cure de campagne," in *The Films of Robert Bresson*, ed. Ian Cameron (New York: Praeger, 1970), pp. 46–47. Durgnat's assumption that the couple's embrace is seen by the priest is undermined by his inaccurate description of the sequence. Unless he has seen a different or corrupt print, "the opening shot" is not of the couple, and the shot of the couple embracing, then separating, is not behind a "grille" of any sort, but an unobstructed medium close-up. Nor is the second shot of the couple walking away seen through a grille. The iron fence, which no doubt is what Durgnat is alluding to, is seen in the shots before and after the first shot of the couple, and

what we see on the other side of it is the priest in long shot, looking left and right but not in the direction of the iron fence, behind which the couple (off-screen) would be standing. Before VHS or DVD became available for checking such things, it was easier to make errors.

36. Nor is there any equivalent scene in the novel that might justify our seeing the count and Mlle. Louise embrace at this point in the story. The priest does not even suspect that there is anything between them until halfway through the novel, when Chantal comes to see him.

37. Some forty-five minutes of footage was apparently cut from the final release version to appease the film's producer, but according to André Bazin, in his review of the film, Bresson was "delighted to have to do so." "*Le Journal d'un curé de campagne* and the Stylistics of Robert Bresson," p. 128. Stills of some of this material are reproduced in René Briot's *Robert Bresson* (Paris: Les Editions du Cerf, 1957), but it is unclear whether these are studio photographs or actual footage that was later eliminated.

38. Bernanos, *Diary,* pp. 76, 96.

39. "Le cinéma selon Pasolini: Entretien avec Pier Paolo Pasolini par Bernardo Bertolucci et Jean-Louis Comolli," *Cahiers du cinema,* no. 160 (August 1965): 25.

Chapter 3

1. The integration of self-contained expository action, in which the depiction of tasks often approaches the level of documentary, was not commonly seen in narrative films and predates both the cinéma vérité movement in France by a few years as well as the inclusion of quasi-documentary passages in films such as Godard's *Vivre sa vie* (*My Life to Live,* 1962) and *Une femme mariée* (*A Married Woman,* 1964).

2. D. W. Winnicott was one of the foremost exponents of the object relations school of psychoanalysis and conceived the terms *false self* and *true self* in respect to the degree to which an individual is in touch with his or her creative or inner character.

3. The central thesis of Harold Bloom's *The Anxiety of Influence* is that in order for great poets to make a place for their work, they had to "forget" those who came before and deeply altered the form through equally radical acts of the artistic will.

4. Devigny's memoir was published in two parts, on November 20 and 27, 1954. This version, not the book, was the source of the film. It was titled "Les lecons de l'énergie: un condamné à mort s'est échappé" (The Lessons of Strength: A Man Condemned to Death Has Escaped). More on this later.

5. Charles Thomas Samuels, "Interview with Robert Bresson," 1970, in *Encountering Directors* (New York: G. P. Putnam and Sons, 1972). According to the critic Jonathan Rosenbaum, however, Bresson was a POW for nine months in a German internment camp in the period 1940–41. "The Last Filmmaker: A Local, Interim Report," in James Quandt, ed., *Robert Bresson* (1998; Toronto: Toronto International Film Festival Group, 2000), p. 22.

6. Bresson, cited in *Telerama,* no. 334, according to Leo Murray in his essay on the film, "*Un condamné à mort s'est échappé,*" in *The Films of Robert Bresson,* ed. Ian Cameron (New York: Praeger, 1970).

7. In the spirit of the film's interest in authenticity, the original French trailer is composed entirely of long shots of this building, some seen in the film itself. A narrator describes what we see and tells us it is the setting of Bresson's film. There are no excerpts from the escape operation, in fact no people at all. It ends on a very long take of the same wall against which the credits of the film are superimposed, but which here is only accompanied by Mozart's Mass in C-minor. The trailer is included in the New Yorker DVD of the film.

8. Leo Murray, "*Un condamné à mort s'est échappé,*" p. 69.

9. This is not the impression one gets from reading Devigny, who does express his hatred of the Germans and in the escape sequence provides violent details of his murder of a guard as an act of vengeance.

10. Bresson's comments, made at a press conference at the Cannes Film Festival on the occasion of the film's premiere in May 1957, are quoted by Jean Sémolué in *Bresson ou L'Acte pur des Métamorphoses* (Paris: Flammarion, 1993), pp. 73–74, my translation.

11. The book, entitled *A Man Escaped,* was translated into English by Peter Green and published in 1958. It was reissued by Lyons Press (Guilford, Connecticut) in 2002.

12. Nevertheless because the more extended descriptions in the book of Devigny's behavior and situations are reflected in Bresson's film and the character of Fontaine, this work will be cited when relevant.

13. The book breaks the spell cast by the subjective focus in one chapter midway in which Devigny reconstructs things going on outside the prison at the same time. He describes his father's persistent efforts to visit him through appeals to Colonel Barbier, who in reality was Klaus Barbie, the infamous commandant of the prison, as well as the risky maneuvers of a fellow prisoner's sister, who carried letters from the prisoners to the outside. Although these are not firsthand experiences, they may have been based on events Devigny learned of after his release and in any case provide a sense of how the locals interacted with the Gestapo and how familiar a presence the prison was in everyday life in Lyon.

14. The phrase forms part of Jesus' response to Nicodemus, who asks how one can be "born again": "That which is born of the flesh is flesh; and that which is born of the Spirit is spirit. Do not wonder that I said to thee, 'You must be born again.' The wind blows where it will, and thou hearest its sound but dost not know where it comes from or where it goes. So is everyone who is born of the Spirit."

15. Devigny, *A Man Escaped,* p. 83.

16. An allusion to the title of Devigny's original article. See note 4.

17. Devigny, *A Man Escaped,* pp. 99, 133.

18. In Devigny's book the idea of escape does not enter his thoughts seriously until one-third of the way through the story. He sees his actions more as desperate attempts to avoid boredom and despair.

19. It would be interesting to consider Fontaine's character in the light of existentialism, a dominant philosophy of French culture at the time Bresson made the film. Although the convictions that underlie Fontaine's beliefs are clearly opposed

to those of a Sartrean existentialist, for whom the individual lives in an absurd world without God or a preexistent meaning to existence, they are in the spirit of such Catholic existentialists as Gabriel Marcel. Fontaine's actions, his commitment to freedom, and his determination to affect his condition and not wait for intervention, God's or otherwise, resembles that of an existentialist hero. This is a complicated question that deserves more investigation and space than can be accommodated here.

20. The film's credits appear over the prison wall on which are inscribed words commemorating those who died fighting with the French Resistance against German occupation, and on which the phrase "Lyon, 1943" is superimposed. However, neither this wall nor the building is the setting of the opening sequence and so do not establish that sequence within the parameters of the classical narrative system.

21. Robert Bresson, *Notes on Cinematography*, trans. Jonathan Griffin (New York: Urizen Books, 1975), p. 2.

22. Ibid., p. 51.

23. Ibid., p. 18.

24. François Leterrier, "Robert Bresson l'insaisissable," *Cahiers du Cinéma,* special issue on the actor, 11, no. 66 (1956): 34–36. Although Leterrier was a philosophy student and not an actor, he does appear to have continued work in film. The credits of Louis Malle's film, *Elevator to the Gallows* (1958), list him as second assistant director. It is not hard to imagine his contribution since the film involves the detailed, intricate efforts of the male protagonist to escape from the elevator in which he is trapped for almost the entire film. The footage devoted to these efforts has an obvious affinity with Bresson's film.

25. Bresson, *Notes on Cinematography,* p. 44.

26. Samuels, "Interview with Robert Bresson." It would be interesting to learn why and under what circumstances Bresson was imprisoned, but he does not discuss that in this interview, nor, as far as I know, in any other published work.

27. Leterrier, "Robert Bresson l'insaisissable," p. 36.

28. Ponge was a friend of Bresson's and wrote many pieces on the nature of the object as well as short poems on both natural and man-made objects (often ignoring or denying any distinction), including the orange, the oyster, the pebble, the snail, the crate, the candle, and the cigarette. These made up a volume titled *Le parti des choses,* published in 1942. An English translation by Lee Fahnestock was published as *The Nature of Things* (New York: Red Dust, 2000).

29. Devigny, *A Man Escaped,* pp. 177–78.

30. D. W. Winnicott, "Creativity and Its Origins," in *Playing and Reality* (New York: Tavistock, 1984), p. 65.

31. Robert Bresson, "Entretien avec Christian Defaye," Television Suisse Romande, 1983, included in the DVD of *L'Argent.*

32. The three principal actors in *Pickpocket*—Martin La Salle (Michel), Marika Green (Jeanne), and Pierre Leymarie (Jacques)—were tracked down and interviewed by Babette Mangolte in her film, *The Models of Pickpocket* (2005), an important contribution to Bresson scholarship, discussed in the Introduction. Much of what we know of Bresson's working methods with actors is recounted firsthand by all three.

33. P. Adams Sitney, "Cinematography vs. the Cinema: Bresson's Figures," in *Modernist Montage: The Obscurity of Vision in Cinema and Literature* (New York: Columbia University Press, 1990), reprinted in James Quandt, ed. *Robert Bresson* (Toronto: Toronto International Film Festival Group, 1998).

34. T. Jefferson Kline, "Picking Dostoevsky's Pocket: Bresson's Sl(e)ight of Screen," in *Screening the Text: Intertextuality in New Wave French Cinema* (Baltimore: Johns Hopkins University Press, 1992), reprinted in Quandt, *Robert Bresson*.

35. Richard Peace, introduction to Feodor Dostoevsky, *Crime and Punishment*, trans. Jessie Coulson (Oxford: Oxford University Press, 1993), p. x.

36. "It is clear and intelligible to the point of obviousness that evil lies deeper in human beings than our socialist-physicians suppose; that no social structure will eliminate evil; that the human soul will remain as it always has been; that abnormality and sin arise from the soul itself." Feodor Dostoevsky, *A Writer's Diary*, trans. by Kenneth Lantz (Evanston, Ill.: Northwestern University Press, 1994), July–August 1877, p. 905.

37. See H. Stuart Hughes, *The Obstructed Path: French Social Thought in the Years of Desperation 1930–1960* (New York: Harper and Row, 1966). Hughes notes that unlike Germany and the United States, France resisted Freud and his theories partly because of its being predominantly Catholic rather than Protestant or Jewish, and partly because it prided itself on being "the classic home of the examination of conscience," and had already a figure, Bergson, whose ideas "liberated the study of human behavior from the tyranny of rationalistic, ready-made explanations," thus performing a function similar to the one Freud did (pp. 9–10).

38. In fact Raskolnikov kills two people. His primary target is the moneylender Alena Ivanovna, but when her half-sister Lizaveta comes in and sees him, he immediately kills her with the same axe.

39. Though there is no diary in the novel, Dostoevsky's original plan was to write the novel in the first person in the form of a journal. In his notebooks to *Crime and Punishment* there are entries that reflect this eventually discarded idea to compose it as a confession.

40. Ernest Jones, "The God Complex," in *Essays in Applied Psychoanalysis* (New York: International Universities Press, Inc., 1964), vol. 2, p. 247.

41. This film features two sequences on a subway where a pickpocket uses newspapers. Since Fuller was among the Hollywood auteurs celebrated by the *politique des auteurs* in France during the late 1950s and 1960s, it is altogether possible that Bresson saw the film. The huge close-ups of a lady's handbag, opened beyond the spatial logic of the setting in order to flaunt the sense of violation and the boldness with which such an act can be perpetrated in a public space, resemble the effects created in *Pickpocket*.

42. See Babette Mangolte's film, *The Models of Pickpocket*, available on the Criterion disc of the film.

43. This was the position taken by Freud, Otto Fenichel, and many subsequent theorists. See Charles W. Socarides, *Homosexuality: Psychoanalytic Therapy* (Northvale, N.J.: Jason Aronson, 1978). It should be noted that contrary to what many believe, Freud remained skeptical of any conclusive determination of how and why people become homosexuals. He believed that such an outcome was neither innate nor acquired, and that understanding the nature of homosexuality would require

enormous research by future clinicians and a "full understanding of its etiology" (p. 13). Current psychoanalytic theories of homosexuality have not entirely resolved the question of innate vs. acquired, nor do they explain to everyone's satisfaction the etiology of the kind of homosexual "acting out" that I am suggesting characterizes Michel's behavior. But this is not the place to explore this complex issue.

44. The actor is Kassagi, a known pickpocket in Tunisia and later a magician in Paris, who Bresson employed as technical advisor on the film. Pierre Gabaston, *Pickpocket* (Crisnée, Belgium: Editions Yellow Now, 1990), p. 31. Kassagi appeared on French television in the 1960s performing his tricks.

45. Notably P. Adams Sitney in his chapter on Bresson in *Modernist Montage: The Obscurity of Vision in Cinema and Literature* (New York: Columbia University Press, 1990), pp. 95–96.

46. Socarides, *Homosexuality,* p. 37.

47. This is basically the thesis of Paul Schrader's *Transcendental Style in Film: Ozu, Bresson, Dreyer* (Berkeley: University of California Press, 1972).

48. Thomas Aquinas, *On the Truth of the Catholic Faith, Summa Contra Gentiles, Book One: God,* trans. Anton C. Pegis (Garden City, N.Y.: Image Books, 1955), p. 265.

49. Dostoevsky, *Crime and Punishment,* p. 400.

50. Mikhail Bakhtin, *Problems of Dostoevsky's Poetics,* trans. Caryl Emerson (Minneapolis: University of Minnesota Press, 1984), p. 168.

51. See the discussion of grace, its categories and its effects, in chapter 1.

52. Jonathan Rosenbaum, who greatly admires the film, finds Michel's sudden redemption "unbelievable," but does not appear to attribute this to the acting. See "The Last Filmmaker: A Local, Interim Report," in Quandt, *Robert Bresson,* p. 20.

53. Theodor Reik, *Listening with the Third Ear* (1948; New York: Farrar, Straus and Giroux, 1983), p. 84. Reik describes the excerpt by Dalal al-Din Rumi in the epigraph as "one of the ghazals [by] the greatest of the Persian mystical poets [who lived] about seven hundred years before our time" (p. 83).

54. Ibid., p. 8.

55. Sigmund Freud, *Beyond the Pleasure Principle,* 1920, trans. and ed. James Strachey (New York: W. W. Norton, 1961), p. 49.

Chapter 4

1. Mario Beunat, interview with Robert Bresson, extract from "Page cinéma," 1962, included in the MK2 DVD of *Procès de Jeanne d'Arc.*

2. Tolstoy's theory of history is discussed in Isaiah Berlin's essay "The Hedgehog and the Fox," in *Russian Thinkers* (London: Penguin Books, 1994).

3. Yves Kovacs, "Entretien avec Robert Bresson," *Cahiers du cinéma,* Feb. 1963, p. 8, my translation.

4. As described by Jean Guitton, a philosopher and historian interviewed after the screening of the film at the Cannes Film Festival in 1962, included on the MK2 DVD of the film.

5. Although it did win the Special Jury Prize at the Cannes Film Festival in 1962 and ranked first in Jean-Luc Godard's list of the Ten Best Films of 1963. *Godard on Godard,* trans. Tom Milne (New York: Viking Press, 1972), p. 205.
6. For many stage actresses of the twentieth century, Shaw's *Saint Joan* became as challenging and desirable a role as Hamlet for male actors. See Holly Hill, *Playing Joan* (New York: Theatre Communications Group, 1987).
7. This is discussed by, among others, Marina Warner, *Joan of Arc: The Image of Female Heroism* (New York: Knopf, 1981), pp. 160–61; and Nadia Margolis, "Trial by Passion: Philology, Film, and Ideology in the Portrayal of Joan of Arc (1900–1930)," *Journal of Medieval and Early Modern Studies* 27, no. 3 (1997).
8. For a more complete list, see Robin Blaetz, *Visions of the Maid: Joan of Arc in American Culture* (Charlottesville: University Press of Virginia, 2001).
9. Pierre Champion, "On the Trial of Jeanne d'Arc," trans. Coley Taylor and Ruth H. Kerr, in *The Trial of Jeanne d'Arc,* trans. from the original Latin and French documents by W. P. Barrett (New York: Gotham House, 1932), pp. 475–540.
10. Champion, "On the Trial of Jeanne d'Arc," p. 479.
11. Ibid., p. 480.
12. *Trial,* p. 105.
13. This was especially so because there were three popes at the time and considerable dispute over which was the true one.
14. Régine Pernoud, *The Retrial of Joan of Arc: The Evidence at the Trial for Her Rehabilitation 1450–1456,* trans. J. M. Cohen (New York: Harcourt, Brace, 1955), p. 25. In the Beunat interview, Bresson cites this book, published originally in French in the decade prior to his film.
15. Although the effect is that of an uninterrupted shot of Joan's mother in black seen from the back, a keen eye will detect that in fact there are two nearly invisible cuts in the course of the credits.
16. Robert Bresson, *Procès de Jeanne d'Arc* [the text of the film] (Paris: René Juilliard, 1962), p. 13, my translation.
17. Pernoud, *The Retrial of Joan of Arc,* pp. 37–38. The family name was d'Arc or Darc. According to Jules Michelet, "The name Romée was often assumed in the [Middle Ages] by those who made the pilgrimage to Rome." *The Life of Joan of Arc* in *History of France* [1844] (New York: The Spencer Press, 1937), p. 3.
18. Kovacs, "Entretien avec Robert Bresson," p. 5.
19. Bresson, Beunat interview.
20. Champion, "On the Trial of Jeanne d'Arc," p. 515.
21. Eileen Atkins, quoted in Hill, *Playing Joan,* p. 197.
22. Michelet, *The Life of Joan of Arc,* p. 30.
23. Ibid., p. 44.
24. Bresson's treatment of the trial's text predates and perhaps influenced those films of Jean-Marie Straub and Danielle Huillet in which actors reciting preexistent texts is the primary, even exclusive aesthetic of the work.
25. The pronounced effect of shot-countershot in *Joan* was no doubt what led the French scholar Jean-Pierre Oudart to cite it as an illustration of what he called "suture," the process by which a film is "stitched together" by the spectator who replaces or acts as a surrogate for the absent figure in each shot by way of an alternating process of automatic and unconscious identification, thus participating in

turning the film into a coherent whole. I don't find this notion illuminating of Bresson's film for the reason given above. Oudart's essay, "La suture," appeared in *Cahiers du Cinéma,* no. 611 (April 1969) 36–39; reprinted in "Cinema and Suture," in *Screen* 18, no. 4 (1977–78). An excellent appraisal of suture can be found in Noël Carroll, *Mystifying Movies* (New York: Columbia University Press, 1988), pp. 183–99; a discussion of it in relation to Bresson is provided in P. Adams Sitney, *Modernist Montage* (New York: Columbia University Press, 1990).

26. Dreyer did the opposite with his exclusionary shots, creating a space around Joan that makes it difficult to discern her position in relation to the court and invites us to see her as spiritually insulated. Incursions into her space are experienced as assaults, charged with psychological and sexual implications.

27. Dreyer constructed his film in imitation of the Passion of Christ, of the final hours of his arrest, trial, torture, and crucifixion. Compressing the many weeks of Joan's trial into what seems a day or two, he likens the agonies to which she is subjected to the Stations of the Cross that mark the long night and day of Jesus's ordeal. The analogy is capped when Joan is taunted by soldiers with a mock crown of thorns in a manner evoking paintings of Christ hailed as "king of the Jews" at Pilate's court. Dreyer induces the feeling of the Passion through a more sensual rendering of Joan's sufferings and by dwelling on the physical features of her tormentors.

28. Kovacs, "Entretien avec Robert Bresson," p. 6, my translation.

29. Michelet, *The Life of Joan of Arc,* p. 43.

30. See Thomas Aquinas's definition of grace in the section on *Les Anges du péché* in chapter 1.

31. Michelet, *The Life of Joan of Arc,* p. 43.

32. Ibid., p. 59.

33. Ibid., p. 64. Bresson's treatment is further supported by the historian George Duby's assertion that it is not clear what happened in the end, that it only "seemed" that Joan recanted and then retracted. Duby interviewed by Laure Adler for the program *Brûlures de l'histoire* (Burning Issues of History, 1994), extracted for the MK2 edition of the DVD.

34. There is not a word about Joan's virginity in the trial scene of Shaw's play *Saint Joan.* In the Tchaikovsky and Verdi operas, Joan's virginity is effectively denied since in both it is implied that she consummates her love, with a soldier in the former, and with the dauphin in the latter. Delteil's description in the epigraph is not of Joan, but of St. Margaret when she appears to Joan in his vivid, often surrealistic account. *Joan of Arc,* trans. Malcolm Cowley (New York: Minton, Balch, 1926), p. 55.

35. *The Works of Voltaire,* trans. William F. Fleming (Paris: E. R. Dumont, 1901), vol. 40, canto 2, p. 83.

36. *Trial,* p. 130.

37. Before Joan was permitted to lead the siege at Orléans, she was examined by theologians at Poitiers to determine whether her prophetic gifts were God-given or demonic. One archbishop declared that "God frequently revealed to virgins" and that "the demon could not make a covenant with a virgin." Upon examination Joan was found to be a virgin, clearing the way for her remarkable career. Michelet, *The Life of Joan of Arc,* p. 12.

38. A belief that prevailed before and after Joan was that a maiden would come to save France, and, according to Michelet, nearly every province at the time had its candidate. The notion that celibacy and virginity gave one privileged access to God was reinforced at the Council of Trent (1563) in its efforts to contest the declarations of the Reformation. "If anyone says that it is not better and more godly to live in virginity or in the unmarried state than to marry, let him be anathema." Quoted in Uta Ranke-Heinemann, *Eunuchs for the Kingdom of Heaven: Women, Sexuality, and the Catholic Church*, trans. Peter Heinegg (New York: Doubleday, 1990), p. 114.

39. Nevertheless there is only one spy hole in Bresson's and Dreyer's films, whereas several historical accounts indicate that there were several slits and peepholes in the wall so the guards could keep watch on Joan from every angle.

40. Instances indicated in the screenplay that are either not in the film or are incorrectly placed by the printer appear on pages 73, 76, and 85.

41. Given the proximity, this could be a misprint.

42. As Leo Murray observes in his essay, "*Le Procès de Jeanne D'Arc,*" in *The Films of Robert Bresson*, ed. Ian Cameron (New York: Praeger, 1970), p. 100.

43. There is a spy hole in *A Man Escaped,* but there are no point-of-view shots of the prisoner from a guard's point of view. One wonders if Bresson's extensive use of the spy hole for erotic implications does not owe something to Jean Genet's homoerotic shots of male prisoners in *Un Chant d'amour* (1950). That film also cuts between shots of the funnel-shaped hole in each cell door with the eye of the leering guard in the center with point-of-view shots of the men, but these images are not reshaped by the aperture as are the images of Joan.

44. Some have speculated that Joan was a lesbian, based on her wearing male garb and supported by the fact that she often slept with female friends and acquaintances. Marina Warner suggests that such readings are naïve, ignoring the historical, social, and cultural conditions of the time, when transvestism "often provided a device for a woman to make something of herself, a figure of speech to lay claim to greatness beyond the expected potential of her sex." *Joan of Arc,* p. 149.

45. Florence Delay, "Postface," *Procès de Jeanne d'Arc* (Paris: Mercure de France, 2002), p. 137.

46. Bresson, interviewed at the Cannes premiere of the film in 1962, included on the MK2 DVD of the film.

47. Interview with Florence Delay, conducted in 2000 for inclusion in the MK2 DVD release of the film.

48. See *The Models of Pickpocket*, mentioned in the preceding chapter and the Introduction.

49. Susan Sontag, "Spiritual Style in the Films of Robert Bresson," in *Against Interpretation* (New York: Dell Laurel Books, 1969), pp. 194, 191, 187, 197.

50. Interview with Beunat.

51. Georges Bernanos, *Sanctity Will Out: An Essay on St Joan,* trans. R. Batchelor (London: Sheed and Ward, 1947), pp. 46–47.

52. George Steiner, *Antigones* (New York: Oxford University Press, 1984), p. 279. In characterizing Antigone's final exchange with the chorus in Sophocles' play in these terms, Steiner adds, "Similar movements occur in the Gospel narratives of the agony in the Garden or in what we know of Joan of Arc's momentary recantation."

53. In response to a question about the gown, Bresson said, "Her garment makes her walk ridiculously, like a little girl. It seems that she's running to the stake." "Interview with Ian Cameron," *Movie*, no. 7 (1963), reprinted in Andrew Sarris, *Interviews with Film Directors* (New York: Avon Books, 1967), p. 48.

54. As opposed to very short pans and tilts of the camera at many junctures.

55. Kovacs, "Entretien avec Robert Bresson," p. 6.

Chapter 5

1. Perusing Jane Sloan's *Robert Bresson: A Guide to References and Resources* (Boston: G. K. Hall, 1983), we find that British, French, and German reviewers upon the film's release found it "an alarmingly pessimistic work." Martin Ripkins, "Zum Beispiel Balthazar," *Filmkritik*, July 1966, pp. 396–97; Andree Tournes, "*Au hasard, Balthazar*," *Jeune Cinema*, Sept.–Oct. 1966, pp. 22–23; Louis Chauvet, "Les Films: *Au hasard, Balthazar*," *Le Figaro*, May 27, 1966, p. 30. Raymond Durgnat considered it "a minor film" for Bresson. *Films and Feeling*, Dec. 1966, pp. 18, 51–52. Some critics used the occasion of its release to lambaste Bresson's cinema in general: Robert Benayoun of *Positif* "attacked Bresson's audience as a passive minority who wish to turn the cinema into a 'sort of non-Actor's Studio for neurasthenic zombies'" (Oct. 1966, pp. 81–82); Robert Drouget described Bresson as a "minimalist...condemn[ed] to making the same film over and over" (*Robert Bresson*, premier plan no. 42 [Lyon: Societé d'Etudes, 1966]). The American critic Richard Roud, a Bresson enthusiast, found his first six films superior to those from *Balthazar* on because of the latter's preoccupation with "despair and suicide." *Cinema: A Critical Dictionary: The Major Filmmakers*, vol. 1 (New York: Viking, 1978), pp. 141–53.

   On the positive side, Henri Chapier discussed its "important place in film history due to its pure and direct language and implicit critique of film structure" ("Avec *Au hasard Balthazar*, Robert Bresson donne au cinema son premier film libre de toute influence," *Combat*, May 20, 1966, p. 11); Clive Denton noted "an awareness of paradox new to Bresson's work and pleads against 'the probable neglect of an immeasurably fine and beautiful film'" ("*Au hasard Balthazar*," *Take One* 1, no. 5 (1967): 33); Charles Barr considered it "profoundly ambivalent" ("*Au hasard Balthazar*," in *The Films of Robert Bresson*, ed. by Ian Cameron [London: Studio Vista, pp. 106–14]).

   On its American release in 1970, Roger Greenspun called it "the only essential moviegoing in New York" ("The Screen: *Au hasard Balthazar*," *New York Times*, Feb. 20, 1970, p. 31); and Andrew Sarris "a very morbidly beautiful flower of cinematic art...[that] stands by itself as one of the loftiest pinnacles of artistically realized emotional experiences" ("Films in Focus," *Village Voice*, Feb. 19, 1970, pp. 55, 60).

2. William Gaddis, *The Recognitions* (New York: Avon Books, 1974), p. 13.

3. A phrase coined by P. Adams Sitney in *Modernist Montage* (New York: Columbia University Press, 1990) to describe the work of Carl Dreyer, but which I think is especially appropriate to the Bresson of *Balthazar*.

4. Philippe Arnaud, *Robert Bresson* (Paris: Cahiers du Cinéma Collection "Auteurs," 1986), p. 182. "'What a simple-minded fellow you are' [*Chrestos ei*]—were the very

words which Pontius Pilate addressed in scorn to Jesus on the morning of the crucifixion." Robert Graves, *King Jesus* (New York: Farrar, Straus and Giroux, 1946), p. 3.

5. See Robert J. Miller, ed., *The Complete Gospels: Annotated Scholars Version* (San Francisco: Harper Collins, 1994), James 17:10 (p. 392); Matthew 21:2–7 (p. 95); and John 12:14–15 (p. 227).

6. As recounted in Matthew 2:1–17 (ibid., pp. 60–62), the figures from the East are called astrologers; other editions call them magi, "a priestly caste of ancient Persia," as described in *The Columbia Encyclopedia* (New York: Columbia University Press, 1954), p. 1195. But it is Christian tradition, not the New Testament, that considered them "wise men," "set their number as three," and "[gave] them [the] names, Caspar, Melchior, and Balthazar" (*Columbia Encyclopedia*, p. 2162).

7. Cornelius Agrippa, *De incertitudine et vanitate scientiarum atque atrium* (1530), quoted in Ioan P. Couliano, *Eros and Magic in the Renaissance*, trans. Margaret Cook (Chicago: University of Chicago Press, 1987), pp. 197–98. Notably, Couliano adds, "This passage reveals the Christian tradition that must have inspired Robert Bresson to film *Au hasard Balthazar*" (p. 198).

8. P. G. Walsh, introduction to Apuleius, *The Golden Ass*, trans. by P. G. Walsh (New York: Oxford University Press, 1999), p. xxxix.

9. I base this description of the style on two English translations: that of P. G. Walsh in the 1999 Oxford reissue of a 1995 World's Classics edition; and that of E. J. Kenney for the Penguin Books edition of 1998.

10. Feodor Dostoevsky, *The Idiot*, trans. David Magarshack (New York: Penguin Books), 1955, p. 79. *The Idiot* is a rich source of many of the ideas and images in *Balthazar*. Coincidentally both works fall at a critical juncture of each artist's career; *Balthazar* is not only Bresson's middle film (the seventh of thirteen), but like *The Idiot*, it represents a significant shift, with attendant compositional challenges, from narratives focused more intensely on a single protagonist (*Notes from the Underground, Crime and Punishment,* and *The Gambler* in Dostoevsky's case; everything prior to *Balthazar* in Bresson's) to those that encompass a broader spectrum of characters and situations (*The Idiot, Demons,* and *The Brothers Karamazov; Balthazar, Lancelot of the Lake,* and *L'Argent*). Bresson's preproduction interview, "Ni vu, ni connu" (1965), was conducted by François Weyergans and used in the television series *Cinéma de notre temps* in 1994.

11. Brian Newbould, *Schubert: The Music and the Man* (Berkeley: University of California Press, 1997), p. 333. In Chantal Akerman's video portrait of pianist Alfred Brendel, he expounds on this irrational quality of Schubert's score.

12. David Magarshack, introduction to *The Idiot*, p. 9.

13. Bresson's Christ figure mirrors Mrs. Yepanchin's unwitting conflation of Prince Myshkin with the donkey. *The Idiot*, p. 243.

14. Harold Bloom, following Bakhtin, judges this to be "Dostoevsky's main contribution to narrative form … in which the struggle to assert a voice of one's own parallels the struggle to affirm a unifying novelistic identity." *Modern Critical Views: Fyodor Dostoevsky*, ed. Harold Bloom (New York: Chelsea House, 1988). Bakhtin, in fact, traces many aspects of Dostoevsky's style back to the genre of menippean satire and to the "carnivalesque" in literature, two lines that also include Apuleius

and *The Golden Ass.* Mikhail Bakhtin, *Problems of Dostoevsky's Poetics,* ed. and trans. Caryl Emerson (Minneapolis: University of Minnesota Press, 1984). Although the overall sense in which this is realized in the extensive stories and "explanations" in which characters are permitted to indulge in *The Idiot* is by no means analogous to the spareness of Bresson's style, the shifting attention and focus in *Balthazar* from primary to secondary characters was certainly a new—and, for many, confounding—development in Bresson's experiment with narrative form.

15. *The Idiot,* p. 138.

16. Gabriel Vahanian, *The Death of God: The Culture of Our Post-Christian Era* (New York: George Braziller, 1957), p. 131.

17. In addition to the sources discussed, Georges Bernanos's novel *Monsieur Ouine* (first translated into English by Geoffrey Dunlop as *The Open Mind* [London: The Bodley Head, 1945], more recently translated by William S. Bush under its original title [Lincoln: University of Nebraska Press, 2000]) has been suggested by at least two film scholars as an inspirational source of *Au hasard Balthazar;* the first is P. Adams Sitney in conversation with the author; the second is Jean Collet, "Le Drole de chemin de Bresson a Balthazar," *Etudes,* no. 325 (July–Aug. 1966): 80–91.

18. Jessie Corrigan Pegis, *A Practical Catholic Dictionary* (New York: All Saints Press, 1961), pp. 24, 45.

19. Among the attempts to create a more human, socially inscribed Jesus are Pier Paolo Pasolini's *The Gospel According to St. Matthew* (1966) and Martin Scorsese's *The Last Temptation of Christ* (1988). The former creates an unglamorous image of Jesus as a social reformer always on the move; the latter, in the spirit of the Nikos Kazantzakis novel, tries to break the mold by superimposing vulnerable traits onto the godly stereotype. It is arguable, however, whether in either case the character fully escapes the entrenched cultural images that have prevailed throughout the centuries.

20. I say this despite Bresson's remarks on the behavior and training of the donkey throughout the interview, "The Question," *Cahiers du Cinéma in English,* no. 8 (Feb. 1967), since it's not clear that he would have divulged anything to the contrary even had he been asked by his interviewers (Godard and Michel Dela-haye), which, curiously enough, he was not. In Anne Wiazemsky's fictionalized account of her work with Bresson on the film (*Jeune Fille* [Paris: Gallimard, 2007]), it is implied that there was only one animal.

21. In conversation, fellow Bresson admirer P. Adams Sitney suggested that the circus animals passage could be read as an illustration of what is referred to in Catholic doctrine as works of mercy, acts of "Christian charity performed for the good of one's neighbor's soul [spiritual works] and body [corporal works]." The latter, which include feeding the hungry and visiting the imprisoned (Pegis, *A Practical Catholic Dictionary,* pp. 146–47), would thus be seen as the purpose of Balthazar's visits and the meaning of his exchanges with the animals, consistent with the Christological analogies in the film.

22. Of course there are frontal shots of Balthazar indicating that something has gotten his attention; for example, in the midst of his arithmetic performance at

the circus, he suddenly brays and bolts when he notices the arrival of the drunken Arnold. This is a humorous moment in one of the film's few public scenes and is in long shot, whereas the careful framing and editing I am referring to is reserved for serious implications and close shots.

23. Julian Barnes, *Flaubert's Parrot* (New York: Knopf, 1985), pp. 66–67.

24. Evelyn Waugh, "Sloth," in *The Seven Deadly Sins,* introduction by Raymond Mortimer (New York: William Morrow, 1962), pp. 57, 61.

25. "The Question," pp. 5–27.

26. Bresson uses this term when he reads the passage from *The Idiot* in which, following Myshkin's account of how the donkey affected him, General Yepanchin's wife observes, "'A donkey?...That's strange. Still,' she went on, looking angrily at her laughing daughters, 'there's nothing strange about it. I shouldn't be surprised if one of us fell in love with a donkey. It happened in mythology'" (*The Idiot,* pp. 78–79), cited by Bresson, "Ni vu, ni connu." Indeed book 10 of the Apuleius includes a physically graphic account of sexual copulation between the donkey and a woman who becomes enamored of him and purchases him precisely because of his physical endowment.

27. Apuleius, *The Golden Ass* (Walsh translation), book 7, pp. 130–32.

28. This is a reasonable assumption based on the combination of the image of Marie wrapped in a blanket and seated on the merchant's lap, his words that he expects pleasure from their interaction, and the ellipsis followed by a shot of Marie dressing the next morning. However, when asked about this by the interviewer Roger Stephane, Bresson, typically evasive, said that after their conversation, he "doesn't know whether she spends the night with the miser or simply spends the night in a chair waiting for daylight." "Un metteur en ordre: Robert Bresson," interview for the television series *Pour le plaisir,* May 11, 1966, included on the DVD of the film.

29. James Quandt astutely observes that the sequence with the corn merchant (played by the writer and de Sade expert Pierre Klossowski) "briefly takes the film into Bunuel territory as he [the merchant] surveys the shivering Marie, who swats his hand away from her neck and hungrily spoons compote from a jar." See his essay on the DVD Criterion disc of the film, adapted from an original essay in *The Hidden God: Film and Faith,* ed. Mary Lea Bandy and Antonio Monda (New York: Museum of Modern Art, 2003).

30. An unsolved murder, along with the cross section of many characters and the ambience of French provincial life suggest the film's affinity with *Monsieur Ouine.* See note 17 above.

31. "When the news of Marie's return spread through the village, everyone ran to have a look at her....Marie was lying on the ground at the old woman's feet, hungry and in rags, and she was crying. When they all crowded into the cottage, she buried her face in her disheveled hair and lay huddled up face downwards on the floor. They all looked at her as if she had been something too vile to be regarded with anything but profound disgust" (p. 91). She is publically blamed for her mother's death by the pastor of the church, "marked by the finger of God...a living warning to those who lose their virtue!" (*The Idiot,* p. 92).

32. See Wallace Stevens, "Effects of Analogy," in *The Necessary Angel* (New York: Vintage Books, 1942), p. 109.

33. "Ni vu, ni connu." This version of the painting is housed in the Musee-Jacquemart-Andre in Paris.

34. Even portraits are analyzed in this fashion by Eisenstein, as in the case of Valentin Serov's portrait of the actress Yermolova. "Yermolova," in *Eisenstein, Volume 2: Towards a Theory of Montage*, ed. Michael Glenny and Richard Taylor, trans. Michael Glenny (London: BFI Publishing, 1991), pp. 82–105.

35. Bresson alludes to this figure as a lady. In many treatments of the subject she is an allegorical or symbolic figure. Breughel depicts her as "Virtue" in his graphic drawings, *The Seven Virtues*. Manfred Wundram identifies her as a princess in *Paintings of the Renaissance*, ed. Ingo F. Walther (Cologne: Benedikt Taschen Verlag, 1997), p. 26.

36. In the second (1456) version, the dragon is on the left, head bowed and mouth bleeding from the spear still in him at a sharp downward thrust by St. George on the right; around the creature's neck is a delicate chain, slackly held by the lady on the left, who is remarkably close to the dragon, the hem of her garment visibly touching the creature's right foot. She and the dragon are further linked by the backdrop that frames them, the large blackened interior of the cave. Although the dragon no longer seems to pose a threat, the proximity is alarming, especially since St. George's position on the right has not altered.

37. It is perhaps the security of her faith that allows the lady to stand so close to the still active dragon in the 1456 version, and a sign of its effect that the chain she holds so daintily requires no strain.

38. The trope continues in *Mouchette*, who knocks a cup of coffee on the floor, and in *L'Argent*, when Yvon propels a soup skimmer noisily across the floor in prison.

39. In an interview conducted by Roger Stéphane for the television series *Pour le plaisir* on May 11, 1966, on the occasion of *Balthazar*'s release. It can be found on the DVD Criterion disc of the film.

40. The Gallery of Modern Art in Palermo, devoted to Sicilian painters, includes *Landscape with Donkey* (1891) by Giovanni Lombardo Calamia, which could easily have inspired this shot. The donkey stands on a foreground slope of a mountain facing left and looking outward to the horizon, his head set against a distant, grander mountain view. Entirely alone, his pose is striking, independent of any activity, his stance in some way both dwarfed by the vastness of the scene and partaking of its majesty. Although it is certainly not impossible that Bresson was familiar with this work, given his interest in art, my point is that it conveys the same spirit and kindred feeling about donkeys that we see in the film and hear about in Dostoevsky's novel and in the Mark Twain quote that heads this chapter.

41. See Paul Schrader's *Transcendental Style in Film: Ozu, Bresson, Dreyer* (Berkeley: University of California Press, 1972).

42. Joseph Frank, *Dostoevsky: The Miraculous Years, 1865–1871* (Princeton: Princeton University Press, 1995), p. 327.

43. Gold, frankincense, and myrrh were the gifts brought by the three magi to the infant Jesus. The incense appears in the scene just before Balthazar is packed for his last journey, in which he participates in an unexplained religious ceremony and a priest, censer in hand, appears to be blessing him, a gesture that parallels the baptism at the beginning and closes the circle of his "spiritual" life.

44. *The Idiot*, p. 243.

45. E. M. Cioran, "Thinking against Oneself," in *The Temptation to Exist*, trans. Richard Howard (New York: Quartet Books, 1987), p. 41.

46. Frank, *Dostoevsky*, p. 327.

47. Aileen Kelly, "The Two Dostoyevskys," a review of Joseph Frank's *Dostoevsky: The Mantle of the Prophet, 1871–1881, New York Review of Books*, Mar. 27, 2003, p. 24.

48. "The Question," p. 25.

Chapter 6

1. Alex Preminger and T. V. F. Brogan, eds., *The New Princeton Encyclopedia of Poetry and Poetics* (Princeton: Princeton University Press, 1993), p. 818.

2. Georges Bernanos, *Mouchette*, trans. Colin Whitehouse (New York: PAG, 1987), p. 65. All quotations are from this edition.

3. Bernanos, quoted in Robert Speaight, *Georges Bernanos: A Study of the Man and the Writer* (New York: Liveright, 1974), pp. 57, 71–72, 66. Bernanos is writing to a friend in 1918 just before the end of the First World War.

4. Georges Bernanos, *Le Crepuscule des Vieux*, 1956, quoted in Speaight, *Georges Bernanos*, p. 68.

5. I am thinking especially of Henry James's method in *What Maisie Knew*, where he tells the story in the third person as if standing directly behind the young protagonist, seeing what she sees but giving her experiences words and meanings she is too young to articulate.

6. Two such references are made by the old woman who keeps vigils over the dead. She implies that her ideas about the dead are superior to the curé's, but she doesn't want to contradict him. In the same context, she somewhat mocks his rituals when she says, "What's he want to walk around the coffin for, with his holy water and incense! He just thinks the body is something to get rid of, like an empty bag. You should treat a dead person better than a sweetheart and be nice to it and spoil it before it goes off to purify itself under the ground" (Bernanos, *Mouchette*, pp. 62, 70, and 71).

7. Robert Gould, "Suicide Problems in Children and Adolescents" (1965), in Aaron H. Esman, *The Psychology of Adolescents: Essential Readings* (New York: International Universities Press, 1975).

8. Magdalene washes Jesus' feet at the last supper and Veronica wipes his face with her veil as he carries the cross.

9. In an interview with André Parinau in *Arts*, cited by Leo Murray, "*Le Procès de Jeanne d'Arc*," in Ian Cameron, *The Films of Robert Bresson* (New York: Praeger, 1970), p. 96.

10. Yves Kovacs, "Entretien avec Robert Bresson," *Cahiers du Cinéma*, no. 140 (February 1963), p. 7, my translation.

11. Other examples of thematic associations will be cited later in relation to the classroom sequence, the song Mouchette's classmates sing, and the play on the number three in the film.

12. Bernanos, *Mouchette*, p. 3.

13. Ibid., p. 80.
14. Charles Barr, "*Mouchette,*" in Cameron, *The Films of Robert Bresson,* p. 125.
15. Feodor Dostoevsky, *Demons,* trans. Richard Pevear and Larissa Volokhonsky (New York: Knopf, 2000), pp. 696, 699.
16. Melanie Klein, "A Contribution to the Psychogenesis of Manic Depressive States" (1935), in *Selected Melanie Klein,* ed. Juliet Mitchell (New York: Free Press, 1986), p. 131.
17. This English translation of the Latin text, "Deposuit potentes de sede et exaltavit humiles," appears in the booklet accompanying a recording of three Monteverdi works. The *Magnificat (II)* is a version for six voices, edited by Clifford Bartlett. Bach Collegium Japan Chorus and Orchestra, directed by Masaaki Suzuki (BIS CD 1071/1072 DIGITAL).

Chapter 7

1. One scholar equally convinced of this is Mireille Latil Le Dantec, whose "Bresson, Dostoevsky" appears in James Quandt, ed. *Robert Bresson* (1998; Toronto: Toronto International Film Festival Group, 2000).
2. In 1891 Konstantin Stanislavsky, founder and director of the Moscow Art Theater, adapted *The Village of Stepanchikovo,* an early work of Dostoevsky, for the stage, which he also acted in and directed.
3. Joseph Frank, *Dostoevsky: The Mantle of the Prophet, 1871–1881* (Princeton: Princeton University Press, 2002), p. 345. I will refer to the story by its familiar title, as it is published in *The Best Short Stories of Dostoevsky,* trans. David Magarshack (New York: Modern Library, n.d.). Unless otherwise noted, all quotations will be taken from this edition. Other citations will be taken from "The Meek One: A Fantastic Story," in Dostoevsky's *A Writer's Diary,* vol. 1, 1873–1876, trans. and annotated by Kenneth Lantz (Evanston, Ill.: Northwestern University Press, 1994).
4. Frank, *Dostoevsky*, p. 345.
5. Dostoevsky, author's foreword to "The Meek One," p. 677.
6. The age disparity may startle a contemporary sensibility, but one finds many examples in nineteenth-century Russian literature of teenage girls marrying much older men.
7. Heinz Kohut, *The Analysis of the Self* (New York: International Universities Press, 1971).
8. Dostoevsky, "The Meek One," p. 704.
9. Ibid., p. 702.
10. The edge of contempt for the narrator's connection to money in both the story and the film has its genesis, in part, from Dostoevsky's hatred of his brother-in-law, Peter Karepin, who, like the pawnbroker, was also forty when he married the seventeen-year-old Varvara, Dostoevsky's sister. Karepin was in charge of the family estate after the death of Dr. Dostoevsky and refused to give Dostoevsky the money he wanted in exchange for surrendering his part of the estate. Enraged

and humiliated, Dostoevsky, according to Joseph Frank, most likely parodied this second "father figure" in his first novel, *Poor Folk*. Joseph Frank, *Dostoevsky: The Seeds of Revolt 1821–1849* (Princeton: Princeton University Press, 1976).

11. Charles Thomas Samuels, "Interview with Robert Bresson," in *Encountering Directors* (New York: G. P. Putnam's Sons, 1972).

12. *Hamlet,* ed. Harold Jenkins, The Arden Shakespeare (London: Thomas Nelson and Sons, 1997), act III, scene 2, lines 347–63, p. 309.

13. Samuels, "Interview with Robert Bresson."

14. Michael Dempsey, "Despair Abounding: The Recent Films of Robert Bresson," in Quandt, *Robert Bresson,* p. 377.

15. In contrast, for example, to the mirror reflection of Gérard in the bar scene of *Au hasard Balthazar,* which involves no before or after internal reflection of the character looking into it before shattering it, and is a fleeting instant of his overall destructive behavior. Following *Une femme douce* a mirror shot in *Four Nights of a Dreamer* (1972) shows Marthe discovering her body in response to the attentions of the tenant; in *Lancelot of the Lake* (1974) Guinevere gazes into a small mirror as she stands in her bath and readies herself for Lancelot. Since both of these involve a woman awaiting a lover, we might wonder if death plays a similar role for the young wife in *Une femme douce.*

16. George Steiner, *Antigones* (New York: Oxford University Press, 1984), p. 242.

17. Although "the idea of Christ as revolutionary was quite standard in [Russia] in the 1840s," seeing him as the "divine harbinger of man's freedom from the shackles of historical determinism was much less conventional." For Dostoevsky, Christ "would always remain not only the traditional Savior from the bonds of sin and death, but also the sacred pledge of the possibility of moral freedom." Frank, *Dostoevsky: The Seeds of Revolt,* p. 210.

18. Mario Beunat, interview with Bresson, "Page cinema," included on the DVD of *Procès de Jeanne d'Arc,* in the boxed set produced by MK2, 2005.

19. This is a 20-minute short in the comic mode mastered by René Clair in the late 1920s, early 1930s. Although I have seen the film twice, it was unavailable to me for any extensive study while I was working on this book. A description of it by William Johnson can be found in Quandt's anthology, pp. 189–91.

20. All references to "White Nights" are to the version in *The Best Short Stories of Dostoevsky,* trans. David Magarshack (New York: Modern Library, n.d.).

21. Geoffrey Nowell-Smith, *Visconti* (Garden City, N.Y.: Doubleday and Co., 1968).

22. Michael Dempsey, "Despair Abounding: The Recent Films of Robert Bresson," in Quandt, *Robert Bresson,* p. 389.

23. Allegedly authored by Louis Aragon in 1928 under the more graphic title, *Le Con d'Irène* (*Irene's Cunt*), the book was rediscovered and republished in 1962.

24. Albert de Routisie, *Irène,* trans. Lowell Blair (New York: Grove Press, 1969), p. 74.

25. Ibid., pp. 51–52.

26. This characteristic of Bresson's is extensively described in Anne Wiazemsky's novel *Jeune Fille* (Paris: Editions Gallimard, 2007), concerning her relationship with Bresson during the filming of *Au hasard Balthazar.* According to her, Bresson assumed the role of parental authority and restricted her freedom while she was on location for the film.

27. Kovacs, "Entretien avec Robert Bresson," p. 7, my translation.

Chapter 8

1. Because the names of the characters are as well, if not better known in their Anglicized forms, I use these instead of the French names. Thus Guinevere, not Guenièvre; Gawain, not Gauvain; Arthur, not Artus.

2. Laura Duke Condominas, the young woman who plays Guinevere, is the daughter of the late Niki de Saint-Phalle, a French sculptor, painter, and filmmaker, who was apparently Bresson's original choice to play the part more than two decades earlier, until she became pregnant. (Personal conversations with individuals who knew Bresson in the 1950s.) According to Anne Wiazemsky, Bresson asked her to play the role near the end of filming of *Au hasard Balthazar* in 1965, claiming she "would be a marvelous Guinevere." He insisted, however, that she not appear in any other director's films in the interim, but she did. *Jeune Fille* (Paris: Gallimard, 2007), p. 197, my translation.

3. Josephin Peladan, a dabbler in occult mysteries, who on a visit to the Holy Land, claimed to have found Jesus' tomb, remarked that the artist should be "a knight in armor, eagerly engaged in the symbolic quest for the Holy Grail." Michael Baigent, Richard Leigh, and Henry Lincoln, *Holy Blood, Holy Grail* (New York: Delta Trade Paperback, 2004), 155–56. The filmmaker Michael Haneke, who acknowledges Bresson as an important influence, sees art as an idealized pursuit "in a world in which God is dead." See the interview that accompanies the DVD of his film *71 Fragments of a Chronology of Chance* (1994).

4. This is unlike other versions of the tales, such as *Excalibur* (John Boorman, 1981) and *King Arthur* (Antoine Fuqua, 2004), in which battles and violence are more conventionally integrated throughout. Interestingly the latter is perhaps the first film to set the legend in the fifth century, when a figure named Arturius fought against the Roman Empire.

5. See Marshall McLuhan and Quentin Fiore, *War and Peace in the Global Village* (1968; Corte Madera, CA: Gingko Press, 2001), an interesting description of the way emerging technologies changed the nature of warfare. None of this changes the fact that armor and stirrups were not in use in the fifth century, when Arthur and his knights presumably existed; like the literature, Bresson's retelling sets the events in the late medieval period, when such accouterments were integral to the armature of warriors. According to Jonathan Rosenbaum, citing Michel Estève, "neither the tents nor the Round Table nor the chess game nor the wooden tub in which Guenièvre bathes belongs to the period, all of them constituting conscious anachronisms on Bresson's part." "Bresson's *Lancelot du Lac*," *Sight and Sound*, 43, no. 3 (1974), p. 129.

6. Heinrich Oskar Sommer, ed., *The Vulgate Version of the Arthurian Romances*, 7 vols. (Washington, D.C.: Carnegie Institution, 1908–16).

7. Carol J. Clover, *The Medieval Saga* (Ithaca: Cornell University Press, 1982).

8. *The Complete Romances of Chrétien de Troyes*, trans. David Staines (Bloomington: Indiana University Press, 1993).

9. *The Quest of the Holy Grail*, trans. and introduced by P. M. Matarasso (London: Penguin Books, 1969); *The Death of King Arthur*, trans. and introduced by James Cable (London: Penguin Books, 1971); *From Camelot to Joyous Guard: The Old French* La Mort le Roi Artu, trans. J. Neale Carman (Lawrence: University Press of

Kansas, 1974); Sir Thomas Malory, *Le Morte D'Arthur*, 2 vols. (London: Penguin Books, 1969); Thomas Malory, *Le Morte D'Arthur*, a rendition by Keith Baines (New York: New American Library, 1962).

10. James Cable, introduction to *The Death of King Arthur*, p. 9.

11. It is beyond the purpose and scope of this discussion to consider the alternative versions of this story that derive from the Gnostic gospels, such as the one of Mary Magdalen, and studies devoted to it.

12. P. M. Matarasso, introduction to *The Quest of the Holy Grail*, p. 12.

13. Ibid, pp. 13, 15, 15–17.

14. *Quest*, p. 174; Malory (Baines rendition), *Le Morte D'Arthur*, p. 396.

15. Matarasso, introduction to *Quest*, p. 15.

16. The Arthurian legends were and are more commonly taught in French schools than in English and are very familiar to French audiences.

17. Chrétien de Troyes's *The Story of the Grail* begins with a description of five knights riding through the "Desolate Forest," heard from a distance by a youth who has never seen a knight and with an accent on the clamor of their armor that fully accords with Bresson's treatment (*Complete Romances*, p. 340).

18. J. Laplanche and J. B. Pontalis, *The Language of Psychoanalysis*, trans. Donald Nicholson-Smith (New York: Norton, 1973), pp. 74–75.

19. *Complete Romances*, p. 344; Sigmund Freud, *Group Psychology and the Analysis of the Ego*, 1921, trans. and ed. James Strachey (New York: Norton, 1959), pp. 6, 10.

20. Sigmund Freud, *Beyond the Pleasure Principle*, 1920, trans. and ed. James Strachey (New York: Norton, 1961), p. 33.

21. John Boorman's *Excalibur* relishes and compounds these insinuations by making Mordred the spawn of Arthur's bewitched intercourse with his sister, Morgan le Fay.

22. Malory, *Le Morte D'Arthur*, p. 462.

23. There is some irony concerning the affair's link to the court's unity in that the Round Table was a wedding gift to Arthur from Guinevere's father, who had gotten it from Arthur's father, Uther Pendragon (Malory, *Le Morte D'Arthur*, pp. 57–58), rendering its full-circle symbolism as pregnant with meaning as any Sophoclean turn of fate. Arthur himself, the illegitimate product of Uther's unlawful seduction of his rival's wife, seems to have been besieged by adulterous relationships since conception.

24. *Complete Romances*, pp. 344–47.

25. Malory (Baines rendition), *Le Morte D'Arthur*, p. 127.

26. As the knights move through the forest in *The Story of the Grail*, "their armor made a loud clamor since branches of oaks and hornbeams often struck against their equipment. All the hauberks jingled; the lances knocked against the shields; the wood of the lances resounded; and the steel of the shields and hauberks reverberated" (*Complete Romances*, p. 340)

27. Kristin Thompson, "The Sheen of Armour, the Whinnies of Horses: Sparse Parametric Style in *Lancelot du Lac*," in *Breaking the Glass Armor: Neoformalist Film Analysis* (Princeton: Princeton University Press, 1988), reprinted in James Quandt, ed., *Robert Bresson* (Toronto: Toronto International Film Festival Group, 1998).

28. From an interview excerpted in the official press book of the film, p. 15, translated by Jon Lomax, for the website robert-bresson.com.

29. As one finds, for example, in such Hollywood treatments as *Ivanhoe* (1952) and *Knights of the Round Table* (1953).
30. This event almost takes place in the literature, although in a different context, following a trap whereby Lancelot is discovered in Guinevere's bedroom and she is condemned to die.
31. Editor's note, in *The Complete Gospels,* ed. Robert J. Miller (San Francisco: Harper, 1994), p. 361.

Chapter 9

1. Jonathan Rosenbaum, "The Last Filmmaker: A Local, Interim Report," in James Quandt, ed., *Robert Bresson* (1998; Toronto: Toronto International Film Festival Group, 2000), p. 19.
2. The use of stock footage is unprecedented in Bresson's work unless we count the glimpses of documentaries and car races on a television in *Une femme douce.*
3. Cited by Richard Roud, "*The Devil Probably:* The Redemption of Despair," in Quandt, *Robert Bresson,* p. 405.
4. Bresson shared his feelings in the 1965 interview with Francois Weyergans, "Ni vu, ni connu."
5. As in such films as *Ordinary People* (1980) and *Good Will Hunting* (1997).
6. Appian, *The Civil Wars,* trans. John Carter (London: Penguin Books, 1996), book 2 (99), p. 122. Cato, unlike Charles, did not assign the task to anyone else. Also see Joseph Addison, *Cato: A Tragedy,* ed. Christine Dunn Henderson and Mark E. Yellin (Indianapolis, Ind.: Liberty Funds, 2004).
7. Joseph Frank, *Dostoevsky: The Seeds of Revolt, 1821–1849* (Princeton: Princeton University Press, 1976), p. 104.
8. Bresson, interviewed by Christian Defaye, Television Suisse Romande, 1983, included on the DVD of *L'Argent* produced by New Yorker Video; Serge Daney and Serge Toubiana, interview with Bresson, *Cahiers du cinema,* nos. 348–49 (June/July 1983).
9. According to Victor Shklovksy, however, Tolstoy's charitable Christian concerns were already evident in his late teens, when he also became convinced that the purpose of literature was to teach. *Lev Tolstoy,* trans. Olga Shartse (Moscow: Progress Publishers, 1978), pp. 87, 95.
10. Leo Tolstoy, "The Forged Coupon," in *The Kreutzer Sonata and Other Stories,* trans. David McDuff (New York: Penguin Books, 1985), p. 253.
11. Leo Tolstoy, *What Is Art?,* trans. Almyer Maude (New York: Bobbs Merrill, 1960), p. 150.
12. This is to use the word *exchange* somewhat broadly, since reciprocity seems utterly absent in many of these instances, yet there is a history of such uses of the word, which according to the OED is also used "in senses more correctly expressed by 'change.'"
13. R. A. Shoaf, *Dante, Chaucer, and the Currency of the Word: Money, Images, and Reference in Late Medieval Poetry* (Norman, Okla.: Pilgrim Books, 1983), p. 27.
14. My use of this term should not be taken in the sense noted by Oudart as a way of positioning the subject or viewer in relation to the film, as discussed in chapter 4.

15. Jean Sémolué reminds us that the phrase recalls Grushenka's in Dostoevsky's *The Brothers Karamazov:* "If I were God, I would pardon the whole world." *Robert Bresson ou L'Acte des Metamorphoses* (Paris: Flammarion, 1993), p. 250.
16. When he turns himself in, he says he "has killed an entire family." However, the last shot of the child shows him crying in bed while Yvon appears to have moved into the woman's room.
17. "The evidence is undeniable, that on some level, this woman, who houses a man who has confessed to two entirely gratuitous murders, who feeds him and exchanges confidences with him, and who refuses to turn him over to the police or warn her loved ones, is asking to be murdered, putting an end to a life of hardship for herself and her family." Kent Jones, *L'Argent* (London: British Film Institute, 1999), pp. 84, 86. Although this reading has undeniable psychological merit, I don't think it accounts for all that the final sequence implies.
18. Flannery O'Connor, "A Good Man Is Hard to Find," in *A Good Man Is Hard to Find, Collected Works* (New York: Library of America, 1988), p. 152.
19. E. M. Cioran, "A People of Solitaries," in *The Temptation to Exist*, trans. Richard Howard (London: Quartet Books, 1987), p. 86.
20. Diderot's *Jacques the Fatalist* is the source for *Les Dames du bois de Boulogne*.

Afterword

1. "The Question," Interview by Jean-Luc Godard and Michel Delahaye, in *Cahiers du Cinéma in English*, no. 8 (February 1967).

Filmography

All Films Directed by Robert Bresson

Affaires Publiques (1934)

Production Company: Arc-Film. Screenplay: Robert Bresson. Cinematography (b&w): Nicolas Toporkoff. Editor: Bresson. Art Director: Pierre Charbonnier. Sound Engineer: Girardot. Music: Jean Wiener, Roger Désormière.

Cast: Beby (the chancellor of Crocandie); Andrée Servilanges (the princess of Miremie); Marcel Dalio (the speaker, the sculptor, the fire captain, the admiral); Gilles Margaritis (the chauffeur); Simone Cressier (Christiane); Franck Maurice (a sailor).

Les Anges du péché (1943)

Production Company: Synops-Roland Tual. Screenplay: Robert Bresson, R. L. Bruckberger. Dialogue: Jean Giraudoux. Cinematography (b&w): Philippe Agostini. Editor: Yvonne Martin. Art Director: René Renoux. Sound Engineer: René Louge. Assistant Director: Frédéric Liotier. Music: Jean-Jacques Grünenwald.

Cast: Renée Faure (Anne-Marie); Jany Holt (Thérèse); Sylvie (the prioress); Mila Parèly (Madeleine); Marie-Hélène Dasté (Mother Saint-Jean); Yolande Laffon (Anne-Marie's mother); Paula Dehelly (Mother Dominique); Silvia Monfort (Agnès); Gilberte Terbon (Sister Marie-Joseph); Louis Seigner (Director of the prison).

Les Dames du bois de Boulogne (1945)

Production Company: Les Films Raoul Ploquin. Screenplay: Robert Bresson, based on *Jacques the Fatalist and His Master* by Denis Diderot. Dialogue: Jean Cocteau. Cinematography (b&w): Philippe Agostini. Editor: Jean Feyte. Art Director: Max Douy. Sound Engineers: René Louge, Robert Ivonnet, Lucien Legrand. Assistant Directors: Roger Spiri-Mercanton, Raymond Bailly, Paul Barbellion. Music: Jean-Jacques Grünenwald.

Cast: Maria Casarès (Hélène); Èlina Labourdette (Agnès); Paul Bernard (Jean); Lucienne Bogaert (Agnès' mother); Jean Marchat (Jacques).

Journal d'un curé de Campagne (1951)

Production Company: Union Générale Cinématographique. Screenplay: Robert Bresson, based on the novel by Georges Bernanos. Cinematography (b&w): Léonce-Henri Burel. Editor: Paulette Robert. Art Director: Pierre Charbonnier. Sound Engineer: Jean Rieul. Assistant Director: Guy Lefranc. Music: Jean-Jacques Grünenwald.

Cast: Claude Laydu (the curé of Ambricourt); Armand Guibert (the curé of Torcy); Marie-Monique Arkell (the countess); Jean Riveyre (the count); Nicole Ladmiral (Chantal); Nicole Maurey (Mlle. Louise); Martine Lemaire (Séraphita); Antoine Balpêtré (Dr. Delbende); Leon Arvel (Fabregard); Jean Danet (Olivier); Gaston Severin (the canon of Motte-Beuvron); Bernard Hubrenne (Louis Dufréty); Yvette Étiévant (Dufréty's female companion).

Un Condamné à mort s'est échappé (1956)

Production Company: Jean Poiré, Jean Thuillier (Gaumont, Nouvelles Éditions de films). Screenplay: Robert Bresson, based on the account by André Devigny. Cinematography (b&w): Léoncé-Henri Burel. Editor: Raymond Lamy. Art Director: Pierre Charbonnier. Sound Engineer: Pierre-André Bertrand. Assistant Directors: Jacques Ballanche, Michel Clément. Music: Wolfgang Amadeus Mozart.

Cast: Francois Letterier (Lt. Fontaine); Charles Le Clainche (Francois Jost); Maurice Beerblock (Blanchet); Roland Monod (Pastor Deleyris); Jacques Ertaud (Orsini); Roger Tréherne (Terry).

Pickpocket (1959)

Production Company: Agnès Delahaie. Screenplay: Robert Bresson. Cinematography (b&w): Léoncé-Henri Burel. Art Director: Pierre Charbonnier. Editor: Raymond Lamy. Sound Engineer: Antoine Archimbaud. Assistant Directors: Jacques Ballanche, Michel Clément. Music: Jean-Baptiste Lully.

Cast: Martin La Salle (Michel); Marika Green (Jeanne); Pierre Leymarie (Jacques); Jean Pelegri (the police inspector); Kassagi (the expert pickpocket who teaches Michel); Dolly Scal (Michel's mother); Pierre Étaix (thief accomplice).

Procès de Jeanne D'Arc (1962)

Production Company: Agnès Delahaie. Screenplay: Robert Bresson, based on the official texts of the Trial of Condemnation and accounts of the Trial of Rehabilitation. Cinematography (b&w): Léonce-Henri Burel. Editor: Germaine Artus. Art Director: Pierre Charbonnier. Costumes: Lucilla Mussini. Sound Engineer: Antoine Archimbaud. Assistant Directors: Marcel Ugols, Alain Ferrari, Serge Roullet, Hugo Santiago. Music: Francis Seyrig.

Cast: Florence Carrez, later Delay (Joan); Jean-Claude Fourneaux (Bishop Cauchon); Roger Honorat (Jean Beaupère); Jean Gillibert (Jean de Chatillon); André Regnier (d'Éstivet); Michel Herubel (Brother Isambart); Philippe Dreux (Brother Martin Ladvenu); Richard Pratt (Warwick); Andre Maurice (doctor); Harry Sommers (Bishop of Winchester).

Au hasard Balthazar (1966)

Production Companies: Parc Film, Argos Films, Athos Films, Swedish Film Institute, Svensk Filmindustri. Screenplay: Robert Bresson. Cinematography (b&w): Ghislain Cloquet. Editor: Raymond Lamy. Art Director: Pierre Charbonnier. Sound Engineers: Antoine Archimbaud, Jacques Carrère. Assistant Directors: Sven Frostenson, Jacques Kébadian, Claude Miller. Music: Franz Schubert, Jean Wiener.

Cast: Anne Wiazemsky (Marie); Francois Lafarge (Gérard); Walter Green (Jacques); Philippe Asselin (Marie's father); Nathalie Joyaut (Marie's mother); Jean-Claude Guilbert (Arnold); Pierre Klossowski (the grain merchant); Marie-Claire Frémont (the baker's wife); Jean-Joël Barbier (the priest); Francois Sullerot (the baker).

Mouchette (1967)

Production Companies: Argos Films; Parc Film. Screenplay: Robert Bresson, based on *Nouvelle histoire de Mouchette* by Georges Bernanos. Cinematography (b&w): Ghislain Cloquet. Editor: Raymond Lamy. Art Director: Pierre Guffroy. Sound Engineers: Séverin Frankiel, Jacques Carrère. Assistant Directors: Mylène Van der Mersch, Jacques Kébadian. Music: Claudio Monteverdi, Jean Wiener.

Cast: Nadine Nortier (Mouchette); Jean-Claude Guilbert (Arsène); Jean Vimenet (Mathieu); Marie Cardinal (Mouchette's mother); Paul Hébert (Mouchette's father); Martine Trichet (Louisa); Liliane Princet (the teacher); Raymonde Chabrun (the grocer); Marie Susini (Mathieu's wife); Suzanne Huguenin (the old woman who tends the dead).

Une femme douce (1969)

Production Companies: Parc Film; Marianne Production. Screenplay: Robert Bresson, based on the story, *A Gentle Creature* by Feodor Dostoevsky. Cinematography (color):

Ghislain Cloquet. Editor: Raymond Lamy. Art Director: Pierre Charbonnier. Sound Engineers: Jacques Lebreton, Urbain Loiseau. Assistant Directors: Mylène Van der Mersch, Jacques Kébadian. Music: Henry Purcell, Jean Wiener.

Cast: Dominique Sanda (the gentle woman); Guy Frangin (the husband); Jane Lobre (Anna).

Quatre Nuits d'un rêveur (1971)

Production Companies: Albina Productions, Victoria Film, I Film dell'orso. Screenplay: Robert Bresson, based on the story, *White Nights* by Feodor Dostoevsky. Cinematography (color): Pierre Lhomme; Ghislain Cloquet, for the gangster film, *Bonds of Love*. Editor: Raymond Lamy. Art Director: Pierre Charbonnier. Sound Engineer: Roger Letellier. Assistant Directors: Mylène Van der Mersch, André Bitoun, Jean-Pierre Ghys, Munni Kabir. Music: Michel Magne; Groupe Batuki; Christopher Hayward; Louis Guitar; F. R. David.

Cast: Isabelle Weingarten (Marthe); Guillaume des Forêts (Jacques); Jean-Maurice Monnoyer (the lodger); Jérôme Massart (Jacques' visitor from art school); Lydia Biondi (Marthe's mother); Patrick Jouanné (the gangster in *Bonds of Love*); Giorgio Maulini.

Lancelot du Lac (1974)

Production Companies: Jean-Pierre Rassam, Francois Rochas, Jean Yanne (Mara-Films, Laser Productions, ORTF, Gerico Sound). Screenplay: Robert Bresson. Cinematography (color): Pasqualino De Santis. Editor: Germaine Lamy. Art Director: Pierre Charbonnier. Sound Engineers: Bernard Bats, Jacques Carrère. Assistant Directors: Mylène Van der Mersch, Robert Baroody, Bernard Cohn. Music: Philippe Sarde.

Cast: Luc Simon (Lancelot); Laura Duke Condominas (Queen Guinevere); Humbert Balsan (Gawain); Wladimir Antolek-Oresek (King Arthur); Patrick Bernard (Mordred); Arthur de Montalembert (Lionel); Marie-Louise Buffet (the old woman in the forest); Marie-Gabrielle Carton (the young girl in the forest).

Le Diable probablement (1977)

Production Companies: Stéphane Tchalgadjieff (Sunchild GMF/Michel Chanderli). Screenplay: Robert Bresson. Cinematography (color): Pasqualino De Santis. Editor: Germaine Lamy. Art Director: Éric Simon. Sound Engineer: Georges Prat. Assistant Directors: Mylène Van der Mersch, Humbert Balsan, Thierry Bodin. Music: Claudio Monteverdi, Wolfgang Amadeus Mozart.

Cast: Antoine Monnier (Charles); Tina Irrisari (Alberte); Henri de Maublanc (Michel); Laetitia Carcano (Edwige); Régis Hanrion (the psychoanalyst); Nicolas Deguy (Valentin); Geoffrey Gaussen (the bookseller); Roger Honorat (police officer).

L'Argent (1983)

Production Company: Jean-Marie Henchoz (Marion Films); Eos Films; FR3. Screenplay: Robert Bresson, based on the novella *The Forged Coupon* by Leo Tolstoy.

Cinematography (color): Pasqualino De Santis, Emmanuel Machuel. Editor: Jean-Francois Naudon. Art Director: Pierre Guffroy. Sound Engineers: Jean-Louis Ughetto, Luc Yersin. Assistant Directors: Mylène Van der Mersch, Thierry Bodin, Pascal Bony. Music: Johann Sebastian Bach.

Cast: Christian Patey (Yvon Targe); Caroline Lang (Élise); Sylvie Van den Elsen (the widow); Michel Briguet (the widow's father); Vincent Risterucci (Lucien); Béatrice Tabourin (photo shop owner wife); Didier Baussy (photo shop owner husband); Marc-Ernest Fourneau (Norbert); André Cler (Norbert's father); Claude Cler (Norbert's mother)'; Bruno Lapeyre (Martial); Francois-Marie Banier (Yvon's philosophical cellmate); Jeanne Aptekman (Yvette).

Index

Delteil, Joseph, *Joan of Arc* 156, 170

De Mille, Cecil B., 156

Denton, Clive, 383n1

De Santis, Pasqualino, 321

De Sica, Vittorio, 111, 124, *Bicycle Thieves* (1948), 18

Devigny, André (See *A Man Escaped*)

Devil Probably, The, 2, 3, 7, 9, 17, 25, 29, 70, 89, 202, 217, 258, 260, 281, 308, 309–30, 336, 338, 361, 362, 397

Diable probablement, Le (See *The Devil Probably*)

Diary of a Country Priest, 3, 6, 10, 13, 17–19, 29, 43, 55, 62, 68, 69–97, 100, 114, 116, 119, 154, 164, 174, 176, 178, 183, 189, 194, 196, 209, 213, 217, 241, 266, 278–79, 281, 305, 326, 332, 360, 361, 362, 371n32, 395

Diderot, Denis, 9, 49, 51–55, 60–64, 66, 98, 180, 358, 371n31

Dostoevky, Feodor, 6, 9, 196, 233–34, 258, 331, 356, 389nn1, 2, 10, 390n17, *The Brothers Karamazov,* 319, 394n15, *Crime and Punishment,* 9, 27, 104, 126–28, 130, 134–35, 148–50, 373n18, *Demons,* 230–31, 310, 329, "A Gentle Creature," 236–41, 247, 249, 251, 253–54, 257, *The Idiot,* 9, 29, 186–87, 189, 192, 195–96, 205–07, 384nn10, 13, 14, 386nn26, 31, "White Nights," 234, 261–63, 275, 390n20, *A Writer's Diary*, 236, 238, 378n36, 389n3

Dreyer, Carl Theodor, 1, *Day of Wrath* (1943), 13–14, *La Passion de Jeanne d'Arc* (1928), 70, 83, 154,156, 164–65, 166–69, 170, 172, 175, 180, 381n27

Duby, George, 381n33

Duchesse de Langeais, La, 33

Duguay, Christian, *Joan of Arc* (1999), 156

Durgnat, Raymond, 374n35

Eisenstein, Sergei, 22, 200, 387n34, *Battleship Potemkin* (1925), 297, *Ivan the Terrible* (1943), 111, 124

ellipsis, 368–369n9

Epstein, Jean, 22

Escholier, Marc, 69

Estève, Michel, 391n5

Existentialism, 376–77n19

Falconetti, Renée, 372n8

Faure, Renée, 42

Fellini, Federico, 2

Femme douce, Une, 3, 16, 18, 27, 29, 67, 234–60, 266–67, 270, 274, 276, 278, 298, 309, 310, 314, 323, 326, 329, 346, 361, 362, 370n27, 397

Fenichel, Otto, 378n43

Flaherty, Robert, 111

Flaubert, Gustave, 4–5, *Sentimental Education,* 5

Fleming, Victor, *Joan of Arc* (1948), 156

Ford, John, 18, *The Fugitive* (1947), 372n2

Forêts, Guillaume des, 267–68, 276

Fourneau, Jean-Claude, 174

Four Nights of a Dreamer, 17, 27, 29, 234, 260–79, 309, 312–14, 323, 326, 328, 361, 397, 366n7

France, Anatole, 156

Frangin, Guy, 241

Frank, Joseph, 207, 389n3, 10, 390n17

Freud, Anna, 373n22

Freud, Sigmund, 25, 284, 348, 378n43, *Beyond the Pleasure Principle*, 152, 289, *Group Psychology and the Ego*, 289

Fuller, Samuel, *Pickup on South Street* (1953), 135, 378n41

Fuqua, Antoine, *King Arthur* (2004), 391n4

Gaddis, William, *The Recognitions*, 145

Genet, Jean, *Un Chant d'amour* (1950), 382n43

Geoffrey of Monmouth, 284

Gilson, Étienne, 286

Gilson, René, 370n25

Giradoux, Jean, 9, 32–33, 46

Godard, Jean-Luc, 2, 204, 315, 366n16, 374n1, 379n5, 385n20

Graves, Robert, 384n4

Green, Marika, 19, 21, 124, 367n32, 378n32

Greenberg, Clement, 11

Greene, Graham, 188

Photo Credits

Photos were taken from a variety of sources. Frame blow-ups from 35mm prints of *Les Dames du bois de Boulogne, A Man Escaped, Pickpocket, Au hasard Balthazar, Mouchette,* and *Une femme douce* are courtesy of Anthology Film Archives. Frame blow-ups from a 16mm print of *Les Anges du péché* are courtesy of a private collection. Other frames from *Une femme douce* are from a VHS. Stills from *Four Nights of a Dreamer* are courtesy of Photofest, New York, as is the photo of Bresson on the title page. Additional images from *A Man Escaped* and all other photos are frame seizures from DVDs. Because DVD and VHS formats do not represent correct aspect ratios of the films, it was decided to standardize all reproductions as they appear on the glossy inserts.